Constitutional Torts

ANDERSON'S
Law School Publications

ADMINISTRATIVE LAW ANTHOLOGY
by Thomas O. Sargentich

ADMINISTRATIVE LAW: CASES AND MATERIALS
by Daniel J. Gifford

APPELLATE ADVOCACY: PRINCIPLES AND PRACTICE
Cases and Materials
by Ursula Bentele and Eve Cary

A CAPITAL PUNISHMENT ANTHOLOGY
by Victor L. Streib

CASES AND PROBLEMS IN CRIMINAL LAW
by Myron Moskovitz

THE CITATION WORKBOOK
by Maria L. Ciampi, Rivka Widerman and Vicki Lutz

COMMERCIAL TRANSACTIONS: PROBLEMS AND MATERIALS
Vol. 1: Secured Transactions Under the Uniform Commercial Code
Vol. 2: Sales Under the Uniform Commercial Code and the Convention on
International Sale of Goods
Vol. 3: Negotiable Instruments Under the Uniform Commercial Code
and the United Nations Convention on International
Bills of Exchange and International Promissory Notes
by Louis F. Del Duca, Egon Guttman and Alphonse M. Squillante

A CONSTITUTIONAL LAW ANTHOLOGY
by Michael J. Glennon

CONSTITUTIONAL TORTS
by Sheldon H. Nahmod, Michael L. Wells, and Thomas A. Eaton

CONTRACTS
Contemporary Cases, Comments, and Problems
by Michael L. Closen, Richard M. Perlmutter and Jeffrey D. Wittenberg

A CONTRACTS ANTHOLOGY
by Peter Linzer

A CRIMINAL LAW ANTHOLOGY
by Arnold H. Loewy

CRIMINAL LAW: CASES AND MATERIALS
by Arnold H. Loewy

CRIMINAL PROCEDURE: TRIAL AND SENTENCING
by Arthur B. LaFrance and Arnold H. Loewy

ECONOMIC REGULATION
Cases and Materials
by Richard J. Pierce, Jr.

ELEMENTS OF LAW
by Eva H. Hanks, Michael E. Herz and Steven S. Nemerson

ENDING IT: DISPUTE RESOLUTION IN AMERICA
Descriptions, Examples, Cases and Questions
by Susan M. Leeson and Bryan M. Johnston

ENVIRONMENTAL LAW
Vol. 1: Environmental Decisionmaking: NEPA and the Endangered Species Act
Vol. 2: Water Pollution; Vol. 3: Air Pollution; Vol. 4: Hazardous Wastes
by Jackson B. Battle, Mark Squillace, Maxine I. Lipeles and Robert L. Fischman

Continued

FEDERAL INCOME TAXATION OF PARTNERSHIPS AND OTHER PASS-THRU ENTITIES
by Howard E. Abrams

FEDERAL RULES OF EVIDENCE
Rules, Legislative History, Commentary and Authority
by Glen Weissenberger

FIRST AMENDMENT ANTHOLOGY
by Donald E. Lively, Dorothy E. Roberts and Russell L. Weaver

INTERNATIONAL HUMAN RIGHTS: LAW, POLICY AND PROCESS
Problems and Materials
by Frank Newman and David Weissbrodt

INTERNATIONAL LAW ANTHOLOGY
by Anthony D'Amato

INTERNATIONAL LAW COURSEBOOK
by Anthony D'Amato

INTRODUCTION TO THE STUDY OF LAW: CASES AND MATERIALS
by John Makdisi

JUSTICE AND THE LEGAL SYSTEM
A Coursebook
by Anthony D'Amato and Arthur J. Jacobson

THE LAW OF MODERN PAYMENT SYSTEMS AND NOTES
by Fred H. Miller and Alvin C. Harrell

PATIENTS, PSYCHIATRISTS AND LAWYERS
Law and the Mental Health System
by Raymond L. Spring, Roy B. Lacoursiere, M.D., and Glen Weissenberger

PROBLEMS AND SIMULATIONS IN EVIDENCE
by Thomas F. Guernsey

PROFESSIONAL RESPONSIBILITY ANTHOLOGY
by Thomas B. Metzloff

A PROPERTY ANTHOLOGY
by Richard H. Chused

THE REGULATION OF BANKING
Cases and Materials on Depository Institutions and Their Regulators
by Michael P. Malloy

A SECTION 1983 CIVIL RIGHTS ANTHOLOGY
by Sheldon H. Nahmod

SPORTS LAW: CASES AND MATERIALS
by Raymond L. Yasser, James R. McCurdy and C. Peter Goplerud

A TORTS ANTHOLOGY
by Lawrence C. Levine, Julie A. Davies and Ted Kionka

TRIAL PRACTICE
Text by Lawrence A. Dubin and Thomas F. Guernsey
Problems and Case Files with *Video* Presentation
by Edward R. Stein and Lawrence A. Dubin

CONSTITUTIONAL TORTS

SHELDON H. NAHMOD

MICHAEL L. WELLS

THOMAS A. EATON

ANDERSON PUBLISHING COMPANY

CONSTITUTIONAL TORTS

Library of Congress Cataloging-in-Publication Data

Constitutional torts / Sheldon H. Nahmod, Michael L. Wells,
    Thomas A. Eaton.
        p.   cm.
    ISBN 0-87084-903-4
    1. Constitutional torts—United States—Cases.   2. State action (Civil rights)—
United States—Cases. I. Nahmod, Sheldon H., 1940- .   II. Eaton, Thomas A.,
1950- .   III. Wells, Michael L.
KF1306.C64C66   1995
342.73'088—dc20
[347.30288]   94-43425
                                                                              CIP

Contents

Table of Cases	xiii
Preface	xv

CHAPTER 1   CONSTITUTIONAL TORTS: A FIRST LOOK   **1**

I. The Text of Section 1983 and Its Jurisdictional Counterpart   1

II. History and Purposes of Section 1983   2

III. *Monroe v. Pape*, the Seminal Decision   3
    Monroe v. Pape   3

IV. Constitutional Torts and Exhaustion of Judicial Remedies   14
    Habeas Corpus   14
    Due Process   14
    Prospective Relief and the *Younger* Rule   14

V. Constitutional Torts and Exhaustion of Administrative Remedies   15
    State Prisoners and Exhaustion of Administrative Remedies   16

VI. Constitutional Torts of Federal Officials: *Bivens* Actions   16
    Bivens v. Six Unknown Named Agents of the Federal Bureau of Nacotics   16

VII. The Current Status of *Bivens* Actions   22
    Schweiker v. Chilicky   22

CHAPTER 2   "UNDER COLOR OF" STATE LAW   **33**

I. The Meaning of "Under Color of"   33
    A.   *Monroe* and "Under Color of"   33
    B.   The Boundaries of "Under Color of"   33

II. "Under Color of" and State Action   35
    Lugar v. Edmondson Oil Co.   35

III. Suing Private Actors Under Section 1983   42
    A.   Self-Help Remedies   42
        Flagg Bros., Inc. v. Brooks   42
    B.   Contracting Out and Other Symbiotic Relationships   48
        Burton v. Wilmington Parking Authority   48
        Rendell-Baker v. Kohn   51
    C.   "Conspiracies" Between Public Officers and Private Actors   59
        National Collegiate Athletic Association v. Tarkanian   59

**CHAPTER 3   "SECURED BY THE CONSTITUTION AND LAWS" THE DOMAIN OF
SECTION 1983 AND CONSTITUTIONAL TORT**   **69**

I. Procedural Due Process and Substantive Due Process   70
    Parratt v. Taylor   70
    Zinermon v. Burch   75

CHAPTER 3 – *continued*

II. The Scope of Substantive Due Process 87
  A. State of Mind 87
     Daniels v. Williams 87
     Farmer v. Brennan 93
  B. Abuse of Power 98
     Collins v. City of Harker Heights 98
  C. Alternatives to Substantive Due Process 104
     Graham v. Connor 104

**CHAPTER 4   "SECURED BY THE CONSTITUTION AND LAWS": AFFIRMATIVE
             CONSTITUTIONAL DUTIES AND RIGHTS SECURED BY
             FEDERAL "LAWS"** 111

I. Affirmative Duties 111
  A. The Supreme Court's Framework 112
     DeShaney v. Winnebago County Department of Social Services 112
  B. Affirmative Duties and State Created Danger 121
     L. W. v. Grubbs 121

II. Section 1983 and Federal "Laws" 127
     Wilder v. Virginia Hospital Association 127
     Suter v. Artist M. 137

CHAPTER 5   "EVERY PERSON": GOVERNMENTAL LIABILITY 145

I. What Governmental Bodies Are Persons? 145
  A. The Prior Law Under *Monroe* 145
  B. The Change in *Monell* 146
     Monell v. Department of Social Services 146
  C. The Status of States as "Persons": *Will* 153
     Will v. Michigan Department of State Police 153

II. The Immunities of Governmental Bodies 160
  A. Qualified Immunity and Compensatory Damages: *Owen* 160
     Owen v. City of Independence, Missouri 160
  B. A Note on *Facts Concerts* and Absolute Immunity From Punitive
     Damage Liability 165

III. How Does One Sue a Governmental Body? 165
  A. Pleading Requirements: *Leatherman* 165
     Leatherman v. Tarrant County Narcotics Unit 165
  B. The Crucial Distinction Between Official and Individual Capacity
     Damages Actions 167
  C. The Requirement of a Constitutional Violation: *Heller* 169

IV. The First Route to Governmental Liability: The Government Itself Acts 169
  A. Formal Official Policy 169
  B. Custom 170

V. The Second Route to Governmental Liability: Attribution Through Policymakers 170
  A. *Pembaur*: The Court's First Encounter With Attribution 170
     Pembaur v. City of Cincinnati 170
  B. *Praprotnik*: The Court's Second Encounter With Attribution 177
     City of St. Louis v. Praprotnik 177
  C. *Jett*: Most (But Not All) of the Questions Resolved 184
  D. Application of the Attribution Rules 185

CHAPTER 5 – *continued*

VI. The Third Route to Governmental Liability: Failure to Train   186
  A. Failure to Train and Single Incidents   186
  B. *City of Canton*   187
      City of Canton, Ohio v. Harris   187
  C. Supervisory Liability and Deliberate Indifference After *City of Canton*
      and *Farmer*   192

VII. Ethical Considerations   193
     Dunton v. County of Suffolk, State of New York   193

CHAPTER 6   "[S]UBJECTS OR CAUSES TO BE SUBJECTED. . .": CAUSATION 199

I. Cause in Fact   199
  A. Mixed Motives   200
      Mt. Healthy City School District Board of Education v. Doyle   200
  B. Governmental and Supervisory Liability   205
      1. Causation and Municipal Policy   206
          Buffington v. Baltimore County   206
      2. Causation and Supervisory Liability   212
          LaMarca v. Turner   212

II. Proximate or Legal Cause   216
  A. Remote Consequences   216
      Martinez v. California   216
  B. Intervening Acts   219
      Barts v. Joyner   219

CHAPTER 7   "EVERY PERSON": ABSOLUTE IMMUNITY   225

I. Absolute Legislative Immunity   225
  A. *Tenney*: The Seminal Case on Absolute Legislative Immunity   225
      Tenney v. Brandhove   225
  B. The Functional Approach of *Lake Country Estates*: Local and
      Regional Legislators   229
  C. A Note on Prospective Relief   231

II. Absolute Judicial Immunity   233
  A. The Common Law Immunity Background in 1871: *Bradley*   233
  B. *Pierson*: The Seminal Case on Absolute Judicial Immunity   234
  C. The Broad Scope of Absolute Judicial Immunity: *Stump*   235
      Stump v. Sparkman   235
  D. The Functional Approach to Judicial Immunity as a Double-Edged Sword:
      Judges, Court Reporters and Prison Disciplinary Hearing Offices   239
  E. *Pulliam* and Prospective Relief   240
  F. A Note on Witness Immunity and Its Connection to Judicial
      Immunity: *Briscoe*   241

III. Absolute Prosecutorial Immunity   242
  A. *Imbler*: The Seminal Absolute Prosecutorial Immunity Case   242
      Imbler v. Pachtman   242
  B. *Burns*: The Prosecutor as Legal Advisor   246
      Burns v. Reed   246
  C. Circuit Court Cases   250
  D. A Note on Prospective Relief   251

CHAPTER 7 – *continued*

IV. Procedural Aspects of Absolute Immunity   251
   A. The Burden of Pleading   251
   B. A Note on Appeal From Denial of an Absolute Immunity Motion to
       Dismiss or for Summary Judgment   252

CHAPTER 8   "EVERY PERSON": QUALIFIED IMMUNITY   **253**

  I. The Origins of Qualified Immunity   253
   A. *Pierson*: The Seminal Qualified Immunity Case and the Two-Part Test   253
      Pierson v. Ray   253
   B. A Note on the Application and Further Elaboration of the Two-Part Test
       to Governors, Mental Health Officials, Prison Officials and School Officials   256

  II. The Transformation of Qualified Immunity   257
   A. *Harlow*   257
      Harlow v. Fitzgerald   257
   B. A Note on *Celolex* and Summary Judgment Practice
       Under Rule 56   262
   C. *Anderson*:   *Harlow* Modified?   262
      Anderson v. Creighton   262
   D. *Siegert*: The Qualified Immunity Inquiry into the Merits of the Prima
       Facie Case   266

  III. The Clearly Settled Law Inquiry   267
   A. What Is Clearly Settled Law?   267
   B. Whose Decisions Determine Clearly Settled Law?   268
   C. Are Some Constitutional Violations Automatically Violations of Clearly
       Settled Law as Well?   269

  IV. Procedural Aspects of Qualified Immunity   270
   A. A Note on Pleading   270
   B. Burden of Proof and Clearly Settled Law   271
   C. The Roles of Court and Jury in the Qualified Immunity Determination   271
      Hunter v. Bryant   272
   D. Interlocutory Appeals and *Mitchell*   276
      Mitchell v. Forsyth   277

  V. Who Is Protected by Qualified Immunity?   280
   A. A Refresher Note on the Functional Approach   280
   B. The Status of Private Persons Who Act Under Color of Law   280
      Wyatt v. Cole   281
   C. Tension with the Functional Approach   286
   D. The Aftermath of *Wyatt*   287
   E. Concluding Questions   288

**CHAPTER 9   "[S]HALL BE LIABLE TO THE PARTY INJURED IN AN ACTION
         AT LAW, SUIT IN EQUITY OR OTHER PROPER PROCEEDING
         FOR REDRESS": CONSTITUTIONAL TORT REMEDIES**   **289**

  I. Damages   289
   A. Compensatory Damages   289
      Carey v. Piphus   289
      Memphis Community School District v. Stachura   296
   B. Punitive Damages   305
      Smith v. Wade   305
      Soderbeck v. Burnett County   314

CHAPTER 9 – *continued*

   C. Survival, Wrongful Death, and Other Damages Issues Ordinarily
      Addressed by Statutes   319
      Robertson v. Wegmann   319
      Berry v. City of Muscogee   326

  II. Prospective Relief   328
     City of Los Angeles v. Lyons   329

CHAPTER 10   PROCEDURAL DEFENSES   **339**

  I. Statutes of Limitations   339
     Wilson v. Garcia   339

  II. Release-Dismissal Agreements   346
     Town of Newton v. Rumery   346

  III. Issue and Claim Preclusion   354
     Migra v. Warren City School District Board of Education   355
     University of Tennessee v. Elliot   360

  IV. Exhaustion of Remedies   364

CHAPTER 11   LITIGATING SECTION 1983 CLAIMS IN STATE COURTS   **371**

  I. Must State Courts Hear Section 1983 Claims?   371
     Howlett v. Rose   371
     Notes on the Choice Between Federal and State Courts   381

  II. The Choice Between State and Federal Law   381
     Felder v. Casey   381

CHAPTER 12   ATTORNEY'S FEES   **391**

  I. Legislative History   391
     The Civil Rights Attorney's Fees Awards Act of 1976, Senate Report No. 94-1011   391

  II. When Is a Party Entitled to Attorney's Fees Under 42 U.S.C. § 1988?   394
     Farrar v. Hobby   394

  III. What is a "Reasonable" Fee?   403
     Hensley v. Eckerhart   403
     Jane L. v. Bangerter   410

  IV. Strategic and Ethical Aspects of Attorney's Fee Awards   422
     Evans v. Jeff D.   423

Table of Cases

Anderson v. Creighton, 262

Barts v. Joyner, 219
Berry v. City of Muscogee, 326
Bivens v. Six Unknown Named Agents of Federal Bureau of Narcotics, 16
Buffington v. Baltimore County, 206
Burns v. Reed, 246
Burton v. Wilmington Parking Authority, 48

Canton, Ohio, City of v. Harris, 187
Carey v. Piphus, 289
Collins v. City of Harker Heights, 98

Daniels v. Williams, 87
DeShaney v. Winnebago County Department of Social Services, 112
Dunton v. County of Suffolk, State of New York, 193

Evans v. Jeff D., 423

Farmer v. Brennan, 93
Farrar v. Hobby, 394
Felder v. Casey, 381
Flagg Bros., Inc. v. Brooks, 42

Graham v. Connor, 104

Harlow v. Fitzgerald, 257
Hensley v. Eckerhart, 403
Howlett v. Rose, 371
Hunter v. Bryant, 272

Imbler v. Pachtman, 242

Jane L. v. Bangerter, 410

LaMarca v. Turner, 212
Leatherman v. Tarrant County Narcotics Unit, 165
Los Angeles, City of v. Lyons, 329
Lugar v. Edmondson Oil Co., 35
L. W. v. Grubbs, 121

Martinez v. California, 216
Memphis Community School District v. Stachura, 296
Migra v. Warren City School District Board of Education, 355
Mitchell v. Forsyth, 277

Monnell v. Department of Social Services, 146
Monroe v. Pape, 3
Mt. Healthy City School District Board of Education v. Doyle, 200

National Collegiate Athletic Association v. Tarkanian, 59
Newton, Town of v. Rumery, 346

Owen v. City of Independence, Missouri, 160

Parratt v. Taylor, 70
Pembaur v. City of Cincinnati, 170
Pierson v. Ray, 253

Rendell-Baker v. Kohn, 51
Robertson v. Wegmann, 319

St. Louis, City of v. Praprotnik, 177
Schweiker v. Chilicky, 22
Smith v. Wade, 305
Soderbeck v. Burnett County, 314
Stump v. Sparkman, 235
Suter v. Artist M., 137

Tenney v. Brandhove, 225

University of Tennessee v. Elliot, 360

Wilder v. Virginia Hospital Association, 127
Will v. Michigan Department of State Police, 153
Wilson v. Garcia, 339
Wyatt v. Cole, 281

Zinermon v. Burch, 75

Preface

CONSTITUTIONAL TORTS: CASES, COMMENTS AND QUESTIONS

Constitutional Torts is the first casebook to focus exclusively on constitutional tort damages actions brought against governments and their officials under 42 U.S.C. section 1983 and the United States Constitution (*Bivens* actions). A course in constitutional torts allows students to integrate their knowledge of torts, constitutional law, federal courts and civil procedure and apply it to a dynamic field of litigation. We also include materials addressing strategic and ethical decisions facing those who litigate those issues. Our primary objective is to offer materials that teach the underlying theories of constitutional tort liability while at the same time providing a solid foundation for practicing in the field.

This casebook is unique in several other respects. Unlike other casebooks dealing with related topics, *Constitutional Torts* emphasizes important circuit court decisions together with relevant Supreme Court case law. This enables students to see how principles articulated in Supreme Court decisions are implemented by lower courts. The casebook also addresses affirmative duties, constitutional tort actions in state courts and attorney's fees, topics that are frequently slighted in civil rights and federal courts casebooks and courses. Further, *Constitutional Torts* is organized around the statutory language of section 1983, thereby driving home the crucial distinction between prima facie case and constitutional tort immunities and defenses.

The notes, comments and questions that precede and follow the cases are vital components of this casebook. These materials are carefully designed to lead students to understand the cases they read, to consider the implications of those cases, to perceive the questions left unanswered and to force students to connect what they have just finished reading to issues they previously encountered. These materials often raise difficult theoretical questions that must be confronted if constitutional torts are to be understood. As a result, insightful ideas and perspectives contained in treatises and law review articles play a prominent role in *Constitutional Torts*.

Constitutional Torts can be used in both introductory and advanced courses meeting either two hours or three hours weekly. What is covered obviously depends on the number of hours allotted. Our experience is that each chapter requires at least two hours of classroom time for adequate coverage. However, some difficult chapters will profit from twice that, while others can be covered in somewhat less time with selective deletions.

Each of the authors carefully read and is jointly responsible for the entire manuscript. However, we individually assumed primary responsiblity for the following chapters: Nahmod, chapters 1, 5, 7, and 8; Wells, chapters 2, 3, part of 4, 9 and 11; and Eaton, part of 4, 6, 10 and 12.

We wish to express our appreciation to our law schools for their support of this project. We thank Professors Kathryn Urbonya and Dan Coenen for their helpful comments on an earlier draft of these materials. We also want to thank Ashley Sexton, Derick Gilbert and Jay Nohr for their valuable research assistance.

Please feel free to contact any of us by phone or by email via the Internet.

Sheldon H. Nahmod
Distinguished Professor of Law
Chicago-Kent College of Law
Illinois Institute of Technology
312.906.5261
{snahmod@mail.kentlaw.edu}

Michael L. Wells
J. Alton Hosch Professor of Law
University of Georgia School of Law
706.542.5142
{wells@jd.lawsch.uga.edu}

Thomas A. Eaton
J. Alton Hosch Professor of Law
University of Georgia School of Law
706.542.5177
{eaton@jd.lawsch.uga.edu}

CHAPTER ONE

Constitutional Torts: A First Look

Constitutional torts are actions brought against governments and their officials and employees seeking damages for the violation of federal constitutional rights, particularly those arising under the Fourteenth Amendment and the Bill of Rights. Tens of thousands of such actions are filed annually in the federal courts, with some in the state courts as well. See generally Eisenberg and Schwab, *The Reality of Constitutional Tort Litigation*, 72 Corn. L. Rev. 641 (1987). In addition, hardly a term of the United States Supreme Court goes by without at least a half-dozen important constitutional tort-related decisions handed down. The overwhelming majority of these actions are brought against state and local governments and their officials and employees under 42 U.S.C. § 1983, probably the most resorted-to federal civil rights statute. A minority are brought against federal officials pursuant to *Bivens v. Six Unknown Named Agents*, 403 U.S. 388 (1971).

Constitutional torts are of considerable practical significance. They represent attempts to render governments and their officials and employees accountable in damages for the constitutional harm they cause. Large sums of money are frequently at stake, a factor that is accentuated by the availability of attorney's fees to prevailing plaintiffs under the Civil Rights Attorney's Fees Awards Act of 1976, 42 U.S.C. § 1988, as discussed in Chapter 12. Constitutional tort actions are thus often bitterly contested.

Constitutional torts raise fascinating and difficult theoretical issues of constitutional and statutory interpretation. Indeed, some of these issues are captured by the term "constitutional torts" itself. For example, what is the connection between tort concepts of accountability and the proper interpretation of section 1983? To what extent does the possibility of damages liability for constitutional torts affect judicial decisions on constitutional issues? Constitutional torts raise different questions as well. For example, federalism concerns are deeply impli-cated in many constitutional tort cases because in such cases federal courts interpret and apply federal law to the conduct of state and local governments and their officials and employees. Government efficiency is also implicated in constitutional tort litigation because the specter of liability may overdeter government officials and employees in the performance of their government duties. Moreover, there is the often-stated position (especially by some federal judges) that federal courts are being overburdened by constitutional tort cases of questionable merit.

It will prove helpful as you go through these materials to envision the structure (*not* the substance) of constitutional torts in tort-like terms. From this structural perspective, the doctrine of constitutional torts can be divided into two parts: the elements of the prima facie case—including duty, basis of liability and causation—on the one hand, and various immunities and defenses on the other. These are extensively considered in this casebook. There are subsidiary doctrines relating to federal court jurisdiction, procedural defenses such as statutes of limitations and preclusion and state court constitutional tort actions that also are addressed. These doctrines, interesting in their own right, often have a good deal of practical significance in the real world of constitutional torts and, together with attorney's fees issues, must therefore be mastered.

I. The Text of Section 1983 and Its Jurisdictional Counterpart

42 U.S.C. § 1983 reads as follows:

Every person who, under color of any statute, ordinance, regulation, custom, or usage, of any State or Territory or the District of Columbia, subjects, or causes to be subjected, any citizen of the United States or other person within the jurisdiction thereof to the deprivation of any rights, privileges, or immunities secured by the Constitution and laws, shall be liable to the party injured in an action at law, suit in equity, or other proper proceeding for redress. For the purposes of this section, any Act of Congress applicable exclusively to the District of Columbia shall be considered to be a statute of the District of Columbia.

28 U.S.C. § 1343(3) reads in relevant part as follows:

(a) The district courts shall have original jurisdiction of any civil action authorized by law to be commenced by any person: . . .

(3) To redress the deprivation, under color of any State law, statute, ordinance, regulation, custom or usage, of any right, privilege or immunity secured by the Constitution of the United States or by any Act of Congress providing for equal rights of citizens or of all persons within the jurisdiction of the United States; . . .

(b) For purposes of this section—

(1) the District of Columbia shall be considered to be a State; and

(2) any Act of Congress applicable exclusively to the District of Columbia shall be considered to be a statute of the District of Columbia.

II. History and Purposes of Section 1983

Section 1983 is modeled on section 2 of the Civil Rights Act of 1866, which made criminal certain acts committed by persons "under color of any law, statute, ordinance, regulation, or custom." Section 2 of the 1866 Act is the predecessor of 18 U.S.C. § 242, the criminal counterpart of section 1983 recently used as the basis for the federal criminal prosecutions of various Los Angeles police officers involved in the Rodney King controversy. See *Adickes v. Kress*, 398 U.S. 144, 162–63 (1970). Section 1983 and its jurisdictional counterpart, 28 U.S.C. § 1343(3), specifically began as section 1 of the Ku Klux Klan Act of April 20, 1871, which was enacted by Congress pursuant to

section 5 of the Fourteenth Amendment in order to enforce that amendment. See *Monroe v. Pape*, 365 U.S. 167, 171 (1961). This purpose is clear from the title of section 1, "An Act to enforce the Provisions of the Fourteenth Amendment to the Constitution of the United States, and for other Purposes." 17 Stat. 13 (1871).

In 1874 Congress codified existing law and, as a result, the substantive portion of section 1 of the 1871 Act became a separate section identical to the present section 1983. The section's coverage also was expanded beyond constitutionally secured rights, privileges, and immunities to include those secured by federal laws as well. Ultimately, the jurisdictional counterpart became 28 U.S.C. § 1343(3). See *Lynch v. Household Finance Corp.*, 405 U.S. 538, 543 n.7 (1972).

The Supreme Court has broadly described the primary purpose of section 1983 in the following terms:

As a result of the new structure of law that emerged in the post-Civil War era— and especially of the Fourteenth Amendment, which was its centerpiece—the role of the Federal Government as a guarantor of basic federal rights against state power was clearly established. Section 1983 opened the federal courts to private citizens, offering a uniquely federal remedy against incursions under the claimed authority of state law upon rights secured by the Constitution and laws of the Nation

. . . .

The very purpose of section 1983 was to interpose the federal courts between the States and the people, as guardians of the people's federal rights—to protect the people from unconstitutional action under color of state law, "whether that action be executive, legislative, or judicial."

Mitchum v. Foster, 407 U.S. 225, 238–39, 242 (1972). The Court has also indicated that section 1983 was designed both to prevent the states from violating the Fourteenth Amendment and certain federal statutes and to compensate injured plaintiffs for deprivations of their federal rights. *Carey v. Piphus*, 435 U.S. 247 (1978).

Section 1983 is directed not only at unconstitutional laws, but also at affording protection of "a federal right in federal courts because, by reason of prejudice, passion, neglect, intolerance or otherwise, state laws might not be enforced and the claims of citizens to the enjoyment of rights, privileges and immunities guaranteed by the Fourteenth Amendment might be denied by the state agencies." *Monroe v. Pape*, 365 U.S. 167, 180 (1961).

III. *Monroe v. Pape,* The Seminal Decision

Although section 1983 was enacted in 1871, it was largely dormant for ninety years for various reasons. One was the restrictive application of the state action doctrine as exemplified in the *Civil Rights Cases*, 109 U.S. 3 (1883). A second was the narrow reading of the Fourteenth Amendment's privileges and immunities clause and section 1983's jurisdictional counterpart. See *Slaughter-House Cases*, 83 U.S. 36 (1873) and *Hague v. CIO*, 307 U.S. 496, 531 (1939) (concurring opinion of Justice Stone). Still another was the Supreme Court's initial refusal to incorporate completely the provisions of the Bill of Rights, *e.g., Adamson v. California*, 332 U.S. 46 (1947), although the Supreme Court has since selectively incorporated most of those provisions. See, on the importance of this last factor, Weinberg, *The* Monroe *Mystery Solved: Beyond the "Unhappy History" Theory of Civil Rights Litigation*, 1991 B.Y.U. L. Rev. 737. However, in 1961 a sea change occurred in the status of section 1983 with the seminal decision in *Monroe v. Pape*. In that year, there were approximately 150 non-prisoner section 1983 cases filed, while twenty-five years later, in 1986, there were approximately 10,000! See *id* at 738, n.9.

Monroe v. Pape

365 U.S. 167 (1961)

Mr. Justice **Douglas** delivered the opinion of the Court.

This case presents important questions concerning the construction of R.S. § 1979, 42 U.S.C. § 1983, which reads as follows:

"Every person who, under color of any statute, ordinance, regulation, custom, or usage, of any State or Territory, subjects, or causes to be subjected, any citizen of the United States or other person within the jurisdiction thereof to the deprivation of any rights, privileges, or immunities secured by the Constitution and laws, shall be liable to the party injured in an action at law, suit in equity, or other proper proceeding for redress."

The complaint alleges that 13 Chicago police officers broke into petitioners' home in the early morning, routed them from bed, made them stand naked in the living room, and ransacked every room, emptying drawers and ripping mattress covers. It further alleges that Mr. Monroe was then taken to the police station and detained on "open" charges for 10 hours, while he was interrogated about a two-day-old murder, that he was not taken before a magistrate, though one was accessible, that he was not permitted to call his family or attorney, that he was subsequently released without criminal charges being preferred against him. It is alleged that the officers had no search warrant and no arrest warrant and that they acted "under color of the statutes, ordinances, regulations, customs and usages" of Illinois and of the City of Chicago. Federal jurisdiction was asserted under R.S. § 1979, which we have set out above, and 28 U.S.C. § 1343 and 28 U.S.C. § 1331.

The City of Chicago moved to dismiss the complaint on the ground that it is not liable under the Civil Rights Acts nor for acts committed in performance of its governmental functions. All defendants moved to dismiss, alleging that the complaint alleged no cause of action under those Acts or under the Federal Constitution. The District Court dismissed the complaint. The Court of Appeals affirmed, relying on its earlier decision, *Stift v. Lynch*. The case is here on a writ of certiorari which we granted because of a seeming conflict of that ruling with our prior cases.

I

Petitioners claim that the invasion of their home and the subsequent search without a warrant and the arrest and detention of Mr.

Monroe without a warrant and without arraignment constituted a deprivation of their "rights, privileges, or immunities secured by the Constitution" within the meaning of R.S. § 1979. It has been said that when 18 U.S.C. § 241 made criminal a conspiracy "to injure, oppress, threaten, or intimidate any citizen in the free exercise or enjoyment of any right or privilege secured to him by the Constitution," it embraced only rights that an individual has by reason of his relation to the central government, not to state governments. But the history of the section of the Civil Rights Act presently involved does not permit such a narrow interpretation.

Section 1979 came onto the books as § 1 of the Ku Klux Act of April 20, 1871. It was one of the means whereby Congress exercised the power vested in it by § 5 of the Fourteenth Amendment to enforce the provisions of that Amendment. Senator Edmunds, Chairman of the Senate Committee on the Judiciary, said concerning this section:

"The first section is one that I believe nobody objects to, as defining the rights secured by the Constitution of the United States when they are assailed by any State law or under color of any State law, and it is merely carrying out the principles of the civil rights bill, which has since become a part of the Constitution," the Fourteenth Amendment.

Its purpose is plain from the title of the legislation, "An Act to enforce the Provisions of the Fourteenth Amendment to the Constitution of the United States, and for other Purposes." Allegation of facts constituting a deprivation under color of state authority of a right guaranteed by the Fourteenth Amendment satisfies to that extent the requirement of R.S. § 1979. So far petitioners are on solid ground. For the guarantee against unreasonable searches and seizures contained in the Fourth Amendment has been made applicable to the States by reason of the Due Process Clause of the Fourteenth Amendment.

II

There can be no doubt at least since *Ex parte Virginia*, that Congress has the power to enforce provisions of the Fourteenth Amendment against those who carry a badge of authority of a State and represent it in some capacity, whether they act in accordance with their authority or misuse it. The question with which we now deal is the narrower one of whether Congress, in enacting § 1979, meant to give a remedy to parties deprived of constitutional rights, privileges and immunities by an official's abuse of his position. We conclude that it did so intend.

It is argued that "under color of" enumerated state authority excludes acts of an official or policeman who can show no authority under state law, state custom, or state usage to do what he did. In this case it is said that these policemen, in breaking into petitioners' apartment, violated the Constitution and laws of Illinois. It is pointed out that under Illinois law a simple remedy is offered for that violation and that, so far as it appears, the courts of Illinois are available to give petitioners that full redress which the common law affords for violence done to a person; and it is earnestly argued that no "statute, ordinance, regulation, custom or usage" of Illinois bars that redress.

The Ku Klux Act grew out of a message sent to Congress by President Grant on March 23, 1871, reading:

"A condition of affairs now exists in some States of the Union rendering life and property insecure and the carrying of the mails and the collection of the revenue dangerous. The proof that such a condition of affairs exists in some localities is now before the Senate. That the power to correct these evils is beyond the control of State authorities I do not doubt; that the power of the Executive of the United States, acting within the limits of existing laws, is sufficient for present emergencies is not clear. Therefore, I urgently recommend such legislation as in the judgment of Congress shall effectually secure life, liberty, and property, and the enforcement of law in all parts of the United States. . . ."

The legislation—in particular the section with which we are now concerned—had several purposes. There are threads of many thoughts running through the debates. One who reads them in their entirety sees that the present section had three main aims.

First, it might, of course, override certain kinds of state laws. Mr. Sloss of Alabama, in opposition, spoke of that object and emphasized that it was irrelevant because there were no such laws:

"The first section of this bill prohibits any invidious legislation by States against the rights or privileges of citizens of the United States. The object of this section is not very clear, as it is not pretended by its advocates on this floor that any State has passed any laws endangering the rights or privileges of the colored people."

Second, it provided a remedy where state law was inadequate. That aspect of the legislation was summed up as follows by Senator Sherman of Ohio:

". . . it is said the reason is that any offense may be committed upon a negro by a white man, and a negro cannot testify in any case against a white man, so that the only way by which any conviction can be had in Kentucky in those cases is in the United States courts, because the United States courts enforce the United States laws by which negroes may testify."

But the purposes were much broader. The third aim was to provide a federal remedy where the state remedy, though adequate in theory, was not available in practice. The opposition to the measure complained that "It overrides the reserved powers of the States," just as they argued that the second section of the bill "absorb[ed] the entire jurisdiction of the States over their local and domestic affairs."

* * *

It was precisely that breadth of the remedy which the opposition emphasized. Mr. Kerr of Indiana referring to the section involved in the present litigation said:

"This section gives to any person who may have been injured in any of his rights, privileges, or immunities of person or property, a civil action for damages against the wrongdoer in the Federal courts. The offenses committed against him may be the common violations of the municipal law of his State. It may give rise to numerous vexations and outrageous prosecutions, inspired by mere mercenary considerations, prosecuted in a spirit of plunder, aided by the crimes of perjury and subornation of perjury, more reckless and dangerous to society than the alleged offenses out of which the cause of action may have arisen. It is a covert attempt to transfer another large portion of jurisdiction from the State tribunals, to which it of right belongs, to those of the United States. It is neither authorized nor expedient, and is not calculated to bring peace, or order,

or domestic content and prosperity to the disturbed society of the South. The contrary will certainly be its effect."

Mr. Voorhees of Indiana, also speaking in opposition, gave it the same construction:

"And now for a few moments let us inspect the provisions of this bill, inspired as it is by the waning and decaying fortunes of the party in power, and called for, as I have shown, by no public necessity whatever. The first and second sections are designed to transfer all criminal jurisdiction from the courts of the States to the courts of the United States. This is to be done upon the assumption that the courts of the southern States fail and refuse to do their duty in the punishment of offenders against the law."

Senator Thurman of Ohio spoke in the same vein about the section we are now considering:

"It authorizes any person who is deprived of any right, privilege, or immunity secured to him by the Constitution of the United States, to bring an action against the wrong-doer in the Federal courts, and that without any limit whatsoever as to the amount in controversy. The deprivation may be of the slightest conceivable character, the damages in the estimation of any sensible man may not be five dollars or even five cents; they may be what lawyers call merely nominal damages; and yet by this section jurisdiction of that civil action is given to the Federal courts instead of its being prosecuted as now in the courts of the States."

The debates were long and extensive. It is abundantly clear that one reason the legislation was passed was to afford a federal right in federal courts because, by reason of prejudice, passion, neglect, intolerance or otherwise, state laws might not be enforced and the claims of citizens to the enjoyment of rights, privileges, and immunities guaranteed by the Fourteenth Amendment might be denied by the state agencies.

* * *

Although the legislation was enacted because of the conditions that existed in the South at that time, it is cast in general language and is as applicable to Illinois as it is to the States whose names were mentioned over and again in the debates. It is no answer that the State has a law which if enforced would give relief. The federal remedy is supplementary to the state remedy, and the latter need not be first sought and refused before the federal one is invoked. Hence the fact that Illinois by its constitution and laws outlaws unreasonable searches and seizures is no barrier to the present suit in the federal court.

We had before us in *United States v. Classic*, § 20 of the Criminal Code, which provides a criminal punishment for anyone who "under color of any law, statute, ordinance, regulation, or custom" subjects any inhabitant of a State to the deprivation of "any rights, privileges, or immunities secured or protected by the Constitution or laws of the United States." Section 242 first came into the law as § 2 of the Civil Rights Act, 1866. After passage of the Fourteenth Amendment, this provision was re-enacted and amended by §§ 17, 18, Act of May 31, 1870. The right involved in the *Classic* case was the right of voters in a primary to have their votes counted. The laws of Louisiana required the defendants "to count the ballots, to record the result of the count, and to certify the result of the election." But according to the indictment they did not perform their duty. In an opinion written by Mr. Justice (later Chief Justice) Stone, in which Mr. Justice Roberts, Mr. Justice Reed, and MR. JUSTICE FRANKFURTER joined, the Court ruled, "Misuse of power, possessed by virtue of state law and made possible only because the wrongdoer is clothed with the authority of state law, is action taken 'under color of' state law." There was a dissenting opinion; but the ruling as to the meaning of "under color of" state law was not questioned.

That view of the meaning of the words "under color of" state law, was reaffirmed in *Screws v. United States*. The acts there complained of were committed by state officers in performance of their duties, making an arrest effective. It was urged there, as it is here, that "under color of" state law should not be construed to duplicate in federal law what was an offense under state law. It was said there, as it is here, that the ruling in the Classic case as to the meaning of "under color of" state law was not in focus and was ill-advised. It was argued there, as it is here, that "under color of" state law included only action taken by officials pursuant to state law. We rejected that view.

* * *

Mr. Shellabarger, reporting out the bill which became the Ku Klux Act, said of the provision with which we now deal:

"The model for it will be found in the second section of the act of April 9, 1866, known as the 'civil rights act.' . . . This section of this bill, on the same state of facts, not only provides a civil remedy for persons whose former condition may have been that of slaves, but also to all people where, under color of State law, they or any of them may be deprived of rights . . . ."

Thus, it is beyond doubt that this phrase should be accorded the same construction in both statutes—in § 1979 and in 18 U.S.C. § 242.

* * *

We conclude that the meaning given "under color of" law in the *Classic* case and in the *Screws* and *Williams* cases was the correct one; and we adhere to it.

In the *Screws* case we dealt with a statute that imposed criminal penalties for acts "wilfully" done. We construed that word in its setting to mean the doing of an act with "a specific intent to deprive a person of a federal right." We do not think that gloss should be placed on § 1979 which we have here. The word "wilfully" does not appear in § 1979. Moreover, § 1979 provides a civil remedy, while in the *Screws* case we dealt with a criminal law challenged on the ground of vagueness. Section 1979 should be read against the background of tort liability that makes a man responsible for the natural consequences of his actions.

So far, then, the complaint states a cause of action. There remains to consider only a defense peculiar to the City of Chicago.

III

The City of Chicago asserts that it is not liable under § 1979. We do not stop to explore the whole range of questions tendered us on this issue at oral argument and in the briefs. For we are of the opinion that Congress did not undertake to bring municipal corporations within the ambit of § 1979.

When the bill that became the Act of April 20, 1871, was being debated in the Senate, Senator Sherman of Ohio proposed an amendment which would have made "the inhabitants of the county, city, or parish" in which certain acts of violence occurred liable "to pay full compensation" to the person damaged or his widow or legal representative. The amendment was adopted by the Senate. The House, however, rejected it. The Conference Committee reported another version. The House rejected the Conference report. In a second conference the Sherman amendment was dropped and in its place § 6 of the Act of April 20, 1871, was substituted. This new section, which is now R.S. § 1981, dropped out all provision for municipal liability and extended liability in damages to "any person or persons, having knowledge that any" of the specified wrongs are being committed. Mr. Poland, speaking for the House Conferees about the Sherman proposal to make municipalities liable, said:

"We informed the conferees on the part of the Senate that the House had taken a stand on that subject and would not recede from it; that that section imposing liability upon towns and counties must go out or we should fail to agree."

The objection to the Sherman amendment stated by Mr. Poland was that "the House had solemnly decided that in their judgment Congress had no constitutional power to impose any obligation upon county and town organizations, the mere instrumentality for the administration of state law." The question of constitutional power of Congress to impose civil liability on municipalities was vigorously debated with powerful arguments advanced in the affirmative.

Much reliance is placed on the Act of February 25, 1871, entitled "An Act prescribing the Form of the enacting and resolving Clauses of Acts and Resolutions of Congress, and Rules for the Construction thereof." Section 2 of this Act provides that "the word 'person' may extend and be applied to bodies politic and corporate." It should be noted, however, that this definition is merely an allowable, not a mandatory, one. It is said that doubts should be resolved in favor of municipal liability because private remedies against officers for illegal searches and seizures are conspicuously ineffective, and because municipal liability will not only afford plaintiffs responsible defendants but cause those defendants to eradicate abuses that exist at the police level. We do not reach those policy considerations. Nor do we reach the constitutional question whether Congress has the power to make municipalities liable for acts of its officers that violate the civil rights of individuals.

The response of the Congress to the proposal to make municipalities liable for certain actions being brought within federal purview by the Act of April 20, 1871, was so antagonistic that we cannot believe that the word "person" was used in this particular Act to include them.

Accordingly we hold that the motion to dismiss the complaint against the City of Chicago was properly granted. But since the complaint should not have been dismissed against the officials the judgment must be and is

Reversed.

Mr. Justice **Frankfurter**, dissenting except insofar as the Court holds that this action cannot be maintained against the City of Chicago.

Abstractly stated, this case concerns a matter of statutory construction. So stated, the problem before the Court is denuded of illuminating concreteness and thereby of its far-reaching significance for our federal system. Again abstractly stated, this matter of statutory construction is one upon which the Court has already passed. But it has done so under circumstances and in settings that negative those considerations of social policy upon which the doctrine of stare decisis, calling for the controlling application of prior statutory construction, rests.

* * *

Of course, if Congress by appropriate statutory language attempted to reach every act which could be attributed to the States under the Fourteenth Amendment's prohibition: "No State shall . . .," the reach of the statute would be the reach of the Amendment itself. Relevant to the enforcement of such a statute would be not only the concept of state action as this Court has developed it, but also considerations of the power of Congress, under the Amendment's Enforcement Clause, to determine what is "appropriate legislation" to protect the rights which the Fourteenth Amendment secures. In this supposed case we would arrive at the question of what Congress could do only after we had determined what it was that Congress had done. So, in the case before us now, we must ask what Congress did in 1871. We must determine what Congress meant by "under color" of enumerated state authority.

Congress used that phrase not only in R.S. § 1979, but also in the criminal provisions of § 2 of the First Civil Rights Act of April 9, 1866, from which is derived the present 18 U.S.C. § 242, and in both cases used it with the same purpose. During the seventy years which followed these enactments, cases in this Court in which the "under color" provisions were invoked uniformly involved action taken either in strict pursuance of some specific command of state law or within the scope of executive discretion in the administration of state laws. The same is true, with two exceptions, in the lower federal courts. In the first of these two cases it was held that § 1979 was not directed to instances of lawless police brutality, although the ruling was not put on "under color" grounds. In the second, an indictment charging a county tax collector with depriving one Ah Koo of a federally secured right under color of a designated California law, set forth in the indictment, was held insufficient against a demurrer. The court wrote:

"The indictment contains no averment that Ah Koo was a foreign miner, and within the provisions of the state law. If this averment be unnecessary . . . the act of congress would then be held to apply to a case of illegal extortion by a tax collector from any person, though such exaction might be wholly unauthorized by the law under which the officer pretended to act.

"We are satisfied that it was not the design of congress to prevent or to punish such abuse of authority by state officers. The object of the act was, not to prevent illegal exactions, but to forbid the execution of state laws, which, by the act itself, are made void. . . .

"It would seem, necessarily, to follow, that the person from whom the tax was exacted must have been a person from whom, under the provisions of the state law, the officer was authorized to exact it. The statute requires that a party shall be subjected to a deprivation of right secured by the statute under color of some law, statute, order or custom; but if this exaction, although made by a tax collector, has been levied upon a person not within the provisions of the state law, the exaction can-

not be said to have been made 'under color of law,' any more than a similar exaction from a Chinese miner, made by a person wholly unauthorized, and under the pretense of being a tax collector."

Throughout this period, the only indication of this Court's views on the proper interpretation of the "under color" language is a dictum in the *Civil Rights Cases*. There, in striking down other Civil Rights Act provisions which, as the Court regarded them, attempted to reach private conduct not attributable to state authority, Mr. Justice Bradley contrasted those provisions with § 2 of the Act of 1866: "This [latter] law is clearly corrective in its character, intended to counteract and furnish redress against State laws and proceedings, and customs having the force of law, which sanction the wrongful acts specified."

A sharp change from this uniform application of seventy years was made in 1941, but without acknowledgment or indication of awareness of the revolutionary turnabout from what had been established practice. The opinion in *United States v. Classic*, accomplished this. The case presented an indictment under § 242 charging certain local Commissioners of Elections with altering ballots cast in a primary held to nominate candidates for Congress. Sustaining the sufficiency of the indictment in an extensive opinion concerned principally with the question whether the right to vote in such a primary was a right secured by the Constitution, Mr. Justice Stone wrote that the alteration of the ballots was "under color" of state law. This holding was summarily announced without exposition; it had been only passingly argued. Of the three authorities cited to support it, two did not involve the "under color" statutes, and the third, *Hague v. C.I.O.*, was a case in which high-ranking municipal officials claimed authorization for their actions under municipal ordinances (here held unconstitutional) and under the general police powers of the State. All three of these cases had dealt with "State action" problems, and it is "State action," not the very different question of the "under color" clause, that Mr. Justice Stone appears to have considered. (I joined in this opinion without having made an independent examination of the legislative history of the relevant legislation or of the authorities drawn upon for the *Classic* construction. Acquiescence so founded does not preclude the responsible recognition of error disclosed by subsequent study.) When, however, four years later the Court was called on to review the conviction under § 242 of a Georgia County Sheriff who had beaten a Negro prisoner to death, the opinion of four of the six Justices who believed that the statute applied merely invoked *Classic* and stare decisis and did not reconsider the meaning which that case had uncritically assumed was to be attached to the language, "under color" of state authority. The briefs in the *Screws* case did not examine critically the legislative history of the Civil Rights Acts. The only reference to this history in the plurality opinion, insofar as it bears on the interpretation of the clause "under color of . . . law," is contained in a pair of sentences discounting two statements by Senators Trumbull and Sherman regarding the Civil Rights Acts of 1866 and 1870, cited by the minority. The bulk of the plurality opinion's treatment of the issue consists of the argument that "under color" had been construed in Classic and that the construction there put on the words should not be abandoned or revised. The case of *Williams v. United States*, reaffirmed *Screws* and applied it to circumstances of third-degree brutality practiced by a private detective who held a special police officer's card and was accompanied by a regular policeman.

"The rule of stare decisis, though one tending to consistency and uniformity of decision, is not inflexible." It is true, of course, that the reason for the rule is more compelling in cases involving inferior law, law capable of change by Congress, than in constitutional cases, where this Court—although even in such cases a wise consciousness of the limitations of individual vision has impelled it always to give great weight to prior decisions—nevertheless bears the ultimate obligation for the development of the law as institutions develop. But the Court has not always declined to re-examine cases whose outcome Congress might have changed.

And with regard to the Civil Rights Acts there are reasons of particular urgency which authorize the Court—indeed, which make it the Court's responsibility—to reappraise in the hitherto skimpily considered context of R.S. § 1979 what was decided in *Classic*, *Screws* and *Williams*. This is not an area of commercial law in which, presumably, individuals may have arranged their affairs in reliance on the expected stability of decision. Nor is it merely a mine-run statutory question involving a narrow compass of individual rights and duties. The issue in the present case concerns directly a basic problem of American federalism: the relation of the Nation to the States in the critically important sphere of municipal law administration. In this aspect, it has significance approximating constitutional dimension. Necessarily, the construction of the Civil Rights Acts raises issues fundamental to our institutions. This imposes on this Court a corresponding obligation to exercise its power within the fair limits of its judicial discretion. "We recognize that stare decisis embodies an important social policy. It represents an element of continuity in law, and is rooted in the psychologic need to satisfy reasonable expectations. But stare decisis is a principle of policy and not a mechanical formula of adherence to the latest decision, however recent and questionable . . . ."

Now, while invoking the prior decisions which have given "under color of [law]" a content that ignores the meaning fairly comported by the words of the text and confirmed by the legislative history, the Court undertakes a fresh examination of that legislative history. The decision in this case, therefore, does not rest on stare decisis, and the true construction of the statute may be thought to be as free from the restraints of that doctrine as though the matter were before us for the first time. Certainly, none of the implications which the Court seeks to draw from silences in the minority reports of congressional committees in 1956, 1957, and 1960, or from the use of "under color" language in the very different context of the Act of May 6, 1960,—concerned, in relevant part, with the preservation of election records and with the implementation of the franchise—serves as an impressive bar to re-examination of the true scope of R.S. § 1979 itself in its pertinent legislative setting.

This case squarely presents the question whether the intrusion of a city policeman for which that policeman can show no such authority at state law as could be successfully interposed in defense to a state-law action against him, is nonetheless to be regarded as "under color" of state authority within the meaning of R.S. § 1979. Respondents, in breaking into the Monroe apartment, violated the laws of the State of Illinois. Illinois law appears to offer a civil remedy for unlawful searches; petitioners do not claim that none is available. Rather they assert that they have been deprived of due process of law and of equal protection of the laws under color of state law, although from all that appears the courts of Illinois are available to give them the fullest redress which the common law affords for the violence done them, nor does any "statute, ordinance, regulation, custom, or usage" of the State of Illinois bar that redress. Did the enactment by Congress of § 1 of the Ku Klux Act of 1871 encompass such a situation?

* * *

The general understanding of the legislators unquestionably was that, as amended, the Ku Klux Act did "not undertake to furnish redress for wrongs done by one person upon another in any of the States . . . in violation of their laws, unless he also violated some law of the United States, nor to punish one person for an ordinary assault and battery . . . ." Even those who—opposing the constitutional objectors—found sufficient congressional power in the Enforcement Clause of the Fourteenth Amendment to give this kind of redress, deemed inexpedient the exercise of any such power: "Convenience and courtesy to the States suggest a sparing use, and never so far as to supplant the State authorities except in cases of extreme necessity, and when the State governments criminally refuse or neglect those duties which are imposed upon them." Extreme Radicals, those who believed that the remedy for the oppressed Unionists in the South was a general expansion of federal judicial jurisdiction so that "loyal men could have the privilege of having their causes, civil and criminal, tried in the Federal courts," were disappointed with the Act as passed.

Finally, it is significant that the opponents of the Act, exhausting ingenuity to discover constitutional objections to every provision of it, also construed § 1 as addressed only to conduct authorized by state law, and therefore within the admitted permissible reach of Fourteenth Amendment federal power. "The first section of this bill prohibits any invidious legislation by States against the rights or privileges of citizens of the United States," one such opponent paraphrased the provision.

And Senator Thurman, who insisted vociferously on the absence of federal power to penalize a conspiracy of individuals to violate state law ("that is a case of mere individual violence, having no color whatsoever of authority of law, either Federal or State; and to say that you can punish men for that mere conspiracy, which is their individual act, and which is a crime against the State laws themselves, punishable by the State laws, is simply to wipe out all the State jurisdiction over crimes and transfer it bodily to the Congress"), admitted without question the constitutionality of § 1 ("It refers to a deprivation under color of law, either statute law or 'custom or usage' which has become common law").

The Court now says, however, that "It was not the unavailability of state remedies but the failure of certain States to enforce the laws with an equal hand that furnished the powerful momentum behind this 'force bill.'" Of course, if the notion of "unavailability" of remedy is limited to mean an absence of statutory, paper right, this is in large part true. Insofar as the Court undertakes to demonstrate—as the bulk of its opinion seems to do—that § 1979 was meant to reach some instances of action not specifically authorized by the avowed, apparent, written law inscribed in the statute books of the States, the argument knocks at an open door. No one would or could deny this, for by its express terms the statute comprehends deprivations of federal rights under color of any "statute, ordinance, regulation, custom, or usage" of a State. The question is, what class of cases other than those involving state statute law were meant to be reached. And, with respect to this question, the Court's conclusion is undermined by the very portions of the legislative debates which it cites. For surely the misconduct of individual municipal police officers, subject to the effective oversight of appropriate state administrative and judicial authorities, presents a situation which differs toto coelo from one in which "Immunity is given to crime, and the records of the public tribunals are searched in vain for any evidence of effective redress," or in which murder rages while a State makes "no successful effort to bring the guilty to punishment or afford protection or redress," or in which the "State courts . . . [are] unable to enforce the criminal laws . . . or to suppress the disorders existing," or in which, in a State's "judicial tribunals one class is unable to secure that enforcement of their rights and punishment for their infraction which is accorded to another," or "of . . . hundreds of outrages . . . not one [is] punished," or "the courts of the . . . States fail and refuse to do their duty in the punishment of offenders against the law," or in which a "class of officers charged under the laws with their administration permanently and as a rule refuse to extend [their] protection." These statements indicate that Congress—made keenly aware by the post-bellum conditions in the South that States through their authorities could sanction offenses against the individual by settled practice which established state law as truly as written codes—designed § 1979 to reach, as well, official conduct which, because engaged in "permanently and as a rule," or "systematically," came through acceptance by law-administering officers to constitute "custom, or usage" having the cast of law. They do not indicate an attempt to reach, nor does the statute by its terms include, instances of acts in defiance of state law and which no settled state practice, no systematic pattern of official action or inaction, no "custom, or usage, of any State," insulates from effective and adequate reparation by the State's authorities.

Rather, all the evidence converges to the conclusion that Congress by § 1979 created a civil liability enforceable in the federal courts only in instances of injury for which redress was barred in the state courts because some "statute, ordinance, regulation, custom, or usage" sanctioned the grievance complained of. This purpose, manifested even by the so-called "Radical" Reconstruction Congress in 1871, accords with the presuppositions of our federal system. The jurisdiction which Article III of the Constitution conferred on the national judiciary reflected the assumption that the state courts, not the federal courts, would remain the primary guardians of that fundamental security of person and property which the long evolution of the common law had secured to one individual as against other individuals. The Fourteenth Amendment did not alter this basic aspect of our federalism. Its commands were addressed to the States. Only when the States, through their responsible organs for the formulation and administra-

tion of local policy, sought to deny or impede access by the individual to the central government in connection with those enumerated functions assigned to it, or to deprive the individual of a certain minimal fairness in the exercise of the coercive forces of the State, or without reasonable justification to treat him differently than other persons subject to their jurisdiction, was an overriding federal sanction imposed. As between individuals, no corpus of substantive rights was guaranteed by the Fourteenth Amendment, but only "due process of law" in the ascertainment and enforcement of rights and equality in the enjoyment of rights and safeguards that the States afford. This was the base of the distinction between federal citizenship and state citizenship drawn by the Slaughter-House Cases. This conception begot the "State action" principle on which, from the time of the Civil Rights Cases, this Court has relied in its application of Fourteenth Amendment guarantees. As between individuals, that body of mutual rights and duties which constitute the civil personality of a man remains essentially the creature of the legal institutions of the States.

But, of course, in the present case petitioners argue that the wrongs done them were committed not by individuals but by the police as state officials. There are two senses in which this might be true. It might be true if petitioners alleged that the redress which state courts offer them against the respondents is different than that which those courts would offer against other individuals, guilty of the same conduct, who were not the police. This is not alleged. It might also be true merely because the respondents are the police—because they are clothed with an appearance of official authority which is in itself a factor of significance in dealings between individuals. Certainly the night-time intrusion of the man with a star and a police revolver is a different phenomenon than the night-time intrusion of a burglar. The aura of power which a show of authority carries with it has been created by state government. For this reason the national legislature, exercising its power to implement the Fourteenth Amendment, might well attribute responsibility for the intrusion to the State and legislate to protect against such intrusion. The pretense of authority alone might seem to Congress sufficient basis for creating an exception to the ordinary rule that it is to the state tribunals that individuals within a State must look for redress against other individuals within that State. The same pretense of authority might suffice to sustain congressional legislation creating the exception. But until Congress has declared its purpose to shift the ordinary distribution of judicial power for the determination of causes between co-citizens of a State, this Court should not make the shift. Congress has not in § 1979 manifested that intention.

* * *

[The concurring opinion of Justices Harlan and Stewart is omitted.]

NOTES

1. What constitutional violations are the defendants accused of? Are these Fourteenth Amendment violations, Bill of Rights violations or both? What difference does it make? Why did the plaintiff seek damages and not prospective relief?

2. What is the defendants' argument regarding "color of law?" Is their argument one of statutory interpretation or is it based on Congressional power under section 5 of the Fourteenth Amendment?

3. In *Monroe*, what is the connection between section 1983's "color of law" language and the Fourteenth Amendment's state action requirement? According to the Court, are they coextensive? According to Justice Frankfurter? *Monroe* indicates that color of law is for the most part coextensive with state action under the Fourteenth Amendment. Color of law and state action are discussed in detail in Chapter 2.

4. Who is more persuasive on the color of law argument, the Court or Justice Frankfurter? For extensive discussions, contrast Zagrans, *"Under Color Of" What Law: A Reconstructed Model of Section 1983 Liability*, 71 Va. L. Rev. 499 (1985), arguing that Justice Frankfurter was correct, reprinted in Nahmod, *A Section 1983 Civil Rights Anthology* 19 (1993) [hereafter referred to as *Section 1983 Anthology*] and Winter, *The Meaning of "Under Color of" Law*, 91 Mich. L. Rev. 323 (1992), maintaining that the Court was correct and that "color" means "pretense." Suppose Justice Frankfurter had prevailed? What would that have done to the

scope of section 1983? What would the relation between state law and section 1983 have been? What would the *Monroe* plaintiff's remedy have been?

5. *Monroe* rejects a specific intent requirement and declares that section 1983 is to be interpreted against a "background of tort liability" that makes a person responsible for the consequences of his or her conduct. What could this mean: Does it refer to duty? To causation in fact? To proximate cause? Whatever it means, is *Monroe* itself an easy or hard case in which to hold the defendants accountable in damages?

6. What intentional torts did the *Monroe* defendants allegedly commit? If intent in the tort sense is present, does it automatically follow that the defendants should be liable in damages for constitutional harm caused? *Restatement (Second) of Torts* § 8A (1965) defines intent ". . . to denote that the actor desires to cause the consequences of his act, or that he believes that the consequences are substantially certain to result from it." Is this what the Court means by the "background of tort liability"?

7. The "background of tort liability" language in *Monroe* proved troublesome for a time. Some federal courts began to talk in terms of section 1983 "negligence" actions and section 1983 "recklessness" actions, on the assumption that *Monroe* articulated some kind of state of mind requirement for the section 1983 prima facie case *as a matter of statutory interpretation*. This position is described and rebutted in Nahmod, *Section 1983 and the "Background" of Tort Liability*, 50 Ind. L.J. 5 (1974), reprinted in *Section 1983 Anthology* 14. Thereafter, the Supreme Court rejected this position in *Parratt v. Taylor*, 451 U.S. 527 (1981), where it held that section 1983 does not contain a state of mind requirement for the prima facie case.

Parratt, a very important case in several respects, is analyzed in a due process context in Chapter 3. For present purposes, you should keep in mind that while section 1983 in fact does not have its own state of mind requirement for the prima facie case, certain constitutional provisions do have particular state of mind requirements *as a matter of constitutional interpretation*. For example, at least deliberate indifference is necessary to make out an Eighth Amendment violation, *Estelle v. Gamble*, 429

U.S. 97 (1976); purposeful discrimination is necessary for an equal protection violation, *Washington v. Davis*, 426 U.S. 229 (1976); and negligence is not enough for a due process violation, *Daniels v. Williams*, 474 U.S. 327 (1986). Thus, a section 1983 plaintiff claiming an equal protection violation must allege and prove purposeful discrimination; one claiming an Eighth Amendment violation must allege and prove at least deliberate indifference; and so on.

8. The "background of tort liability" is important in another respect: To what extent, if at all, is section 1983 doctrine to be determined by tort law? Should tort concepts of responsibility, including, for example, causation in fact, proximate cause, joint and several liability and damages, govern section 1983 liability? Should these tort concepts govern constitutional interpretation in a section 1983 setting? See Abernathy, *Section 1983 and Constitutional Torts*, 77 Geo. L.J. 1441 (1989). What is the role, if any, of *fault*? See Jeffries, *Compensation for Constitutional Torts: Reflections of the Significance of Fault*, 88 Mich. L. Rev. 82 (1989), arguing that the section 1983 damages remedy is predominantly based on fault.

Notice that the characterization "constitutional tort" appears to give prominence to the noun "tort" and to make the adjective "constitutional" secondary. For the argument that the use of tort rhetoric in section 1983 cases does in fact tend improperly to encourage tort-like approaches to section 1983 liability while minimizing the significance of section 1983's constitutional dimension, see Nahmod, *Section 1983 Discourse: The Move from Constitution to Tort*, 77 Geo. L.J. 1719, reprinted in *Section 1983 Anthology* 278.

Whether this argument is correct or not, the nature of the relationship among constitutional interpretation, section 1983 interpretation and tort law pervades all of section 1983 doctrine. See, by way of example, Chapter 6 on causation, Chapter 7 on absolute immunity, Chapter 8 on qualified immunity and Chapter 9 on remedies.

9. What is the scope of section 1983 damages actions after *Monroe*? Does it include *all* Fourteenth Amendment violations, whether due process, equal protection or incorporated provisions of the Bill of Rights, and however "trivial"? Consider Shapo, *Constitutional Tort:* Monroe v. Pape *and the Frontiers Beyond*, 60 Nw. U. L. Rev. 277 (1965), reprinted in *Section 1983 Anthology* 4, which argues that the proper standard of section 1983 liability should be "outrageous conduct" going beyond the garden variety tort action.

10. Section 1983 is intended to promote compliance with the Fourteenth Amendment as well as to compensate for harm caused by Fourteenth Amendment violations. Does *Monroe*'s remedial scheme, in which government officials and employees are personally liable while local governments are not, effectively promote compliance with the Fourteenth Amendment? Does it effectively promote the compensation function of section 1983? Or might this scheme sometimes *overdeter* state and local government officials and employees by discouraging them from exercising independent judgment because of the fear of liability?

The concern with overdeterrence is especially implicated in section 1983 case law dealing with immunities, as discussed extensively in Chapters 7 and 8. In this connection, notice that the language of section 1983 does not on its face refer to the availability of affirmative defenses to individual liability. Yet it turns out that the Supreme Court, relying on the "background of tort liability," has found absolute and qualified immunity applicable to certain persons sued under section 1983. The first such immunity case, *Tenney v. Brandhove*, 341 U.S. 367 (1951), analyzed in Chapter 7, applied absolute legislative immunity ten years before *Monroe* was decided.

11. Can you imagine situations in which the regulation of conduct function and the compensation function of section 1983 are in conflict? Consider that the portion of *Monroe* holding that local governments are not suable persons under section 1983 was overruled by the Supreme Court in 1978 in *Monell v. Department of Social Services*, 436 U.S. 658 (1978). Did that change render section 1983 more effective by providing a deep pocket defendant so that constitutionally damaged persons would have a greater incentive to sue? *Monell* and local government liability in general are considered at length in Chapter 5.

IV. Constitutional Torts and Exhaustion of Judicial Remedies

Monroe makes clear that a plaintiff who has a section 1983 cause of action for damages need not exhaust or pursue state judicial remedies before filing in a federal forum. (Why should this be?) The Court rejected the arguments of the defendants in *Monroe* that the plaintiff should proceed in state court. It asserted: "It is no answer that the State has a law which if enforced would give relief. The federal remedy is supplementary to the state remedy, and the latter need not first be sought and refused before the federal one is invoked." Significantly, *Monroe*'s choice of judicial forum rule applies irrespective of the adequacy of the state judicial remedy. There are, however, several important qualifications of this no-exhaustion rule that you should be aware of.

Habeas Corpus. A prisoner, like other section 1983 plaintiffs, need not exhaust state judicial remedies as, for example, in challenging prison procedures or conditions, or the acts of prison authorities generally. However, the Supreme Court held in *Preiser v Rodriguez*, 411 U.S. 475 (1973), that a prisoner's section 1983 challenge to the *fact or duration of his or her confinement* is in substance a petition for habeas corpus and must be treated as such by the federal courts. Because the federal habeas corpus statute requires exhaustion of state judicial remedies, 28 U.S.C. § 2254, the effect of treating the section 1983 claim as federal habeas corpus is the dismissal of that claim from the federal forum altogether in situations where state judicial remedies have not yet been pursued. As a practical matter, if a prisoner challenges both the conditions of confinement and its length or fact, the latter challenge, being in the nature of habeas corpus, will be dismissed and the prisoner sent to the state courts. However, the former claim can still be pursued in federal court while state judicial proceedings are being conducted.

In its most recent section 1983 habeas corpus-related decision, the Supreme Court held in *Heck v. Humphrey*, 114 S. Ct. 2364 (1994) that "in order to recover damages for allegedly unconstitutional conviction or imprisonment, or for other harm caused by actions whose unlawfulness would render a conviction or sentence invalid, a § 1983 plaintiff must prove that the conviction or sentence has been reversed on direct appeal, expunged by executive order, declared invalid by a state tribunal authorized to make such a determination, or called into question by a federal court's issuance of a writ of habeas corpus." See Chapter 10 for a fuller discussion of *Heck*.

Due Process. In certain cases a decision adverse to a plaintiff's due process challenge amounts to a *de facto* requirement that state judicial remedies be exclusively pursued. For example, in *Paul v Davis*, 424 U.S. 693 (1976), the Supreme Court held that a section 1983 claim based on the due process clause was not stated where the plaintiff sought relief from being listed as an active shoplifter by police authorities. The Court held that no liberty or property interest was implicated; plaintiff's sole legal remedy was an action for defamation in the state courts. Similarly, in *Ingraham v Wright*, 430 U.S. 651 (1977), the Court held that procedural due process was not violated when school authorities imposed corporal punishment on students because students against whom excessive force was used would have a tort cause of action in the state courts. Finally, in *Hudson v Palmer*, 468 U.S. 517 (1984), the Court held that, in certain circumstances, intentional deprivations of property do not violate procedural due process where adequate post-deprivation remedies are available.

Indeed, these cases go well beyond a *de facto* exhaustion of judicial remedies requirement in holding that no section 1983 cause of action is stated at all; the federal forum is rendered totally unavailable at any time. This rule is broader than an exhaustion of judicial remedies requirement which would only *postpone* access to the federal forum. Procedural due process is addressed in Chapter 3.

Prospective Relief and the Younger *Rule.* Mention should be made of yet another qualification of this rule of no exhaustion of judicial remedies: where a section 1983 plaintiff seeks not damages but prospective relief. When state criminal judicial proceedings are already pending, a federal plaintiff seeking declaratory or injunctive relief against their continuation will typically be barred from the federal forum by reason of the Supreme Court's decision in *Younger v. Harris*, 401 U.S. 37 (1971). Barring the federal plaintiff amounts to a de facto exhaustion of judicial remedies requirement. Furthermore, the *Younger* rule has since been extended by the Supreme Court to include equitable relief against state judicial proceedings between private litigants where important state interests are implicated, *e.g.*, *Pennzoil Co. v. Texaco, Inc.*, 481 U.S. 1 (1987), as well as pending state administrative proceedings, *e.g.*, *Ohio Civil Rights Commission v. Dayton Christian Schools*, 477 U.S. 619 (1986), where important state interests are involved and there is a full and fair opportunity to litigate any constitutional claims upon state judicial review of that proceeding. The *Younger* rule and its progeny are extensively treated in most federal courts courses. See chapter 10.

Do these qualifications of the no-exhaustion rule tend to undermine the effectiveness of section 1983 in enforcing the Fourteenth Amendment? Or do they promote federalism and other important values? For an answer from the bench, see Blackmun, *Section 1983 and Federal Protection of Individual Rights— Will the Statute Remain Alive or Fade Away?*, 60 N.Y.U. L. Rev. 1 (1985), reprinted in *Section 1983 Anthology* 37.

V. Constitutional Torts and Exhaustion of Administrative Remedies

Suppose that a state provides an administrative proceeding which a prospective section 1983 plaintiff can use in an attempt to be made whole. Is the plaintiff required to exhaust that administrative remedy as a condition precedent to filing a section 1983 action in federal (or state) court? Might it not make sense to submit the plaintiff's claim first to an administrative tribunal which possesses expertise and experience in such matters? Although *Monroe* does not specifically address that question, consider the suggestion that it would have been anomalous to hold that exhaustion of judicial remedies is *not* required while at the same time ruling that exhaustion of administrative remedies *is* required. It would appear that a state administrative tribunal should be entitled to no more deference than that accorded a state judicial tribunal. In fact, the Supreme Court repeatedly asserted, beginning with *McNeese v. Board of*

Education, 373 U.S. 668 (1963), that state administrative remedies, like judicial remedies, need not be exhausted before maintaining a section 1983 action in federal court. In addition, the Court never in fact required exhaustion of state administrative remedies in a section 1983 case.

However, it was not until 1982, when the Court decided *Patsy v. Florida Board of Regents,* 457 U.S. 496 (1982), that the Supreme Court definitively ruled that exhaustion of administrative remedies is not a condition precedent to filing a section 1983 action. *Patsy* involved a section 1983 race and sex discrimination action brought by a secretary against a state university. Taking what it called a "flexible" approach, the Fifth Circuit had emphasized that exhaustion of administrative remedies should be required in section 1983 cases where an orderly system of review is provided; the agency is able to grant the relief requested; relief is available promptly; agency procedures are fair, not unduly burdensome, and not used to harass; and interim relief is available to preserve the litigant's section 1983 rights until the administrative process is concluded.

The Supreme Court reversed in an opinion by Justice Marshall. At the outset the Court asserted that the no-exhaustion requirement was not an issue of first impression but rather had not been deviated from for 19 years. Next, the Court rejected the argument that an exhaustion requirement should be adopted. It emphasized that section 1983's legislative history shows that "Congress assigned to the federal courts a paramount role in protecting constitutional rights"; that the "1871 Congress would not have wanted to impose an exhaustion requirement"; and that many legislators interpreted section 1983 as "enabling the plaintiff to choose the forum in which to seek relief." The Court then went on to reject the defendants' contention that various policy considerations, including federal court burdens, comity, and improved federal-state relations, warranted an exhaustion requirement. According to the Court, the policy considerations respecting the existence of such a requirement, besides being complex, did not all cut in the same direction. Furthermore, the design and scope of an exhaustion requirement were equally difficult, and included categories of section 1983 claims, standards for evaluating administrative procedures, tolling and limitations problems, res judicata and collateral estoppel issues, and the like.

State Prisoners and Exhaustion of Administrative Remedies. As mentioned above, a prisoner's section 1983 claim is sometimes treated as federal habeas corpus and thereby becomes subject to an exhaustion of state judicial remedies requirement. In contrast, a section 1983 claim attacking prison conditions and events unrelated to the fact and duration of confinement is not, as a matter of section 1983 interpretation, subject to an exhaustion of administrative remedies requirement. However, Congress has legislated an exhaustion of administrative remedies requirement in certain circumstances for persons institutionalized in state or local government correctional facilities. The statute, the Civil Rights of Institutionalized Persons Act, is codified as 42 U.S.C. § 1997e. Among other things, the Act specifically provides that an inmate who sues under section 1983 shall, if appropriate and the interests of justice warrant, have his or her case continued by the court for 90 days so that the inmate may exhaust "such plain, speedy, and effective administrative remedies as are available."

Exhaustion under the Act may only be ordered, however, where the applicable administrative procedures are either certified by the Attorney General or are determined by the court to comply substantially with certain minimum acceptable standards. These standards, promulgated by the Attorney General and published in the Code of Federal Regulations, 28 C.F.R. §§ 4.01–.22 (pt. 40), include an advisory role for the inmates; time limits for written replies to inmate grievances; priority processing of emergency grievances; safeguards to avoid reprisals; and independent review of the disposition of grievances.

Why, as a matter of policy, should prisoners alone be subject to an exhaustion of administrative remedies requirement? See chapter 10.

VI. Constitutional Torts of Federal Officials: *Bivens* Actions

Suppose *federal* law enforcement officers violate a person's Fourth Amendment rights. Is a section 1983 damages remedy available? The clear answer is that it is *not* because section 1983 governs only conduct under color of state law, *not* federal law. Does it therefore follow that there is no damages remedy available? Consider carefully the following very important and influential Supreme Court decision.

Bivens v. Six Unknown Named Agents of Federal Bureau of Narcotics

403 U.S. 388 (1988)

Mr. Justice **Brennan** delivered the opinion of the Court.

The Fourth Amendment provides that:

"The right of the people to be secure in their persons, houses, papers, and effects, against unreasonable searches and seizures, shall not be violated . . . ."

In *Bell v. Hood*, we reserved the question whether violation of that command by a federal agent acting under color of his authority gives rise to a cause of action for damages consequent upon his unconstitutional conduct. Today we hold that it does.

This case has its origin in an arrest and search carried out on the morning of November 26, 1965. Petitioner's complaint alleged that on that day respondents, agents of the Federal Bureau of Narcotics acting under claim of federal authority, entered his apartment and arrested him for alleged narcotics violations. The agents manacled petitioner in front of his wife and children, and threatened to arrest the entire family. They searched the apartment from stem to stern. Thereafter, petitioner was taken to the federal courthouse in Brooklyn, where he was interrogated, booked, and subjected to a visual strip search.

On July 7, 1967, petitioner brought suit in Federal District Court. In addition to the allegations above, his complaint asserted that the arrest and search were effected without a warrant, and that unreasonable force was employed in making the arrest; fairly read, it alleges as well that the arrest was made without probable cause. n1 Petitioner claimed to have suffered great humiliation, embarrassment, and mental suffering as a result of the agents' unlawful conduct, and sought $15,000 damages from each of them. The District Court, on respondents' motion, dismissed the complaint on the ground, inter alia, that it failed to state a cause of action. The Court of Appeals, one judge concurring specially, affirmed on that basis. We granted certiorari.

We reverse.

I

Respondents do not argue that petitioner should be entirely without remedy for an unconstitutional invasion of his rights by federal agents. In respondents' view, however, the rights that petitioner asserts—primarily rights of privacy—are creations of state and not of federal law. Accordingly, they argue, petitioner may obtain money damages to redress invasion of these rights only by an action in tort, under state law, in the state courts. In this scheme the Fourth Amendment would serve merely to limit the extent to which the agents could defend the state law tort suit by asserting that their actions were a valid exercise of federal power: if the agents were shown to have violated the Fourth Amendment, such a defense would be lost to them and they would stand before the state law merely as private individuals. Candidly admitting that it is the policy of the Department of Justice to remove all such suits from the state to the federal courts for decision, respondents nevertheless urge that we uphold dismissal of petitioner's complaint in federal court, and remit him to filing an action in the state courts in order that the case may properly be removed to the federal court for decision on the basis of state law. We think that respondents' thesis rests upon an unduly restrictive view of the Fourth Amendment's protection against unreasonable searches and seizures by federal agents, a view that has consistently been rejected by this Court. Respondents seek to treat the relationship between a citizen and a federal agent unconstitutionally exercising his authority as no different from the relationship between two private citizens. In so doing, they ignore the fact that power, once granted, does not disappear like a magic gift when it is wrongfully used. An agent acting—albeit unconstitutionally—in the name of the United States possesses a far greater capacity for harm than an individual trespasser exercising no authority other than his own. Accordingly, as our cases make clear, the Fourth Amendment operates as a limitation upon the exercise of federal power regard-

less of whether the State in whose jurisdiction that power is exercised would prohibit or penalize the identical act if engaged in by a private citizen. It guarantees to citizens of the United States the absolute right to be free from unreasonable searches and seizures carried out by virtue of federal authority. And "where federally protected rights have been invaded, it has been the rule from the beginning that courts will be alert to adjust their remedies so as to grant the necessary relief."

First. Our cases have long since rejected the notion that the Fourth Amendment proscribes only such conduct as would, if engaged in by private persons, be condemned by state law. Thus in *Gambino v. United States*, petitioners were convicted of conspiracy to violate the National Prohibition Act on the basis of evidence seized by state police officers incident to petitioners' arrest by those officers solely for the purpose of enforcing federal law. Notwithstanding the lack of probable cause for the arrest, it would have been permissible under state law if effected by private individuals. It appears, moreover, that the officers were under direction from the Governor to aid in the enforcement of federal law. Accordingly, if the Fourth Amendment reached only to conduct impermissible under the law of the State, the Amendment would have had no application to the case. Yet this Court held the Fourth Amendment applicable and reversed petitioners' convictions as having been based upon evidence obtained through an unconstitutional search and seizure. Similarly, in *Byars v. United States*, the petitioner was convicted on the basis of evidence seized under a warrant issued, without probable cause under the Fourth Amendment, by a state court judge for a state law offense. At the invitation of state law enforcement officers, a federal prohibition agent participated in the search. This Court explicitly refused to inquire whether the warrant was "good under the state law . . . since in no event could it constitute the basis for a federal search and seizure." And our recent decisions regarding electronic surveillance have made it clear beyond peradventure that the Fourth Amendment is not tied to the niceties of local trespass laws. In light of these cases, respondents' argument that the Fourth Amendment serves only as a limitation on federal defenses to a state law claim, and not as an independent limitation upon the exercise of federal power, must be rejected.

Second. The interests protected by state laws regulating trespass and the invasion of privacy, and those protected by the Fourth Amendment's guarantee against unreasonable searches and seizures, may be inconsistent or even hostile. Thus, we may bar the door against an unwelcome private intruder, or call the police if he persists in seeking entrance. The availability of such alternative means for the protection of privacy may lead the State to restrict imposition of liability for any consequent trespass. A private citizen, asserting no authority other than his own, will not normally be liable in trespass if he demands, and is granted, admission to another's house. But one who demands admission under a claim of federal authority stands in a far different position. The mere invocation of federal power by a federal law enforcement official will normally render futile any attempt to resist an unlawful entry or arrest by resort to the local police; and a claim of authority to enter is likely to unlock the door as well. 'In such cases there is no safety for the citizen, except in the protection of the judicial tribunals, for rights which have been invaded by the officers of the government, professing to act in its name. There remains to him but the alternative of resistance, which may amount to crime." Nor is it adequate to answer that state law may take into account the different status of one clothed with the authority of the Federal Government. For just as state law may not authorize federal agents to violate the Fourth Amendment, neither may state law undertake to limit the extent to which federal authority can be exercised. The inevitable consequence of this dual limitation on state power is that the federal question becomes not merely a possible defense to the state law action, but an independent claim both necessary and sufficient to make out the plaintiff's cause of action.

Third. That damages may be obtained for injuries consequent upon a violation of the Fourth Amendment by federal officials should hardly seem a surprising proposition. Historically, damages have been regarded as the ordinary remedy for an invasion of personal interests in liberty. Of course, the Fourth Amendment does not in so many words provide for its enforcement by an award of money damages for the consequences of its violation. But "it is . . . well settled that where legal rights have been invaded, and a federal statute provides for a general right to sue for such invasion, federal courts may use any available remedy to make good the wrong done." The present case involves no special factors counselling hesitation in the absence of affirmative action by Congress. We are not dealing with a question of "federal fiscal policy," as in *United States v. Standard Oil Co.* In that case we refused to infer from the Government-soldier relationship that the United States could recover damages from one who negligently injured a soldier and thereby caused the Government to pay his medical expenses and lose his services during the course of his hospitalization. Noting that Congress was normally quite solicitous where the federal purse was involved, we pointed out that "the United States [was] the party plaintiff to the suit. And the United States has power at any time to create the liability." Nor are we asked in this case to impose liability upon a congressional employee for actions contrary to no constitutional prohibition, but merely said to be in excess of the authority delegated to him by the Congress. Finally, we cannot accept respondents' formulation of the question as whether the availability of money damages is necessary to enforce the Fourth Amendment. For we have here no explicit congressional declaration that persons injured by a federal officer's violation of the Fourth Amendment may not recover money damages from the agents, but must instead be remitted to another remedy, equally effective in the view of Congress. The question is merely whether petitioner, if he can demonstrate an injury consequent upon the violation by federal agents of his Fourth Amendment rights, is entitled to redress his injury through a particular remedial mechanism normally available in the federal courts. "The very essence of civil liberty certainly consists in the right of every individual to claim the protection of the laws, whenever he receives an injury." Having concluded that petitioner's complaint states a cause of action under the Fourth Amendment, we hold that petitioner is entitled to recover money damages for any injuries he has suffered as a result of the agents' violation of the Amendment.

II

In addition to holding that petitioner's complaint had failed to state facts making out a cause of action, the District Court ruled that in any event respondents were immune from liability by virtue of their official position. This question was not passed upon by the Court of Appeals, and accordingly we do not consider here. The judgment of the Court of Appeals is reversed and the case is remanded for further proceedings consistent with this opinion.

So ordered.

Mr. Justice **Harlan**, concurring in the judgment.

* * *

For the reasons set forth below, I am of the opinion that federal courts do have the power to award damages for violation of "constitutionally protected interests" and I agree with the Court that a traditional judicial remedy such as damages is appropriate to the vindication of the personal interests protected by the Fourth Amendment.

I

I turn first to the contention that the constitutional power of federal courts to accord Bivens damages for his claim depends on the passage of a statute creating a "federal cause of action." Although the point is not entirely free of ambiguity, I do not understand either the Government or my dissenting Brothers to maintain that Bivens' contention that he is entitled to be free from the type of official conduct prohibited by the Fourth Amendment depends on a decision by the State in which he resides to accord him a remedy. Such a position would be incompatible with the presumed availability of federal equitable relief, if a proper showing can be made in terms of the ordinary principles governing equitable remedies. However broad a federal court's discretion concerning equitable remedies, it is absolutely clear—at least after *Erie R. Co. v. Tompkins* —that in a non-diversity suit a federal court's power to grant even equitable relief depends on the presence of a substantive right derived from federal law.

Thus the interest which Bivens claims—to be free from official conduct in contravention of the Fourth Amendment—is a federally protected interest. Therefore, the question of judicial *power* to grant Bivens damages is not a problem of the "source" of the "right"; instead, the question is whether the power to authorize damages as a judicial remedy for the vindication of a federal constitutional right is placed by the Constitution itself exclusively in Congress' hands.

* * *

III

The major thrust of the Government's position is that, where Congress has not expressly authorized a particular remedy, a federal court should exercise its power to accord a traditional form of judicial relief at the behest of a litigant, who claims a constitutionally protected interest has been invaded, only where the remedy is "essential," or "indispensable for vindicating constitutional rights." While this "essentiality" test is most clearly articulated with respect to damage remedies, apparently the Government believes the same test explains the exercise of equitable remedial powers. It is argued that historically the Court has rarely exercised the power to accord such relief in the absence of an express congressional authorization and that "[i]f Congress had thought that federal officers should be subject to a law different than state law, it would have had no difficulty in saying so, as it did with respected to state officers * * *." Although conceding that the standard of determining whether a damage remedy should be utilized to effectuate statutory polices is one of "necessity" or "appropriateness," the Government contends that questions concerning congressional discretion to modify judicial remedies relating to constitutionally protected interests warrant a more stringent constraint on the exercise of judicial power with respect to this class of legally protected interests.

These arguments for a more stringent test to govern the grant of damages in constitutional cases seem to be adequately answered by the point that the judiciary has a particular responsibility to assure the vindication of constitutional interests such as those embraced by the Fourth Amendment. To be sure, "it must be remembered that legislatures are ultimate guardians of the liberties and welfare of the people in quite as great a degree as the courts." But it must also be recognized that the Bill of Rights is particularly intended to vindicate the interests of the individual in the face of the popular will as expressed in legislative majorities; at the very least, it strikes me as no more appropriate to await express congressional authorization of traditional judicial relief with regard to these legal interests than with respect to interests protected by federal statutes.

The question then, is, as I see it, whether compensatory relief is "necessary" or "appropriate" to the vindication of the interest asserted. In resolving that question, it seems to me that the range of policy considerations we may take into account is at least as broad as the range of a legislature would consider with respect to an express statutory authorization of a traditional remedy. In this regard I agree with the Court that the appropriateness of according Bivens compensatory relief does not turn simply on the deterrent effect liability will have on federal official conduct. Damages as a traditional form of compensation for invasion of a legally protected interest may be entirely appropriate even if no substantial deterrent effects on future official lawlessness might be thought to result. Bivens, after all, has invoked judicial processes claiming entitlement to compensation for injuries resulting from allegedly lawless official behavior, if those injuries are properly compensable in money damages. I do not think a court of law—vested with the power to accord a remedy—should deny him his relief simply because he cannot show that future lawless conduct will thereby be deterred.

And I think it is clear that Bivens advances a claim of the sort that, if proved, would be properly compensable in damages. The personal interests protected by the fourth Amendment are those we attempt to capture by the notion of "privacy"; while the Court today properly points out that the type of harm which officials can inflict when they invade protected zones of an individual's life are different from the types of harm private citizens inflict on one another, the experience of judges in dealing with private trespass and false imprisonment claims supports the conclusion that courts of law are capable of making the types of judgment concerning causation and magnitude of injury necessary to accord meaningful compensation of invasion of Fourth Amendment rights.

On the other hand, the limitation on state remedies for violation of common-law rights by private citizens argue in favor of federal damages remedy. The injuries inflicted by officials action under color of law, while no less compensable in damages than those inflicted by private parties, are substantially different in kind, as the Court's opinion today discusses in detail. See *Monroe v. Pape* (Harlan, J., concurring). It seems to me entirely proper that these injuries be compensable according to uniform rules of federal law, especially in light of the very large element of federal law which must in any event control the scope of official defenses to liability. Certainly, there is very little to be gained from the standpoint of federalism by preserving different rules of liability for federal officers dependent on the State where the injury occurs.

Putting aside the desirability of leaving the problem of federal official liability to the vagaries of common-law actions, it is apparent that some form of damages is the only possible remedy for someone in Bivens' alleged position. It will be a rare case indeed in which an individual in Bivens' position will be able to obviate the harm by securing injunctive relief from any court. However desirable a direct remedy against the Government might be as a substitute for individual official liability, the sovereign still remains immune to suit. Finally, assuming Bivens' innocence of the crime charged, the "exclusionary rule" is simply irrelevant. For the people in Bivens' shoes, it is damages or nothing.

The only substantial policy consideration advanced against recognition of a federal cause of action for violation of Fourth Amendment rights by federal officials is the incremental expenditure of judicial resources that will be necessitated by this class of litigation. There is, however, something ultimately self-defeating about this argument. For if, as the Government contends, damages will rarely be realized by plaintiffs in these cases because of jury hostility, the limited resources of the official concerned, etc., then I am not ready to assume that there will be a significant increase in the expenditure of judicial resources on these claims. Few responsible lawyers and plaintiffs are likely to choose the course of litigation if the statistical chances of success are truly *de minimis*. And I simply cannot agree with my Brother BLACK that the possibility of "frivolous" claims—if defined simply as claims with no legal merit—warrants closing the courthouse doors to people in Bivens' situation. There are other ways, short of that, of coping with frivolous lawsuits.

On the other hand, if—as I believe is the case with respect, at least, to the most flagrant abuses of official power—damages to some degree will be available when the option of litigation is chosen, then the question appears to be how Fourth Amendment interests rank on a scale of social values compared with, for example, the interests of stockholders defrauded by misleading proxies. Judicial resources, I am well aware, are increasingly scarce these days. Nonetheless, when we automatically close the courthouse door solely on this basis, we implicitly express a value judgement on the comparative importance of classes of legally protected interests. And current limitations upon the effective functioning of the courts arising from budgetary inadequacies should not be permitted to stand in the way of the recognition of otherwise sound constitutional principles.

Of course, for a variety of reasons, the remedy may not often be sought. And the countervailing interests in efficient law enforcement of course argue for a protective zone with respect to many types of Fourth Amendment violations. But, while I express no view on the immunity defense offered in the instant case, I deem it proper to venture the thought that at the very least such a remedy would be available for the most flagrant and patently unjustified sorts of police conduct. Although litigants may not often choose to seek relief, it is important, in a civilized society, that the judicial branch of the Nation's government stand ready to afford a remedy in these circumstances. It goes without saying that I intimate no view on the merits of petitioner's underlying claim.

[The dissenting opinions of Chief Justice Burger and Justices Black and Blackmun are omitted.]

NOTES

1. Why does the plaintiff in *Bivens* seek damages? Was any other remedy available?

2. What is the purpose of a *Bivens* Fourth Amendment damages remedy? To compensate? To deter? To punish?

3. Why not a state tort remedy? Is a Fourth Amendment damages remedy more effective? Does it protect different interests? Does it provide surer access to a federal forum? Do the Court and Justice Harlan differ on these matters?

4. Recall the Court's "background of tort liability" approach to interpreting section 1983 in *Monroe*. Does the Court adopt a similar approach to the nature and scope of Fourth Amendment damages actions in *Bivens*? Does Justice Harlan?

5. What is the role of Congress, according to the *Bivens* majority? According to Justice Harlan? What if Congress had provided a constitutional damages remedy against federal officials or the United States itself in such cases? Would that have made a difference in the outcome? Should it have? Is the creation of a constitutional damages action against federal officials primarily within the discretion with the Court?

6. Notice the implicit use in *Bivens* of 28 U.S.C. § 1331, the general federal question jurisdiction statute which at the time had a $10,000 amount in controversy requirement. In contrast, section 1983 has its own jurisdictional counterpart, 28 U.S.C. § 1343(3). Currently, section 1983 plaintiffs can use either section 1343(3) or section 1331, which no longer has an amount in controversy requirement.

7. Recall that *Monroe v. Pape* made clear that section 1983 creates a damages actions against state and local government officials and employees for their Fourteenth Amendment violations. What if there were no section 1983, or if section 1983 were repealed? Is it plausible to maintain, based on *Bivens*, that a Fourteenth Amendment damages action could be implied? Whatever your answer to this question, it appears that currently no such damages action is available apart from section 1983. Indeed, Justice Powell so declared in his concurring opinion in *Monell v. Department of Social Services*, 436 U.S. 658, 713–14 (1978). See, to the same effect, *Thomas v. Shipka*, 818 F.2d 496, 499 (6th Cir. 1987), *vacated on other grounds and remanded*, 488 U.S. 1036 (1989) and *Williams v. Bennett*, 689 F.2d 1370, 1390 (11th Cir. 1982). Compare *Lake Nacimiento Ranch Co. v. San Luis Obispo County*, 841 F.2d 872, 880 (9th Cir. 1988) which left the question undecided after noting that the Supreme Court had not resolved the matter.

VII. The Current Status of *Bivens* Actions

Eight years after *Bivens* the Supreme Court confronted a similar issue in *Davis v. Passman*, 442 U.S. 228 (1979), which held, in reliance on *Bivens*, that the plaintiff, a female deputy administrative assistant to a United States congressman, had a Fifth Amendment damages action against the congressman for his alleged violation of her right to be free from gender discrimination. The Court observed that a damages remedy was appropriate in the case before it; there were no "special concerns counselling hesitation"; there was no explicit congressional declaration that money damages should not be available; and there was little likelihood that the federal courts would be deluged with claims. Chief Justice Burger and Justices Powell and Rehnquist dissented, arguing among other things that separation of powers concerns, buttressed by congressional refusal to provide damages remedies to its staff employees, warranted a contrary result. *Davis* was shortly thereafter followed by *Carlson v. Green*, 446 U.S. 14 (1980), which similarly implied an Eighth Amendment damages action against federal prison officials, even though there was a damages remedy against the United States under the Federal Tort Claims Act, 60 Stat. 812, 842 (1946).

The tide began to turn in *Chappell v. Wallace*, 462 U.S. 296 (1983), where the Court unanimously ruled against enlisted personnel who, alleging racial discrimination in job assignments, sought damages from their commanding officers under the Constitution. The Court emphasized the existence of special factors counseling hesitation: control over the military and the command structure. Significantly, even though *Chappell*'s refusal to extend *Bivens* could have been limited to the special situation of the military, it quickly became clear that this would not be the case. Thus, in *Bush v. Lucas*, 462 U.S. 367 (1983), the Court ruled that there was no damages remedy for a federal employee who sued his supervisor for disciplining him for the exercise of his First Amendment rights. As in *Chappell*, here, too, there were "special

factors counseling hesitation in the absence of affirmative action by Congress," namely, that the federal employment relationship "is governed by comprehensive procedural and substantive provisions giving meaningful remedies against the United States." *Bush v. Lucas*, 462 U.S. at 368.

Consider the following case.

Schweiker v. Chilicky

487 U.S. 412 (1988)

Justice **O'Connor** delivered the opinion of the Court.

This case requires us to decide whether the improper denial of Social Security disability benefits, allegedly resulting from violations of due process by government officials who administered the federal Social Security program, may give rise to a cause of action for money damages against those officials. We conclude that such a remedy, not having been included in the elaborate remedial scheme devised by Congress, is unavailable.

I

A

Under Title II of the Social Security Act (Act), the Federal Government provides disability benefits to individuals who have contributed to the Social Security program and who, because of a medically determinable physical or mental impairment, are unable to engage in substantial gainful work. A very similar program for disabled indigents is operated under Title XVI of the Act, but those provisions are technically not at issue in this case. Title II, which is administered in conjunction with state welfare agencies, provides benefits only while an individual's statutory disability persists. In 1980, Congress noted that existing administrative procedures provided for reexamination of eligibility "only under a limited number of circumstances." Congress responded by enacting legislation requiring that most disability determinations be reviewed at least once every three years. Although the statute did not require this program for "continuing disability review" (CDR) to become effective before January 1,

1982, the Secretary of Health and Human Services initiated CDR in March 1981.

The administration of the CDR program was at first modeled on the previous procedures for reexamination of eligibility. Under these procedures, an individual whose case is selected for review bears the burden of demonstrating the continuing existence of a statutory disability. The appropriate state agency performs the initial review, and persons who are found to have become ineligible are generally provided with administrative review similar to the review provided to new claimants. Under the original CDR procedures, benefits were usually terminated after a state agency found a claimant ineligible, and were not available during administrative appeals.

Finding that benefits were too often being improperly terminated by state agencies, only to be reinstated by a federal administrative law judge (ALJ), Congress enacted temporary emergency legislation in 1983. This law provided for the continuation of benefits, pending review by an ALJ, after a state agency determined that an individual was no longer disabled. In the Social Security Disability Benefits Reform Act of 1984 (1984 Reform Act), Congress extended this provision until January 1, 1988, and provided for a number of other significant changes in the administration of CDR. In its final form, this legislation was enacted without a single opposing vote in either Chamber.

The problems to which Congress responded so emphatically were widespread. One of the cosponsors of the 1984 Reform Act, who had conducted hearings on the administration of CDR, summarized evidence from the General Accounting Office as follows: "[T]he message perceived by the State agencies, swamped with cases, was to deny, deny, deny, and, I might add, to process cases faster and faster and faster. In the name of efficiency, we have scanned our computer terminals, rounded up the disabled workers in the country, pushed the discharge button, and let them go into a free [f]all toward economic chaos."

Other legislators reached similar conclusions. Such conclusions were based, not only on anecdotal evidence, but on compellingly forceful statistics. The Social Security Administration itself apparently reported that about 200,000 persons were wrongfully terminated, and then reinstated, between March 1981 and April 1984. In the first year of CDR, half of those who were terminated appealed the decision, and "an amazing two-thirds of those who appealed were being reinstated."

Congress was also made aware of the terrible effects on individual lives that CDR had produced. The chairman of the Senate's Special Committee on Aging pointed out that "[t]he human dimension of this crisis—the unnecessary suffering, anxiety, and turmoil—has been graphically exposed by dozens of congressional hearings and in newspaper articles all across the country." Termination could also lead to the cut-off of Medicare benefits, so that some people were left without adequate medical care. There is little doubt that CDR led to many hardships and injuries that could never be adequately compensated.

B

Respondents are three individuals whose disability benefits under Title II were terminated pursuant to the CDR program in 1981 and 1982. Respondents Spencer Harris and Dora Adelerte appealed these determinations through the administrative process, were restored to disabled status, and were awarded full retroactive benefits. Respondent James Chilicky did not pursue these administrative remedies. Instead, he filed a new application for benefits about a year and a half after his benefits were stopped. His application was granted, and he was awarded one year's retroactive benefits; his application for the restoration of the other six months' benefits is apparently still pending. Because the terminations in these three cases occurred before the 1983 emergency legislation was enacted, respondents experienced delays of many months in receiving disability benefits to which they were entitled. All the respondents had been wholly dependent on their disability benefits, and all allege that they were unable to maintain themselves or their families in even a minimally adequate fashion after they were declared ineligible. Respondent James Chilicky was in the hospital recovering from open-heart surgery when he was informed that his heart condition was no longer disabling.

In addition to pursuing administrative remedies, respondents (along with several other individuals who have since withdrawn from the case) filed this lawsuit in the United States District Court for the District of Arizona.

They alleged that petitioners—one Arizona and two federal officials who had policy making roles in the administration of the CDR program—had violated respondents' due process rights. The thrust of the complaint, which named petitioners in their official and individual capacities, was that petitioners had adopted illegal policies that led to the wrongful termination of benefits by state agencies. Among the allegations were claims that petitioners improperly accelerated the starting date of the CDR program; illegally refused to acquiesce in decisions of the United States Court of Appeals for the Ninth Circuit; failed to apply uniform written standards in implementing the CDR program; failed to give effect to dispositive evidence in particular cases; and used an impermissible quota system under which state agencies were required to terminate predetermined numbers of recipients. Respondents sought injunctive and declaratory relief, and money damages for "emotional distress and for loss of food, shelter and other necessities proximately caused by [petitioners'] denial of benefits without due process."

The District Court dismissed the case on the ground that petitioners were protected by a qualified immunity. Their alleged conduct, the court concluded, did not violate "'clearly established statutory or constitutional rights of which a reasonable person would have known.'" Although the court discussed only the claims involving acceleration of the starting date for CDR and nonacquiescence in Ninth Circuit decisions, its qualified immunity holding apparently applied to respondents' other claims as well.

Respondents appealed, pressing only their claims for money damages against petitioners in their individual capacities. These claims, noted the Court of Appeals, are "predicated on the constitutional tort theory of *Bivens v. Six Unknown Named Agents*. Petitioners argued that the District Court lacked subject matter jurisdiction because the procedures set forth in 42 U.S.C. § 405(g), which do not authorize judicial review in a case like this one, provide the exclusive means of judicial redress for actions "arising under" the relevant provisions of the Act. The Court of Appeals rejected this argument, holding that subject matter jurisdiction existed because respondents' claims for emotional distress "arose under" the Due Process Clause of the Fifth Amendment rather than under the statute. The Court of Appeals went on to affirm the District Court to the extent that it dismissed the claims involving acceleration of the CDR program and nonacquiescence in Ninth Circuit decisions. As to respondents' other claims, however, the Court of Appeals concluded that "[i]t cannot be determined as a matter of law that [respondents] could prove no state of facts . . . that resulted in violations of their due process rights and consequent damages." The case was accordingly remanded for further proceedings, including a trial if necessary.

The petition for certiorari presented one question: "Whether a Bivens remedy should be implied for alleged due process violations in the denial of social security disability benefits."

We granted the petition, and now reverse.

II

A

The Constitution provides that federal courts may be given original jurisdiction over "all Cases, in Law and Equity, arising under this Constitution, the Laws of the United States, and Treaties made, or which shall be made, under their Authority." Since 1875, Congress has provided the federal trial courts with general jurisdiction over such cases. The statute currently provides that the "district courts shall have original jurisdiction of all civil actions arising under the Constitution, laws, or treaties of the United States."

In 1971, this Court held that the victim of a Fourth Amendment violation by federal officers acting under color of their authority may bring suit for money damages against the officers in federal court. *Bivens v. Six Unknown Fed. Narcotics Agents.* The Court noted that Congress had not specifically provided for such a remedy and that "the Fourth Amendment does not in so many words provide for its enforcement by an award of money damages for the consequences of its violation." Nevertheless, finding "no special factors counselling hesitation in the absence of affirmative action by Congress," and "no explicit congressional declaration" that money damages may not be awarded, the majority relied on the rule that "'where legal rights have been invaded, and a federal statute provides for a general right to sue for such invasion, federal courts may use any available remedy to make good the wrong done.'"

So-called *"Bivens* actions" for money damages against federal officers have subsequently been permitted under § 1331 for violations of the Due Process Clause of the Fifth Amendment, *Davis v. Passman*, and the Cruel and Unusual Punishments Clause of the Eighth Amendment, *Carlson v. Green*, In each of these cases, as in *Bivens* itself, the Court found that there were no "special factors counselling hesitation in the absence of affirmative action by Congress," no explicit statutory prohibition against the relief sought, and no exclusive statutory alternative remedy.

Our more recent decisions have responded cautiously to suggestions that Bivens remedies be extended into new contexts. The absence of statutory relief for a constitutional violation, for example, does not by any means necessarily imply that courts should award money damages against the officers responsible for the violation. Thus, in *Chappell v. Wallace*, we refused—unanimously—to create a *Bivens* action for enlisted military personnel who alleged that they had been injured by the unconstitutional actions of their superior officers and who had no remedy against the Government itself:

> The special nature of military life—the need for unhesitating and decisive action by military officers and equally disciplined responses by enlisted personnel—would be undermined by a judicially created remedy exposing officers to personal liability at the hands of those they are charged to command. . . .

> "Also, Congress, the constitutionally authorized source of authority over the military system of justice, has not provided a damages remedy for claims by military personnel that constitutional rights have been violated by superior officers. Any action to provide a judicial response by way of such a remedy would be plainly inconsistent with Congress' authority in this field.

> "Taken together, the unique disciplinary structure of the Military Establishment and Congress' activity in the field constitute 'special factors' which dictate that it would be inappropriate to provide enlisted mili-

tary personnel a Bivens-type remedy against their superior officers."

Similarly, we refused—again unanimously—to create a *Bivens* remedy for a First Amendment violation "aris[ing] out of an employment relationship that is governed by comprehensive procedural and substantive provisions giving meaningful remedies against the United States." *Bush v. Lucas*. In that case, a federal employee was demoted, allegedly in violation of the First Amendment, for making public statements critical of the agency for which he worked. He was reinstated through the administrative process, with retroactive seniority and full backpay, but was not permitted to recover for any loss due to emotional distress or mental anguish, or for attorney's fees. Concluding that the administrative system created by Congress "provides meaningful remedies for employees who may have been unfairly disciplined for making critical comments about their agencies," the Court refused to create a Bivens action even though it assumed a First Amendment violation and acknowledged that "existing remedies do not provide complete relief for the plaintiff." The Court stressed that the case involved policy questions in an area that had received careful attention from Congress. Noting that the Legislature is far more competent than the Judiciary to carry out the necessary "balancing [of] governmental efficiency and the rights of employees," we refused to "decide whether or not it would be good policy to permit a federal employee to recover damages from a supervisor who has improperly disciplined him for exercising his First Amendment rights."

In sum, the concept of "special factors counselling hesitation in the absence of affirmative action by Congress" has proved to include an appropriate judicial deference to indications that congressional inaction has not been inadvertent. When the design of a Government program suggests that Congress has provided what it considers adequate remedial mechanisms for constitutional violations that may occur in the course of its administration, we have not created additional *Bivens* remedies.

B

The administrative structure and procedures of the Social Security system, which affects virtually every American, "are of a size and extent difficult to comprehend." Millions of claims are filed every year under the Act's disability benefits programs alone, and these claims are handled under "an unusually protective [multi]-step process for the review and adjudication of disputed claims."

The steps provided for under Title II are essentially identical for new claimants and for persons subject to CDR. An initial determination of a claimant's eligibility for benefits is made by a state agency, under federal standards and criteria. Next, a claimant is entitled to de novo reconsideration by the state agency, and additional evidence may be presented at that time. If the claimant is dissatisfied with the state agency's decision, review may then be had by the Secretary of Health and Human Services, acting through a federal ALJ; at this stage, the claimant is again free to introduce new evidence or raise new issues. If the claimant is still dissatisfied, a hearing may be sought before the Appeals Council of the Social Security Administration. Once these elaborate administrative remedies have been exhausted, a claimant is entitled to seek judicial review, including review of constitutional claims. The Act, however, makes no provision for remedies in money damages against officials responsible for unconstitutional conduct that leads to the wrongful denial of benefits. As respondents concede, claimants whose benefits have been fully restored through the administrative process would lack standing to invoke the Constitution under the statute's administrative review provision.

The case before us cannot reasonably be distinguished from *Bush v. Lucas.* Here, exactly as in Bush, Congress has failed to provide for "complete relief": respondents have not been given a remedy in damages for emotional distress or for other hardships suffered because of delays in their receipt of Social Security benefits. The creation of a *Bivens* remedy would obviously offer the prospect of relief for injuries that must now go unredressed. Congress, however, has not failed to provide meaningful safeguards or remedies for the rights of persons situated as respondents were. Indeed, the system for protecting their rights is, if anything, considerably more elaborate than the civil service system considered in *Bush.* The prospect of personal liability for

official acts, moreover, would undoubtedly lead to new difficulties and expense in recruiting administrators for the programs Congress has established. Congressional competence at "balancing governmental efficiency and the rights of [individuals]," *Bush* is no more questionable in the social welfare context than it is in the civil service context.

Congressional attention to problems that have arisen in the administration of CDR (including the very problems that gave rise to this case) has, moreover, been frequent and intense. Congress itself required that the CDR program be instituted. Within two years after the program began, Congress enacted emergency legislation providing for the continuation of benefits even after a finding of ineligibility by a state agency. Less than two years after passing that law, and fully aware of the results of extensive investigations of the practices that led to respondents' injuries, Congress again enacted legislation aimed at reforming the administration of CDR; that legislation again specifically addressed the problem that had provoked the earlier emergency legislation. At each step, Congress chose specific forms and levels of protection for the rights of persons affected by incorrect eligibility determinations under CDR. At no point did Congress choose to extend to any person the kind of remedies that respondents seek in this lawsuit. Thus, congressional unwillingness to provide consequential damages for unconstitutional deprivations of a statutory right is at least as clear in the context of this case as it was in *Bush.*

Respondents nonetheless contend that *Bush* should be confined to its facts, arguing that it applies only in the context of what they call "the special nature of federal employee relations." Noting that the parties to this case did "not share the sort of close, collaborative, continuing juridical relationship found in the federal civil service," respondents suggest that the availability of *Bivens* remedies would create less "inconvenience" to the Social Security system than it would in the context of the civil service. Petitioners are less sanguine, arguing that the creation of *Bivens* remedy in this context would lead to "a complete disruption of [a] carefully crafted and constantly monitored congressional scheme."

We need not choose between these competing predictions, which have little bearing on the applicability of *Bush* to this case. The decision in *Bush* did not rest on this Court's belief that *Bivens* actions would be more disruptive of the civil service than they are in other contexts where they have been allowed, such as federal law enforcement agencies (*Bivens* itself) or the federal prisons (*Carlson v. Green*). Rather, we declined in Bush "'to create a new substantive legal liability . . .' because we are convinced that Congress is in a better position to decide whether or not the public interest would be served by creating it." That reasoning applies as much, or more, in this case as it did in itself.

Respondents also suggest that this case is distinguishable from *Bush* because the plaintiff in that case received compensation for the constitutional violation itself, while these respondents have merely received that to which they would have been entitled had there been no constitutional violation. The *Bush* opinion, however, drew no distinction between compensation for a "constitutional wrong" and the restoration of statutory rights that had been unconstitutionally taken away. Nor did it suggest that such labels would matter. Indeed, the Court appeared to assume that civil service employees would get "precisely the same thing whether or not they were victims of constitutional deprivation." *Bush* thus lends no support to the notion that statutory violations caused by unconstitutional conduct necessarily require remedies in addition to the remedies provided generally for such statutory violations. Here, as in *Bush*, it is evident that if we were "to fashion an adequate remedy for every wrong that can be proved in a case . . . [the complaining party] would obviously prevail." In neither case, however, does the presence of alleged unconstitutional conduct that is not separately remedied under the statutory scheme imply that the statute has provided "no remedy" for the constitutional wrong at issue.

The remedy sought in *Bush* was virtually identical to the one sought by respondents in this case: consequential damages for hardships resulting from an allegedly unconstitutional denial of a statutory right (Social Security benefits in one instance and employment in a particular Government job in the other). In light of the comprehensive statutory schemes involved, the harm resulting from the alleged constitutional violation can in neither case be separated from the harm resulting from the denial of the statutory right. Respondents' effort to separate the two does not distinguish this case from *Bush* in any analytically meaningful sense.

In the end, respondents' various arguments are rooted in their insistent and vigorous contention that they simply have not been adequately recompensed for their injuries. They say, for example:

> Respondents are disabled workers who were dependent upon their Social Security benefits when petitioners unconstitutionally terminated them. Respondents needed those benefits, at the time they were wrongfully withheld, to purchase food, shelter, medicine, and life's other necessities. The harm they suffered as a result bears no relation to the dollar amount of the benefits unjustly withheld from them. For the Government to offer belated restoration of back benefits in a lump sum and attempt to call it quits, after respondents have suffered deprivation for months on end, is not only to display gross insensitivity to the damage done to respondents' lives, but to trivialize the seriousness of petitioners' offense."

We agree that suffering months of delay in receiving the income on which one has depended for the very necessities of life cannot be fully remedied by the "belated restoration of back benefits." The trauma to respondents, and thousands of others like them, must surely have gone beyond what anyone of normal sensibilities would wish to see imposed on innocent disabled citizens. Nor would we care to "trivialize" the nature of the wrongs alleged in this case. Congress, however, has addressed the problems created by state agencies' wrongful termination of disability benefits. Whether or not we believe that its response was the best response, Congress is the body charged with making the inevitable compromises required in the design of a massive and complex welfare benefits program. Congress has discharged that responsibility to the extent that it affects the case before us, and we see no legal basis that would allow us to revise its decision.

Because the relief sought by respondents is unavailable as a matter of law, the case must be dismissed. The judgment of the Court of Appeals to the contrary is therefore Reversed.

Justice **Brennan**, with whom Justice **Marshall** and Justice **Blackmun** join, dissenting.

Respondents are three individuals who, because they are unable to engage in gainful employment as a result of certain disabilities, rely primarily or exclusively on disability benefits awarded under Title II of the Social Security Act, for their support and that of their families. Like hundreds of thousands of other such recipients, in the early 1980's they lost this essential source of income following state implementation of a federally mandated "continuing disability review" process (CDR), only to have an administrative law judge (ALJ) ultimately reinstate their benefits after appeal, or to regain them, as respondent James Chilicky did, by filing a new application for benefits. Respondents allege that the initial benefit termination resulted from a variety of unconstitutional actions taken by state and federal officials responsible for administering the CDR program. They further allege, and petitioners do not dispute, that as a result of these deprivations, which lasted from 7 to 19 months, they suffered immediate financial hardship, were unable to purchase food, shelter, and other necessities, and were unable to maintain themselves in even a minimally adequate fashion.

The Court today reaffirms the availability of a federal action for money damages against federal officials charged with violating constitutional rights. Acknowledging that the trauma respondents and others like them suffered as a result of the allegedly unconstitutional acts of state and federal officials "must surely have gone beyond what anyone of normal sensibilities would wish to see imposed on innocent disabled citizens," the Court does not for a moment suggest that the retroactive award of benefits to which respondents were always entitled remotely approximates full compensation for such trauma. Nevertheless, it refuses to recognize a *Bivens* remedy here because the "design of [the disability insurance] program suggests that Congress has provided what it considers adequate remedial mechanisms for constitutional violations that may occur in the course of its administration."

I agree that in appropriate circumstances we should defer to a congressional decision to substitute alternative relief for a judicially created remedy. Neither the design of Title

II's administrative review process, however, nor the debate surrounding its reform contains any suggestion that Congress meant to preclude recognition of a *Bivens* action for persons whose constitutional rights are violated by those charged with administering the program, or that Congress viewed this process as an adequate substitute remedy for such violations. Indeed, Congress never mentioned, let alone debated, the desirability of providing a statutory remedy for such constitutional wrongs. Because I believe legislators of "normal sensibilities" would not wish to leave such traumatic injuries unrecompensed, I find it inconceivable that Congress meant by mere silence to bar all redress for such injuries.

* * *

In *Bivens* itself, we noted that, although courts have the authority to provide redress for constitutional violations in the form of an action for money damages, the exercise of that authority may be inappropriate where Congress has created another remedy that it regards as equally effective, or where "special factors counse[l] hesitation [even] in the absence of affirmative action by Congress." Among the "special factors" the Court divines today in our prior cases is "an appropriate judicial deference to indications that congressional inaction has not been inadvertent." Describing congressional attention to the numerous problems the CDR process spawned as "frequent and intense," the Court concludes that the very design of that process "suggests that Congress has provided what it considers adequate remedial mechanisms for constitutional violations that may occur in the course of its administration." The cases setting forth the "special factors" analysis upon which the Court relies, however, reveal, by way of comparison, both the inadequacy of Title II's "remedial mechanism" and the wholly inadvertent nature of Congress' failure to provide any statutory remedy for constitutional injuries inflicted during the course of previous review proceedings.

In *Chappell v. Wallace*, where we declined to permit an action for damages by enlisted military personnel seeking redress from their superior officers for constitutional injuries, we noted that Congress, in the exercise of its "plenary constitutional authority over the military, has enacted statutes regulating military life, and has established a comprehensive internal system of justice to regulate military life . . . . The resulting system provides for the review and remedy of complaints and grievances such as [the equal protection claim] presented by respondents." That system not only permits aggrieved military personnel to raise constitutional challenges in administrative proceedings, it authorizes recovery of significant consequential damages, notably retroactive promotions. Similarly, in *Bush v. Lucas*, we concluded that, in light of the "elaborate, comprehensive scheme" governing federal employment relations, recognition of any supplemental judicial remedy for constitutional wrongs was inappropriate. Under that scheme—which Congress has "constructed step-by-step, with careful attention to conflicting policy considerations," over the course of nearly 100 years—"[c]onstitutional challenges . . . are fully cognizable" and prevailing employees are entitled not only to full backpay, but to retroactive promotions, seniority, pay raises, and accumulated leave. Indeed, Congress expressly "intended [to] put the employee in the same position he would have been in had the unjustified or erroneous personnel action not taken place.'"

It is true that neither the military justice system nor the federal employment relations scheme affords aggrieved parties full compensation for constitutional injuries; nevertheless, the relief provided in both is far more complete than that available under Title II's review process. Although federal employees may not recover damages for any emotional or dignitary harms they might suffer as a result of a constitutional injury, they, like their military counterparts, are entitled to redress for most economic consequential damages, including, most significantly, consequential damage to their Government careers. Here, by stark contrast, Title II recipients cannot even raise constitutional challenges to agency action in any of the four tiers of administrative review, and if they ultimately prevail on their eligibility claims in those administrative proceedings they can recover no consequential damages whatsoever. The only relief afforded persons unconstitutionally deprived of their disability benefits is retroactive payment of the very benefits they should have received all along. Such an award, of course, fails miserably to

compensate disabled persons illegally stripped of the income upon which, in many cases, their very subsistence depends.

The inadequacy of this relief is by no means a product of "the inevitable compromises required in the design of a massive and complex welfare benefits program." In Chappell and, we dealt with elaborate administrative systems in which Congress anticipated that federal officials might engage in unconstitutional conduct, and in which it accordingly sought to afford injured persons a form of redress as complete as the Government's institutional concerns would allow. In the federal employment context, for example, Congress carefully "balanc[ed] governmental efficiency and the rights of employees," paying "careful attention to conflicting policy considerations," and in the military setting it "established a comprehensive internal system of justice to regulate military life, taking into account the special patterns that define the military structure."

Here, as the legislative history of the 1984 Reform Act makes abundantly clear, Congress did not attempt to achieve a delicate balance between the constitutional rights of Title II beneficiaries on the one hand, and administrative concerns on the other. Rather than fine-tuning "an elaborate remedial scheme that ha[d] been constructed step-by-step" over the better part of a century, Congress confronted a paralyzing breakdown in a vital social program, which it sought to rescue from near-total anarchy. Although the legislative debate surrounding the 1984 Reform Act is littered with references to "arbitrary," "capricious," and "wrongful" terminations of benefits, it is clear that neither Congress nor anyone else identified unconstitutional conduct by state agencies as the cause of this paralysis. Rather, Congress blamed the systemic problems it faced in 1984 on SSA's determination to control the cost of the disability insurance program by accelerating the CDR process and mandating more restrictive reviews. Legislators explained that, "[b]ecause of the abrupt acceleration of the reviews, . . . [s]tate disability determinations offices were forced to accept a three-fold increase in their workloads," yet despite this acceleration, SSA took no steps to "assur[e] that the State agencies had the resources to handle the greatly increased workloads," and instead put "pressure upon [those] agencies to make inaccurate and unfair decisions.

Legislating in a near-crisis atmosphere, Congress saw itself as wrestling with the Executive Branch for control of the disability insurance program. It emphatically repudiated SSA's policy of restrictive, illiberal, and hasty benefit reviews, and adopted a number of prospective measures designed "to prevent further reckless reviews," and to ensure that recipients dependent on disability benefits for their sustenance would be adequately protected in any future review proceedings.

At no point during the lengthy legislative debate, however, did any Member of Congress so much as hint that the substantive eligibility criteria, notice requirements, and interim payment provisions that would govern future disability reviews adequately redressed the harms that beneficiaries may have suffered as a result of the unconstitutional actions of individual state and federal officials in past proceedings, or that the constitutional right of those unjustly deprived of benefits in the past had to be sacrificed in the name of administrative efficiency or any other governmental interest. The Court today identifies no legislative compromise, "inevitable" or otherwise, in which lawmakers expressly declined to afford a remedy for such past wrongs. Nor can the Court point to any legislator who suggested that state and federal officials should be shielded from liability for any unconstitutional acts taken in the course of administering the review program, or that exposure to liability for such acts would be inconsistent with Congress' comprehensive and carefully crafted remedial scheme.

[The concurring opinion of Justice Stevens is omitted.]

NOTES

1. Does the remedy provided by Congress adequately compensate individuals like the plaintiff in *Chilicky*? Do the majority and dissenters disagree on the answer to this question? If they do not, what accounts for their different views on the *Bivens* issue?

2. Did Congress explicitly preclude the availability of a constitutional tort action against federal Social Security officials accused of violating procedural due process? Did it do so implicitly? Whatever your answers to these questions, does the Court's decision in *Chilicky* make sense in terms of the sound administration of the Social Security disability system?

3. Along parallel lines, can Congress preempt particular section 1983 *constitutionally based* claims by providing a different damages remedy? Consider *Smith v. Robinson*, 468 U.S. 992 (1984), where the Supreme Court held that Congress, in enacting the Education of the Handicapped Act (EHA), 20 U.S.C. § 1401 *et seq*, intended to exclude from section 1983's coverage independent equal protection claims identical to claims covered by the Act. Thus, according to the Court, the Act was the exclusive avenue for such claims. Congress responded to *Smith* by amending the EHA to provide explicitly that parallel equal protection and other constitutional claims are not preempted by the EHA and can in fact accompany claims based on the Act. However, such preemption issues continue to be litigated in the circuits. See, for example, *Pfeiffer v. School Board for Marion Center Area*, 917 F.2d 779 (3rd Cir. 1990), where the Third Circuit relied on *Smith* in ruling that a former high school student's section 1983 sex discrimination claims were preempted by Title IX of the Education Amendments of 1972, 20 U.S.C. § 1681 *et seq.*

4. Are issues of Congressional intent and the administration of federal regulatory schemes that are implicated in *Bivens* actions comparable to those implicated in section 1983 "laws" actions, that is, actions based on state and local government violations of certain federal statutes? Should they be? After all, *Bivens* actions are based on the Constitution while "laws" actions are based on federal statutes. See Chapter 4 on "laws" actions.

5. When *Chilicky* is read with *Chappell* and *Bush*, does it indicate that the development of *Bivens* actions has come to a halt? If so, is that necessarily a bad thing, given that Congress can create *Bivens*-like remedies for constitutional violations by federal officials similar to those provided by section 1983 for constitutional violations by state and local government officials? Consider that the Federal Tort Claims Act, noted above, provides damages remedies against the United States for certain wrongful conduct of its employees and officials, including "any claim . . . arising out of assault, battery, false imprisonment, false arrest, abuse of process or malicious prosecution [committed through the] acts or omissions of investigative or law enforcement officers of the United States government . . . ." This Act, whose study is beyond the scope of this casebook, should be consulted whenever a damages action against federal officials is contemplated.

6. Should a *Bivens* action be available against a federal *agency*? In *F.D.I.C. v. Meyer*, 114 S. Ct. 996 (1994), the Supreme Court unanimously answered in the negative. The Court observed that *Bivens* itself was premised on the *absence* of a damages remedy against a federal agency. Thus, it would be illogical to extend *Bivens* to federal agencies. The Court also reasoned that such an extension would allow plaintiffs to bypass federal officials with qualified immunity and go directly after the federal agency. This would undermine the deterrent effect of *Bivens* actions, according to the Court. Do you agree with the latter argument? Compare local government liability, discussed in Chapter 5.

7. Keep in mind that in situations where *Bivens* actions are available, many of the legal rules applicable to section 1983 damages actions are similarly applicable to *Bivens* actions. For example, section 1983's absolute and qualified immunity rules govern *Bivens* actions. See *Butz v. Economou*, 438 U.S. 478 (1978), applying immunity rules and the functional approach to *Bivens* actions. See also *Mitchell v. Forsyth*, 472 U.S. 511 (1985), *Harlow v. Fitzgerald*, 457 U.S. 800 (1982) and *Anderson v. Creighton*, 483 U.S. 635 (1987), which developed complicated qualified immunity rules in *Bivens* settings and announced that those rules equally apply to section 1983 actions. Chapters 7 and 8 address absolute and qualified immuni-

ty. It is also likely that section 1983 damages rules apply to *Bivens* actions as well. See Chapter 9 on section 1983 remedies.

On the other hand, there is at least one situation in which *Bivens* immunity rules do *not* apply to section 1983. A state governor, a state's highest ranking executive official, is protected only by qualified immunity in section 1983 cases, but the President of the United States, the nation's highest ranking executive official, is protected by absolute immunity. Compare *Scheuer v. Rhodes*, 416 U.S. 232 (1974) (governor) with *Nixon v. Fitzgerald*, 457 U.S. 731 (1982) (President).

Quaere: suppose a President of the United States is sued under section 1983 for damages for constitutional violations allegedly committed by him when he was governor of a state. In addition to qualified immunity for his gubernatorial conduct, should some kind of presidential immunity be available in order to prevent the disruption of, and interference with, his presidential duties?

As you proceed through the rest of this casebook you might ask yourself whether Congress should do for constitutional tort actions against federal officials (and perhaps the United States as an entity) what it did over one hundred years ago for Fourteenth Amendment violations committed by state and local government officials and employees and local governments themselves. See Nichol, *Bivens, Chilicky and Constitutional Damages Claims*, 75 Va. L. Rev. 1117 (1989). Recall also, as you study the rest of these materials, the underlying structure of all constitutional tort actions: (1) the elements of the *prima facie* case, including duty, basis of liability and causation, and (2) available immunities and defenses.

CHAPTER TWO

"Under Color of" State Law

Section 1983 grants a remedy only for acts taken "under color of any statute, ordinance, regulation, custom, or usage, of any State or Territory or the District of Columbia." The Fourteenth Amendment, which furnishes the substantive law for most section 1983 suits, declares that "[n]o *State* shall . . . deprive any person of life, liberty, or property, without due process of law; nor deny to any person . . . the equal protection of the laws." (emphasis added). This chapter addresses three questions raised by these provisions: (1) Which acts of public officials are covered by the statute, and which are not? (2) What is the relationship between "under color of" and the "state action" requirement for application of the fourteenth amendment? (3) When may a plaintiff sue private actors under section 1983?

Part I takes up the first of these questions, Part II the second, and Part III the third. Although the first two inquiries are of great theoretical importance and sometimes present difficult issues, the third is the most complex of the three and receives the most attention here.

I. The Meaning of "Under Color of"

A. *Monroe* and "Under Color of"

The Supreme Court construed the statutory term "under color of [state law]" in the seminal section 1983 case, *Monroe v. Pape*. That case is discussed at length in Chapter 1. The Court held that actions by state officers that violate state law may still be "under color of" state law. According to the Court, "it is no answer that the state has a law which if enforced would give relief. The federal remedy is supplementary to the state remedy, and the latter need not be first sought and refused before the federal one is invoked." Quoting an earlier case construing

the same phrase in a criminal civil rights statute, the Court said the phrase "under color of" embraces "[m]isuse of power, possessed by virtue of state law and made possible only because the wrongdoer is clothed with the authority of state law." *Monroe v. Pape*, 365 U.S. 167, 184, quoting *United States v. Classic*, 313 U.S. 299, 326 (1941).

B. The Boundaries of "Under Color of"

Though officers whose conduct is proscribed by state law nonetheless act under color of law, it does not follow that every single action taken by a state officer is actionable under section 1983. A distinction must be drawn between cases where the actor's official status is more or less irrelevant, and those where, however personal the officer's aims, his use of the authority or accoutrements of office contributes significantly to the harm he is able to do. Some cases are easy. A high school principal who shoots his neighbor in the course of an argument over a noisy stereo does not act under color of state law. A policeman who, in the course of an arrest, carries out a personal grudge by beating a helpless suspect does act under color of state law. Here are some cases that present harder line-drawing problems:

1. A recurring fact-pattern features an off-duty policeman who injures someone. "While it is clear that 'personal pursuits' of police officers do not give rise to section 1983 liability, there is no bright line test for distinguishing 'personal pursuits' from activities taken under color of law." *Pitchell v. Callan*, 13 F.3d 545, 548 (2d Cir. 1994). If the officer uses some piece of police equipment, and is doing police business, courts generally hold that the policeman acts under color of law. See, e.g., *Layne v. Sampley*, 627 F.2d 12 (6th Cir. 1980); *Stengel v. Belcher*, 522 F.2d 438 (6th Cir. 1975). Suppose the off-duty officer violently attacks someone for purely personal reasons? If he uses a weapon that belongs to him and is not doing police business, the act is not under color of law. See, e.g., *Pitchell v. Callan*, supra. Compare *Bonsignore v. City of New York*, 683 F.2d 635 (2d Cir. 1982) (although the officer was required to carry a gun at all times, his off-duty, personal use of a weapon was not under color of law) with *United States v. Tarpley*, 945 F.2d 806, 809 (5th Cir. 1991) (prosecution under the criminal counterpart of section 1983; defendant assaulted his former wife's lover using his service weapon; then he and another officer ran the victim out of town in a squad car; this amounted to action under color of law).

On the other hand, when officers on duty pursue their private ends, they are often, though not always, deemed to act under color of law. Compare *Cassady v. Tackett*, 938 F.2d 693, 695 (6th Cir. 1991) (defendant, an elected county jailor, allegedly threatened to kill the plaintiff, the executive director of the jail, on jail premises; defendant "had the authority or power to carry the gun in the jail only because he was the elected jailor of [the county]). That [defendant] acted against a fellow employee is of no matter. . . ."; with *Delcambre v. Delcambre*, 635 F.2d 407 (5th Cir. 1981) (on-duty policeman who assaulted his sister-in-law did not act under color of law when the impetus for the attack was a family and political dispute and plaintiff was not threatened with arrest).

2. What result if a police officer who was suspended as mentally unfit for duty, yet was permitted to keep his gun and ammunition, shoots someone with the gun? *Gibson v. City of Chicago*, 910 F.2d 1510, 1517–18 (7th Cir. 1990) holds that he is not a state actor. "[W]hether Novit acted under color of law turns primarily on the legal effect of the March 3 order that directed Novit not to carry a weapon or exercise any police powers. . . While it is no doubt true that an officer who, motivated by personal animus, misuses his lawfully possessed authority to injure the plaintiff may be found to be acting under 'pretense' of law, we have found no authority for expanding this concept of 'pretense' of law to encompass the actions of an official who possessed *absolutely no authority* to act but nonetheless assumed the position of an imposter in pretending that he did." (emphasis in original). Is this reasoning

compatible with *Monroe*? Suppose the officer kept his uniform as well?

Under the reasoning of *Gibson*, would a game warden who has no power generally to enforce state law act under color of law when he calls a deputy sheriff to have the plaintiff arrested? See *Hughes v. Meyer*, 880 F.2d 967, 972 (7th Cir. 1989) (not state action). Would an officer act under color of state law when the terms of his employment provide that he is under no obligation to intervene while off-duty, but he does so anyway? Suppose he is forbidden to intervene while off duty?

Does it follow from *Gibson* that the city cannot be held liable for permitting Novit to keep his gun and ammunition? The court rejected the city's argument against liability. Compare *Martinez v. California*, 444 U.S. 277 (1980), where a parolee killed the plaintiffs' decedent five months after his release. The Court dismissed the section 1983 case against parole board members. Among other reasons, the Court said that the requisite state action was missing, since the parolee and not state officers killed the victim. Is *Gibson* consistent with *Martinez*? Does the opinion in *Martinez* reflect an accurate understanding of the plaintiff's theory of recovery? Note that the *Martinez* Court also held that the death was "too remote a consequence of the parole officers' action to hold them responsible under the federal civil rights law." 444 U.S. at 285. That aspect of *Martinez* is addressed in Chapter 6. Which rationale provides a more persuasive ground for the result?

3. Police officers sometimes take second jobs as security guards. Are their actions under color of law? See, e.g., *Griffin v. Maryland*, 378 U.S. 130 (1964); *Lusby v. TG&Y Stores, Inc.*, 749 F.2d 1423 (10th Cir. 1984); *Traver v. Meshriy*, 627 F.2d 934 (9th Cir. 1980) (holding that they are). In all three cases the policeman's work as a security guard was related to his official status. *Griffin* found state action when an amusement park security guard had been deputized as a county sheriff and identified himself as a deputy sheriff when arresting the plaintiffs. The officer in *Traver* identified himself as a police officer when he stopped the plaintiff, and had obtained his job through a police department program. In *Lusby*, the officer "flashed his badge and identified himself as a

Lawton police officer working as a security guard for T.G.&Y." 749 F.2d at 1429.

Would the result be different if the officer makes no pretense that he is acting under state authority? See *Watkins v. Oaklawn Jockey Club*, 183 F.2d 440, 443 (8th Cir. 1950) (no state action). What if the plaintiff knows that the officer is acting as a private guard, even though he is in police uniform? *Robinson v. Davis*, 447 F.2d 753, 758–59 (4th Cir. 1971) holds that the officer does not act under color of state law. Sound?

II. "Under Color of" and State Action

The relation between "under color of" law and state action is addressed in the following case. This case is relevant as well to Part III, which discusses the use of section 1983 to sue private actors.

Lugar v. Edmondson Oil Co.

457 U.S. 922 (1982)

Justice **White** delivered the opinion of the Court.

The Fourteenth Amendment of the Constitution provides in part:

"No State shall make or enforce any law which shall abridge the privileges or immunities of citizens of the United States; nor shall any State deprive any person of life, liberty, or property, without due process of law; nor deny to any person within its jurisdiction the equal protection of the laws."

Because the Amendment is directed at the States, it can be violated only by conduct that may be fairly characterized as "state action."

Title 42 U.S.C. § 1983 provides a remedy for deprivations of rights secured by the Constitution and laws of the United States when that deprivation takes place "under color of any statute, ordinance, regulation, custom, or usage, of any State or Territory. . . ." This case concerns the relationship between the § 1983 requirement of action

under color of state law and the Fourteenth Amendment requirement of state action.

I

In 1977, petitioner, a lessee-operator of a truckstop in Virginia, was indebted to his supplier, Edmondson Oil Co., Inc. Edmondson sued on the debt in Virginia state court. Ancillary to that action and pursuant to state law, Edmondson sought prejudgment attachment of certain of petitioner's property. The prejudgment attachment procedure required only that Edmondson allege, in an ex parte petition, a belief that petitioner was disposing of or might dispose of his property in order to defeat his creditors. Acting upon that petition, a Clerk of the state court issued a writ of attachment, which was then executed by the County Sheriff. This effectively sequestered petitioner's property, although it was left in his possession. Pursuant to the statute, a hearing on the propriety of the attachment and levy was later conducted. Thirty-four days after the levy, a state trial judge ordered the attachment dismissed because Edmondson had failed to establish the statutory grounds for attachment alleged in the petition.

Petitioner subsequently brought this action under 42 U.S.C. § 1983 against Edmondson and its president. His complaint alleged that in attaching his property respondents had acted jointly with the State to deprive him of his property without due process of law. The lower courts construed the complaint as alleging a due process violation both from a misuse of the Virginia procedure and from the statutory procedure itself. He sought compensatory and punitive damages for specified financial loss allegedly caused by the improvident attachment . . .

[The Court of Appeals] distinguished between the acts directly chargeable to respondents and the larger context within which those acts occurred, including the direct levy by state officials on petitioner's property. While the latter no doubt amounted to state action, the former was not so clearly action under color of state law. The court held that a private party acts under color of state law within the meaning of § 1983 only when there is a usurpation or corruption of official power by the private litigant or a surrender of judicial power to the private litigant in such a way that the independence of the enforcing officer has been compromised to a significant degree. Because the court thought none of these elements was present here, the complaint failed to allege conduct under color of state law.

Because this construction of the under-color-of-state-law requirement appears to be inconsistent with prior decisions of this Court, we granted certiorari.

II

Although the Court of Appeals correctly perceived the importance of *Flagg Brothers v. Brooks*, to a proper resolution of this case, it misread that case. It also failed to give sufficient weight to that line of cases, beginning with *Sniadach v. Family Finance Corp.*, in which the Court considered constitutional due process requirements in the context of garnishment actions and prejudgment attachments. See *North Georgia Finishing, Inc. v. Di-Chem, Inc., Mitchell v. W.T. Grant Co., Fuentes v. Shevin*. Each of these cases involved a finding of state action as an implicit predicate of the application of due process standards. *Flagg Brothers* distinguished them on the ground that in each there was overt, official involvement in the property deprivation; there was no such overt action by a state officer in *Flagg Brothers*. Although this case falls on the *Sniadach*, and not the *Flagg Brothers*, side of this distinction, the Court of Appeals thought the garnishment and attachment cases to be irrelevant because none but *Fuentes* arose under 42 U.S.C. § 1983 and because *Fuentes* was distinguishable. It determined that it could ignore all of them because the issue in this case was not whether there was state action, but rather whether respondents acted under color of state law.

As we see it, however, the two concepts cannot be so easily disentangled. Whether they are identical or not, the state-action and the under-color-of-state-law requirements are obviously related.[8] Indeed, until recently this

---

[8] The Court of Appeals itself recognized this when it stated that in two of three basic patterns of § 1983 litigation—that in which the defendant is a public official and that in which he is a private party—there is no distinction between state action and action under color of state law. Only when there is joint action by private parties and state officials, the court stated, could a distinction arise between these two requirements.

Court did not distinguish between the two requirements at all.

A

In *United States v. Price* we explicitly stated that the requirements were identical: "In cases under § 1983, 'under color' of law has consistently been treated as the same thing as the 'state action' required under the Fourteenth Amendment." In support of this proposition the Court cited *Smith v. Allwright* and *Terry v. Adams*. In both of these cases black voters in Texas challenged their exclusion from party primaries as a violation of the Fifteenth Amendment and sought relief under 8 U.S.C. § 43 (1946 ed.). In each case, the Court understood the problem before it to be whether the discriminatory policy of a private political association could be characterized as "state action within the meaning of the Fifteenth Amendment." *Smith*, supra. Having found state action under the Constitution, there was no further inquiry into whether the action of the political associations also met the statutory requirement of action " under color of state law."

Similarly, it is clear that in a § 1983 action brought against a state official, the statutory requirement of action "under color of state law" and the "state action" requirement of the Fourteenth Amendment are identical. The Court's conclusion in *United States v. Classic* that "[misuse] of power, possessed by virtue of state law and made possible only because the wrongdoer is clothed with the authority of state law, is action taken 'under color of' state law," was founded on the rule announced in *Ex parte Virginia* that the actions of a state officer who exceeds the limits of his authority constitute state action for purposes of the Fourteenth Amendment . . .

To read the "under color of any statute" language of the Act in such a way as to impose a limit on those Fourteenth Amendment violations that may be redressed by the § 1983 cause of action would be wholly inconsistent with the purpose of § 1 of the Civil Rights Act of 1871, from which § 1983 is derived. The Act was passed "for the express purpose of [enforcing] the Provisions of the Fourteenth Amendment." *Lynch v. Household Finance Corp.* The history of the Act is replete with statements indicating that Congress thought it was creating a remedy as broad as the protection that the Fourteenth Amendment affords the individual. Perhaps the most direct statement of this was that of Senator Edmunds, the manager of the bill in the Senate: "[Section 1 is] so very simple and really [reenacts] the Constitution." Cong. Globe, 42d Cong., 1st Sess., 569 (1871). Representative Bingham similarly stated that the bill's purpose was "the enforcement . . . of the Constitution on behalf of every individual citizen of the Republic . . . to the extent of the rights guarantied to him by the Constitution."

In sum, the line drawn by the Court of Appeals is inconsistent with our prior cases and would substantially undercut the congressional purpose in providing the § 1983 cause of action. If the challenged conduct of respondents constitutes state action as delimited by our prior decisions, then that conduct was also action under color of state law and will support a suit under § 1983.[18]

---

[18] Our conclusion in this case is not inconsistent with the statement in Flagg Brothers that "these two elements [state action and action under color of state law] denote two separate areas of inquiry." First, although we hold that conduct satisfying the state-action requirement of the Fourteenth Amendment satisfies the statutory requirement of action under color of state law, it does not follow from that that all conduct that satisfies the under-color-of-state-law requirement would satisfy the Fourteenth Amendment requirement of state action. If action under color of state law means nothing more than that the individual act "with the knowledge of and pursuant to that statute," Adickes v. S.H. Kress & Co. then clearly under Flagg Brothers that would not, in itself, satisfy the state-action requirement of the Fourteenth Amendment. Second, although we hold in this case that the under-color-of-state-law requirement does not add anything not already included within the state-action requirement of the Fourteenth Amendment, § 1983 is applicable to other constitutional provisions and statutory provisions that contain no state-action requirement. Where such a federal right is at issue, the statutory concept of action under color of state law would be a distinct element of the case not satisfied implicitly by a finding of a violation of the particular federal right.

Nor is our decision today inconsistent with Polk County v. Dodson. In Polk County, we held that a public defender's actions, when performing a lawyer's traditional functions as counsel in a state criminal proceeding, would not support a § 1983 suit. Although we analyzed the public defender's conduct in light of the requirement of action "under color of state law," we specifically stated that it was not necessary in that case to consider whether that requirement was identical to the "state action" requirement of the Fourteenth Amendment: "Although this Court has sometimes

III

As a matter of substantive constitutional law the state-action requirement reflects judicial recognition of the fact that "most rights secured by the Constitution are protected only against infringement by governments," *Flagg Brothers*. As the Court said in *Jackson v. Metropolitan Edison Co.:*
"In 1883, this Court in the *Civil Rights Cases* affirmed the essential dichotomy set forth in [the Fourteenth] Amendment between deprivation by the State, subject to scrutiny under its provisions, and private conduct, 'however discriminatory or wrongful,' against which the Fourteenth Amendment offers no shield."

Careful adherence to the "state action" requirement preserves an area of individual freedom by limiting the reach of federal law and federal judicial power. It also avoids imposing on the State, its agencies or officials, responsibility for conduct for which they cannot fairly be blamed. A major consequence is to require the courts to respect the limits of their own power as directed against state governments and private interests. Whether this is good or bad policy, it is a fundamental fact of our political order.

Our cases have accordingly insisted that the conduct allegedly causing the deprivation of a federal right be fairly attributable to the State. These cases reflect a two-part approach to this question of "fair attribution." First, the deprivation must be caused by the exercise of some right or privilege created by the State or by a rule of conduct imposed by the State or by a person for whom the State is responsible. In *Sniadach, Fuentes, W. T. Grant,* and *North*

---

treated the questions as if they were identical, we need not consider their relationship in order to decide this case." We concluded there that a public defender, although a state employee, in the day-to-day defense of his client, acts under canons of professional ethics in a role adversarial to the State. Accordingly, although state employment is generally sufficient to render the defendant a state actor under our analysis, infra, it was "peculiarly difficult" to detect any action of the State in the circumstances of that case. In Polk County, we also rejected respondent's claims against governmental agencies because he "failed to allege any policy that arguably violated his rights under the Sixth, Eighth, or Fourteenth Amendments." Because respondent failed to challenge any rule of conduct or decision for which the State was responsible, his allegations would not support a claim of state action under the analysis proposed below. Thus, our decision today does not suggest a different outcome in Polk County.

Georgia, for example, a state statute provided the right to garnish or to obtain prejudgment attachment, as well as the procedure by which the rights could be exercised. Second, the party charged with the deprivation must be a person who may fairly be said to be a state actor. This may be because he is a state official, because he has acted together with or has obtained significant aid from state officials, or because his conduct is otherwise chargeable to the State. Without a limit such as this, private parties could face constitutional litigation whenever they seek to rely on some state rule governing their interactions with the community surrounding them.

Although related, these two principles are not the same. They collapse into each other when the claim of a constitutional deprivation is directed against a party whose official character is such as to lend the weight of the State to his decisions. See *Monroe v. Pape.* The two principles diverge when the constitutional claim is directed against a party without such apparent authority, i.e., against a private party. The difference between the two inquiries is well illustrated by comparing *Moose Lodge No. 107 v. Irvis* with *Flagg Brothers,* supra.

In *Moose Lodge*, the Court held that the discriminatory practices of the appellant did not violate the Equal Protection Clause because those practices did not constitute "state action." The Court focused primarily on the question of whether the admittedly discriminatory policy could in any way be ascribed to a governmental decision. The inquiry, therefore, looked to those policies adopted by the State that were applied to appellant. The Court concluded as follows:

"We therefore hold, that with the exception hereafter noted, the operation of the regulatory scheme enforced by the Pennsylvania Liquor Control Board does not sufficiently implicate the State in the discriminatory guest policies of Moose Lodge to . . . make the latter 'state action' within the ambit of the Equal Protection Clause of the Fourteenth Amendment."

In other words, the decision to discriminate could not be ascribed to any governmental decision; those governmental decisions that

did affect Moose Lodge were unconnected with its discriminatory policies.[20]

Flagg Brothers focused on the other component of the state-action principle. In that case, the warehouseman proceeded under New York Uniform Commercial Code, § 7-210, and the debtor challenged the constitutionality of that provision on the grounds that it violated the Due Process and Equal Protection Clauses of the Fourteenth Amendment. Undoubtedly the State was responsible for the statute. The response of the Court, however, focused not on the terms of the statute but on the character of the defendant to the § 1983 suit: Action by a private party pursuant to this statute, without something more, was not sufficient to justify a characterization of that party as a "state actor." The Court suggested that that "something more" which would convert the private party into a state actor might vary with the circumstances of the case. This was simply a recognition that the Court has articulated a number of different factors or tests in different contexts: e.g., the "public function" test, see *Terry v. Adams*; *Marsh v. Alabama*; the "state compulsion" test, see *Adickes v. S.H. Kress & Co.*; the "nexus" test, see *Jackson v. Metropolitan Edison Co.*; *Burton v. Wilmington Parking Authority*; and, in the case of prejudgment attachments, a "joint action test," *Flagg Brothers.* Whether these different tests are actually different in operation or simply different ways of characterizing the necessarily fact-bound inquiry that confronts the Court in such a situation need not be resolved here. See *Burton,* supra, ("Only by sifting facts and weighing circumstances can the nonobvious involvement of the State in private conduct be attributed its true significance").

IV

Turning to this case, the first question is whether the claimed deprivation has resulted from the exercise of a right or privilege having its source in state authority. The second

---

[20] The "one exception" further illustrates this point. The Court enjoined enforcement of a state rule requiring Moose Lodge to comply with its own constitution and bylaws insofar as they contained racially discriminatory provisions. State enforcement of this rule, either judicially or administratively, would, under the circumstances, amount to a governmental decision to adopt a racially discriminatory policy.

question is whether, under the facts of this case, respondents, who are private parties, may be appropriately characterized as "state actors."

Both the District Court and the Court of Appeals noted the ambiguous scope of petitioner's contentions: 'There has been considerable confusion throughout the litigation on the question whether Lugar's ultimate claim of unconstitutional deprivation was directed at the Virginia statute itself or only at its erroneous application to him." Both courts held that resolution of this ambiguity was not necessary to their disposition of the case: both resolved it, in any case, in favor of the view that petitioner was attacking the constitutionality of the statute as well as its misapplication. In our view, resolution of this issue is essential to the proper disposition of the case.

Petitioner presented three counts in his complaint. Count three was a pendent claim based on state tort law; counts one and two claimed violations of the Due Process Clause. Count two alleged that the deprivation of property resulted from respondents' 'malicious, wanton, willful, oppressive [sic], [and] unlawful acts." By "unlawful," petitioner apparently meant "unlawful under state law." To say this, however, is to say that the conduct of which petitioner complained could not be ascribed to any governmental decision; rather, respondents were acting contrary to the relevant policy articulated by the State. Nor did they have the authority of state officials to put the weight of the State behind their private decision, i.e., this case does not fall within the abuse of authority doctrine recognized in *Monroe v. Pape*. That respondents invoked the statute without the grounds to do so could in no way be attributed to a state rule or a state decision. Count two, therefore, does not state a cause of action under § 1983 but challenges only private action.

Count one is a different matter. That count describes the procedures followed by respondents in obtaining the prejudgment attachment as well as the fact that the state court subsequently ordered the attachment dismissed because respondents had not met their burden under state law. Petitioner then summarily states that this sequence of events deprived him of his property without due process. Although it is not clear whether petitioner is referring to the state-created

procedure or the misuse of that procedure by respondents, we agree with the lower courts that the better reading of the complaint is that petitioner challenges the state statute as procedurally defective under the Fourteenth Amendment.

While private misuse of a state statute does not describe conduct that can be attributed to the State, the procedural scheme created by the statute obviously is the product of state action. This is subject to constitutional restraints and properly may be addressed in a § 1983 action, if the second element of the state-action requirement is met as well.

As is clear from the discussion in Part II, we have consistently held that a private party's joint participation with state officials in the seizure of disputed property is sufficient to characterize that party as a "state actor" for purposes of the Fourteenth Amendment . . .

In summary, petitioner was deprived of his property through state action; respondents were, therefore, acting under color of state law in participating in that deprivation. Petitioner did present a valid cause of action under § 1983 insofar as he challenged the constitutionality of the Virginia statute; he did not insofar as he alleged only misuse or abuse of the statute.

NOTES

1. Why is it that the statutory "under color of" requirement and the constitutional "state action" requirement turn out to be coextensive, or virtually so? Does the convergence stem more from the intentions of the framers of the fourteenth amendment and section 1983, or from modern Supreme Court policy-making?

In 1871, at the time section 1983 was enacted, Congress seems to have given little attention to the possibility that a "state action" requirement may significantly limit the reach of the fourteenth amendment. That constitutional provision had just been enacted and there was much uncertainty about its proper interpretation. The debates on section 1983 itself indicate that many members of Congress viewed it as a means by which to regulate the conduct of private citizens. Indeed, the central aim of the Civil Rights Act of 1871 was to provide means by which federal officers and federal courts could fight Ku Klux Klan terrorism against blacks and their white supporters. See Wells, *The Past and the Future of Constitutional Tort*, 19 Conn. L. Rev. 53, 65–68 (1986).

Similar observations have been made about other Reconstruction-Era statutes. According to Professor Eisenberg, "Congress' enactment and the Court's invalidation of the Civil Rights Act of 1875 . . . and of other nineteenth century civil rights laws suggest that the Reconstruction Congresses did not anticipate the broad outlines of the state action doctrine." Eisenberg, *Section 1983: Doctrinal Foundations and an Empirical Study*, 67 Cornell L. Rev. 482, 509 n.108 (1982).

2. One circumstance in which the "under color of state law" requirement has teeth independent of "state action" arises when someone tries to sue a federal official under section 1983. Only where the federal officials have collaborated with state officers will they be deemed to have acted under color of *state* law. Otherwise, the plaintiff is required to find some other statute authorizing suit against the federal officer, or else to bring a *Bivens* suit. On the latter see Chapter 1.

A recent example of the application of "color of law" doctrine to federal officials is *Cabrera v. Martin*, 973 F.2d 735 (9th Cir. 1992). Labor organizations and private employers challenged a decision by the governor of California to unilaterally request the United States Secretary of Labor to withdraw approval of California's occupational safety and health plan. Besides the Governor and other state officials, they sued the Secretary of Labor and two other federal Labor Department officials seeking injunctive relief prohibiting the Secretary from accepting the Governor's request.

The court held that the federal officials did not act under color of state law, despite a lower court finding that they had engaged in "'significant and substantial cooperation' with the Governor in accepting his withdrawal of Cal-OSHA." In particular, the district court "placed special emphasis on the fact that the Secretary changed his policy in mid-stream by deciding in September 1987 to accept Governor Deukmejian's letter of withdrawal and assume exclusive jurisdiction over California's occupational safety matters." 973 F.2d at 742.

[Even so,] [f]ederal officials do not become state actors unless [t]he State has so far insinuated itself into a position of interdependence with . . . [the federal officials] that it must be recognized as a joint participant in the challenged activity . . . To transform a federal official into a state actor, the appellee must show there is a symbiotic relationship between the [federal defendant] and the state such that the challenged action can fairly be attributed to the state . . . The Secretary actively opposed Governor Deukmejian's attempt to terminate Cal-OSHA as evidenced by the fact that he refused to withdraw approval when the Governor first notified DOL of his plan in February 1987. The Secretary did not finally approve Deukmejian's request and assume exclusive federal jurisdiction in California until after the California legislature adjourned on September 11, 1987, without either providing additional funds for Cal-OSHA or overriding the Governor's line-item veto. The evidence demonstrates, in other words, that the Governor and the federal defendants were involved in an antagonistic relationship, not a "symbiotic" venture. The Governor induced the federal defendants to terminate Cal-OSHA; they did not 'act in concert' with him . . .

[Even though] . . . the federal defendants met with Governor Deukmejian's agents on several occasions and cooperated with the Governor to fill the gap created by his veto of funding for Cal-OSHA, we do not agree that the federal defendants' contacts and discussions . . . transformed them into state actors whose actions could fairly be attributed to the state. This was not a case where federal officials conspired or cooperated with state agents to deprive individuals of their federal rights. The federal defendants only resumed jurisdiction over California's occupational health matters out of a need to fill the gap in coverage left by [the termination] and to ensure that California's workers would be adequately protected by federal safety standards. Far from being a symbiotic participant, whose actions could fairly be attributed to the State, we hold as a matter of law that the federal defendants' decision to resume exclusive federal jurisdiction over the

State's occupational health and safety matters was taken under color of federal law and that the state played no significant role in the challenged activity."

973 F.2d at 742–43.

The court distinguished *Hampton v. Hanrahan*, 600 F.2d 600, 623 (7th Cir. 1979) (federal officers who collaborated with the Chicago police in a raid on the Black Panther Party acted under color of state law because the action was the "joint product of the exercise of a State power and of a non-State power" and the State and its officials played a "significant role in the result.")

3. Conversely, state officials sometimes administer federal programs. They may be deemed to be acting under color of federal law and hence not amenable to suit under section 1983. See, e.g., *Rosas v. Brooks*, 826 F.2d 1004, 1007 (11th Cir. 1987) (Florida disaster relief workers acted under color of federal law when they denied a claim of compensation under federal guidelines). Similarly, when state police officers are assigned to work with federal agencies on a full-time basis, courts have held that they act under color of federal law, even though they are paid by the state. See, e.g., *Askew v. Bloemker*, 548 F.2d 673, 677 (1976).

For an example from a different context, see *Ellis v. Blum*, 643 F.2d 68, 83 & n.17 (2d Cir. 1981), where state officials were charged with employing improper termination procedures for Social Security benefits. '[T]he funds are entirely of federal origin and the state agencies function solely as agents of the Secretary [of Health and Human Services] in making determinations of disability, applying federal law and federal regulations in accordance with procedures prescribed by her." Section 1983 was therefore unavailable and the plaintiffs were required to pursue a *Bivens* suit.

4. National guard activities give rise to similar problems, for the guards have both state and federal characteristics. According to the Seventh Circuit, "[n]o set formula exists for determining whether the representatives of an agency with both state and federal characteristics act under color of law. Our evaluation of whether particular conduct constitutes action taken under color of state law focuses on the nature of the action and functional capacity of the actor." *Knutson v. Wisconsin Air National Guard*, 995 F.2d 765, 767 (7th Cir. 1993). In

Knutson, the Adjutant General of the Guard dismissed plaintiff from the guard on account of bad performance evaluations. This was done "under color of" state law in spite of "the overarching scheme of federal authorization for the guard [and] the fact that Wisconsin adopts and WIANG opts to utilize federal substantive and procedural rules in the exercise of its authority . . . No one is claiming that the guard had been called into service by the federal government at the time of the termination. Moreover, WIANG is a part of the Wisconsin militia, with the governor serving as commander-in-chief. The adjutant general, an appointee of the governor, effected the termination of Knutson." Id. at 768. See also *Johnson v. Orr*, 780 F.2d 386 (3rd Cir. 1986) (reaching the same result on similar facts).

Suppose two states, with the approval of Congress, create an interstate compact to carry out certain common goals. Do those officials act under color of state or federal law? See *Lake Country Estates, Inc. v. Tahoe Regional Planning Agency*, 440 U.S. 391 (1979) (holding that they act under color of state law).

5. Since *Lugar*, lower courts have treated the statutory "under color of state law" and the constitutional "state action" requirements as equivalent in the typical constitutional tort case where the plaintiff relies on the Fourteenth Amendment (including the rights the Supreme Court has incorporated into that amendment) to establish a breach of constitutional duty. Does the Court rule that the two inquiries are *always* identical? See footnote 18. Why is the Court reluctant to take that step? Will it ever be necessary to develop an independent body of doctrine for deciding "under color of" issues? Consider two possibilities:

(a) Almost all constitutional provisions are directed at the state. The Thirteenth Amendment is the sole exception. It outlaws slavery whether or not the state sponsors or condones the practice. Suppose a farm worker kept on the land through intimidation and blackmail by the landowner brought a section 1983 suit to recover damages and obtain injunctive relief, and the court agrees that the landowner's practices amount to slavery. Suppose further that the landowner's practices violate state law. Would the victim still fail on account of his failure to meet the "under color of" requirement?

(b) Section 1983 grants a cause of action not only to enforce constitutional provisions but also to redress violations of federal "laws". The Court's doctrine on whether a given federal statute may be enforced through a section 1983 suit is examined in chapter 4. Suppose that the Court were to hold (as it has not yet done) that a federal statute directed at private conduct (as opposed to one regulating the actions of state and local governments) can be enforced under section 1983. Cf. *Hobbs v. Hawkins*, 968 F.2d 471 (5th Cir. 1992) where the plaintiff unsuccessfully argued that section 1983 should be available for disputes between union organizers and employers in connection with an organizing campaign. If the plaintiff had prevailed on that issue, would he then have to overcome the "under color of" hurdle as well?

6. The limitations on civil rights remedies addressed in this chapter apply only to suits brought under section 1983. Some civil rights statutes do not require a showing of state action. E.g., 42 U.S.C. § 1981 provides that "[a]ll persons within the jurisdiction of the United States shall have the same right in every State and Territory to make and enforce contracts, to sue, be parties, give evidence, and to the full and equal benefit of all laws and proceedings for the security of persons and property as is enjoyed by white citizens . . ." No showing of state action is required in order to state a cause of action under this provision. See Runyon v. McCrary, 427 U.S. 160 (1976).

III. Suing Private Actors Under Section 1983

Lugar illustrates that in the proper circumstances private persons commit "state action", act "under color of" state law, and thus may be sued under section 1983 for Fourteenth Amendment violations. Persons who employ self-help remedies, like the defendant in *Lugar*, are but one of several groups who may be vulnerable to section 1983 suits. Others include private individuals or firms to whom the state has contracted out some function that would otherwise be performed by state employees

and persons who conspire with public officers to deprive the plaintiff of federal rights.

A. Self-Help Remedies

Flagg Bros., Inc. v. Brooks

436 U.S. 149 (1978)

Mr. Justice **Rehnquist** delivered the opinion of the Court.

The question presented by this litigation is whether a warehouseman's proposed sale of goods entrusted to him for storage, as permitted by New York Uniform Commercial Code § 7–210 is an action properly attributable to the State of New York. The District Court found that the warehouseman's conduct was not that of the State, and dismissed this suit for want of jurisdiction under 28 U.S.C. § 1343(3). The Court of Appeals for the Second Circuit, in reversing the judgment of the District Court, found sufficient state involvement with the proposed sale to invoke the provisions of the Due Process Clause of the Fourteenth Amendment. We agree with the District Court, and we therefore reverse.

I

According to her complaint, the allegations of which we must accept as true, respondent Shirley Brooks and her family were evicted from their apartment in Mount Vernon, N.Y., on June 13, 1973. The city marshal arranged for Brooks' possessions to be stored by petitioner Flagg Brothers, Inc., in its warehouse. Brooks was informed of the cost of moving and storage, and she instructed the workmen to proceed, although she found the price too high. On August 25, 1973, after a series of disputes over the validity of the charges being claimed by petitioner Flagg Brothers, Brooks received a letter demanding that her account be brought up to date within 10 days "or your furniture will be sold." App. 13a. A series of subsequent letters from respondent and her attorneys produced no satisfaction.

Brooks thereupon initiated this class action in the District Court under 42 U.S.C. § 1983, seeking damages, an injunction against the threatened sale of her belongings, and the declaration that such a sale pursuant to § 7–210 would violate the Due Process and Equal Protection Clauses of the Fourteenth Amendment . . .

II

A claim upon which relief may be granted to respondents against Flagg Brothers under § 1983 must embody at least two elements. Respondents are first bound to show that they have been deprived of a right "secured by the Constitution and the laws" of the United States. They must secondly show that Flagg Brothers deprived them of this right acting "under color of any statute" of the State of New York. It is clear that these two elements denote two separate areas of inquiry.

Respondents allege in their complaints that "the threatened sale of the goods pursuant to New York Uniform Commercial Code § 7–210" is an action under color of state law. We have previously noted, with respect to a private individual, that "[whatever] else may also be necessary to show that a person has acted 'under color of [a] statute' for purposes of § 1983, . . . we think it essential that he act with the knowledge of and pursuant to that statute." Certainly, the complaints can be fairly read to allege such knowledge on the part of Flagg Brothers. However, we need not determine whether any further showing is necessary, since it is apparent that neither respondent has alleged facts which constitute a deprivation of any right "secured by the Constitution and laws" of the United States.

A moment's reflection will clarify the essential distinction between the two elements of a § 1983 action. Some rights established either by the Constitution or by federal law are protected from both governmental and private deprivation. See, e.g., *Jones v. Alfred H. Mayer Co.* (discussing 42 U.S.C. § 1982). Although a private person may cause a deprivation of such a right, he may be subjected to liability under § 1983 only when he does so under color of law. However, most rights secured by the Constitution are protected only against infringement by governments. Here, respondents allege that Flagg Brothers has deprived them of their right, secured by the Fourteenth Amendment, to be free from state deprivations of property without due process of law. Thus, they must establish not only that

Flagg Brothers acted under color of the challenged statute, but also that its actions are properly attributable to the State of New York.

It must be noted that respondents have named no public officials as defendants in this action. The city marshal, who supervised their evictions, was dismissed from the case by the consent of all the parties.[5] This total absence of overt official involvement plainly distinguishes this case from earlier decisions imposing procedural restrictions on creditors' remedies such as *North Georgia Finishing, Inc. v. Di-Chem, Inc.*; *Fuentes v. Shevin*; *Sniadach v. Family Finance Corp.* In those cases, the Court was careful to point out that the dictates of the Due Process Clause "[attach] only to the deprivation of an interest encompassed within the Fourteenth Amendment's protection." While as a factual matter any person with sufficient physical power may deprive a person of his property, only a State or a private person whose action "may be fairly treated as that of the State itself," may deprive him of "an interest encompassed within the Fourteenth Amendment's protection." Thus, the only issue presented by this case is whether Flagg Brothers' action may fairly be attributed to the State of New York. We conclude that it may not.

III

Respondents' primary contention is that New York has delegated to Flagg Brothers a power "traditionally exclusively reserved to the State." They argue that the resolution of private disputes is a traditional function of civil government, and that the State in § 7–210 has delegated this function to Flagg Brothers. Respondents, however, have read too much into the language of our previous cases. While many functions have been traditionally performed by governments, very few have been "exclusively reserved to the State."

One such area has been elections. While the Constitution protects private rights of associa-

---

[5] Of course, where the defendant is a public official, the two elements of a § 1983 action merge. 'The involvement of a state official . . . plainly provides the state action essential to show a direct violation of petitioner's Fourteenth Amendment . . . rights, whether or not the actions of the police were officially authorized, or lawful." Adickes v. S.H. Kress & Co. (citations omitted).

tion and advocacy with regard to the election of public officials, our cases make it clear that the conduct of the elections themselves is an exclusively public function. This principle was established by a series of cases challenging the exclusion of blacks from participation in primary elections in Texas . . . The doctrine does not reach to all forms of private political activity, but encompasses only state-regulated elections or elections conducted by organizations which in practice produce "the uncontested choice of public officials." . . .

A second line of cases under the public-function doctrine originated with *Marsh v. Alabama*, . . . [T]he Gulf Shipbuilding Corp. performed all the necessary municipal functions in the town of Chickasaw, Ala., which it owned. Under those circumstances, the Court concluded it was bound to recognize the right of a group of Jehovah's Witnesses to distribute religious literature on its streets . . .

These two branches of the public-function doctrine have in common the feature of exclusivity. Although the elections held by the Democratic Party and its affiliates were the only meaningful elections in Texas, and the streets owned by the Gulf Shipbuilding Corp. were the only streets in Chickasaw, the proposed sale by Flagg Brothers under § 7–210 is not the only means of resolving this purely private dispute. Respondent Brooks has never alleged that state law barred her from seeking a waiver of Flagg Brothers' right to sell her goods at the time she authorized their storage. Presumably, respondent Jones, who alleges that she never authorized the storage of her goods, could have sought to replevy her goods at any time under state law. The challenged statute itself provides a damages remedy against the warehouseman for violations of its provisions. This system of rights and remedies, recognizing the traditional place of private arrangements in ordering relationships in the commercial world, can hardly be said to have delegated to Flagg Brothers an exclusive prerogative of the sovereign.

Whatever the particular remedies available under New York law, we do not consider a more detailed description of them necessary to our conclusion that the settlement of disputes between debtors and creditors is not traditionally an exclusive public function. Creditors and debtors have had available to them historically a far wider number of choices than has one who would be an elected public official, or a member of Jehovah's Witnesses who wished to distribute literature in Chickasaw, Ala., at the time Marsh was decided. Our analysis requires no parsing of the difference between various commercial liens and other remedies to support the conclusion that this entire field of activity is outside the scope of Terry and Marsh. This is true whether these commercial rights and remedies are created by statute or decisional law. To rely upon the historical antecedents of a particular practice would result in the constitutional condemnation in one State of a remedy found perfectly permissible in another.

Thus, even if we were inclined to extend the sovereign-function doctrine outside of its present carefully confined bounds, the field of private commercial transactions would be a particularly inappropriate area into which to expand it. We conclude that our sovereign-function cases do not support a finding of state action here . . .

[W]e would be remiss if we did not note that there are a number of state and municipal functions not covered by our election cases or governed by the reasoning of Marsh which have been administered with a greater degree of exclusivity by States and municipalities than has the function of so-called "dispute resolution." Among these are such functions as education, fire and police protection, and tax collection. We express no view as to the extent, if any, to which a city or State might be free to delegate to private parties the performance of such functions and thereby avoid the strictures of the Fourteenth Amendment. The mere recitation of these possible permutations and combinations of factual situations suffices to caution us that their resolution should abide the necessity of deciding them.

IV

Respondents further urge that Flagg Brothers' proposed action is properly attributable to the State because the State has authorized and encouraged it in enacting § 7–210. Our cases state "that a State is responsible for the . . . act of a private party when the State, by its law, has compelled the act." This Court, however, has never held that a State's mere acquiescence in a private action converts that

action into that of the State. The Court rejected a similar argument in *Jackson*:
"Approval by a state utility commission of such a request from a regulated utility, where the commission has not put its own weight on the side of the proposed practice by ordering it, does not transmute a practice initiated by the utility and approved by the commission into 'state action.'" . . .

The clearest demonstration of this distinction appears in *Moose Lodge No. 107 v. Irvis* which held that the Commonwealth of Pennsylvania, although not responsible for racial discrimination voluntarily practiced by a private club, could not by law require the club to comply with its own discriminatory rules. These cases clearly rejected the notion that our prior cases permitted the imposition of Fourteenth Amendment restraints on private action by the simple device of characterizing the State's inaction as "authorization" or "encouragement."

It is quite immaterial that the State has embodied its decision not to act in statutory form. If New York had no commercial statutes at all, its courts would still be faced with the decision whether to prohibit or to permit the sort of sale threatened here the first time an aggrieved bailor came before them for relief. A judicial decision to deny relief would be no less an "authorization" or "encouragement" of that sale than the legislature's decision embodied in this statute. It was recognized in the earliest interpretations of the Fourteenth Amendment "that a State may act through different agencies,—either by its legislative, its executive, or its judicial authorities; and the prohibitions of the amendment extend to all action of the State" infringing rights protected thereby. If the mere denial of judicial relief is considered sufficient encouragement to make the State responsible for those private acts, all private deprivations of property would be converted into public acts whenever the State, for whatever reason, denies relief sought by the putative property owner.

Not only is this notion completely contrary to that "essential dichotomy," between public and private acts, but it has been previously rejected by this Court. In *Evans v. Abney* our Brother Brennan in dissent contended that a Georgia statutory provision authorizing the establishment of trusts for racially restricted parks conferred a "special power" on testators taking advantage of the provision. The Court nevertheless concluded that the State of Georgia was in no way responsible for the purely private choice involved in that case. By the same token, the State of New York is in no way responsible for *Flagg Brothers'* decision, a decision which the State in § 7–210 permits but does not compel, to threaten to sell these respondents' belongings.

Here, the State of New York has not compelled the sale of a bailor's goods, but has merely announced the circumstances under which its courts will not interfere with a private sale. Indeed, the crux of respondents' complaint is not that the State has acted, but that it has refused to act. This statutory refusal to act is no different in principle from an ordinary statute of limitations whereby the State declines to provide a remedy for private deprivations of property after the passage of a given period of time.

We conclude that the allegations of these complaints do not establish a violation of these respondents' Fourteenth Amendment rights by either petitioner Flagg Brothers or the State of New York. The District Court properly concluded that their complaints failed to state a claim for relief under 42 U.S.C. § 1983. The judgment of the Court of Appeals holding otherwise is

Reversed.

[Justice Marshall's dissent is omitted.]

Mr. Justice **Stevens,** with whom Mr. Justice **White** and Mr. Justice **Marshall** join, dissenting . . .

There is no question in this case but that respondents have a property interest in the possessions that the warehouseman proposes to sell. It is also clear that, whatever power of sale the warehouseman has, it does not derive from the consent of the respondents. The claimed power derives solely from the State, and specifically from § 7–210 of the New York Uniform Commercial Code. The question is whether a state statute which authorizes a private party to deprive a person of his property without his consent must meet the requirements of the Due Process Clause of the Fourteenth Amendment. This question must be answered in the affirmative unless the State has virtually unlimited power to transfer interests in private property without any procedural protections . . .

The test of what is a state function for purposes of the Due Process Clause has been variously phrased. Most frequently the issue is presented in terms of whether the State has delegated a function traditionally and historically associated with sovereignty. In this Court, petitioners have attempted to argue that the nonconsensual transfer of property rights is not a traditional function of the sovereign. The overwhelming historical evidence is to the contrary, however, and the Court wisely does not adopt this position. Instead, the Court reasons that state action cannot be found because the State has not delegated to the warehouseman an exclusive sovereign function. This distinction, however, is not consistent with our prior decisions on state action; is not even adhered to by the Court in this case; and, most importantly, is inconsistent with the line of cases beginning with *Sniadach v. Family Finance Corp.*

Since *Sniadach* this Court has scrutinized various state statutes regulating the debtor-creditor relationship for compliance with the Due Process Clause. See also *North Georgia Finishing, Inc. v. Di-Chem, Inc.; Mitchell v. W.T. Grant Co.; Fuentes v. Shevin.* In each of these cases a finding of state action was a prerequisite to the Court's decision. The Court today seeks to explain these findings on the ground that in each case there was some element of "overt official involvement." Given the facts of those cases, this explanation is baffling. In *North Georgia Finishing,* for instance, the official involvement of the State of Georgia consisted of a court clerk who issued a writ of garnishment based solely on the affidavit of the creditor. The clerk's actions were purely ministerial, and, until today, this Court had never held that purely ministerial acts of "minor governmental functionaries" were sufficient to establish state action. The suggestion that this was the basis for due process review in *Sniadach, Shevin,* and *North Georgia Finishing* marks a major and, in my judgment, unwise expansion of the state-action doctrine. The number of private actions in which a governmental functionary plays some ministerial role is legion; to base due process review on the fortuity of such governmental intervention would demean the majestic purposes of the Due Process Clause.

Instead, cases such as *North Georgia Finishing* must be viewed as reflecting this Court's recognition of the significance of the State's role in defining and controlling the debtor-creditor relationship. The Court's language to this effect in the various debtor-creditor cases has been unequivocal. In *Fuentes v. Shevin* the Court stressed that the statutes in question "[abdicated] effective state control over state power." And it is clear that what was of concern in Shevin was the private use of state power to achieve a nonconsensual resolution of a commercial dispute. The state statutes placed the state power to repossess property in the hands of an interested private party, just as the state statute in this case places the state power to conduct judicially binding sales in satisfaction of a lien in the hands of the warehouseman.

"Private parties, serving their own private advantage, may unilaterally invoke state power to replevy goods from another. No state official participates in the decision to seek a writ; no state official reviews the basis for the claim to repossession; and no state official evaluates the need for immediate seizure. There is not even a requirement that the plaintiff provide any information to the court on these matters." . . .

Yet the very defect that made the statutes in *Shevin* and *North Georgia Finishing* unconstitutional—lack of state control—is, under today's decision, the factor that precludes constitutional review of the state statute. The Due Process Clause cannot command such incongruous results. If it is unconstitutional for a State to allow a private party to exercise a traditional state power because the state supervision of that power is purely mechanical, the State surely cannot immunize its actions from constitutional scrutiny by removing even the mechanical supervision.

Not only has the State removed its nominal supervision in this case, it has also authorized a private party to exercise a governmental power that is at least as significant as the power exercised in *Shevin* or *North Georgia Finishing.* In *Shevin,* the Florida statute allowed the debtor's property to be seized and held pending the outcome of the creditor's action for repossession. The property would not be finally disposed of until there was an adjudication of the underlying claim. Similarly, in *North Georgia Finishing*, the state statute provided for a garnishment procedure which deprived the debtor of the use of property in the garnishee's hands pending the outcome of litigation. The warehouseman's power under § 7–210 is far broader, as the Court of Appeals pointed out: 'After giving the bailor specified notice, . . . the warehouseman is entitled to sell the stored goods in satisfaction of whatever he determines the storage charges to be. The warehouseman, unquestionably an interested party, is thus authorized by law to resolve any disputes over storage charges finally and unilaterally."

Whether termed "traditional," "exclusive," or "significant," the state power to order binding, nonconsensual resolution of a conflict between debtor and creditor is exactly the sort of power with which the Due Process Clause is concerned. And the State's delegation of that power to a private party is, accordingly, subject to due process scrutiny. This, at the very least, is the teaching of *Sniadach, Shevin*, and *North Georgia Finishing . . .*

[T]his conclusion does not even remotely suggest that "all private deprivations of property [will] be converted into public acts whenever the State, for whatever reason, denies relief sought by the putative property owner." The focus is not on the private deprivation but on the state authorization . . . My analysis in this case thus assumes that petitioner Flagg Brothers' proposed sale will conform to the procedure specified by the state legislature and that respondents' challenge therefore will be to the constitutionality of that process. It is only what the State itself has enacted that they may ask the federal court to review in a § 1983 case. If there should be a deviation from the state statute—such as a failure to give the notice required by the state law—the defect could be remedied by a state court and there would be no occasion for § 1983 relief . . .

[I]t is obviously true that the overwhelming majority of disputes in our society are resolved in the private sphere. But it is no longer possible, if it ever was, to believe that a sharp line can be drawn between private and public actions. The Court today holds that our examination of state delegations of power should be limited to those rare instances where the State has ceded one of its "exclusive" powers. As indicated, I believe that this limitation is

neither logical nor practical. More troubling, this description of what is state action does not even attempt to reflect the concerns of the Due Process Clause, for the state-action doctrine is, after all, merely one aspect of this broad constitutional protection.

In the broadest sense, we expect government "to provide a reasonable and fair framework of rules which facilitate commercial transactions. . . ." This "framework of rules" is premised on the assumption that the State will control nonconsensual deprivations of property and that the State's control will, in turn, be subject to the restrictions of the Due Process Clause. The power to order legally binding surrenders of property and the constitutional restrictions on that power are necessary correlatives in our system. In effect, today's decision allows the State to divorce these two elements by the simple expedient of transferring the implementation of its policy to private parties. Because the Fourteenth Amendment does not countenance such a division of power and responsibility, I respectfully dissent.

NOTES

1. In *Lugar*, the Court distinguished *Flagg Brothers* as a case in which there was no state involvement in the property deprivation. State law allowed the warehouseman to exercise his lien without any action by officials. Is it sensible to have the availability of constitutional restrictions on the deprivation of property turn on whether the state statute at issue mandates that a private actor enlist officials in his effort to deprive another of property? Why should constitutional restrictions apply to the disposition of property under systems where state officials perform strictly administrative functions, exercising no judgment? Is it wise to find the constitution inapplicable to state regimes under which state authorities play no role in the deprivation? Is the effect of the ruling in *Flagg Brothers* to insulate the UCC provision authorizing a warehouseman's lien from judicial review on constitutional grounds?

For that matter, is there any real difference between the two kinds of cases, in terms of the state's involvement? For an argument that there is not, see Brest, *State Action and Liberal*

Theory: A Casenote on Flagg Brothers v. Brooks, 130 U. Pa. L. Rev. 1296, 1312–15 (1982).

2. In *Jackson v. Metropolitan Edison Co.,* 419 U.S. 345, 357 (1974) the Court held that a private utility's termination of service was not state action subject to due process constraints. The plaintiff pointed out that state regulators had authorized termination without notice and hearing, and argued that this amounted to state action. The Court said that "[a]pproval by a state utility commission of . . . a request by a regulated utility, where the commission has not put its own weight on the side of the proposed practice by ordering it, does not transmute a practice initiated by the utility and approved by the commission into 'state action.'"

The utility in *Jackson* terminated service for lack of payment. Would the result have been different if the electric company had refused to serve blacks? Consider that question in connection with the next case.

B. Contracting Out and Other Symbiotic Relationships

Burton v. Wilmington Parking Authority

365 U.S. 715 (1961)

Mr. Justice **Clark** delivered the opinion of the Court.

In this action for declaratory and injunctive relief it is admitted that the Eagle Coffee Shoppe, Inc., a restaurant located within an off-street automobile parking building in Wilmington, Delaware, has refused to serve appellant food or drink solely because he is a Negro. The parking building is owned and operated by the Wilmington Parking Authority, an agency of the State of Delaware, and the restaurant is the Authority's lessee. Appellant claims that such refusal abridges his rights under the Equal Protection Clause of the Fourteenth Amendment to the United States Constitution. The Supreme Court of Delaware has held that Eagle was acting in "a purely private capacity" under its lease; that its action was not that of the Authority and was

not, therefore, state action within the contemplation of the prohibitions contained in that Amendment. It also held that under [Delaware law] . . . Eagle was a restaurant, not an inn, and that as such it "is not required . . . to serve any and all persons entering its place of business." . . . [W]e . . . conclude[] that the exclusion of appellant under the circumstances shown to be present here was discriminatory state action in violation of the Equal Protection Clause of the Fourteenth Amendment.

The Authority was created . . . to provide adequate parking facilities for the convenience of the public . . . To this end the Authority is granted wide powers including that of constructing or acquiring by lease, purchase or condemnation, lands and facilities, and that of leasing "portions of any of its garage buildings or structures for commercial use by the lessee, where, in the opinion of the Authority, such leasing is necessary and feasible for the financing and operation of such facilities." The Act provides that the rates and charges for its facilities must be reasonable and are to be determined exclusively by the Authority "for the purposes of providing for the payment of the expenses of the Authority, the construction, improvement, repair, maintenance, and operation of its facilities and properties, the payment of the principal of and interest on its obligations, and to fulfill the terms and provisions of any agreements made with the purchasers or holders of any such obligations or with the city." The Authority has no power to pledge the credit of the State of Delaware but may issue its own revenue bonds which are tax exempt. Any and all property owned or used by the Authority is likewise exempt from state taxation.

The first project undertaken by the Authority was the erection of a parking facility on Ninth Street in downtown Wilmington. The tract consisted of four parcels, all of which were acquired by negotiated purchases from private owners. Three were paid for in cash, borrowed from Equitable Security Trust Company, and the fourth, purchased from Diamond Ice and Coal Company, was paid for "partly in Revenue Bonds of the Authority and partly in cash [$934,000] donated by the City of Wilmington, pursuant to 22 Del. C. c. 5. . . . Subsequently, the City of Wilmington gave the Authority $1,822,827.69 which sum the Authority applied to the redemption of the Revenue Bonds delivered to Diamond Ice & Coal Co. and to the repayment of the Equitable Security Trust Company loan."

Before it began actual construction of the facility, the Authority was advised by its retained experts that the anticipated revenue from the parking of cars and proceeds from sale of its bonds would not be sufficient to finance the construction costs of the facility. Moreover, the bonds were not expected to be marketable if payable solely out of parking revenues. To secure additional capital needed for its "debt-service" requirements, and thereby to make bond financing practicable, the Authority decided it was necessary to enter long-term leases with responsible tenants for commercial use of some of the space available in the projected "garage building." The public was invited to bid for these leases.

In April 1957 such a private lease, for 20 years and renewable for another 10 years, was made with Eagle Coffee Shoppe, Inc., for use as a "restaurant, dining room, banquet hall, cocktail lounge and bar and for no other use and purpose." The multi-level space of the building which was let to Eagle, although "within the exterior walls of the structure, has no marked public entrance leading from the parking portion of the facility into the restaurant proper . . . [whose main entrance] is located on Ninth Street." In its lease the Authority covenanted to complete construction expeditiously, including completion of "the decorative finishing of the leased premises and utilities therefor, without cost to Lessee," including necessary utility connections, toilets, hung acoustical tile and plaster ceilings; vinyl asbestos, ceramic tile and concrete floors; connecting stairs and wrought iron railings; and wood-floored show windows. Eagle spent some $220,000 to make the space suitable for its operation and, to the extent such improvements were so attached to realty as to become part thereof, Eagle to the same extent enjoys the Authority's tax exemption.

The Authority further agreed to furnish heat for Eagle's premises, gas service for the boiler room, and to make, at its own expense, all necessary structural repairs, all repairs to exterior surfaces except store fronts and any repairs caused by lessee's own act or neglect. The Authority retained the right to place any directional signs on the exterior of the let space which would not interfere with or obscure Eagle's display signs. Agreeing to pay an annual rental of $28,700, Eagle covenanted to "occupy and use the leased premises in accordance with all applicable laws, statutes, ordinances and rules and regulations of any federal, state or municipal authority." Its lease, however, contains no requirement that its restaurant services be made available to the general public on a nondiscriminatory basis, in spite of the fact that the Authority has power to adopt rules and regulations respecting the use of its facilities except any as would impair the security of its bondholders.

Other portions of the structure were leased to other tenants, including a bookstore, a retail jeweler, and a food store. Upon completion of the building, the Authority located at appropriate places thereon official signs indicating the public character of the building, and flew from mastheads on the roof both the state and national flags.

In August 1958 appellant parked his car in the building and walked around to enter the restaurant by its front door on Ninth Street. Having entered and sought service, he was refused it . . .

The *Civil Rights Cases*, "embedded in our constitutional law" the principle "that the action inhibited by the first section [Equal Protection Clause] of the Fourteenth Amendment is only such action as may fairly be said to be that of the States. That Amendment erects no shield against merely private conduct, however discriminatory or wrongful." . . . Because the virtue of the right to equal protection of the laws could lie only in the breadth of its application, its constitutional assurance was reserved in terms whose imprecision was necessary if the right were to be enjoyed in the variety of individual-state relationships which the Amendment was designed to embrace. For the same reason, to fashion and apply a precise formula for recognition of state responsibility under the Equal Protection Clause is an "impossible task" which "This Court has never attempted." Only by sifting facts and weighing circumstances can the nonobvious involvement of the State in private conduct be attributed its true significance . . .

[T]he Delaware Supreme Court seems to have placed controlling emphasis on its conclusion, as to the accuracy of which there is doubt, that only some 15% of the total cost of the facility was "advanced" from public funds; that the cost of the entire facility was allocated three-fifths to the space for commercial leasing and two-fifths to parking space; that anticipated revenue from parking was only some 30.5% of the total income, the balance of which was expected to be earned by the leasing; that the Authority had no original intent to place a restaurant in the building, it being only a happenstance resulting from the bidding; that Eagle expended considerable moneys on furnishings; that the restaurant's main and marked public entrance is on Ninth Street without any public entrance direct from the parking area; and that "the only connection Eagle has with the public facility . . . is the furnishing of the sum of $28,700 annually in the form of rent which is used by the Authority to defray a portion of the operating expense of an otherwise unprofitable enterprise." While these factual considerations are indeed validly accountable aspects of the enterprise upon which the State has embarked, we cannot say that they lead inescapably to the conclusion that state action is not present. Their persuasiveness is diminished when evaluated in the context of other factors which must be acknowledged.

The land and building were publicly owned. As an entity, the building was dedicated to "public uses" in performance of the Authority's "essential governmental functions." The costs of land acquisition, construction, and maintenance are defrayed entirely from donations by the City of Wilmington, from loans and revenue bonds and from the proceeds of rentals and parking services out of which the loans and bonds were payable . . . [T]he commercially leased areas were not surplus state property, but constituted a physically and financially integral and, indeed, indispensable part of the State's plan to operate its project as a self-sustaining unit. Upkeep and maintenance of the building, including necessary repairs, were responsibilities of the Authority and were payable out of public funds. It cannot be doubted that the peculiar relationship of the restaurant to the parking facility in which it is located confers on each an incidental variety of mutual benefits. Guests of the restaurant are afforded a convenient place to park their automobiles, even if

they cannot enter the restaurant directly from the parking area. Similarly, its convenience for diners may well provide additional demand for the Authority's parking facilities. Should any improvements effected in the leasehold by Eagle become part of the realty, there is no possibility of increased taxes being passed on to it since the fee is held by a tax-exempt government agency. Neither can it be ignored, especially in view of Eagle's affirmative allegation that for it to serve Negroes would injure its business, that profits earned by discrimination not only contribute to, but also are indispensable elements in, the financial success of a governmental agency.

Addition of all these activities, obligations and responsibilities of the Authority, the benefits mutually conferred, together with the obvious fact that the restaurant is operated as an integral part of a public building devoted to a public parking service, indicates that degree of state participation and involvement in discriminatory action which it was the design of the Fourteenth Amendment to condemn. It is irony amounting to grave injustice that in one part of a single building, erected and maintained with public funds by an agency of the State to serve a public purpose, all persons have equal rights, while in another portion, also serving the public, a Negro is a second-class citizen, offensive because of his race, without rights and unentitled to service, but at the same time fully enjoys equal access to nearby restaurants in wholly privately owned buildings. As the Chancellor pointed out, in its lease with Eagle the Authority could have affirmatively required Eagle to discharge the responsibilities under the Fourteenth Amendment imposed upon the private enterprise as a consequence of state participation. But no State may effectively abdicate its responsibilities by either ignoring them or by merely failing to discharge them whatever the motive may be. It is of no consolation to an individual denied the equal protection of the laws that it was done in good faith. Certainly the conclusions drawn in similar cases by the various Courts of Appeals do not depend upon such a distinction. By its inaction, the Authority, and through it the State, has not only made itself a party to the refusal of service, but has elected to place its power, property and prestige behind the admitted discrimination. The State has so far insinuated itself into a position of interdependence with Eagle that it must be recognized as a joint participant in the challenged activity, which, on that account, cannot be considered to have been so "purely private" as to fall without the scope of the Fourteenth Amendment.

Because readily applicable formulae may not be fashioned, the conclusions drawn from the facts and circumstances of this record are by no means declared as universal truths on the basis of which every state leasing agreement is to be tested. Owing to the very "largeness" of government, a multitude of relationships might appear to some to fall within the Amendment's embrace, but that, it must be remembered, can be determined only in the framework of the peculiar facts or circumstances present. Therefore respondents' prophecy of nigh universal application of a constitutional precept so peculiarly dependent for its invocation upon appropriate facts fails to take into account "Differences in circumstances [which] beget appropriate differences in law." Specifically defining the limits of our inquiry, what we hold today is that when a State leases public property in the manner and for the purpose shown to have been the case here, the proscriptions of the Fourteenth Amendment must be complied with by the lessee as certainly as though they were binding covenants written into the agreement itself . . .

Reversed and remanded.

NOTES

Would *Burton* have come out differently if the substantive complaint were that employees of the coffee shop were entitled to the same procedural due process rights as public employees? For a suggestion that it would have, see Friendly, *The Public-Private Penumbra—Fourteen Years Later*, 130 U. Pa. L. Rev. 1289, 1291, 1294 (1982). See also Glennon & Nowak, *A Functional Analysis of the Fourteenth Amendment "State Action" Requirement*, 1976 Sup. Ct. Rev. 221; 1 S. Nahmod, *Civil Rights and Civil Liberties Litigation* 63 (3d ed. 1991) ("[T]he Court may in effect be using a balancing test in its state action cases. If this is so, then the perceived importance of the section 1983 plaintiff's constitutional claim will be a significant

factor in the Supreme Court's state action determination. From this perspective, state action is not a unitary concept, but arises depending on the constitutional violation asserted.")

In recent years the Court has increasingly employed a "nexus" test for resolving cases where the government has contracted with a private party. It is not enough that there be a mutually beneficial relationship between the state and the private party, or that the private party is heavily regulated. "[T]he inquiry must be whether there is a sufficiently close nexus between the State and the challenged action of the regulated entity so that the action of the latter may be fairly treated as that of the State itself." *Jackson v. Metropolitan Edison Co.,* 419 U.S. 345 (1974). This approach is illustrated by the following case.

Rendell-Baker v. Kohn

457 U.S. 830 (1982)

Chief Justice **Burger** delivered the opinion of the Court.

We granted certiorari to decide whether a private school, whose income is derived primarily from public sources and which is regulated by public authorities, acted under color of state law when it discharged certain employees.

I

A

Respondent Kohn is the director of the New Perspectives School, a nonprofit institution located on privately owned property in Brookline, Massachusetts. The school was founded as a private institution and is operated by a board of directors, none of whom are public officials or are chosen by public officials. The school specializes in dealing with students who have experienced difficulty completing public high schools; many have drug, alcohol, or behavioral problems, or other special needs. In recent years, nearly all of the students at the school have been referred to it by the Brookline or Boston School Committees, or by the Drug Rehabilitation Division of the Massachusetts Department of Mental

Health. The school issues high school diplomas certified by the Brookline School Committee.

When students are referred to the school by Brookline or Boston under Chapter 766 of the Massachusetts Acts of 1972, the School Committees in those cities pay for the students' education. The school also receives funds from a number of other state and federal agencies. In recent years, public funds have accounted for at least 90%, and in one year 99%, of respondent school's operating budget. There were approximately 50 students at the school in those years and none paid tuition.

To be eligible for tuition funding under Chapter 766, the school must comply with a variety of regulations, many of which are common to all schools. The State has issued detailed regulations concerning matters ranging from record-keeping to student-teacher ratios. Concerning personnel policies, the Chapter 766 regulations require the school to maintain written job descriptions and written statements describing personnel standards and procedures, but they impose few specific requirements.

The school is also regulated by Boston and Brookline as a result of its Chapter 766 funding. By its contract with the Boston School Committee, which refers to the school as a "contractor," the school must agree to carry out the individualized plan developed for each student referred to the school by the Committee. The contract specifies that school employees are not city employees.

The school also has a contract with the State Drug Rehabilitation Division. Like the contract with the Boston School Committee, that agreement refers to the school as a "contractor." It provides for reimbursement for services provided for students referred to the school by the Drug Rehabilitation Division, and includes requirements concerning the services to be provided. Except for general requirements, such as an equal employment opportunity requirement, the agreement does not cover personnel policies.

While five of the six petitioners were teachers at the school, petitioner Rendell-Baker was a vocational counselor hired under a grant from the federal Law Enforcement Assistance Administration, whose funds are distributed in Massachusetts through the State Committee on Criminal Justice. As a condition of the grant, the Committee on Criminal Justice must approve the school's initial hiring decisions. The purpose of this requirement is to insure that the school hires vocational counselors who meet the qualifications described in the school's grant proposal to the Committee; the Committee does not interview applicants for counselor positions.

B

Rendell-Baker was discharged by the school in January 1977, and the five other petitioners were discharged in June 1978. Rendell-Baker's discharge resulted from a dispute over the role of a student-staff council in making hiring decisions. A dispute arose when some students presented a petition to the school's board of directors in December 1976, seeking greater responsibilities for the student-staff council. Director Kohn opposed the proposal, but Rendell-Baker supported it and so advised the board. On December 13, Kohn notified the State Committee on Criminal Justice, which funded Rendell-Baker's position, that she intended to dismiss Rendell-Baker and employ someone else. Kohn notified Rendell-Baker of her dismissal in January 1977 . . .

In the spring of 1978, students and staff voiced objections to Kohn's policies. The five petitioners other than Rendell-Baker, who were all teachers at the school, wrote a letter to the board of directors urging Kohn's dismissal. When the board affirmed its confidence in Kohn, students from the school picketed the home of the president of the board. The students were threatened with suspension; a local newspaper then ran a story about the controversy at the school. In response to the story, the five petitioners wrote a letter to the editor in which they stated that they thought the prohibition of picketing was unconstitutional. On the day the letter to the editor appeared, the five teachers told the president of the board that they were forming a union. Kohn discharged the teachers the next day. They brought suit against the school and its directors in December 1978. Like Rendell-Baker, they sought relief under § 1983, alleging that their rights under the First, Fifth, and Fourteenth Amendments had been violated . . .

II

A

[I]t is fundamental that the First Amendment prohibits governmental infringement on the right of free speech. Similarly, the Fourteenth Amendment, which prohibits the states from denying federal constitutional rights and which guarantees due process, applies to acts of the states, not to acts of private persons or entities. And § 1983, which was enacted pursuant to the authority of Congress to enforce the Fourteenth Amendment, prohibits interference with federal rights under color of state law . . .

The core issue presented in this case is not whether petitioners were discharged because of their speech or without adequate procedural protections, but whether the school's action in discharging them can fairly be seen as state action. If the action of the respondent school is not state action, our inquiry ends.

B

In *Blum v. Yaretsky* the Court analyzed the state action requirement of the Fourteenth Amendment. The Court considered whether certain nursing homes were state actors for the purpose of determining whether decisions regarding transfers of patients could be fairly attributed to the State, and hence be subjected to Fourteenth Amendment due process requirements. The challenged transfers primarily involved decisions, made by physicians and nursing home administrators, to move patients from "skilled nursing facilities" to less expensive "health-related facilities." Like the New Perspectives School, the nursing homes were privately owned and operated . . . The Court held that, "a State normally can be held responsible for a private decision only when it has exercised coercive power or has provided such significant encouragement, either overt or covert, that the choice must in law be deemed to be that of the State." In determining that the transfer decisions were not actions of the State, the Court considered each of the factors alleged by petitioners here to make the discharge decisions of the New Perspectives School fairly attributable to the State.

First, the nursing homes, like the school, depended on the State for funds; the State subsidized the operating and capital costs of the nursing homes, and paid the medical expenses of more than 90% of the patients. Here the Court of Appeals concluded that the fact that virtually all of the school's income was derived from government funding was the strongest factor to support a claim of state action. But in *Blum v. Yaretsky*, we held that the similar dependence of the nursing homes did not make the acts of the physicians and nursing home administrators acts of the State, and we conclude that the school's receipt of public funds does not make the discharge decisions acts of the State.

The school, like the nursing homes, is not fundamentally different from many private corporations whose business depends primarily on contracts to build roads, bridges, dams, ships, or submarines for the government. Acts of such private contractors do not become acts of the government by reason of their significant or even total engagement in performing public contracts.

The school is also analogous to the public defender found not to be a state actor in *Polk County v. Dodson*. There we concluded that, although the State paid the public defender, her relationship with her client was "identical to that existing between any other lawyer and client." Here the relationship between the school and its teachers and counselors is not changed because the State pays the tuition of the students.

A second factor considered in *Blum v. Yaretsky* was the extensive regulation of the nursing homes by the State. There the State was indirectly involved in the transfer decisions challenged in that case because a primary goal of the State in regulating nursing homes was to keep costs down by transferring patients from intensive treatment centers to less expensive facilities when possible. Both state and federal regulations encouraged the nursing homes to transfer patients to less expensive facilities when appropriate. The nursing homes were extensively regulated in many other ways as well . . . The Court relied on *Jackson* where we held that state regulation, even if "extensive and detailed," did not make a utility's actions state action.

Here the decisions to discharge the petitioners were not compelled or even influenced by any state regulation. Indeed, in contrast to the extensive regulation of the school generally, the various regulators showed relatively little interest in the school's personnel matters. The most intrusive personnel regulation promulgated by the various government agencies was the requirement that the Committee on Criminal Justice had the power to approve persons hired as vocational counselors. Such a regulation is not sufficient to make a decision to discharge, made by private management, state action . . .

The third factor asserted to show that the school is a state actor is that it performs a "public function." However, our holdings have made clear that the relevant question is not simply whether a private group is serving a "public function." We have held that the question is whether the function performed has been "traditionally the *exclusive* prerogative of the State." *Jackson*, supra; quoted in *Blum v. Yaretsky* (emphasis added). There can be no doubt that the education of maladjusted high school students is a public function, but that is only the beginning of the inquiry. Chapter 766 of the Massachusetts Acts of 1972 demonstrates that the State intends to provide services for such students at public expense. That legislative policy choice in no way makes these services the exclusive province of the State. Indeed, the Court of Appeals noted that until recently the State had not undertaken to provide education for students who could not be served by traditional public schools. That a private entity performs a function which serves the public does not make its acts state action.[7]

Fourth, petitioners argue that there is a "symbiotic relationship" between the school and the State similar to the relationship involved in *Burton v. Wilmington Parking Authority*. Such a claim is rejected in *Blum v. Yaretsky*, and we reject it here. In *Burton*, the Court held that the refusal of a restaurant located in a public parking garage to serve Negroes constituted state action. The Court stressed that the restaurant was located on public property and that the rent from the restaurant contributed to the support of the garage. In response to the argument that the restaurant's profits, and hence the State's financial position, would suffer if it did not discriminate, the Court concluded that this showed that the State profited from the restaurant's discriminatory conduct. The Court viewed this as support for the conclusion that

the State should be charged with the discriminatory actions. Here the school's fiscal relationship with the State is not different from that of many contractors performing services for the government. No symbiotic relationship such as existed in *Burton* exists here.

C

We hold that petitioners have not stated a claim for relief under 42 U.S.C. § 1983; accordingly, the judgment of the Court of Appeals for the First Circuit is

Affirmed.

Justice White, concurring in the judgments.[1]

The issue in *Blum v. Yaretsky* is whether a private nursing home's decision to discharge or transfer a Medicaid patient satisfies the state-action requirement of the Fourteenth Amendment. To satisfy this requirement, respondents must show that the transfer or discharge is made on the basis of some rule of decision for which the State is responsible. *Lugar v. Edmondson Oil Co.* It is not enough to show that the State takes certain actions in response to this private decision. The rule of decision implicated in the actions at issue here appears to be nothing more than a medical judgment. This is the clear import of the majority's conclusion that the "decisions ultimately turn on medical judgments made by private parties according to professional standards that are not established by the State," with which I agree.

Similarly, the allegations of the petitioners in *Rendell-Baker v. Kohn*, fail to satisfy the state-action requirement. In this case, the question of state action focuses on an employment decision made by a private school that receives most of its funding from public sources and is subject to state regulation in certain respects. For me, the critical factor is the absence of any allegation that the employment decision was itself based upon some rule of conduct or policy put forth by the State. As the majority states, "in contrast to the extensive regulation of the school generally, the various regulators showed relatively little interest in the school's personnel matters." The employment decision remains, therefore, a

---

[7] There is no evidence that the State has attempted to avoid its constitutional duties by a sham arrangement which attempts to disguise provision of public services as acts of private parties. Cf. Evans v. Newton (private trustees appointed to manage previously public park for white persons only).

[1] [This opinion applies also to . . . Blum v. Yaretsky.]

private decision not fairly attributable to the State.

Accordingly, I concur in the judgments.

Justice Marshall, with whom Justice Brennan joins, dissenting. . .

II

The decisions of this Court clearly establish that where there is a symbiotic relationship between the State and a privately owned enterprise, so that the State and a privately owned enterprise are participants in a joint venture, the actions of the private enterprise may be attributable to the State. "Conduct that is formally 'private' may become so entwined with governmental policies or so impregnated with a governmental character" that it can be regarded as governmental action . . . The question whether such a relationship exists "can be determined only in the framework of the peculiar facts or circumstances present." Here, an examination of the facts and circumstances leads inexorably to the conclusion that the actions of the New Perspectives School should be attributed to the State; it is difficult to imagine a closer relationship between a government and a private enterprise.

The New Perspectives School receives virtually all of its funds from state sources. This financial dependence on the State is an important indicium of governmental involvement. The school's very survival depends on the State. If the State chooses, it may exercise complete control over the school's operations simply by threatening to withdraw financial support if the school takes action that it considers objectionable.

The school is heavily regulated and closely supervised by the State. This fact provides further support for the conclusion that its actions should be attributed to the State. The school's freedom of decisionmaking is substantially circumscribed by the Massachusetts Department of Education's guidelines and the various contracts with state agencies. For example, the school is required to develop and comply with written rules for hiring and dismissal of personnel. Almost every decision the school makes is substantially affected in some way by the State's regulations.

The fact that the school is providing a substitute for public education is also an important indicium of state action. The provision of education is one of the most important tasks performed by government: it ranks at the very apex of the function of a State. Of course, as the majority emphasizes, performance of a public function is by itself sufficient to justify treating a private entity as a state actor only where the function has been "traditionally the exclusive prerogative of the State." But the fact that a private entity is performing a vital public function, when coupled with other factors demonstrating a close connection with the State, may justify a finding of state action.

The school's provision of a substitute for public education deserves particular emphasis because of the role of Chapter 766. Under this statute, the State is required to provide a free education to all children, including those with special needs. Clearly, if the State had decided to provide the service itself, its conduct would be measured against constitutional standards. The State should not be permitted to avoid constitutional requirements simply by delegating its statutory duty to a private entity. In my view, such a delegation does not convert the performance of the duty from public to private action when the duty is specific and the private institution's decisionmaking authority is significantly curtailed.

When an entity is not only heavily regulated and funded by the State, but also provides a service that the State is required to provide, there is a very close nexus with the State. Under these circumstances, it is entirely appropriate to treat the entity as an arm of the State. Here, since the New Perspectives School exists solely to fulfill the State's obligations under Chapter 766, I think it fully reasonable to conclude that the school is a state actor.

Indeed, I would conclude that the actions challenged here were under color of state law, even if I believed that the sole basis for state action was the fact that the school was providing Chapter 766 services. Petitioners claim that they were discharged because they supported student demands for increased responsibilities in school affairs, that is, because they criticized the school's educational policies. If petitioners' allegations are true, then the school has adopted a specific view of the sort of education that should be provided under the statute, and refuses to tolerate departures from that view. The State, by refusing to intervene, has effectively endorsed that view of its duties under Chapter 766. In short, because petitioners' criticism was directly addressed to the State's responsibilities under Chapter 766, a finding of state action is justified.

The majority repeatedly compares the school to a private contractor that "depends primarily on contracts to build roads, bridges, dams, ships, or submarines for the government." The New Perspectives School can be readily distinguished, however. Although shipbuilders and dambuilders, like the school, may be dependent on government funds, they are not so closely supervised by the government. And unlike most private contractors, the school is performing a statutory duty of the State.

The majority also focuses on the fact that the actions at issue here are personnel decisions. It would apparently concede that actions directly affecting the students could be treated as under color of state law, since the school is fulfilling the State's obligations to those children under Chapter 766. It suggests, however, that the State has no interest in personnel decisions. As I have suggested, I do not share this narrow view of the school's obligations; the personnel decisions challenged here are related to the provision of Chapter 766 education. In any event, since the school is funded almost entirely by the State, is closely supervised by the State, and exists solely to perform the State's statutory duty to educate children with special needs—since the school is really just an arm of the State—its personnel decisions may appropriately be considered state action.

III

Even though there are myriad indicia of state action in this case, the majority refuses to find that the school acted under color of state law when it discharged petitioners. The decision in this case marks a return to empty formalism in state action doctrine. Because I believe that the state action requirement must be given a more sensitive and flexible interpretation than the majority offers, I dissent.

NOTES

1. Charles Black once described state action doctrine as "a conceptual disaster area."

Black, *The Supreme Court 1966 Term—Foreword: "State Action," Equal Protection, and California's Proposition 14*, 81 Harv. L. Rev. 69, 95 (1967). See also Schnieder, *State Action—Making Sense Out of Chaos—A Historical Approach*, 37 U. Fla. L. Rev. 737, 737 (1985). One reason it is hard to make sense of state action doctrine is that the Court identifies a number of factors that matter, but does not apply the standards consistently from one case to the next. It sometimes seems as though the Court uses the factors more to rationalize a result it reaches on unstated grounds than to guide its decisionmaking in the first place.

Are *Rendell-Baker* and *Blum* consistent with *Lugar*? (The opinions were all handed down on the same day.) If schools and hospitals are not "traditionally the exclusive province of the state", then neither is the enforcement of security interests in property, is it? See *Flagg Bros. v. Brooks*, supra.

2. The Court cites *Polk County v. Dodson*, 454 U.S. 312 (1981) in support of its decision. *Dodson* held that a public defender did not act under color of state law, even though he was a state employee.

Compare *West v. Atkins*, 487 U.S. 42 (1988), where the state had contracted with Atkins, an orthopedic surgeon, to spend two days a week seeing patients at a state prison. West, a prisoner, tore an Achilles tendon and received medical care from Atkins. Unsatisfied with the results of the treatment, West sued Atkins under section 1983, alleging that Atkins acted with "deliberate indifference", in violation of the cruel and unusual punishment clause of the Eighth Amendment. The Fourth Circuit held that persons like Atkins, acting "within the bounds of traditional professional discretion and judgment", do not act under color of state law.

The Supreme Court reversed. Although the Fourth Circuit had relied upon *Dodson*, that case was inapposite, in the Court's view. '[I]n contrast to the public defender, Doctor Atkins' professional and ethical obligation to make independent medical judgments did not set him in conflict with the State and other prison authorities. Indeed, his relationship with other prison authorities was cooperative . . . [The Court of Appeals] appears to have misread *Polk County* as establishing a general principle that professionals do not act under color of state law when they act in their professional capacities . . . To the extent this Court in *Polk County* relied on the fact that the public defender is a 'professional' in concluding that he was not engaged in state action, the case turned on the particular professional obligation of the criminal defense attorney to be an adversary of the State, not on the independence and integrity generally applicable to professionals as a class."

3. Suppose Dr. Atkins had worked for a private corporation that had contracted with the state to provide medical services for prison inmates. *Calvert v. Sharp*, 748 F.2d 861 (4th Cir. 1984) held that the conduct of the physician was not under color of state law. Is *Calvert* still good law after *West*?

Can a private pharmacy that supplies prescription drugs to a state prison be sued under section 1983 if its products cause harm to inmates? See *Kost v. Kozakiewicz*, 1 F.3d 176, 184 (3rd Cir. 1993) (no). Here the pharmacy, Gatti, sold the drugs not to the prison directly, but through private third party, Corrections Medical Systems, Inc. "Had Gatti contracted directly with the [jail] or Allegheny County to provide off-site prescription filling services, . . . a sufficient connection [might have] existed between a state actor and Gatti to . . . [establish state action]. Gatti contracted, however, with a private, intermediary third party; it had no contact whatsoever with a state actor and was not one itself." What result if the prisoners had sued Corrections Medical Systems (which they did not do)?

In recent years some states have contracted with private businesses to administer prisons. Must these prisons comply with the eighth amendment and other constitutional constraints? For an argument that they must, see Robbins, *The Legal Dimensions of Private Incarceration*, 38 Am. U.L. Rev. 531, 577–604 (1989).

4. Compare *Black v. Indiana Area School District*, 985 F.2d 707 (3rd Cir. 1993). The school district had contracted school bus service to a private company. Plaintiffs were school children who charged that they were molested by a school bus driver while being driven to and from school. They sued the driver, the school district, school officials, and the bus company. Relying on *Rendell-Baker*, the court rejected liability against the private defendants for lack of state action. *West*, it said, was different. "Because the State, through incarcer-

ation, had deprived the inmates of access to medical care, it had a non-delegable constitutional duty to provide medical care on its own." 985 F.2d at 711. Are the school children less vulnerable than prisoners to abuse by private contractors hired by the state? Is it a sufficient answer that children are not legally *required* to ride the bus?

5. Are *Blum* and *Rendell-Baker* consistent with *West*? In each case the state contracted out its governmental responsibilities to private entities. Why is the act of a self-employed doctor at a state prison properly deemed state action while the act of a hospital administrator whose patients are funded by the state or a private school administrator at a school, most of whose students' tuitions are paid by the state, is not?

In *Jackson v. Metropolitan Edison Co.*, 419 U.S. 345, 350 (1974), the Court said that the complaining party must show that "there is a sufficiently close nexus between the State and the challenged action of the regulated entity so that the action of the latter may be fairly treated as that of the State itself." In *Blum* it added that "[t]he purpose of this requirement is to assure that constitutional standards are invoked only when it can be said that the State is *responsible* for the specific conduct of which the plaintiff complains. The importance of this assurance is evident when, as in this case, the complaining party seeks to hold the State liable for the actions of private parties." 457 U.S. at 1004.

Is the difference between *West* and the other cases that the doctor is carrying out the state's constitutional obligation to care for its prisoners, while the acts complained of in *Rendell-Baker*—firing teachers—are not closely related to the state's obligations to the students? In *Blum* the act complained of was transferring Medicaid patients to facilities offering a lower level of care. Is this act any less closely connected to the state's obligations than the doctor's acts in *West*? Is *West* distinguishable from *Blum* on the ground that the provision of medical services for the poor is not a constitutional requirement but is undertaken at the state's discretion? Is it relevant in this regard that the state voluntarily participated in the federal Medicaid program as a means of delivering those services?

6. Rather than sending patients to a private hospital at public expense, the government sometimes maintains a public hospital but con-

tracts with a private business for management services. Under such an arrangement all the hospital employees are employees of the private firm. Are they state actors? See, e.g., *Carnes v. Parker*, 922 F.2d 1506, 1509 (10th Cir. 1991) (yes). Is *Carnes* consistent in principle with *Blum*? See also *Chalfant v. Wilmington Inst.*, 574 F.2d 739 (3rd Cir. 1978) (discharge of employee from library system was state action where the state is extensively involved in support and operations of the library).

Chalfant and *Carnes* rely on *Burton*. Is *Burton* good law after *Blum* and *Rendell-Baker*? Is the test set forth in *Burton*, "sifting facts and weighing circumstances", the equivalent of the inquiry undertaken in *Blum* and *Rendell-Baker*? Those cases consider four factors in deciding whether a private actor was engaged in state action: (a) the entity's source of funding, (b) how extensively it is regulated by the state, (c) whether there is a symbiotic relationship between the state and the private entity, and (d) whether it performs a traditionally governmental function. Note that in *Rendell-Baker* the Court does not quote *Burton*'s "sifting facts and weighing circumstances" language, but characterizes the case as one in which there was a "symbiotic" relationship between government and the coffee shop. *Blum* and *Rendell-Baker* further illustrate that the plaintiff will often fail even if she can establish some of these factors, as the funding test is met in both those cases, yet the plaintiff loses.

Do these cases represent an effort to narrow the scope of *Burton*? If so, why didn't the Court say so? In any event, lower courts do continue to rely on *Burton*, typically in cases like *Chalfant* and *Carnes* where they end up finding state action.

7. The preceding notes are addressed primarily to the problem of whether and when someone to whom the state has contracted out a task acts under color of state law. *Blum* also adverts to another theme that sometimes surfaces in the cases: The private defendant may act under color of state law if he performs an "exclusive public function".

Is a volunteer fire department whose building, fire trucks, and equipment are furnished by the state, and that receives some of this financing from the city a state actor? *Yeager v. City of MacGregor*, 980 F.2d 337 (5th Cir. 1993) holds that it is not. Firefighting is not an "exclusive public function" because Texas law did not *require* municipalities to provide fire protection," and "only half the population of the United States is served by exclusive government fire protection." 980 F.2d at 341.

By contrast, *Haavistola v. Community Fire Co. of Rising Sun*, 6 F.3d 211 (4th Cir. 1993), denied the fire company's motion of summary judgment. Firefighting might be a "public function". But "the determination is a factually intense analysis; and . . . its outcome hinges on how a given state itself views the conduct of the function by the private entity . . . Haavistola and the Fire Company should be allowed to introduce evidence as to the function of fire protection in Maryland." Id. at 218. By using the phrase "the function of fire protection" the court meant the extent of government involvement in volunteer fire departments and the functions served by volunteer fire departments.

C. "Conspiracies" Between Public Officers and Private Actors

National Collegiate Athletic Association v. Tarkanian

488 U.S. 179 (1988)

Justice **Stevens** delivered the opinion of the Court.

When he became head basketball coach at the University of Nevada, Las Vegas (UNLV), in 1973, Jerry Tarkanian inherited a team with a mediocre 14–14 record. App. 188, 205. Four years later the team won 29 out of 32 games and placed third in the championship tournament sponsored by the National Collegiate Athletic Association (NCAA), to which UNLV belongs.

Yet in September 1977 UNLV informed Tarkanian that it was going to suspend him. No dissatisfaction with Tarkanian, once described as "the 'winningest' active basketball coach," id., at 19, motivated his suspension. Rather, the impetus was a report by the NCAA detailing 38 violations of NCAA rules by UNLV personnel, including 10 involving Tarkanian. The NCAA had placed the university's basketball team on probation for two years and ordered UNLV to show cause why the NCAA should not impose further penalties unless UNLV severed all ties during the probation between its intercollegiate athletic program and Tarkanian.

Facing demotion and a drastic cut in pay, Tarkanian brought suit in Nevada state court, alleging that he had been deprived of his Fourteenth Amendment due process rights in violation of 42 U.S.C. § 1983. Ultimately Tarkanian obtained injunctive relief and an award of attorney's fees against both UNLV and the NCAA. NCAA's liability may be upheld only if its participation in the events that led to Tarkanian's suspension constituted "state action" prohibited by the Fourteenth Amendment and was performed "under color of" state law within the meaning of § 1983. We granted certiorari to review the Nevada Supreme Court's holding that the NCAA engaged in state action when it conducted its investigation and recommended that Tarkanian be disciplined. We now reverse.

[I]t is useful to begin with a description of the relationship among the three parties—Tarkanian, UNLV, and the NCAA.

Tarkanian initially was employed on a year-to-year basis but became a tenured professor in 1977. He receives an annual salary with valuable fringe benefits, and his status as a highly successful coach enables him to earn substantial additional income from sports-related activities such as broadcasting and the sponsorship of products.

UNLV is a branch of the University of Nevada, a state-funded institution. The university is organized and operated pursuant to provisions of Nevada's State Constitution, statutes, and regulations. In performing their official functions, the executives of UNLV unquestionably act under color of state law.

The NCAA is an unincorporated association of approximately 960 members, including virtually all public and private universities and 4-year colleges conducting major athletic programs in the United States. Basic policies of the NCAA are determined by the members at annual conventions. Between conventions, the Association is governed by its Council, which appoints various committees to implement specific programs.

One of the NCAA's fundamental policies "is to maintain intercollegiate athletics as an integral part of the educational program and the athlete as an integral part of the student body, and by so doing, retain a clear line of demarcation between college athletics and professional sports." It has therefore adopted rules, which it calls "legislation," governing the conduct of the intercollegiate athletic programs of its members. This NCAA legislation applies to a variety of issues, such as academic standards for eligibility, admissions, financial aid, and the recruiting of student athletes. By joining the NCAA, each member agrees to abide by and to enforce such rules.

The NCAA's bylaws provide that its enforcement program shall be administered by a Committee on Infractions. The Committee supervises an investigative staff, makes factual determinations concerning alleged rule violations, and is expressly authorized to "impose appropriate penalties on a member found to be in violation, or recommend to the Council suspension or termination of membership." In particular, the Committee may order a member institution to show cause why that member should not suffer further penalties unless it imposes a prescribed discipline on an employee; it is not authorized, however, to sanction a member institution's employees directly. The bylaws also provide that representatives of member institutions "are expected to cooperate fully" with the administration of the enforcement program . . .

On November 28, 1972, the Committee on Infractions notified UNLV's president that it was initiating a preliminary inquiry into alleged violations of NCAA requirements by UNLV. As a result of that preliminary inquiry, some three years later the Committee decided that an "Official Inquiry" was warranted and so advised the UNLV president on February 25, 1976. That advice included a series of detailed allegations concerning the recruitment of student athletes during the period between 1971 and 1975. Many of the allegations implicated Tarkanian. It requested UNLV to investigate and provide detailed information concerning each alleged incident.

With the assistance of the Attorney General of Nevada and private counsel, UNLV conducted a thorough investigation of the charges. On October 27, 1976, it filed a comprehensive response containing voluminous exhibits and sworn affidavits. The response denied all of the allegations and specifically concluded that Tarkanian was completely innocent of wrongdoing . . . Ultimately the Committee [found] 38 violations of NCAA rules, including 10 committed by Tarkanian. Most serious was the finding that Tarkanian had violated the University's obligation to provide full cooperation with the NCAA investigation . . .

The Committee proposed [and the Council approved] a series of sanctions against UNLV, including a 2-year period of probation during which its basketball team could not participate in postseason games or appear on television. The Committee also requested UNLV to show cause why additional penalties should not be imposed against UNLV if it failed to discipline Tarkanian by removing him completely from the University's intercollegiate athletic program during the probation period . . .

Promptly after receiving the NCAA report, the president of UNLV directed the Universi-

ty's vice president to schedule a hearing to determine whether the Committee's recommended sanctions should be applied. Tarkanian and UNLV were represented at that hearing; the NCAA was not. Although the vice president expressed doubt concerning the sufficiency of the evidence supporting the Committee's findings, he concluded that "given the terms of our adherence to the NCAA we cannot substitute—biased as we must be—our own judgment on the credibility of witnesses for that of the infractions committee and the Council." . . . [The president of the university suspended Tarkanian.]

Tarkanian filed [a section 1983 suit] in Nevada state court for declaratory and injunctive relief against UNLV and a number of its officers. He alleged that these defendants had . . . deprived him of property and liberty without . . . due process of law . . . [T]he trial court enjoined UNLV from suspending Tarkanian on the ground that he had been denied procedural and substantive due process of law. UNLV appealed.

The NCAA, which had not been joined as a party, filed an amicus curiae brief arguing that . . . the trial court had exceeded its jurisdiction by effectively invalidating the enforcement proceedings of the NCAA, even though the Association was not a party to the suit. Should a controversy exist, the NCAA argued, it was a necessary party to litigate the scope of any relief . . . The Nevada Supreme Court . . . agreed that the NCAA was a necessary party and therefore reversed and remanded to permit joinder of the NCAA . . .

[T]he trial judge . . . concluded that NCAA's conduct constituted state action for jurisdictional and constitutional purposes, and that its decision was arbitrary and capricious. It reaffirmed its earlier injunction barring UNLV from disciplining Tarkanian or otherwise enforcing the Confidential Report. Additionally, it enjoined the NCAA from conducting "any further proceedings against the University," from enforcing its show-cause order, and from taking any other action against the University that had been recommended in the Confidential Report . . .

[The trial court ordered both defendants to pay Tarkanian's attorneys fees, apportioning 90% to the NCAA and 10% to UNLV.] The NCAA appealed both the injunction and the fee order. Not surprisingly, UNLV, which had scored a total victory except for its obligation to pay a fraction of Tarkanian's fees, did not appeal.

[The Nevada Supreme Court modified but largely affirmed the judgment.]

Embedded in our Fourteenth Amendment jurisprudence is a dichotomy between state action, which is subject to scrutiny under the Amendment's Due Process Clause, and private conduct, against which the Amendment affords no shield, no matter how unfair that conduct may be. As a general matter the protections of the Fourteenth Amendment do not extend to "private conduct abridging individual rights."

"Careful adherence to the 'state action' requirement preserves an area of individual freedom by limiting the reach of federal law" and avoids the imposition of responsibility on a State for conduct it could not control. When Congress enacted § 1983 as the statutory remedy for violations of the Constitution, it specified that the conduct at issue must have occurred "under color of" state law; thus, liability attaches only to those wrongdoers "who carry a badge of authority of a State and represent it in some capacity, whether they act in accordance with their authority or misuse it." *Monroe v. Pape* . . .

In this case Tarkanian argues that the NCAA was a state actor because it misused power that it possessed by virtue of state law. He claims specifically that UNLV delegated its own functions to the NCAA, clothing the Association with authority both to adopt rules governing UNLV's athletic programs and to enforce those rules on behalf of UNLV. Similarly, the Nevada Supreme Court held that UNLV had delegated its authority over personnel decisions to the NCAA. Therefore, the court reasoned, the two entities acted jointly to deprive Tarkanian of liberty and property interests, making the NCAA as well as UNLV a state actor.

These contentions fundamentally misconstrue the facts of this case. In the typical case raising a state-action issue, a private party has taken the decisive step that caused the harm to the plaintiff, and the question is whether the State was sufficiently involved to treat that decisive conduct as state action. This may occur if the State creates the legal framework governing the conduct, if it delegates its authority to the private actor, or sometimes if

it knowingly accepts the benefits derived from unconstitutional behavior. Thus, in the usual case we ask whether the State provided a mantle of authority that enhanced the power of the harm-causing individual actor.

This case uniquely mirrors the traditional state-action case. Here the final act challenged by Tarkanian—his suspension—was committed by UNLV. A state university without question is a state actor. When it decides to impose a serious disciplinary sanction upon one of its tenured employees, it must comply with the terms of the Due Process Clause of the Fourteenth Amendment to the Federal Constitution. Thus when UNLV notified Tarkanian that he was being separated from all relations with the university's basketball program, it acted under color of state law within the meaning of 42 U.S.C. § 1983.

The mirror image presented in this case requires us to step through an analytical looking glass to resolve the case. Clearly UNLV's conduct was influenced by the rules and recommendations of the NCAA, the private party. But it was UNLV, the state entity, that actually suspended Tarkanian. Thus the question is not whether UNLV participated to a critical extent in the NCAA's activities, but whether UNLV's actions in compliance with the NCAA rules and recommendations turned the NCAA's conduct into state action.

We examine first the relationship between UNLV and the NCAA regarding the NCAA's rulemaking. UNLV is among the NCAA's members and participated in promulgating the Association's rules; it must be assumed, therefore, that Nevada had some impact on the NCAA's policy determinations. Yet the NCAA's several hundred other public and private member institutions each similarly affected those policies. Those institutions, the vast majority of which were located in States other than Nevada, did not act under color of Nevada law. It necessarily follows that the source of the legislation adopted by the NCAA is not Nevada but the collective membership, speaking through an organization that is independent of any particular State.[13] Cf. *Allied*

---

[13] The situation would, of course, be different if the membership consisted entirely of institutions located within the same State, many of them public institutions created by the same sovereign. See *Clark v. Arizona Interscholastic Association, Louisiana High*

Tube & Conduit Corp. v. Indian Head, Inc. ("Whatever de facto authority the [private standard-setting] Association enjoys, no official authority has been conferred on it by any government . . .").

State action nonetheless might lie if UNLV, by embracing the NCAA's rules, transformed them into state rules and the NCAA into a state actor. UNLV engaged in state action when it adopted the NCAA's rules to govern its own behavior, but that would be true even if UNLV had taken no part in the promulgation of those rules. In *Bates v. State Bar of Arizona* we established that the State Supreme Court's enforcement of disciplinary rules transgressed by members of its own bar was state action. Those rules had been adopted in toto from the American Bar Association Code of Professional Responsibility. It does not follow, however, that the ABA's formulation of those disciplinary rules was state action. The State Supreme Court retained plenary power to reexamine those standards and, if necessary, to reject them and promulgate its own. So here, UNLV retained the authority to withdraw from the NCAA and establish its own standards. The university alternatively could have stayed in the Association and worked through the Association's legislative process to amend rules or standards it deemed harsh, unfair, or unwieldy. Neither UNLV's decision to adopt the NCAA's standards nor its minor role in their formulation is a sufficient reason for concluding that the NCAA was acting under color of Nevada law when it promulgated standards governing athlete recruitment, eligibility, and academic performance.

Tarkanian further asserts that the NCAA's investigation, enforcement proceedings, and consequent recommendations constituted state action because they resulted from a delegation of power by UNLV. UNLV, as an NCAA member, subscribed to the statement in the Association's bylaws that NCAA "enforcement procedures are an essential part of the intercollegiate athletic program of each member institution." It is, of course, true that a State may delegate authority to a private

School Athletic Association v. St. Augustine High School. The dissent apparently agrees that the NCAA was not acting under color of state law in its relationships with private universities, which constitute the bulk of its membership.

party and thereby make that party a state actor. Thus, we recently held that a private physician who had contracted with a state prison to attend to the inmates' medical needs was a state actor. *West v. Atkins.* But UNLV delegated no power to the NCAA to take specific action against any university employee. The commitment by UNLV to adhere to NCAA enforcement procedures was enforceable only by sanctions that the NCAA might impose on UNLV itself.

Indeed, the notion that UNLV's promise to cooperate in the NCAA enforcement proceedings was tantamount to a partnership agreement or the transfer of certain university powers to the NCAA is belied by the history of this case. It is quite obvious that UNLV used its best efforts to retain its winning coach—a goal diametrically opposed to the NCAA's interest in ascertaining the truth of its investigators' reports. During the several years that the NCAA investigated the alleged violations, the NCAA and UNLV acted much more like adversaries than like partners engaged in a dispassionate search for the truth. The NCAA cannot be regarded as an agent of UNLV for purposes of that proceeding. It is more correctly characterized as an agent of its remaining members which, as competitors of UNLV, had an interest in the effective and evenhanded enforcement of the NCAA's recruitment standards. Just as a state-compensated public defender acts in a private capacity when he or she represents a private client in a conflict against the State, *Polk County v. Dodson*, the NCAA is properly viewed as a private actor at odds with the State when it represents the interests of its entire membership in an investigation of one public university.

The NCAA enjoyed no governmental powers to facilitate its investigation.[17] It had no

---

[17] In Dennis v. Sparks, on which the dissent relies, the parties had entered into a corrupt agreement to perform a judicial act. As we explained: "[H]ere the allegations were that an official act of the defendant judge was the product of a corrupt conspiracy involving bribery of the judge. Under these allegations, the private parties conspiring with the judge were acting under color of state law; and it is of no consequence in this respect that the judge himself is immune from damages liability. Immunity does not change the character of the judge's action or that of his co-conspirators. Indeed, his immunity is dependent on the challenged conduct being an official judicial act

power to subpoena witnesses, to impose contempt sanctions, or to assert sovereign authority over any individual. Its greatest authority was to threaten sanctions against UNLV, with the ultimate sanction being expulsion of the university from membership. Contrary to the premise of the Nevada Supreme Court's opinion, the NCAA did not—indeed, could not—directly discipline Tarkanian or any other state university employee. The express terms of the Confidential Report did not demand the suspension unconditionally; rather, it requested "the University . . . to show cause" why the NCAA should not impose additional penalties if UNLV declines to suspend Tarkanian. Even the university's vice president acknowledged that the Report gave the university options other than suspension: UNLV could have retained Tarkanian and risked additional sanctions, perhaps even expulsion from the NCAA, or it could have withdrawn voluntarily from the Association.

Finally, Tarkanian argues that the power of the NCAA is so great that the UNLV had no practical alternative to compliance with its demands. We are not at all sure this is true, but even if we assume that a private monopolist can impose its will on a state agency by a threatened refusal to deal with it, it does not follow that such a private party is therefore acting under color of state law. Cf. *Jackson* (State's conferral of monopoly status does not convert private party into state actor).

In final analysis the question is whether "the conduct allegedly causing the deprivation of a federal right [can] be fairly attributable to the State." It would be ironic indeed to conclude that the NCAA's imposition of sanctions against UNLV—sanctions that UNLV and its counsel, including the Attorney General of Nevada, steadfastly opposed during

---

within his statutory jurisdiction, broadly construed. Private parties who corruptly conspire with a judge in connection with such conduct are thus acting under color of law. . . ." In this case there is no suggestion of any impropriety respecting the agreement between the NCAA and UNLV. Indeed the dissent seems to assume that the NCAA's liability as a state actor depended not on its initial agreement with UNLV, but on whether UNLV ultimately accepted the NCAA's recommended discipline of Tarkanian. In contrast, the conspirators in Dennis became state actors when they formed the corrupt bargain with the judge, and remained so through completion of the conspiracy's objectives . . .

protracted adversary proceedings—is fairly attributable to the State of Nevada. It would be more appropriate to conclude that UNLV has conducted its athletic program under color of the policies adopted by the NCAA, rather than that those policies were developed and enforced under color of Nevada law.

The judgment of the Nevada Supreme Court is reversed, and the case is remanded to that court for further proceedings not inconsistent with this opinion.

It is so ordered.

Justice **White**, with whom Justice **Brennan**, Justice **Marshall**, and Justice **O'Connor** join, dissenting.

All agree that UNLV, a public university, is a state actor, and that the suspension of Jerry Tarkanian, a public employee, was state action. The question here is whether the NCAA acted jointly with UNLV in suspending Tarkanian and thereby also became a state actor. I would hold that it did.

I agree with the majority that this case is different on its facts from many of our prior state-action cases. As the majority notes, in our "typical case raising a state-action issue, a private party has taken the decisive step that caused the harm to the plaintiff."

In this case, however, which in the majority's view "uniquely mirrors the traditional state-action case," the final act that caused the harm to Tarkanian was committed, not by a private party, but by a party conceded to be a state actor. Because of this difference, the majority finds it necessary to "step through an analytical looking glass" to evaluate whether the NCAA was a state actor.

But the situation presented by this case is not unknown to us and certainly is not unique. In both *Adickes v. S.H. Kress & Co.* and *Dennis v. Sparks*, we faced the question whether private parties could be held to be state actors in cases in which the final or decisive act was carried out by a state official. In both cases we held that the private parties could be found to be state actors, if they were "jointly engaged with state officials in the challenged action."

The facts of *Dennis* are illustrative. In *Dennis*, a state trial judge enjoined the production of minerals from oil leases owned by the plaintiff. The injunction was later dissolved on appeal as having been issued illegally. The plaintiff then filed suit under 42 U.S.C. § 1983, alleging that the judge had conspired with the party seeking the original injunction—a private corporation—the sole owner of the corporation, and the two sureties on the injunction bond to deprive the plaintiff of due process by corruptly issuing the injunction. We held unanimously that under the facts as alleged the private parties were state actors because they were "willful participant[s] in joint action with the State or its agents." See also *Adickes,* supra, (plaintiff entitled to relief under § 1983 against private party if she can prove that private party and police officer "reached an understanding" to cause her arrest on impermissible grounds).

On the facts of the present case, the NCAA acted jointly with UNLV in suspending Tarkanian. First, Tarkanian was suspended for violations of NCAA rules, which UNLV embraced in its agreement with the NCAA. As the Nevada Supreme Court found in its first opinion in this case, "[a]s a member of the NCAA, UNLV contractually agrees to administer its athletic program in accordance with NCAA legislation." Indeed, NCAA rules provide that NCAA "enforcement procedures are an essential part of the intercollegiate athletic program of each member institution."

Second, the NCAA and UNLV also agreed that the NCAA would conduct the hearings concerning violations of its rules. Although UNLV conducted its own investigation into the recruiting violations alleged by the NCAA, the NCAA procedures provide that it is the NCAA Committee on Infractions that "determine[s] facts related to alleged violations," subject to an appeal to the NCAA Council. As a result of this agreement, the NCAA conducted the very hearings the Nevada Supreme Court held to have violated Tarkanian's right to procedural due process.

Third, the NCAA and UNLV agreed that the findings of fact made by the NCAA at the hearings it conducted would be binding on UNLV. By becoming a member of the NCAA, UNLV did more than merely "promise to cooperate in the NCAA enforcement proceedings." It agreed, as the university hearing officer appointed to rule on Tarkanian's suspension expressly found, to accept the NCAA's "findings of fact as in some way superior to [its] own." By the terms of UNLV's membership in the NCAA, the

NCAA's findings were final and not subject to further review by any other body, and it was for that reason that UNLV suspended Tarkanian, despite concluding that many of those findings were wrong.

In short, it was the NCAA's findings that Tarkanian had violated NCAA rules, made at NCAA-conducted hearings, all of which were agreed to by UNLV in its membership agreement with the NCAA, that resulted in Tarkanian's suspension by UNLV. On these facts, the NCAA was "jointly engaged with [UNLV] officials in the challenged action," and therefore was a state actor.

The majority's objections to finding state action in this case were implicitly rejected by our decision in Dennis. Initially, the majority relies on the fact that the NCAA did not have any power to take action directly against Tarkanian as indicating that the NCAA was not a state actor. But the same was true in Dennis: the private parties did not have any power to issue an injunction against the plaintiff. Only the trial judge, using his authority granted under state law, could impose the injunction.

Next, the majority points out that UNLV was free to withdraw from the NCAA at any time. Indeed, it is true that when considering UNLV's options, the university hearing officer noted that one of those options was to "[p]ull out of the NCAA completely." But of course the trial judge in Dennis could have withdrawn from his agreement at any time as well. That he had that option is simply irrelevant to finding that he had entered into an agreement. What mattered was not that he could have withdrawn, but rather that he did not do so.

Finally, the majority relies extensively on the fact that the NCAA and UNLV were adversaries throughout the proceedings before the NCAA. The majority provides a detailed description of UNLV's attempts to avoid the imposition of sanctions by the NCAA. But this opportunity for opposition, provided for by the terms of the membership agreement between UNLV and the NCAA, does not undercut the agreement itself. Surely our decision in Dennis would not have been different had the private parties permitted the trial judge to seek to persuade them that he should not grant the injunction before finally holding the judge to his agreement with them to do so. The key there, as with any conspiracy, is that ultimately the parties agreed to take the action.

The majority states in conclusion that "[i]t would be ironic indeed to conclude that the NCAA's imposition of sanctions against UNLV—sanctions that UNLV and its counsel, including the Attorney General of Nevada, steadfastly opposed during protracted adversary proceedings—is fairly attributable to the State of Nevada." I agree. Had UNLV refused to suspend Tarkanian, and the NCAA responded by imposing sanctions against UNLV, it would be hard indeed to find any state action that harmed Tarkanian. But that is not this case. Here, UNLV did suspend Tarkanian, and it did so because it embraced the NCAA rules governing conduct of its athletic program and adopted the results of the hearings conducted by the NCAA concerning Tarkanian, as it had agreed that it would. Under these facts, I would find that the NCAA acted jointly with UNLV and therefore is a state actor.

I respectfully dissent.

NOTES

1. *Dennis v. Sparks*, 449 U.S. 24 (1980) concerned the liability of private actors who conspire with state officials to deprive the plaintiffs of constitutional rights. A state judge had enjoined the plaintiffs from producing oil from their leases. Although the order was overturned on appeal, the holders of the leases lost two years of production because of it. They brought a suit under section 1983 against the judge who issued the injunction and the private actors who had obtained the injunction, alleging that the defendants had corruptly conspired to deprive them of property without due process of law. The judge was immune from suit on account of absolute judicial immunity, a doctrine that is discussed in Chapter 7. The private defendants maintained that they, too, must be dismissed, on account of the dismissal of the case against their alleged co-conspirator.

The Court disagreed. Before disposing of the private defendant's immunity claim, it addressed the "under color" issue.

[T]o act "under color of" state law for section 1983 purposes does not require that the defendant be an officer of the State. It is enough that he is a wilful participant in joint action with the State or its agents. Private persons, jointly engaged with state officials in the challenged action, are acting "under color" of law for purposes of section 1983 actions. Of course, merely resorting to the courts and being on the winning side of a lawsuit does not make a party a co-conspirator or a joint actor with the judge. But here the allegations were that an official act of the defendant judge was the product of a corrupt conspiracy involving bribery of the judge. Under these allegations, the private parties conspiring with the judge were acting under color of state law; and it is of no consequence in this respect that the judge himself is immune from damages liability. Immunity does not change the character of the judge's action or that of his co-conspirators.

449 U.S. at 28.

In *Tower v. Glover*, 467 U.S. 914 (1984) the plaintiff, a prisoner, sued the public defender who had represented him at his robbery trial, claiming that the public defender had conspired with state judges and other state officials to obtain the plaintiff's conviction. Citing *Dennis*, the Court allowed the suit to go forward. Is this holding consistent with *Polk County v. Dodson*, p. 56 *supra*.?

2. Justice Stevens in *Tarkanian* distinguishes *Dennis* as a case where there was a "corrupt" agreement between the private entity and the state. Why should the purpose of the agreement matter, so long as the two cooperate in pursuing a common end? Keep in mind that many constitutional violations can be made out without a showing of malice.

Tarkanian also stresses that the university and the NCAA were actually antagonists. Were they really? As the Court points out, no one is forcing UNLV to remain a member. Would it not be more accurate to characterize their relationship as one in which UNLV felt it had more to gain than to lose by maintaining the relationship at the cost of taking an action it would have preferred to avoid—firing Tarkanian? Beneath the friction isn't there an underlying commonality of interests between UNLV and the NCAA?

3. In *Arnold v. IBM*, 637 F.2d 1350 (9th Cir. 1981) the plaintiff, a former employee of IBM, had been charged by the government with theft of IBM documents. Later the charges were dropped after a judge granted Arnold's motion to suppress evidence seized in a search of his house. Arnold sued IBM, alleging that it

> failed to disclose to the law enforcement officials evidence that would have been exculpatory to him in the criminal investigation, and that they caused the preparation of the arrest and search warrants, knowing that the affidavits in support of those warrants contained misstatements of facts and failed to disclose the true facts.

The court affirmed summary judgment for the defendants because Arnold could not show that IBM caused the illegal arrest.

> If Arnold could point to any fact that would tend to show that defendants had some control or power over the [police] Task Force, and that defendants directed the Task Force to take action against Arnold, there would certainly be a dispute of material fact on the issue of proximate cause sufficient to reverse the summary judgment. Arnold has, however, failed to show this.

637 F.2d at 1356–57.

After *Tarkanian* would a plaintiff who can make the requisite causal showing be able to sue IBM in constitutional tort? Suppose that IBM had insisted that Arnold was innocent but had nevertheless furnished the police with the information necessary to make an illegal search and arrest, information without which the arrest would not have been made?

4. What evidence is needed in order to establish a conspiracy? In *Mershon v. Beasley*, 994 F.2d 449, 451 (8th Cir. 1993), the Mershon brothers had borrowed money from the Missouri Farmers Association. The MFA made a criminal complaint against the Mershons, claiming that they had defrauded a creditor. The state initiated a prosecution. but later dropped the charges. The Mershons then brought a section 1983 suit against the MFA and their employees, including William Beasley. Beasley sought dismissal on the ground that he did not act under color of state law and so could not be

sued under section 1983. The Eighth Circuit agreed.

In its order denying a JNOV to Mr. Beasley on this issue, the trial court referred to evidence that the county prosecutor was the son of a "substantial client" of the MFA, that the county prosecutor himself was an officer of a corporation that did "considerable business with [the] MFA," that multiple communications had taken place between Mr. Beasley and the county prosecutor, and that a check hat implicated the Mershons at the state probable cause hearing had been altered by another employee at the MFA. The trial court concluded that "the totality of the evidence" established a submissible case on Mr. Beasley's alleged conspiracy with the county prosecutor. We disagree . . .

[A] plaintiff seeking to hold a private party liable under section 1983 must allege, at the very least, that there was a mutual understanding, or a meeting of the minds, between the private party and the state actor . . . [E]vidence must be produced from which reasonable jurors could conclude that such an agreement was come to . . . [Here] the evidence was insufficient as a matter of law on the question of a mutual understanding, or a meeting of the minds, between Mr. Beasley and the county prosecutor . . . It is undisputed that there were multiple contacts between Mr. Beasley and the county prosecutor . . . The MFA was, however, the complaining party in the criminal case. We do not believe that the fact of these contacts, by themselves and without more, allows the inference that Mr. Beasley and the county prosecutor eve reached any mutual understanding that the MFA would use the criminal process for the purpose of collecting its civil debt. The Mershons offered no evidence, for example, that the MFA had sought criminal prosecution of other defaulting debtors in the past or, indeed, that the county prosecutor had filed criminal charges in the past against other debtors who had defaulted on loans from the MFA.

The Mershons' theory as to why the county prosecutor would agree to misuse the power of his office seems to have been that a criminal conviction of the

Mershons would have precluded the discharge in bankruptcy off the debt to the MFA that was secured by the crops sold, that the count prosecutor and his father were owed a debt that was secured by the same crops, and that a criminal conviction of the Mershons would therefore generate a similar exception to bankruptcy discharge of the debt owed to the county prosecutor and his father . . . We consider extremely attenuated . . . any connection, based on this theory, between the decision to prosecute and the personal benefit the county prosecutor might have realized from pursuing the criminal action against the Mershons. Any inference of a mutual understanding that would be drawn from this tenuous connection between the county prosecutor and Mr. Beasley, in our view, could be the result only of "mere conjecture and speculation."

Id. at 451–52. See also *Cinel v. Connick*, 15 F.3d 1338, 1343–44 (5th Cir. 1994).

5. May a conspiracy exist where state officers take no harmful action toward the plaintiff, but simply fail to protect him against private violence? *Dwares v. City of New York*, 985 F.2d 94 (2d Cir. 1993) arose when "skinheads" beat the plaintiffs, who were burning an American flag. The plaintiffs alleged that the police had told the skinheads that, should they beat the plaintiffs, the police would not intervene, "unless they got totally out of control." 985 F.2d at 99. According to the second circuit, this allegation stated a constitutional claim against the skinheads and the police.

Is this holding compatible with *DeShaney v. Winnebago Co. Dep't of Social Services*? See Chapter 4.

How would *Dwares* come out if the evidence showed that the police never spoke to the skinheads, but the skinheads inferred from the passivity of the officers that the police would not intervene? Recall from *Mershon*, supra, that "a plaintiff seeking to hold a private party liable under section 1983 must allege, at the very least, that there was a mutual understanding, or a meeting of the minds, between the private party and the state actor." Would this standard be met on the hypothesized facts?

6. Do not be misled by our decision to treat *Dennis* in notes, rather than featuring it as a main case. The opinion is terse and elliptical, and not a particularly good teaching vehicle. Yet from a litigator's point of view, *Dennis* is far more important than *Tarkanian*. There are not too many arrangements like the one between UNLV and the NCAA, and so not much litigation over them. *Dennis*, on the other hand, provides the main doctrinal vehicle for plaintiffs seeking to sue private actors under section 1983. Unless the case concerns a self-help remedy like the ones at issue in *Lugar* and *Flagg Brothers*, the plaintiff will frequently need to show a conspiracy between private and public actors in order to maintain his section 1983 case against the private party. If he survives a "state action"/"color of law" challenge, his case against the private defendant may be far stronger than his other claims, for many private actors will not be able to escape damages liability by asserting an immunity defense. See Chapter 8.

7. Private security guards may be state actors if they cooperate with the police. See, e.g., *Woodward & Lothrop v. Hillary* 598 A.2d 1142, 1144–46 (D.C. Ct. App. 1991) (the guards had been specially commissioned as police officers under a code provision designed to grant security guards the power to make arrests on the premises where they work, and they had acted in that role when they arrested the plaintiff); *El Fundi v. Deroche*, 625 F.2d 195, 196 (8th Cir. 1980) (cooperation between private guard and police). By contrast, *White v. Scrivner Corp.*, 594 F.2d 140, 143–44 (5th Cir. 1979) found that the guard did not act under color of law where the police department had a policy of independently investigating before making arrests for shoplifting.

8. Are private individuals who accept money from the police in exchange for information government actors? See *Ghandi v. Police Department of the City of Detroit*, 823 F.2d 959, 963–64 (6th Cir. 1987) (refusing to make a general rule that they are state actors; in affirming a dismissal of the case the court relied upon the district courts findings that this informant acted "on his own behalf").

CHAPTER THREE

"Secured by the Constitution and Laws" The Domain of Section 1983 and Constitutional Tort

Section 1983 authorizes suits against persons acting "under color of" state law, to redress "the deprivation of any rights, privileges, or immunities secured by the Constitution and laws." The "implied constitutional cause of action" line of cases, beginning with *Bivens v. Six Unknown Named Agents*, 403 U.S. 388 (1971), grants a remedy to persons seeking relief for constitutional violations committed by federal officers. What wrongs may be vindicated under these statutory and judge-made causes of action? This chapter examines the general issues that arise when litigants use section 1983 and *Bivens* to sue for constitutional violations. The next chapter discusses the special problems that come up when a plaintiff claims that government owes him an affirmative constitutional duty or sues for deprivation of federal statutory rights.

Bivens suits and section 1983 suits cover the full range of constitutional rights. A *Bivens* remedy may be denied on account of the availability of statutory remedies or perhaps other "special factors counseling hesitation", as discussed in Chapter 1. Either a *Bivens* suit or a section 1983 suit may falter on account of official immunity, as discussed in Chapters 7 & 8. But the Supreme Court, in its elaboration of either of these doctrines, has never distinguished among constitutional rights, finding some of them cognizable and others not.

Many section 1983 suits rely upon the specifics of the Bill of Rights. Prominent themes in section 1983 litigation include actions brought to enforce (a) the free speech clause of the First Amendment, by public employees who have been fired or disciplined on account of something they said; (b) the "unreasonable search and seizure" clause of the Fourth Amendment, by persons who think the police went too far in going through homes or their belongings; and (c) the "cruel and unusual punishment" clause of the Eighth Amendment, by prisoners claiming that prison conditions or disciplinary measures are too harsh.

Dennis v. Higgins, 498 U.S. 439 (1991), illustrates the breadth of section 1983. The plaintiff used section 1983 as the vehicle for raising a claim that state taxation violated the commerce clause. Noting that section 1983 covered all constitutional rights, and citing a well-established principle that commerce clause violations are violations of constitutional rights, the Court allowed the suit to go forward. See Note, *Doctrinal Foundations of Section 1983 and the Resurgent Dormant Commerce Clause*, 77 Iowa L. Rev. 1249 (1992).

In each of these kinds of litigation, the Court has articulated and applied the constitutional standards governing the substantive issues by reference to the general principles of constitutional doctrine. When a public employee is fired for writing a letter to the newspaper, and sues to get her job back, the governing principles are found in the Court's general first amendment jurisprudence. When someone sues to recover damages for a police search, courts look to the fourth amendment standards developed over the years, primarily in criminal prosecutions where the defendant seeks to exclude evidence obtained through the challenged search. In *Dennis*, the resolution of the dormant commerce clause issue turns on the Court's case law regarding the level and kinds of state taxation that place an undue burden on interstate commerce. A casebook on constitutional torts and section 1983 has nothing to add to the discussions of these matters found in casebooks on constitutional law. The reader seeking guidance on the resolution of First

Amendment issues arising in constitutional tort cases is advised to study the Court's whole body of First Amendment cases. Specialized and general constitutional law casebooks are full of materials on the First, Fourth, and Eighth Amendments, the Dormant Commerce Clause, and most other constitutional provisions whose claimed violation may form the basis for a section 1983 suit. A constitutional torts casebook can safely focus on other issues not already well-covered by other materials.

There are exceptions to the general principle that the constitutional rules governing constitutional tort exist separate and independent from the constitutional tort context. The most important and complex one relates to the Due Process Clause of the Fourteenth Amendment: "[N]or shall any State deprive any person of life, liberty, or property without due process of law." This provision had a long and checkered history before *Monroe* and the growth of constitutional tort, and some of that history has a bearing on the difficulties courts have faced in applying it to constitutional tort cases. At the same time, distinctive questions have arisen in the constitutional tort context. Does the Due Process Clause protect persons solely against procedural errors by state government, or does it include a substantive component as well? What is the difference between "procedural" and 'substantive' violations in connection with constitutional torts? Assuming substantive rights are guaranteed by the Due Process Clause, what is the content of the substantive protection it affords?

I. Procedural Due Process and Substantive Due Process

Parratt v. Taylor

451 U.S. 527 (1981)

Justice **Rehnquist** delivered the opinion of the Court . . .

I

The facts underlying this dispute are not seriously contested. Respondent paid for the hobby materials he ordered with two drafts drawn on his inmate account by prison officials. The packages arrived at the complex and were signed for by two employees who worked in the prison hobby center. One of the employees was a civilian and the other was an inmate. Respondent was in segregation at the time and was not permitted to have the hobby materials. Normal prison procedures for the handling of mail packages is that upon arrival they are either delivered to the prisoner who signs a receipt for the package or the prisoner is notified to pick up the package and to sign a receipt. No inmate other than the one to whom the package is addressed is supposed to sign for a package. After being released from segregation, respondent contacted several prison officials regarding the whereabouts of his packages. The officials were never able to locate the packages or to determine what caused their disappearance.

In 1976, respondent commenced this action against the petitioners, the Warden and Hobby Manager of the prison, in the District Court seeking to recover the value of the hobby materials which he claimed had been lost as a result of the petitioners' negligence. Respondent alleged that petitioners' conduct deprived him of property without due process of law in violation of the Fourteenth Amendment of the United States Constitution. Respondent chose to proceed in the United States District Court under 28 U.S.C. § 1343 and 42 U.S.C. § 1983, even though the State of Nebraska had a tort claims procedure which provided a remedy to persons who suffered tortious losses at the hands of the State.

On October 25, 1978, the District Court granted respondent's motion for summary judgment. The District Court ruled that negligent actions by state officials can be a basis for an action under 42 U.S.C. § 1983; petitioners were not immune from damages actions of this kind; and the deprivation of the hobby kit "[implicated] due process rights." The District Court explained:

> "This is not a situation where prison officials confiscated contraband. The negligence of the officials in failing to follow their own policies concerning the distribution of mail resulted in a loss of personal property for [respondent], which loss should not go without redress."

II

[In this part of the opinion the Court ruled that negligent deprivations of liberty and property could support a claim for relief under section 1983. That holding was later overruled in *Daniels v. Williams*, infra.]

[Prior cases] suggest that § 1983 affords a "civil remedy" for deprivations of federally protected rights caused by persons acting under color of state law without any express requirement of a particular state of mind. Accordingly, in any § 1983 action the initial inquiry must focus on whether the two essential elements to a § 1983 action are present: (1) whether the conduct complained of was committed by a person acting under color of state law; and (2) whether this conduct deprived a person of rights, privileges, or immunities secured by the Constitution or laws of the United States.

III

Since this Court's decision in *Monroe v. Pape*, it can no longer be questioned that the alleged conduct by the petitioners in this case satisfies the "under color of state law" requirement. Petitioners were, after all, state employees in positions of considerable authority. They do not seriously contend otherwise. Our inquiry, therefore, must turn to the second requirement—whether respondent has been deprived of any right, privilege, or immunity secured by the Constitution or laws of the United States.

The only deprivation respondent alleges in his complaint is that "his rights under the Fourteenth Amendment of the Constitution of the United States were violated. That he was deprived of his property and Due Process of Law." As such, respondent's claims differ from the claims which were before us in *Monroe v. Pape*, supra, which involved violations of the Fourth Amendment, and the claims presented in *Estelle v. Gamble*, which involved alleged violations of the Eighth Amendment. Both of these Amendments have been held applicable to the States by virtue of the adoption of the Fourteenth Amendment. Respondent here refers to no other right, privilege, or immunity secured by the Constitution or federal laws other than the Due Process Clause of the Fourteenth Amendment simpliciter. The pertinent text of the Fourteenth Amendment provides:

"Section 1. All persons born or naturalized in the United States, and subject to the jurisdiction thereof, are citizens of the United States and the State wherein they reside. No State shall make or enforce any law which shall abridge the privileges or immunities of citizens of the United States; *nor shall any State deprive any person of life, liberty, or property, without due process of law;* nor deny to any person within its jurisdiction the equal protection of the laws." (Emphasis supplied [by the Court].)

Unquestionably, respondent's claim satisfies three prerequisites of a valid due process claim: the petitioners acted under color of state law; the hobby kit falls within the definition of property; and the alleged loss, even though negligently caused, amounted to a deprivation. Standing alone, however, these three elements do not establish a violation of the Fourteenth Amendment. Nothing in that Amendment protects against all deprivations of life, liberty, or property by the State. The Fourteenth Amendment protects only against deprivations "without due process of law." Our inquiry therefore must focus on whether the respondent has suffered a deprivation of property without due process of law. In particular, we must decide whether the tort remedies which the State of Nebraska provides as a means of redress for property deprivations satisfy the requirements of procedural due process.

This Court has never directly addressed the question of what process is due a person when an employee of a State negligently takes his property. In some cases this Court has held that due process requires a predeprivation hearing before the State interferes with any liberty or property interest enjoyed by its citizens. In most of these cases, however, the deprivation of property was pursuant to some established state procedure and "process" could be offered before any actual deprivation took place. For example, in *Mullane v. Central Hanover Trust Co.* the Court struck down on due process grounds a New York statute that allowed a trust company, when it sought a judicial settlement of its trust accounts, to give notice by publication to all beneficiaries even if the whereabouts of the beneficiaries were known. The Court held that personal notice in such situations was required and stated that "when notice is a person's due, process which is a mere gesture is not due process." More recently, in *Bell v. Burson*, we reviewed a state statute which provided for the taking of the driver's license and registration of an uninsured motorist who had been involved in an accident. We recognized that a driver's license is often involved in the livelihood of a person and as such could not be summarily taken without a prior hearing. In *Fuentes v. Shevin* we struck down the Florida prejudgment replevin statute which allowed secured creditors to obtain writs in ex parte proceedings. We held that due process required a prior hearing before the State authorized its agents to seize property in a debtor's possession. In all these cases, deprivations of property were authorized by an established state procedure and due process was held to require predeprivation notice and hearing in order to serve as a check on the possibility that a wrongful deprivation would occur.

We have, however, recognized that postdeprivation remedies made available by the State can satisfy the Due Process Clause. In such cases, the normal predeprivation notice and opportunity to be heard is pretermitted if the State provides a postdeprivation remedy. In *North American Cold Storage Co. v. Chicago* we upheld the right of a State to seize and destroy unwholesome food without a preseizure hearing. The possibility of erroneous destruction of property was outweighed by the fact that the public health emergency justified immediate action and the owner of the property could recover his damages in an action at law after the incident. In *Ewing v. Mytinger & Casselberry, Inc.* we upheld under the Fifth Amendment Due Process Clause the summary seizure and destruction of drugs without a preseizure hearing. Similarly, in *Fahey v. Mallonee* we recognized that the protection of the public interest against economic harm can justify the immediate seizure of property without a prior hearing when substantial questions are raised about the competence of a bank's management. In *Bowles v. Willingham* we upheld in the face of a due process challenge the authority of the Administrator of the Office of Price Administration to issue rent control orders without providing a hearing to landlords before the order or regulation fixing rents became effective. These cases recognize that either the necessity of quick action by the State or the impracticality of providing any meaningful predeprivation pro-

cess, when coupled with the availability of some meaningful means by which to assess the propriety of the State's action at some time after the initial taking, can satisfy the requirements of procedural due process . . .

Our past cases mandate that some kind of hearing is required at some time before a State finally deprives a person of his property interests. The fundamental requirement of due process is the opportunity to be heard and it is an "opportunity which must be granted at a meaningful time and in a meaningful manner." *Armstrong v. Manzo*. However, as many of the above cases recognize, we have rejected the proposition that "at a meaningful time and in a meaningful manner" always requires the State to provide a hearing prior to the initial deprivation of property. This rejection is based in part on the impracticability in some cases of providing any preseizure hearing under a state-authorized procedure, and the assumption that at some time a full and meaningful hearing will be available.

The justifications which we have found sufficient to uphold takings of property without any predeprivation process are applicable to a situation such as the present one involving a tortious loss of a prisoner's property as a result of a random and unauthorized act by a state employee. In such a case, the loss is not a result of some established state procedure and the State cannot predict precisely when the loss will occur. It is difficult to conceive of how the State could provide a meaningful hearing before the deprivation takes place. The loss of property, although attributable to the State as action under "color of law," is in almost all cases beyond the control of the State. Indeed, in most cases it is not only impracticable, but impossible, to provide a meaningful hearing before the deprivation. That does not mean, of course, that the State can take property without providing a meaningful postdeprivation hearing. The prior cases which have excused the prior-hearing requirement have rested in part on the availability of some meaningful opportunity subsequent to the initial taking for a determination of rights and liabilities . . .

IV

Application of the principles recited above to this case leads us to conclude the respondent has not alleged a violation of the Due

Process Clause of the Fourteenth Amendment. Although he has been deprived of property under color of state law, the deprivation did not occur as a result of some established state procedure. Indeed, the deprivation occurred as a result of the unauthorized failure of agents of the State to follow established state procedure. There is no contention that the procedures themselves are inadequate nor is there any contention that it was practicable for the State to provide a predeprivation hearing. Moreover, the State of Nebraska has provided respondent with the means by which he can receive redress for the deprivation. The State provides a remedy to persons who believe they have suffered a tortious loss at the hands of the State. See Neb. Rev. Stat. § 81–8,209 et seq. (1976). Through this tort claims procedure the State hears and pays claims of prisoners housed in its penal institutions. This procedure was in existence at the time of the loss here in question but respondent did not use it. It is argued that the State does not adequately protect the respondent's interests because it provides only for an action against the State as opposed to its individual employees, it contains no provisions for punitive damages, and there is no right to a trial by jury. Although the state remedies may not provide the respondent with all the relief which may have been available if he could have proceeded under § 1983, that does not mean that the state remedies are not adequate to satisfy the requirements of due process. The remedies provided could have fully compensated the respondent for the property loss he suffered, and we hold that they are sufficient to satisfy the requirements of due process.

Our decision today is fully consistent with our prior cases. To accept respondent's argument that the conduct of the state officials in this case constituted a violation of the Fourteenth Amendment would almost necessarily result in turning every alleged injury which may have been inflicted by a state official acting under "color of law" into a violation of the Fourteenth Amendment cognizable under § 1983. It is hard to perceive any logical stopping place to such a line of reasoning. Presumably, under this rationale any party who is involved in nothing more than an automobile accident with a state official could allege a constitutional violation under § 1983. Such reasoning "would make of the Four-

teenth Amendment a font of tort law to be superimposed upon whatever systems may already be administered by the States." *Paul v. Davis.* We do not think that the drafters of the Fourteenth Amendment intended the Amendment to play such a role in our society . . .

[Concurring opinions by Justices Stewart, White, and Blackmun, Justice Powell's opinion concurring in the result, and Justice Marshall's opinion concurring in part and dissenting in part, are omitted.]

NOTES

1. Due process consists of both procedural and substantive dimensions, and we must distinguish between them in order to make sense of and evaluate *Parratt* as well as later developments. A person may concede that the state is empowered to deprive him of life, liberty or property, and find fault with the procedures used to accomplish the deprivation, on the ground that he did not receive notice or a hearing, for example. But even where officials employ a flawless procedure, an injured person may maintain that their actions are constitutionally impermissible, because they are arbitrary or abusive or shock the conscience. The contours of substantive due process in the constitutional tort context are discussed in detail later in this chapter.

The Court in *Parratt* frequently uses the language (as well as the case law) of procedural due process. As an exercise in applying procedural due process principles, the case is unexceptionable. There are many instances where circumstances require urgent action or a predeprivation hearing is impossible, so that a post-deprivation remedy provides the process that is due.

The difficulty with this reading of the case is that Taylor was not really claiming that the mail room workers would have been entitled to lose his hobby materials, provided they followed proper procedures. The more plausible way to understand the claim for lost hobby materials is that the mail room carelessness violates the prisoner's substantive rights. See Wells & Eaton, *Substantive Due Process and the Scope of Constitutional Torts*, 18 Ga. L. Rev. 201, 222–23 (1984); see also Fallon, *Some Confusions About Due Process, Judicial Review, and*

Constitutional Remedies, 93 Colum. L. Rev. 309, 341–42 (1993). (Whether this is a viable claim is a separate issue. *Daniels v. Williams*, infra, holds that negligence does not make out a substantive due process violation.)

Viewed as a substantive due process ruling, *Parratt* raises some thorny issues:

(a) A respected scholar has asserted that *Parratt* and *Monroe v. Pape* "are on an obvious collision course." Bator, *Some Thoughts on Applied Federalism*, 6 Harv. J.L. & Pub. Pol'y 51, 56 (1982). Do you agree? There is a tension between the two cases, in that *Monroe* opens the federal courts even where adequate state remedies are available, yet *Parratt* closes them to (at least) some due process claims if state remedies are adequate. Are the cases reconcilable on the ground that *Monroe* is an interpretation of section 1983, while *Parratt* is a constitutional ruling? Does *Parratt* make sense in terms of the policies underlying *Monroe*?

(b) Is *Parratt* consistent with *Home Telephone & Telegraph Co. v. City of Los Angeles*, 227 U.S. 278 (1913)? That case was a challenge by the telephone company to a city ordinance fixing its rates at levels it judged to be confiscatory, and hence in violation of the due process clause. The city pointed out that state law provided a remedy, in that the state constitution also proscribed confiscatory takings. In the city's view, the existence of state action violating the fourteenth amendment would depend on whether the state courts gave the plaintiff's claim the respect it deserved. The Court rejected the city's argument.

By the proposition [advanced by the city] the prohibitions and guaranties of the [Fourteenth] Amendment are addressed to and control the states only in their complete governmental capacity, and as a result give no authority to exert Federal judicial power until, by the decision of a court of last resort of a state, acts complained of under the 14th Amendment have been held valid, and therefore state acts in the fullest sense. To the contrary, the provisions of the Amendment as conclusively fixed by previous decisions are generic in their terms, are addressed, of course, to the states, but also to every person, whether natural or juridical, who is the repository of state power. By this construction the reach of the Amendment is shown to be coextensive with any exercise by a state of power, in whatever form exerted . . .

To speak broadly, the difference between the proposition insisted upon and the true meaning of the Amendment is this: that the one assumes that the Amendment virtually contemplates alone wrongs authorized by a state, and gives only power accordingly, while in truth the Amendment contemplates the possibility of state officers abusing the powers lawfully conferred upon them by doing wrongs prohibited by the Amendment.

Home Telephone is a prominent case in the law of constitutional remedies, establishing that a constitutional violation may be found even though the state provides remedies for the challenged conduct. Should *Parratt v. Taylor* be read as having partially overruled *Home Telephone*, without ever mentioning the earlier case? See Monaghan, *State Law Wrongs, State Law Remedies, and the Fourteenth Amendment*, 86 Colum. L. Rev. 979, 990–91 (1986); Alexander, *Constitutional Torts, The Supreme Court, and the Law of Noncontradiction: An Essay on* Zinermon v. Burch, 87 Nw. U.L. Rev. 576, 581–83 (1993)(describing the tension between *Parratt* and *Home Telephone*).

(c) Professor Fallon interprets *Parratt* rather differently. He thinks "*Parratt* would best fit into the surrounding doctrinal framework if it were recharacterized as launching a body of federal abstention doctrine, under which federal courts should sometimes decline to exercise jurisdiction in cases that lie within the literal terms of their statutory authority." Fallon, *Some Thoughts About Due Process, Judicial Review, and Constitutional Remedies*, 93 Colum. L. Rev. 309, 345 (1993). Would this reading of *Parratt* avoid a collision with *Home Telephone*? Would it conflict with *Monroe*? See Fallon, supra, at 354–55.

2. Reread the last paragraph of *Parratt. Paul v. Davis* held that someone complaining of defamation by government officials could not sue under section 1983 for a constitutional violation, but must instead resort to state tort remedies. Another pre-*Parratt* case, *Ingraham v. Wright*, 430 U.S. 651 (1977), emphasizes the availability of state remedies in rejecting eighth amendment and procedural due process challenges brought by public school students complaining of severe corporal punishment. *Baker v. McCollan*, 443 U.S. 137 (1979) denied relief to an innocent man who had been incarcerated for three days on account of mistaken identity, with the observation that he could pursue a state law action for false imprisonment.

Whatever differences there may be among these cases, they have in common a sensitivity to state prerogatives, a desire on the Court's part not to allow the due process clause to intrude too far into the realm of state tort law. To the extent they are based on a judgment that state interests in setting the rules for recovery are more compelling than the plaintiff's interest in having a constitutional trump to play against state law, they are instances of a common theme in constitutional litigation over the scope of individual rights in the Supreme Court over the past two decades. In this regard, note that in remitting plaintiffs to state remedies the Court does not guarantee that state remedies will provide relief. *Paul*, for example, arose in Kentucky, where state defamation law effectively immunized officials and governments from liability.

3. *Parratt* sowed much confusion in the lower federal courts. Among other issues, courts divided over the issue that underlies the preceding notes: whether *Parratt* applied to substantive due process claims or solely to procedural ones. Courts also split over whether *Parratt* only applied to property claims, or to deprivations of liberty as well. In addition, courts puzzled over the meaning of *Parratt's* category of "random and unauthorized" deprivations for which pre-deprivation process was impracticable. These issues are addressed in the next case.

Zinermon v. Burch

494 U.S. 113 (1990)

Justice **Blackmun** delivered the opinion of the Court.

I

Respondent Darrell Burch brought this suit under 42 U.S.C. § 1983 (1982 ed.) against the 11 petitioners, who are physicians, administrators, and staff members at Florida State Hospital (FSH) in Chattahoochee, and others. Respondent alleges that petitioners deprived him of his liberty, without due process of law, by admitting him to FSH as a "voluntary" mental patient when he was incompetent to give informed consent to his admission. Burch contends that in his case petitioners should have afforded him procedural safeguards required by the Constitution before involuntary commitment of a mentally ill person, and that petitioners' failure to do so violated his due process rights. Petitioners argue that Burch's complaint failed to state a claim under § 1983 because, in their view, it alleged only a random, unauthorized violation of the Florida statutes governing admission of mental patients. Their argument rests on *Parratt v. Taylor* (overruled in part not relevant here, by *Daniels v. Williams* and *Hudson v. Palmer*, where this Court held that a deprivation of a constitutionally protected property interest caused by a state employee's random, unauthorized conduct does not give rise to a § 1983 procedural due process claim, unless the State fails to provide an adequate postdeprivation remedy. The Court in those two cases reasoned that in a situation where the State cannot predict and guard in advance against a deprivation, a postdeprivation tort remedy is all the process the State can be expected to provide, and is constitutionally sufficient . . .

[The District Court granted petitioners' motion to dismiss] pointing out that Burch did not contend that Florida's statutory procedure for mental health placement was inadequate to ensure due process, but only that petitioners failed to follow the state procedure. Since the State could not have anticipated or prevented this unauthorized deprivation of Burch's liberty, the District Court reasoned, there was no feasible predeprivation remedy, and, under Parratt and Hudson, the State's postdeprivation tort remedies provided Burch with all the process that was due him.

[The Eleventh Circuit first affirmed the dismissal and then, after rehearing en banc, reversed and remanded the case.]

This Court granted certiorari to resolve the conflict—so evident in the divided views of the judges of the Eleventh Circuit—that has arisen in the Courts of Appeals over the proper scope of the *Parratt* rule.

Because this case concerns the propriety of a [motion to dismiss the complaint], the question before us is a narrow one. We decide only whether the *Parratt* rule necessarily means that Burch's complaint fails to allege any deprivation of due process, because he was constitutionally entitled to nothing more than what he received—an opportunity to sue petitioners in tort for his allegedly unlawful confinement. The broader questions of what procedural safeguards the Due Process Clause requires in the context of an admission to a mental hospital, and whether Florida's statutes meet these constitutional requirements, are not presented in this case . . .

A

For purposes of review of a [motion to dismiss the complaint], the factual allegations of Burch's complaint are taken as true. Burch's complaint, and the medical records and forms attached to it as exhibits, provide the following factual background: . . .

[Burch alleged that someone found him wandering along a highway, evidently hurt and disoriented. He was taken to a mental hospital and asked to sign forms giving his consent to admission and treatment. He signed these forms, and later signed other forms agreeing to admission and treatment at another hospital. He remained in state custody for five months without ever getting a hearing regarding his hospitalization and treatment.]

In February 1985, Burch filed a complaint in the United States District Court for the Northern District of Florida. He alleged, among other things, that ACMHS and the 11 individual petitioners, acting under color of Florida law, and "by and through the authority of their respective positions as employees at FSH . . . as part of their regular and official employment at FSH, took part in admitting Plaintiff to FSH as a 'voluntary' patient." Specifically, he alleged:

"Defendants, and each of them, knew or should have known that Plaintiff was incapable of voluntary, knowing, understanding and informed consent to admission and treatment at FSH. Nonetheless, Defendants, and each of them, seized Plaintiff and against Plaintiff's will confined him and imprisoned him and subjected him to involuntary commitment and treatment for the period from December 10, 1981, to May 7, 1982. For said period of 149 days, Plaintiff was without the benefit of counsel and no hearing of any sort was held at which he could have challenged his involuntary admission and treatment at FSH.

". . . Defendants, and each of them, deprived Plaintiff of his liberty without due process of law in contravention of the Fourteenth Amendment to the United States Constitution. Defendants acted with willful, wanton and reckless disregard of and indifference to Plaintiff's Constitutionally guaranteed right to due process of law."

Id., at 201–202.

B

Burch's complaint thus alleges that he was admitted to and detained at FSH for five months under Florida's statutory provisions for "voluntary" admission. These provisions are part of a comprehensive statutory scheme under which a person may be admitted to a mental hospital in several different ways.

First, Florida provides for short-term emergency admission . . .

Second, under a court order a person may be detained at a mental health facility for up to five days for evaluation . . .

Third, a person may be detained as an involuntary patient, if he meets the same criteria as for evaluation, and if the facility administrator and two mental health professional recommend involuntary placement. Before involuntary placement, the patient has a right to notice, a judicial hearing, appointed counsel, access to medical records and personnel, and an independent expert examination. If the court determines that the patient meets the criteria for involuntary placement, it then decides whether the patient is competent to consent to treatment. If not, the court appoints a guardian advocate to make treatment decisions. After six months, the facility must either release the patient, or seek a court order for continued placement by stating the reasons therefor, summarizing the patient's treatment to that point, and submitting a plan for future treatment.

Finally, a person may be admitted as a voluntary patient. Mental hospitals may admit for treatment any adult "making application by express and informed consent," if he is "found to show evidence of mental illness and to be suitable for treatment." "Express and informed consent" is defined as "consent voluntarily given in writing after sufficient explanation and disclosure . . . to enable the person . . . to make a knowing and willful decision without any element of force, fraud, deceit, duress, or other form of constraint or coercion." A voluntary patient may request discharge at any time. If he does, the facility administrator must either release him within three days or initiate the involuntary placement process. At the time of his admission and each six months thereafter, a voluntary patient and his legal guardian or representatives must be notified in writing of the right to apply for a discharge.

Burch, in apparent compliance with [Florida law], was admitted by signing forms applying for voluntary admission. He alleges, however, that petitioners violated this statute in admitting him as a voluntary patient, because they knew or should have known that he was incapable of making an informed decision as to his admission. He claims that he was entitled to receive the procedural safeguards provided by Florida's involuntary placement procedure, and that petitioners violated his due process rights by failing to initiate this procedure. The question presented is whether these allegations suffice to state a claim under § 1983, in light of *Parratt* and *Hudson*.

III

A

To understand the background against which this question arises, we return to the interpretation of § 1983 articulated in *Monroe v. Pape*. [Under *Monroe*] . . . overlapping state remedies are generally irrelevant to the question of the existence of a cause of action under § 1983. A plaintiff, for example, may bring a § 1983 action for an unlawful search and seizure despite the fact that the search and seizure violated the State's Constitution or statutes, and despite the fact that there are common-law remedies for trespass and conversion. As was noted in *Monroe*, in many cases there is "no quarrel with the state laws on the books,"; instead, the problem is the way those laws are or are not implemented by state officials.

This general rule applies in a straightforward way to two of the three kinds of § 1983 claims that may be brought against the State under the Due Process Clause of the Fourteenth Amendment. First, the Clause incorporates many of the specific protections defined in the Bill of Rights. A plaintiff may bring suit under § 1983 for state officials' violation of his rights to, e.g., freedom of speech or freedom from unreasonable searches and seizures. Second, the Due Process Clause contains a substantive component that bars certain arbitrary, wrongful government actions "regardless of the fairness of the procedures used to implement them." *Daniels v. Williams*. As to these two types of claims, the constitutional violation actionable under § 1983 is complete when the wrongful action is taken. A plaintiff, under *Monroe v. Pape*, may invoke § 1983 regardless of any state-tort remedy that might be available to compensate him for the deprivation of these rights.

The Due Process Clause also encompasses a third type of protection, a guarantee of fair procedure. A § 1983 action may be brought for a violation of procedural due process, but here the existence of state remedies is relevant in a special sense. In procedural due process claims, the deprivation by state action of a constitutionally protected interest in "life, liberty, or property" is not in itself unconstitutional; what is unconstitutional is the deprivation of such an interest without due process of law. The constitutional violation actionable under § 1983 is not complete when the deprivation occurs; it is not complete unless and until the State fails to provide due process. Therefore, to determine whether a constitutional violation has occurred, it is necessary to ask what process the State provided, and whether it was constitutionally adequate. This inquiry would examine the procedural safeguards built into the statutory or administrative procedure of effecting the deprivation, and any remedies for erroneous deprivations provided by statute or tort law.

In this case, Burch does not claim that his confinement at FSH violated any of the specific guarantees of the Bill of Rights. Burch's complaint could be read to include a substantive due process claim, but that issue was not raised in the petition for certiorari, and we express no view on whether the facts Burch alleges could give rise to such a claim. The claim at issue falls within the third, or procedural, category of § 1983 claims based on the Due Process Clause.

B

Due process, as this Court often has said, is a flexible concept that varies with the particular situation. To determine what procedural protections the Constitution requires in a particular case, we weigh several factors:

"First, the private interest that will be affected by the official action; second, the risk of an erroneous deprivation of such interest through the procedures used, and the probable value, if any, of additional or substitute procedural safeguards; and finally, the Government's interest, including the function involved and the fiscal and administrative burdens that the additional or substitute procedural requirement would entail."

Mathews v. Eldridge.

Applying this test, the Court usually has held that the Constitution requires some kind of a hearing before the State deprives a person of liberty or property. . . .

In some circumstances, however, the Court has held that a statutory provision for a postdeprivation hearing, or a common-law tort remedy for erroneous deprivation, satisfies due process. . . .

This is where the *Parratt* rule comes into play. *Parratt* and *Hudson* represent a special case of the general *Mathews v. Eldridge* analysis, in which postdeprivation tort remedies are all the process that is due, simply because they are the only remedies the State could be expected to provide. In *Parratt*, a state prisoner brought a § 1983 action because prison employees negligently had lost materials he had ordered by mail.[14] The prisoner did not dispute that he had a postdeprivation remedy. Under state law, a tort-claim procedure was available by which he could have recovered the value of the materials. This Court ruled

that the tort remedy was all the process the prisoner was due, because any predeprivation procedural safeguards that the State did provide, or could have provided, would not address the risk of this kind of deprivation. The very nature of a negligent loss of property made it impossible for the State to predict such deprivations and provide predeprivation process. The Court explained:

"The justifications which we have found sufficient to uphold takings of property without any predeprivation process are applicable to a situation such as the present one involving a tortious loss of a prisoner's property as a result of a random and unauthorized act by a state employee. In such a case, the loss is not a result of some established state procedure and the State cannot predict precisely when the loss will occur. It is difficult to conceive of how the State could provide a meaningful hearing before the deprivation takes place."

Given these special circumstances, it was clear that the State, by making available a tort remedy that could adequately redress the loss, had given the prisoner the process he was due. Thus, *Parratt* is not an exception to the *Mathews* balancing test, but rather an application of that test to the unusual case in which one of the variables in the *Mathews* equation—the value of predeprivation safeguards—is negligible in preventing the kind of deprivation at issue. Therefore, no matter how significant the private interest at stake and the risk of its erroneous deprivation, the State cannot be required constitutionally to do the impossible by providing predeprivation process.

In *Hudson*, the Court extended this reasoning to an intentional deprivation of property. A prisoner alleged that, during a search of his prison cell, a guard deliberately and maliciously destroyed some of his property, including legal papers. Again, there was a tort remedy by which the prisoner could have been compensated. In *Hudson*, as in *Parratt*, the state official was not acting pursuant to any established state procedure, but, instead, was apparently pursuing a random, unauthorized personal vendetta against the prisoner. The Court pointed out: "The state can no more anticipate and control in advance the random and unauthorized intentional conduct of its

---

[14] Parratt was decided before this Court ruled, in Daniels v. Williams that a negligent act by a state official does not give rise to § 1983 liability.

employees than it can anticipate similar negligent conduct." Of course, the fact that the guard's conduct was intentional meant that he himself could "foresee" the wrongful deprivation and could prevent it simply by refraining from his misconduct. Nonetheless, the Court found that an individual state employee's ability to foresee the deprivation is "of no consequence," because the proper inquiry under *Parratt* is "whether the *state* is in a position to provide for predeprivation process." (emphasis added).

C

Petitioners argue that the dismissal under Rule 12(b)(6) was proper because, as in *Parratt* and *Hudson*, the State could not possibly have provided predeprivation process to prevent the kind of "random, unauthorized" wrongful deprivation of liberty Burch alleges, so the postdeprivation remedies provided by Florida's statutory and common law necessarily are all the process Burch was due.[15]

Before turning to that issue, however, we must address a threshold question raised by Burch. He argues that *Parratt* and *Hudson* cannot apply to his situation, because those cases are limited to deprivations of property, not liberty.

Burch alleges that he was deprived of his liberty interest in avoiding confinement in a mental hospital without either informed consent or the procedural safeguards of the involuntary placement process. Petitioners do not seriously dispute that there is a substantial liberty interest in avoiding confinement in a mental hospital. Burch's confinement at FSH for five months without a hearing or any other procedure to determine either that he validly had consented to admission, or that he met the statutory standard for involuntary placement, clearly infringes on this liberty interest.

---

[15] Burch does not dispute that he had remedies under Florida law for unlawful confinement. Florida's mental health statutes provide that a patient confined unlawfully may sue for damages. § 394.459(13) ("Any person who violates or abuses any rights or privileges of patients" is liable for damages, subject to good-faith immunity but not immunity for negligence). Also, a mental patient detained at a mental health facility, or a person acting on his behalf, may seek a writ of habeas corpus to "question the cause and legality of such detention and request . . . release." § 394.459(10)(a). Finally, Florida recognizes the common-law tort of false imprisonment. Johnson v. Weiner.

Burch argues that postdeprivation tort remedies are never constitutionally adequate for a deprivation of liberty, as opposed to property, so the *Parratt* rule cannot apply to this case. We, however, do not find support in precedent for a categorical distinction between a deprivation of liberty and one of property. . . .

It is true that *Parratt* and *Hudson* concerned deprivations of property. It is also true that Burch's interest in avoiding six months' confinement is of an order different from inmate Parratt's interest in mail-order materials valued at $23.50. But the reasoning of *Parratt* and *Hudson* emphasizes the State's inability to provide predeprivation process because of the random and unpredictable nature of the deprivation, not the fact that only property losses were at stake. In situations where the State feasibly can provide a predeprivation hearing before taking property, it generally must do so regardless of the adequacy of a postdeprivation tort remedy to compensate for the taking. Conversely, in situations where a predeprivation hearing is unduly burdensome in proportion to the liberty interest at stake, or where the State is truly unable to anticipate and prevent a random deprivation of a liberty interest, postdeprivation remedies might satisfy due process. Thus, the fact that a deprivation of liberty is involved in this case does not automatically preclude application of the *Parratt* rule.

To determine whether, as petitioners contend, the *Parratt* rule necessarily precludes § 1983 liability in this case, we must ask whether predeprivation procedural safeguards could address the risk of deprivations of the kind Burch alleges. To do this, we examine the risk involved. The risk is that some persons who come into Florida's mental health facilities will apparently be willing to sign forms authorizing admission and treatment, but will be incompetent to give the "express and informed consent" required for voluntary placement under [Florida law]. Indeed, the very nature of mental illness makes it foreseeable that a person needing mental health care will be unable to understand any proffered "explanation and disclosure of the subject matter" of the forms that person is asked to sign, and will be unable "to make a knowing and willful decision" whether to consent to admission. A person who is willing to sign forms but is incapable of making an informed decision is, by the same token, unlikely to benefit from the voluntary patient's statutory right to request discharge. Such a person thus is in danger of being confined indefinitely without benefit of the procedural safeguards of the involuntary placement process, a process specifically designed to protect persons incapable of looking after their own interests. Persons who are mentally ill and incapable of giving informed consent to admission would not necessarily meet the statutory standard for involuntary placement, which requires either that they are likely to injure themselves or others, or that their neglect or refusal to care for themselves threatens their well-being. The involuntary placement process serves to guard against the confinement of a person who, though mentally ill, is harmless and can live safely outside an institution. Confinement of such a person not only violates Florida law, but also is unconstitutional. *O'Connor v. Donaldson* (there is no constitutional basis for confining mentally ill persons involuntarily "if they are dangerous to no one and can live safely in freedom"). Thus, it is at least possible that if Burch had an involuntary placement hearing, he would not have been found to meet the statutory standard for involuntary placement and would not have been confined at FSH. Moreover, even assuming that Burch would have met the statutory requirements for involuntary placement, he still could have been harmed by being deprived of other protections built into the involuntary placement procedure, such as the appointment of a guardian advocate to make treatment decisions and periodic judicial review of placement.[19]

The very risks created by the application of the informed-consent requirement to the special context of mental health care are borne out by the facts alleged in this case. It appears from the exhibits accompanying Burch's com-

plaint that he was simply given admission forms to sign by clerical workers, and, after he signed, was considered a voluntary patient. Burch alleges that petitioners knew or should have known that he was incapable of informed consent. This allegation is supported, at least as to petitioner Zinermon, by the psychiatrist's admission notes, described above, on Burch's mental state. Thus, the way in which Burch allegedly was admitted to FSH certainly did not ensure compliance with the statutory standard for voluntary admission.

We now consider whether predeprivation safeguards would have any value in guarding against the kind of deprivation Burch allegedly suffered. Petitioners urge that here, as in *Parratt* and *Hudson*, such procedures could have no value at all, because the State cannot prevent its officials from making random and unauthorized errors in the admission process. We disagree.

The Florida statutes, of course, do not allow incompetent persons to be admitted as "voluntary" patients. But the statutes do not direct any member of the facility staff to determine whether a person is competent to give consent, nor to initiate the involuntary placement procedure for every incompetent patient. A patient who is willing to sign forms but incapable of informed consent certainly cannot be relied on to protest his "voluntary" admission and demand that the involuntary placement procedure be followed. The staff are the only persons in a position to take notice of any misuse of the voluntary admission process and to ensure that the proper procedure is followed.

Florida chose to delegate to petitioners a broad power to admit patients to FSH, i.e., to effect what, in the absence of informed consent, is a substantial deprivation of liberty. Because petitioners had state authority to deprive persons of liberty, the Constitution imposed on them the State's concomitant duty to see that no deprivation occurs without adequate procedural protections.

It may be permissible constitutionally for a State to have a statutory scheme like Florida's, which gives state officials broad power and little guidance in admitting mental patients.

But when those officials fail to provide constitutionally required procedural safeguards to a person whom they deprive of liberty, the state officials cannot then escape

---

[19] Hence, Burch might be entitled to actual damages, beyond the nominal damages awardable for a procedural due process violation unaccompanied by any actual injury, see Carey v. Piphus 435 U.S. 247, 266–267 (1978), if he can show either that if the proper procedure had been followed he would have remained at liberty and that he suffered harm by being confined, or that even if he would have been committed anyway under the involuntary placement procedure, the lack of this procedure harmed him in some way.

liability by invoking *Parratt* and *Hudson*. It is immaterial whether the due process violation Burch alleges is best described as arising from petitioner's failure to comply with state procedures for admitting involuntary patients, or from the absence of a specific requirement that petitioners determine whether a patient is competent to consent to voluntary admission. Burch's suit is neither an action challenging the facial adequacy of a State's statutory procedures, nor an action based only on state officials' random and unauthorized violation of state laws. Burch is not simply attempting to blame the State for misconduct by its employees. He seeks to hold state officials accountable for their abuse of their broadly delegated, uncircumscribed power to effect the deprivation at issue.

This case, therefore, is not controlled by *Parratt* and *Hudson*, for three basic reasons:

First, petitioners cannot claim that the deprivation of Burch's liberty was unpredictable. Under Florida's statutory scheme, only a person competent to give informed consent may be admitted as a voluntary patient. There is, however, no specified way of determining, before a patient is asked to sign admission forms, whether he is competent. It is hardly unforeseeable that a person requesting treatment for mental illness might be incapable of informed consent, and that state officials with the power to admit patients might take their apparent willingness to be admitted at face value and not initiate involuntary placement procedures. Any erroneous deprivation will occur, if at all, at a specific, predictable point in the admission process—when a patient is given admission forms to sign.

This situation differs from the State's predicament in *Parratt*. While it could anticipate that prison employees would occasionally lose property through negligence, it certainly "cannot predict precisely when the loss will occur." Likewise, in Hudson, the State might be able to predict that guards occasionally will harass or persecute prisoners they dislike, but cannot "know when such deprivations will occur."

Second, we cannot say that predeprivation process was impossible here. Florida already has an established procedure for involuntary placement. The problem is only to ensure that this procedure is afforded to all patients who cannot be admitted voluntarily, both those who are unwilling and those who are unable to give consent.

In *Parratt*, the very nature of the deprivation made predeprivation process "impossible." It would do no good for the State to have a rule telling its employees not to lose mail by mistake, and it "borders on the absurd to suggest that a State must provide a hearing to determine whether or not a corrections officer should engage in negligent conduct." *Daniels* (Stevens, J., concurring in judgments). In Hudson, the errant employee himself could anticipate the deprivation since he intended to effect it, but the State still was not in a position to provide predeprivation process, since it could not anticipate or control such random and unauthorized intentional conduct. Again, a rule forbidding a prison guard to maliciously destroy a prisoner's property would not have done any good; it would be absurd to suggest that the State hold a hearing to determine whether a guard should engage in such conduct.

Here, in contrast, there is nothing absurd in suggesting that, had the State limited and guided petitioners' power to admit patients, the deprivation might have been averted. Burch's complaint alleges that petitioners "knew or should have known" that he was incompetent, and nonetheless admitted him as a voluntary patient in "willful, wanton, and reckless disregard" of his constitutional rights. Understood in context, the allegation means only that petitioners disregarded their duty to ensure that the proper procedures were followed, not that they, like the prison guard in Hudson, were bent upon effecting the substantive deprivation and would have done so despite any and all predeprivation safeguards. Moreover, it would indeed be strange to allow state officials to escape § 1983 liability for failing to provide constitutionally required procedural protections by assuming that those procedures would be futile because the same state officials would find a way to subvert them.

Third, petitioners cannot characterize their conduct as "unauthorized" in the sense the term is used in *Parratt* and *Hudson*. The State delegated to them the power and authority to effect the very deprivation complained of here, Burch's confinement in a mental hospital, and also delegated to them the concomitant duty to initiate the procedural safeguards set up by state law to guard against unlawful confinement. In *Parratt* and *Hudson*, the state employees had no similar broad authority to deprive prisoners of their personal property, and no similar duty to initiate (for persons unable to protect their own interests) the procedural safeguards required before deprivations occur. The deprivation here is "unauthorized" only in the sense that it was not an act sanctioned by state law, but, instead, was a "deprivation of constitutional rights . . . by an official's abuse of his position." *Monroe*.

We conclude that petitioners cannot escape § 1983 liability by characterizing their conduct as a "random, unauthorized" violation of Florida law which the State was not in a position to predict or avert, so that all the process Burch could possibly be due is a postdeprivation damages remedy. Burch, according to the allegations of his complaint, was deprived of a substantial liberty interest without either valid consent or an involuntary placement hearing, by the very state officials charged with the power to deprive mental patients of their liberty and the duty to implement procedural safeguards. Such a deprivation is foreseeable, due to the nature of mental illness, and will occur, if at all, at a predictable point in the admission process. Unlike *Parratt* and *Hudson*, this case does not represent the special instance of the *Mathews* due process analysis where postdeprivation process is all that is due because no predeprivation safeguards would be of use in preventing the kind of deprivation alleged.

We express no view on the ultimate merits of Burch's claim; we hold only that his complaint was sufficient to state a claim under § 1983 for violation of his procedural due process rights.

Justice **O'Connor**, with whom The Chief Justice, Justice **Scalia**, and Justice **Kennedy** join, dissenting.

Without doubt, respondent Burch alleges a serious deprivation of liberty; yet equally clearly he alleges no violation of the Fourteenth Amendment. The Court concludes that an allegation of state actors' wanton, unauthorized departure from a State's established policies and procedures, working a deprivation of liberty, suffices to support a procedural due process claim even though the State provides adequate postdeprivation remedies

for that deprivation. The Court's opinion unnecessarily transforms well-established procedural due process doctrine and departs from controlling precedent. I respectfully dissent.

Parratt v. Taylor and *Hudson v. Palmer* should govern this case. Only by disregarding the gist of Burch's complaint—that state actors' wanton and unauthorized departure from established practice worked the deprivation—and by transforming the allegations into a challenge to the adequacy of Florida's admissions procedures can the Court attempt to distinguish this case from *Parratt* and *Hudson*.

Burch alleges a deprivation occasioned by petitioners' contravention of Florida's established procedures. Florida allows the voluntary admission process to be employed to admit to its mental hospitals only patients who have made "application by express and informed consent for admission," and requires that the elaborate involuntary admission process be used to admit patients requiring treatment and incapable of giving such consent. Burch explicitly disavows any challenge to the adequacy of those established procedural safeguards accompanying Florida's two avenues of admission to mental hospitals . . . Nor does the complaint allege any widespread practice of subverting the State's procedural safeguards. Burch instead claims that in his case petitioners wrongfully employed the voluntary admission process deliberately or recklessly to deny him the hearing that Florida requires state actors to provide, through the involuntary admission process, to one in his position. He claims that petitioners "knew or should have known" that he was incapable of consent but "with willful, wanton and reckless disregard of and indifference to" his constitutional rights "subjected him to involuntary commitment" without any hearing "at which he could have challenged his involuntary admission and treatment." . . . Consistent with his disavowal of any attack upon the adequacy of the State's established procedures, Burch alleges that petitioners flagrantly and at least recklessly contravened those requirements. In short, Burch has alleged that petitioners' unauthorized actions worked the deprivation of his liberty.

Parratt and *Hudson* should readily govern procedural due process claims such as respondent's. Taken together, the decisions indicate that for deprivations worked by such random and unauthorized departures from otherwise unimpugned and established state procedures the State provides the process due by making available adequate postdeprivation remedies. In *Parratt*, the Court addressed a deprivation which "occurred as a result of the unauthorized failure of agents of the State to follow established state procedure." The random nature of the state actor's unauthorized departure made it not "practicable for the State to provide a predeprivation hearing," and adequate postdeprivation remedies available through the State's tort system provided the process due under the Fourteenth Amendment. *Hudson* applied this reasoning to intentional deprivations by state actors and confirmed the distinction between deprivation pursuant to "an established state procedure" and that pursuant to "random and unauthorized action." In *Hudson*, the Court explained that the *Parratt* doctrine was applicable because "the state cannot possibly know in advance of a negligent deprivation of property," and that "the controlling inquiry is solely whether the state is in a position to provide for predeprivation process."

Application of *Parratt* and *Hudson* indicates that respondent has failed to state a claim allowing recovery under 42 U.S.C. § 1983. Petitioners' actions were unauthorized: they are alleged to have wrongly and without license departed from established state practices. Florida officials in a position to establish safeguards commanded that the voluntary admission process be employed only for consenting patients and that the involuntary hearing procedures be used to admit unconsenting patients. Yet it is alleged that petitioners "with willful, wanton and reckless disregard of and indifference to" Burch's rights contravened both commands. As in *Parratt*, the deprivation "occurred as a result of the unauthorized failure of agents of the State to follow established state procedure." The wanton or reckless nature of the failure indicates it to be random. The State could not foresee the particular contravention and was hardly "in a position to provide for predeprivation process," to ensure that officials bent upon subverting the State's requirements would in fact follow those procedures. For this wrongful deprivation resulting from an unauthorized departure from established state practice, Florida provides adequate post-

deprivation remedies, as two courts below concluded, and which the Court and respondent do not dispute. *Parratt* and *Hudson* thus should govern this case and indicate that respondent has failed to allege a violation of the Fourteenth Amendment.

The allegedly wanton nature of the subversion of the state procedures underscores why the State cannot in any relevant sense anticipate and meaningfully guard against the random and unauthorized actions alleged in this case. The Court suggests that the State could foresee "that a person requesting treatment for mental illness might be incapable of informed consent." While foreseeability of that routine difficulty in evaluating prospective patients is relevant in considering the general adequacy of Florida's voluntary admission procedures, *Parratt* and *Hudson* address whether the State can foresee and thus be required to forestall the deliberate or reckless departure from established state practice. Florida may be able to predict that over time some state actors will subvert its clearly implicated requirements. Indeed, that is one reason that the State must implement an adequate remedial scheme. But Florida "cannot predict precisely when the loss will occur," and the Due Process Clause does not require the State to do more than establish appropriate remedies for any wrongful departure from its prescribed practices.

The Court attempts to avert the force of *Parratt* and *Hudson* by characterizing petitioners' alleged failures as only the routine but erroneous application of the admissions process. According to the Court, Burch suffered an "erroneous deprivation," and the "risk of deprivations of the kind Burch alleges" is that incompetent "persons who come into Florida's mental health facilities will apparently be willing to sign forms," prompting officials to "make random and unauthorized errors in the admission process." The Court's characterization omits petitioners' alleged wrongful state of mind and thus the nature and source of the wrongful deprivation . . .

The unauthorized and wrongful character of the departure from established state practice makes additional procedures an "impracticable" means of preventing the deprivation . . . The Court suggests that additional safeguards surrounding the voluntary admission process would have quite possibly reduced the risk of deprivation. This reasoning conflates the value of procedures for preventing error in the repeated and usual case (evaluated according to the test set forth in *Mathews v. Eldridge*) with the value of additional predeprivation procedures to forestall deprivations by state actors bent upon departing from, or indifferent to, complying with established practices. Unsurprisingly, the Court is vague regarding how its proffered procedures would prevent the deprivation Burch alleges, and why the safeguards would not form merely one more set of procedural protections that state employees could willfully, recklessly, and wantonly subvert. Indeed, Burch alleges that, presented with the clearest evidence of his incompetence, petitioners nonetheless wantonly or recklessly denied him the protections of the State's admission procedures and requirements. The state actor so indifferent to guaranteed protections would be no more prevented from working the deprivation by additional procedural requirements than would the mail handler in *Parratt* or the prison guard in *Hudson* . . . In all three cases, the unpredictable, wrongful departure is beyond the State's reasonable control. Additional safeguards designed to secure correct results in the usual case do not practicably forestall state actors who flout the State's command and established practice.

Even indulging the Court's belief that the proffered safeguards would provide "some" benefit, *Parratt* and *Hudson* extend beyond circumstances in which procedural safeguards would have had "negligible" value. In *Parratt* and *Hudson* additional measures would conceivably have had some benefit in preventing the alleged deprivations. A practice of barring individual or unsupervised shakedown searches, a procedure of always pairing or monitoring guards, or a requirement that searches be conducted according to "an established policy" (the proposed measure rejected as unnecessary in *Hudson*) might possibly have helped to prevent the type of deprivation considered in *Hudson*. More sensible staffing practices, better training, or a more rigorous tracking procedure may have averted the deprivation at issue in *Parratt*. In those cases, like this one, the State knew the exact context in which the wrongful deprivation would occur. Yet the possibility of implementing such marginally beneficial measures, in light

of the type of alleged deprivation, did not alter the analysis. The State's inability to foresee and to forestall the wrongful departure from established procedures renders additional predeprivation measures "impracticable" and not required by the dictates of due process.

Every command to act imparts the duty to exercise discretion in accord with the command and affords the opportunity to abuse that discretion. The *Mathews* test measures whether the State has sufficiently constrained discretion in the usual case, while the *Parratt* doctrine requires the State to provide a remedy for any wrongful abuse. The Court suggests that this case differs from *Parratt* and *Hudson* because petitioners possessed a sort of delegated power. Yet petitioners no more had the delegated power to depart from the admission procedures and requirements than did the guard in *Hudson* to exceed the limits of his established search and seizure authority, or the prison official in *Parratt* wrongfully to withhold or misdeliver mail. Petitioners' delegated duty to act in accord with Florida's admissions procedures is akin to the mailhandler's duty to follow and implement the procedures surrounding delivery of packages, or the guard's duty to conduct the search properly. In the appropriate circumstances and pursuant to established procedures, the guard in *Hudson* was charged with seizing property pursuant to a search. The official in *Parratt* no doubt possessed some power to withhold certain packages from prisoners. *Parratt* and *Hudson* distinguish sharply between deprivations caused by unauthorized acts and those occasioned by established state procedures. The delegation argument blurs this line and ignores the unauthorized nature of petitioners' alleged departure from established practices . . .

The Court's reliance upon the State's inappropriate delegation of duty also creates enormous line-drawing problems. Today's decision applies to deprivations occasioned by state actors given "little guidance" and "broadly delegated, uncircumscribed power" to initiate required procedures. At some undefined point, the breadth of the delegation of power requires officials to channel the exercise of that power or become liable for its misapplications. When guidance is provided and the power to effect the deprivation circumscribed, no liability arises. And routine exercise of the power must be sufficiently fraught with the danger of "erroneous deprivation." In the absence of this broadly delegated power that carries with it pervasive risk of wrongful deprivation, *Parratt* and *Hudson* still govern. In essence, the Court's rationale applies when state officials are loosely charged with fashioning effective procedures or ensuring that required procedures are not routinely evaded. In a roundabout way, this rationale states the unexceptional conclusion that liability exists when officials' actions amount to the established state practice, a rationale unasserted in this case and, otherwise, appropriately analyzed under the *Mathews* test . . .

I respectfully dissent.

NOTES

1. *Zinermon* provides straightforward answers to two of the questions raised in the notes before the case: *Parratt* does apply to liberty as well as property claims, and it does not apply to substantive due process claims. Does the dissent take issue with either of these propositions?

As discussed in the first note after *Parratt*, that case itself seems better characterized as a substantive due process claim. One commentator has argued that *Zinermon* is "mistaken" in limiting *Parratt* to procedural due process claims. *Fallon*, supra, at 341 n.184.

In what sense does the Court commit a mistake when it interprets (or modifies) its own decisions? Would it be appropriate to interpret *Zinermon* as having cleared up some of the confusion and incoherence *Parratt* would create if *Parratt* applied to substantive due process cases?

2. According to the Court, Burch, the plaintiff in *Zinermon*, made a procedural due process claim. He did not assert that the state is forbidden, under the due process clause, to confine persons who consent to confinement or who pose a danger to themselves or others. He challenged the process by which it was decided that he had validly consented to confinement, and in particular the broad discretion afforded administrators to determine whether someone could validly consent, with no procedural safeguards against errors on their part. But the Fourteenth Amendment does not always re-

quire pre-deprivation process. Sometimes the circumstances justify state actions taken with no prior procedural safeguards, followed by a postdeprivation procedure for determining the propriety of the state's action. The majority opinion in *Zinermon* listed some examples: "See. e.g., *Logan v. Zimmerman Brush Co.*, 455 U.S. 422, 436 (1982) ("'The necessity of quick action by the State or the impracticality of providing any predeprivation process'" may mean that a postdeprivation remedy is constitutionally adequate, quoting *Parratt*, 451 U.S., at 539); *Memphis Light*, 436 U.S., at 19 ("Where the potential length or severity of the deprivation does not indicate a likelihood of serious loss and where the procedures . . . are sufficiently reliable to minimize the risk of erroneous determination," a prior hearing may not be required); *Ingraham v. Wright*, 430 U.S. 651, 682 (1977) (hearing not required before corporal punishment of junior high school students); *Mitchell v. W.T. Grant Co.*, 416 U.S. 600, 619–620 (1974) (hearing not required before issuance of writ to sequester debtor's property)." *Zinermon v. Burch*, 494 U.S. at 128.

3. In determining the process that is due in a given set of circumstances, courts generally follow *Mathews v. Eldridge*, 424 U.S. 319 (1976), where the Court said:

> [I]dentification of the specific dictates of due process generally requires consideration of three distinct factors: First, the private interest that will be affected by the official action; second, the risk of an erroneous deprivation of such interest through the procedures used, and the probable value, if any, of additional or substitute procedural safeguards; and finally, the Government's interest, including the function involved and the fiscal and administrative burdens that the additional or substitute procedural requirement would entail.

Id. at 335.

4. If the circumstances justify waiting until later to afford a remedy, the question arises whether the state's post-deprivation remedies are adequate. In *Flatford v. City of Monroe*, 17 F.3d 162 (6th Cir. 1994) tenants were evacuated from their apartment without a prior hearing due to a fire hazard, and sued for deprivation of property without due process. The landlord, but not the tenants, were informed of administrative remedies. Though the emergency justified the evacuation without a pre-deprivation hearing, plaintiffs were entitled to a post-deprivation remedy, and "post deprivation state tort remedies [were] neither timely nor sufficiently remedial for emergency evacuees. Fundamental fairness expects more of a state than mere tort remedies where government dispossesses its citizens from their homes . . . [F]undamental fairness requires notice in short order of the right to an administrative hearing, including the manner designated for obtaining timely review." Id. at 169.

5. Professor Larry Alexander is not so sure that Burch's complaint was directed at procedural due process:

> Burch's complaint was ambiguous regarding whether the alleged denial of due process was procedural or substantive. If Burch was claiming that (1) his "consent" was involuntary *and* that (2) he was neither a danger to himself nor a danger to others, then he was claiming a deprivation of substantive due process, namely, that Florida and its officials had no sufficient reason *in fact* to commit him to a mental hospital. On the other hand, if Burch was not denying that he was in fact constitutionally committable, either involuntarily or voluntarily, but only that the procedures the defendants employed were neither sufficient to commit him involuntarily . . . nor sufficient, given the evidence that he might not understand what he was doing, to commit him as a voluntary patient, then his complaint sounded in procedural due process.

Alexander, *Constitutional Torts, the Supreme Court, and the Law of Noncontradiction: An Essay on* Zinermon v. Burch, 87 Nw. U.L. Rev. 576, 589–90 (1993). Should the district court have required Burch to rewrite his complaint? Should the Supreme Court have so required?

6. Does *Zinermon* merely apply *Parratt*, as the majority insists, or significantly modify the *Parratt* test for determining whether post-deprivation remedies are adequate, as the dissent claims? Consider Judge Easterbrook's view:

> *Zinermon* . . . is inconsistent with the foundations of *Parratt v. Taylor* and *Hudson v. Palmer*. *Zinermon* said that if errors

in the implementation of a state's scheme for civil commitment are foreseeable, then process after the fact is inadequate, and it "distinguished" *Parratt* and *Hudson* on the ground that the wrongs committed in those cases were not foreseeable. This is no distinction at all. It is always foreseeable that there will be some errors in the implementation of any administrative system, and it is never foreseeable which occasions will give rise to those errors. It was foreseeable that some prison guards would lose the prisoners' property (*Parratt*), just as it was foreseeable that some persons would be committed without proper authorization (*Zinermon*); in neither case could the state or a court know in advance just when the errors would occur. If foreseeability of the *category* of blunders requires process in advance, then *Parratt* and *Hudson* were wrongly decided; if the inability to foresee the *particular* blunder makes subsequent remedies all the process "due", then *Zinermon* was wrongly decided.

Easter House v. Felder, 910 F.2d 1387, 1408 (7th Cir. 1990) (en banc) (concurring opinion).

7. Despite the tension between the two cases, *Zinermon* did not overrule *Parratt*; indeed, it claimed that the two cases were compatible. As a result, some lower courts sympathetic to post-deprivation state remedies have been able to rationalize their decisions requiring resort to them in circumstances where *Zinermon* suggests a contrary ruling. For example, *Easter House*, supra, was a case the Supreme Court had remanded for reconsideration in light of *Zinermon*. The seventh circuit, sitting en banc, found post-deprivation remedies sufficient for due process where the plaintiff alleged a conspiracy between public officers and private actors to deprive it of its state license to operate an adoption agency. This conspiracy was "random and unauthorized" and hence within *Parratt*, rather than "predictable" (and controlled by *Zinermon*) because, among other reasons, "[t]he state had no opportunity to discover that the [defendants] were disregarding the established state procedures for renewing licenses." 910 F.2d at 1399.

As for Judge Easterbrook, he thought that adherence to *Zinermon* would forbid federal dismissal, yet he joined the majority. Since

Zinermon did not overrule *Parratt*, it seemed to him unlikely that *Zinermon* represented a stable equilibrium. The majority opinion here "offers the best estimate of the course a majority of the Court will take." 910 F.2d at 1409.

A later Seventh Circuit case, *Cushing v. City of Chicago*, 3 F.3d 1156 (7th Cir. 1993), fell on the *Zinermon* side of the ledger. A city fireman disabled by heart disease left his job. The city continued to pay his medical expenses for a few months, then stopped. In Cushing's section 1983 suit he claimed that he had a property interest in continuing medical coverage, and that the decision to deny benefits was made without adequate procedural safeguards, in violation of his fourteenth amendment due process rights. Defendants argued that

> the City had no practicable way to anticipate the deprivation . . . and to provide Cushing with pre-deprivation notice and a hearing. Consequently, the existence of a postdeprivation remedy (presumably in the form of a tort claim against the City officials in state court) supplies Cushing with adequate process and thus precludes section 1983 liability.

3 F.3d at 1164.

But the court held otherwise.

> The defendants' argument that the City could not have anticipated the deprivation . . . and thus could not have provided him with predeprivation process, is unconvincing. As the defendants concede, "[i]f the City paid the expenses in full for some time it did so mistakenly, and discontinued payments when it determined that Cushing's illness was not duty related." This admission belies the claim that any termination of Cushing's medial benefits was the result of random conduct that would have made a postdeprivation hearing impossible, or even unduly burdensome.

3 F.3d at 1165.

Is this reasoning consistent with *Easter House*? The *Cushing* court thought so, because the officials' actions in *Easter House* violated state law, and "the adoption agency could "point to nothing which would indicate that the state knew or should have known that the [defendants] or other state employees had

disregarded, or were likely to disregard the state's established procedure for processing renewal applications.'" In *Cushing*, "[b]y contrast, the City does not disavow knowledge of Tully's and Knorr's actions, and does not suggest either individual contravened the provisions of the collective bargaining agreement, much less municipal or state law. The defendants' contentions that their actions were of a piece and were entirely proper thus take this case out of the ambit of *Easter House*." Id.

See also *Caine v. Hardy*, 943 F.2d 1406 (5th Cir. 1991) (applying *Parratt* to dismiss a claim by a doctor who lost his staff privileges at a public hospital, allegedly in violation of procedural due process; *Zinermon* did not apply because there the plaintiff "was afforded *no* predeprivation process", id. at 1413 (emphasis in original) while here the hospital had "precise and detailed regulations", id., and the plaintiff's allegation was that they were not followed).

For a discussion of post-*Zinermon* cases, in which the lower federal courts take divergent views of *Zinermon* and its effect on the *Parratt* doctrine, see Oren, *Signing Into Heaven*: Zinermon v. Burch, *Federal Rights, and State Remedies Thirty Years After* Monroe v. Pape, 40 Emory L.J. 1, 55–69 (1991).

II.   The Scope of Substantive Due Process

A.   State of Mind

Daniels v. Williams

474 U.S. 327 (1986)

Justice **Rehnquist** delivered the opinion of the Court.

In *Parratt v. Taylor* a state prisoner sued under 42 U.S.C. § 1983, claiming that prison officials had negligently deprived him of his property without due process of law. After deciding that § 1983 contains no independent state-of-mind requirement, we concluded that although petitioner had been "deprived" of property within the meaning of the Due Process Clause of the Fourteenth Amendment, the State's postdeprivation tort remedy provided the process that was due. Petitioner's claim in this case, which also rests on an alleged Fourteenth Amendment "deprivation" caused by the negligent conduct of a prison official, leads us to reconsider our statement in *Parratt* that "the alleged loss, even though negligently caused, amounted to a deprivation." Id., at 536–537. We conclude that the Due Process Clause is simply not implicated by a negligent act of an official causing unintended loss of or injury to life, liberty, or property.

In this § 1983 action, petitioner seeks to recover damages for back and ankle injuries allegedly sustained when he fell on a prison stairway. He claims that, while an inmate at the city jail in Richmond, Virginia, he slipped on a pillow negligently left on the stairs by respondent, a correctional deputy stationed at the jail. Respondent's negligence, the argument runs, "deprived" petitioner of his "liberty" interest in freedom from bodily injury, see *Ingraham v. Wright*; because respondent maintains that he is entitled to the defense of sovereign immunity in a state tort suit, petitioner is without an "adequate" state remedy, cf. *Hudson v. Palmer*. Accordingly, the deprivation of liberty was without "due process of law."

Because of the inconsistent approaches taken by lower courts in determining when tortious conduct by state officials rises to the level of a constitutional tort, and the apparent lack of adequate guidance from this Court, we granted certiorari.

In *Parratt v. Taylor*, we granted certiorari, as we had twice before, "to decide whether mere negligence will support a claim for relief under § 1983." After examining the language, legislative history, and prior interpretations of the statute, we concluded that § 1983, unlike its criminal counterpart, 18 U.S.C. § 242, contains no state-of-mind requirement independent of that necessary to state a violation of the underlying constitutional right. We adhere to that conclusion. But in any given § 1983 suit, the plaintiff must still prove a violation of the underlying constitutional right; and depending on the right, merely negligent conduct may not be enough to state a claim. See, e. g., *Arlington Heights v. Metropolitan Housing Dev. Corp.* (invidious discriminatory purpose required for claim of

racial discrimination under the Equal Protection Clause); Estelle v. Gamble, 429 U.S. 97, 105 (1976) ("deliberate indifference" to prisoner's serious illness or injury sufficient to constitute cruel and unusual punishment under the Eighth Amendment).

In *Parratt*, before concluding that Nebraska's tort remedy provided all the process that was due, we said that the loss of the prisoner's hobby kit, "even though negligently caused, amounted to a deprivation [under the Due Process Clause]." Justice Powell, concurring in the result, criticized the majority for "[passing] over" this important question of the state of mind required to constitute a "deprivation" of property. He argued that negligent acts by state officials, though causing loss of property, are not actionable under the Due Process Clause. To Justice Powell, mere negligence could not "[work] a deprivation in the constitutional sense." Not only does the word "deprive" in the Due Process Clause connote more than a negligent act, but we should not "open the federal courts to lawsuits where there has been no affirmative abuse of power." Id.; see also id. (Stewart, J., concurring) ("To hold that this kind of loss is a deprivation of property within the meaning of the Fourteenth Amendment seems not only to trivialize, but grossly to distort the meaning and intent of the Constitution"). Upon reflection, we agree and overrule *Parratt* to the extent that it states that mere lack of due care by a state official may "deprive" an individual of life, liberty, or property under the Fourteenth Amendment.

The Due Process Clause of the Fourteenth Amendment provides: "[Nor] shall any State deprive any person of life, liberty, or property, without due process of law." Historically, this guarantee of due process has been applied to deliberate decisions of government officials to deprive a person of life, liberty, or property. E.g., *Davidson v. New Orleans* (assessment of real estate); *Rochin v. California* (stomach pumping); *Bell v. Burson* (suspension of driver's license); *Ingraham v. Wright* (paddling student); *Hudson v. Palmer* (intentional destruction of inmate's property).

The decision of this Court before *Parratt* supported the view that negligent conduct by a state official, even though causing injury, constitutes a deprivation under the Due Process Clause. This history reflects the traditional and common-sense notion that the Due Process Clause, like its forebear in the Magna Carta, was "'intended to secure the individual from the arbitrary exercise of the powers of government,'" *Hurtado v. California* (quoting *Bank of Columbia v. Okely*). See also *Wolff v. McDonnell* ("The touchstone of due process is protection of the individual against arbitrary action of government, *Dent v. West Virginia*"); *Parratt*, supra (Powell, J., concurring in result). By requiring the government to follow appropriate procedures when its agents decide to "deprive any person of life, liberty, or property," the Due Process Clause promotes fairness in such decisions. And by barring certain government actions regardless of the fairness of the procedures used to implement them, e.g., *Rochin*, supra, it serves to prevent governmental power from being "used for purposes of oppression," *Murray's Lessee v. Hoboken Land & Improvement Co.* (discussing Due Process Clause of Fifth Amendment).

We think that the actions of prison custodians in leaving a pillow on the prison stairs, or mislaying an inmate's property, are quite remote from the concerns just discussed. Far from an abuse of power, lack of due care suggests no more than a failure to measure up to the conduct of a reasonable person. To hold that injury caused by such conduct is a deprivation within the meaning of the Fourteenth Amendment would trivialize the centuries-old principle of due process of law.

The Fourteenth Amendment is a part of a Constitution generally designed to allocate governing authority among the Branches of the Federal Government and between that Government and the States, and to secure certain individual rights against both State and Federal Government. When dealing with a claim that such a document creates a right in prisoners to sue a government official because he negligently created an unsafe condition in the prison, we bear in mind Chief Justice Marshall's admonition that "we must never forget, that it is a constitution we are expounding," *McCulloch v. Maryland* (emphasis in original). Our Constitution deals with the large concerns of the governors and the governed, but it does not purport to supplant traditional tort law in laying down rules of conduct to regulate liability for injuries that attend living together in society. We have previously rejected reasoning that "'would make of the Fourteenth Amendment a font of tort law to be superimposed upon whatever systems may already be administered by the States,'" *Paul v. Davis.*

The only tie between the facts of this case and anything governmental in nature is the fact that respondent was a sheriff's deputy at the Richmond city jail and petitioner was an inmate confined in that jail. But while the Due Process Clause of the Fourteenth Amendment obviously speaks to some facets of this relationship, we do not believe its protections are triggered by lack of due care by prison officials. "Medical malpractice does not become a constitutional violation merely because the victim is a prisoner," *Estelle v. Gamble*, and "false imprisonment does not become a violation of the Fourteenth Amendment merely because the defendant is a state official." *Baker v. McCollan.* Where a government official's act causing injury to life, liberty, or property is merely negligent, "no procedure for compensation is constitutionally required." Parratt, supra (Powell, J., concurring in result) (emphasis added).

That injuries inflicted by governmental negligence are not addressed by the United States Constitution is not to say that they may not raise significant legal concerns and lead to the creation of protectible legal interests. The enactment of tort claim statutes, for example, reflects the view that injuries caused by such negligence should generally be redressed. It is no reflection on either the breadth of the United States Constitution or the importance of traditional tort law to say that they do not address the same concerns.

In support of his claim that negligent conduct can give rise to a due process "deprivation," petitioner makes several arguments, none of which we find persuasive. He states, for example, that "it is almost certain that some negligence claims are within § 1983," and cites as an example the failure of a State to comply with the procedural requirements of *Wolff v. McDonnell* before depriving an inmate of good-time credit. We think the relevant action of the prison officials in that situation is their deliberate decision to deprive the inmate of good-time credit, not their hypothetically negligent failure to accord him the procedural protections of the Due Process Clause. But we need not rule out the possibility that there are other constitutional provisions that would be violated by mere lack of care in order to hold, as we do, that such conduct does not implicate the Due Process Clause of the Fourteenth Amendment.

Petitioner also suggests that artful litigants, undeterred by a requirement that they plead more than mere negligence, will often be able to allege sufficient facts to support a claim of intentional deprivation. In the instant case, for example, petitioner notes that he could have alleged that the pillow was left on the stairs with the intention of harming him. This invitation to "artful" pleading, petitioner contends, would engender sticky (and needless) disputes over what is fairly pleaded. What's more, requiring complainants to allege something more than negligence would raise serious questions about what "more" than negligence—intent, recklessness, or "gross negligence"—is required,[3] and indeed about what these elusive terms mean. But even if accurate, petitioner's observations do not carry the day. In the first place, many branches of the law abound in nice distinctions that may be troublesome but have been thought nonetheless necessary . . . More important, the difference between one end of the spectrum—negligence—and the other—intent—is abundantly clear. See O. Holmes, *The Common Law* 3 (1923). In any event, we decline to trivialize the Due Process Clause in an effort to simplify constitutional litigation. . . .

---

[3] Despite his claim about what he might have pleaded, petitioner concedes that respondent was at most negligent. Accordingly, this case affords us no occasion to consider whether something less than intentional conduct, such as recklessness or "gross negligence," is enough to trigger the protections of the Due Process Clause.

NOTES

1. In *Davidson v. Cannon*, 474 U.S. 344 (1986), a companion case to *Daniels*, a prisoner sued prison officials for failing to protect him against assault by McMillian, another inmate. After being threatened by the attacker, the plaintiff had explained the situation to Cannon, the assistant superintendent of the prison, who passed it on to James, a corrections sergeant. Yet nothing was done to ensure his safety. Two days later McMillian attacked him. Applying the standard it had set forth in *Daniels*, the Court held that this failure did not amount to "deliberate indifference".

> Respondents' lack of due care in this case led to serious injury, but that lack of care simply does not approach the sort of abusive government conduct that the Due Process Clause was designed to prevent. Far from abusing governmental power, or employing it as an instrument of oppression, respondent Cannon mistakenly believed that the situation was not particularly serious, and respondent James simply forgot about the note. The guarantee of due process has never been understood to mean that the State must guarantee due care on the part of its officials . . . Petitioner's claim, based on respondents' negligence, is quite different from one involving injuries caused by an unjustified attack by prison guards themselves or by another prisoner where officials simply stood by and permitted the attack to proceed . . .

474 U.S. at 347–48.

In dissent, Justice Blackmun took issue with the Court's sweeping holding

> that negligent activity can *never* implicate the concerns of the Due Process Clause . . . In some cases, by any reasonable standard, governmental negligence is an abuse of power. This is one of those cases. It seems to me that when a State assumes sole responsibility for one's physical security and then ignores his call for help, the State cannot claim that it did not know a subsequent injury was likely to occur . . . In the context of prisons this means that once the State has taken away an inmate's means of protecting himself from attack by other inmates, a prison official's negligence in providing protection can amount to a deprivation of the inmate's liberty . . . In *Daniels*, the negligence was only coincidentally connected to an inmate-guard relationship; the same incident could have occurred on any staircase . . . In contrast, where the State renders a person vulnerable and strips him of his ability to defend himself, an injury that results from a state official's negligence in performing his duty is pecul-

iarly related to the governmental function . . . The deliberate decision not to protect Davidson from a known threat was directly related to the often violent life of prisoners.

474 U.S. at 353–56.

2. The Court in *Davidson* and *Daniels* addressed substantive due process claims, yet the *Davidson* opinion concludes with the sweeping pronouncement that "the protections of the Due Process Clause, *whether procedural or substantive*, are just not triggered by lack of due care by prison officials." 474 U.S. at 348. See also *Daniels*, 474 U.S. at 333–34.

Did the Court mean to say that procedural due process is not violated unless the defendant is at least grossly negligent, if not reckless?

But this seems too preposterous to take seriously. Appellate courts routinely reverse trial courts for errors of procedural due process, many of which presumably are attributable to negligence but are due process violations nonetheless. I would similarly suppose that school officials who negligently suspended a student without providing the constitutionally required hearing would violate the Constitution by doing so and that the suspension could be challenged successfully in a suit for an injunction, if not one for damages.

Fallon, *Some Confusions About Due Process, Judicial Review, and Constitutional Remedies*, 93 Colum. L. Rev. 309, 365 n.307 (1993).

Fallon himself seems to assume that negligence is necessary to make out a procedural due process violation. But surely some of the trial court errors to which he adverts are not even negligent. Any time an appellate court decides to change the law after the lower court has acted, the "mistake" cannot be fairly characterized as negligent, yet appellate courts reverse these innocent mistakes anyway.

For another example of the same theme in a different context, see *Owen v. City of Independence*, 445 U.S. 622 (1980). The Court there held that municipal governments are not entitled to a qualified immunity defense based on the reasonable belief of their officials that their action was constitutional. The violation at issue was procedural due process, specifically the

city's failure to give proper notice and hearing before firing the police chief. But the Supreme Court did not establish that procedural due process required these protections until *after* the firing occurred, hence the issue with regard to qualified immunity. If a procedural due process violation required negligence, would any violation have occurred here? Would it have been necessary to reach the immunity issue? *Owen* is discussed in Chapter 5.

3. Critics of substantive due process point out that the term is an oxymoron, "a contradiction in terms—sort of like 'green pastel redness.'" J. Ely, *Democracy and Distrust* 18 (1980). The grammatical incoherence of the phrase, they say, suggests more fundamental objections to the whole notion of using the due process clause as a source of substantive constraints on government. They claim that the text of the constitution ought to control its interpretation, and say that no plausible reading of "due process of law" could produce *substantive* limitations on government. Substantive due process acquired a bad reputation, from which it has never fully recovered, in the late nineteenth and early twentieth centuries when the Court used it as its tool for striking down social legislation like minimum wage and maximum hour laws. See G. Gunther, *Constitutional Law* 444–45 (1991). After going underground in the wake of the constitutional revolution of the 1930s, substantive due process was revived by the Warren Court. See *Griswold v. Connecticut*, 381 U.S. 479 (1965); *Roe v. Wade*, 410 U.S. 113 (1973).

However inelegant the term may be, and however checkered its history, substantive due process has managed to survive the efforts to remove it from our constitutional tradition. In particular, it is an important element of constitutional torts. Conservative Justices rail against the substantive due process decision in *Roe*. Why did Justice Rehnquist not take the opportunity afforded by *Daniels* to banish it from the constitutional lexicon altogether?

4. In the constitutional tort context, substantive due process is the Court's means for addressing wrongs that do not fit within any of the specifics of the bill of rights, yet are sufficiently egregious to call for a remedy as a matter of constitutional law. The Court has as yet made little progress in defining the scope of substantive due process in this context. Its cases focus more on what is *not* a constitutional violation rather than what government conduct is prohibited.

Daniels holds that negligence on the part of government actors is not sufficient to make out a substantive due process claim. Is the Court right to demand more than negligence?

> Consider some of the principles of negligence law. Negligence is an objective standard of care that is met whenever the defendant's conduct does not measure up to that of the mythical reasonable person. Typically, it does not imply a moral judgment of blameworthyness. It does not denote ill will or subjective lack of concern for the plaintiff's welfare, and it cannot support an award of punitive damages signifying societal disapproval of the defendant. When the plaintiff carelessly disregards his own safety, recovery of even compensatory damages will be diminished or barred entirely. More or less arbitrary rules of proximate cause and concededly arbitrary limits on damages for emotional harm further restrict recovery for negligence. All of these principles operate even when the plaintiff's injuries are severe. Taken together, these principles show that negligence is not commonly viewed as a particularly grave intrusion. Mislaying an inmate's property, failing to enforce the speed limit, and building dangerous streets are rather far removed from the Constitution's focus on individual autonomy against abuse of government power. This kind of government conduct shows no particular lack of concern and respect for the individual.

Wells & Eaton, *Substantive Due Process and the Scope of Constitutional Torts*, 18 Ga. L. Rev. 201, 239–40 (1984).

Do you agree? Keep in mind that the common law and the democratic process often (but not always) yield more or less effective remedies for governmental negligence. In constitutional tort the issue is whether the Supreme Court should mandate a federal remedy. Should such a remedy be reserved solely for the very worst cases of governmental misconduct? Does the tension between judicial lawmaking and democratic theory require that constitutional tort be reserved for extraordinary wrongs?

5. If negligence is not enough to justify constitutional sanctions, is "gross negligence" or "recklessness" sufficiently egregious? The courts of appeals are split on gross negligence. See *Manarite v. City of Springfield*, 957 F.2d 953 n.7 (1st Cir. 1992) and cases cited therein; *Salas v. Carpenter*, 980 F.2d 299, 307 n.6 (5th Cir. 1992).

Introducing gross negligence and recklessness into constitutional tort obliges courts to define these terms. Does their content differ here from other tort cases? One court says that in the constitutional tort context the criminal definition of recklessness must be met. *DeRosario v. Moran*, 949 F.2d 15, 19 (1st Cir. 1991) (plaintiff must "prove that the defendant had a culpable state of mind and intended wantonly to inflict pain . . . While this mental state can aptly be described as "recklessness', it is recklessness not in the tort-law sense but in the appreciably stricter criminal law sense, requiring actual knowledge [or wilful blindness] of impending harm, easily preventable"). Another says that "[a]n act is reckless when it reflects a wanton or obdurate disregard or complete indifference to risk, for example when the actor does not care whether the other person lives or dies, despite knowing that there is a significant risk of death or grievous bodily injury." *Medina v. City and County of Denver*, 960 F.2d 1493, 1496 (10th Cir. 1992).

6. In common law torts there is no consensus as to what gross negligence and recklessness mean, and what the difference is between them. Gross negligence, in particular, is notoriously elastic. Do courts run the risk of nullifying *Daniels* by allowing juries to find for the plaintiff based on gross negligence? May the problem be solved by imposing Rule 11 sanctions against lawyers who plead gross negligence or recklessness when all they can prove is negligence?

7. Often courts in constitutional tort cases favor the phrase "deliberate indifference", especially when the alleged tort occurs in a custodial setting. See, e.g., *Menarite v. City of Springfield*, 957 F.2d 953 (1st Cir. 1992). Deliberate indifference originated in eighth amendment law, as the test for whether inadequate medical treatment amounts to a constitutional violation. See *Estelle v. Gamble*, 429 U.S. 97 (1976). When the Supreme Court extended constitutional protection beyond prisoners to other persons held in state custody, such as pretrial detainees and mental patients, it justified its rules in terms of substantive due process. See, e.g., *Youngberg v. Romeo*, 457 U.S. 307 (1982); *Revere v. Massachusetts General Hospital*, 463 U.S. 239 (1983). Circuit courts have extended the analysis to other contexts where government officers exercise some control over individuals. See, e.g., *Gates v. Unified School District No. 449*, 996 F.2d 1035 (10th Cir. 1993) (public school).

Lower courts often have often used the terms "gross negligence", "recklessness", and "deliberate indifference" without carefully defining them. Consider the proper meaning of these terms in the light of a recent Supreme Court decision.

Farmer v. Brennan

114 S. Ct. 1970 (1994)

Justice **Souter** delivered the opinion of the Court.

A prison official's "deliberate indifference" to a substantial risk of serious harm to an inmate violates the Eighth Amendment. This case requires us to define the term "deliberate indifference," as we do by requiring a showing that the official was subjectively aware of the risk.

I

[Plaintiff, a transexual with a feminine appearance, was beaten and raped shortly after being placed in the general population at a federal prison.] Acting without counsel, petitioner then filed a *Bivens* complaint, alleging a violation of the Eighth Amendment. See *Bivens v. Six Unknown Fed. Narcotics Agents*; *Carlson v. Green*. As defendants, petitioner named respondents [several prison officials]. . . [T]he complaint alleged that respondents either transferred petitioner to USP-Terre Haute or placed petitioner in its general population despite knowledge that the penitentiary had a violent environment and a history of inmate assaults, and despite knowledge that petitioner, as a transsexual who "projects feminine characteristics," would be particularly vulnerable to sexual attack by some USP-Terre Haute inmates. This allegedly amounted to a deliberately indifferent failure to protect petitioner's safety, and thus to a violation of petitioner's Eighth Amendment rights. Petitioner sought compensatory and punitive damages, and an injunction barring future confinement in any penitentiary, including USP-Terre Haute . . .

[T]he District Court . . . granted summary judgment to respondents, concluding that there had been no deliberate indifference to petitioner's safety . . . The failure of prison officials to prevent inmate assaults violates the Eighth Amendment, the court stated, only if prison officials were "reckless in a criminal sense," meaning that they had "actual knowledge" of a potential danger. Respondents, however, lacked the requisite knowledge, the court found. "[Petitioner] never expressed any concern for his safety to any of [respondents]. Since [respondents] had no knowledge of any potential danger to [petitioner], they were not deliberately indifferent to his safety."

The . . . Court of Appeals . . . summarily affirmed without opinion. We granted certiorari because Courts of Appeals had adopted inconsistent tests for "deliberate indifference." Compare, for example, *McGill v. Duckworth* (holding that "deliberate indifference" requires a "subjective standard of recklessness"), with *Young v. Quinlan* (CA3 1992) ("[A] prison official is deliberately indifferent when he knows or should have known of a sufficiently serious danger to an inmate").

II

A

. . . In its prohibition of "cruel and unusual punishments," the Eighth Amendment places restraints on prison officials, who may not, for example, use excessive physical force against prisoners. The Amendment also imposes duties on these officials, who must provide humane conditions of confinement; prison officials must ensure that inmates receive adequate food, clothing, shelter and medical care, and must "take reasonable measures to guarantee the safety of the inmates".

In particular, as the lower courts have uniformly held, and as we have assumed, "prison officials have a duty . . . to protect prisoners from violence at the hands of other prisoners." . . .

It is not, however, every injury suffered by one prisoner at the hands of another that translates into constitutional liability for prison officials responsible for the victim's safety . . . To violate the Cruel and Unusual Punishments Clause, a prison official must have a "sufficiently culpable state of mind." In prison-conditions cases that state of mind is one of "deliberate indifference" to inmate health or safety, a standard the parties agree governs the claim in this case. The parties disagree, however, on the proper test for deliberate indifference, which we must therefore undertake to define.

B

1

Although we have never paused to explain the meaning of the term "deliberate indifference," the case law is instructive. The term first appeared in the United States Reports in *Estelle v. Gamble,* and its use there shows that deliberate indifference describes a state of mind more blameworthy than negligence. In considering the inmate's claim in *Estelle* that inadequate prison medical care violated the Cruel and Unusual Punishments Clause, we distinguished "deliberate indifference to serious medical needs of prisoners," from "negligence in diagnosing or treating a medical condition," holding that only the former violates the Clause. We have since read Estelle for the proposition that Eighth Amendment liability requires "more than ordinary lack of due care for the prisoner's interests or safety." *Whitley v. Albers.*

While *Estelle* establishes that deliberate indifference entails something more than mere negligence, the cases are also clear that it is satisfied by something less than acts or omissions for the very purpose of causing harm or with knowledge that harm will result. That point underlies the ruling that "application of the deliberate indifference standard is inappropriate" in one class of prison cases: when "officials stand accused of using excessive physical force." In such situations, where the decisions of prison officials are typically made "'in haste, under pressure, and frequently without the luxury of a second chance,'" an Eighth Amendment claimant must show more than "indifference," deliberate or otherwise. The claimant must show that officials applied force "maliciously and sadis-

tically for the very purpose of causing harm," or, as the Court also put it, that officials used force with "a knowing willingness that [harm] occur". This standard of purposeful or knowing conduct is not, however, necessary to satisfy the mens rea requirement of deliberate indifference for claims challenging conditions of confinement; "the very high state of mind prescribed by *Whitley* does not apply to prison conditions cases."

With deliberate indifference lying somewhere between the poles of negligence at one end and purpose or knowledge at the other, the Courts of Appeals have routinely equated deliberate indifference with recklessness.[4] It is, indeed, fair to say that acting or failing to act with deliberate indifference to a substantial risk of serious harm to a prisoner is the equivalent of recklessly disregarding that risk.

That does not, however, fully answer the pending question about the level of culpability deliberate indifference entails, for the term recklessness is not self-defining. The civil law generally calls a person reckless who acts or (if the person has a duty to act) fails to act in the face of an unjustifiably high risk of harm that is either known or so obvious that it should be known. The criminal law, however, generally permits a finding of recklessness only when a person disregards a risk of harm of which he is aware. The standards proposed by the parties in this case track the two approaches (though the parties do not put it that way): petitioner asks us to define deliberate indifference as what we have called civil-law recklessness, and respondents urge us to adopt an approach consistent with recklessness in the criminal law.

We reject petitioner's invitation to adopt an objective test for deliberate indifference. We hold instead that a prison official cannot be found liable under the Eighth Amendment for denying an inmate humane conditions of confinement unless the official knows of and disregards an excessive risk to inmate health or safety; the official must both be aware of

---

[4] Between the poles lies "gross negligence" too, but the term is a "nebulous" one, in practice typically meaning little different from recklessness as generally understood in the civil law (which we discuss later in the text). See W. KEETON, D. DOBBS, R. KEETON & D. OWEN, PROSSER AND KEETON ON LAW OF TORTS 34, p. 212 (5th ed. 1984) (hereinafter PROSSER AND KEETON).

facts from which the inference could be drawn that a substantial risk of serious harm exists, and he must also draw the inference. This approach comports best with the text of the Amendment as our cases have interpreted it. The Eighth Amendment does not outlaw cruel and unusual "conditions"; it outlaws cruel and unusual "punishments." An act or omission unaccompanied by knowledge of a significant risk of harm might well be something society wishes to discourage, and if harm does result society might well wish to assure compensation. The common law reflects such concerns when it imposes tort liability on a purely objective basis. But an official's failure to alleviate a significant risk that he should have perceived but did not, while no cause for commendation, cannot under our cases be condemned as the infliction of punishment . . .

To be sure, the reasons for focussing on what a defendant's mental attitude actually was (or is), rather than what it should have been (or should be), differ in the Eighth Amendment context from that of the criminal law. Here, a subjective approach isolates those who inflict punishment; there, it isolates those against whom punishment should be inflicted. But the result is the same: to act recklessly in either setting a person must "consciously disregard" a substantial risk of serious harm. Model Penal Code, supra, § 2.02(2)(c) . . . [S]ubjective recklessness as used in the criminal law is a familiar and workable standard that is consistent with the Cruel and Unusual Punishments Clause as interpreted in our cases, and we adopt it as the test for "deliberate indifference" under the Eighth Amendment.

2

Our decision that Eighth Amendment liability requires consciousness of a risk is thus based on the Constitution and our cases, not merely on a parsing of the phrase "deliberate indifference." And we do not reject petitioner's arguments for a thoroughly objective approach to deliberate indifference without recognizing that on the crucial point (whether a prison official must know of a risk, or whether it suffices that he should know) the term does not speak with certainty. Use of "deliberate," for example, arguably requires nothing more than an act (or omission) of indifference to a serious risk that is voluntary, not accidental. And even if "deliberate" is better read as implying knowledge of a risk, the concept of constructive knowledge is familiar enough that the term "deliberate indifference" would not, of its own force, preclude a scheme that conclusively presumed awareness from a risk's obviousness . . .

We are [not] . . . persuaded by petitioner's argument that, without an objective test for deliberate indifference, prison officials will be free to ignore obvious dangers to inmates. Under the test we adopt today, an Eighth Amendment claimant need not show that a prison official acted or failed to act believing that harm actually would befall an inmate; it is enough that the official acted or failed to act despite his knowledge of a substantial risk of serious harm. We doubt that a subjective approach will present prison officials with any serious motivation "to take refuge in the zone between 'ignorance of obvious risks' and actual knowledge of risks.'" Whether a prison official had the requisite knowledge of a substantial risk is a question of fact subject to demonstration in the usual ways, including inference from circumstantial evidence . . . and a factfinder may conclude that a prison official knew of a substantial risk from the very fact that the risk was obvious . . . For example, if an Eighth Amendment plaintiff presents evidence showing that a substantial risk of inmate attacks was "longstanding, pervasive, well-documented, or expressly noted by prison officials in the past, and the circumstances suggest that the defendant-official being sued had been exposed to information concerning the risk and thus 'must have known' about it, then such evidence could be sufficient to permit a trier of fact to find that the defendant-official had actual knowledge of the risk."[5]

---

[5] While the obviousness of a risk is not conclusive and a prison official may show that the obvious escaped him, he would not escape liability if the evidence showed that he merely refused to verify underlying facts that he strongly suspected to be true, or declined to confirm inferences of risk that he strongly suspected to exist (as when a prison official is aware of a high probability of facts indicating that one prisoner has planned an attack on another but resists opportunities to obtain final confirmation; or when a prison official knows that some diseases are communicable and that a single needle is being used to

Nor may a prison official escape liability for deliberate indifference by showing that, while he was aware of an obvious, substantial risk to inmate safety, he did not know that the complainant was especially likely to be assaulted by the specific prisoner who eventually committed the assault. The question under the Eighth Amendment is whether prison officials, acting with deliberate indifference, exposed a prisoner to a sufficiently substantial "risk of serious damage to his future health," and it does not matter whether the risk comes from a single source or multiple sources, any more than it matters whether a prisoner faces an excessive risk of attack for reasons personal to him or because all prisoners in his situation face such a risk. If, for example, prison officials were aware that inmate "rape was so common and uncontrolled that some potential victims dared not sleep [but] instead . . . would leave their beds and spend the night clinging to the bars nearest the guards' station," it would obviously be irrelevant to liability that the officials could not guess beforehand precisely who would attack whom . . .

Because, however, prison officials who lacked knowledge of a risk cannot be said to have inflicted punishment, it remains open to the officials to prove that they were unaware even of an obvious risk to inmate health or safety. That a trier of fact may infer knowledge from the obvious, in other words, does not mean that it must do so. Prison officials charged with deliberate indifference might show, for example, that they did not know of the underlying facts indicating a sufficiently substantial danger and that they were therefore unaware of a danger, or that they knew the underlying facts but believed (albeit unsoundly) that the risk to which the facts gave rise was insubstantial or nonexistent.

In addition, prison officials who actually knew of a substantial risk to inmate health or safety may be found free from liability if they

responded reasonably to the risk, even if the harm ultimately was not averted. A prison official's duty under the Eighth Amendment is to ensure "reasonable safety," a standard that incorporates due regard for prison officials' "unenviable task of keeping dangerous men in safe custody under humane conditions." Whether one puts it in terms of duty or deliberate indifference, prison officials who act reasonably cannot be found liable under the Cruel and Unusual Punishments Clause . . .

III

A

Against this backdrop, we consider whether the District Court's disposition of petitioner's complaint, summarily affirmed without briefing by the Court of Appeals for the Seventh Circuit, comports with Eighth Amendment principles. We conclude that the appropriate course is to remand.

In granting summary judgment to respondents . . . the District Court may have placed decisive weight on petitioner's failure to notify respondents of a risk of harm. That petitioner "never expressed any concern for his safety to any of [respondents]," was the only evidence the District Court cited for its conclusion that there was no genuine dispute about respondents' assertion that they "had no knowledge of any potential danger to [petitioner]". But . . . the failure to give advance notice is not dispositive. Petitioner may establish respondents' awareness by reliance on any relevant evidence.

The summary judgment record does not so clearly establish respondent's entitlement to judgment as a matter of law on the issue of subjective knowledge that we can simply assume the absence of error below. For example, in papers filed in opposition to respondents' summary-judgment motion, petitioner pointed to respondents' admission that petitioner is a "non-violent" transsexual who, because of petitioner's "youth and feminine appearance" is "likely to experience a great deal of sexual pressure" in prison. And petitioner recounted a statement by one of the respondents, then warden of the penitentiary in Lewisburg, Pennsylvania, who told petitioner that there was "a high probability that [petitioner] could not safely function at USP-Lewisburg," an

administer flu shots to prisoners but refuses to listen to a subordinate who he strongly suspects will attempt to explain the associated risk of transmitting disease). When instructing juries in deliberate indifference cases with such issues of proof, courts should be careful to ensure that the requirement of subjective culpability is not lost. It is not enough merely to find that a reasonable person would have known, or that the defendant should have known, and juries should be instructed accordingly.

incident confirmed in a published District Court opinion . . .

We cannot, moreover, be certain that additional evidence is unavailable to petitioner because in denying petitioner's Rule 56(f) motion for additional discovery the District Court may have acted on a mistaken belief that petitioner's failure to notify was dispositive. Petitioner asserted in papers accompanying the Rule 56(f) motion that the requested documents would show that "each defendant had knowledge that USP-Terre Haute was and is, a violent institution with a history of sexual assault, stabbings, etc., [and that] each defendant showed reckless disregard for my safety by designating me to said institution knowing that I would be sexually assaulted." But in denying the Rule 56(f) motion, the District Court stated that the requested documents were "not shown by plaintiff to be necessary to oppose defendants' motion for summary judgment," a statement consistent with the erroneous view that failure to notify was fatal to petitioner's complaint.

Because the District Court may have mistakenly thought that advance notification was a necessary element of an Eighth Amendment failure-to-protect claim, we think it proper to remand for reconsideration of petitioner's Rule 56(f) motion and, whether additional discovery is permitted or not, for application of the Eighth Amendment principles explained above . . .

[Justice Blackmun's concurring opinion, Justice Stevens' concurring opinion, and Justice Thomas's opinion concurring in the judgment, are omitted.]

NOTES

1. Does *Farmer* help to clarify the meaning, in the constitutional tort context, of the terms "deliberate indifference", "recklessness", and "gross negligence"?

2. *Farmer* is an Eighth Amendment case. What are its implications for substantive due process litigation? Are there differences between the two contexts that would justify broader or narrower liability in the substantive due process context than in the Eighth Amendment context? Should courts apply *Farmer*'s definition of "deliberate indifference" in determining whether a state official has violated the plaintiff's substantive due process rights? How will the Supreme Court likely resolve the split among the circuits, referred to in note 5 before *Farmer*, as to whether gross negligence is sufficient to make out a substantive due process claim? Are the pre-*Farmer* cases that allow recovery on a showing of recklessness still good law after *Farmer*?

The term "deliberate indifference" figures in another constitutional tort issue: governmental liability. In a part of the *Farmer* opinion that is omitted here, the Court indicated that the term should be defined differently when the issue is governmental liability. See Chapter 5.

3. Is there a danger that courts applying the "deliberate indifference" standard will inevitably slide down a slippery slope into negligence? Consider the following comments:

Lower federal courts . . . have managed quite well to apply the deliberate indifference standard so as to avoid the slippery slope. In resolving inmate complaints concerning the adequacy of medical care, lower courts have been able to distinguish between simple malpractice and deliberate indifference. Through the traditional process of case-by-case determination, general principles have emerged. To establish a constitutional claim an inmate must allege and prove that the defendant deliberately failed to respond to the inmate's serious medical needs of which he was aware. Thus, refusing to provide prescribed treatment or denying the inmate's access to medical personnel qualified to evaluate his condition can be considered deliberate indifference. On the other hand, disagreements as to diagnosis and treatment do not rise to the level of a constitutional claim.

To be sure, the line separating simple negligence from deliberate indifference is fine, and the resolution of particular claims will necessarily turn on the facts of each case. Requiring an inmate to wait two and one-half days to be examined by the regularly scheduled physician does not violate constitutional standards when the inmate does not manifest outward signs of physical injury. By contrast, a defendant who delays a few hours in providing care to an inmate he knows is stabbed or shot may be properly labeled as deliberately indifferent.

To say that the distinction between constitutional and common law claims turns on the facts of particular cases does not mean that every case must be resolved by a jury. Courts have demonstrated ample ability to summarily dispose of eighth amendment claims that fail to allege or substantiate deliberate indifference."

Eaton & Wells, *Governmental Inaction as a Constitutional Tort:* DeShaney *and Its Aftermath*, 66 Wash. L. Rev. 107, 164–65 (1991).

Are you convinced that the "deliberate indifference" standard gives rise to no danger of a slide down the slippery slope?

4. While *Daniels* ruled that negligence is insufficient to make out a substantive due process claim, the *Daniels* rule is not universal across the range of constitutional claims. Sometimes, as with the Fourth Amendment's proscription of "unreasonable" searches and seizures, a showing of negligence is enough for the plaintiff to prevail. In contrast to the subjective test required by substantive due process, the Fourth Amendment standard is an objective one. See *Graham v. Conner*, infra. Other constitutional claims may, in effect, require no showing of fault. For example, an official may quite reasonably think that the First Amendment permits him to deny a parade permit and yet be deemed to have violated the Constitution. In such a case, state of mind enters the case only when the defendant asserts immunity. Even if immunity is successfully asserted against the award of damages, it will not bar prospective relief for constitutional violations. See Chapters 7 & 8 infra.

On the other hand, substantive due process and cruel and unusual punishment are not the *sole* constitutional wrongs that depend on the defendant's state of mind. The Equal Protection Clause is violated only if the defendant intended to discriminate. See *Arlington Heights v. Metropolitan Housing Corp.*, 429 U.S. 252 (1977); *Washington v. Davis*, 426 U.S. 229 (1976).

State of mind apparently enters into some first amendment cases as well. According to a fragmented Court in *Waters v. Churchill*, 114 S. Ct. 1878 (1994), a public employer that disciplines an employee on account of the employee's speech commits a First Amendment violation only if the employer's investigation into the circumstances is not reasonable. A governmental employer that mistakenly, but reasonably, concludes that the employee made disruptive, unprotected comments, and disciplines the employee for them, commits no constitutional violation.

B. Abuse of Power

Is it necessary for the plaintiff to show anything beyond recklessness or deliberate indifference in order to make out a good substantive due process claim in constitutional tort? Consider that question in connection with the following case.

Collins v. City of Harker Heights

112 S.Ct. 1061 (1992)

Justice **Stevens** delivered the opinion of the Court.

The question presented is whether § 1 of the Civil Rights Act of 1871, 42 U.S.C. § 1983, provides a remedy for a municipal employee who is fatally injured in the course of his employment because the city customarily failed to train or warn its employees about known hazards in the workplace. Even though the city's conduct may be actionable under state law, we hold that § 1983 does not apply because such conduct does not violate the Due Process Clause.

On October 21, 1988, Larry Michael Collins, an employee in the sanitation department of the city of Harker Heights, Texas, died of asphyxia after entering a manhole to unstop a sewer line. Petitioner, his widow, brought this action alleging that Collins "had a constitutional right to be free from unreasonable risks of harm to his body, mind and emotions and a constitutional right to be protected from the city of Harker Heights' custom and policy of deliberate indifference toward the safety of its employees." Her complaint alleged that the city violated that right by following a custom and policy of not training its employees about the dangers of working in sewer lines and manholes, not providing safety equipment at job sites, and not providing safety warnings. The complaint also alleged that a prior incident had given the city notice of the risks of entering the sewer lines and that the city had systematically and intentionally failed to provide the equipment and training required by a Texas statute. The District Court dismissed the complaint on the ground that a constitutional violation had not been alleged. The Court of Appeals for the Fifth Circuit affirmed on a different theory. It did not reach the question whether the city had violated Collins' constitutional rights because it denied recovery on the ground that there had been no abuse of governmental power," which the Fifth Circuit had found to be a necessary element of a § 1983 action.

The contrary decision in *Ruge v. City of Bellevue* together with our concern about the Court of Appeals' interpretation of the statute, prompted our grant of certiorari.

I

Our cases do not support the Court of Appeals' reading of § 1983 as requiring proof of an abuse of governmental power separate and apart from the proof of a constitutional violation. Although the statute provides the citizen with an effective remedy against those abuses of state power that violate federal law, it does not provide a remedy for abuses that do not violate federal law. More importantly, the statute does not draw any distinction between abusive and nonabusive federal violations.

The Court of Appeals' analysis rests largely on the fact that the city had, through allegedly tortious conduct, harmed one of its employees rather than an ordinary citizen over whom it exercised governmental power. The employment relationship, however, is not of controlling significance. On the one hand, if the city had pursued a policy of equally deliberate indifference to the safety of pedestrians that resulted in a fatal injury to one who inadvertently stepped into an open manhole, the Court of Appeals' holding would not speak to this situation at all, although it would seem that a claim by such a pedestrian should be analyzed in a similar manner as the claim by this petitioner. On the other hand, a logical application of the holding might also bar potentially meritorious claims by employees if, for example, the city had given an employee

a particularly dangerous assignment in retaliation for a political speech, or because of his or her gender. The First Amendment, the Equal Protection and Due Process Clauses of the Fourteenth Amendment, and other provisions of the Federal Constitution afford protection to employees who serve the government as well as to those who are served by them, and § 1983 provides a cause of action for all citizens injured by an abridgement of those protections. Neither the fact that petitioner's decedent was a government employee nor the characterization of the city's deliberate indifference to his safety as something other than an "abuse of governmental power" is a sufficient reason for refusing to entertain petitioner's federal claim under § 1983.

Nevertheless, proper analysis requires us to separate two different issues when a § 1983 claim is asserted against a municipality: (1) whether plaintiff's harm was caused by a constitutional violation, and (2) if so, whether the city is responsible for that violation. Because most of our opinions discussing municipal policy have involved the latter issue, it is appropriate to discuss it before considering the question whether petitioner's complaint has alleged a constitutional violation.

[The Court's discussion of municipal policy is omitted. See Chapter 5 for materials bearing on that issue.]

III

Petitioner's constitutional claim rests entirely on the Due Process Clause of the Fourteenth Amendment. The most familiar office of that Clause is to provide a guarantee of fair procedure in connection with any deprivation of life, liberty, or property by a State. Petitioner, however, does not advance a procedural due process claim in this case. Instead, she relies on the substantive component of the Clause that protects individual liberty against "certain government actions regardless of the fairness of the procedures used to implement them." *Daniels v. Williams.*

As a general matter, the Court has always been reluctant to expand the concept of substantive due process because guideposts for responsible decisionmaking in this unchartered area are scarce and open-ended. The doctrine of judicial self-restraint requires us to exercise the utmost care whenever we are asked to break new ground in this field. It is important, therefore, to focus on the allegations in the complaint to determine how petitioner describes the constitutional right at stake and what the city allegedly did to deprive her husband of that right.

A fair reading of petitioner's complaint does not charge the city with a wilful violation of Collins' rights. Petitioner does not claim that the city or any of its agents deliberately harmed her husband. In fact, she does not even allege that his supervisor instructed him to go into the sewer when the supervisor knew or should have known that there was a significant risk that he would be injured. Instead, she makes the more general allegation that the city deprived him of life and liberty by failing to provide a reasonably safe work environment. Fairly analyzed, her claim advances two theories: that the Federal Constitution imposes a duty on the city to provide its employees with minimal levels of safety and security in the workplace, or that the city's "deliberate indifference" to Collins' safety was arbitrary government action that must "shock the conscience" of federal judges. Cf. *Rochin v. California.*

Neither the text nor the history of the Due Process Clause supports petitioner's claim that the governmental employer's duty to provide its employees with a safe working environment is a substantive component of the Due Process Clause. "The Due Process Clause of the Fourteenth Amendment was intended to prevent government from abusing [its] power, or employing it as an instrument of oppression.'" *DeShaney v. Winnebago County Department of Social Services* (quoting *Davidson v. Cannon*). As we recognized in *DeShaney,*

> "The Clause is phrased as a limitation on the State's power to act, not as a guarantee of certain minimal levels of safety and security. It forbids the State itself to deprive individuals of life, liberty, or property without due process of law,' but its language cannot fairly be extended to impose an affirmative obligation on the State to ensure that those interests do not come to harm through other means. Nor does history support such an expansive reading of the constitutional text." 489 U.S., at 195.

Petitioner's submission that the city violated a federal constitutional obligation to provide its employees with certain minimal levels of safety and security is unprecedented. It is quite different from the constitutional claim advanced by plaintiffs in several of our prior cases who argued that the State owes a duty to take care of those who have already been deprived of their liberty. We have held, for example, that apart from the protection against cruel and unusual punishment provided by the Eighth Amendment, the Due Process Clause of its own force requires that conditions of confinement satisfy certain minimal standards for pretrial detainees, for persons in mental institutions, for convicted felons, and for persons under arrest. The "process" that the Constitution guarantees in connection with any deprivation of liberty thus includes a continuing obligation to satisfy certain minimal custodial standards. Petitioner cannot maintain, however, that the city deprived Collins of his liberty when it made, and he voluntarily accepted, an offer of employment.

We also are not persuaded that the city's alleged failure to train its employees, or to warn them about known risks of harm, was an omission that can properly be characterized as arbitrary, or conscience-shocking, in a constitutional sense. Petitioner's claim is analogous to a fairly typical state law tort claim: The city breached its duty of care to her husband by failing to provide a safe work environment. Because the Due Process Clause "does not purport to supplant traditional tort law in laying down rules of conduct to regulate liability for injuries that attend living together in society," *Daniels v. Williams,* we have previously rejected claims that the Due Process Clause should be interpreted to impose federal duties that are analogous to those traditionally imposed by state tort law. The reasoning in those cases applies with special force to claims asserted against public employers because state law, rather than the Federal Constitution, generally governs the substance of the employment relationship.

Our refusal to characterize the city's alleged omission in this case as arbitrary in a constitutional sense rests on the presumption that the administration of Government programs is based on a rational decisionmaking process that takes account of competing social, political, and economic forces. Decisions concerning the allocation of resources to individual programs, such as sewer maintenance, and to particular aspects of those programs, such as the training and compensation of employees, involve a host of policy choices that must be made by locally elected representatives, rather than by federal judges interpreting the basic charter of Government for the entire country. The Due Process Clause "is not a guarantee against incorrect or ill-advised personnel decisions." Nor does it guarantee municipal employees a workplace that is free of unreasonable risks of harm. . . .

In sum, we conclude that the Due Process Clause does not impose an independent federal obligation upon municipalities to provide certain minimal levels of safety and security in the workplace and the city's alleged failure to train or to warn its sanitation department employees was not arbitrary in a constitutional sense. The judgment of the Court of Appeals is therefore affirmed.

NOTES

1. Is it necessary, under *Collins*, for the plaintiff to show an abuse of power in order to win on a first or fourth amendment claim?

Does *Collins* stand for the principle that, in addition to the state-of-mind requirement imposed in *Daniels*, the availability of constitutional tort for violation of substantive due process should turn on whether the plaintiff can show an abuse of power by government officials? Does that principle explain why some "pretrial detainees, . . . persons in mental institutions, . . . convicted felons, and . . . persons under arrest" have greater substantive due process rights than government employees exposed to hazardous working conditions?

Is *Collins* limited to claims brought by government employees? Suppose someone is injured in an accident on a government owned transit system an can show deliberate indifference to passenger safety in the inspection and maintenance of the trains. Will constitutional tort liability be available after *Collins*? See *Searles v. SEPTA*, 990 F.2d 789 (3rd Cir. 1993) (no).

2. The Supreme Court has recognized a substantive due process right to "personal security from bodily injury", see *Ingraham v. Wright*, 430 U.S. 651, 673–74 (1977). Using this right as their premise, bystanders injured in the course of high speed police chases have tried to recover damages for substantive due process violations. Even when plaintiffs plead recklessness, they often find their claims dismissed on the ground that something more is required for liability. See, e.g., *Fagan v. City of Vineland*, 22 F.3d 1296 (3rd Cir. 1994) (en banc) (*Collins* imposes a "shock the conscience" standard for non-custodial cases, and that standard is not met in the circumstances of the police chase at issue here). But cf. *Medina v. City and County of Denver*, 960 F.2d 1493, 1496–98 (10th Cir. 1992) (holding that, though a reckless police chase can give rise to constitutional tort liability, defendants here were entitled to qualified immunity because the right was not clearly established at the time they acted).

In light of *Collins*, which side of this argument is the Supreme Court likely to take? Is recklessness enough for liability in such a case, or must the plaintiff also establish that it shocks the conscience or is an abuse of power? Can a high speed chase amount to an abuse of power toward an innocent bystander? Does anyone ever have a Fourth Amendment claim arising out of a police chase?

The majority and dissenting opinions in *Fagan*, supra, address much more than the police chase at issue there. They contain lengthy discussions of *Collins*, the "shock the conscience" test, the "recklessness" test, and the lower court cases that choose one or the other as a test of substantive due process liability.

3. Does corporal punishment of public school students violate substantive due process? *Ingraham v. Wright*, supra, was a corporal punishment case. Besides establishing the central premise of the plaintiff's claim here and in other personal injury suits, that "personal security" is an element of Fourteenth Amendment liberty, the Court also held that state tort remedies meet the requirements of *procedural* due process. But the *Ingraham* court did not address the criteria for determining which instances of corporal punishment violate the substantive component of due process.

Courts generally deal with the issue on a case by case basis, considering "such factors as the need for application of force, the relationship between the need and the amount of force that was used, the extent of injury inflicted, and whether force was applied in a good faith effort to maintain or restore discipline or maliciously and sadistically, for the very purpose of causing harm." *Metzger v. Osbeck*, 841 F.2d 518, 520. (3rd Cir. 1988).

For most courts a few whacks with a paddle are constitutionally permissible. See, e.g., *Woodard v. Los Fresnos Ind. Sch. District*, 732 F.2d 1243 (5th Cir. 1984) (three whacks; no constitutional violation); *Hale v. Pringle*, 562 F.Supp. 598 (Ala. 1983) (three to five whacks; no constitutional violation); Rhodus v. Dumiller, 552 F.Supp. 425 (D. La. 1982) (eight whacks, no constitutional violation). How many whacks does it take to make a constitutional violation? Does the answer depend on the offense? Would the plaintiff make out a constitutional claim in these cases if he could show that the school official violated school regulations or other provisions of state law?

When school officials inflict injuries other than with a paddle applied to the buttocks, they are often found liable. See, e.g., *Hall v. Tawney*, 621 F.2d 607 (4th Cir. 1980) (plaintiff injured while struggling to evade punishment, complaint upheld against a motion to dismiss); *Garcia v. Miera*, 817 F.2d 650 (10th Cir. 1987) (similar). In *Metzger*, supra, where a teacher allegedly broke the plaintiff's nose, the court said the student stated a good claim. But see *Brooks v. Richmond School Board*, 569 F. Supp. 1534 (E.D. Va. 1983) (piercing student's arm with a straight pin is not a substantive due process violation).

4. Are threats of physical harm, directed at the plaintiff by police officers or prison guards, enough to make out a constitutional claim? Most courts say no. Compare *Bender v. Brumley*, 1 F.3d 271 (5th Cir. 1993) (threats not sufficient); and *Swoboda v. Dubach*, 992 F.2d 286 (10th Cir. 1993) (even threats to kill plaintiff are not sufficient) with *McDowell v. Jones*, 990 F.2d 433 (8th Cir. 1993) (threats generally not sufficient but terrorizing prisoner with threats of death would be). Cf. *Hopson v. Fredericksen*, 961 F.2d 1374, 1378–79 (8th Cir. 1992) (police officer's threat to knock the plaintiff's teeth out does not come within the eighth circuit's rule that terrorizing the plaintiff with threats of death is actionable).

5. In *Paul v. Davis*, 424 U.S. 693 (1976), the Court refused to allow constitutional tort suits for defamation, because to do so would risk

turning the Fourteenth Amendment into a "font of tort law", replacing state tort law with federal law in a way that threatens the primacy of state law in personal injury litigation. What if the plaintiff offers to show that the defendant officer not only defamed him, but did so maliciously, knowing that the charges were false and intending to destroy the plaintiff's reputation out of malice? Would this be a sufficient abuse of power to justify a constitutional tort suit? In *Siegert v. Gilley*, 500 U.S. 226 (1991) the Court held that such allegations fail to state a constitutional tort claim: "Our decision in *Paul v. Davis* did not turn . . . on the state of mind of the defendant, but on the lack of any constitutional protection for the interest in reputation."

Is this ruling consistent with the principle underlying *Collins*?

Defamation is not simply irrelevant to constitutional tort litigation. But plaintiff's "loss of reputation must be coupled with some other tangible element in order to rise to the level of a protectible liberty interest." *Valmonte v. Bane*, 8 F.3d 992, 999 (2d Cir. 1994), citing *Paul v. Davis*, 424 U.S. at 701. In *Valmonte*, the court characterized this as a "stigma plus" requirement, and held that the "plus" requirement was met. Not only was Valmonte's name put on a list of suspected child abusers, but prospective employers in the child care field were required by law to consult the list and

> if they do wish to hire her, those employers are required by law to explain the reasons why in writing. This is not just the intangible deleterious effect that flows from a bad reputation. Rather, it is a specific deprivation of her opportunity to seek employment caused by a statutory impediment established by the state.

Id. at 1001.

6. In *Baker v. McCollan*, 443 U.S. 137 (1979) the plaintiff had been arrested and incarcerated by mistake. Officials discovered the error three days later and released him. He sued for deprivation of liberty without due process of law, but the Supreme Court rejected his claim. The opinion suggests that three days in jail is not long enough to make out a constitutional violation. It said that "mere detention pursuant to a valid warrant but in the face of repeated protests of innocence will after the lapse of a

certain amount of time deprive the accused of "liberty without due process of law.'" Do you agree that three days incarceration is too short a time to warrant constitutional sanction? Would it be better, especially after *Daniels*, to read the case as one in which the original mistake plus the three day delay amounted to no more than negligence on the part of the jailors? Suppose the jailor knew that he had the wrong man, and kept the plaintiff locked up for three days out of spite? Three hours?

Is it the case that the longer a jailor keeps a prisoner without investigating his claims of innocence, the easier it is to find the jailor guilty of gross negligence or recklessness? In *Simmons v. McIlvain*, 846 F.2d 337 (5th Cir. 1988) the plaintiff was incarcerated for eight months, on account of the failure of the police properly to investigate a lead that would have proven his innocence. Yet he lost his constitutional tort claim, because in the court's view, the conduct of the police "simply [did] not exceed the level of negligence." Id. at 339. Compare *Sanders v. English*, 950 F.2d 1152, 1162 (5th Cir. 1992), where the Fifth Circuit distinguished *Simmons*. Here, "unlike *Simmons*, the plaintiff has come forward with evidence which, if credited by the fact-finder, would establish that the defendant knowingly and willfully ignored substantial exculpatory evidence." The court allowed a constitutional tort suit for illegal detention.

See also *Cannon v. Macon County*, 1 F.3d 1558, 1563 (11th Cir. 1993) (upholding a jury verdict for plaintiff incarcerated for seven days due to mistaken identity, under a deliberate indifference standard); *Moore v. Tartler*, 986 F.2d 682 (3rd Cir. 1993). Here there was a six month delay in plaintiff's release from prison, but the court found no eighth amendment violation since the delay did not result from deliberate indifference to the inmate's liberty interest.

[A]n investigation, however slow and incompetent was conducted by [parole board employees], pursuant to standard parole board operating procedures. Significant was the fact that the parole board did not reject Moore's initial complaint outright, or suspend its search once it was begun. Based on these undisputed facts, the district court concluded that there was no evidence that the defendant's acts constituted deliberate indiffer-

ence and refused to infer deliberate indifference from the fact that it took parole board officials approximately five months to investigate Moore's claim. . . We cannot say that this investigation was so inept or ineffectual that deliberate indifference on the part of the parole board officials may be inferred from the evidence here.

Id. at 687. Is the court's understanding of "deliberate indifference" consistent with *Farmer*?

7. Apart from the cases dealing with personal injury, defamation, and confinement, what kinds of harms inflicted by government actors violate substantive due process and thereby give rise to constitutional tort liability? Officials do things that harm individuals every day, by firing someone from a government job, denying a business license, refusing a zoning variance, and so on. If the action is done on account of race or some other invidious classification, the injured person may make out an equal protection claim. If it is done in retaliation for the exercise of first amendment or some other constitutional right, the plaintiff will be able to make out a claim for violation of that right.

Suppose neither of these avenues is available, but the plaintiff can show that the government acted arbitrarily. Do any of these actions violate substantive due process? The Supreme Court has had little to say on this issue, leaving the development of the law here to the lower courts.

Some courts have held that substantive due process is violated by arbitrary or badly motivated actions taken against the plaintiff. See, e.g., *Parkway Garage, Inc. v. City of Philadelphia*, 5 F.3d 685, 692 (3rd Cir. 1993) ("Substantive due process protects citizens from arbitrary and irrational acts of government. A violation of substantive due process rights is proven: (1) if the government's actions were not rationally related to a legitimate government interest; or (2) if the government's actions in a particular case were in fact motivated by bias, bad faith, or improper motive.") See also *Bateson v. Dempsey*, 857 F.2d 1300 (9th Cir. 1988) (badly motivated refusal to grant a building permit is a substantive due process violation); *Kimbrough v. O'Neil*, 545 F.2d 1059 (7th Cir. 1976) (conversion of property is actionable in a section 1983 suit if it is done intentionally).

On the other hand, some courts are reluctant to recognize substantive due process violations even for badly motivated actions. See, e.g., *McKinney v. Pate*, 20 F.3d 1550, 1553 (11th Cir. 1994) (someone claiming that he was dismissed from a government job "by an arbitrary and capricious non-legislative government action" states only a procedural and not a substantive due process claim); *Kauth v. Hartford Ins. Co.* 852 F.2d 951 (7th Cir. 1988) (state deprivation of property through its attachment laws is not a substantive due process violation even if officials act arbitrarily); *Chesterfield Development Corp. v. City of Chesterfield*, 963 F.2d 1102, 1105 (8th Cir. 1992) (developer's substantive due process rights were not violated by the city enforcing an invalid zoning plan against it; the court said that its "decision would be the same even if the city had knowingly enforced the invalid zoning ordinance in bad faith and had no claim that St. Louis County zoning applied to the property").

C. Alternatives to Substantive Due Process

One of the most frequent fact patterns in constitutional tort litigation is an altercation between the plaintiff and the police that gives rise to a claim of police brutality. Should these cases be resolved according to the substantive due process standards described above, or under some other rubric?

Graham v. Connor

490 U.S. 386 (1989)

Chief Justice **Rehnquist** delivered the opinion of the Court.

This case requires us to decide what constitutional standard governs a free citizen's claim that law enforcement officials used excessive force in the course of making an arrest, investigatory stop, or other "seizure" of his person. We hold that such claims are properly analyzed under the Fourth Amendment's "objective reasonableness" standard, rather than under a substantive due process standard.

In this action under 42 U.S.C. § 1983, petitioner Dethorne Graham seeks to recover damages for injuries allegedly sustained when law enforcement officers used physical force against him during the course of an investigatory stop. Because the case comes to us from a decision of the Court of Appeals affirming the entry of a directed verdict for respondents, we take the evidence hereafter noted in the light most favorable to petitioner. On November 12, 1984, Graham, a diabetic, felt the onset of an insulin reaction. He asked a friend, William Berry, to drive him to a nearby convenience store so he could purchase some orange juice to counteract the reaction. Berry agreed, but when Graham entered the store, he saw a number of people ahead of him in the checkout line. Concerned about the delay, he hurried out of the store and asked Berry to drive him to a friend's house instead.

Respondent Connor, an officer of the Charlotte, North Carolina, Police Department, saw Graham hastily enter and leave the store. The officer became suspicious that something was amiss and followed Berry's car. About one-half mile from the store, he made an investigative stop. Although Berry told Connor that Graham was simply suffering from a "sugar reaction," the officer ordered Berry and Graham to wait while he found out what, if anything, had happened at the convenience store. When Officer Connor returned to his patrol car to call for backup assistance, Graham got out of the car, ran around it twice, and finally sat down on the curb, where he passed out briefly.

In the ensuing confusion, a number of other Charlotte police officers arrived on the scene in response to Officer Connor's request for backup. One of the officers rolled Graham over on the sidewalk and cuffed his hands tightly behind his back, ignoring Berry's pleas to get him some sugar. Another officer said: "I've seen a lot of people with sugar diabetes that never acted like this. Ain't nothing wrong with the M.F. but drunk. Lock the S.B. up." Several officers then lifted Graham up from behind, carried him over to Berry's car, and placed him face down on its hood. Regaining consciousness, Graham asked the officers to check in his wallet for a diabetic decal that he carried. In response, one of the officers told him to "shut up" and shoved his face down against the hood of the car. Four officers grabbed Graham and threw him headfirst into the police car. A friend of Graham's brought some orange juice to the car, but the officers refused to let him have it. Finally, Officer Connor received a report that Graham had done nothing wrong at the convenience store, and the officers drove him home and released him.

At some point during his encounter with the police, Graham sustained a broken foot, cuts on his wrists, a bruised forehead, and an injured shoulder; he also claims to have developed a loud ringing in his right ear that continues to this day. He commenced this action under 42 U.S.C. § 1983 against the individual officers involved in the incident, all of whom are respondents here, alleging that they had used excessive force in making the investigatory stop, in violation of "rights secured to him under the Fourteenth Amendment to the United States Constitution and 42 U.S.C. § 1983." The case was tried before a jury. At the close of petitioner's evidence, respondents moved for a directed verdict. In ruling on that motion, the District Court considered the following four factors, which it identified as "the factors to be considered in determining when the excessive use of force gives rise to a cause of action under § 1983": (1) the need for the application of force; (2) the relationship between that need and the amount of force that was used; (3) the extent of the injury inflicted; and (4) "whether the force was applied in a good faith effort to maintain and restore discipline or maliciously and sadistically for the very purpose of causing harm." Finding that the amount of force used by the officers was "appropriate under the circumstances," that "there was no discernable injury inflicted," and that the force used "was not applied maliciously or sadistically for the very purpose of causing harm," but in "a good faith effort to maintain or restore order in the face of a potentially explosive situation," the District Court granted respondents' motion for a directed verdict.

A divided panel of the Court of Appeals for the Fourth Circuit affirmed. The majority ruled first that the District Court had applied the correct legal standard in assessing petitioner's excessive force claim. Without attempting to identify the specific constitutional provision under which that claim arose, the majority endorsed the four-factor test applied by the District Court as generally applicable to all claims of "constitutionally excessive force" brought against governmental officials. The majority rejected petitioner's argument, based on Circuit precedent, that it was error to require him to prove that the allegedly excessive force used against him was applied "maliciously and sadistically for the very purpose of causing harm." Finally, the majority held that a reasonable jury applying the four-part test it had just endorsed to petitioner's evidence "could not find that the force applied was constitutionally excessive." The dissenting judge argued that this Court's decisions in *Terry v. Ohio* and *Tennessee v. Garner* required that excessive force claims arising out of investigatory stops be analyzed under the Fourth Amendment's "objective reasonableness" standard. We granted certiorari and now reverse.

Fifteen years ago, in *Johnson v. Glick . . .* the Second Circuit addressed a § 1983 damages claim filed by a pretrial detainee who claimed that a guard had assaulted him without justification. In evaluating the detainee's claim, Judge Friendly applied neither the Fourth Amendment nor the Eighth, the two most textually obvious sources of constitutional protection against physically abusive governmental conduct. Instead, he looked to "substantive due process," holding that "quite apart from any 'specific' of the Bill of Rights, application of undue force by law enforcement officers deprives a suspect of liberty without due process of law." As support for this proposition, he relied upon our decision in *Rochin v. California* which used the Due Process Clause to void a state criminal conviction based on evidence obtained by pumping the defendant's stomach. If a police officer's use of force which "shocks the conscience" could justify setting aside a criminal conviction, Judge Friendly reasoned, a correctional officer's use of similarly excessive force must give rise to a due process violation actionable under § 1983. Judge Friendly went on to set forth four factors to guide courts in determining "whether the constitutional line has been crossed" by a particular use of force—the same four factors relied upon by the courts below in this case.

In the years following *Johnson v. Glick*, the vast majority of lower federal courts have applied its four-part "substantive due process" test indiscriminately to all excessive force claims lodged against law enforcement and prison officials under § 1983, without considering whether the particular application of force might implicate a more specific constitutional right governed by a different standard. Indeed, many courts have seemed to assume, as did the courts below in this case, that there is a generic "right" to be free from excessive force, grounded not in any particular constitutional provision but rather in "basic principles of § 1983 jurisprudence."

We reject this notion that all excessive force claims brought under § 1983 are governed by a single generic standard. As we have said many times, § 1983 "is not itself a source of substantive rights," but merely provides "a method for vindicating federal rights elsewhere conferred." In addressing an excessive force claim brought under § 1983, analysis begins by identifying the specific constitutional right allegedly infringed by the challenged application of force. In most instances, that will be either the Fourth Amendment's prohibition against unreasonable seizures of the person, or the Eighth Amendment's ban on cruel and unusual punishments, which are the two primary sources of constitutional protection against physically abusive governmental conduct. The validity of the claim must then be judged by reference to the specific constitutional standard which governs that right, rather than to some generalized "excessive force" standard. See *Tennessee v. Garner*, supra, (claim of excessive force to effect arrest analyzed under a Fourth Amendment standard); *Whitley v. Albers* (claim of excessive force to subdue convicted prisoner analyzed under an Eighth Amendment standard).

Where, as here, the excessive force claim arises in the context of an arrest or investigatory stop of a free citizen, it is most properly characterized as one invoking the protections of the Fourth Amendment, which guarantees citizens the right "to be secure in their persons . . . against unreasonable . . . seizures" of the person. This much is clear from our decision in *Tennessee v. Garner*, supra. In *Garner*, we addressed a claim that the use of deadly force to apprehend a fleeing suspect who did not appear to be armed or otherwise dangerous violated the suspect's constitutional rights, notwithstanding the existence of

probable cause to arrest. Though the complaint alleged violations of both the Fourth Amendment and the Due Process Clause, we analyzed the constitutionality of the challenged application of force solely by reference to the Fourth Amendment's prohibition against unreasonable seizures of the person, holding that the "reasonableness" of a particular seizure depends not only on when it is made, but also on how it is carried out. Today we make explicit what was implicit in *Garner's* analysis, and hold that all claims that law enforcement officers have used excessive force—deadly or not—in the course of an arrest, investigatory stop, or other "seizure" of a free citizen should be analyzed under the Fourth Amendment and its "reasonableness" standard, rather than under a "substantive due process" approach. Because the Fourth Amendment provides an explicit textual source of constitutional protection against this sort of physically intrusive governmental conduct, that Amendment, not the more generalized notion of "substantive due process," must be the guide for analyzing these claims.

Determining whether the force used to effect a particular seizure is "reasonable" under the Fourth Amendment requires a careful balancing of "'the nature and quality of the intrusion on the individual's Fourth Amendment interests'" against the countervailing governmental interests at stake. Our Fourth Amendment jurisprudence has long recognized that the right to make an arrest or investigatory stop necessarily carries with it the right to use some degree of physical coercion or threat thereof to effect it. Because "the test of reasonableness under the Fourth Amendment is not capable of precise definition or mechanical application," however, its proper application requires careful attention to the facts and circumstances of each particular case, including the severity of the crime at issue, whether the suspect poses an immediate threat to the safety of the officers or others, and whether he is actively resisting arrest or attempting to evade arrest by flight . . .

The "reasonableness" of a particular use of force must be judged from the perspective of a reasonable officer on the scene, rather than with the 20/20 vision of hindsight. The Fourth Amendment is not violated by an arrest based on probable cause, even though the wrong person is arrested, nor by the mistaken execution of a valid search warrant on the wrong premises. With respect to a claim of excessive force, the same standard of reasonableness at the moment applies: "Not every push or shove, even if it may later seem unnecessary in the peace of a judge's chambers," *Johnson v. Glick*, violates the Fourth Amendment. The calculus of reasonableness must embody allowance for the fact that police officers are often forced to make split-second judgments—in circumstances that are tense, uncertain, and rapidly evolving—about the amount of force that is necessary in a particular situation.

As in other Fourth Amendment contexts, however, the "reasonableness" inquiry in an excessive force case is an objective one: the question is whether the officers' actions are "objectively reasonable" in light of the facts and circumstances confronting them, without regard to their underlying intent or motivation. . . An officer's evil intentions will not make a Fourth Amendment violation out of an objectively reasonable use of force; nor will an officer's good intentions make an objectively unreasonable use of force constitutional.

Because petitioner's excessive force claim is one arising under the Fourth Amendment, the Court of Appeals erred in analyzing it under the four-part *Johnson v. Glick* test. That test, which requires consideration of whether the individual officers acted in "good faith" or "maliciously and sadistically for the very purpose of causing harm," is incompatible with a proper Fourth Amendment analysis. We do not agree with the Court of Appeals' suggestion, that the "malicious and sadistic" inquiry is merely another way of describing conduct that is objectively unreasonable under the circumstances. Whatever the empirical correlations between "malicious and sadistic" behavior and objective unreasonableness may be, the fact remains that the "malicious and sadistic" factor puts in issue the subjective motivations of the individual officers, which our prior cases make clear has no bearing on whether a particular seizure is "unreasonable" under the Fourth Amendment. Nor do we agree with the Court of Appeals' conclusion, that because the subjective motivations of the individual officers are of central importance in deciding whether force used against a convicted prisoner violates the Eighth Amend-

ment, it cannot be reversible error to inquire into them in deciding whether force used against a suspect or arrestee violates the Fourth Amendment. Differing standards under the Fourth and Eighth Amendments are hardly surprising: the terms "cruel" and "punishment" clearly suggest some inquiry into subjective state of mind, whereas the term "unreasonable" does not. Moreover, the less protective Eighth Amendment standard applies "only after the State has complied with the constitutional guarantees traditionally associated with criminal prosecutions." The Fourth Amendment inquiry is one of "objective reasonableness" under the circumstances, and subjective concepts like "malice" and "sadism" have no proper place in that inquiry.[12]

Because the Court of Appeals reviewed the District Court's ruling on the motion for directed verdict under an erroneous view of the governing substantive law, its judgment must be vacated and the case remanded to that court for reconsideration of that issue under the proper Fourth Amendment standard.

It is so ordered.

Justice **Blackmun**, with whom Justice **Brennan** and Justice **Marshall** join, concurring in part and concurring in the judgment.

I join the Court's opinion insofar as it rules that the Fourth Amendment is the primary tool for analyzing claims of excessive force in the prearrest context, and I concur in the judgment remanding the case to the Court of Appeals for reconsideration of the evidence under a reasonableness standard. In light of respondents' concession, however, that the pleadings in this case properly may be con-

---

[12]Of course, in assessing the credibility of an officer's account of the circumstances that prompted the use of force, a factfinder may consider, along with other factors, evidence that the officer may have harbored ill-will toward the citizen. Similarly, the officer's objective "good faith"—that is, whether he could reasonably have believed that the force used did not violate the Fourth Amendment—may be relevant to the availability of the qualified immunity defense to monetary liability under § 1983. See *Anderson v. Creighton*. Since no claim of qualified immunity has been raised in this case, however, we express no view on its proper application in excessive force cases that arise under the Fourth Amendment.

strued as raising a Fourth Amendment claim, I see no reason for the Court to find it necessary further to reach out to decide that prearrest excessive force claims are to be analyzed under the Fourth Amendment rather than under a substantive due process standard. I also see no basis for the Court's suggestion that our decision in *Tennessee v. Garner* implicitly so held. Nowhere in *Garner* is a substantive due process standard for evaluating the use of excessive force in a particular case discussed; there is no suggestion that such a standard was offered as an alternative and rejected.

In this case, petitioner apparently decided that it was in his best interest to disavow the continued applicability of substantive due process analysis as an alternative basis for recovery in prearrest excessive force cases. His choice was certainly wise as a matter of litigation strategy in his own case, but does not (indeed, cannot be expected to) serve other potential plaintiffs equally well. It is for that reason that the Court would have done better to leave that question for another day. I expect that the use of force that is not demonstrably unreasonable under the Fourth Amendment only rarely will raise substantive due process concerns. But until I am faced with a case in which that question is squarely raised, and its merits are subjected to adversary presentation, I do not join in foreclosing the use of substantive due process analysis in prearrest cases.

NOTES

1. *Graham* was foreshadowed by *Tennessee v. Garner*, 471 U.S. 1 (1984), where the Court spurned substantive due process in favor of a Fourth Amendment "objective reasonableness" standard for evaluating police use of deadly force against suspects who flee or resist arrest. "Where the officer has probable cause to believe that the suspect poses a threat of serious physical harm, either to the officer or to others, it is not constitutionally unreasonable to prevent escape by using deadly force." Id. at 11. See, e.g., *Krueger v. Fuhr*, 991 F.2d 435, 439 (8th Cir. 1993) (where "a man fitting Krueger's description was suspected of committing an armed assault . . . probably had a

knife and was inebriated", it was objectively reasonable to use deadly force against him even if he did not actually have a weapon and even though the officer shot him in the back).

2. *Graham*'s theme of supplanting a substantive due process standard by Fourth Amendment analysis is echoed in *Albright v. Oliver*, 114 S.Ct. 807 (1994). The plaintiff had earlier won dismissal of a state criminal charge against him on the ground that the charge did not state an offense under state law. In his section 1983 suit, he sought to recover for under a substantive due process theory that he had a "right to be free of prosecution without probable cause." 114 S.Ct. at 112. A fragmented Court held that "it is the Fourth Amendment, and not substantive due process, under which . . . Albright's claims must be judged." 114 S.Ct. at 811 (4 justices), id. at 817 (2 justices).

Before *Albright*, some lower courts had recognized a constitutional tort suit roughly paralleling the common law tort of malicious prosecution. See 114 S. Ct. at 811 n.4. Though there is no majority opinion, *Albright* evidently does away with this theory of recovery.

3. *Graham* removes from the domain of substantive due process a significant number of cases, for encounters with the police produce more complaints of governmental abuse of power than any other aspect of the relationship between citizens and the government. Under *Graham*, will plaintiffs be able to recover from policemen who act maliciously, but whose conduct is objectively reasonable? If not, isn't the holding in *Graham* at odds with the theory of constitutional tort underlying *Daniels* and *Collins*, that a constitutional cause of action should be available for abuses of government power? Is malicious or otherwise improperly motivated police conduct any less reprehensible just because some other policeman could quite reasonably have done the same thing?

On the other hand, how often is objectively reasonable conduct likely to be badly motivated? If the answer is "not very often", then *Graham* can be defended as a means of simplifying trials and providing helpful guidance to police departments and the lower courts, even if it does not cover every single case that deserves a constitutional remedy. That cost may be worth the benefit of having a predictable and dependable rule to apply, rather than engaging into a consideration of all the circumstances in each case. On the costs and benefits of rule-based decision-making in general, see F. Schauer, *Playing by the Rules: An Examination of Rule-Based Decision-Making in Law and in Life* (1991).

4. The Court suggests that plaintiffs are better off under *Graham* than under the eighth amendment standard of *Whitley v. Albers*, which emphasizes state of mind. Do you agree?

Granted that a bad motive will not establish a constitutional violation under *Graham*, is the plaintiff's attorney actually precluded from introducing evidence of bad motive? See footnote 12 in the *Graham* opinion.

5. Is *Graham* consistent in principle with the cases on substantive due process in connection with pretrial detainees, corporal punishment, land use decisions, and the like? Why should one kind of official conduct be singled out for treatment under an objective standard, while other officials are liable for badly motivated conduct?

(a) Because the Court is wary of substantive due process in general? Consider Justice Souter's comments in *Albright v. Oliver*, supra, 114 S. Ct. at 820: "We are . . . required by '[t]he doctrine of judicial self-restraint . . . to exercise the utmost care whenever we are asked to break new ground in [the] field of substantive due process [citing *Collins*]. Just as the concept of due process does not protect against insubstantial impositions on liberty, neither should the 'rational continuum' be reduced to the mere duplication of protections adequately addressed by other constitutional provisions. . . [W]e are not free to infer that it was meant to be applied without thereby adding a substantial increment to protection otherwise available. The importance of recognizing [this] . . . limitation is underscored by pragmatic concerns about subjecting government actors to two (potentially inconsistent) standards for the same conduct and needlessly imposing on trial courts the unenviable burden of reconciling well-established jurisprudence under the Fourth and Eighth Amendments with the ill-defined contours of some novel due process right." (Souter, J., concurring in the judgment).

See also Fallon, *Some Confusions About Due Process, Judicial Review, and Constitutional Remedies*, 93 Colum. L. Rev. 309, 349

n.226 (1993) (suggesting that the Court's discomfort with substantive due process influenced its decision in *Graham*).

(b) Because it thinks the police will win more often under the Fourth Amendment standard? If that is the reason, then we will not know whether the regime initiated by *Graham* favors the police or plaintiffs until we know more about the content of the Fourth Amendment "unreasonableness" standard, which will be elaborated in future cases.

(c) Because an objective standard will avoid or at least minimize inquiries into state of mind and thereby simplify trials and discovery? Cf. Chapters 7 & 8, discussing the contemporary law of official immunity, a body of doctrine strongly influenced by this concern.

Judge Richard Posner wrote the decision affirmed in *Graham*. Posner disapproves generally of legal rules that require state of mind inquiries. Noting that we cannot observe mental states, he maintains that they "are entities of distinctly dubious ontology" (that is, it is not clear whether they exist). See R. Posner, *The Problems of Jurisprudence* 167 (1991). He suggests "that we often use the word 'mind' . . . not to name a thing, not to make an ontological assertion, but to cover our ignorance of certain causal relationships." Id. at 166. "[A]s human beings learn more about the world, the number of posited mental entities or states diminishes." Id. at 167.

Do you think that malice, caprice, ill-will, arrogance, and the like are "entities of distinctly dubious ontology", and are therefore best avoided in formulating legal doctrine?

6. One consequence of the proliferation of standards governing police use of force is that it becomes necessary to determine the plaintiff's status at the time force was used. *Graham* holds that Fourth Amendment law applies during the arrest. At some point, the arrestee becomes a pretrial detainee and (apparently) substantive due process governs his rights against his jailors. See, e.g., *Valencia v. Wiggins*, 981 F.2d 1440 (5th Cir. 1993). Once convicted, he is covered by the Eighth Amendment. When does an arrestee become a pretrial detainee? For diverse views, see the majority and dissenting opinions in *Brothers v. Klevenhagen*, 28 F.3d 452 (5th Cir. 1994).

7. Recall that persons injured due to high speed police chases have generally had little success winning on a substantive due process theory. What if they frame their suits as fourth amendment claims instead?

The starting point for analysis of this problem is *Brower v. Inyo County*, 489 U.S. 593 (1989), where the Court held that someone injured when he ran into a police roadblock may have a Fourth Amendment claim, because the fourth amendment applies when an officer intentionally applies force to the plaintiff, and "it is enough for a seizure that a person be stopped by the very instrumentality set in motion or put in place in order to achieve the result. It was enough here, therefore, that, according to the allegations of the complaint, Brower was meant to be stopped by the physical obstacle of the roadblock—and that he was so stopped." Id. at 599. The Court remanded for consideration of whether the seizure was "unreasonable" in the circumstances.

Lower courts have addressed variants on this theme. See, e.g., Horta v. Sullivan, 4 F.3d 2, 10 (1st Cir. 1993). The court said

> Officer Menino's pursuit of the motorcycle on which Horta was riding, without more, was not a Fourth Amendment seizure . . . If the officer speeds off, pursued by the officer, and a crash ensues, this does not necessarily constitute a seizure, either. Hence, if during the chase here Demoranville's motorcycle had accidentally collided with a tree on Mason Road there would plainly have been no seizure, as Menino would not have terminated Horta's freedom of movement through means intentionally applied, (i.e., Menino did not intentionally cause the motorcycle to strike the tree). . . By the same token, it is not sufficient that Menino pursued and the pursuit resulted in a collision with

another police vehicle . . . to establish that Menino seized her, appellant must show that the collision with Officer Sullivan's cruiser was the means *intended by Menino* to end the pursuit.

The court relied on Brower, 489 U.S. at 596–97 (1989)

> [A] Fourth Amendment seizure does not occur whenever there is a governmentally caused termination of an individual's freedom of movement (the innocent passerby), nor even whenever there is a governmentally caused and governmentally *desired* termination of an individual's freedom of movement (the fleeing felon), but only when there is a governmental termination of freedom of movement *through means intentionally applied.*" (emphasis in original).

Cf. *Donovan v. City of Milwaukee*, 17 F.3d 944, 950–51 (7th Cir. 1994) (intentional striking of plaintiff's vehicle may be Fourth Amendment violation).

Does it seem fair to you that persons injured while fleeing the police have stronger constitutional arguments than do motorists and pedestrians injured by the police while minding their own business?

8. If there is no "seizure" within the meaning of the fourth amendment, lower courts have generally held that a substantive due process claim remains available after *Graham* to someone injured by the police or other officials. See, e.g., *Wilson v. Northcutt*, 987 F.2d 719, 722 (11th Cir. 1993) (plaintiff locked herself in a bedroom and shot herself when deputy sheriffs tried to serve an arrest warrant; applying the standards of *Johnson v. Glick*, a case that is discussed in *Graham*, the court found that in the circumstances of *Wilson* the police were not even grossly negligent).

CHAPTER FOUR

"Secured by the Constitution and Laws": Affirmative Constitutional Duties and Rights Secured by Federal "Laws"

A significant portion of the preceding chapter addressed the question of whether government inflicted injury can be characterized as a denial of substantive or procedural due process. The defendants in those cases actively injured the plaintiffs, and the issue was whether their conduct amounted to a deprivation of life, liberty or property without due process of law. The first part this chapter considers a variation of this issue. The cases below involve defendants who allow the plaintiff to be injured or fail to prevent some third party from injuring the plaintiff, as when a police officer passively observes a citizen being beaten or robbed. A question common to these cases is whether the Constitution imposes any affirmative obligations on government officials to protect persons from harm.

Although the vast majority of section 1983 claims are based on alleged violations of constitutional rights, the statute also provides a remedy for "the deprivation of any rights . . . secured by [federal] laws." What are federal "laws" in this context? Can the violation of federal statutes give rise to a claim under section 1983? Part II of this chapter addresses special issues presented by non-constitutional based claims of violations of federal "laws."

I. Affirmative Duties

The common law tort system has long struggled with the scope of affirmative duties for both private and public actors. The first principle of the common law of affirmative duties is that government, like private individuals, owes no general tort obligation to help anyone. See, e.g., *Riss v. City of New York*, 22 N.Y.2d 579, 240 N.E.2d 860, 293 N.Y.S.2d 897 (1968). The rationale for the no-duty rule differs sharply depending on whether the defendant is public or private. The no-duty rule as applied to private individuals rests primarily on libertarian values. A state-imposed duty to act would seriously impinge upon individual freedom and autonomy. See Richard Epstein, *A Theory of Strict Liability*, 2 J. Legal Stud. 151, 199–200 (1973). When the defendant is the government or its officer, individual autonomy is not an issue. The no-duty rule as applied to governments rests primarily on the need to preserve legislative and executive discretion in the allocation of limited public resources. For a more extended discussion of the tort policies implicated in the governmental affirmative duty context, see Wells and Eaton, *Affirmative Duty and Constitutional Tort*, 16 U. Mich. J.L. Ref. 1, 3–11 (1982).

What additional considerations are involved when the scope of affirmative duties of government is raised in the context of constitutional tort? What are the practical and theoretical consequences of framing the affirmative duty issue in terms of constitutional (in contrast to common law) tort? To what extent can a state legislature modify a common law rule imposing an affirmative duty on a government or its officials? To what extent can a state legislature modify an affirmative duty recognized under constitutional law?

A. The Supreme Court's Framework

DeShaney v. Winnebago County Department of Social Services

489 U.S. 189 (1989)

Chief Justice **Rehnquist** delivered the opinion of the Court.

Petitioner is a boy who was beaten and permanently injured by his father, with whom he lived. Respondents are social workers and other local officials who received complaints that petitioner was being abused by his father and had reason to believe that this was the case, but nonetheless did not act to remove petitioner from his father's custody. Petitioner sued respondents claiming that their failure to act deprived him of his liberty in violation of the Due Process Clause of the Fourteenth Amendment to the United States Constitution. We hold that it did not.

I

The facts of this case are undeniably tragic. Petitioner Joshua DeShaney was born in 1979. In 1980, a Wyoming court granted his parents a divorce and awarded custody of Joshua to his father, Randy DeShaney. The father shortly thereafter moved to Neenah, a city located in Winnebago County, Wisconsin, taking the infant Joshua with him. There he entered into a second marriage, which also ended in divorce.

The Winnebago County authorities first learned that Joshua DeShaney might be a victim of child abuse in January 1982, when his father's second wife complained to the police, at the time of their divorce, that he had previously "hit the boy causing marks and [was] a prime case for child abuse." The Winnebago County Department of Social Services (DSS) interviewed the father, but he denied the accusations, and DSS did not pursue them further. In January 1983, Joshua was admitted to a local hospital with multiple bruises and abrasions. The examining physician suspected child abuse and notified DSS, which immediately obtained an order from a Wisconsin juvenile court placing Joshua in the temporary custody of the hospital. Three days later, the county convened an ad hoc "Child Protection Team"—consisting of a pediatrician, a psychologist, a police detective, the county's lawyer, several DSS caseworkers, and various hospital personnel—to consider Joshua's situation. At this meeting, the Team decided that there was insufficient evidence of child abuse to retain Joshua in the custody of the court. The Team did, however, decide to recommend several measures to protect Joshua, including enrolling him in a preschool program, providing his father with certain counselling services, and encouraging his father's girlfriend to move out of the home. Randy DeShaney entered into a voluntary agreement with DSS in which he promised to cooperate with them in accomplishing these goals.

Based on the recommendation of the Child Protection Team, the juvenile court dismissed the child protection case and returned Joshua to the custody of his father. A month later, emergency room personnel called the DSS caseworker handling Joshua's case to report that he had once again been treated for suspicious injuries. The caseworker concluded that there was no basis for action. For the next six months, the caseworker made monthly visits to the DeShaney home, during which she observed a number of suspicious injuries on Joshua's head; she also noticed that he had not been enrolled in school, and that the girlfriend had not moved out. The caseworker dutifully recorded these incidents in her files, along with her continuing suspicions that someone in the DeShaney household was physically abusing Joshua, but she did nothing more. In November 1983, the emergency room notified DSS that Joshua had been treated once again for injuries that they believed to be caused by child abuse. On the caseworker's next two visits to the DeShaney home, she was told that Joshua was too ill to see her. Still DSS took no action.

In March 1984, Randy DeShaney beat 4-year-old Joshua so severely that he fell into a life-threatening coma. Emergency brain surgery revealed a series of hemorrhages caused by traumatic injuries to the head inflicted over a long period of time. Joshua did not die, but he suffered brain damage so severe that he is expected to spend the rest of his life confined to an institution for the profoundly retarded.

Randy DeShaney was subsequently tried and convicted of child abuse.

Joshua and his mother brought this action under 42 U.S.C. § 1983 in the United States District Court for the Eastern District of Wisconsin against respondents Winnebago County, DSS, and various individual employees of DSS. The complaint alleged that respondents had deprived Joshua of his liberty without due process of law, in violation of his rights under the Fourteenth Amendment, by failing to intervene to protect him against a risk of violence at his father's hands of which they knew or should have known. The District Court granted summary judgment for respondents.

The Court of Appeals for the Seventh Circuit affirmed. . . .

Because of the inconsistent approaches taken by the lower courts in determining when, if ever, the failure of a state or local governmental entity or its agents to provide an individual with adequate protective services constitutes a violation of the individual's due process rights, see *Archie v. Racine* (collecting cases) and the importance of the issue to the administration of state and local governments, we granted certiorari. We now affirm.

II

The Due Process Clause of the Fourteenth Amendment provides that "no State shall . . . deprive any person of life, liberty, or property, without due process of law." Petitioners contend that the State deprived Joshua of his liberty interest in "freedom from . . . unjustified intrusions on personal security," by failing to provide him with adequate protection against his father's violence. The claim is one invoking the substantive rather than the procedural component of the Due Process Clause; petitioners do not claim that the State denied Joshua protection without according him appropriate procedural safeguards but that it was categorically obligated to protect him in these circumstances.[2]

But nothing in the language of the Due Process Clause itself requires the State to protect the life, liberty, and property of its citizens against invasion by private actors. The Clause is phrased as a limitation on the State's power to act, not as a guarantee of certain minimal levels of safety and security. It forbids the State itself to deprive individuals of life, liberty, or property without "due process of law," but its language cannot fairly be extended to impose an affirmative obligation on the State to ensure that those interests do not come to harm through other means. Nor does history support such an expansive reading of the constitutional text. Like its counterpart in the Fifth Amendment, the Due Process Clause of the Fourteenth Amendment was intended to prevent government "from abusing [its] power, or employing it as an instrument of oppression." Its purpose was to protect the people from the State, not to ensure that the State protected them from each other. The Framers were content to leave the extent of governmental obligation in the latter area to the democratic political processes.

Consistent with these principles, our cases have recognized that the Due Process Clauses generally confer no affirmative right to governmental aid, even where such aid may be necessary to secure life, liberty, or property interests of which the government itself may not deprive the individual. See, e. g., *Harris v. McRae* (no obligation to fund abortions or other medical services) (discussing Due Process Clause of Fifth Amendment); *Lindsey v. Normet* (no obligation to provide adequate housing) (discussing Due Process Clause of Fourteenth Amendment); see also *Youngberg v. Romeo*, supra, ("As a general matter, a State is under no constitutional duty to provide substantive services for those within its border"). As we said in *Harris v. McRae*: "Although the liberty protected by the Due Process Clause affords protection against unwarranted government interference . . . , it does not confer an entitlement to such [governmental aid] as may be necessary to realize all the

---

[2] Petitioners also argue that the Wisconsin child protection statutes gave Joshua an "entitlement" to receive protective services in accordance with the terms of the statute, an entitlement which would enjoy due process protection against state deprivation under our decision in Board of Regents of State Colleges v. Roth. Brief for Petitioners 24–29. But this argument is made for the first time in petitioners' brief to this Court: it was not pleaded in the complaint, argued to the Court of Appeals as a ground for reversing the District Court, or raised in the petition for certiorari. We therefore decline to consider it here. . . .

advantages of that freedom." 448 U.S., at 317–318 (emphasis added). If the Due Process Clause does not require the State to provide its citizens with particular protective services, it follows that the State cannot be held liable under the Clause for injuries that could have been averted had it chosen to provide them.[3] As a general matter, then, we conclude that a State's failure to protect an individual against private violence simply does not constitute a violation of the Due Process Clause. Petitioners contend, however, that even if the Due Process Clause imposes no affirmative obligation on the State to provide the general public with adequate protective services, such a duty may arise out of certain "special relationships" created or assumed by the State with respect to particular individuals. Petitioners argue that such a "special relationship" existed here because the State knew that Joshua faced a special danger of abuse at his father's hands, and specifically proclaimed, by word and by deed, its intention to protect him against that danger. Having actually undertaken to protect Joshua from this danger—which petitioners concede the State played no part in creating—the State acquired an affirmative "duty," enforceable through the Due Process Clause, to do so in a reasonably competent fashion. Its failure to discharge that duty, so the argument goes, was an abuse of governmental power that so "shocks the conscience," as to constitute a substantive due process violation.

We reject this argument. It is true that in certain limited circumstances the Constitution imposes upon the State affirmative duties of care and protection with respect to particular individuals. In *Estelle v. Gamble* we recognized that the Eighth Amendment's prohibition against cruel and unusual punishment, made applicable to the States through the Fourteenth Amendment's Due Process Clause, requires the State to provide adequate medical care to incarcerated prisoners. We reasoned that because the prisoner is unable "by reason of the deprivation of his liberty [to] care for himself," it is only "just" that the State be required to care for him.

In *Youngberg v. Romeo* we extended this analysis beyond the Eighth Amendment setting, holding that the substantive component of the Fourteenth Amendment's Due Process Clause requires the State to provide involuntarily committed mental patients with such services as are necessary to ensure their "reasonable safety" from themselves and others (dicta indicating that the State is also obligated to provide such individuals with "adequate food, shelter, clothing, and medical care"). As we explained: "If it is cruel and unusual punishment to hold convicted criminals in unsafe conditions, it must be unconstitutional [under the Due Process Clause] to confine the involuntarily committed—who may not be punished at all—in unsafe conditions." See also *Revere v. Massachusetts General Hospital* (holding that the Due Process Clause requires the responsible government or governmental agency to provide medical care to suspects in police custody who have been injured while being apprehended by the police).

But these cases afford petitioners no help. Taken together, they stand only for the proposition that when the State takes a person into its custody and holds him there against his will, the Constitution imposes upon it a corresponding duty to assume some responsibility for his safety and general well-being. The rationale for this principle is simple enough: when the State by the affirmative exercise of its power so restrains an individual's liberty that it renders him unable to care for himself, and at the same time fails to provide for his basic human needs—e. g., food, clothing, shelter, medical care, and reasonable safety— it transgresses the substantive limits on state action set by the Eighth Amendment and the Due Process Clause. The affirmative duty to protect arises not from the State's knowledge of the individual's predicament or from its expressions of intent to help him, but from the limitation which it has imposed on his freedom to act on his own behalf. In the substantive due process analysis, it is the State's affirmative act of restraining the individual's freedom to act on his own behalf—through incarceration, institutionalization, or other similar restraint of personal liberty—which is the "deprivation of liberty" triggering the protections of the Due Process Clause, not its

---

[3] The State may not, of course, selectively deny its protective services to certain disfavored minorities without violating the Equal Protection Clause. See Yick Wo v. Hopkins. But no such argument has been made here.

failure to act to protect his liberty interests against harms inflicted by other means.

The *Estelle-Youngberg* analysis simply has no applicability in the present case. Petitioners concede that the harms Joshua suffered did not occur while he was in the State's custody, but while he was in the custody of his natural father, who was in no sense a state actor.[9] While the State may have been aware of the dangers that Joshua faced in the free world, it played no part in their creation, nor did it do anything to render him any more vulnerable to them. That the State once took temporary custody of Joshua does not alter the analysis, for when it returned him to his father's custody, it placed him in no worse position than that in which he would have been had it not acted at all; the State does not become the permanent guarantor of an individual's safety by having once offered him shelter. Under these circumstances, the State had no constitutional duty to protect Joshua.

It may well be that, by voluntarily undertaking to protect Joshua against a danger it concededly played no part in creating, the State acquired a duty under state tort law to provide him with adequate protection against that danger. See Restatement (Second) of Torts § 323 (1965) (one who undertakes to render services to another may in some circumstances be held liable for doing so in a negligent fashion); see generally W. Keeton, D. Dobbs, R. Keeton, & D. Owen, Prosser and Keeton on the Law of Torts § 56 (5th ed. 1984) (discussing "special relationships" which may give rise to affirmative duties to act under the

common law of tort). But the claim here is based on the Due Process Clause of the Fourteenth Amendment, which, as we have said many times, does not transform every tort committed by a state actor into a constitutional violation. A State may, through its courts and legislatures, impose such affirmative duties of care and protection upon its agents as it wishes. But not "all common-law duties owed by government actors were . . . constitutionalized by the Fourteenth Amendment." Because, as explained above, the State had no constitutional duty to protect Joshua against his father's violence, its failure to do so—though calamitous in hindsight—simply does not constitute a violation of the Due Process Clause.[10]

Judges and lawyers, like other humans, are moved by natural sympathy in a case like this to find a way for Joshua and his mother to receive adequate compensation for the grievous harm inflicted upon them. But before yielding to that impulse, it is well to remember once again that the harm was inflicted not by the State of Wisconsin, but by Joshua's father. The most that can be said of the state functionaries in this case is that they stood by and did nothing when suspicious circumstances dictated a more active role for them. In defense of them it must also be said that had they moved too soon to take custody of the son away from the father, they would likely have been met with charges of improperly intruding into the parent-child relationship, charges based on the same Due Process Clause that forms the basis for the present charge of failure to provide adequate protection.

The people of Wisconsin may well prefer a system of liability which would place upon the State and its officials the responsibility for failure to act in situations such as the present

---

[9] Complaint para. 16, App. 6 ("At relevant times to and until March 8, 1984, [the date of the final beating,] Joshua DeShaney was in the custody and control of Defendant Randy DeShaney"). Had the State by the affirmative exercise of its power removed Joshua from free society and placed him in a foster home operated by its agents, we might have a situation sufficiently analogous to incarceration or institutionalization to give rise to an affirmative duty to protect. Indeed, several Courts of Appeals have held, by analogy to Estelle and Youngberg, that the State may be held liable under the Due Process Clause for failing to protect children in foster homes from mistreatment at the hands of their foster parents. See Doe v. New York City Dept. of Social Services. Catholic Home Bureau v. Doe; Taylor ex rel. Walker v. Ledbetter, cert. pending Ledbetter v. Taylor. We express no view on the validity of this analogy, however, as it is not before us in the present case.

[10] Because we conclude that the Due Process Clause did not require the State to protect Joshua from his father, we need not address respondents' alternative argument that the individual state actors lacked the requisite "state of mind" to make out a due process violation. See Daniels v. Williams. Similarly, we have no occasion to consider whether the individual respondents might be entitled to a qualified immunity defense, see Anderson v. Creighton, or whether the allegations in the complaint are sufficient to support a § 1983 claim against the county and DSS under Monell v. New York City Dept. of Social Services, and its progeny.

one. They may create such a system, if they do not have it already, by changing the tort law of the State in accordance with the regular lawmaking process. But they should not have it thrust upon them by this Court's expansion of the Due Process Clause of the Fourteenth Amendment.

Affirmed.

Dissent: Justice **Brennan**, with whom Justice **Marshall** and Justice **Blackmun** join, dissenting.

. . .

It may well be, as the Court decides that the Due Process Clause as construed by our prior cases creates no general right to basic governmental services. That, however, is not the question presented here; indeed, that question was not raised in the complaint, urged on appeal, presented in the petition for certiorari, or addressed in the briefs on the merits. No one, in short, has asked the Court to proclaim that, as a general matter, the Constitution safeguards positive as well as negative liberties.

This is more than a quibble over dicta; it is a point about perspective, having substantive ramifications. In a constitutional setting that distinguishes sharply between action and inaction, one's characterization of the misconduct alleged under § 1983 may effectively decide the case. Thus, by leading off with a discussion (and rejection) of the idea that the Constitution imposes on the States an affirmative duty to take basic care of their citizens, the Court foreshadows—perhaps even preordains—its conclusion that no duty existed even on the specific facts before us. This initial discussion establishes the baseline from which the Court assesses the DeShaneys' claim that, when a State has—"by word and by deed,"—announced an intention to protect a certain class of citizens and has before it facts that would trigger that protection under the applicable state law, the Constitution imposes upon the State an affirmative duty of protection.

The Court's baseline is the absence of positive rights in the Constitution and a concomitant suspicion of any claim that seems to depend on such rights. From this perspective, the DeShaneys' claim is first and foremost about inaction (the failure, here, of respondents to take steps to protect Joshua), and only tangentially about action (the establishment of a state program specifically designed to help children like Joshua). And from this perspective, holding these Wisconsin officials liable—where the only difference between this case and one involving a general claim to protective services is Wisconsin's establishment and operation of a program to protect children—would seem to punish an effort that we should seek to promote.

I would begin from the opposite direction. I would focus first on the action that Wisconsin has taken with respect to Joshua and children like him, rather than on the actions that the State failed to take. Such a method is not new to this Court. Both *Estelle v. Gamble* and *Youngberg v. Romeo* began by emphasizing that the States had confined J. W. Gamble to prison and Nicholas Romeo to a psychiatric hospital. This initial action rendered these people helpless to help themselves or to seek help from persons unconnected to the government. . . . Cases from the lower courts also recognize that a State's actions can be decisive in assessing the constitutional significance of subsequent inaction. For these purposes, moreover, actual physical restraint is not the only state action that has been considered relevant. See, e. g., *White v. Rochford* (police officers violated due process when, after arresting the guardian of three young children, they abandoned the children on a busy stretch of highway at night).

Because of the Court's initial fixation on the general principle that the Constitution does not establish positive rights, it is unable to appreciate our recognition in *Estelle* and *Youngberg* that this principle does not hold true in all circumstances. . . . I do not mean to suggest that "the State's affirmative act of restraining the individual's freedom to act on his own behalf," was irrelevant in *Youngberg*; rather, I emphasize that this conduct would have led to no injury, and consequently no cause of action under § 1983, unless the State then had failed to take steps to protect Romeo from himself and from others. In addition, the Court's exclusive attention to state—imposed restraints of "the individual's freedom to act on his own behalf," suggests that it was the State that rendered Romeo unable to care for himself, whereas in fact—with an I. Q. of between 8 and 10, and the mental capacity of an 18-month-old child—he had been quite incapable of taking care of himself long before the State stepped into his life. Thus, the fact of hospitalization was critical in *Youngberg* not because it rendered Romeo helpless to help himself, but because it separated him from other sources of aid that, we held, the State was obligated to replace. Unlike the Court, therefore, I am unable to see in *Youngberg* a neat and decisive divide between action and inaction.

Moreover, to the Court, the only fact that seems to count as an "affirmative act of restraining the individual's freedom to act on his own behalf" is direct physical control. Ante, at 200, (listing only "incarceration, institutionalization, [and] other similar restraint of personal liberty" in describing relevant "affirmative acts"). I would not, however, give *Youngberg* and *Estelle* such a stingy scope. I would recognize, as the Court apparently cannot, that "the State's knowledge of [an] individual's predicament [and] its expressions of intent to help him" can amount to a "limitation of his freedom to act on his own behalf" or to obtain help from others. Thus, I would read *Youngberg* and *Estelle* to stand for the much more generous proposition that, if a State cuts off private sources of aid and then refuses aid itself, it cannot wash its hands of the harm that results from its inaction.

Youngberg and *Estelle* are not alone in sounding this theme. In striking down a filing fee as applied to divorce cases brought by indigents, see *Boddie v. Connecticut*, and in deciding that a local government could not entirely foreclose the opportunity to speak in a public forum, see, e. g., *Schneider v. State*; *Hague v. Committee for Industrial Organization*; *United States v. Grace*, we have acknowledged that a State's actions—such as the monopolization of a particular path of relief—may impose upon the State certain positive duties. Similarly, *Shelley v. Kraemer* and *Burton v. Wilmington Parking Authority* suggest that a State may be found complicit in an injury even if it did not create the situation that caused the harm.

Wisconsin has established a child-welfare system specifically designed to help children like Joshua. Wisconsin law places upon the local departments of social services such as respondent (DSS or Department) a duty to investigate reported instances of child abuse. While other governmental bodies and private persons are largely responsible for the reporting of possible cases of child abuse, Wisconsin law channels all such reports to the local departments of social services for evaluation and, if necessary, further action. Even when it is the sheriff's office or police department that receives a report of suspected child abuse, that report is referred to local social services departments for action; the only exception to this occurs when the reporter fears for the child's immediate safety. In this way, Wisconsin law invites—indeed, directs—citizens and other governmental entities to depend on local departments of social services such as respondent to protect children from abuse.

The specific facts before us bear out this view of Wisconsin's system of protecting children. Each time someone voiced a suspicion that Joshua was being abused, that information was relayed to the Department for investigation and possible action. When Randy DeShaney's second wife told the police that he had "hit the boy causing marks and [was] a prime case for child abuse," the police referred her complaint to DSS. When, on three separate occasions, emergency room personnel noticed suspicious injuries on Joshua's body, they went to DSS with this information. When neighbors informed the police that they had seen or heard Joshua's father or his father's lover beating or otherwise abusing Joshua, the police brought these reports to the attention of DSS. And when respondent Kemmeter, through these reports and through her own observations in the course of nearly 20 visits to the DeShaney home, compiled growing evidence that Joshua was being abused, that information stayed within the Department–chronicled by the social worker in detail that seems almost eerie in light of her failure to act upon it. (As to the extent of the social worker's involvement in, and knowledge of, Joshua's predicament, her reaction to the news of Joshua's last and most devastating injuries is illuminating: "I just knew the phone would ring some day and Joshua would be dead.")

Even more telling than these examples is the Department's control over the decision whether to take steps to protect a particular child from suspected abuse. While many different people contributed information and advice to this decision, it was up to the people at DSS to make the ultimate decision (subject to the approval of the local government's corporation counsel) whether to disturb the family's current arrangements. When Joshua first appeared at a local hospital with injuries signaling physical abuse, for example, it was DSS that made the decision to take him into temporary custody for the purpose of studying his situation—and it was DSS, acting in conjunction with the corporation counsel, that returned him to his father. Unfortunately for Joshua DeShaney, the buck effectively stopped with the Department.

In these circumstances, a private citizen, or even a person working in a government agency other than DSS, would doubtless feel that her job was done as soon as she had reported her suspicions of child abuse to DSS. Through its child-welfare program, in other words, the State of Wisconsin has relieved ordinary citizens and governmental bodies other than the Department of any sense of obligation to do anything more than report their suspicions of child abuse to DSS. If DSS ignores or dismisses these suspicions, no one will step in to fill the gap. Wisconsin's child-protection program thus effectively confined Joshua DeShaney within the walls of Randy DeShaney's violent home until such time as DSS took action to remove him. Conceivably, then, children like Joshua are made worse off by the existence of this program when the persons and entities charged with carrying it out fail to do their jobs.

It simply belies reality, therefore, to contend that the State "stood by and did nothing" with respect to Joshua. Through its child-protection program, the State actively intervened in Joshua's life and, by virtue of this intervention, acquired ever more certain knowledge that Joshua was in grave danger. These circumstances, in my view, plant this case solidly within the tradition of cases like *Youngberg* and *Estelle*.

. . .

I do not suggest that such irrationality was at work in this case; I emphasize only that we do not know whether or not it was. I would allow Joshua and his mother the opportunity to show that respondents' failure to help him arose, not out of the sound exercise of professional judgment that we recognized in *Youngberg* as sufficient to preclude liability, . . ., but from the kind of arbitrariness that we have in the past condemned.

. . .

As the Court today reminds us, "the Due Process Clause of the Fourteenth Amendment was intended to prevent government 'from abusing [its] power, or employing it as an instrument of oppression.'" My disagreement with the Court arises from its failure to see that inaction can be every bit as abusive of power as action, that oppression can result when a State undertakes a vital duty and then ignores it. Today's opinion construes the Due Process Clause to permit a State to displace private sources of protection and then, at the critical moment, to shrug its shoulders and turn away from the harm that it has promised to try to prevent. Because I cannot agree that our Constitution is indifferent to such indifference, I respectfully dissent.

Justice **Blackmun**, dissenting.

. . .

The Court . . . attempts to draw a sharp and rigid line between action and inaction. But such formalistic reasoning has no place in the interpretation of the broad and stirring Clauses of the Fourteenth Amendment. Indeed, I submit that these Clauses were designed, at least in part, to undo the formalistic legal reasoning that infected antebellum jurisprudence . . .

Like the antebellum judges who denied relief to fugitive slaves, the Court today claims that its decision, however harsh, is compelled by existing legal doctrine. On the contrary, the question presented by this case is an open one, and our Fourteenth Amendment precedents may be read more broadly or narrowly depending upon how one chooses to read them. Faced with the choice, I would adopt a "sympathetic" reading, one which comports with dictates of fundamental justice and recognizes that compassion need not be exiled from the province of judging. . . .

Poor Joshua! Victim of repeated attacks by an irresponsible, bullying, cowardly, and intemperate father, and abandoned by respondents who placed him in a dangerous predicament and who knew or learned what was going on, and yet did essentially nothing except, as the Court revealingly observes, ante, at 193, "dutifully recorded these incidents in [their] files." It is a sad commentary upon American life, and constitutional principles—so full of late of patriotic fervor and proud proclamations about "liberty and justice for all," that this child, Joshua DeShaney, now is assigned to live out the remainder of his life profoundly retarded. Joshua and his mother, as petitioners here, deserve—but now are denied by this Court—the opportunity to have the facts of their case considered in the light of the constitutional protection that 42 U.S.C. § 1983 is meant to provide.

NOTES

1. Would the result in *DeShaney* be any different if the social worker did nothing to protect Joshua while actually observing the beatings?

2. The Supreme Court has recognized the constitutional right of a parent to retain custody of a minor child. This "fundamental right" is limited by a "compelling state interest" in protecting a minor child from imminent danger of abuse or neglect. *Santosky v. Kramer*, 455 U.S. 745 (1982). Would Randy DeShaney have had a section 1983 claim if the DSS caseworker had taken action to remove Joshua from his custody? Should caseworkers be immune from such claims? Some courts have held that caseworkers are absolutely immune for actions taken in initiating or prosecuting child abuse cases while others recognize only a qualified immunity. Compare *Meyers v. Contra Costa County Department of Social Services*, 812 F.2d 1154 (9th Cir. 1987) (absolute immunity) with *Millspaugh v. County Department of Public Welfare*, 937 F.2d 1172 (7th Cir. 1991) (qualified immunity). See Chapters 7 and 8. Local governments, on the other hand, have no immunity when their official policies or customs cause a constitutional violation. See Chapter 5. How would these various immunity doctrines affect litigation strategies? What effect would these immunity doctrines likely have on caseworkers' decisions on whether to intervene in a particular case? How does the "no duty" rationale of *DeShaney* affect the incentives for action or inaction in close cases?

3. How useful is the "act/omission" distinction as a principle of adjudication? Some critics maintain that since government plays some role in virtually every aspect of daily life, it is formalistic and naive to accord decisive weight to the difference between active and passive

defaults of government officials. Consider Professor Tribe's critique of *DeShaney*:

> My trouble is with the majority's quite primitive vision of the state of Wisconsin as some sort of distinct object, a kind of machine that must be understood to act upon a pre-political, natural order of private life. From the majority's perspective, the state of Wisconsin operates as a thing, its arms exerting force from a safe distance upon a sometimes unpleasant natural world, in which the abuse of children is an unfortunate, yet external, ante-legal and pre-political fact of our society. Courts, as passive and detached observers, may reach in to offer a helping hand only when another arm of the state has reached out and shattered this natural, pre-political order by itself directly harming a young child.
>
> . . . [T]here is no hint that the hand of the observing state may itself have played a major role in shaping the world it observes. . . [T]he Supreme Court majority. . . did not inquire whether the hand of the state may have altered an already political landscape in a way that encouraged such child-beating to go uncorrected. The majority's question in *DeShaney* was simply, "did the State of Wisconsin beat up that child?", and not, "did the law of Wisconsin, taken in its entirety, warp the legal landscape so that it in effect deflected the assistance otherwise available to Joshua DeShaney?"

Laurence H. Tribe, *The Curvature of Constitutional Space: What Lawyers Can Learn From Modern Physics*, 103 Harv. L. Rev. 1, 9–10 (1989). If Professor Tribe's point of view were to prevail, what limits would there be on recognizing affirmative constitutional duties under the due process clause?

4. One problem inherent in the act/omission distinction is that of characterization. Labeling misconduct as active or passive may turn on how one poses the question. Assume, for example, a policeman impounds a car, arrests the driver and leaves the children-passengers stranded on a busy highway. Are the children endangered by the officer's *acts* of impounding the car and arresting the driver, or by the *failure to rescue* the children? Cf. *White v. Rochford*,

592 F.2d 381 (7th Cir. 1979). How difficult is it for courts to ascertain whether a particular claim actually turns on an act or omission?

5. The majority in *DeShaney* notes that the due process clause "generally confer[s] no affirmative right to governmental aid" and cites cases in which the government was found to have no obligation to provide housing or to fund abortions or other medical services. The dissenting Justices discuss other cases that they believe could support recognizing a duty to protect Joshua. Professor Currie has identified several lines of cases in which the Court has found the state to have a constitutional obligation to act in some positive way. In addition to cases like *Youngberg* and *Estelle* dealing with the protection of the involuntarily confined, Currie notes the constitutional obligations to provide legal counsel for the indigent charged with crimes, to enforce contracts, and to provide access to certain information and to public forums. See David P. Currie, *Positive and Negative Constitutional Rights*, 53 U.Chi. L. Rev. 864, 872–880 (1986). Professor Currie also cites *Truax v. Corrigan*, 257 U.S. 312 (1921) in which the court ruled that a state law restricting the use of injunctions in labor disputes deprived the employer of property without due process of law. Does *Truax* support the proposition that the Due Process Clause may require the state to protect persons from the acts of private parties? While Professor Currie dismisses as "profoundly ahistorical" the notion that the Constitution offers a positive right to basic welfare services, he warns that "it would be dangerous to read too much, even at the theoretical level, into the generally valid principle that ours. . .is a Constitution of negative rather than positive liberties." 53 U.Chi.L.Rev. at 878 and 887. Given the conflicting strains of cases, what is the proper role of precedent in deciding cases like *DeShaney* presenting novel issues regarding the scope of constitutional protection and obligation?

6. When the person who actively injures the plaintiff is a private party, the affirmative duty issue sometimes becomes confused with the "under color of" state law element of a section 1983 claim. As discussed in Chapter 2, Section 1983 grants a remedy only for acts taken "under color of" state law. Where, as in *DeShaney*, the active wrongdoer is a private citizen, some courts have denied liability on the grounds that the injury was not the product of

state action. In *Milburn v. Anne Arundel Department of Social Services*, 871 F.2d 474 (4th Cir. 1989), for example, the court reasoned that the abusive acts of the state approved foster parents of a voluntarily placed infant were not state action. The fourth circuit drew support for this conclusion from Supreme Court decisions finding private action adversely affecting liberty or property is not subject to the demands of procedural due process despite some involvement of the state. E.g., *Blum v. Yaretsky*, 457 U.S. 991 (1982); *Rendell-Baker v. Kohn*, 457 U.S. 830 (1982); *Jackson v. Metropolitan Edison Co.*, 419 U.S. 345 (1974).

The issue of state action, however, is only marginally relevant to issue of affirmative duty in the constitutional tort context. On a superficial level, both lines of cases raise the question of whether the state bears any responsibility for the conduct of a nominally private actor. On closer examination, however, the two lines of cases address distinctly different issues. The affirmative duty cases raise the question of whether a state official owes an obligation to protect the plaintiff from some peril—not whether the peril itself can be said to be that of the state. State action is often a key issue in cases where the defendant is a government official, but the relationship between his governmental status and the injury is called into question. Claims arising from the off-duty actions of police officers and school teachers are commonly analyzed in terms of state action. E.g., *Gibson v. City of Chicago*, 910 F.2d 1510 (7th Cir. 1990) (shooting by suspended police officer was not under color of law); *D.T by M.T. v. Independent School Dist. No. 16*, 894 F.2d 1176 (10th Cir. 1990) (molestation of a child by a teacher during summer months was not under color of state law). See Chapter 2.

7. Despite the broad rhetoric of *DeShaney*, a large number of cases continue to raise issues of affirmative constitutional duties. The explanation for this may be twofold. First, state involvement in the affairs of its citizens is pervasive and may induce reliance on government for protection and other basic services. Thus, demand for affirmative duties remains high. Second, ambiguity within the *DeShaney* opinion leaves open several doctrinal bases for recognizing such duties. The majority opinion appears to leave open the possibility that "special relationships" giving rise to an affirmative constitutional duty of protection might be recognized under other circumstances. See generally Eaton and Wells, *Governmental Inaction as a Constitutional Tort. DeShaney and Its Aftermath*, 66 Wash. L. Rev. 107 (1991).

The following case explores the viability of affirmative duty constitutional tort claims after *DeShaney.*

B.   Affirmative Duties and State Created Danger

L. W. v. Grubbs

974 F.2d 119 (9th Cir. 1992)

Goodwin, Circuit Judge:

L. W., a registered nurse employed by the State of Oregon at a medium security custodial institution for young male offenders, was raped and terrorized by an inmate. She sued under 42 U.S.C. § 1983 for damages, and appeals the district court's judgment of dismissal under Fed. R. Civ. P. 12 (b) (6) for failure to state a claim against defendants Dee Grubbs, Thomas Nelson, Marlin Hutton, Richard Hill and James Mason (collectively, "Defendants"). We reverse.

Defendants are state employees who served as L.W.'s supervisors at the custodial institution. According to L.W.'s complaint, which, for Rule 12 purposes, we must accept as true, Defendants hired her to work in the institution's medical clinic and led her to believe that she would not be required to work alone with violent sex offenders. On August 15, 1989, however, Defendants selected inmate David Blehm to work with L.W. alone in the clinic. Blehm was a violent sex offender who had failed all treatment programs at the institution. According to his files, Blehm was considered very likely to commit a violent crime if placed alone with a female. Once alone with L.W. in the clinic, Blehm assaulted, battered, kidnapped and raped her. He also stole certain of her personal belongings.

In her complaint, L.W. alleged that the foregoing facts constituted conduct, under color of state law, which deprived her of her right to liberty without due process of law.

L.W. sued on the theory that the government actors violated her constitutional rights by intentionally placing her in a position of known danger, that is, in unguarded proximity with an inmate whose record they knew included attacks upon women.

Defendants moved to dismiss the case for failure to state a claim, arguing that no due process right of L.W. was affected because she was not in custody. The district court granted the motion, agreeing that only a person in official custody could state a section 1983 claim when injured by a third party.

. . .

I.   Section 1983 and Third Party Harm

To state a section 1983 claim, the plaintiff must allege that (1) the conduct complained of was committed by a person acting under color of state law; and (2) the conduct deprived the plaintiff of a constitutional right. In this case involving harm inflicted by a third party who was not a state actor, Defendants argue that L.W.'s claim is barred for three reasons. First, Defendants assert that, under *DeShaney v. Winnebago County, Dep't of Social Servs.*, the absence of a custodial relationship between L.W. and the Defendants bars her claim. Second, Defendants argue that, under *Collins v. City of Harker Heights*, L.W.'s status as an employee of the Defendants bars her claim. Finally, Defendants argue that L.W.'s complaint is insufficient because it alleges "mere negligence."

A.   Custody

Relying on *DeShaney*, the district court ruled that victim custody was a prerequisite to L.W.'s claim. In so ruling, the court misread *DeShaney* and overlooked circuit case law to the contrary.

As a general rule, members of the public have no constitutional right to sue state employees who fail to protect them against harm inflicted by third parties. *DeShaney, Ketchum v. County of Alameda.*

This general rule is modified by two exceptions: (1) the "special relationship" exception; and (2) the "danger creation" exception. Although some cases have blended the two exceptions together, see, e.g., *Ketchum*, the distinction is important.

After the state has created a special relationship with a person, as in the case of custody or involuntary hospitalization, cases have imposed liability under a due process theory, premised on an abuse of that special relationship. See, e.g., *Youngberg v. Romeo* (patient in custodial facility for the mentally retarded denied protection from violence); *Estelle v. Gamble* (prisoner denied Eighth Amendment right to medical care).

The "danger creation" basis for a claim, by contrast, necessarily involves affirmative conduct on the part of the state in placing the plaintiff in danger. *DeShaney* did not rule that custody was required where the state affirmatively causes the harm. In addition to pointing out that Joshua DeShaney was not in state custody when injured, the Court noted that "while the State may have been aware of the dangers that Joshua faced in the free world, it played no part in their creation, nor did it do anything to render him any more vulnerable to them." *DeShaney*. *DeShaney* thus suggests that had the state created the danger, Joshua might have recovered even though he was not in custody.

In the Ninth Circuit, the law concerning the "danger creation" exception begins with *Wood [v. Ostrander.]* In *Wood* (decided after *DeShaney*), we held that a woman who was raped by a third party could hold a police officer liable under section 1983. In that case, the officer had stopped the car in which the plaintiff was riding, arrested and removed the driver, impounded the car, and left the plaintiff stranded in a high crime area. She was subsequently raped. Even though the plaintiff had not been in state custody, we allowed her claim to go forward because the jury could have found that the defendant officer had affirmatively created the particular danger that exposed her to third party violence.

Similarly, in the present case, the actions of the Defendants created the danger to which L.W. fell victim by elevating Blehm to cart boy status. According to the complaint, the Defendants knowingly assigned Blehm to work with L.W. despite their knowledge that: (1) Blehm was not qualified to serve as a cart boy; (2) Blehm had an extraordinary history of unrepentant violence against women and girls; (3) Blehm was likely to assault a female if left alone with her; (4) L.W. would be alone with Blehm during her rounds; and (5) L.W. would not be prepared to defend against or take steps to avert an attack because she had not been

informed at hiring that she would be left alone with violent offenders. The Defendants, like the officer in *Wood*, thus used their authority as state correctional officers to create an opportunity for Blehm to assault L.W. that would not otherwise have existed. The Defendants also enhanced L.W.'s vulnerability to attack by misrepresenting to her the risks attending her work.

These allegations support section 1983 liability. L.W. is not seeking to hold Defendants liable for Blehm's violent proclivities. Rather, L.W. seeks to make Defendants answer for their acts that independently created the opportunity for and facilitated Blehm's assault on her. Cf. *Wood*; see also *Cornelius v. Town of Highland Lake* (City and prison officials' actions in operating prisoner work squad in populated area could form basis for section 1983 liability where, despite knowledge of prisoners' violent dispositions, officials failed to exercise adequate control and supervision, resulting in kidnapping and terrorizing of a city resident; the officials "significantly increased both the risk of harm to the plaintiff, and the opportunity for the inmates to commit the harm"), cert. denied.

Because custody is not a prerequisite to the "danger creation" basis for a section 1983 third party harm claim, and because Defendants affirmatively created the dangerous situation which resulted in L.W.'s assault, the district court erred in dismissing L.W.'s claim for a failure to allege a custodial relationship between her and the Defendants.

B. Employment

Defendants next argue that L.W.'s status as a state employee should bar her claim. Defendants mistakenly rely on *Collins*.

In *Collins*, city sanitation employee Collins died of asphyxia after entering a manhole. Collins' estate subsequently sued the city under section 1983 for violation of his due process rights.

. . .

In rejecting Collins' claim, the Court held that Collins had not alleged affirmative culpable acts by the city. According to the Court, Collins' complaint alleged merely that "the city deprived him of life and liberty by failing to provide a reasonably safe work environment." *Id.* (footnote omitted). The Court pointed out that Collins had *not* alleged that "his supervisor instructed him to go into the sewer when the supervisor knew or should have know that there was a significant risk that he would be injured." *Id.*

Under *Collins*, we cannot dismiss L.W.'s claim against Defendants merely because she was an employee supervised by them. Moreover, the shortcomings identified by the Court in Collins' complaint do not exist in L.W.'s complaint. Unlike Collins, L.W. alleges that the Defendants took affirmative steps to place her at significant risk, and that they knew of the risks. Contrary to Defendants' arguments, Collins actually supports L.W.'s claim.

C. "Mere Negligence"

Finally, Defendants argue that L.W.'s claim is barred because it alleges "mere negligence" and section 1983 does not permit such claims. *Davidson v. Cannon.* Defendants misread L.W.'s complaint, however. Neither the Supreme Court nor this court has stated what mental state beyond "mere negligence" is required for due process third party harm claims. The Supreme Court and this court have observed that not every tort claim automatically becomes a constitutional wrong. Something more than an ordinary tort is required. We need not address the hypothetical boundaries here, however, because L.W. has alleged facts demonstrating official deliberate indifference in creating the danger. See *Wood.* L.W. has alleged that Defendants knew that Blehm was a violent sex offender who had failed all treatment and was likely to assault a woman if alone with her, and that, even knowing this, Defendants intentionally assigned Blehm to work alone with L.W. in the clinic.

D. L.W. Has Stated a Claim Under Section 1983

L.W. has alleged that she was deprived of her liberty because Defendants, acting in their capacity as state correctional officers, affirmatively created a significant risk of harm to her, and did so with a sufficiently culpable mental state. Accordingly, we hold that L.W. has stated a claim under section 1983 for violation of her due process rights.

. . .

REVERSED and REMANDED.

NOTES

1. Is *Grubbs* consistent with *DeShaney*? Did the defendants in *Grubbs* contribute to the L.W.'s need for protection in a way that materially differed from the conduct of the welfare authorities in *DeShaney*? Recall from Chapter 3 that in *Collins v. City of Harker Heights*, 112 S. Ct. 1061 (1992), the Court affirmed the dismissal of a complaint that alleged that the city had a policy and custom of deliberate indifference toward the safety of its employees. The complaint focused on the city's alleged "custom and policy of not training its employees about the dangers of working in sewer lines and manhole, not providing safety equipment at job sites, and not providing safety warnings." *Collins*, 112 S. Ct. at 1064. These allegations were not actionable under § 1983 because they could not "properly be characterized as arbitrary or conscience-shocking, in a constitutional sense." *Collins*, 112 S. Ct. at 1170. What specific allegations in L.W's complaint elevate her claim to a constitutional status? Is artful pleading the difference between Collin's failure to survive a motion to dismiss and L.W.'s success?

2. Lower courts agree in principle that state creation of danger can provide the basis for recognizing a constitutional duty of protection. As explained by Judge Posner, "[i]if a state puts a man in a position of danger from private persons and then fails to protect him, it will not be heard to say that its role is merely passive; it is as much an active tort-feasor as if it had thrown him into a snake pit." *Bowers v. DeVito*, 686 F.2d 616, 618 (7th Cir. 1982). The primary point of disagreement is whether the alleged conduct was sufficient to trigger the duty. A rich pattern of cases has emerged.

(a) One line of claims arise from governmental action that enhances the ability of a third party over whom the defendant has some control to injure the plaintiff. Conduct that simply contributes to a nonparticularized increase in danger is generally insufficient to trigger a constitutional duty to protect. Thus, courts routinely deny claims brought by those suffering at the hands of inmates released by parole, furlough or escape. E.g., *Martinez v. California*, 444 U.S. 277 (1980) (parole); *Estate of Gilmore v. Buckley*, 787 F.2d 714 (1st Cir. 1986) (furlough); *Ketchum v. Alameda County*, 811 F.2d 1243 (9th Cir.

1987) (escape). However, several courts have recognized a constitutional duty when the defendant's actions create a particular opportunity for an assault by a person in the defendant's custody. In addition to *Grubbs*, see *Cornelius v. Town of Highland Lake*, 880 F.2d 348 (11th Cir. 1989) (state-created danger in assigning prison inmates with known violent propensities to work near city hall; town clerk abducted); *Nishiyama v. Dickson County*, 814 F.2d 277 (6th Cir. 1987) (state-created danger in giving trusty inmate unsupervised use patrol car; trusty stopped and murdered the plaintiff's daughter).

Why is it that state officials may not be held liable in constitutional tort for the criminal acts of a parolee (*Martinez*), but may be held responsible for the criminal acts of trusty inmates (*Nishiyama*) or inmates assigned to work release (*Cornelius*)?

(b) A related group of cases focus on state action that encourages private violence. *DeShaney* makes clear that "[n]othing in the Due Process Clause itself requires the State to protect the life, liberty, and property of its citizens against invasions by private actors." *DeShaney*, 489 U.S. at 195. Accordingly, it is not a denial of due process for a police officer to sit in his patrol car and passively observe the robbing or beating of a citizen. E.g., *Tucker v. Callahan*, 867 F.2d 909 (6th Cir. 1989). Suppose, however, the plaintiff alleges the police were not merely indifferent to an assault, but encouraged it? In *Dwares v. City of New York*, 985 F.2d 94 (2d Cir. 1993), the plaintiff was beaten up by a group of "skinheads" on the fourth of July, during a demonstration at which an American flag was burned. In reversing the district court's dismissal of a section 1983 claim against individual police officers and the city, the court stated

> The complaint in the present case was unlike that in *DeShaney* because it went well beyond allegations that the defendant officers merely stood by and did nothing, and that the circumstances were merely suspicious. It alleged that the officers conspired with the "skinheads" to permit the latter to beat up flag burners with relative impunity, assuring the "skinheads" that

> unless they got totally out of control they would not be impeded or arrested. It requires no stretch to infer that such prior assurances would have increased the likelihood that the "skinheads" would assault demonstrators.

Dwares, 785 F.2d at 99. See also, *Freeman v. Ferguson*, 911 F.2d 52 (8th Cir. 1990) (police chief enhanced the plaintiff's exposure to danger by instructing officers not to enforce protective order against plaintiff's estranged husband who was also the chief's friend). Cf. *Horton v. Flenory*, 889 F.2d 454 (3rd Cir. 1989) (official policy of allowing private clubs to handle on-premise disturbances created an enhanced risk of beating by club's security personnel).

Should the police or prosecutors have a constitutional duty to protect persons who cooperate in criminal investigations? See *Ying Jing Gan v. City of New York*, 996 F.2d 522 (2d Cir. 1993) (no duty to protect witness who identified gang members as perpetrators of a robbery).

(c) Another line of cases involves the claims of persons placed in peril as a result of state action taken against another party, as when a passenger is endangered by the arrest of the driver and the impounding of the car. Several courts have ruled that the actions of the police in arresting the driver and impounding the car trigger some constitutional obligations towards the passengers. E.g., *Wood v. Ostrander*, 879 F.2d 583 (9th Cir. 1989) (female passenger was raped by a third party after police arrested the driver, impounded the car and left her stranded in a high crime area at 2:30 a.m.); *White v. Rochford*, 592 F.2d 381 (7th Cir. 1979) (police arrested the driver and left small children stranded on a busy highway). But see *Walton v. City of Southfield*, 995 F.2d 1331, (6th Cir. 1993) (fifteen year old and two year old children left stranded by the police following the arrest of the driver of the car; the defendants were entitled to qualified immunity because at the time of the incident "there was no clearly established right to personal security forbidding the police from abandoning passengers"; *White v. Rochford* was distinguished on the grounds that the "children in [*White*] were left in a more dangerous situation."); *Hillard v. City and*

County of Denver, 930 F.2d 1516 (10th Cir. 1991) (passenger left stranded in a high crime area after the arrest of the driver was sexually assaulted; notwithstanding *Wood v. Ostrander* and *White v. Rochford*, "we are not persuaded. . .that the plaintiff here has articulated the deprivation of a constitutional right, much less a "clearly established" constitutional right"; the defendants were entitled to qualified immunity).

Suppose the police arrest the driver of a car in which intoxicated adult passengers are riding. Do the police owe a constitutional duty to the passengers or others who might be injured should the intoxicated passengers attempt to drive the car away? See *Reed v. Gardner*, 986 F.2d 1122 (7th Cir. 1993) (plaintiffs were injured in an automobile collision with a drunk driver; allegation that police arrested a sober driver and left the car in the control of a intoxicated passenger who then drove the car was sufficient to state a claim under section 1983). Would it matter whether the arrested driver was also intoxicated? See also *Gregory v. City of Rogers*, 974 F.2d 1006 (8th Cir. 1992) (6:5 en banc) (police arrested the "designated driver", who gave the keys to his car to an intoxicated passenger, who, in turn, drove the car and subsequently were involved in a fatal accident; the police were entitled to summary judgment because (1) there was insufficient evidence that the police knew the passengers were intoxicated; and (2) even if the police were aware, they owed no duty to protect the passengers from their own recklessness).

Are *Wood*, *White* and *Reed* consistent with *Collins v. City of Harker Heights*, set out in Chapter 3?

(d) Suppose a person drowns after police instruct private citizens not to attempt a rescue. Could the police be said to have denied the drowning man liberty or life without due process? See *Ross v. United States*, 910 F.2d 1422, 1431 (7th Cir. 1990) ("the county had a policy of arbitrarily cutting off private rescue without providing a meaningful alternative"). Would it make any difference if the person drowning was fleeing arrest and could be considered dangerous? See *Andrews v. Wilkins*, 934 F.2d 1267 (D.C. Cir. 1991) (no constitutional duty to rescue fleeing suspect; interference with

private rescue that might endanger the rescuer does not violate any constitutional rights of the fleeing suspect). See also *Rogers v. City of Port Huron*, 833 F.Supp. 1212 (E.D. Mich. 1993) (police officers instructed bystanders to let a man lying on the side of a road "sleep it off"; the man was later found injured; summary judgment granted to the defendants).

3. The court in *Grubbs* briefly mentions that government officials may have a constitutional duty to protect persons involuntarily placed in governmental custody. *DeShaney* expressly reaffirmed this principle in the context of incarceration and the involuntary confinement of the mentally ill. Footnote 9 in *DeShaney* suggests that there may be situations "sufficiently analogous to incarceration or institutionalization to give rise to an affirmative duty to protect." Is a child's compulsory attendance in public school or placement in a foster home "sufficiently analogous" to incarceration or institutionalization to trigger a constitutional duty of protection? In what sense is compulsory school attendance or placement in a foster home analogous to or different from incarceration? What are the appropriate points of comparison?

A majority of courts to consider the issue have concluded that children attending public schools under state compulsory attendance laws are not in state "custody" so as to trigger a constitutional duty for school officials to protect students from physical or sexual assaults by teachers or other students. Many of these decisions emphasize that school attendance, unlike penal confinement, does not reduce the plaintiff's ability to protect herself. For a thorough discussion of this issue, see *D.R. v. Middle Bucks Area Vocational Technical School*, 972 F.2d 1364 (3rd Cir. 1992) (en banc). See also, *Dorothy J. v. Little Rock School Dist.*, 7 F.3d 729 (8th Cir. 1993); *Graham v. Independent School Dist. No. 1–89*, 1994 U.S. App. Lexis 8143 (10th Cir. 1994) (collecting cases). A panel of the Fifth Circuit Court of Appeals recently expressed a contrary view. In *Walton v. Alexander*, 20 F.3d 1350 (5th Cir. 1994), reh'g, en banc granted, 1994 U.S. App. Lexis 11083 (5th Cir 1994) a student at a state school for the deaf sued the superintendent alleging that the superintendent failed to protect him from sexual assault by another student. A majority of the court found that a special relationship triggering a duty of protection existed because (1) the school had 24 hour custody of the students; (2) the deaf child lacked basic communication skills; and (3) the family had no other viable option for the education of their child. The court, however, granted summary judgment to the defendant due to the lack of evidence that the superintendent was deliberately indifferent to the child's need for protection.

4. In contrast to the cases dealing with school children, most lower courts have concluded that children involuntarily placed in foster homes are entitled to a constitutional duty of protection. E.g., *Norfleet v. Arkansas Department of Human Services*, 989 F.2d 289 (8th Cir. 1993) (collecting cases); *Taylor v. Ledbetter*, 818 F.2d 791 (11th Cir. 1987) (en banc); *Doe v. New York City Department of Social Services*, 649 F.2d 134 (2d Cir. 1981).

Why do government officials have a constitutional obligation to protect children involuntarily placed in foster homes, but not children who attend public schools under state mandatory attendance laws? In what respect is foster care analogous to incarceration or involuntary commitment in a mental health facility? How is it different? Why is there is no constitutional obligation when welfare officials return a child to the custody of a parent they know or suspect is abusive, but there is a constitutional obligation when the child is placed in an abusive foster home?

5. Courts often phrase the level of state involvement necessary to trigger a constitutional affirmative duty in terms of "involuntary" custody. Some courts have stated that there is no constitutional affirmative duty towards those who are voluntarily placed in the state's custody. E.g., *Monahan v. Dorchester Counseling Center, Inc.*, 961 F.2d 987 (1st Cir. 1992) (no constitutional duty to protect a voluntary placed mentally ill patient); *Milburn v. Anne Arundel County Department of Social Services*, 871 F.2d 474 (4th Cir. 1989) (no affirmative duty to protect a child voluntarily placed in a foster home); *Fialkowski v. Greenwich Home for Children*, 921 F.2d 459 (3rd Cir. 1990) (no affirmative duty to protect a mentally impaired adult man voluntarily placed in a group home). But see, *The Estate of Cassara v. Illinois*, 853 F.Supp 411 (N.D. Ill. 1994) (state mental health officials owe a duty to protect voluntarily committed suicidal patient).

Why is the voluntariness of custody considered to be significant in determining the existence of a constitutional duty? Is there any meaningful difference in the level of state involvement in voluntary and involuntary placement of children in state supervised foster homes? Is there any less need for protection in the two situations? Is deliberate indifference by supervising welfare officials to the security of the voluntarily placed foster child any less abusive than deliberate indifference to the needs of the involuntarily placed child?

6. Claims that could be framed in terms of affirmative duty under the due process clause may also be analyzed under other constitutional theories. An equal protection claim may exist, for example, if the police deny protection to classes of persons on a constitutionally impermissible basis. Victims of domestic violence sometimes sue government officials under an equal protection theory, alleging that police customarily disregard the domestic violence reports of women. E.g., *Brown v. Grabowski*, 922 F.2d 1097 (3rd Cir. 1991). In *Dwares v. City of New York*, 785 F.2d 94 (2d Cir. 1993), the plaintiffs also were allowed to proceed under a theory that the police denied them equal protection by intentionally discriminating against "flag burners" in providing protection from assaults.

In some circumstances the standard rules governing supervisory and governmental liability for the acts of subordinates will suffice to provide the basis for a claim. Under *Monell v. Department of Social Services*, 436 U.S. 658 (1978), governmental entities are not vicariously liable for the unconstitutional acts of subordinates. They may, however, be held liable for their own deficiencies in supervision or training. See, *City of Canton v. Harris*, 489 U.S. 378 (1989) (discussed in detail in Chapter 5). A concrete example of how governmental and supervisory liability theories can circumvent the limitations on affirmative duties is found in two circuit court opinions addressing the potential constitutional tort liability of school officials for sexual abuse inflicted on a student by the school's band director. In a ruling issued before *DeShaney*, the third circuit held that the case could proceed to trial under a theory that school officials had a constitutional affirmative duty under *Youngberg v. Romeo*, 457 U.S. 307 (1982) to protect the student from the abuse of the band director. See, *Stoneking v. Bradford Area School District*, 856 F.2d 594 (3rd Cir.

1988). In a post-*DeShaney* reconsideration of this decision, the court affirmed the result, but on a different ground. Instead of relying on a theory of affirmative duty, the court characterized the claim in terms of the school officials' own actions in adopting and maintaining a practice, custom, or policy of reckless indifference to instances of known or suspected sexual abuse of students by teachers." *Stoneking v. Bradford Area School District*, 882 F.2d 720, 724–25 (3rd Cir. 1989). To the same effect, see *Doe v. Taylor Independent School Dist.*, 17 F.3rd 443 (5th Cir. 1994) (en banc) affirming 975 F.2d 137 (5th Cir. 1992).

Suppose that a handcuffed prisoner is beaten by one police officer while another officer observes. See, *O'Neill v. Krzeminski*, 839 F.2d 9 (2d Cir. 1988). How could the prisoner plead claims against the two officers and their municipal employer? How might the underlying theories of liability differ if the passive officer is subordinant or superior to the officer engaged in the active beating? Would it matter if the beating occurred prior to a formal arrest, after arrest but before confinement, while the plaintiff was in jail awaiting trial, or after conviction? How would an allegation of racial motivation affect the claim?

7. The principle focus of the post-*DeShaney* cases has been on whether the state was sufficiently involved with the plaintiff's need for protection to trigger a constitutional affirmative duty. The majority in *DeShaney* concluded that there was insufficient state involvement to trigger an affirmative constitutional duty. Accordingly, they did not reach the issue of whether the defendants had a sufficiently culpable state of mind to warrant labeling their inaction an abuse of governmental authority. It is important to remember that where, as in *Grubbs*, state involvement is sufficient to support a constitutional duty, the court must also consider the defendant's state of mind. Thus, the court in *Grubbs* emphasized that "deliberate indifference" and not "mere negligence" is essential tò support a substantive due process claim. Consequently, even when the level of state involvement is clearly sufficient to trigger a duty of protection, the claim will fail if the plaintiff can not prove deliberate indifference. See e.g., *Brownell v. Figel*, 950 F.2d 1285 (7th Cir. 1991) (deliberate indifference not shown when police reasonably concluded that arrestee was intoxicated and not seriously ill); *McGill v.*

Duckworth, 944 F.2d 344 (7th Cir. 1991) (prison officials not liable for sexual assault of inmate; deliberate indifference not shown since defendants did not know of threats against the inmate). The contours of deliberate indifference are discussed in Chapters 3 and 5.

II. Section 1983 and Federal "Laws"

Under the terms of section 1983, suit may be brought not only for constitutional wrongs, but also for violations of federal "laws". Questions arise as to the scope of this provision. The Supreme Court has never permitted plaintiffs to use section 1983 indiscriminately, to redress *any* violation of federal statutory or common law. On the other hand, the decisions contain varying statements regarding the conditions under which section 1983 suits are proper, and some of the cases are more liberal than others in allowing section 1983 suits.

Wilder v. Virginia Hospital Association

496 U.S. 498 (1990)

Brennan, J. This case requires us to determine whether a health care provider may bring an action under 42 U.S.C. § 1983 to challenge the method by which a State reimburses health care providers under the Medicaid Act. More specifically, the question presented is whether the Boren Amendment to the Act, which requires reimbursement according to rates that a "State finds, and makes assurances satisfactory to the Secretary, are reasonable and adequate to meet the costs which must be incurred by efficiently and economically operated facilities," is enforceable in an action pursuant to § 1983.

A

Medicaid is a cooperative federal-state program through which the Federal Government provides financial assistance to States so that they may furnish medical care to needy individuals. Although participation in the program is voluntary, participating States must comply with certain requirements imposed by the Medicaid Act (Act) and regulations promulgated by the Secretary of Health and Human Services (Secretary). To qualify for federal assistance, a State must submit to the Secretary and have approved "a plan for medical assistance," that contains a comprehensive statement describing the nature and scope of the State's Medicaid program. The state plan is required to establish, among other things, a scheme for reimbursing health care providers for the medical services provides to needy individuals.

Section 1902(a)(13) of the Act sets out the requirements for reimbursement of health care providers. As amended in 1980 (Boren Amendment), the section provides that

> "a" State plan for medical assistance must . . . . "provide . . . for payment . . . of hospital services, nursing facility services, and services in an intermediate care facility for the mentally retarded provided under the plan through the use of rates (determined in accordance with methods and standards developed by the State . . .) which the State funds, and makes assurances satisfactory to the Secretary, are reasonable and adequate to meet the costs which must be incurred by efficiently and economically operated facilities in order to provide care and services in conformity with applicable State and Federal laws, regulations, and quality and safety standards and to assure that individuals eligible for medical assistance have reasonable access . . . to inpatient hospital services of adequate quality." (emphasis added).

The Commonwealth of Virginia's State Plan for Medical Assistance was approved by the Secretary in 1982 and again in 1986 after an amendment was made. Under the Plan, health care providers are reimbursed for services according to a prospective formula—that is, reimbursement rates for various types of medical services and procedures are fixed in advance. Specially, providers are divided into "peer groups" based on their size and location and reimbursed according to a formula based on the median cost of medical care for that peer group.

In 1986, respondent Virginia Hospital Association (VHA), a nonprofit corporation composed of both public and private hospitals operating in Virginia, filed suit in the United States District Court for the Eastern District of Virginia against several state officials including the Governor, the Secretary of Human Resources, and the members of the State Department of Medical Assistance Services (the state agency that administers the Virginia Medicaid System). Respondent contends that Virginia's Plan for reimbursement violates the Medicaid Act because the "rates are not reasonable and adequate to meet the economically and efficiently incurred cost of providing care to Medicaid patients in hospitals and do not assure access to inpatient care." [Respondent argues that] "the per diem reimbursement rates . . . have not reasonably nor adequately met the costs incurred by efficiently and economically operated hospitals in providing care and services in conformity with applicable state and federal laws, regulations, and quality and safety standards").[3] Respondent seeks declaratory and injunctive relief including an order requiring petitioners to promulgate a new state Plan providing new rates and, in the interim, to reimburse Medicaid providers at rates commensurate with payments under the Medicare program.

Petitioners filed a motion to dismiss or in the alternative a motion for summary judgment on the ground that 42 U.S.C. § 1983 does not afford respondent a cause of action to challenge the Commonwealth's compliance

---

[3] Virginia's current formula for reimbursement rates takes the median cost of care for each peer group as computed for 1982 and adjusts the costs annually to account for inflation. The figures for the median cost of care in 1982 were calculated by determining the per diem median cost of care for Medicaid patient in the year 1981 and then adjusting for inflation through the use of the Consumer Price Index (CPI). Until 1986, to determine the annual reimbursement rates, the 1982 baseline figures were adjusted by the CPI. In 1986, however, the Plan was amended so that these baseline figures are adjusted by an inflation index that is tied to medical care costs.

Respondent argues that this method of calculating the payment rates is not tied to the costs incurred by an efficient and economical hospital. More specifically, respondent challenges: (1) the method of computing the baseline median costs for 1982; (2) the use of the CPI rather than an index tied to medical care costs to adjust the rates in the years 1982–1986; and (3) the way in which the medical care cost index was used after 1986. In addition, respondent contends that the appeals procedure established by the state Plan is inadequate under the Medicaid Act in part because it excludes challenges to the principles of reimbursement.

with the Medicaid Act. The District Court denied the motion. The Court of Appeals for the Fourth Circuit affirmed, concluding that health care providers may sue state officials for declaratory and injunctive relief under § 1983 to ensure compliance with the Medicaid Act. More specifically, the court held that the language and legislative history of the Boren Amendment demonstrate that it creates "enforceable rights" and that Congress did not intend to foreclose a private remedy for the enforcement of those rights. We granted certiorari.

B

In order to determine whether the Boren Amendment is enforceable under § 1983, it is useful first to consider the history of the reimbursement provision. When enacted in 1965, the Act required States to provide reimbursement for the "reasonable cost" of hospital services actually provided, measured according to standards adopted by the Secretary. Congress became concerned, however, that the Secretary wielded too much control over reimbursement rates. Congress therefore amended the Act in 1972 to give States more flexibility to develop methods and standards for reimbursement, but Congress retained the ultimate requirement that the rates reimburse the "reasonable cost" of the services provided. The new law required States to pay "the reasonable cost of inpatient hospital services . . . as determined in accordance with methods and standards which shall be developed by the State and reviewed and approved by the Secretary."

In response to rapidly rising Medicaid costs, Congress in 1981 extended the Boren Amendment to hospitals. Congress blamed mounting Medicaid costs on the complexity and rigidity of the Secretary's reimbursement regulations. Although the previous version of the Act in theory afforded States some degree of flexibility to adopt their own methods for determining reimbursement rates, Congress found that, in fact the regulations promulgated by the Secretary had essentially forced States to adopt Medicaid rates based on Medicare "reasonable cost" principles. Congress "recognized the inflationary nature of the [then] current cost reimbursement system and intended to give States greater latitude in developing and implementing alternative reimbursement methodologies that promote the efficient and economical delivery of such services." The Amendment "deleted the current provision requiring States to reimburse hospitals on a reasonable cost basis [and] substituted a provision requiring States to reimburse hospitals at rates . . . that are reasonable and adequate to meet the cost which must be incurred by efficiently and economically operated facilities in order to meet applicable laws and quality and safety standards." Thus, while Congress affirmed its desire that state reimbursement rates be "reasonable," it afforded States greater flexibility in calculating those "reasonable rates." For example, Congress explained that States would be free to establish statewide or classwide rates, establish rates based on a prospective cost,[7] or include incentive provisions to encourage efficient operation. Flexibility was ensured by limiting the oversight role of the Secretary. Thus, the Boren Amendment provides that a State must reimburse providers according to rates that it "finds, and makes assurances satisfactory to the Secretary," are "reasonable and adequate" to meet the costs of "efficiently and economically operated facilities." The State must also assure the Secretary that individuals have "reasonable access" to facilities of "adequate quality."

The Act does not define these terms, and the Secretary has declined to adopt a national definition, concluding that States should determine the factors to be considered in determining what rates are "reasonable and adequate" to meet the costs of "efficiently and economically operated facilities." The regulations require a State to make a finding at least annually that its rates are "reasonable and adequate," though the State is required to submit assurances to that effect to the Secretary only when it makes a change in its reimbursement rates. According to the Secretary, the Boren Amendment "places the re-

---

[7] Before the passage of the Boren Amendment, state plans provided for reimbursement on a retrospective basis; that is, health care providers were reimbursed according to the reasonable cost of the services actually provided. Since the passage of the Boren Amendment in 1981, however, most States have adopted plans that are prospective in nature, whereby providers are paid in advance and payments are calculated according to the State's formula for what such care should cost. The Virginia Plan is a typical prospective plan.

sponsibility for the development of reasonable and adequate payment rates with the States." Thus, he reviews only the reasonableness of the assurances provided by a State and not the State's findings themselves. The Secretary's review focuses "on the assurances which attest to the fact that States' findings do indeed indicate that the payment rates are reasonable" and judges "whether the assurances are satisfactory." Therefore the Secretary does not require States to submit the findings themselves or the underlying data.[8]

II

Section 1983 provides a cause of action for "the deprivation of any rights, privileges, or immunities secured by the Constitution and laws" of the United States. In *Maine v. Thiboutot*, 448 U.S. 1, 4 (1980), we held that § 1983 provides a cause of action for violations of federal statutes as well as the Constitution. We have recognized two exceptions to this rule. A plaintiff alleging a violation of a federal statute will be permitted to sue under § 1983 unless (1) "the statute [does] not create enforceable rights, privileges, or immunities within the meaning of § 1983," or (2) "Congress has foreclosed such enforcement of the statute in the enactment itself." *Wright v. Roanoke Redevelopment and Housing Authority*, 479 U.S. 418, 423 (1987). Petitioners argue first that the Boren Amendment does not create any "enforceable rights" and second, that Congress has foreclosed enforcement of the Act under § 1983. We address these contentions in turn.

A

"Section 1983 speaks in terms of 'rights, privileges, or immunities,' not violations of

---

[8] The state Medicaid agency must submit the following information with the assurances: (1) the amount of the estimated average proposed payment rate for each type of provider, (2) the amount by which the rate is increased or decreased in relation to the preceding year, and (3) an estimate of the short-term, and to the extent feasible, long-term, effect the new rate will have on the availability of services, the type of care furnished, the extent of provider participation, and the degree to which costs are covered in hospitals that serve a disproportionate number of low income patients. The Secretary may, however, request a State to provide additional background information if he believes it is necessary for a complete review of the State's assurances.

federal law." *Golden State Transit Corp. v. Los Angeles*, 493 U.S. 103, 106 (1989) (emphasis added). We must therefore determine whether the Boren Amendment creates a "federal right" that is enforceable under § 1983. Such an inquiry turns on whether "the provision in question was intended to benefit the putative plaintiff." If so, the provision creates an enforceable right unless it reflects merely a "congressional preference" for a certain kind of conduct rather than a binding obligation on the governmental unit, *Pennhurst State School and Hospital v. Halderman*, 451 U.S. 1, 19 (1981), or unless the interest the plaintiff asserts is "'too vague and amorphous'" such that is "'beyond the competence of the judiciary to enforce.'" Under this test, we conclude that the Medicaid Act creates a right enforceable by health care providers under § 1983 to the adoption of reimbursement rates that are reasonable and adequate to meet the costs of an efficiently and economically operated facility that provides care to Medicaid patients. The right is not merely a procedural one that rates be accompanied by findings and assurances (however perfunctory) of reasonableness and adequacy; rather the Act provides a substantive right to reasonable and adequate rates as well.

There can be little doubt that health care providers are the intended beneficiaries of the Boren Amendment. The provision establishes a system for reimbursement of providers and is phrased in terms benefiting health care providers: it requires a state plan to provide for "payment . . . of the hospital services, nursing facility services, and services in an intermediate care facility for the mentally retarded provided under the plan." The question in this case is whether the Boren Amendment imposes a "binding obligation" on the States that gives rise to enforceable rights.

In *Pennhurst*, supra, the Court held that § 6010 of the Developmentally Disabled Assistance and Bill of Rights Act of 1975 did not create rights enforceable under § 1983. That section, entitled "bill of rights," declares that Congress had made certain "findings respecting the rights of persons with developmental disabilities," namely that such persons have a right to "appropriate treatment" in the least restrictive environment and that federal and state governments have an obligation to ensure that institutions failing to provide "appropriate treatment" do not receive federal funds. The Court concluded that the context of the entire statute and its legislative history revealed that Congress intended neither to create new substantive rights nor to require State to recognize such rights; instead, Congress intended only to indicate a preference for "appropriate treatment." The Court examined the language of the provision and determined that a general statement of "findings" was "too thin a reed to support" a creation of rights and obligations. Moreover, since neither the statute nor the corresponding regulations made compliance with the provision a condition of receipt of federal funding, the Court reasoned that "the provisions of § 6010 were intended to be hortatory, not mandatory." The Court refused to infer congressional intent to condition federal funding on compliance because "Congress must express clearly its intent to impose conditions on the grant of federal funds so that the States can knowingly decide whether or not to accept those funds."

More recently, in *Wright*, supra, however, we found that the Brooke Amendment to the Housing Act of 1937, and its implementing regulations did create rights enforceable under § 1983. The Brooke Amendment limits the amount of rent a public housing tenant can be charged, and the regulations adopted pursuant to the statute require inclusion of a "reasonable" allowance for utilities in the rent. We reasoned that both the statute and the regulations were "mandatory limitations focusing on the individual family and its income." In addition, we rejected the argument that the provision for a reasonable utility allotment was too vague to create an enforceable right. Because the regulations set out guidelines for the housing authorities to follow in determining the utility allowance, the right was "sufficiently specific and definite to qualify as [an] enforceable right under Pennhurst and § 1983 [and was] not . . . beyond the competence of the judiciary to enforce."

In light of *Pennhurst* and *Wright*, we conclude that the Boren Amendment imposes a binding obligation on States participating in the Medicaid program to adopt reasonable and adequate rates and that this obligation is enforceable under § 1983 by health care providers. The Boren Amendment is cast in mandatory rather than precatory terms: the

state plan "must" "provide for payment . . . of hospitals" according to rates the State finds are reasonable and adequate. (emphasis added). Moreover, provision of federal funds is expressly conditioned on compliance with the Amendment and the Secretary is authorized to withhold funds for noncompliance with this provision. The Secretary has expressed his intention to withhold funds if the state plan does not comply with the statute or if there is "noncompliance in practice." . . . "The [Boren Amendment's] language succinctly sets forth a congressional command, which is wholly uncharacteristic of a mere suggestion or 'nudge.'"

Petitioners concede that the Boren Amendment requires a State to provide some level of reimbursement to health care providers and that a cause of action would lie under § 1983 if a State failed to adopt any reimbursement provision whatsoever. Petitioners also concede, as they must, that a State is required to find that its rates are reasonable and adequate and to make assurances to that effect to the Secretary. The dissent, although acknowledging that the State has these obligations, apparently would hold that the only right enforceable under § 1983 is the right to compel compliance with these bare procedural requirements. We think the Amendment cannot be so limited. Any argument that the requirements of findings and assurances are procedural requirements only and do not require the State to adopt rates that are actually reasonable and adequate is nothing more than an argument that the State's findings and assurances need not be correct.

We reject that argument because it would render the statutory requirements of findings and assurances, and thus the entire reimbursement provision, essentially meaningless. It would make little sense for Congress to require a State to make findings without requiring those findings to be correct. In addition, there would be no reason to require a State to submit assurances to the Secretary if the statute did not require the State's findings to be reviewable in some manner by the Secretary. We decline to adopt an interpretation of the Boren Amendment that would render it a dead letter.

Petitioners acknowledge that a State may not make, or submit assurances based on, a patently false finding, but insist that Congress left it to the Secretary, and not the federal courts, to ensure that the State's rates are not based on such false findings. To the extent that this argument bears on the question whether the Boren Amendment creates enforceable rights (as opposed to whether Congress intended to foreclose private enforcement of the statute pursuant to § 1983, see [Part B] infra . . ., it supports the conclusion that the provision does create enforceable rights. If the Secretary is entitled to reject a state plan upon concluding that a State's assurances of compliance are unsatisfactory, a State is on notice that it cannot adopt any rates it chooses and that the requirement that it make "findings" is not a mere formality. Rather, the only plausible interpretation of the Amendment is that by requiring a State to find that its rates are reasonable and adequate, the statute imposes the concomitant obligation to adopt reasonable and adequate rates.

Any doubt that Congress intended to require States to adopt rates that actually are reasonable and adequate is quickly dispelled by a review of the legislative history of the Boren Amendment. The primary objective of the Amendment was to free States from reimbursement according to Medicare "reasonable cost" principles as had been required by prior regulation. The Amendment "deleted the . . . provision requiring States to reimburse hospitals on a reasonable cost basis. It substituted a provision requiring States to reimburse hospitals at rates . . . that are reasonable and adequate to meet the cost which must be incurred by efficiently and economically operated facilities in order to meet applicable laws and quality and safety standards." In passing the Boren Amendment, Congress sought to decentralize the method for determining rates, but not to eliminate a State's fundamental obligation to pay reasonable rates. . . . In other words, while Congress gave States leeway in adopting a method of computing rates—they can choose between retrospective and prospective rate-setting methodologies, for example—Congress retained the underlying requirement of "reasonable and adequate" rates . . .

Moreover, it is clear that prior to the passage of the Boren Amendment, Congress intended that health care providers be able to sue in federal court for injunctive relief to ensure that they were reimbursed according to reasonable rates. During the 1970's, provider suits in the federal court were commonplace. In addition, in response to several States freezing their Medicaid payments to health care providers, Congress amended the Act in 1975 to require States to waive any Eleventh Amendment immunity from suit for violations of the Act. Congress believed the waiver necessary because the existing means of enforcement—noncompliance procedures instituted by the Secretary or suits for injunctive relief by health care providers—were insufficient to deal with the problem of outright noncompliance because they included no compensation for past underpayments. The amendment required the Secretary to withhold 10% of federal Medicaid funds from any State that had not executed a waiver of its immunity by March 31, 1976. The provision generated a great deal of opposition from the States and was repealed in the next session of Congress. But Congress explained that it did not intend the repeal to "be construed as in any way contravening or constraining the rights of the providers of Medicaid services, the State Medicaid agencies, or the Department to seek prospective, injunctive relief in a federal or state judicial forum. Neither should the repeal of [the waiver section] be interpreted as placing constraints on the rights of the parties involved to seek prospective, injunctive relief."

This experience demonstrates clearly that Congress and the States both understood the Act to grant health care providers enforceable rights both before and after repeal of the ill-fated waiver requirement. Given this background, it is implausible to conclude that by substituting the requirements of "findings" and "assurances," Congress intended to deprive health care providers of their right to challenge rates under § 1983. Instead, as the legislative history shows, the requirements of "findings" and "assurances" prescribe the respective roles of a State and the Secretary and do not, as petitioners suggest, eliminate a State's obligation to adopt reasonable rates.

Nevertheless, petitioners argue that because the Boren Amendment gives a State flexibility to adopt any rates it finds are reasonable and adequate, the obligation imposed by the Amendment is too "vague and amorphous" to be judicially enforceable. We reject this argument. As in Wright, the statute and regulation set out factors which a State must consider in adopting its rates. In addition, the statute requires the State, in making its findings, to judge the reasonableness of its rates against the objective benchmark of an "efficiently and economically operated facility" providing care in compliance with federal and state standards while at the same time ensuring "reasonable access" to eligible participants. That the Amendment gives the States substantial discretion in choosing among reasonable methods of calculating rates may affect the standard under which a court reviews whether the rates comply with the Amendment, but it does not render the Amendment unenforceable by a court. While there may be a range of reasonable rates, there certainly are some rates outside that range that no State could ever find to be reasonable and adequate under the Act. Although some knowledge of the hospital industry might be required to evaluate a State's findings with respect to the reasonableness of its rates, such an inquiry is well within the competence of the judiciary.

B

Petitioners also argue that Congress has foreclosed enforcement of the Medicaid Act under § 1983. We find little merit in this argument. "We do not lightly conclude that Congress intended to preclude reliance on § 1983 as a remedy' for the deprivation of a federally secured right." The burden is on the State to show "by express provision or other specific evidence from the statute itself that Congress intended to foreclose such private enforcement." Petitioners concede that the Medicaid Act does not expressly preclude resort to § 1983. In the absence of such an express provision, we have found private enforcement foreclosed only when the statute itself creates a remedial scheme that is "sufficiently comprehensive . . . to demonstrate congressional intent to preclude the remedy of suits under § 1983."

On only two occasions have we found a remedial scheme established by Congress sufficient to displace the remedy provided in § 1983. In *Sea Clammers*, supra, we held that the comprehensive enforcement scheme found in the Federal Water Pollution Control Act (FWPCA)—which granted the Environmental Protection Agency considerable enforcement power through the use of noncompliance orders, civil suits, and criminal penalties, and which included two citizen-suit provisions— evidenced a congressional intent to foreclose reliance on § 1983. Similarly in *Smith v. Robinson*, supra at 1010–1011, we held that the elaborate administrative scheme set forth in the Education of the Handicapped Act (EHA), manifested Congress' desire to foreclose private reliance on § 1983 as a remedy. The EHA contained a "carefully tailored administrative and judicial mechanism," that included local administrative review and culminated in a right to judicial review.

The Medicaid Act contains no comparable provision for private judicial or administrative enforcement. Instead, the Act authorizes the Secretary to withhold approval of plans, or to curtail federal funds to States whose plans are not in compliance with the Act. In addition, the Act requires States to adopt a procedure for postpayment claims review to "ensure the proper and efficient payment of claims and management of the program." By regulation, the States are required to adopt an appeals procedure by which individual providers may obtain administrative review of reimbursement rates. The Commonwealth of Virginia has adopted a three-tiered administrative scheme within the state Medicaid agency to comply with these regulations.

This administrative scheme cannot be considered sufficiently comprehensive to demonstrate a congressional intent to withdraw the private remedy of § 1983. In *Wright*, we concluded that the "generalized powers" of HUD to audit and cut off federal funds were insufficient to foreclose reliance on § 1983 to vindicate federal rights. We noted that HUD did not exercise its auditing power frequently, and the statute did not require, nor did HUD provide, any mechanism for individuals to bring problems to the attention of HUD. Such a conclusion is even more appropriate in the context of the Medicaid Act since as explained above, a primary purpose of the Boren Amendment was to reduce the role of the Secretary in determining methods for calculating payment rates. It follows that the Secretary's limited oversight is insufficient to demonstrate an intent to foreclose relief altogether in the courts under § 1983.

We also reject petitioners' argument that the existence of administrative procedures whereby health care providers can obtain review of individual claims for payment evidences an intent to foreclose a private remedy in the federal courts. The availability of state administrative procedures ordinarily does not foreclose resort to § 1983. See *Patsy v. Board of Regents of Florida*, 457 U.S. 496, 516 (1982). Nor do we find any indication that Congress specifically intended that this administrative procedure replace private remedies available under § 1983. The regulations allow States to limit the issues that may be raised in the administrative proceeding. Most States, including Virginia, do not allow health care providers to challenge the overall method by which rates are determined. Such limited state administrative procedures cannot be considered a "comprehensive" scheme that manifests a congressional intent to foreclose reliance on § 1983. See *Wright*, 479 U.S., at 429 (availability of grievance procedure did not prevent resort to § 1983). Thus, we conclude that Congress did not foreclose a private judicial remedy under § 1983.

III

The Boren Amendment to the Medicaid Act creates a right, enforceable in a private cause of action pursuant to § 1983, to have the State adopt rates that it finds are reasonable and adequate rates to meet the costs of an efficient and economical health care provider. The judgment of the Court of Appeals is accordingly Affirmed.

Chief Justice **Rehnquist**, with whom Justice **O'Connor**, Justice Scalia, and Justice **Kennedy** join, dissenting.

The relevant portion of the Boren Amendment requires States to reimburse Medicaid services providers using rates

> "(determined in accordance with methods and standards developed by the State . . .) which the State finds, and makes assurances satisfactory to the Secretary, are reasonable and adequate to meet the costs which must be incurred by efficiently and economically operated facilities. . . ."

The Court notes in its opinion that respondent seeks permanent relief under § 1983 in the form of court-ordered reimbursement at new rates. Respondent also seeks, as interim relief, reimbursement at rates commensurate

with payments under the Medicare program. And though respondent's prayer for relief is only one example of a good claim for relief under today's decision, every § 1983 action hereafter brought by providers to enforce [the Boren Amendment] will inevitably seek the substitution of a rate system preferred by the provider for the rate system chosen by the State. Thus, whenever a provider prevails in such an action, the defendant State will be enjoined to implement a system of rates other than the rates "determined in accordance with methods and standards developed by the State," which the "State finds . . . are reasonable and adequate," and with respect to which the State made assurances to the Secretary that the Secretary found "satisfactory." The court orders entered in such actions therefore will require the States to adopt reimbursement rate systems different from those Congress expressly required them to adopt by the above-quoted language.

The Court reasons that the policy underlying the Boren Amendment would be thwarted if judicial review under § 1983 were unavailable to challenge the reasonableness and adequacy of rates established by States for reimbursing Medicaid services providers. This sort of reasoning, however, has not hitherto been thought an adequate basis for deciding that Congress conferred an enforceable right on a party.

Before *Maine v. Thiboutot*, a plaintiff seeking to judicially enforce a provision in a federal statute was required to demonstrate that the statute contained an implied cause of action. Satisfaction of the now familiar standards was the means for making the requisite showing. The Court's general practice was "to imply a cause of action where the language of the statute explicitly conferred a right directly on a class of persons that included the plaintiff in the case." It was thus crucial to a demonstration of the existence of an implied action for the statute to contain a right "in favor of" the particular plaintiff. . . . The plaintiff then would have to satisfy three additional standards to establish that the statute contained an implied judicial remedy for vindicating that right. In *Maine v. Thiboutot*, the Court essentially removed the burden of making the latter three showings by holding that § 1983 generally (with an exception subsequently developed in Middlesex County Sewerage Authority v. National Sea Clammers Assn. supplies the remedy for vindication of rights arising from federal statutes.

But while the Court's holding in *Thiboutot* rendered obsolete some of the case law pertaining to implied rights of action, a significant area of overlap remained. For relief to be had either under § 1983 or by implication . . . the language used by Congress must confer identifiable enforceable rights. . . . In this regard, the Court in *Wright* said that a § 1983 action does not lie where Congress did not intend for the statutory provision "to rise to the level of an enforceable right."

In *Cannon [v. University of Chicago]* the Court said that "the right- or duty-creating language of the statute has generally been the most accurate indicator of the propriety of implication of a cause of action." This statement is suggestive of the traditional rule that the first step in our exposition of a statute always is to look to the statute's text and to stop there if the text fully reveals its meaning. . . . There is no apparent reason to deviate from this sound rule when the question is whether a federal statute confers substantive rights on a § 1983 plaintiff. Yet the Court virtually ignores the relevant text of the Medicaid statute in this case.

The Medicaid statute provides for appropriations of federal funds to States that submit, and have approved by the Secretary of Health and Human Services, "State plans for medical assistance." The next provision in the statute specifies requirements for the contents of State medical assistance plans. The provision in issue here is simply a part of the thirteenth listed requirement for such plans. In light of the placement of [the Boren Amendment] within the structure of the statute . . ., one most reasonably would conclude that [the Boren Amendment] is addressed to the States and merely establishes one of many conditions for receiving Federal Medicaid funds; the text does not clearly confer any substantive rights on Medicaid services providers. This structural evidence is buttressed by the absence in the statute of any express "focus" on providers as a beneficiary class of the provision. See *Wright*, supra, at 430 (finding a provision in the statute "focusing" on the plaintiff class dispositive evidence of Congress' intent in the Brooke Amendment to create rights in favor of the plaintiff class).

Even if one were to assume that the terms of [the Boren Amendment] confer a substantive right on providers in the nature of a guarantee of "reasonable and adequate" rates, the statute places its own limitation on that right in very plain language. [The Boren Amendment] establishes a procedure for establishing such rates of reimbursement. The first step requires the States to make certain findings. The second and only other step requires the States to make certain assurances to the Secretary and the Secretary—not the courts—to review those assurances. Under the logic of our case law, respondent arguably may bring a § 1983 action to require that rates be set according to that process. Indeed, establishment of rates in accordance with that process is the only discernible right accruing to anyone under [the Boren Amendment]. But as this case illustrates, Medicaid providers bring § 1983 actions to avoid the process rather than to seek its implementation. The Court approves such challenges despite the fact that a plaintiff's success in such a suit results in the displacement of rates created in accordance with the statutory process by rates established pursuant to court order. To support its decision, the Court looks beyond the unambiguous terms of the statute and relies on policy considerations purportedly derived from legislative history and superseded versions of the statute.

The Court concludes that the contrary position equates with the proposition that the States are not obligated to adopt reasonable rates. Indeed, the theme of much of the Court's argument is that without judicial enforceability, the States cannot be trusted to implement [the Boren Amendment]'s command of creating rate systems that are reasonable and adequate. The Court states at one point that "it would make little sense for Congress to require a State to make findings without requiring those findings to be correct. . . . We decline to adopt an interpretation of the Boren Amendment that would render it a dead letter."

The interpretation to which the Court refers, however, would scarcely render the Boren Amendment a "dead letter." It is, instead, the Court's own reading that nullifies the "letter" of the Amendment. Apart from its displacement of the statutory rate setting process noted previously, the Court's suggestion that the States would deliberately disregard the requirements of the statute ignores the Secretary's oversight incorporated into the statute and does less than justice to the States. The Court itself recognizes that the basic purpose of the Boren Amendment was to allow the States more latitude in establishing Medicaid reimbursement rates. In light of that fact, the Court's interpretation takes far more liberties with the statutory language than does the position advanced by petitioners. I would reverse the judgment of the Court of Appeals.

NOTES

1. A litigant may wish to proceed under the section 1983 cause of action for any number of reasons. One is that successful plaintiffs may recover attorney's fees in successful section 1983 cases, see Chapter 12. In addition, the statute creating the substantive law on which the plaintiff relies may authorize remedies that the plaintiff finds inadequate. For example, it may make no provision for recovery of damages.

Some federal statutes do not specifically authorize any suits by private individuals. A plaintiff must then either ask the court to "imply" a cause of action from the statute, or else rely on section 1983. Before 1975 the Court freely implied causes of action, but then, in *Cort v. Ash*, 422 U.S. 66 (1975), the Court began to tighten the rules considerably, requiring litigants seeking to imply a statutory cause of action to show that Congress intended to create one. This test is typically met only when the statute was itself enacted during the pre-*Cort* years and the legislative history shows that Congress did not bother to insert a cause-of-action provision, simply because it knew the Court would imply one. See, e.g., *Touche Ross & Co. v. Redington*, 442 U.S. 560 (1979); *Merrill Lynch, Pierce, Fenner & Smith v. Curran*, 456 U.S. 353 (1982).

In a footnote to *Wilder* the Court distinguished the issue presented when a plaintiff seeks to sue under section 1983 from the implied-cause-of-action issue. It said:

This is a different inquiry than that involved in determining whether a private right of action can be implied from a particular statute. See *Cort v. Ash*, 422

U.S. 66 (1975). In implied right of action cases, we employ the four-factor *Cort* test to determine "whether Congress intended to create the private remedy asserted for the violation of statutory rights." This test reflects a concern, grounded in separation of powers, that Congress rather than the courts controls the availability of remedies for violations of statutes. Because section 1983 provides an "alternative source of express congressional authorization of private suits," these separation of powers concerns are not present in a section 1983 case. Consistent with this view, we recognize an exception to the general rule that section 1983 provides a remedy for violation of federal statutory rights only when Congress has affirmatively withdrawn the remedy.

In view of the legislative history and political background of section 1983, discussed in Chapter 1, does the existence of this statute simply do away with separation of powers concerns? If Congress meant for persons suing under the Medicaid statute to have the opportunity to recover attorney's fees, then wouldn't it have explicitly extended to such cases the coverage of the Civil Rights Attorney's Fees Awards Act?

2. *Maine v. Thiboutot*, 448 U.S. 1 (1980), is the first major case on the scope of "laws" within the domain of section 1983. The issue was whether suits to enforce provisions of the Social Security Act could be brought under section 1983. Justice Brennan's opinion for the Court adopted a "plain meaning" approach to interpreting the statute. "The question before us is whether the phrase 'and laws,' as used in section 1983, means what it says, or whether it should be limited to some subset of laws. Given that Congress attached no modifiers to the phrase, the plain language of the statute undoubtedly embraces respondents' claim that petitioners violated the Social Security Act." Does the Court always follow the "plain meaning" approach to interpreting section 1983? If not, why does it shift from one interpretive theory to another as it moves from case to case?

3. After *Thiboutot*, in *Middlesex County Sewerage Authority v. National Sea Clammers Assn*, 453 U.S. 1 (1981), the Court restricted the availability of section 1983 for enforcement of federal statutes in two ways. Section 1983 would not be available if (a) "Congress had foreclosed private enforcement" of the statute on which the plaintiff sought to base the substance of the lawsuit, or if (b) "the statute at issue was [not] the kind that created enforceable 'rights' under section 1983." After *Middlesex* lower courts often found it inappropriate to allow a section 1983 suit to enforce federal statutes. See Brown, *Whither Thiboutot?: Section 1983, Private Enforcement, and the Damages Dilemma*, 33 DePaul L. Rev. 31, 46–53 (1983).

4. Later Supreme Court cases, however, have read these two limits rather narrowly. For example, in *Wright v. Roanoke Redevelopment and Housing Authority*, 479 U.S. 418 (1987) the Court addressed the first exception. It allowed low-income housing tenants to sue under section 1983 to enforce federal housing laws that specified how the local housing authority should calculate their rent, even though federal housing laws authorized the Department of Housing and Urban Development to enforce the benefits due tenants. The Court said this was not enough to foreclose private suits: "Not only are the Brooke Amendment and its legislative history devoid of any express indication that exclusive enforcement authority was vested in HUD, but there have also been both congressional and agency actions indicating that enforcement authority is not centralized and that private actions were anticipated. Neither, in our view, are the remedial mechanisms provided sufficiently comprehensive and effective to raise a clear inference that Congress intended to foreclose a section 1983 cause of action for the enforcement of tenants' rights secured by federal law." 479 U.S. at 424–25. See also *Marshall v. Switzer*, 10 F.3d 925, 930 (2d Cir. 1993) (under *Wright*, federal agency oversight and review of state vocational rehabilitation plans do not preclude section 1983 suit to enforce rights under the Rehabilitation Act of 1973).

Courts do sometimes continue to hold that Congressionally provided remedies foreclose the section 1983 action. See, e.g., *Grady v. El Paso Community College*, 979 F.2d 1111 (5th Cir. 1992) (Veterans Reemployment Rights Act); cf. *Williams v. School District of Bethlehem*, 998 F.2d 168, 176 (3rd Cir. 1993) (Title IX, which prohibits sex discrimination in education-

al programs, subsumes constitutional claims, so that a section 1983 suit is inappropriate). Is *Williams* consistent with the principle of *Monroe v. Pape*, discussed in Chapter 1?

5. *Wilder* addressed the second exception. The issue dividing the Justices was the proper characterization of a statutory provision that requires reimbursement according to rates that a "State finds, and makes assurances satisfactory to the Secretary, are reasonable and adequate to meet the costs which must be incurred by efficiently and economically operated facilities." The issue was whether this created "enforceable rights". Does the holding suggest that the Court will approach this inquiry with a presumption in favor of locating "enforceable rights" in the statute?

Before answering that question, consider the following case.

Suter v. Artist M.

112 S. Ct. 1360 (1992).

Rehnquist, C.J. [The Adoption Assistance and Child Welfare Act of 1980 reimburses states for some expenses of administering foster care and adoption services, provided they satisfy the requirements of the act. In order to receive funds, states must submit a plan for approval by the Secretary. The plan must provide "that the plan shall be in effect in all political subdivisions of the State, and, if administered by them, be mandatory upon them; [and that] in each case, reasonable efforts will be made (A) prior to the placement of a child in foster care, to prevent or eliminate the need for removal of the child from his home, and (B) to make it possible for the child to return to his home . . ." 42 U.S.C. section 671 (a)(3), (15). The statute does not authorize a private cause of action to enforce these provisions. These plaintiffs sought to sue under section 1983, alleging that state welfare officials "failed to make reasonable efforts to prevent removal of children from their homes and to facilitate reunification of families where removal had occurred. [According to the plaintiffs] this failure occurred . . . because [state officials] failed promptly to assign caseworkers to children placed in [their] custody and promptly to reassign cases when caseworkers were on leave . . ." The Court held that this statute created no "enforceable rights".]

As recognized by petitioners, respondents, and the courts below, the Act is mandatory in its terms. However, . . . we must examine exactly what is required of States by the Act. Here, the terms of § 671(a) are clear; "In order for a State to be eligible for payments under this part, it shall have a plan approved by the Secretary." Therefore the Act does place a requirement on the States, but that requirement only goes so far as to ensure that the State have a plan approved by the Secretary which contains the 16 listed features.

Respondents do not dispute that Illinois in fact has a plan approved by the Secretary which provides that reasonable efforts at prevention and reunification will be made. Respondents argue, however, that § 1983 allows them to sue in federal court to obtain enforcement of this particular provision of the state plan. This argument is based, at least in part, on the assertion that 42 U.S.C. § 671(a)(3) requires that the State has a plan which is "in effect." This section states that the state plan shall "provide that the plan shall be in effect in all political subdivisions of the State, and, if administered by them, be mandatory upon them." But we think that "in effect" is directed to the requirement that the plan apply to all political subdivisions of the State, and is not intended to otherwise modify the word "plan."

In *Wilder*, the underlying Medicaid legislation similarly required participating States to submit to the Secretary of Health and Human Services a plan for medical assistance describing the State's Medicaid program. But in that case we held that the Boren Amendment actually required the States to adopt reasonable and adequate rates, and that this obligation was enforceable by the providers. We relied in part on the fact that the statute and regulations set forth in some detail the factors to be considered in determining the methods for calculating rates.

In the present case, however, the term "reasonable efforts" to maintain an abused or neglected child in his home, or return the child to his home from foster care, appears in quite a different context. No further statutory guidance is found as to how "reasonable efforts"

are to be measured. This directive is not the only one which Congress has given to the States, and it is a directive whose meaning will obviously vary with the circumstances of each individual case. How the State was to comply with this directive, and with the other provisions of the Act, was, within broad limits, left up to the State.

Other sections of the Act provide enforcement mechanisms for the reasonable efforts clause of 42 U.S.C. § 671(a)(15). The Secretary has the authority to reduce or eliminate payments to a State on finding that the State's plan no longer complies with § 671(a) or that "there is a substantial failure" in the administration of a plan such that the State is not complying with its own plan. § 671(b). The Act also requires that in order to secure federal reimbursement for foster care payments made with respect to a child involuntarily removed from his home the removal must be "the result of a judicial determination to the effect that continuation [in the child's home] would be contrary to the welfare of such child and (effective October 1, 1983) that reasonable efforts of the type described in section 671(a)(15) of this title have been made." § 672(a)(1). While these statutory provisions may not provide a comprehensive enforcement mechanism so as to manifest Congress' intent to foreclose remedies under § 1983, they do show that the absence of a remedy to private plaintiffs under § 1983 does not make the reasonable efforts clause a dead letter.[12]

The regulations promulgated by the Secretary to enforce the Adoption Act do not evidence a view that § 671(a) places any requirement for state receipt of federal funds other than the requirement that the State submit a plan to be approved by the Secre-

----

[12] The language of other sections of the Act also shows that Congress knew how to impose precise requirements on the States aside from the submission of a plan to be approved by the Secretary when it intended to. For example, 42 U.S.C. § 672(e) provides that "no Federal payment may be made under this part" for a child voluntarily placed in foster care for more than 180 days unless within that period there is a judicial determination that the placement is in the best interest of the child. That the "reasonable efforts" clause is not similarly worded buttresses a conclusion that Congress had a different intent with respect to it.

tary.[13] The regulations provide that to meet the requirements of § 671(a)(15) the case plan for each child must "include a description of the services offered and the services provided to prevent removal of the child from the home and to reunify the family." Another regulation, entitled "requirements and submittal", provides that a state plan must specify "which preplacement preventive and reunification services are available to children and families in need." 1357.15(e)(1). What is significant is that the regulations are not specific, and do not provide notice to the States that failure to do anything other than submit a plan with the requisite features, to be approved by the Secretary, is a further condition on the receipt of funds from the Federal Government. Respondents contend that "neither [petitioners] nor amici supporting them present any legislative history to refute the evidence that Congress intended 42 U.S.C. § 671(a)(15) to be enforceable." To the extent such history may be relevant, our examination of it leads us to conclude that Congress was concerned that the required reasonable efforts be made by the States, but also indicated that the Act left a great deal of discretion to them.

Careful examination of the language relied upon by respondents, in the context of the entire Act, leads us to conclude that the "reasonable efforts" language does not unambiguously confer an enforceable right upon the Act's beneficiaries. The term "reasonable efforts" in this context is at least as plausibly read to impose only a rather generalized duty on the State, to be enforced not by private individuals, but by the Secretary in the manner previously discussed . . ."

The judgment of the Court of Appeals is therefore

Reversed.

[Justice **Blackmun**, joined by Justice **Stevens**, dissented. He thought the holding] plainly inconsistent with . . . *Wilder*, in which we found enforceable under § 1983 a functionally identical provision of the Medicaid Act requiring 'reasonable' reimbursements to health care providers. More troubling still, the Court reaches its conclusion without even stating, much less applying, the principles our precedents have used to determine whether a statute has created a right enforceable under § 1983 . . .

In determining the scope of the first exception [to the *Thiboutot* rule]—whether a federal statute creates an "enforceable right"—the Court has developed and repeatedly applied a three-part test. We have asked (1) whether the statutory provision at issue "was intended to benefit the putative plaintiff." If so, then the provision creates an enforceable right unless (2) the provision "reflects merely a 'congressional preference' for a certain kind of conduct rather than a binding obligation on the governmental unit," or unless (3) the plaintiff's interest is so "vague and amorphous" as to be "beyond the competence of the judiciary to enforce." . . . The Court today has little difficulty concluding that the plaintiff children in this case have no enforceable rights, because it does not mention—much less apply—this firmly established analytic framework . . .

[P]etitioners] . . . argue that the "reasonable efforts" clause of the Adoption Act is too "vague and amorphous" to be judicially enforced. Aware that *Wilder* enforced an apparently similar "reasonableness" clause, they argue that this clause is categorically different.

According to petitioners, the Court would not have found the Boren Amendment's reasonableness clause enforceable had the statute not provided an "objective benchmark" against which "reasonable and adequate" reimbursement rates could be measured. Reasonable and adequate rates, the Boren Amendment provides, are those that meet the costs that would be incurred by "an 'efficiently and economically operated facility' providing care in compliance with federal and state standards while at the same time ensuring 'reasonable access' to eligible participants." Petitioners claim that, given this benchmark, "reasonable and adequate" rates can be ascertained by "monetary calculations easily determined based on prevailing rates in the market." By contrast, they observe, there is "no market for 'reasonable efforts' to keep or return a child

---

[13] Compare Wright v. Roanoke Redevelopment and Housing Authority (statute providing that tenants in low-income housing could only be charged 30% of their income as rent, in conjunction with regulations providing that "reasonable utilities" costs were included in the rental figure, created right under § 1983 to not be charged more than a "reasonable" amount for utilities).

home, and such 'reasonable efforts' cannot be calculated or quantified.

Petitioners misunderstand the sense in which the "benchmark" in Wilder is "objective." The Boren Amendment does not simply define "reasonable and adequate" rates as market rates. Rather, it defines a "reasonable and adequate" rate by referring to what would be provided by a hypothetical facility—one that operates "efficiently and economically," "complies with federal and state standards," and "ensures 'reasonable access' to eligible participants." Whether particular existing facilities meet those criteria is not a purely empirical judgment that requires only simple "monetary calculations." Indeed, the Boren Amendment's specification of the words "reasonable and adequate" ultimately refers us to a second reasonableness clause: The "benchmark" facility, we are told, is one that "ensures 'reasonable access' to eligible participants." This second reasonableness clause is left undefined. Contrary to petitioners' suggestions, then, the "reasonable and adequate" rates provision of the Boren Amendment is not "objective" in the sense of being mechanically measurable. The fact that this Court found the provision judicially enforceable demonstrates that an asserted right is not "vague and amorphous" simply because it cannot be easily "calculated or quantified."

Petitioners also argue that the right to "reasonable efforts" is "vague and amorphous" because of substantial disagreement in the child-welfare community concerning appropriate strategies. Furthermore, they contend, because the choice of a particular strategy in a particular case necessarily will depend upon the facts of that case, a court-enforced right to reasonable efforts either will homogenize very different situations or else will fragment into a plurality of "rights" that vary from State to State. For both of these reasons, petitioners contend, Congress left the question of what efforts are "reasonable" to state juvenile courts, the recognized experts in such matters.

Here again, comparison with Wilder is instructive. The Court noted the lack of consensus concerning which of various possible methods of calculating reimbursable costs would best promote efficient operation of health care facilities. The Court further noted that Congress chose a standard that leaves the States considerable autonomy in selecting the methods they will use to determine which reimbursement rates are "reasonable and adequate." The result, of course, is that the "content" of the federal right to reasonable and adequate rates—the method of calculating reimbursement and the chosen rate—varies from State to State. And although federal judges are hardly expert either in selecting methods of Medicaid cost reimbursement or in determining whether particular rates are "reasonable and adequate," neither the majority nor the dissent found that the right to reasonable and adequate reimbursement was so vague and amorphous as to be "beyond the competence of the judiciary to enforce." State flexibility in determining what is "reasonable," we held,

> may affect the standard under which a court reviews whether the rates comply with the amendment, but it does not render the amendment unenforceable by a court. While there may be a range of reasonable rates, there certainly are some rates outside that range that no State could ever find to be reasonable and adequate under the Act.'

The same principles apply here. There may be a "range" of "efforts" to prevent unnecessary removals or secure beneficial reunifications that are "reasonable." Id., at 520. It may also be that a court, in reviewing a State's strategies of compliance with the "reasonable efforts" clause, would owe substantial deference to the State's choice of strategies. That does not mean, however, that no State's efforts could ever be deemed "unreasonable." As in Wilder, the asserted right in this case is simply not inherently "beyond the competence of the judiciary to enforce." . . .

The Court, without acknowledgement, has departed from our precedents in yet another way. In our prior cases, the existence of other enforcement mechanisms has been relevant not to the question whether the statute at issue creates an enforceable right, but to whether the second exception to § 1983 enforcement applies—whether, that is, "'Congress has foreclosed enforcement of the statute in the enactment itself.'" In determining whether this second exception to § 1983 enforcement applies, we have required the defendant not merely to point to the existence of alternative means of enforcement, but to demonstrate "by express provision or other specific evidence from the statute itself that Congress intended to foreclose [§ 1983] enforcement." We have said repeatedly that we will not "lightly" conclude that Congress has so intended. In only two instances, where we concluded that "the statute itself provides a comprehensive remedial scheme which leaves no room for additional private remedies under § 1983," have we held that Congress has intended to foreclose § 1983 enforcement . . .

The Court does not find these demanding criteria satisfied here. Instead, it simply circumvents them altogether: The Court holds that even if the funding cutoff provision in the Adoption Act is not an "express provision" that "provides a comprehensive remedial scheme" leaving "no room for additional private remedies under § 1983," that provision nevertheless precludes § 1983 enforcement. In so holding, the Court has inverted the established presumption that a private remedy is available under § 1983 unless "Congress has affirmatively withdrawn the remedy."

NOTES

1. Does *Suter* implicitly overrule *Wilder?* In *Stowell v. Ives*, 976 F.2d 65 (1st Cir. 1992) the first circuit commented that in *Suter* "the old regime fell on hard times." 976 F.2d at 68. Yet the court chose to read *Suter* as modifying rather than abandoning *Wilder*. "In *Suter* the Court held that an intended recipient of programmatic benefits could not sue under section 1983 if the federal statute merely required that the state submit a plan to a federal agency satisfying certain criteria, because such a 'requirement only goes so far as to ensure that the State have a plan approved by the Secretary which contains [the listed criteria.]' Thus, *Suter* instructs that, when a provision in a statute fails to impose a direct obligation on the States, instead placing the onus of compliance with the statute's substantive provisions on the federal government, no cause of action under section 1983 can flourish." Id. at 70. In *Albiston v. Maine Commissioner of Human Services*, 7 F.3d 258, 263 (1st Cir. 1993), the court elaborated on this language: "Since *Suter*, section 1983 cognizability in the ambiguous context of

shared state-federal obligations contemplates that the alleged breach of statutory rights shall have resulted from some impermissible '*state action*,' rather than from a mere default in the performance of a federally-retained obligation." Id. at 263.

In *Resident Council of Allen Parkway Village v. HUD*, 980 F.2d 1043 (5th Cir. 1993), the court relied on *Stowell* in denying a section 1983 cause of action to residents of a public housing project seeking to enjoin the Housing Authority of the City of Houston from demolishing the project. They relied upon a federal statute, the Frost-Leland Amendment, that directed the federal Department of Housing and Urban Development not to demolish the project. "Although stated in mandatory terms, the Frost-Leland Amendment is an appropriations rider directed solely to HUD, a federal agency. In our view, Congress, by directing its command to HUD, expressed its intent that HUD—not private individuals such as the residents of [the project]—should enforce the prohibition against using federal funds to demolish the specified public housing projects. Indeed, it is difficult to believe that Congress would impose a binding obligation on the states in an amendment to a bill appropriating funds to a federal agency." Id. at 1052.

2. The issue in *Procopio v. Johnson*, 994 F.2d 325 (7th Cir. 1993), was whether section 1983 could be used by foster parents to enforce a section 675(5)(C) of the AACWA that assures each foster child under state supervision a hearing as to his disposition within eighteen months of the original placement. "The plaintiffs contend that section 675(5)(C) is distinguishable from the provision considered in *Artist M.* and *does* create a federal right enforceable under section 1983. . ." The court disagreed. After setting out the *Wilder* factors, and endorsing *Stowell*'s view that *Wilder* survives *Suter*, the court found that the language of the provision for hearings, with its emphasis on "assur[ing] each child in foster care . . . of a dispositional hearing", 42 U.S.C. § 675(5)(C), "indicates a clear intent to benefit the children," not foster parents. In addition, "*Artist M.* seemed to hold that the AACWA provision *does not* create such enforceable rights in part because the requirement it imposes on the states 'only goes so far as to ensure that the State have a plan approved by the Secretary

which contains the listed . . . features.'" Id. at 330–31 (quoting *Suter*) (emphasis in original).

Compare *Howe v. Ellenbecker*, 8 F.3d 1258 (8th Cir. 1993). Here the statute at issue was a provision of the Social Security Act that regulates child support enforcement by the states. This statute creates enforceable rights against state officers because it places several specific obligations on state agencies. Among other things, they must provide for programs to establish paternity, notify a family of the amount of child support collected on its behalf, make their services available to non-AFDC families, "give the first fifty dollars collected from each absent parent to the family without a corresponding reduction in their monthly AFDC payment", "attempt to locate absent parents, . . . periodically review and adjust child support orders. . . and enforce support obligations for the children. . .The mandates of Title IV-D are particular and specific enough to impose binding obligations on South Dakota, and accordingly, create substantive enforceable rights in the class." 8 F.3d at 1262–63.

3. Suppose federal law preempts state regulation of some area. May the preemption create "enforceable rights"? The Court in *Golden State Transit Corp. v. City of Los Angeles*, 493 U.S. 103 (1989) held that it could. At an earlier stage of the litigation the Court had decided that the city violated federal labor law by requiring Golden State to settle a labor dispute with its union as a condition of renewing Golden State's taxicab license. On remand Golden State sought both injunctive relief and damages, relying on section 1983 for its cause of action to recover damages. The district court enjoined the city but refused to allow the section 1983 suit for damages, on the ground that "the supremacy clause does not create enforceable rights that may be vindicated in an action for damages under Section 1983." The Supreme Court agreed that the supremacy clause "of its own force, does not create rights enforceable under section 1983." 493 U.S. at 107. Here, however, Golden State "was the intended beneficiary of a statutory scheme that prevents governmental interference with the collective-bargaining process and . . . the NLRA gives it rights enforceable against governmental interference in an action under section 1983." 493 U.S. at 109. The Court continued:

In the NLRA, Congress has not just "occupied the field" with legislation that is passed solely with the interests of the general public in mind. In such circumstances, when congressional pre-emption benefits particular parties only as an incident of the federal scheme of regulation, a private damages remedy under section 1983 may not be available. The NLRA, however, creates rights in labor and management both against one another and against the State. By its terms, the Act confers certain rights "generally on employees and not merely as against the employer." We have thus stated that "[i]f the state law regulates conduct that is actually protected by federal law, . . . preemption follows . . . as a matter of substantive right . . ."

The Court went on to explain that the city had violated Golden State's substantive right "to make use of 'economic weapons, not explicitly set forth in the Act, free of governmental interference." 493 U.S. at 111.

4. In *Livadas v. Bradshaw*, 114 S. Ct. 2068 (1994) a unanimous Court followed *Golden State* in holding that a federal preemption claim may be raised in a section 1983 suit. As in *Golden State*, the plaintiff relied upon the National Labor Relations Act. The Court said:

Having determined that the Commissioner's policy is in fact pre-empted by federal law, we find strong support in our precedents for the position taken by both courts below that Livadas is entitled to seek relief under 42 U.S.C. § 1983 for the Commissioner's abridgment of her NLRA rights. . . We have, it is true, recognized that even the broad statutory text [of section 1983] does not authorize a suit for every alleged violation of federal law. A particular statutory provision, for example, may be so manifestly precatory that it could not fairly be read to impose a "binding obligation[]" on a governmental unit, or its terms may be so "vague and amorphous" that determining whether a "deprivation" might have occurred would strain judicial competence. And Congress itself might make it clear that violation of a statute will not give rise to liability under § 1983, either by express words or by providing a comprehensive alternative enforcement scheme. But apart from these exceptional cases, § 1983 remains a generally and presumptively available remedy for claimed violations of federal law. . .

Our conclusion that Livadas is entitled to seek redress under § 1983 is, if not controlled outright, at least heavily foreshadowed by our decision in Golden State II. . .

The right Livadas asserts, to complete the collective-bargaining process and agree to an arbitration clause, is, if not provided in so many words in the NLRA, at least as imminent in its structure as the right of the cab company in Golden State II. And the obligation to respect it on the part of the Commissioner and others acting under color of law is no more "vague and amorphous" than the obligation in Golden State. Congress, of course, has given no more indication of any intent to foreclose actions like Livadas's than the sort brought by the cab company. Finding no cause for special caution here, we hold that Livadas's claim is properly brought under § 1983. . .''

Is the Court's summary of the principles governing access to section 1983 to enforce federal law compatible with its decision in *Sutor*?

5. Justice Kennedy dissented in *Golden State*. He said:

The Court should not interpret section 1983 to give a cause of action for damages when the only wrong committed by the State or its local entities is misapprehending the precise location of the boundaries between state and federal power. The dispute over the taxicab franchise involves no greater transgression than this . . . Although the NLRA does not provide in any detailed way how a city should act when renewing an operating franchise, the statute does have a preemptive effect under the Supremacy Clause . . . [A]lthough the NLRB affords the States the power to regulate activities within its peripheral concern, the States have no such power or authority to influence the substantive terms of collective bargaining agreements. [At the earlier stage of this litigation] we held that the city has no power to interfere with the

NLRA by conditioning Golden State's franchise renewal upon settlement of a labor dispute.

The city's lack of power gives rise to a correlative legal interest in Golden State that we did not discuss in Golden State I. The majority has chosen to call the interest a right. I would prefer to follow the familiar Hohfeldian terminology and say that Golden State has an immunity from the city's interference with the NLRA. This terminology best reflects Congress' intent to create [a] free zone of bargaining
. . .

Section 1983 uses the word 'secure' to mean 'protect' or 'make certain,' in the sense of securing to 'any person, any individual rights'. The section thus distinguishes secured rights, privileges, and immunities from those interests merely resulting from the allocation of power between the State and Federal Governments . . .

Pre-emption concerns the federal structure of the Nation rather than the securing of rights, privileges, and immunities to individuals . . . Golden state does not and cannot contend that a federal statute protects it from the city's primary conduct apart from its governmental character . . . [The pre-emption at issue here] rests upon the allocation of power rather than upon individual rights, privileges, or immunities. The dispute between Golden State and the city exists because the Federal Government has exercised its power under the Commerce Clause to regulate Golden State's labor relations under the NLRA and thus has deprived the city of the power to effect its own regulations of these relations . . .

Why did Justice Kennedy go along with *Livadas*? Has he thrown in the towel on this issue, or is *Livadas* an easier case for access to section 1983?

6. In *Livadas*, the Court reiterated an important distinction it had made in *Golden State*: "[N]ot every instance of federal pre-emption gives rise to a § 1983 cause of action[.] [T]o decide the availability of § 1983 relief a court must look to the nature of the federal law accorded pre-emptive effect and the character of the interest claimed under it." In a footnote, the court explained: "Thus, *Golden State II* observed that an NLRA pre-emption claim grounded in the need to vindicate the primary jurisdiction of the NLRB, . . . is 'fundamentally different' from one stemming from state abridgement of a protected individual interest, a difference that might prove relevant to cognizability under § 1983." 114 S. Ct. at 2083 and n. 27.

7. The foregoing materials demonstrate that, at least so far, the question of whether persons may use section 1983 as a vehicle for enforcing federal statutes is adjudicated on an ad hoc, highly contextual basis, in which the features of the particular statute at issue dominate the analysis. The disparate results in *Wilder* and *Suter* suggest that subtle differences between two statutes can be determinative. For a defense and elaboration of this approach, see Sunstein, *Section 1983 and the Private Enforcement of Federal Law*, 49 U. Chi. L. Rev. 394 (1982).

Is there any strong objection to contextual analysis of these issues? The alternative is to devise per se rules, such as a rule that section 1983 will (or will not) be available unless Congress explicitly states otherwise. Would such a rule not simplify litigation and avoid doctrinal complexity, like the rule announced in *Graham v. Connor*, supra? Why should the courts occupy themselves with issues that Congress could, by careful drafting, put to rest without litigation?

Besides efficiency in litigation, another advantage of rules over case-by-case adjudication is that under a regime of rules persons are better able to know what is required of them before they act and can rely on a stable body of law in arranging their affairs. How important are stability and predictability in this area? Would any strong social policy be served by per se rules one way or the other, in an area where the issue is not the substantive law governing official behavior but the remedies available for state officials' violations of federal law? Are there good reasons for preferring rule-based adjudication in the circumstances of *Graham v. Connor*, and yet resorting to case-by-case application of standards in determining when section 1983 may be used to enforce federal statutes?

CHAPTER FIVE

"Every Person": Governmental Liability

The preceding chapters deal generally with the elements of every section 1983 prima facie case. This chapter focuses in particular on the important subject of section 1983 governmental liability which requires that the plaintiff allege and prove even more elements in order to make out a prima facie case. Supervisory liability and ethical considerations are also addressed. Specifically, this chapter is organized around the following questions: (1) what governmental bodies are "persons" suable under section 1983? (2) why sue a governmental body under section 1983? (3) how does one sue a governmental body? (4) what are the various theories of governmental liability under section 1983?

The purpose of this chapter is to teach you about the requirements of section 1983 governmental liability at both the theoretical and practical levels so that you understand and are comfortable with this kind of litigation.

I. What Governmental Bodies Are Persons?

The short answer to the question of what governmental bodies are suable persons under section 1983 is that after *Monell v. Department of Social Services*, 436 U.S. 658 (1978), set out later, *all* local governmental bodies, whether general or special purpose, are. In contrast, *state* governmental bodies are not. However, the long answer is considerably more complex.

A. The Prior Law Under *Monroe*

Before the Supreme Court decided *Monell* in 1978, the rule was that governmental bodies were not "persons" within the meaning of section 1983. This rule derived from the Court's decision in *Monroe v. Pape*, 365 U.S. 167 (1961), discussed earlier in Chapter 1, which held that the City of Chicago could not be sued under section 1983. The plaintiff there sued individual police officers as well as the City of Chicago under a respondeat superior theory. Writing for the Court, Justice Douglas purported to rely solely on particular legislative debates for its conclusion that "we are of the opinion that Congress did not undertake to bring municipal corporations within the ambit of [section 1983]." *Id* at 187.

In *Monroe*, the plaintiff made various policy arguments supporting governmental liability: the compensation of injured plaintiffs, the encouragement of compliance with the Fourteenth Amendment and the provision of a federal forum for section 1983 claims. Interestingly, the Court in *Monroe* simply did not address these arguments, relying instead on its reading of legislative history.

This holding was much criticized. *See, e.g.,* Levin, *The Section 1983 Municipal Immunity Doctrine,* 65 Geo. L.J. 1483 (1977); Kates & Kouba, *Liability of Public Entities Under Section 1983 of the Civil Rights Act,* 45 S. Cal. L. Rev. 131 (1972); *Developments in the Law—Section 1983 and Federalism,* 90 Harv. L. Rev. 1133 (1977). Nevertheless, the outcome was not in question. A local (and state) governmental body was not liable in damages for the unconstitutional conduct of its officials or employees. In addition, the Court later ruled that local governments could not be sued in their own names for injunctive relief either. *City of Kenosha v. Bruno,* 412 U.S. 507 (1973). Thus, section 1983 plaintiffs had a remedy only against individual defendants who, unless they were covered by insurance or governmentally provided indemnification, would often be judgment proof.

This all changed dramatically in 1978 when the Court decided *Monell v. Department of Social Services.*

B. The Change in *Monell*

Monell v. Department of Social Services

436 U.S. 658 (1978)

Mr. Justice **Brennan** delivered the opinion of the Court.

Petitioners, a class of female employees of the Department of Social Services and of the Board of Education of the city of New York, commenced this action under 42 U.S.C. § 1983 in July 1971. The gravamen of the complaint was that the Board and the Department had as a matter of official policy compelled pregnant employees to take unpaid leaves of absence before such leaves were required for medical reasons. *Cf. Cleveland Board of Education v. LaFleur.* The suit sought injunctive relief and backpay for periods of unlawful forced leave. Named as defendants in the action were the Department and its Commissioner, the Board and its Chancellor, and the city of New York and its Mayor. In each case, the individual defendants were sued solely in their official capacities.

* * *

We granted certiorari in this case to consider "Whether local governmental officials and/or local independent school boards are 'persons' within the meaning of 42 U.S.C. § 1983 when equitable relief in the nature of back pay is sought against them in their official capacities?"

Although, after plenary consideration, we have decided the merits of over a score of cases brought under § 1983 in which the principal defendant was a school board and, indeed, in some of which § 1983 and its jurisdictional counterpart, 28 U.S.C. § 1343, provided the only basis for jurisdiction—we indicated in *Mt. Healthy City Board of Education v. Doyle* last Term that the question presented here was open and would be decided "another day." That other day has come and we now overrule *Monroe v. Pape, supra,* insofar as it holds that local governments are wholly immune from suit under § 1983.

I

In *Monroe v. Pape,* we held that "Congress did not undertake to bring municipal corpora-

tions within the ambit of [§ 1983]." The sole basis for this conclusion was an inference drawn from Congress' rejection of the "Sherman amendment" to the bill which became the Civil Rights Act of 1871, the precursor of § 1983. The amendment would have held a municipal corporation liable for damage done to the person or property of its inhabitants by private persons "riotously and tumultuously assembled." Although the Sherman amendment did not seek to amend § 1 of the Act, which is now § 1983, and although the nature of the obligation created by that amendment was vastly different from that created by § 1, the Court nonetheless concluded in *Monroe* that Congress must have meant to exclude municipal corporations from the coverage of § 1 because "'the House [in voting against the Sherman amendment] had solemnly decided that in their judgment Congress had no constitutional power to impose any *obligation* upon county and town organizations, the mere instrumentality for the administration of state law.'" This statement, we thought, showed that Congress doubted its "constitutional power . . . to impose civil liability on municipalities," and that such doubt would have extended to any type of civil liability.

A fresh analysis of the debate on the Civil Rights Act of 1871, and particularly of the case law which each side mustered in its support, shows, however, that *Monroe* incorrectly equated the "obligation" of which Representative Poland spoke with "civil liability."

A. An Overview

There are three distinct stages in the legislative consideration of the bill which became the Civil Rights Act of 1871. On March 28, 1871, Representative Shellabarger, acting for a House select committee, reported H. R. 320, a bill "to enforce the provisions of the fourteenth amendment to the Constitution of the United States, and for other purposes." H. R. 320 contained four sections. Section 1, now codified as 42 U.S.C. § 1983, was the subject of only limited debate and was passed without amendment. Sections 2 through 4 dealt primarily with the "other purpose" of suppressing Ku Klux Klan violence in the Southern States. The wisdom and constitutionality of these sections—not § 1, now § 1983—were the subject of almost all congressional debate and each of these sections was amended. The

House finished its initial debates on H. R. 320 on April 7, 1871, and one week later the Senate also voted out a bill. Again, debate on § 1 of the bill was limited and that section was passed as introduced.

Immediately prior to the vote on H.R. 320 in the Senate, Senator Sherman introduced his amendment. This was *not* an amendment to § 1 of the bill, but was to be added as § 7 at the end of the bill. Under the Senate rules, no discussion of the amendment was allowed and, although attempts were made to amend the amendment, it was passed as introduced. In this form, the amendment did *not* place liability on municipal corporations, but made any inhabitant of a municipality liable for damage inflicted by persons "riotously and tumultuously assembled."

The House refused to acquiesce in a number of amendments made by the Senate, including the Sherman amendment, and the respective versions of H. R. 320 were therefore sent to a conference committee. Section 1 of the bill, however, was not a subject of this conference since, as noted, it was passed verbatim as introduced in both Houses of Congress.

On April 18, 1871, the first conference committee completed its work on H. R. 320. The main features of the conference committee draft of the Sherman amendment were these:

First, a cause of action was given to persons injured by

"any persons riotously and tumultuously assembled together . . . with intent to deprive any person of any right conferred upon him by the Constitution and laws of the United States, or to deter him or punish him for exercising such right, or by reason of his race, color, or previous condition of servitude . . . ."

Second, the bill provided that the action would be against the county, city, or parish in which the riot had occurred and that it could be maintained by either the person injured or his legal representative. Third, unlike the amendment as proposed, the conference substitute made the government defendant liable on the judgment if it was not satisfied against individual defendants who had committed the violence. If a municipality were liable, the judgment against it could be collected

"by execution, attachment, mandamus, garnishment, or any other proceeding in aid of execution or applicable to the enforcement of judgments against municipal corporations; and such judgment [would become] a lien as well upon all moneys in the treasury of such county, city, or parish, as upon the other property thereof."

In the ensuing debate on the first conference report, which was the first debate of any kind on the Sherman amendment, Senator Sherman explained that the purpose of his amendment was to enlist the aid of persons of property in the enforcement of the civil rights laws by making their property "responsible" for Ku Klux Klan damage. Statutes drafted on a similar theory, he stated, had long been in force in England and were in force in 1871 in a number of States. Nonetheless there were critical differences between the conference substitute and extant state and English statutes: The conference substitute, unlike most state riot statutes, lacked a short statute of limitations and imposed liability on the government defendant whether or not it had notice of the impending riot, whether or not the municipality was authorized to exercise a police power, whether or not it exerted all reasonable efforts to stop the riot, and whether or not the rioters were caught and punished.

The first conference substitute passed the Senate but was rejected by the House. House opponents, within whose ranks were some who had supported § 1, thought the Federal Government could not, consistent with the Constitution, obligate municipal corporations to keep the peace if those corporations were neither so obligated nor so authorized by their state charters. And, because of this constitutional objection, opponents of the Sherman amendment were unwilling to impose damages liability for nonperformance of a duty which Congress could not require municipalities to perform. This position is reflected in Representative Poland's statement that is quoted in *Monroe*.

Because the House rejected the first conference report a second conference was called and it duly issued its report. The second conference substitute for the Sherman amendment abandoned municipal liability and, instead, made "any person or persons having knowledge [that a conspiracy to violate civil rights was afoot], and having power to prevent or aid in preventing the same," who did not attempt to stop the same, liable to any person injured by the conspiracy. The amendment in this form was adopted by both Houses of Congress and is now codified as 42 U.S.C. § 1986.

The meaning of the legislative history sketched above can most readily be developed by first considering the debate on the report of the first conference committee. This debate shows conclusively that the constitutional objections raised against the Sherman amendment—on which our holding in *Monroe* was based—would not have prohibited congressional creation of a civil remedy against state municipal corporations that infringed federal rights. Because § 1 of the Civil Rights Act does not state expressly that municipal corporations come within its ambit, it is finally necessary to interpret § 1 to confirm that such corporations were indeed intended to be included within the "persons" to whom that section applies.

* * *

C. Debate on § 1 of the Civil Rights Bill

From the foregoing discussion, it is readily apparent that nothing said in debate on the Sherman amendment would have prevented holding a municipality liable under § 1 of the Civil Rights Act for its own violations of the Fourteenth Amendment. The question remains, however, whether the general language describing those to be liable under § 1—"any person"—covers more than natural persons. An examination of the debate on § 1 and application of appropriate rules of construction show unequivocally that § 1 was intended to cover legal as well as natural persons. Representative Shellabarger was the first to explain the function of § 1:

"[Section 1] not only provides a civil remedy for persons whose former condition may have been that of slaves, but also to all people where, under color of State law, they or any of them may be deprived of rights to which they are entitled under the Constitution by reason and virtue of their national citizenship."

By extending a remedy to all people, including whites, § 1 went beyond the mischief to which

the remaining sections of the 1871 Act were addressed. Representative Shellabarger also stated without reservation that the constitutionality of § 2 of the Civil Rights Act of 1866 controlled the constitutionality of § 1 of the 1871 Act, and that the former had been approved by "the supreme courts of at least three States of this Union" and by Mr. Justice Swayne, sitting on circuit, who had concluded: "We have no doubt of the constitutionality of every provision of this act." Representative Shellabarger then went on to describe how the courts would and should interpret § 1:

"This act is remedial, and in aid of the preservation of human liberty and human rights. All statutes and constitutional provisions authorizing such statutes are liberally and beneficently construed. It would be most strange and, in civilized law, monstrous were this not the rule of interpretation. As has been again and again decided by your own Supreme Court of the United States, and everywhere else where there is wise judicial interpretation, the largest latitude consistent with the words employed is uniformly given in construing such statutes and constitutional provisions as are meant to protect and defend and give remedies for their wrongs to all the people. . . . Chief Justice Jay and also Story say: "'Where a power is remedial in its nature there is much reason to contend that it ought to be construed liberally, and it is generally adopted in the interpretation of laws.'"

The sentiments expressed in Representative Shellabarger's opening speech were echoed by Senator Edmunds, the manager of H. R. 320 in the Senate:

"The first section is one that I believe nobody objects to, as defining the rights secured by the Constitution of the United States when they are assailed by any State law or under color of any State law, and it is merely carrying out the principles of the civil rights bill [of 1866], which have since become a part of the Constitution."

"[Section 1 is] so very simple and really [reenacts] the Constitution."

And he agreed that the bill "[secured] the rights of white men as much as of colored men."

In both Houses, statements of the supporters of § 1 corroborated that Congress, in enacting § 1, intended to give a broad remedy for violations of federally protected civil rights. Moreover, since municipalities through their official acts could, equally with natural persons, create the harms intended to be remedied by § 1, and, further, since Congress intended § 1 to be broadly construed, there is no reason to suppose that municipal corporations would have been excluded from the sweep of § 1. *Cf., e. g., Ex parte Virginia; Home Tel. & Tel. Co. v. Los Angeles.* One need not rely on this inference alone, however, for the debates show that Members of Congress understood "persons" to include municipal corporations.

Representative Bingham, for example, in discussing § 1 of the bill, explained that he had drafted § 1 of the Fourteenth Amendment with the case of *Barron v. Mayor of Baltimore* especially in mind. "In [that] case the city had taken private property for public use, without compensation . . . , and there was no redress for the wrong . . . ." Bingham's further remarks clearly indicate his view that such takings by cities, as had occurred in Barron, would be redressable under § 1 of the bill. More generally, and as Bingham's remarks confirm, § 1 of the bill would logically be the vehicle by which Congress provided redress for takings, since that section provided the only civil remedy for Fourteenth Amendment violations and that Amendment unequivocally prohibited uncompensated takings. Given this purpose, it beggars reason to suppose that Congress would have exempted municipalities from suit, insisting instead that compensation for a taking come from an officer in his individual capacity rather than from the government unit that had the benefit of the property taken.

In addition, by 1871, it was well understood that corporations should be treated as natural persons for virtually all purposes of constitutional and statutory analysis. This had not always been so. When this Court first considered the question of the status of corporations, Mr. Chief Justice Marshall, writing for the Court, denied that corporations "as such" were persons as that term was used in Art. III and the Judiciary Act of 1789. See *Bank of the United States v. Deveaux.* By 1844,

however, the *Deveaux* doctrine was unhesitatingly abandoned:

> "[A] corporation created by and doing business in a particular state, is to be deemed to all intents and purposes as a person, although an artificial person, . . . capable of being treated as a citizen of that state, as much as a natural person." *Louisville R. Co. v. Letson.*

And only two years before the debates on the Civil Rights Act, in *Cowles v. Mercer County*, the *Letson* principle was automatically and without discussion extended to municipal corporations. Under this doctrine, municipal corporations were routinely sued in the federal courts and this fact was well known to Members of Congress.

That the "usual" meaning of the word "person" would extend to municipal corporations is also evidenced by an Act of Congress which had been passed only months before the Civil Rights Act was passed. This Act provided that

> "in all acts hereafter passed . . . the word 'person' may extend and be applied to bodies politic and corporate . . . unless the context shows that such words were intended to be used in a more limited sense."

Municipal corporations in 1871 were included within the phrase "bodies politic and corporate" and, accordingly, the "plain meaning" of § 1 is that local government bodies were to be included within the ambit of the persons who could be sued under § 1 of the Civil Rights Act. Indeed, a Circuit Judge, writing in 1873 in what is apparently the first reported case under § 1, read the Dictionary Act in precisely this way in a case involving a corporate plaintiff and a municipal defendant. See *Northwestern Fertilizing Co. v. Hyde Park.*

II

Our analysis of the legislative history of the Civil Rights Act of 1871 compels the conclusion that Congress did intend municipalities and other local government units to be included among those persons to whom § 1983 applies.[54] Local governing bodies,[55] therefore,

---

[54] There is certainly no constitutional impediment to municipal liability. "The Tenth Amendment's reservation of nondelegated powers to the States is not

can be sued directly under § 1983 for monetary, declaratory, or injunctive relief where, as
here, the action that is alleged to be unconstitutional implements or executes a policy statement, ordinance, regulation, or decision officially adopted and promulgated by that body's
officers. Moreover, although the touchstone of
the § 1983 action against a government body
is an allegation that official policy is responsible for a deprivation of rights protected by the
Constitution, local governments, like every
other § 1983 "person," by the very terms of
the statute, may be sued for constitutional
deprivations visited pursuant to governmental
"custom" even though such a custom has not
received formal approval through the body's
official decision-making channels. As Mr. Justice Harlan, writing for the Court, said in
Adickes v. S. H. Kress & Co.: "Congress
included customs and usages [in § 1983] because of the persistent and widespread discriminatory practices of state officials . . . .
Although not authorized by written law, such
practices of state officials could well be so
permanent and well settled as to constitute a
'custom or usage' with the force of law."

On the other hand, the language of § 1983,
read against the background of the same
legislative history, compels the conclusion
that Congress did not intend municipalities to
be held liable unless action pursuant to official
municipal policy of some nature caused a
constitutional tort. In particular, we conclude
that a municipality cannot be held liable solely
because it employs a tortfeasor—or, in other

words, a municipality cannot be held liable
under § 1983 on a respondeat superior theory.

We begin with the language of § 1983 as
originally passed:

> "[Any] person who, under color of any law,
> statute, ordinance, regulation, custom, or
> usage of any State, shall subject, or cause to
> be subjected, any person . . . to the depri-
> vation of any rights, privileges, or immuni-
> ties secured by the Constitution of the
> United States, shall, any such law, statute,
> ordinance, regulation, custom, or usage of
> the State to the contrary notwithstanding,
> be liable to the party injured in any action
> at law, suit in equity, or other proper
> proceeding for redress . . . ."

The italicized language plainly imposes liability on a government that, under color of some
official policy, "causes" an employee to violate another's constitutional rights. At the
same time, that language cannot be easily read
to impose liability vicariously on governing
bodies solely on the basis of the existence of
an employer-employee relationship with a
tortfeasor. Indeed, the fact that Congress did
specifically provide that A's tort became B's
liability if B "caused" A to subject another to
a tort suggests that Congress did not intend
§ 1983 liability to attach where such causation
was absent. See *Rizzo v. Goode.*

Equally important, creation of a federal law
of respondeat superior would have raised all
the constitutional problems associated with
the obligation to keep the peace, an obligation
Congress chose not to impose because it
thought imposition of such an obligation
unconstitutional. To this day, there is disagreement about the basis for imposing liability on an employer for the torts of an employee
when the sole nexus between the employer
and the tort is the fact of the employer-employee relationship. See W. Prosser, *Law of
Torts* § 69, p. 459 (4th ed. 1971). Nonetheless,
two justifications tend to stand out. First is
the common-sense notion that no matter how
blameless an employer appears to be in an
individual case, accidents might nonetheless
be reduced if employers had to bear the cost of
accidents. See, e. g., ibid.; 2 F. Harper & F.
James, *Law of Torts*, § 26.3, pp. 1368–1369
(1956). Second is the argument that the cost of
accidents should be spread to the community

---

implicated by a federal-court judgment enforcing the
express prohibitions of unlawful state conduct enacted
by the Fourteenth Amendment." *Milliken v. Bradley;*
see *Ex parte Virginia.* For this reason, *National League
of Cities v. Usery* is irrelevant to our consideration of
this case. Nor is there any basis for concluding that the
Eleventh Amendment is a bar to municipal liability.
See, e. g., *Fitzpatrick v. Bitzer; Lincoln County v.
Luning.* Our holding today is, of course, limited to
local government units which are not considered part
of the State for Eleventh Amendment purposes.

[55] Since official-capacity suits generally represent
only another way of pleading an action against an
entity of which an officer is an agent—at least where
Eleventh Amendment considerations do not control
analysis—our holding today that local governments
can be sued under § 1983 necessarily decides that local
government officials sued in their official capacities
are "persons" under § 1983 in those cases in which, as
here, a local government would be suable in its own
name.

as a whole on an insurance theory. See, e. g., id., § 26.5; Prosser, supra, at 459.[58]

The first justification is of the same sort that was offered for statutes like the Sherman amendment: "The obligation to make compensation for injury resulting from riot is, by arbitrary enactment of statutes, affirmatory law, and the reason of passing the statute is to secure a more perfect police regulation." This justification was obviously insufficient to sustain the amendment against perceived constitutional difficulties and there is no reason to suppose that a more general liability imposed for a similar reason would have been thought less constitutionally objectionable. The second justification was similarly put forward as a justification for the Sherman amendment: "we do not look upon [the Sherman amendment] as a punishment. . . . It is a mutual insurance." Again, this justification was insufficient to sustain the amendment.

We conclude, therefore, that a local government may not be sued under § 1983 for an injury inflicted solely by its employees or agents. Instead, it is when execution of a government's policy or custom, whether made by its lawmakers or by those whose edicts or acts may fairly be said to represent official policy, inflicts the injury that the government as an entity is responsible under § 1983. Since this case unquestionably involves official policy as the moving force of the constitutional violation found by the District Court, we must reverse the judgment below. In so doing, we have no occasion to address, and do not address, what the full contours of municipal liability under § 1983 may be. We have attempted only to sketch so much of the § 1983 cause of action against a local government as is apparent from the history of the 1871 Act and our prior cases, and we expressly leave further development of this action to another day.

---

[58] A third justification, often cited but which on examination is apparently insufficient to justify the doctrine of respondeat superior, see, e. g., 2 F. Harper & F. James, § 26.3, is that liability follows the right to control the actions of a tortfeasor. By our decision in *Rizzo v. Goode* we appear to have decided that the mere right to control without any control or direction having been exercised and without any failure to supervise is not enough to support § 1983 liability.

* * *

IV

Since the question whether local government bodies should be afforded some form of official immunity was not presented as a question to be decided on this petition and was not briefed by the parties or addressed by the courts below, we express no views on the scope of any municipal immunity beyond holding that municipal bodies sued under § 1983 cannot be entitled to an absolute immunity, lest our decision that such bodies are subject to suit under § 1983 "be drained of meaning," *Scheuer v. Rhodes.*

V

For the reasons stated above, the judgment of the Court of Appeals is

Reversed.

[The concurring opinions of Justices Powell and Stevens, and the dissenting opinion of Justice Rehnquist and Chief Justice Burger are omitted.]

NOTES

1. Is the Court's reading of the legislative history of section 1983 convincing? What was wrong with its prior reading of that very same legislative history in *Monroe v. Pape*?

2. Why did the Court reject respondeat superior liability? Apparently, it interpreted section 1983's "subjects, or causes to be subjected" language as precluding respondeat superior liability in *all* section 1983 cases. Is this correct? A negative answer is offered in *Section 1983 Municipal Liability and the Doctrine of Respondeat Superior*, 46 U. Chi. L. Rev. 935 (1979). In any event, does the Court's discussion confuse causation and duty? Consider the following analysis:

In reality, *Monell* held as a matter of *§ 1983 interpretation* that a local government has not necessarily breached a § 1983 duty to a plaintiff just because that plaintiff has been deprived of constitutional rights by that local government's employees. One example of such a no-duty case, according to *Monell*, is where all that can be shown of local governmental involvement in plaintiff's constitutional deprivation is "the mere right to control." Thus, *Monell* is essentially a § 1983 duty case, not a cause in fact case.

This distinction between duty and cause in fact can be made clear by a simple example from tort law. Suppose P is drowning at a public beach; D, readily able to save him, does nothing and P drowns. A cause in fact relationship between D's failure to act and P's drowning exists. However, D is not liable because in the absence of statute or some other basis for imposing a legal obligation, there is no duty to rescue. Now, suppose that D is a hired lifeguard. Again, the necessary cause in fact relationship exists between P's drowning and D's failure to act. This time, though, D will probably be liable because lifeguard status gives rise to a duty to rescue. In short, tort liability requires both duty and a cause in fact relationship between its breach and the plaintiff's injury.

In this light, therefore, while *Monell* spoke of cause in fact in a § 1983 context, what it apparently meant is that, regardless of the existence of a cause in fact relationship between a local government's failure to control an employee and that employee's unconstitutional conduct leading to plaintiff's injury, the local government will ordinarily have no duty to control. Hence there will be no § 1983 liability. Similarly, the rejection in *Monell* of respondeat superior indicates that there is no § 1983 duty running from the local government to the injured plaintiff unless there is something more than an employment relationship between the local government and the employee whose conduct caused the plaintiff's constitutional deprivation. As with tort liability, § 1983 local government liability (and all other § 1983 liability as well) requires the existence of a duty to the plaintiff and a causal relationship between defendant's breach of that duty and plaintiff's constitutional deprivation.

S. Nahmod, 1 *Civil Rights and Civil Liberties Litigation: The Law of Section 1983* 418–19 (3d ed. 1991).

3. *Monell* announces that local governmental liability requires that the "execution of a government's policy or custom . . . inflicts the injury." This is the source of the famous "official policy or custom" requirement that has generated so much confusion and litigation. While we will address this in considerable detail later, ask yourself whether *Monell* is an easy or hard case in which to discern an official policy or custom. Is *Monell* an official policy case? What *is* an official policy? Is it a custom case? What *is* a custom? In this connection, what is the challenged conduct of the local government in *Monell*?

4. What is the connection, if any, between *Monell*'s official policy or custom requirement and *Parratt v. Taylor*'s random and unauthorized conduct standard for procedural due process, discussed in Chapter 3? *See* Bandes, Monell, Parratt, Daniels *and* Davidson: *Distinguishing a Custom or Policy from a Random, Unauthorized Act*, 72 Iowa L. Rev. 101 (1986).

5. *Monell* also declares that an official policy or custom may be "made by . . . lawmakers or by those whose edicts or acts may fairly be said to represent official policy." What could this possibly mean, especially in light of the Court's rejection of respondeat superior liability? The language seems to suggest that certain high ranking local government officials could render their employers liable for damages for their unconstitutional conduct. The question, of course, is which officials make official policy and under what circumstances. To put the matter somewhat differently but more accurately, when is the unconstitutional conduct of a high ranking official *attributed* to the local government itself? See the discussion of policymakers later in this chapter.

6. Obviously, the Court in *Monell* had to hold that local governments are not protected by absolute immunity from compensatory damages liability. A contrary result would have resurrected *Monroe*'s "nonperson" rule. However, the Court left open the question of the possible applicability of qualified immunity to local governments. As it turns out, the Court was to rule in *Owen v. City of Independence*, 445 U.S. 622 (1980), discussed later, that local governments are not so protected from compensatory damages liability. On the other hand, as we shall also see, they are absolutely immune from *punitive damages* liability. *City of Newport v. Fact Concerts*, 453 U.S. 247 (1981).

7. *Monell* involves the affirmative conduct, so to speak, of a local government. Are there circumstances in which a local government can be liable for its *failure to act*? See the discussion later on local government liability for failure to train and *City of Canton v. Harris*, 489 U.S. 378 (1989).

8. Do *Monell*'s official policy or custom requirement and its rejection of respondeat superior liability make economic sense? For a critique, *see* Kramer and Sykes, *Municipal Liability Under Section 1983: A Legal and Economic Analysis*, 1987 Sup. Ct. Rev. 249. They maintain that *Monell*'s official policy or custom requirement is "economically inefficient." Instead, they argue for a negligence approach to local government liability or, in the alternative, for respondeat superior. They also "tentatively" conclude that where the individual local government official or employee is protected by qualified immunity—see Chapter 8—the local government should be similarly protected. As we shall shortly see, however, local governments are *not* protected by qualified immunity.

9. Does the official policy or custom requirement make sense from a tort law and organizational theory perspective? For the argument that it does not, *see* Schuck, *Municipal Liability Under Section 1983: Some Lessons from Tort Law and Organization Theory*, 77 Geo. L.J. 1753 (1989), *reprinted in Section 1983 Anthology* 65.

10. Suppose a private corporation is sued for damages under section 1983 for the allegedly unconstitutional conduct of its employees. If color of law—discussed in Chapter 2—is present, can the corporation be held liable under a respondeat superior theory, or must an official policy or custom be proved? Does the assumption of color of law beg the very question at issue? That is, once there is color of law, does it follow that respondeat superior liability is no longer implicated?

Consider *Sanders v. Sears Roebuck & Company*, 984 F.2d 972 (8th Cir. 1993), where the plaintiff sued a department store for the allegedly unconstitutional conduct of its security guard in detaining him for shoplifting and thereafter turning him over to police. Affirming the district court's dismissal, the Eighth Circuit assumed *arguendo* that the department store acted under color of law, but held that it could be held liable under section 1983 only for its own unconstitutional policies, and not through respondeat superior. The plaintiff did not allege that the defendant had a policy of false arrests

or malicious prosecution; its employment of the security guard, standing alone, was insufficient.

Why should *Monell*'s official policy or custom requirement for local government liability apply to private corporations?

C. The Status of States as "Persons": *Will*

Unlike local governments, states enjoy sovereign immunity from suit in federal courts. U.S. Constitution amend. 11; *Hans v. Louisiana*, 134 U.S. 1 (1890). Congress, though, may abrogate that immunity by a statute containing a "clear statement" that states are subject to suit in a particular kind of case. *Fitzpatrick v. Bitzer*, 427 U.S. 445 (1976); *Pennsylvania v. Union Gas Co.*, 491 U.S. 1 (1989). Prior to *Monell*, the circuits uniformly ruled that section 1983 actions against states and their alter egos were barred by the Eleventh Amendment. The typical judicial reasoning in such cases relied on *Monroe v. Pape*'s holding in concluding: "A municipal corporation is but a political subdivision of a state and if a state's political subdivisions are not 'persons' under the statute, then neither is the state." *Williford v. California*, 352 F.2d 474, 476 (9th Cir. 1965). The subsequent overruling of *Monroe* by *Monell* gave rise to the argument that states, like local governments, should be considered suable persons because section 1983 had abrogated Eleventh Amendment immunity. See *Hutto v. Finney*, 437 U.S. 678 (1978), a Civil Rights Attorney's Fees Act case. That was not to be, however. In *Quern v. Jordan*, 440 U.S. 332 (1979), the Court held that section 1983 was not such a statute.

Nevertheless, despite *Quern*, it was still possible to argue that states were suable in *state court*, since the Eleventh Amendment and the "clear statement" rule applied only to the federal courts. That issue was addressed in *Will v. Michigan Department of State Police*, set out next.

Will v. Michigan Department of State Police

491 U.S. 58 (1989)

Justice **White** delivered the opinion of the Court.

This case presents the question whether a State, or an official of the State while acting in his or her official capacity, is a "person" within the meaning of Rev. Stat. § 1979, 42 U.S.C. § 1983.

Petitioner Ray Will filed suit in Michigan Circuit Court alleging various violations of the United States and Michigan Constitutions as grounds for a claim under § 1983. He alleged that he had been denied a promotion to a data systems analyst position with the Department of State Police for an improper reason, that is, because his brother had been a student activist and the subject of a "red squad" file maintained by respondent. Named as defendants were the Department of State Police and the Director of State Police in his official capacity, also a respondent here.

* * *

The Michigan Supreme Court's holding that a State is not a person under § 1983 conflicts with a number of state and federal court decisions to the contrary. We granted certiorari to resolve the conflict.

Prior to *Monell v. New York City Dept. of Social Services*, the question whether a State is a person within the meaning of § 1983 had been answered by this Court in the negative. In *Monroe v. Pape*, the Court had held that a municipality was not a person under § 1983. "That being the case," we reasoned, § 1983 "could not have been intended to include States as parties defendant." *Fitzpatrick v. Bitzer*.

But in *Monell*, the Court overruled *Monroe*, holding that a municipality was a person under § 1983. Since then, various members of the Court have debated whether a State is a person within the meaning of § 1983, see *Hutto v. Finney* (BRENNAN, J., concurring) (Powell, J., concurring in part and dissenting in part), but this Court has never expressly dealt with that issue.

Some courts, including the Michigan Supreme Court here, have construed our decision in *Quern v. Jordan*, as holding by implication that a State is not a person under § 1983. *Quern* held that § 1983 does not override a State's Eleventh Amendment immunity, a holding that the concurrence suggested was "patently dicta" to the effect that a State is not a person (BRENNAN, J., concurring in judgment).

Petitioner filed the present § 1983 action in Michigan state court, which places the question whether a State is a person under § 1983 squarely before us since the Eleventh Amendment does not apply in state courts. *Maine v. Thiboutot*. For the reasons that follow, we reaffirm today what we had concluded prior to *Monell* and what some have considered implicit in *Quern*: that a State is not a person within the meaning of § 1983.

We observe initially that if a State is a "person" within the meaning of § 1983, the section is to be read as saying that "every person, including a State, who, under color of any statute, ordinance, regulation, custom, or usage, of any State or Territory or the District of Columbia, subjects . . . ." That would be a decidedly awkward way of expressing an intent to subject the States to liability. At the very least, reading the statute in this way is not so clearly indicated that it provides reason to depart from the often-expressed understanding that "'in common usage, the term 'person' does not include the sovereign, [and] statutes employing the [word] are ordinarily construed to exclude it.'" *Wilson v. Omaha Indian Tribe* (quoting *United States v. Cooper Corp.*).

This approach is particularly applicable where it is claimed that Congress has subjected the States to liability to which they had not been subject before. In *Wilson v. Omaha Indian Tribe*, we followed this rule in construing the phrase "white person" contained in 25 U. S. C. § 194, as not including the "sovereign States of the Union." This common usage of the term "person" provides a strong indication that person as used in § 1983 likewise does not include a State.

The language of § 1983 also falls far short of satisfying the ordinary rule of statutory construction that if Congress intends to alter the "usual constitutional balance between the States and the Federal Government," it must make its intention to do so "unmistakably clear in the language of the statute." *Atascadero State Hospital v. Scanlon. Atascadero* was an Eleventh Amendment case, but a similar approach is applied in other contexts. Congress should make its intention "clear and manifest" if it intends to pre-empt the historic powers of the States, or if it intends to impose a condition on the grant of federal moneys. "In traditionally sensitive areas, such as legislation affecting the federal balance, the requirement of clear statement assures that the legislature has in fact faced, and intended to bring into issue, the critical matters involved in the judicial decision." *United States v. Bass.*

Our conclusion that a State is not a person within the meaning of § 1983 is reinforced by Congress' purpose in enacting the statute. Congress enacted § 1 of the Civil Rights Act of 1871, 17 Stat. 13, the precursor to § 1983, shortly after the end of the Civil War "in response to the widespread deprivations of civil rights in the Southern States and the inability or unwillingness of authorities in those States to protect those rights or punish wrongdoers." *Felder v. Casey.* Although Congress did not establish federal courts as the exclusive forum to remedy these deprivations, it is plain that "Congress assigned to the federal courts a paramount role" in this endeavor, *Patsy v. Board of Regents of Florida.*

Section 1983 provides a federal forum to remedy many deprivations of civil liberties, but it does not provide a federal forum for litigants who seek a remedy against a State for alleged deprivations of civil liberties. The Eleventh Amendment bars such suits unless the State has waived its immunity, or unless Congress has exercised its undoubted power under § 5 of the Fourteenth Amendment to override that immunity. That Congress, in passing § 1983, had no intention to disturb the States' Eleventh Amendment immunity and so to alter the federal-state balance in that respect was made clear in our decision in *Quern.* Given that a principal purpose behind the enactment of § 1983 was to provide a federal forum for civil rights claims, and that Congress did not provide such a federal forum for civil rights claims against States, we cannot accept petitioner's argument that Congress intended nevertheless to create a cause of action against States to be brought in state courts, which are precisely the courts Congress sought to allow civil rights claimants to avoid through § 1983.

This does not mean, as petitioner suggests, that we think that the scope of the Eleventh Amendment and the scope of § 1983 are not separate issues. Certainly they are. But in deciphering congressional intent as to the scope of § 1983, the scope of the Eleventh Amendment is a consideration, and we decline to adopt a reading of § 1983 that disregards it.

Our conclusion is further supported by our holdings that in enacting § 1983, Congress did not intend to override well-established immunities or defenses under the common law. "One important assumption underlying the Court's decisions in this area is that members of the 42d Congress were familiar with common-law principles, including defenses previously recognized in ordinary tort litigation, and that they likely intended these common-law principles to obtain, absent specific provisions to the contrary." *Newport v. Fact Concerts, Inc.* The doctrine of sovereign immunity was a familiar doctrine at common law. "The principle is elementary that a State cannot be sued in its own courts without its consent." *Railroad Co. v. Tennessee.* It is an "established principle of jurisprudence" that the sovereign cannot be sued in its own courts without its consent. We cannot conclude that § 1983 was intended to disregard the well-established immunity of a State from being sued without its consent.

The legislative history of § 1983 does not suggest a different conclusion. Petitioner contends that the congressional debates on § 1 of the 1871 Act indicate that § 1983 was intended to extend to the full reach of the Fourteenth Amendment and thereby to provide a remedy "'against all forms of official violation of federally protected rights.'" Brief for Petitioner 16. He refers us to various parts of the vigorous debates accompanying the passage of § 1983 and revealing that it was the failure of the States to take appropriate action that was undoubtedly the motivating force behind § 1983. The inference must be drawn, it is urged, that Congress must have intended to subject the States themselves to liability. But the intent of Congress to provide a remedy for unconstitutional state action does not without more include the sovereign States among those persons against whom § 1983 actions would lie. Construing § 1983 as a remedy for "official violation of federally protected rights" does no more than confirm that the section is directed against state action—action "under color of" state law. It does not suggest that the State itself was a person that Congress intended to be subject to liability.

Although there were sharp and heated debates, the discussion of § 1 of the Bill, which contained the present § 1983, was not extended. And although in other respects the impact on state sovereignty was much talked about, no one suggested that § 1 would subject the States themselves to a damages suit under federal law. There was complaint that § 1 would subject state officers to damages liability, but no suggestion that it would also expose the States themselves. Cong. Globe, 42d Cong., 1st Sess. 366, 385 (1871). We find nothing substantial in the legislative history that leads us to believe that Congress intended that the word "person" in § 1983 included the States of the Union. And surely nothing in the debates rises to the clearly expressed legislative intent necessary to permit that construction.

Likewise, the Act of Feb. 25, 1871, § 2, 16 Stat. 431 (the "Dictionary Act"), on which we relied in *Monell*, does not counsel a contrary conclusion here. As we noted in *Quern*, that Act, while adopted prior to § 1 of the Civil Rights Act of 1871, was adopted after § 2 of the Civil Rights Act of 1866, from which § 1 of the 1871 Act was derived. Moreover, we disagree with JUSTICE BRENNAN that at the time the Dictionary Act was passed "the phrase 'bodies politic and corporate' was understood to include the States." Rather, an examination of authorities of the era suggests that the phrase was used to mean corporations, both private and public (municipal), and not to include the States. In our view, the Dictionary Act, like § 1983 itself and its legislative history, fails to evidence a clear congressional intent that States be held liable.

Finally, *Monell* itself is not to the contrary. True, prior to *Monell* the Court had reasoned that if municipalities were not persons then surely States also were not. *Fitzpatrick v. Bitzer*. And *Monell* overruled *Monroe*, undercutting that logic. But it does not follow that if municipalities are persons then so are States. States are protected by the Eleventh Amendment while municipalities are not, *Monell*, and we consequently limited our holding in *Monell* "to local government units which are not considered part of the State for Eleventh Amendment purposes,". Conversely, our holding here does not cast any doubt on *Monell*, and applies only to States or governmental entities that are considered "arms of the State" for Eleventh Amendment purposes. *See, e. g., Mt. Healthy Bd. of Ed. v. Doyle.*

Petitioner asserts, alternatively, that state officials should be considered "persons" under § 1983 even though acting in their official capacities. In this case, petitioner named as defendant not only the Michigan Department of State Police but also the Director of State Police in his official capacity.

Obviously, state officials literally are persons. But a suit against a state official in his or her official capacity is not a suit against the official but rather is a suit against the official's office. As such, it is no different from a suit against the State itself. We see no reason to adopt a different rule in the present context, particularly when such a rule would allow petitioner to circumvent congressional intent by a mere pleading device.[10]

We hold that neither a State nor its officials acting in their official capacities are "persons" under § 1983. The judgment of the Michigan Supreme Court is affirmed.

Justice **Brennan**, with whom Justice **Marshall**, Justice **Blackmun**, and Justice **Stevens** join, dissenting.

Because this case was brought in state court, the Court concedes, the Eleventh Amendment is inapplicable here. Like the guest who would not leave, however, the Eleventh Amendment lurks everywhere in today's decision and, in truth, determines its outcome.

I

Section 1 of the Civil Rights Act of 1871, 42 U.S.C. § 1983, renders certain "persons" liable for deprivations of constitutional rights. The question presented is whether the word "persons" in this statute includes the States and state officials acting in their official capacities.

One might expect that this statutory question would generate a careful and thorough analysis of the language, legislative history, and general background of § 1983. If this is what one expects, however, one will be disappointed by today's decision. For this case is not decided on the basis of our ordinary

---

[10] Of course a state official in his or her official capacity, when sued for injunctive relief, would be a person under § 1983 because "official-capacity actions for prospective relief are not treated as actions against the State." *Kentucky v. Graham.*

method of statutory construction; instead, the Court disposes of it by means of various rules of statutory interpretation that it summons to its aid each time the question looks close. Specifically, the Court invokes the following interpretative principles: the word "persons" is ordinarily construed to exclude the sovereign; congressional intent to affect the federal-state balance must be "clear and manifest"; and intent to abrogate States' Eleventh Amendment immunity must appear in the language of the statute itself. The Court apparently believes that each of these rules obviates the need for close analysis of a statute's language and history. Properly applied, however, only the last of these interpretative principles has this effect, and that principle is not pertinent to the case before us.

The Court invokes, first, the "often-expressed understanding" that "in common usage, the term 'person' does not include the sovereign, [and] statutes employing the [word] are ordinarily construed to exclude it." This rule is used both to refute the argument that the language of § 1983 demonstrates an intent that States be included as defendants, and to overcome the argument based on the Dictionary Act's definition of "persons" to include bodies politic and corporate. It is ironic, to say the least, that the Court chooses this interpretive rule in explaining why the Dictionary Act is not decisive, since the rule is relevant only when the word "persons" has no statutory definition. When one considers the origins and content of this interpretive guideline, moreover, one realizes that it is inapplicable here and, even if applied, would defeat rather than support the Court's approach and result.

The idea that the word "persons" ordinarily excludes the sovereign can be traced to the "familiar principle that the King is not bound by any act of Parliament unless he be named therein by special and particular words." *Dollar Savings Bank v. United States*. As this passage suggests, however, this interpretive principle applies only to "the enacting sovereign." *United States v. California*. Furthermore, as explained in *United States v. Herron*, even the principle as applied to the enacting sovereign is not without limitations: "Where an act of Parliament is made for the public good, as for the advancement of religion and justice or to prevent injury and wrong, the king is bound by such act, though not particu-

larly named therein; but where a statute is general, and thereby any prerogative, right, title, or interest is divested or taken from the king, in such case the king is not bound, unless the statute is made to extend to him by express words." It would be difficult to imagine a statute more clearly designed "for the public good," and "to prevent injury and wrong," than § 1983.

Even if this interpretive principle were relevant to this case, the Court's invocation of it to the exclusion of careful statutory analysis is in error. As we have made clear, this principle is merely "an aid to consistent construction of statutes of the enacting sovereign when their purpose is in doubt, but it does not require that the aim of a statute fairly to be inferred be disregarded because not explicitly stated." *United States v. California*. Indeed, immediately following the passage quoted by the Court today, to the effect that statutes using the word "person" are "ordinarily construed to exclude" the sovereign, we stated:

> "But there is no hard and fast rule of exclusion. The purpose, the subject matter, the context, the legislative history, and the executive interpretation of the statute are aids to construction which may indicate an intent, by the use of the term, to bring state or nation within the scope of the law.
>
> . . . .
>
> "Decision is not to be reached by a strict construction of the words of the Act, nor by the application of artificial canons of construction. On the contrary, we are to read the statutory language in its ordinary and natural sense, and if doubts remain, resolve them in the light, not only of the policy intended to be served by the enactment, but, as well, by all other available aids to construction." *United States v. Cooper Corp.*.

The second interpretive principle that the Court invokes comes from cases which require a "clear and manifest" expression of congressional intent to change some aspect of federal-state relations. These cases do not, however, permit substitution of an absolutist rule of statutory construction for thorough statutory analysis. Indeed, in each of these decisions the Court undertook a careful and detailed analysis of the statutory language and history under consideration. *Rice v. State Elevator Corp.* is a particularly inapposite source for the interpretive method that the Court today employs, since it observes that, according to conventional pre-emption analysis, a "clear and manifest" intent to pre-empt state legislation may appear in the "scheme" or "purpose" of the federal statute.

The only principle of statutory construction employed by the Court that would justify a perfunctory and inconclusive analysis of a statute's language and history is one that is irrelevant to this case. This is the notion "that if Congress intends to alter the 'usual constitutional balance between the States and the Federal Government,' it must make its intention to do so 'unmistakably clear in the language of the statute.'" As the Court notes, *Atascadero* was an Eleventh Amendment case; the "constitutional balance" to which *Atascadero* refers is that struck by the Eleventh Amendment as this Court has come to interpret it. Although the Court apparently wishes it were otherwise, the principle of interpretation that *Atascadero* announced is unique to cases involving the Eleventh Amendment.

Where the Eleventh Amendment applies, the Court has devised a clear-statement principle more robust than its requirement of clarity in any other situation. Indeed, just today, the Court has intimated that this clear-statement principle is not simply a means of discerning congressional intent. Since this case was brought in state court, however, this strict drafting requirement has no application here. The Eleventh Amendment can hardly be "a consideration," in a suit to which it does not apply.

That this Court has generated a uniquely daunting requirement of clarity in Eleventh Amendment cases explains why *Quern v. Jordan*, did not decide the question before us today. Because only the Eleventh Amendment permits use of this clear-statement principle, the holding of *Quern v. Jordan* that § 1983 does not abrogate States' Eleventh Amendment immunity tells us nothing about the meaning of the term "persons" in § 1983 as a matter of ordinary statutory construction. *Quern's* conclusion thus does not compel, or even suggest, a particular result today.

The singularity of this Court's approach to statutory interpretation in Eleventh Amend-

ment cases also refutes the Court's argument that, given *Quern's* holding, it would make no sense to construe § 1983 to include States as "persons." This is so, the Court suggests, because such a construction would permit suits against States in state but not federal court, even though a major purpose of Congress in enacting § 1983 was to provide a federal forum for litigants who had been deprived of their constitutional rights. In answering the question whether § 1983 provides a federal forum for suits against the States themselves, however, one must apply the clear-statement principle reserved for Eleventh Amendment cases. Since this principle is inapplicable to suits brought in state court, and inapplicable to the question whether States are among those subject to a statute, the answer to the question whether § 1983 provides a federal forum for suits against the States may be, and most often will be, different from the answer to the kind of question before us today. Since the question whether Congress has provided a federal forum for damages suits against the States is answered by applying a uniquely strict interpretive principle, the Court should not pretend that we have, in *Quern*, answered the question whether Congress intended to provide a federal forum for such suits, and then reason backwards from that "intent" to the conclusion that Congress must not have intended to allow such suits to proceed in state court.

In short, the only principle of statutory interpretation that permits the Court to avoid a careful and thorough analysis of § 1983's language and history is the clear-statement principle that this Court has come to apply in Eleventh Amendment cases—a principle that is irrelevant to this state-court action. In my view, a careful and detailed analysis of § 1983 leads to the conclusion that States are "persons" within the meaning of that statute.

* * *

[The dissenting opinion of Justice Stevens is omitted.]

NOTES

1. Is *Will* a statutory interpretation case or an Eleventh Amendment case? Which *should* it be?

2. After *Will*, can a section 1983 plaintiff sue a state for damages in *state court*? After *Will*, can a state waive its Eleventh Amendment immunity under section 1983?

3. Recall that section 1983 was enacted pursuant to section 5 of the Fourteenth Amendment which on its face is directed at *state* action. Is it not therefore anomalous that local governments, the creations of states, are potentially liable under section 1983 while the states themselves, with considerably more power and influence than local governments, are not?

4. *Will* does not change the rule that state officials can be sued for damages under section 1983 in their *individual capacities*. In such cases the defendants may be personally liable but the state is not directly implicated. In contrast, state officials cannot be sued for damages in their *official capacities*. Such suits are considered to be suits against the states themselves and are barred by *Will*. *See* the discussion later on *Hafer v. Melo*, 502 U.S. 21 (1991) and the all-important distinction between *individual capacity* damages actions and *official capacity* damages actions.

5. Following *Will*, the Supreme Court held in *Ngiraingas v. Sanchez*, 495 U.S. 182 (1990), that territories, like states, are not suable persons under section 1983. It determined, upon examination of section 1983's legislative history, that Congress never intended to render territories suable under section 1983. Suppose that a section 1983 plaintiff sues the official of a territory for damages in his or her *official capacity*. What result? What if the suit is brought against the official in his or her *individual capacity*? Is there a different result? Why or why not? Does *Will* help answer these questions?

II. The Immunities of Governmental Bodies

A. Qualified Immunity and Compensatory Damages: *Owen*

Owen v. City of Independence, Missouri

445 U.S. 622 (1980)

Mr. Justice **Brennan** delivered the opinion of the Court.

Monell v. New York City Dept. of Social Services overruled *Monroe v. Pape* insofar as *Monroe* held that local governments were not among the "persons" to whom 42 U.S.C. § 1983 applies and were therefore wholly immune from suit under the statute. *Monell* reserved decision, however, on the question whether local governments, although not entitled to an absolute immunity, should be afforded some form of official immunity in § 1983 suits. In this action brought by petitioner in the District Court for the Western District of Missouri, the Court of Appeals for the Eighth Circuit held that respondent city of Independence, Mo., "is entitled to qualified immunity from liability" based on the good faith of its officials: "We extend the limited immunity the district court applied to the individual defendants to cover the City as well, because its officials acted in good faith and without malice." We granted certiorari. We reverse.

* * *

II

Petitioner named the city of Independence, City Manager Alberg, and the present members of the City Council in their official capacities as defendants in this suit. Alleging that he was discharged without notice of reasons and without a hearing in violation of his constitutional rights to procedural and substantive due process, petitioner sought declaratory and injunctive relief, including a hearing on his discharge, backpay from the date of discharge, and attorney's fees. The District Court, after a bench trial, entered judgment for respondents.

* * *

[T]he Court of Appeals affirmed the judgment of the District Court denying petitioner any relief against the respondent city, stating:

"The Supreme Court's decisions in *Board of Regents v. Roth*, and *Perry v. Sindermann*, crystallized the rule establishing the right to a name-clearing hearing for a government employee allegedly stigmatized in the course of his discharge. The Court decided those two cases two months after the discharge in the instant case. Thus, officials of the City of Independence could not have been aware of [petitioner's] right to a name-clearing hearing in connection with the discharge. The City of Independence should not be charged with predicting the future course of constitutional law. We extend the limited immunity the district court applied to the individual defendants to cover the City as well, because its officials acted in good faith and without malice. We hold the City not liable for actions it could not reasonably have known violated [petitioner's] constitutional rights."

We turn now to the reasons for our disagreement with this holding.

III

Because the question of the scope of a municipality's immunity from liability under § 1983 is essentially one of statutory construction, see *Wood v. Strickland; Tenney v. Brandhove,* the starting point in our analysis must be the language of the statute itself. *Andrus v. Allard; Blue Chip Stamps v. Manor Drug Stores.* By its terms, § 1983 "creates a species of tort liability that on its face admits of no immunities." *Imbler v. Pachtman.* Its language is absolute and unqualified; no mention is made of any privileges, immunities, or defenses that may be asserted. Rather, the Act imposes liability upon "every person" who, under color of state law or custom, "subjects, or causes to be subjected, any citizen of the United States . . . to the deprivation of any rights, privileges, or immunities secured by the Constitution and laws." And *Monell* held that these words were intended to encompass municipal corporations as well as natural "persons."

Moreover, the congressional debates surrounding the passage of § 1 of the Civil Rights Act of 1871, 17 Stat. 13—the forerunner of § 1983—confirm the expansive sweep of the statutory language. Representative Shellabarger, the author and manager of the bill in the House, explained in his introductory remarks the breadth of construction that the Act was to receive:

"I have a single remark to make in regard to the rule of interpretation of those provisions of the Constitution under which all the sections of the bill are framed. This act is remedial, and in aid of the preservation of human liberty and human rights. All statutes and constitutional provisions authorizing such statutes are liberally and beneficently construed. It would be most strange and, in civilized law, monstrous were this not the rule of interpretation. As has been again and again decided by your own Supreme Court of the United States, and everywhere else where there is wise judicial interpretation, the largest latitude consistent with the words employed is uniformly given in construing such statutes and constitutional provisions as are meant to protect and defend and give remedies for their wrongs to all the people."

Similar views of the Act's broad remedy for violations of federally protected rights were voiced by its supporters in both Houses of Congress. See *Monell v. New York City Dept. of Social Services*

However, notwithstanding § 1983's expansive language and the absence of any express incorporation of common-law immunities, we have, on several occasions, found that a tradition of immunity was so firmly rooted in the common law and was supported by such strong policy reasons that "Congress would have specifically so provided had it wished to abolish the doctrine." *Pierson v. Ray*, Thus in *Tenney v. Brandhove, supra,* after tracing the development of an absolute legislative privilege from its source in 16th-century England to its inclusion in the Federal and State Constitutions, we concluded that Congress "would [not] impinge on a tradition so well grounded in history and reason by covert inclusion in the general language" of § 1983.

Subsequent cases have required that we consider the personal liability of various other types of government officials. Noting that "[few] doctrines were more solidly established at common law than the immunity of judges from liability for damages for acts committed within their judicial jurisdiction," *Pierson v. Ray, supra,* held that the absolute immunity traditionally accorded judges was preserved under § 1983. In that same case, local police officers were held to enjoy a "good faith and probable cause" defense to § 1983 suits similar to that which existed in false arrest actions at common law. Several more recent decisions have found immunities of varying scope appropriate for different state and local officials sued under § 1983. See *Procunier v. Navarette* (qualified immunity for prison officials and officers); *Imbler v. Pachtman* (absolute immunity for prosecutors in initiating and presenting the State's case); *O'Connor v. Donaldson* (qualified immunity for superintendent of state hospital); *Wood v. Strickland* (qualified immunity for local school board members); *Scheuer v. Rhodes* (qualified "good-faith" immunity for state Governor and other executive officers for discretionary acts performed in the course of official conduct).

In each of these cases, our finding of § 1983 immunity "was predicated upon a considered inquiry into the immunity historically accorded the relevant official at common law and the interests behind it." *Imbler v. Pachtman.* Where the immunity claimed by the defendant was well established at common law at the time § 1983 was enacted, and where its rationale was compatible with the purposes of the Civil Rights Act, we have construed the statute to incorporate that immunity. But there is no tradition of immunity for municipal corporations, and neither history nor policy supports a construction of § 1983 that would justify the qualified immunity accorded the city of Independence by the Court of Appeals. We hold, therefore, that the municipality may not assert the good faith of its officers or agents as a defense to liability under § 1983.

* * *

In sum, we can discern no "tradition so well grounded in history and reason" that would warrant the conclusion that in enacting § 1 of the Civil Rights Act, the 42d Congress sub silentio extended to municipalities a qualified immunity based on the good faith of their officers. Absent any clearer indication that Congress intended so to limit the reach of a statute expressly designed to provide a "broad remedy for violations of federally protected civil rights," *Monell v. New York City Dept. of Social Services*, we are unwilling to suppose that injuries occasioned by a municipality's unconstitutional conduct were not also meant to be fully redressable through its sweep.

B

Our rejection of a construction of § 1983 that would accord municipalities a qualified immunity for their good-faith constitutional violations is compelled both by the legislative purpose in enacting the statute and by considerations of public policy. The central aim of the Civil Rights Act was to provide protection to those persons wronged by the "[misuse] of power, possessed by virtue of state law and made possible only because the wrongdoer is clothed with the authority of state law." *Monroe v. Pape* (quoting *United States v. Classic*). By creating an express federal remedy, Congress sought to "enforce provisions of the Fourteenth Amendment against those who carry a badge of authority of a State and represent it in some capacity, whether they act in accordance with their authority or misuse it." *Monroe v. Pape*.

How "uniquely amiss" it would be, therefore, if the government itself—"the social organ to which all in our society look for the promotion of liberty, justice, fair and equal treatment, and the setting of worthy norms and goals for social conduct"—were permitted to disavow liability for the injury it has begotten. See *Adickes v. Kress & Co.*. A damages remedy against the offending party is a vital component of any scheme for vindicating cherished constitutional guarantees, and the importance of assuring its efficacy is only accentuated when the wrongdoer is the institution that has been established to protect the very rights it has transgressed. Yet owing to the qualified immunity enjoyed by most government officials, see *Scheuer v. Rhodes*, many victims of municipal malfeasance would be left remediless if the city were also allowed to assert a good-faith defense. Unless countervailing considerations counsel otherwise, the injustice of such a result should not be tolerated.

Moreover, § 1983 was intended not only to provide compensation to the victims of past abuses, but to serve as a deterrent against future constitutional deprivations, as well. The knowledge that a municipality will be liable for all of its injurious conduct, whether committed in good faith or not, should create an incentive for officials who may harbor doubts about the lawfulness of their intended actions to err on the side of protecting citizens' constitutional rights. Furthermore, the threat that damages might be levied against the city may encourage those in a policymaking position to institute internal rules and programs designed to minimize the likelihood of unintentional infringements on constitutional rights. Such procedures are particularly beneficial in preventing those "systemic" injuries that result not so much from the conduct of any single individual, but from the interactive behavior of several government officials, each of whom may be acting in good faith. Cf. Note, *Developments in the Law: Section 1983 and Federalism*, 90 Harv. L. Rev. 1133, 1218–1219 (1977).

Our previous decisions conferring qualified immunities on various government officials are not to be read as derogating the significance of the societal interest in compensating the innocent victims of governmental misconduct. Rather, in each case we concluded that overriding considerations of public policy nonetheless demanded that the official be given a measure of protection from personal liability. The concerns that justified those decisions, however, are less compelling, if not wholly inapplicable, when the liability of the municipal entity is at issue.

In *Scheuer v. Rhodes*, THE CHIEF JUSTICE identified the two "mutually dependent rationales" on which the doctrine of official immunity rested:

> "(1) the injustice, particularly in the absence of bad faith, of subjecting to liability an officer who is required, by the legal obligations of his position, to exercise discretion; (2) the danger that the threat of such liability would deter his willingness to execute his office with the decisiveness and the judgment required by the public good."

The first consideration is simply not implicated when the damages award comes not from the official's pocket, but from the public treasury. It hardly seems unjust to require a municipal defendant which has violated a citizen's constitutional rights to compensate him for the injury suffered thereby. Indeed, Congress enacted § 1983 precisely to provide a remedy for such abuses of official power. Elemental notions of fairness dictate that one who causes a loss should bear the loss.

It has been argued, however, that revenue raised by taxation for public use should not be diverted to the benefit of a single or discrete group of taxpayers, particularly where the municipality has at all times acted in good faith. On the contrary, the accepted view is that stated in *Thayer v. Boston*—"that the city, in its corporate capacity, should be liable to make good the damage sustained by an [unlucky] individual, in consequence of the acts thus done." After all, it is the public at large which enjoys the benefits of the government's activities, and it is the public at large which is ultimately responsible for its administration. Thus, even where some constitutional development could not have been foreseen by municipal officials, it is fairer to allocate any resulting financial loss to the inevitable costs of government borne by all the taxpayers, than to allow its impact to be felt solely by those whose rights, albeit newly recognized, have been violated.

The second rationale mentioned in *Scheuer* also loses its force when it is the municipality, in contrast to the official, whose liability is at issue. At the heart of this justification for a qualified immunity for the individual official is the concern that the threat of personal monetary liability will introduce an unwarranted and unconscionable consideration into the decisionmaking process, thus paralyzing the governing official's decisiveness and distorting his judgment on matters of public policy. The inhibiting effect is significantly reduced, if not eliminated, however, when the threat of personal liability is removed. First, as an empirical matter, it is questionable whether the hazard of municipal loss will deter a public officer from the conscientious exercise of his duties; city officials routinely make decisions that either require a large expenditure of municipal funds or involve a substantial risk of depleting the public fisc.

More important, though, is the realization that consideration of the *municipality's* liability for constitutional violations is quite properly the concern of its elected or appointed officials. Indeed, a decisionmaker would be derelict in his duties if, at some point, he did not consider whether his decision comports with constitutional mandates and did not weigh the risk that a violation might result in an award of damages from the public treasury. As one commentator aptly put it: "Whatever other concerns should shape a particular official's actions, certainly one of them should be the constitutional rights of individuals who will be affected by his actions. To criticize section 1983 liability because it leads decisionmakers to avoid the infringement of constitutional rights is to criticize one of the statute's *raisons d'etre*."

IV

In sum, our decision holding that municipalities have no immunity from damages liability flowing from their constitutional violations harmonizes well with developments in the common law and our own pronouncements on official immunities under § 1983. Doctrines of tort law have changed significantly over the past century, and our notions of governmental responsibility should properly reflect that evolution. No longer is individual "blameworthiness" the acid test of liability; the principle of equitable loss-spreading has joined fault as a factor in distributing the costs of official misconduct.

We believe that today's decision, together with prior precedents in this area, properly allocates these costs among the three principals in the scenario of the § 1983 cause of action: the victim of the constitutional deprivation; the officer whose conduct caused the injury; and the public, as represented by the municipal entity. The innocent individual who is harmed by an abuse of governmental authority is assured that he will be compensated for his injury. The offending official, so long as he conducts himself in good faith, may go about his business secure in the knowledge that a qualified immunity will protect him from personal liability for damages that are more appropriately chargeable to the populace as a whole. And the public will be forced to bear only the costs of injury inflicted by the "execution of a government's policy or custom, whether made by its lawmakers or by those whose edicts or acts may fairly be said to represent official policy." *Monell v. New York City Dept. of Social Services.*

Reversed.

Mr. Justice **Powell**, with whom The Chief Justice, Mr. Justice **Stewart**, and Mr. Justice **Rehnquist** join, dissenting.

The Court today holds that the City of Independence may be liable in damages for violating a constitutional right that was unknown when the events in this case occurred. It finds a denial of due process in the city's failure to grant petitioner a hearing to clear his name after he was discharged. But his dismissal involved only the proper exercise of discretionary powers according to prevailing constitutional doctrine. The city imposed no stigma on petitioner that would require a "name clearing" hearing under the Due Process Clause.

On the basis of this alleged deprivation of rights, the Court interprets 42 U.S.C. § 1983 to impose strict liability on municipalities for constitutional violations. This strict liability approach inexplicably departs from this Court's prior decisions under § 1983 and runs counter to the concerns of the 42d Congress when it enacted the statute. The Court's ruling also ignores the vast weight of common-law precedent as well as the current state law of municipal immunity. For these reasons, and because this decision will hamper local governments unnecessarily, I dissent.

* * *

The Court turns a blind eye to this overwhelming evidence that municipalities have enjoyed a qualified immunity and to the policy considerations that for the life of this Republic have justified its retention. This disregard of precedent and policy is especially unfortunate because suits under § 1983 typically implicate evolving constitutional standards. A good-faith defense is much more important for those actions than in those involving ordinary tort liability. The duty not to run over a pedestrian with a municipal bus is far less likely to change than is the rule as to what process, if any, is due the busdriver if he claims the right to a hearing after discharge.

The right of a discharged government employee to a "name clearing" hearing was not recognized until our decision in *Board of Regents v. Roth.* That ruling was handed down 10 weeks after Owen was discharged and 8 weeks after the city denied his request for a hearing. By stripping the city of any immunity, the Court punishes it for failing to predict our decision in Roth. As a result, local governments and their officials will face the unnerving prospect of crushing damages judgments whenever a policy valid under current law is later found to be unconstitutional. I can see no justice or wisdom in that outcome.

NOTES

1. Does the Court rely on section 1983's legislative history and the common law background? Does it bring to bear theories of liability that were not current in 1871? Is equitable loss spreading one of them? If so, is there anything wrong with that? Why should *Monroe v. Pape*'s "background of tort liability" be frozen in 1871?

2. Does *Owen* promote the compensatory function of section 1983 liability? Does it promote the deterrence or enforcement function of section 1983?

3. How does *Owen* operate in practice? Suppose both a local government and one of its officials are sued for damages under section 1983 and the official turns out to be protected by absolute immunity. Is the local government therefore immune as well? If the answer is no, then suppose the official is protected by qualified immunity. Does the local government now escape liability for compensatory damages?

4. Is the no-qualified-immunity rule fair to local governments? Or is it unjust? Doesn't *Owen* mean that a local government, unlike an official or employee, can be liable for damages in a case of first impression? Does this amount to strict liability (without fault)?

If so, is there any way around this result? *See Chevron Oil Co. v. Huson*, 404 U.S. 97 (1971), setting out equitable guidelines for retroactivity in civil cases. *But see Harper v. Virginia Dept. of Taxation*, 113 S. Ct. 2510 (1993), rejecting equitable guidelines and announcing a universally applicable rule of retroactivity in civil cases. See generally Brown, *The Demise of Constitutional Prospectivity: New Life for Owen?* 79 Iowa L. Rev. 273 (1994).

B. A Note on *Fact Concerts* and Absolute Immunity From Punitive Damages Liability

1. In *City of Newport v. Fact Concerts*, 453 U.S. 247 (1981), the Supreme Court conferred a semblance of immunity on local governments by holding that they are absolutely immune from punitive damages liability. Its approach was straightforward. First, it stated that the common law background suggested absolute immunity from punitive damages. Second, the legislative history of section 1983 did not indicate a Congressional rejection of this common law background. Finally, the Court considered the objectives of punitive damages, considerations of policy and section 1983's purposes. Among other factors, it found significant that compensatory damages awards against local governments provided sufficient incentives for their constitutional compliance and that punitive damages awards against officials and employees are an adequate means of deterring them. The Court also observed that a different result would create serious risks to the financial stability of local governments by exposing them to unpredictable punitive damages awards at the hands of juries.

2. Does *Fact Concerts* undermine *Owen v. City of Independence*? Or, as the Court suggests, is the availability of punitive damages largely irrelevant to constitutional compliance by local governments? What is the connection between compensatory and punitive damages? *See* Chapter 9 on damages.

3. *Fact Concerts* may very well represent the view of the Court that "enough is enough." After all, *Monell* overruled *Monroe* with the result that local governments suddenly became suable persons exposed to significant potential liability, and *Owen* shortly thereafter held that local governments were not even protected by qualified immunity.

4. May a local government *voluntarily* pay a punitive damages award directed at individual defendants? In *Cornwell v. City of Riverside*, 896 F.2d 398, 399 (9th Cir. 1990), the Ninth Circuit asked the following question: "Can a plaintiff successful in an action under 42 U.S.C. § 1983 and awarded punitive damages by the jury compel their payment to be made by the individual defendants rather than by the city that employed them?" It answered: "We agree with the district court that there is no federal prohibition against the city paying the punitive damages." Does this make sense? See the more extensive discussion of damages in Chapter 9.

III. How Does One Sue a Governmental Body?

This section addresses several important threshold questions that must be confronted in every section 1983 damages action against local governments. Recall *Monell*'s official policy or custom requirement. How is an official policy or custom pleaded? Since federal courts are notice pleading forums pursuant to Rule 8 of the Federal Rules of Civil Procedure, is it sufficient that a plaintiff simply allege in conclusory terms that a local government's official policy or custom caused the plaintiff's constitutional deprivation? Or is some form of fact pleading required? Also, how does the plaintiff as a formal matter name the local government? Finally, and apart from pleading, suppose it turns out that there was no constitutional violation to begin with. Might the local government still be liable? Does the absolute or qualified immunity of the official or employee who acted unconstitutionally have anything to do with local government liability?

A. Pleading Requirements: *Leatherman*

Leatherman v. Tarrant County Narcotics Unit

113 S. Ct. 1160 (1993)

Chief Justice **Rehnquist** delivered the opinion of the Court.

We granted certiorari to decide whether a federal court may apply a "heightened pleading standard"—more stringent than the usual pleading requirements of Rule 8(a) of the Federal Rules of Civil Procedure—in civil rights cases alleging municipal liability under Rev. Stat. § 1979, 42 U.S.C. § 1983. We hold it may not.

We review here a decision granting a motion to dismiss, and therefore must accept as true all the factual allegations in the complaint. *United States v. Gaubert.* This action arose out of two separate incidents involving the execution of search warrants by local law enforcement officers. Each involved the forcible entry into a home based on the detection of odors associated with the manufacture of narcotics. One homeowner claimed that he was assaulted by the officers after they had entered; another claimed that the police had entered her home in her absence and killed her two dogs. Plaintiffs sued several local officials in their official capacity and the county and two municipal corporations that employed the police officers involved in the incidents, asserting that the police conduct had violated the Fourth Amendment to the United States Constitution. The stated basis for municipal liability under *Monell v. New York City Dept. of Social Services* was the failure of these bodies adequately to train the police officers involved. *Canton v. Harris.*

The United States District Court for the Northern District of Texas ordered the complaints dismissed, because they failed to meet the "heightened pleading standard" required by the decisional law of the Court of Appeals for the Fifth Circuit. The Fifth Circuit, in turn, affirmed the judgment of dismissal and we granted certiorari to resolve a conflict among the Courts of Appeals concerning the applicability of a heightened pleading standard to § 1983 actions alleging municipal liability. Compare, e. g., *Karim-Panahi v. Los Angeles Police Dept.* ("a claim of municipal liability under section 1983 is sufficient to withstand a motion to dismiss even if the claim is based on nothing more than a bare allegation that the individual officers' conduct conformed to official policy, custom, or practice") We now reverse.

Respondents seek to defend the Fifth Circuit's application of a more rigorous pleading standard on two grounds. First, respondents claim that municipalities' freedom from respondeat superior liability, *supra*, necessarily includes immunity from suit. In this sense, respondents assert, municipalities are no different from state or local officials sued in their individual capacity. Respondents reason that a more relaxed pleading requirement would subject municipalities to expensive and time consuming discovery in every § 1983 case, eviscerating their immunity from suit and disrupting municipal functions.

This argument wrongly equates freedom from liability with immunity from suit. To be sure, we reaffirmed in *Monell* that "a municipality cannot be held liable under § 1983 on a respondeat superior theory." But, contrary to respondents' assertions, this protection against liability does not encompass immunity from suit. Indeed, this argument is flatly contradicted by *Monell* and our later decisions involving municipal liability under § 1983. In *Monell*, we overruled *Monroe v. Pape*, insofar as it held that local governments were wholly immune from suit under § 1983, though we did reserve decision on whether municipalities are entitled to some form of limited immunity. Yet, when we took that issue up again in *Owen v. City of Independence*, we rejected a claim that municipalities should be afforded qualified immunity, much like that afforded individual officials, based on the good faith of their agents. These decisions make it quite clear that, unlike various government officials, municipalities do not enjoy immunity from suit—either absolute or qualified—under § 1983. In short, a municipality can be sued under § 1983, but it cannot be held liable unless a municipal policy or custom caused the constitutional injury. We thus have no occasion to consider whether our qualified immunity jurisprudence would require a heightened pleading in cases involving individual government officials.

Second, respondents contend that the Fifth Circuit's heightened pleading standard is not really that at all. According to respondents, the degree of factual specificity required of a complaint by the Federal Rules of Civil Procedure varies according to the complexity of the underlying substantive law. To establish municipal liability under § 1983, respondents argue, a plaintiff must do more than plead a single instance of misconduct. This requirement, respondents insist, is consistent with a plaintiff's Rule 11 obligation to make a reasonable pre-filing inquiry into the facts.

But examination of the Fifth Circuit's decision in this case makes it quite evident that the "heightened pleading standard" is just what it purports to be: a more demanding rule for pleading a complaint under § 1983 than for pleading other kinds of claims for relief. This rule was adopted by the Fifth Circuit in *Elliott v. Perez* and described in this language:

> "In cases against government officials involving the likely defense of immunity we require of trial judges that they demand that the plaintiff's complaints state with factual detail and particularity the basis for the claim which necessarily includes why the defendant-official cannot successfully maintain the defense of immunity."

In later cases, the Fifth Circuit extended this rule to complaints against municipal corporations asserting liability under § 1983.

We think that it is impossible to square the "heightened pleading standard" applied by the Fifth Circuit in this case with the liberal system of "notice pleading" set up by the Federal Rules. Rule 8(a)(2) requires that a complaint include only "a short and plain statement of the claim showing that the pleader is entitled to relief." In *Conley v. Gibson* we said in effect that the Rule meant what it said:

> "The Federal Rules of Civil Procedure do not require a claimant to set out in detail the facts upon which he bases his claim. To the contrary, all the Rules require is 'a short and plain statement of the claim' that will give the defendant fair notice of what the plaintiff's claim is and the grounds upon which it rests."

Rule 9(b) does impose a particularity requirement in two specific instances. It provides that "in all averments of fraud or mistake, the circumstances constituting fraud or mistake shall be stated with particularity." Thus, the Federal Rules do address in Rule 9(b) the question of the need for greater particularity in pleading certain actions, but do not include among the enumerated actions any reference to complaints alleging municipal liability under § 1983. *Expressio unius est exclusio alterius.*

The phenomenon of litigation against municipal corporations based on claimed constitutional violations by their employees dates from our decision in Monell, supra, where we for the first time construed § 1983 to allow such municipal liability. Perhaps if Rules 8

and 9 were re-written today, claims against municipalities under § 1983 might be subjected to the added specificity requirement of Rule 9(b). But that is a result which must be obtained by the process of amending the Federal Rules, and not by judicial interpretation. In the absence of such an amendment, federal courts and litigants must rely on summary judgment and control of discovery to weed out unmeritorious claims sooner rather than later.

The judgment of the Court of Appeals is reversed, and the case remanded for further proceedings consistent with this opinion.

NOTES

1. What is the precise holding in *Leatherman*? Did the Court leave any pleading question open? If so, why? *See* Justice Kennedy's concurring opinion in *Siegert v. Gilley*, 111 S. Ct. 1789, 1795 (1991) regarding heightened pleading requirements in certain individual liability cases. How should that open question be answered? See Chapter 8 on the procedural aspects of qualified immunity.

2. How would you characterize the tone and reasoning of the Court's opinion? Do that tone and reasoning suggest particular answers to the preceding questions?

3. Why do you suppose that federal courts would ever impose heightened pleading requirements on section 1983 plaintiffs?

B. The Crucial Distinction Between Official and Individual Capacity Damages Actions

A considerable, but unnecessary, source of confusion for lawyers and judges alike in the section 1983 setting is the difference between official and individual capacity damages actions. Official capacity damages actions are actions against the governmental employer. Where an official capacity damages action is brought against a *local government* official or employee, it is a damages action against the local government itself and thus triggers *Monell's* official policy or custom requirement. If an official capacity damages action is brought against a *state* official or employee, it is a damages action against the state itself which, after *Will*, is not permitted.

In contrast, an individual capacity damages action against either a local or state official or employee is a damages action against the official personally. Such a damages action may implicate absolute or qualified immunity, as the case may be, but it does *not* trigger *Monell*'s official policy or custom requirement. It also raises the possibility of a punitive damages award against the individual.

1. The origin of the confusion between the two might be the following:

> Perhaps the major reason that lawyers all too often do not understand this distinction is that they erroneously think that § 1983's "color of law" requirement . . . means that *every* § 1983 damages suit, even one against local government or state officials personally (that is, in their individual capacities), must of necessity be an official capacity damages action as well. These lawyers do not realize that "color of law" is not synonymous with official capacity and that it is typically present in *both* individual capacity *and* official capacity damages actions. The Third Circuit put it this way: "It does not follow that every time a public official acts under color of state law, the suit must of necessity be one against the official in his or her official capacity."

S. Nahmod, 1 *Civil Rights and Civil Liberties Litigation: The Law of Section 1983* 488 (3d ed. 1991) (citations omitted) (quoting *Melo v. Hafer*, 912 F.2d 628, 636 (3rd Cir. 1990), *affd*, 112 S. Ct. 358 (1991)).

2. The distinction is important not only for liability purposes. It can also be significant for attorney's fees purposes as well. For example, in *Kentucky v. Graham*, 473 U.S. 159 (1985), the Court, confronted with a successful damages action against state officials, held that the state could not be held responsible for attorney's fees because under the Eleventh Amendment it could not be held liable on the merits. Consequently, the damages action must have been directed at the defendants solely in their individual or personal capacities, and only they—and not the state—could be responsible for attorney's fees.

3. The Supreme Court revisited this issue in *Hafer v. Melo*, 112 S. Ct. 358 (1991), where it held that state officials sued for damages in their individual capacities are "persons" suable under section 1983 and that such suits are not barred by the Eleventh Amendment. It rejected a reading of *Will v. Michigan Department of State Police* that section 1983 "does not authorize suits against state officers for damages arising out of official acts." The plaintiff sued the Pennsylvania Auditor General for damages in her individual capacity but the defendant argued that under *Will* she could not be held personally liable because the challenged conduct was undertaken in her official capacity. The Supreme Court unanimously disagreed (Justice Thomas did not participate) and, affirming the Third Circuit, explained once again the important differences between individual capacity and official capacity damages actions against state officials. Only the latter were barred by *Will* because they were in effect suits against the state which is not a person. However, individual capacity damages actions were personal capacity suits which sought to impose personal liability on the individuals sued and were therefore not barred by *Will* at all. The Court went on to declare that such individual capacity damages actions against state officials were similarly not barred by the Eleventh Amendment.

4. The best way to avoid confusion about these matters is for plaintiff's attorneys to explicitly sue the relevant individuals and/or local governments without using the language of official capacity damages actions. The complaint should identify the local government as a party defendant and properly allege an official policy or custom, as required by *Monell*.

What happens if a complaint nevertheless speaks in terms of official capacity damages actions? Consider the following warning:

> In order to avoid further confusion on this issue [of potential local government liability where an official is successfully sued for damages in his or her official capacity] in the future, where a complaint alleges that the conduct of a public official acting under color of state law gives rise to liability under Section 1983, we will ordinarily assume that he has been sued in his official capacity and only in that capacity . . . . If a plaintiff intends to sue public

officials in their individual capacities or in both their official and individual capacities . . . he should expressly state so in the complaint.

Kolar v. County of Sangamon, 756 F.2d 564, 568–69 (7th Cir. 1985).

C. The Requirement of a Constitutional Violation: *Heller*

In *City of Los Angeles v. Heller*, 475 U.S. 796 (1986) (per curiam), the Court dealt with a damages action in which the plaintiff sued various defendants, including two police officers and a city, for an allegedly illegal arrest and the use of excessive force against him. Following a bifurcated trial on the claim against one of the police officers—the other had previously been dismissed—there was a jury verdict against the plaintiff followed by dismissal of the action against the city on the ground that the city could not be liable in the absence of a constitutional violation by the police officer. There was no qualified immunity instruction. The Ninth Circuit reversed the dismissal of the city, reasoning that the jury might have applied qualified immunity even without an instruction to that effect. Since there was some ambiguity in the jury verdict, the plaintiff should have an opportunity to prove an official policy based upon police department regulations.

In turn reversing, the Supreme Court noted that the major problem with the Ninth Circuit's reasoning was that no such qualified immunity instruction was ever given. The Court stated that in a § 1983 damages action, "[i]f a person has suffered no constitutional injury at the hands of the individual police officer, the fact that the departmental regulations might have *authorized* the use of constitutionally excessive force is quite beside the point."

Heller makes clear that local government liability must be premised on a constitutional violation by *someone*. Suppose, in contrast to *Heller*, an individual defendant escapes damages liability on either absolute or qualified immunity grounds. Since there could well be a constitutional violation in such circumstances, the local government would not necessarily avoid liability under *Heller*. Only if there is an accompanying determination that there was no constitutional violation in the first place would *Heller* apply.

IV. The First Route to Governmental Liability: The Government Itself Acts

A. Formal Official Policy

Monell v. Department of Social Services was an easy case in which to find official policy because there the challenged conduct was an officially promulgated policy regarding pregnancy leaves. Similarly easy are those cases in which a local government formally and as a body makes a decision which, when executed by the body itself or its employees, gives rise to the alleged constitutional violation. Policy statements, ordinances, regulations and similar decisions are good examples. It does not matter whether the policy or decision is general and in the form of an ordinance or regulation, or is specific and particularized, affecting only one or a few individuals. *See, e.g., Bateson v. Geisse*, 857 F.2d 1300 (9th Cir. 1988) (single decision of city council to withhold building permit). It has also been held that a local government resolution adopted by a city council and directed against a named individual constituted an official policy although it was not an enforceable law. *Little v. City of North Miami*, 805 F.2d 962 (11th Cir. 1986).

Does it really make sense to speak about a local government's "acting"? Do *Monell* and its progeny treat local governments as if they were natural persons? If so, does not such treatment imply that tort concepts developed for individual wrongdoing should similarly govern local government liability? Is this sound? *See* Whitman, *Government Responsibility for Constitutional Torts*, 85 Mich. L. Rev. 226 (1986), reprinted in *Section 1983 Anthology* 52.

B. Custom

Monell declares that a local government may be liable not only for its official policy but for its custom as well. What does "custom" mean? It may be helpful to think of it as a *de facto* official policy, which differs from official policy in that there is no *formal* evidence of its establishment. According to *Monell*, an actionable policy must be persistent and well-settled.

Why should custom give rise to section 1983 local government liability? The Ninth Circuit answered as follows: "The existence of custom as a basis for liability under § 1983 . . . serves a critical role in insuring that local government entities are held responsible for widespread abuses or practices that cannot be affirmatively attributed to the decisions or ratification of an official government policy maker but are so pervasive as to have the force of law." *Thompson v. City of Los Angeles*, 885 F.2d 1439, 1444 (9th Cir. 1989).

Consider in this regard *Webster v. City of Houston*, 689 F.2d 1220 (5th Cir. 1982), *affd*, 739 F.2d 993 (5th Cir. 1984) (en banc), where the court affirmed a jury verdict against a city in favor of the plaintiffs who claimed that police officers unconstitutionally shot and killed plaintiffs' decedent. According to the Fifth Circuit, there was sufficient evidence to show that it was police department policy or custom to use a "throw-down" gun to be put near an unarmed suspect who had been shot by police officers, so as to justify the shooting. Among other things: the throw-down was almost universally used in the police department; recruits learned to protect themselves in this way while still in the police academy; twenty police officers stood around decedent after he was shot and debated the use of a throw-down; the use of throw-downs was widely known to high officials in the police department, but they never told officers to stop using them; and officers knew they could get away with using throw-downs. All of this encouraged police officers in their illegal activities, including the shooting of decedent and the subsequent attempt to cover up by all levels of the police department.

Notice that *Webster* is a case in which lower level employees, here police officers, engaged in a custom that was so pervasive that the local government or its high-ranking officials either knew of it or were reckless with regard to its existence.

V. The Second Route to Governmental Liability: Attribution Through Policymakers

Recall that *Monell* declared without much explanation that local government liability can be premised on the unconstitutional conduct of those "whose edicts or acts may fairly be said to represent official policy." This kind of liability was referred to earlier in this chapter as liability through *attribution*. Until the Supreme Court began to deal with these attribution issues in a series of cases set out next, the general rule in the circuits was that local governments could be held liable through attribution of the conduct of officials who were the *final repository of power* over the kind of conduct challenged. *See, e.g., Rookard v. Health & Hospitals Corp.*, 710 F.2d 41 (2d Cir. 1983) and *Wilson v. Taylor*, 733 F.2d 1539 (11th Cir. 1984). However, in *Bennett v. City of Slidell*, 728 F.2d 762 (5th Cir. 1984) (en banc), *affd*, 735 F.2d 861 (5th Cir. 1984) (per curiam), the Fifth Circuit articulated a *delegation of policymaking authority* approach which eventually became dominant, as we shall see. Under this approach, the inquiry is whether a local government has delegated policymaking authority to the particular official.

A. *Pembaur*: The Court's First Encounter With Attribution

Pembaur v. City of Cincinnati

475 U.S. 469 (1986)

Justice **Brennan** delivered the opinion of the Court, except as to Part II-B.

In *Monell v. New York City Dept. of Social Services* the Court concluded that municipal liability under 42 U.S.C. § 1983 is limited to deprivations of federally protected rights caused by action taken "pursuant to official municipal policy of some nature . . . .". The question presented is whether, and in what circumstances, a decision by municipal policymakers on a single occasion may satisfy this requirement.

I

Bertold Pembaur is a licensed Ohio physician and the sole proprietor of the Rockdale Medical Center, located in the city of Cincinnati in Hamilton County. Most of Pembaur's patients are welfare recipients who rely on government assistance to pay for medical care. During the spring of 1977, Simon Leis, the Hamilton County Prosecutor, began investigating charges that Pembaur fraudulently had accepted payments from state welfare agencies for services not actually provided to patients. A grand jury was convened, and the case was assigned to Assistant Prosecutor William Whalen. In April, the grand jury charged Pembaur in a six-count indictment.

During the investigation, the grand jury issued subpoenas for the appearance of two of Pembaur's employees. When these employees failed to appear as directed, the Prosecutor obtained capiases for their arrest and detention from the Court of Common Pleas of Hamilton County.

On May 19, 1977, two Hamilton County Deputy Sheriffs attempted to serve the capiases at Pembaur's clinic. Although the reception area is open to the public, the rest of the clinic may be entered only through a door next to the receptionist's window. Upon arriving, the Deputy Sheriffs identified themselves to the receptionist and sought to pass through this door, which was apparently open. The receptionist blocked their way and asked them to wait for the doctor. When Pembaur appeared a moment later, he and the receptionist closed the door, which automatically locked from the inside, and wedged a piece of wood between it and the wall. Returning to the receptionist's window, the Deputy Sheriffs identified themselves to Pembaur, showed him the capiases and explained why they were there. Pembaur refused to let them enter, claiming that the police had no legal authority to be there and requesting that they leave. He told them that he had called the Cincinnati police, the local media, and his lawyer. The Deputy Sheriffs decided not to take further action until the Cincinnati police arrived.

Shortly thereafter, several Cincinnati police officers appeared. The Deputy Sheriffs explained the situation to them and asked that they speak to Pembaur. The Cincinnati police told Pembaur that the papers were lawful and

that he should allow the Deputy Sheriffs to enter. When Pembaur refused, the Cincinnati police called for a superior officer. When he too failed to persuade Pembaur to open the door, the Deputy Sheriffs decided to call their supervisor for further instructions. Their supervisor told them to call Assistant Prosecutor Whalen and to follow his instructions. The Deputy Sheriffs then telephoned Whalen and informed him of the situation. Whalen conferred with County Prosecutor Leis, who told Whalen to instruct the Deputy Sheriffs to "go in and get [the witnesses]." Whalen in turn passed these instructions along to the Deputy Sheriffs.

After a final attempt to persuade Pembaur voluntarily to allow them to enter, the Deputy Sheriffs tried unsuccessfully to force the door. City police officers, who had been advised of the County Prosecutor's instructions to "go in and get" the witnesses, obtained an axe and chopped down the door. The Deputy Sheriffs then entered and searched the clinic. Two individuals who fit descriptions of the witnesses sought were detained, but turned out not to be the right persons.

After this incident, the Prosecutor obtained an additional indictment against Pembaur for obstructing police in the performance of an authorized act. Although acquitted of all other charges, Pembaur was convicted for this offense. The Ohio Court of Appeals reversed, reasoning that Pembaur was privileged under state law to exclude the deputies because the search of his office violated the Fourth Amendment. The Ohio Supreme Court reversed and reinstated the conviction. The Supreme Court held that the state-law privilege applied only to bad-faith conduct by law enforcement officials, and that, under the circumstances of this case, Pembaur was obliged to acquiesce to the search and seek redress later in a civil action for damages.

On April 20, 1981, Pembaur filed the present action in the United States District Court for the Southern District of Ohio against the city of Cincinnati, the County of Hamilton, the Cincinnati Police Chief, the Hamilton County Sheriff, the members of the Hamilton Board of County Commissioners (in their official capacities only), Assistant Prosecutor Whalen, and nine city and county police officers. Pembaur sought damages under 42 U.S.C. § 1983, alleging that the county and city police had violated his rights under the Fourth and Fourteenth Amendments. His theory was that, absent exigent circumstances, the Fourth Amendment prohibits police from searching an individual's home or business without a search warrant even to execute an arrest warrant for a third person. We agreed with that proposition in *Steagald v. United States*, decided the day after Pembaur filed this lawsuit. Pembaur sought $ 10 million in actual and $ 10 million in punitive damages, plus costs and attorney's fees.

Much of the testimony at the 4-day trial concerned the practices of the Hamilton County Police in serving capiases. Frank Webb, one of the Deputy Sheriffs present at the clinic on May 19, testified that he had previously served capiases on the property of third persons without a search warrant, but had never been required to use force to gain access. Assistant Prosecutor Whalen was also unaware of a prior instance in which police had been denied access to a third person's property in serving a capias and had used force to gain entry. Lincoln Stokes, the County Sheriff, testified that the Department had no written policy respecting the serving of capiases on the property of third persons and that the proper response in any given situation would depend upon the circumstances. He too could not recall a specific instance in which entrance had been denied and forcibly gained. Sheriff Stokes did testify, however, that it was the practice in his Department to refer questions to the County Prosecutor for instructions under appropriate circumstances and that "it was the proper thing to do" in this case.

* * *

The Court of Appeals affirmed the District Court's dismissal of Pembaur's claim against Hamilton County . . . . The court held that the County Board's lack of control over the Sheriff would not preclude county liability if "the nature and duties of the Sheriff are such that his acts may fairly be said to represent the county's official policy with respect to the specific subject matter." Based upon its examination of Ohio law, the Court of Appeals found it "[clear]" that the Sheriff and the Prosecutor were both county officials authorized to establish "the official policy of Hamilton County" with respect to matters of law

enforcement. Notwithstanding these conclusions, however, the court found that Pembaur's claim against the county had been properly dismissed:

"We believe that Pembaur failed to prove the existence of a county policy in this case. Pembaur claims that the deputy sheriffs acted pursuant to the policies of the Sheriff and Prosecutor by forcing entry into the medical center. Pembaur has failed to establish, however, anything more than that, on this *one occasion*, the Prosecutor and the Sheriff decided to force entry into his office. . . . That single, discrete decision is insufficient, by itself, to establish that the Prosecutor, the Sheriff, or both were implementing a governmental policy." (emphasis in original).

Pembaur petitioned for certiorari to review only the dismissal of his claim against Hamilton County. The decision of the Court of Appeals conflicts with holdings in several other Courts of Appeals, and we granted the petition to resolve the conflict. We reverse.

II

A

Our analysis must begin with the proposition that "Congress did not intend municipalities to be held liable unless action pursuant to official municipal policy of some nature caused a constitutional tort." *Monell v. New York City Dept. of Social Services*. As we read its opinion, the Court of Appeals held that a single decision to take particular action, although made by municipal policymakers, cannot establish the kind of "official policy" required by *Monell* as a predicate to municipal liability under § 1983. The Court of Appeals reached this conclusion without referring to *Monell* —indeed, without any explanation at all. However, examination of the opinion in *Monell* clearly demonstrates that the Court of Appeals misinterpreted its holding.

Monell is a case about responsibility. In the first part of the opinion, we held that local government units could be made liable under § 1983 for deprivations of federal rights, overruling a contrary holding in *Monroe v. Pape*. In the second part of the opinion, we recognized a limitation on this liability and concluded that a municipality cannot be made liable by application of the doctrine of respondeat superior. See *Monell.* In part, this conclusion rested upon the language of § 1983, which imposes liability only on a person who "subjects, or causes to be subjected," any individual to a deprivation of federal rights; we noted that this language "cannot easily be read to impose liability vicariously on government bodies solely on the basis of the existence of an employer-employee relationship with a tortfeasor." Primarily, however, our conclusion rested upon the legislative history, which disclosed that, while Congress never questioned its power to impose civil liability on municipalities for their own illegal acts, Congress did doubt its constitutional power to impose such liability in order to oblige municipalities to control the conduct of others. We found that, because of these doubts, Congress chose not to create such obligations in § 1983. Recognizing that this would be the effect of a federal law of respondeat superior, we concluded that § 1983 could not be interpreted to incorporate doctrines of vicarious liability.

The conclusion that tortious conduct, to be the basis for municipal liability under § 1983, must be pursuant to a municipality's "official policy" is contained in this discussion. The "official policy" requirement was intended to distinguish acts of the municipality from acts of employees of the municipality, and thereby make clear that municipal liability is limited to action for which the municipality is actually responsible. *Monell* reasoned that recovery from a municipality is limited to acts that are, properly speaking, acts "of the municipality"—that is, acts which the municipality has officially sanctioned or ordered.

With this understanding, it is plain that municipal liability may be imposed for a single decision by municipal policymakers under appropriate circumstances. No one has ever doubted, for instance, that a municipality may be liable under § 1983 for a single decision by its properly constituted legislative body—whether or not that body had taken similar action in the past or intended to do so in the future—because even a single decision by such a body unquestionably constitutes an act of official government policy. See, e. g., *Owen v. City of Independence* (City Council passed resolution firing plaintiff without a pretermination hearing); *Newport v. Fact Concerts, Inc.* (City Council canceled license permitting concert because of dispute over content of performance). But the power to establish policy is no more the exclusive province of the legislature at the local level than at the state or national level. *Monell's* language makes clear that it expressly envisioned other officials "whose acts or edicts may fairly be said to represent official policy," *Monell,* and whose decisions therefore may give rise to municipal liability under § 1983.

Indeed, any other conclusion would be inconsistent with the principles underlying § 1983. To be sure, "official policy" often refers to formal rules or understandings—often but not always committed to writing—that are intended to, and do, establish fixed plans of action to be followed under similar circumstances consistently and over time. That was the case in *Monell* itself, which involved a written rule requiring pregnant employees to take unpaid leaves of absence before such leaves were medically necessary. However, as in *Owen* and *Newport,* a government frequently chooses a course of action tailored to a particular situation and not intended to control decisions in later situations. If the decision to adopt that particular course of action is properly made by that government's authorized decisionmakers, it surely represents an act of official government "policy" as that term is commonly understood. More importantly, where action is directed by those who establish governmental policy, the municipality is equally responsible whether that action is to be taken only once or to be taken repeatedly. To deny compensation to the victim would therefore be contrary to the fundamental purpose of § 1983.

B

Having said this much, we hasten to emphasize that not every decision by municipal officers automatically subjects the municipality to § 1983 liability. Municipal liability attaches only where the decisionmaker possesses final authority to establish municipal policy with respect to the action ordered. The fact that a particular official—even a policymaking official—has discretion in the exercise of particular functions does not, without more, give rise to municipal liability based on an exercise of that discretion. See, e. g., *Oklahoma City v. Tuttle.* The official must also be responsible for establishing final government policy respecting such activity before the municipality can be held liable.[12] Authority to make municipal policy may be granted directly by a legislative enactment or may be delegated by an official who possesses such authority, and of course, whether an official had final policymaking authority is a question of state law. However, like other governmental entities, municipalities often spread policymaking authority among various officers and official bodies. As a result, particular officers may have authority to establish binding county policy respecting particular matters and to adjust that policy for the county in changing circumstances. To hold a municipality liable for actions ordered by such officers exercising their policymaking authority is no more an application of the theory of respondeat superior than was holding the municipalities liable for the decisions of the City Councils in *Owen* and *Newport*. In each case municipal liability attached to a single decision to take unlawful action made by municipal policymakers. We hold that municipal liability under § 1983 attaches where—and only where—a deliberate choice to follow a course of action is made from among various alternatives by the official or officials responsible for establishing final policy with respect to the subject matter in question. See *Tuttle* ("'policy' generally implies a course of action consciously chosen from among various alternatives").

C

Applying this standard to the case before us, we have little difficulty concluding that the

---

[12] Thus, for example, the County Sheriff may have discretion to hire and fire employees without also being the county official responsible for establishing county employment policy. If this were the case, the Sheriff's decisions respecting employment would not give rise to municipal liability, although similar decisions with respect to law enforcement practices, over which the Sheriff is the official policymaker, would give rise to municipal liability. Instead, if county employment policy was set by the Board of County Commissioners, only that body's decisions would provide a basis for county liability. This would be true even if the Board left the Sheriff discretion to hire and fire employees and the Sheriff exercised that discretion in an unconstitutional manner; the decision to act unlawfully would not be a decision of the Board. However, if the Board delegated its power to establish final employment policy to the Sheriff, the Sheriff's decisions would represent county policy and could give rise to municipal liability.

Court of Appeals erred in dismissing petitioner's claim against the county. The Deputy Sheriffs who attempted to serve the capiases at petitioner's clinic found themselves in a difficult situation. Unsure of the proper course of action to follow, they sought instructions from their supervisors. The instructions they received were to follow the orders of the County Prosecutor. The Prosecutor made a considered decision based on his understanding of the law and commanded the officers forcibly to enter petitioner's clinic. That decision directly caused the violation of petitioner's Fourth Amendment rights.

Respondent argues that the County Prosecutor lacked authority to establish municipal policy respecting law enforcement practices because only the County Sheriff may establish policy respecting such practices. Respondent suggests that the County Prosecutor was merely rendering "legal advice" when he ordered the Deputy Sheriffs to "go in and get" the witnesses. Consequently, the argument concludes, the action of the individual Deputy Sheriffs in following this advice and forcibly entering petitioner's clinic was not pursuant to a properly established municipal policy.

We might be inclined to agree with respondent if we thought that the Prosecutor had only rendered "legal advice." However, the Court of Appeals concluded, based upon its examination of Ohio law, that both the County Sheriff and the County Prosecutor could establish county policy under appropriate circumstances, a conclusion that we do not question here. Ohio Rev. Code Ann. § 309.09(A) (1979) provides that county officers may "require . . . instructions from [the County Prosecutor] in matters connected with their official duties." Pursuant to standard office procedure, the Sheriff's Office referred this matter to the Prosecutor and then followed his instructions. The Sheriff testified that his Department followed this practice under appropriate circumstances and that it was "the proper thing to do" in this case. We decline to accept respondent's invitation to overlook this delegation of authority by disingenuously labeling the Prosecutor's clear command mere "legal advice." In ordering the Deputy Sheriffs to enter petitioner's clinic the County Prosecutor was acting as the final decisionmaker for the county, and the county may therefore be held liable under § 1983.

The decision of the Court of Appeals is reversed, and the case is remanded for further proceedings consistent with this opinion.

Justice **White**, concurring.

The forcible entry made in this case was not then illegal under federal, state, or local law. The city of Cincinnati frankly conceded that forcible entry of third-party property to effect otherwise valid arrests was standard operating procedure. There is no reason to believe that respondent county would abjure using lawful means to execute the capiases issued in this case or had limited the authority of its officers to use force in executing capiases. Further, the county officials who had the authority to approve or disapprove such entries opted for the forceful entry, a choice that was later held to be inconsistent with the Fourth Amendment. Vesting discretion in its officers to use force and its use in this case sufficiently manifested county policy to warrant reversal of the judgment below.

This does not mean that every act of municipal officers with final authority to effect or authorize arrests and searches represents the policy of the municipality. It would be different if *Steagald v. United States* had been decided when the events at issue here occurred, if the State Constitution or statutes had forbidden forceful entries without a warrant, or if there had been a municipal ordinance to this effect. Local law enforcement officers are expected to obey the law and ordinarily swear to do so when they take office. Where the controlling law places limits on their authority, they cannot be said to have the authority to make contrary policy. Had the Sheriff or Prosecutor in this case failed to follow an existing warrant requirement, it would be absurd to say that he was nevertheless executing county policy in authorizing the forceful entry in this case and even stranger to say that the county would be liable if the Sheriff had secured a warrant and it turned out that he and the Magistrate had mistakenly thought there was probable cause for the warrant. If deliberate or mistaken acts like this, admittedly contrary to local law, expose the county to liability, it must be on the basis of respondent superior and not because the officers' acts represent local policy.

Such results would not conform to Monell and the cases following it. I do not understand

the Court to hold otherwise in stating that municipal liability attaches where "a deliberate choice to follow a course of action is made from among various alternatives by the official or officials responsible for establishing final policy with respect to the subject matter in question." A sheriff, for example, is not the final policymaker with respect to the probable-cause requirement for a valid arrest. He has no alternative but to act in accordance with the established standard; and his deliberate or mistaken departure from the controlling law of arrest would not represent municipal policy.

In this case, however, the Sheriff and the Prosecutor chose a course that was not forbidden by any applicable law, a choice that they then had the authority to make. This was county policy, and it was no less so at the time because a later decision of this Court declared unwarranted forceful entry into third-party premises to be violation of the Fourth Amendment. Hence, I join the Court's opinion and judgment.

Justice **Stevens**, concurring in part and concurring in the judgment.

This is not a hard case. If there is any difficulty, it arises from the problem of obtaining a consensus on the meaning of the word "policy"—a word that does not appear in the text of 42 U.S.C. § 1983, the statutory provision that we are supposed to be construing. The difficulty is thus a consequence of this Court's lawmaking efforts rather than the work of the Congress of the United States.

* * *

Justice **Powell**, with whom **The Chief Justice** and Justice **Rehnquist** join, dissenting.

The Court today holds Hamilton County liable for the forcible entry in May 1977 by Deputy Sheriffs into petitioner's office. The entry and subsequent search were pursuant to capiases for third parties—petitioner's employees—who had failed to answer a summons to appear as witnesses before a grand jury investigating petitioner. When petitioner refused to allow the Sheriffs to enter, one of them, at the request of his supervisor, called the office of the County Prosecutor for instructions. The Assistant County Prosecutor received the call, and apparently was in doubt as to what advice to give. He referred the question to the County Prosecutor, who advised the Deputy Sheriffs to "go in and get them [the witnesses]" pursuant to the capiases.

This five-word response to a single question over the phone is now found by this Court to have created an official county policy for which Hamilton County is liable under § 1983. This holding is wrong for at least two reasons. First, the Prosecutor's response and the Deputies' subsequent actions did not violate any constitutional right that existed at the time of the forcible entry. Second, no official county policy could have been created solely by an offhand telephone response from a busy County Prosecutor.

* * *

In my view, the question whether official policy—in any normal sense of the term—has been made in a particular case is not answered by explaining who has final authority to make policy. The question here is not "could the County Prosecutor make policy?" but rather, "did he make policy?" By focusing on the authority granted to the official under state law, the Court's test fails to answer the key federal question presented. The Court instead turns the question into one of state law. Under a test that focuses on the authority of the decisionmaker, the Court has only to look to state law for the resolution of this case. Here the Court of Appeals found that "both the County Sheriff and the County Prosecutor [had authority under Ohio law to] establish county policy under appropriate circumstances." Apparently that recitation of authority is all that is needed under the Court's test because no discussion is offered to demonstrate that the Sheriff or the Prosecutor actually used that authority to establish official county policy in this case.

Moreover, the Court's reasoning is inconsistent with *Monell*. Today's decision finds that policy is established because a policymaking official made a decision on the telephone that was within the scope of his authority. The Court ignores the fact that no business organization or governmental unit makes binding policy decisions so cavalierly. The Court provides no mechanism for distinguishing those acts or decisions that cannot fairly be construed to create official policy from the normal process of establishing an official policy

that would be followed by a responsible public entity. Thus, the Court has adopted in part what it rejected in *Monell*: local government units are now subject to respondeat superior liability, at least with respect to a certain category of employees, i. e., those with final authority to make policy. See *Monell*; see also *Oklahoma City v. Tuttle* (rejecting theories akin to respondeat superior) (plurality opinion). The Court's reliance on the status of the employee carries the concept of "policy" far beyond what was envisioned in *Monell*.

B

In my view, proper resolution of the question whether official policy has been formed should focus on two factors: (i) the nature of the decision reached or the action taken, and (ii) the process by which the decision was reached or the action was taken.

Focusing on the nature of the decision distinguishes between policies and mere ad hoc decisions. Such a focus also reflects the fact that most policies embody a rule of general applicability. That is the tenor of the Court's statement in *Monell* that local government units are liable under § 1983 when the action that is alleged to be unconstitutional "implements or executes a policy statement, ordinance, regulation, or decision officially adopted and promulgated by that body's officers." The clear implication is that policy is created when a rule is formed that applies to all similar situations—a "governing principle [or] plan." *Webster's New Twentieth Century Dictionary* 1392 (2d ed. 1979). When a rule of general applicability has been approved, the government has taken a position for which it can be held responsible.

Another factor indicating that policy has been formed is the process by which the decision at issue was reached. Formal procedures that involve, for example, voting by elected officials, prepared reports, extended deliberation, or official records indicate that the resulting decisions taken "may fairly be said to represent official policy," *Monell, supra. Owen v. City of Independence* provides an example. The City Council met in a regularly scheduled meeting. One member of the Council made a motion to release to the press certain reports that cast an employee in a bad light. After deliberation, the Council passed the motion with no dissents and one abstention. Although this official action did not establish a rule of general applicability, it is clear that policy was formed because of the process by which the decision was reached.

Applying these factors to the instant case demonstrates that no official policy was formulated. Certainly, no rule of general applicability was adopted. The Court correctly notes that the Sheriff "testified that the Department had no written policy respecting the serving of capiases on the property of third persons and that the proper response in any given situation would depend upon the circumstances." Nor could he recall a specific instance in which entrance had been denied and forcibly gained. The Court's result today rests on the implicit conclusion that the Prosecutor's response— "go in and get them"—altered the prior case-by-case approach of the Department and formed a new rule to apply in all similar cases. Nothing about the Prosecutor's response to the inquiry over the phone, nor the circumstances surrounding the response, indicates that such a rule of general applicability was formed.

Similarly, nothing about the way the decision was reached indicates that official policy was formed. The prosecutor, without time for thoughtful consideration or consultation, simply gave an off-the-cuff answer to a single question. There was no process at all. The Court's holding undercuts the basic rationale of *Monell*, and unfairly increases the risk of liability on the level of government least able to bear it. I dissent.

[The concurring opinion of Justice O'Connor is omitted.]

NOTES

1. What does *Pembaur* tell us about the meaning of the word "policy"?

2. What attribution approach did the Court use? What is the significance of footnote 12 in Justice Brennan's opinion?

3. Does it, or should it, make a difference if the purported policymaker violated state law? What would such a violation have to do with liability through attribution?

4. What is the relevance, if any, of state law to the attribution issue?

5. What questions does *Pembaur* leave open?

B. *Praprotnik*: The Court's Second Encounter With Attribution

City of St. Louis v. Praprotnik

485 U.S. 112 (1988)

Justice **O'Connor** announced the judgment of the Court and delivered an opinion, in which The Chief Justice **Rehnquist**, Justice **White**, and Justice **Scalia** join.

This case calls upon us to define the proper legal standard for determining when isolated decisions by municipal officials or employees may expose the municipality itself to liability under 42 U.S.C. § 1983.

I

The principal facts are not in dispute. Respondent James H. Praprotnik is an architect who began working for petitioner city of St. Louis in 1968. For several years, respondent consistently received favorable evaluations of his job performance, uncommonly quick promotions, and significant increases in salary. By 1980, he was serving in a management-level city planning position at petitioner's Community Development Agency (CDA).

The Director of CDA, Donald Spaid, had instituted a requirement that the agency's professional employees, including architects, obtain advance approval before taking on private clients. Respondent and other CDA employees objected to the requirement. In April 1980, respondent was suspended for 15 days by CDA's Director of Urban Design, Charles Kindleberger, for having accepted outside employment without prior approval. Respondent appealed to the city's Civil Service Commission, a body charged with reviewing employee grievances. Finding the penalty too harsh, the Commission reversed the suspension, awarded respondent back pay, and directed that he be reprimanded for having failed to secure a clear understanding of the rule.

The Commission's decision was not well received by respondent's supervisors at CDA. Kindleberger later testified that he believed respondent had lied to the Commission, and that Spaid was angry with respondent.

Respondent's next two annual job performance evaluations were markedly less favorable than those in previous years. In discussing one of these evaluations with respondent, Kindleberger apparently mentioned his displeasure with respondent's 1980 appeal to the Civil Service Commission. Respondent appealed both evaluations to the Department of Personnel. In each case, the Department ordered partial relief and was upheld by the city's Director of Personnel or the Civil Service Commission.

In April 1981, a new mayor came into office, and Donald Spaid was replaced as Director of CDA by Frank Hamsher. As a result of budget cuts, a number of layoffs and transfers significantly reduced the size of CDA and of the planning section in which respondent worked. Respondent, however was retained.

In the spring of 1982, a second round of layoffs and transfers occurred at CDA. At that time, the city's Heritage and Urban Design Division (Heritage) was seeking approval to hire someone who was qualified in architecture and urban planning. Hamsher arranged with the Director of Heritage, Henry Jackson, for certain functions to be transferred from CDA to Heritage. This arrangement, which made it possible for Heritage to employ a relatively high-level "city planning manager," was approved by Jackson's supervisor, Thomas Nash. Hamsher then transferred respondent to Heritage to fill this position.

Respondent objected to the transfer, and appealed to the Civil Service Commission. The Commission declined to hear the appeal because respondent had not suffered a reduction in his pay or grade. Respondent then filed suit in federal district court, alleging that the transfer was unconstitutional. The city was named as a defendant, along with Kindleberger, Hamsher, Jackson (whom respondent deleted from the list before trial), and Deborah Patterson, who had succeeded Hamsher at CDA.

At Heritage, respondent became embroiled in a series of disputes with Jackson and Jackson's successor, Robert Killen. Respondent was dissatisfied with the work he was assigned, which consisted of unchallenging clerical functions far below the level of responsibilities that he had previously enjoyed. At least one adverse personnel decision was taken against respondent, and he obtained partial relief after appealing that decision.

In December 1983, respondent was laid off from Heritage. The lay off was attributed to a lack of funds, and this apparently meant that respondent's supervisors had concluded that they could create two lower-level positions with the funds that were being used to pay respondent's salary. Respondent then amended the complaint in his lawsuit to include a challenge to the layoff. He also appealed to the Civil Service Commission, but proceedings in that forum were postponed because of the pending lawsuit and have never been completed.

The case went to trial on two theories: (1) that respondent's First Amendment rights had been violated through retaliatory actions taken in response to his appeal of his 1980 suspension; and (2) that respondent's layoff from Heritage was carried out for pretextual reasons in violation of due process. The jury returned special verdicts exonerating each of the three individual defendants, but finding the city liable under both theories. Judgment was entered on the verdicts, and the city appealed.

* * *

III

A

* * *

In the years since *Monell* was decided, the Court has considered several cases involving isolated acts by government officials and employees. We have assumed that an unconstitutional governmental policy could be inferred from a single decision taken by the highest officials responsible for setting policy in that area of the government's business. See, e.g., *Owen v. City of Independence*; *Newport v. Fact Concerts, Inc.*. Cf. *Pembaur*. At the other end of the spectrum, we have held that an unjustified shooting by a police officer cannot, without more, be thought to result from official policy. *Tuttle* (plurality opinion).

Two terms ago, in *Pembaur, supra,* we undertook to define more precisely when a decision on a single occasion may be enough to establish an unconstitutional municipal policy. Although the Court was unable to settle on a general formulation, JUSTICE BRENNAN's plurality opinion articulated several guiding principles. First, a majority of the Court agreed that municipalities may be held liable under § 1983 only for acts for which the municipality itself is actually responsible, "that is, acts which the municipality has officially sanctioned or ordered." Second, only those municipal officials who have "final policymaking authority" may by their actions subject the government to § 1983 liability. Third, whether a particular official has "final policymaking authority" is a question of state law. Fourth, the challenged action must have been taken pursuant to a policy adopted by the official or officials responsible under state law for making policy in that area of the city's business.

The Courts of Appeals have already diverged in their interpretations of these principles. Today, we set out again to clarify the issue that we last addressed in *Pembaur.*

B

We begin by reiterating that the identification of policymaking officials is a question of state law. "Authority to make municipal policy may be granted directly by a legislative enactment or may be delegated by an official who possesses such authority, and of course, whether an official had final policymaking authority is a question of state law." *Pembaur v. Cincinnati* (plurality opinion). Thus the identification of policymaking officials is not a question of federal law and it is not a question of fact in the usual sense. The States have extremely wide latitude in determining the form that local government takes, and local preferences have led to a profusion of distinct forms. Among the many kinds of municipal corporations, political subdivisions, and special districts of all sorts, one may expect to find a rich variety of ways in which the power of government is distributed among a host of different officials and official bodies. Without attempting to canvass the numberless factual scenarios that may come to

light in litigation, we can be confident that state law (which may include valid local ordinances and regulations) will always direct a court to some official or body that has the responsibility for making law or setting policy in any given area of local government's business.

We are not, of course, predicting that state law will always speak with perfect clarity. We have no reason to suppose, however, that federal courts will face greater difficulties here than those that they routinely address in other contexts. We are also aware that there will be cases in which policymaking responsibility is shared among more than one official or body. In the case before us, for example, it appears that the mayor and aldermen are authorized to adopt such ordinances relating to personnel administration as are compatible with the City Charter. The Civil Service Commission, for its part, is required to "prescribe . . . rules for the administration and enforcement of the provisions of this article, and of any ordinance adopted in pursuance thereof, and not inconsistent therewith." Assuming that applicable law does not make the decisions of the Commission reviewable by the mayor and aldermen, or vice versa, one would have to conclude that policy decisions made either by the mayor and aldermen or by the Commission would be attributable to the city itself. In any event, however, a federal court would not be justified in assuming that municipal policymaking authority lies somewhere other than where the applicable law purports to put it. And certainly there can be no justification for giving a jury the discretion to determine which officials are high enough in the government that their actions can be said to represent a decision of the government itself.

As the plurality in *Pembaur* recognized, special difficulties can arise when it is contended that a municipal policymaker has delegated his policymaking authority to another official. If the mere exercise of discretion by an employee could give rise to a constitutional violation, the result would be indistinguishable from respondeat superior liability. If, however, a city's lawful policymakers could insulate the government from liability simply by delegating their policymaking authority to others, § 1983 could not serve its intended purpose. It may not be possible to draw an elegant line that will resolve this conundrum, but certain principles should provide useful guidance.

First, whatever analysis is used to identify municipal policymakers, egregious attempts by local government to insulate themselves from liability for unconstitutional policies are precluded by a separate doctrine. Relying on the language of § 1983, the Court has long recognized that a plaintiff may be able to prove the existence of a widespread practice that, although not authorized by written law or express municipal policy, is "so permanent and well settled as to constitute a custom or usage' with the force of law." *Adickes v. S. H. Kress & Co..* That principle, which has not been affected by *Monell* or subsequent cases, ensures that most deliberate municipal evasions of the Constitution will be sharply limited.

Second, as the *Pembaur* plurality recognized, the authority to make municipal policy is necessarily the authority to make final policy. When an official's discretionary decisions are constrained by policies not of that official's making, those policies, rather than the subordinate's departures from them, are the act of the municipality. Similarly, when a subordinate's decision is subject to review by the municipality's authorized policymakers, they have retained the authority to measure the official's conduct for conformance with their policies. If the authorized policymakers approve a subordinate's decision and the basis for it, their ratification would be chargeable to the municipality because their decision is final.

C

Whatever refinements of these principles may be suggested in the future, we have little difficulty concluding that the Court of Appeals applied an incorrect legal standard in this case. In reaching this conclusion, we do not decide whether the First Amendment forbade the city from retaliating against respondent for having taken advantage of the grievance mechanism in 1980. Nor do we decide whether there was evidence in this record from which a rational jury could conclude either that such retaliation actually occurred or that respondent suffered any compensable injury from whatever retaliatory action may have been taken. Finally, we do not address petitioner's contention that the

jury verdict exonerating the individual defendants cannot be reconciled with the verdict against the city. Even assuming that all these issues were properly resolved in respondent's favor, we would not be able to affirm the decision of the Court of Appeals.

The city cannot be held liable under § 1983 unless respondent proved the existence of an unconstitutional municipal policy. Respondent does not contend that anyone in city government ever promulgated, or even articulated, such a policy. Nor did he attempt to prove that such retaliation was ever directed against anyone other than himself. Respondent contends that the record can be read to establish that his supervisors were angered by his 1980 appeal to the Civil Service Commission; that new supervisors in a new administration chose, for reasons passed on through some informal means, to retaliate against respondent two years later by transferring him to another agency; and that this transfer was part of a scheme that led, another year and a half later, to his lay off. Even if one assumes that all this was true, it says nothing about the actions of those whom the law established as the makers of municipal policy in matters of personnel administration. The mayor and aldermen enacted no ordinance designed to retaliate against respondent or against similarly situated employees. On the contrary, the city established an independent Civil Service Commission and empowered it to review and correct improper personnel actions. Respondent does not deny that his repeated appeals from adverse personnel decisions repeatedly brought him at least partial relief, and the Civil Service Commission never so much as hinted that retaliatory transfers or lay offs were permissible. Respondent points to no evidence indicating that the Commission delegated to anyone its final authority to interpret and enforce the following policy set out in article XVIII of the city's Charter, § 2(a):

> "Merit and fitness. All appointments and promotions to positions in the service of the city and all measures for the control and regulation of employment in such positions, and separation therefrom, shall be on the sole basis of merit and fitness . . . ."

The Court of Appeals concluded that "appointing authorities," like Hamsher and Killen, who had the authority to initiate transfers and layoffs, were municipal "policymakers." The court based this conclusion on its findings (1) that the decisions of these employees were not individually reviewed for "substantive propriety" by higher supervisory officials; and (2) that the Civil Service Commission decided appeals from such decisions, if at all, in a circumscribed manner that gave substantial deference to the original decisionmaker. We find these propositions insufficient to support the conclusion that Hamsher and Killen were authorized to establish employment policy for the city with respect to transfers and layoffs. To the contrary, the City Charter expressly states that the Civil Service Commission has the power and the duty:

"To consider and determine any matter involved in the administration and enforcement of this [Civil Service] article and the rules and ordinances adopted in accordance therewith that may be referred to it for decision by the director [or personnel], or on appeal by any appointing authority, employe, or taxpayer of the city, from any act of the director or of any appointing authority. The decision of the commission in all such matters shall be final, subject, however, to any right of action under any law of the state or of the United States."

This case therefore resembles the hypothetical example in *Pembaur*: "If [city] employment policy was set by the [Mayor and Aldermen and by the Civil Service Commission], only [those] bod[ies'] decisions would provide a basis for [city] liability. This would be true even if the [mayor and aldermen and the Commission] left the [appointing authorities] discretion to hire and fire employees and [they] exercised that discretion in an unconstitutional manner . . . ." . A majority of the Court of Appeals panel determined that the Civil Service Commission's review of individual employment actions gave too much deference to the decisions of appointing authorities like Hamsher and Killen. Simply going along with discretionary decisions made by one's subordinates, however, is not a delegation to them of the authority to make policy. It is equally consistent with a presumption that the subordinates are faithfully attempting to comply with the policies that are supposed to guide them. It would be a different matter if a particular decision by a subordinate was cast in the form of a policy statement and expressly approved by the supervising policymaker. It would also be a different matter if a series of decisions by a subordinate official manifested a "custom or usage" of which the supervisor must have been aware. In both those cases, the supervisor could realistically be deemed to have adopted a policy that happened to have been formulated or initiated by a lower-ranking official. But the mere failure to investigate the basis of a subordinate's discretionary decisions does not amount to a delegation of policymaking authority, especially where (as here) the wrongfulness of the subordinate's decision arises from a retaliatory motive or other unstated rationale. In such circumstances, the purposes of § 1983 would not be served by treating a subordinate employees' decision as if it were a reflection of municipal policy.

Justice Brennan's opinion, concurring in the judgment, finds implications in our discussion that we do not think necessary or correct. We nowhere say or imply, for example, that "a municipal charter's precatory admonition against discrimination or any other employment practice not based on merit and fitness effectively insulates the municipality from any liability based on acts inconsistent with that policy." *Post.* Rather, we would respect the decisions, embodied in state and local law, that allocated policymaking authority among particular individuals and bodies. Refusals to carry out stated policies could obviously help to show that a municipality's actual policies were different from the ones that had been announced. If such a showing were made, we would be confronted with a different case than the one we decide today.

Nor do we believe that we have left a "gaping hole" in § 1983 that needs to be filled with the vague concept of "de facto final policymaking authority." *Post.* Except perhaps as a step towards overruling *Monell* and adopting the doctrine of respondeat superior, ad hoc searches for officials possessing such "de facto" authority would serve primarily to foster needless unpredictability in the application of § 1983.

IV

We cannot accept either the Court of Appeals' broad definition of municipal policymakers or respondent's suggestion that a jury should be entitled to define for itself which officials' decisions should expose a municipality to liability. Respondent has suggested that the record will support an inference that policymaking authority was in fact delegated to individuals who took retaliatory action against him and who were not exonerated by the jury. Respondent's arguments appear to depend on a legal standard similar to the one suggested in JUSTICE STEVENS' dissenting opinion, which we do not accept. Our examination of the record and state law, however, suggests that further review of this case may be warranted in light of the principles we have discussed. That task is best left to the Court of Appeals, which will be free to invite additional briefing and argument if necessary. Accordingly, the decision of the Court of Appeals is reversed, and the case is remanded for further proceedings consistent with this opinion.

Justice **Brennan**, with whom Justice **Marshall** and Justice **Blackmun** join, concurring.

Despite its somewhat confusing procedural background, this case at bottom presents a relatively straightforward question: whether respondent's supervisor at the Community Development Agency, Frank Hamsher, possessed the authority to establish final employment policy for the city of St. Louis such that the city can be held liable under 42 U.S.C. § 1983 for Hamsher's allegedly unlawful decision to transfer respondent to a dead-end job. Applying the test set out two Terms ago by the plurality in *Pembaur v. Cincinnati*, I conclude that Hamsher did not possess such authority and I therefore concur in the Court's judgment reversing the decision below. I write separately, however, because I believe that the commendable desire of today's plurality to "define more precisely when a decision on a single occasion may be enough" to subject a municipality to § 1983 liability has led it to embrace a theory of municipal liability that is both unduly narrow and unrealistic, and one that ultimately would permit municipalities to insulate themselves from liability for the acts of all but a small minority of actual city policymakers.

* * *

In concluding that Frank Hamsher was a policymaker, the Court of Appeals relied on the fact that the City had delegated to him "the authority, either directly or indirectly, to act on [its] behalf," and that his decisions within the scope of this delegated authority were effectively final. In *Pembaur*, however, we made clear that a municipality is not liable merely because the official who inflicted the constitutional injury had the final authority to act on its behalf; rather, as four of us explained, the official in question must possess "final authority to establish municipal policy with respect to the [challenged] action." Thus, we noted, "the fact that a particular official— even a policymaking official—has discretion in the exercise of particular functions does not, without more, give rise to municipal liability based on an exercise of that discretion." By way of illustration, we explained that if, in a given county, the Board of County Commissioners established county employment policy and delegated to the County Sheriff alone the discretion to hire and fire employees, the county itself would not be liable if the Sheriff exercised this authority in an unconstitutional manner, because "the decision to act unlawfully would not be a decision of the Board." We pointed out, however, that in that same county the Sheriff could be the final policymaker in other areas, such as law enforcement practices, and that if so, his or her decisions in such matters could give rise to municipal liability. In short, just as in *Owen* and *Fact Concerts* we deemed it fair to hold municipalities liable for the isolated, unconstitutional acts of their legislative bodies, regardless of whether those acts were meant to establish generally applicable "policies," so too in *Pembaur* four of us concluded that it is equally appropriate to hold municipalities accountable for the isolated constitutional injury inflicted by an executive final municipal policymaker, even though the decision giving rise to the injury is not intended to govern future situations. In either case, as long as the contested decision is made in an area over which the official or legislative body could establish a final policy capable of governing future municipal conduct, it is both fair and consistent with the purposes of § 1983 to treat the decision as that of the municipality itself, and to hold it liable for the resulting constitutional deprivation.

In my view, *Pembaur* controls this case. As an "appointing authority," Hamsher was empowered under the City Charter to initiate lateral transfers such as the one challenged here, subject to the approval of both the Director of Personnel and the appointing authority of the transferee agency. The Charter, however, nowhere confers upon agency heads any authority to establish city policy, final or otherwise, with respect to such transfers. Thus, for example, Hamsher was not authorized to promulgate binding guidelines or criteria governing how or when lateral transfers were to be accomplished. Nor does the record reveal that he in fact sought to exercise any such authority in these matters. There is no indication, for example, that Hamsher ever purported to institute or announce a practice of general applicability concerning transfers. Instead, the evidence discloses but one transfer decision—the one involving respondent—which Hamsher ostensibly undertook pursuant to a city-wide program of fiscal restraint and budgetary reductions. At most, then, the record demonstrates that Hamsher had the authority to determine how best to effectuate a policy announced by his superiors, rather than the power to establish that policy. Like the hypothetical Sheriff in *Pembaur's* footnote 12, Hamsher had discretionary authority to transfer CDA employees laterally; that he may have used this authority to punish respondent for the exercise of his First Amendment rights does not, without more, render the city liable for respondent's resulting constitutional injury. The court below did not suggest that either Killen or Nash, who together orchestrated respondent's ultimate layoff, shared Hamsher's constitutionally impermissible animus. Because the court identified only one unlawfully motivated municipal employee involved in respondent's transfer and layoff, and because that employee did not possess final policymaking authority with respect to the contested decision, the city may not be held accountable for any constitutional wrong respondent may have suffered.

III

These determinations, it seems to me, are sufficient to dispose of this case, and I therefore think it unnecessary to decide, as the plurality does, who the actual policymakers in St. Louis are. I question more than the mere necessity of these determinations, however,

for I believe that in the course of passing on issues not before us, the plurality announces legal principles that are inconsistent with our earlier cases and unduly restrict the reach of § 1983 in cases involving municipalities.

* * *

I cannot endorse the plurality's determination, based on nothing more than its own review of the City Charter, that the mayor, the aldermen, and the CSC are the only policymakers for the city of St. Louis. While these officials may well have policymaking authority, that hardly ends the matter; the question before us is whether the officials responsible for respondent's allegedly unlawful transfer were final policymakers. As I have previously indicated, I do not believe that CDA Director Frank Hamsher possessed any policymaking authority with respect to lateral transfers and thus I do not believe that his allegedly improper decision to transfer respondent could, without more, give rise to municipal liability. Although the plurality reaches the same result, it does so by reasoning that because others could have reviewed the decisions of Hamsher and Killen, the latter officials simply could not have been final policymakers.

This analysis, however, turns a blind eye to reality, for it ignores not only the lower court's determination, nowhere disputed, that CSC review was highly circumscribed and deferential, but that in this very case the Commission refused to judge a propriety of Hamsher's transfer decision because a lateral transfer was not an "adverse" employment action falling within its jurisdiction. Nor does the plurality account for the fact that Hamsher's predecessor, Donald Spaid, promulgated what the city readily acknowledges was a binding policy regarding secondary employment; although the CSC ultimately modified the sanctions respondent suffered as a result of his apparent failure to comply with that policy, the record is devoid of any suggestion that the Commission reviewed the substance or validity of the policy itself. Under the plurality's analysis, therefore, even the hollowest promise of review is sufficient to divest all city officials save the mayor and governing legislative body of final policymaking authority. While clarity and ease of application may commend such a rule, we have remained steadfast in our conviction that Congress intended to hold municipalities accountable for those constitutional injuries inflicted not only by their lawmakers, but "by those whose edicts or acts may fairly be said to represent official policy." *Monell.* Because the plurality's mechanical "finality" test is fundamentally at odds with the pragmatic and factual inquiry contemplated by *Monell,* I cannot join what I perceive to be its unwarranted abandonment of the traditional factfinding process in § 1983 actions involving municipalities.

Finally, I think it necessary to emphasize that despite certain language in the plurality opinion suggesting otherwise, the Court today need not and therefore does not decide that a city can only be held liable under § 1983 where the plaintiff "prov[es] the existence of an unconstitutional municipal policy." Just last Term, we left open for the second time the question whether a city can be subjected to liability for a policy that, while not unconstitutional in and of itself, may give rise to constitutional deprivations. See *Springfield v. Kibbe;* see also *Oklahoma City v. Tuttle.* That question is certainly not presented by this case, and nothing we say today forecloses its future consideration.

* * *

[The dissenting opinion of Justice Stevens is omitted; Justice Kennedy did not participate.]

NOTES

1. What is the holding in *Praprotnik?* Notice that there is no opinion for the Court.

2. What attribution approach does the plurality adopt? Why?

3. Is *Praprotnik* an easier or harder case than *Pembaur* in which to find liability through attribution?

4. What is the function of state law in the policymaker inquiry? Is state law always formal? What is the function of custom?

5. Is federal law relevant to the policymaker question?

6. What is the relevance of the existence of a review mechanism to the policymaker question?

7. What is the role of the jury in the attribution inquiry? Does it depend in part on the answers to the prior questions?

8. What accounts for the split among the justices in *Praprotnik?* What are their respective concerns?

9. The plurality opinion asserts that a local government is liable for the unconstitutional decision of an official or employee only if a policymaker approves *both* the decision *and* the basis for it. 485 U.S. at 127. Under this standard, ratification of a decision, standing alone, is insufficient for local government liability. Why should that be?

C.   *Jett:* Most (But Not All) of the Questions Resolved

In *Jett v. Dallas Independent School District,* 491 U.S. 701 (1989), the plaintiff, a former athletic director and football coach, sued a school district and principal alleging that they had deprived him of his position in violation of equal protection and the First Amendment. The Fifth Circuit initially observed that the instructions to the jury did not comply with its decision in *Bennett v. City of Slidell,* noted earlier, because they did not condition liability of the school district on the delegation of policy-making authority to the superintendent who approved the principal's recommendation to remove plaintiff. The court then went on to consider the possible effect of the Supreme Court's *Pembaur* decision but determined that it did not have to decide whether *Pembaur* should be read to mean that the superintendent's "final exclusive authority to make individual transfer decisions would not alone subject the [school district] to responsibility for his actions in the case of a particular individual transfer decision *unless* he *also* had final authority with respect to general [school district] transfer *policy* applicable to teachers or coaches."

The Fifth Circuit in *Jett* was able to avoid this important issue because it held that even if the superintendent was a policy maker within the meaning of *Bennett,* there was insufficient evidence to show that the superintendent himself was impermissibly motivated in approving the principal's removal recommendation or that he was deliberately indifferent to the allegedly impermissible motivation of the principal. In short, there was insufficient evidence to support a finding that the superintendent's challenged conduct was itself wrongful, a requirement for attribution of that conduct to the school district for liability purposes.

Thereafter, in an opinion by Justice O'Connor which dealt primarily with the relation between § 1983 and 42 U.S.C. § 1981, the Supreme Court remanded to the Fifth Circuit to consider whether the superintendent was a policy maker in light of the plurality opinion in *Praprotnik*. In so doing, the Court made clear that the approach of the *Praprotnik* plurality, with its reliance on state law and the role of the trial judge, was to govern on remand. The Court declared:

> As with other questions of state law relevant to the application of federal law, the identification of those officials whose decisions represent the official policy of the local governmental unit is itself a legal question to be resolved by the trial judge *before* the case is submitted to the jury . . . . Once those officials who have the power to make official policy on a particular issue have been identified [by the trial judge], it is for the jury to determine whether *their* decisions have caused the deprivation of rights at issue by policies which affirmatively command that it occur . . ., or by acquiescence in a longstanding practice or custom which constitutes the "standard operating procedure" of the local governmental entity.

What is significant about *Jett* is that Justice O'Connor's opinion for the Court was joined by four other justices, including Justice Kennedy. This indicates that a majority of the Court has now decided that state law governs the policy maker inquiry. On the other hand, the Court in *Jett* retreated somewhat from the apparent insistence in the *Praprotnik* plurality opinion that state *formal* law alone was determinative of the policy maker issue. This is demonstrated by its reference in *Jett* to a trial court's use of "relevant legal materials, including state and local positive law, as well as 'custom or usage' having the force of law" in deciding the policy maker issue.

1. After *Jett*, what is the role of the jury in the policymaker inquiry?

2. After *Jett*, what attribution questions, if any, are still open?

3. In *Jett v. Dallas Independent School Dist,* 7 F.3d 1241 (5th Cir. 1993), on remand from the Supreme Court, the Fifth Circuit examined Texas law and determined that the school district superintendent did not have final policymaking authority over employee tranfers. Thus, the school district was not liable through attribution. According to the Fifth Circuit, Texas law, both statutory and judicial, made clear that final policymaking authority belonged to the independent school district's board of trustees. The court also rejected the plaintiff's argument that the district delegated policymaking authority as to employee transfers to the superintendent. That the superintendent had been delegated the final decision in individual cases did not mean that he had been delegated the status of policymaker regarding employee transfers in general. There was an all-important distinction between final *decisionmaking* authority and final *policymaking* authority.

D. Application of Attribution Rules

Consider the application of the foregoing attribution rules in the following circuit court cases. Are the cases consistent with *Jett*? With one another?

1. The Ninth Circuit held in *Davis v. Mason County*, 927 F.2d 1473 (9th Cir. 1991), a police excessive force case, that a county sheriff was a policymaker for the county in connection with the training of deputies. Looking at Washington law which provided that the sheriff is the chief executive officer and conservator of the peace of the county, the court concluded that the sheriff's actions regarding training were attributable to the county. Judge Wallace dissented in part, *id.* at 1489, arguing that the final authority for personnel administration rested with the civil service commission, not the sheriff, and that the sheriff was thus not a county policymaker. The majority, distinguishing between hiring and training, contended that the sheriff was a county policymaker for training even if not for hiring.

2. A city was sued by police officers who claimed that a new police superintendent demoted them because of their race and political affiliations. The Seventh Circuit found that the superintendent was not the city's policymaker. It was significant that city ordinances clearly banned racial and political discrimination, and had done so for a long time. In addition, there was an important distinction between legislative and executive functions: the former ordinarily represented official policy while, as to the latter, "[a]uthority to make a final decision need not imply authority to establish rules" and in this city, Chicago, it did not. In short, the superintendent was not a policymaker here because "he violated rather then implemented the policy of Chicago." *Auriemma v. Rice*, 957 F.2d 397, 401 (7th Cir. 1992). Judge Ripple concurred, *id*, pointing out that under state law and custom—which *Jett* declared to be controlling for policymaker purposes—the superintendent's conduct here was not that of the city.

3. In *Johnson v. Moore*, 958 F.2d 92 (5th Cir. 1992), the plaintiff sued a city and a judge alleging that he had been sentenced to jail without benefit of counsel pursuant to an official policy of the city. The Fifth Circuit rejected the plaintiff's contention that because the judge was the final authority on his incarceration, the judge executed city policy. It explained that a city judge "acting in his or her judicial capacity to enforce state law does not act as a municipal official or lawmaker." Here, the plaintiff did not allege that he was sentenced to jail through the judge's exercise of administrative or other non-judicial functions. "Only with respect to actions taken pursuant to his or her administrative role can a judge be said to institute municipal policy under *Pembaur* and *Monell*." *Id*. at 94.

4. In *Manor Healthcare Corp v. Lomelo*, 929 F.2d 633 (11th Cir. 1991), the plaintiff nursing home corporation sued a city alleging that the mayor and president of the city council extorted $30,000 while acting on behalf of the city in connection with a zoning matter. Ruling against the plaintiff and affirming the district court, the Eleventh Circuit found that the mayor was not a policymaker for the city in this case. The city charter gave the city council the power to override the mayor's veto in zoning matter, thereby indicating that the mayor was not the ultimate policymaking authority on such matters. Even if the mayor were considered to have de facto policymaking authority over zoning, the mayor acted as he did to benefit himself and his friends, not the city. Since the city did not adopt or ratify his bribery or extortion activities, "[t]o hold the city liable for [the mayor's] actions in this case would in essence subject the city to vicarious liability. . . ." *Id*. at 638. In addition, the mayor was not executing city policy when he acted contrary to the laws regarding bribery and extortion.

VI.   The Third Route to Governmental Liability: Failure to Train

A.   Failure to Train and Single Incidents

As we have seen, local governments can be liable for their official policies or customs which, when implemented, cause constitutional deprivations. However, for the most part the cases we have considered thus far have dealt with the affirmative conduct of either the local governments themselves or policymakers. Are there circumstances in which local governments are liable for their failure to act? To put this another way: can the failure to act constitute an actionable official policy or custom? It turns out that the answer is yes, at least where a local government or its policymakers, accused of failing to train and/or supervise police officers who act unconstitutionally, are deliberately indifferent to the constitutional rights of persons with whom the police come into contact. See *City of Canton v. Harris*, 489 U.S. 378 (1989), set out below.

However, before *City of Canton* was decided, the Supreme Court struggled with this issue in *City of Oklahoma City v. Tuttle*, 471 U.S. 808 (1985), involving the shooting death of plaintiff's decedent by a police officer where the decedent had no weapon and did not threaten the officer. The plaintiff sued both the police officer and the city, which resulted in a jury verdict in favor of the police officer on the basis of qualified immunity but against the city for failure to train. Affirming the verdict against the city, the Tenth Circuit found that the district court had properly charged the jury that the city could be liable for gross negligence in failing to train if it had "actual or imputed knowledge of the almost inevitable consequences that arise from completely inadequate training or supervision."

There was also sufficient evidence, according to the Tenth Circuit, to support a finding of an official policy or custom of gross negligence and deliberate indifference, even though this finding was largely, if not completely, based on the single incident in question. "The act here was so plainly and grossly negligent that it spoke out very positively on the issue of lack of training." In this connection, the jury had been charged that "a single, unusually excessive use of force may be sufficiently out of the ordinary to warrant an inference that it was attributable to inadequate training or supervision amounting to 'deliberate indifference' or 'gross negligence' on the part of the officials in charge."

The Supreme Court reversed. There was no opinion for the Court, but only Justice Stevens dissented as to the judgment (Justice Powell did not participate). Justice Rehnquist, joined by Chief Justice Burger and Justices White and O'Connor, held that the instruction was reversible error because it allowed the jury, on the basis of a single incident, to find a policy of training and supervising police officers which resulted in inadequate training and the claimed constitutional violations. It was significant that there was no claim that the city had a policy of authorizing its police force to use excessive force in apprehending criminals. Justice Rehnquist concluded:

> Proof of a single incident of unconstitutional activity is not sufficient to impose liability under *Monell*, unless proof of the incident includes proof that it was caused by an existing, unconstitutional municipal policy, which policy can be attributed to a municipal policy maker. Otherwise the existence of the unconstitutional policy, and its origin, must be separately proved. But where the policy relied upon is not itself unconstitutional [as in this case], considerably more proof than the single incident will be necessary in every case to establish both the requisite fault on the part of the municipality, and the causal connection between the "policy" and the constitutional deprivation.

471 U.S. at 823–24. Justices Brennan, Marshall and Blackmun concurred in the judgment, agreeing that the single incident jury instruction was defective.

1. Why were the justices worried about the single incident instruction in *Tuttle*? Recall the rejection of respondeat superior liability in *Monell*.

2. Did *Tuttle* resolve the issue of local government liability for failure to act? Whether you believe it did or not, *Tuttle* set the stage for *City of Canton v. Harris*.

B. *City of Canton*

City of Canton, Ohio v. Harris

489 U.S. 378 (1989)

Justice **White** delivered the opinion of the Court.

In this case, we are asked to determine if a municipality can ever be liable under 42 U.S.C. § 1983 for constitutional violations resulting from its failure to train municipal employees. We hold that, under certain circumstances, such liability is permitted by the statute.

In April 1978, respondent Geraldine Harris was arrested by officers of the Canton Police Department. Mrs. Harris was brought to the police station in a patrol wagon.

When she arrived at the station, Mrs. Harris was found sitting on the floor of the wagon. She was asked if she needed medical attention, and responded with an incoherent remark. After she was brought inside the station for processing, Mrs. Harris slumped to the floor on two occasions. Eventually, the police officers left Mrs. Harris lying on the floor to prevent her from falling again. No medical attention was ever summoned for Mrs. Harris. After about an hour, Mrs. Harris was released from custody, and taken by an ambulance (provided by her family) to a nearby hospital. There, Mrs. Harris was diagnosed as suffering from several emotional ailments; she was hospitalized for one week and received subsequent outpatient treatment for an additional year.

Some time later, Mrs. Harris commenced this action alleging many state-law and constitutional claims against the city of Canton and its officials. Among these claims was one seeking to hold the city liable under 42 U.S.C. § 1983 for its violation of Mrs. Harris' right, under the Due Process Clause of the Fourteenth Amendment, to receive necessary medical attention while in police custody.

A jury trial was held on Mrs. Harris' claims. Evidence was presented that indicated that, pursuant to a municipal regulation, shift commanders were authorized to determine, in their sole discretion, whether a detainee required medical care. In addition, testimony also suggested that Canton shift commanders were not provided with any special training (beyond first-aid training) to make a determination as to when to summon medical care for an injured detainee.

At the close of the evidence, the District Court submitted the case to the jury, which rejected all of Mrs. Harris' claims except one: her § 1983 claim against the city resulting from its failure to provide her with medical treatment while in custody. In rejecting the city's subsequent motion for judgment notwithstanding the verdict, the District Court explained the theory of liability as follows:

"The evidence construed in a manner most favorable to Mrs. Harris could be found by a jury to demonstrate that the City of Canton had a custom or policy of vesting complete authority with the police supervisor of when medical treatment would be administered to prisoners. Further, the jury could find from the evidence that the vesting of such carte blanche authority with the police supervisor without adequate training to recognize when medical treatment is needed was grossly negligent or so reckless that future police misconduct was almost inevitable or substantially certain to result."

On appeal, the Sixth Circuit affirmed this aspect of the District Court's analysis, holding that "a municipality is liable for failure to train its police force, [where] the plaintiff . . . prove[s] that the municipality acted recklessly, intentionally, or with gross negligence." The Court of Appeals also stated that an additional prerequisite of this theory of liability was that the plaintiff must prove "that the lack of training was so reckless or grossly negligent that deprivations of persons' constitutional rights were substantially certain to result." Thus, the Court of Appeals found that there had been no error in submitting Mrs. Harris' "failure to train" claim to the jury. However, the Court of Appeals reversed the judgment

for respondent, and remanded this case for a new trial, because it found that certain aspects of the District Court's jury instructions might have led the jury to believe that it could find against the city on a mere respondeat superior theory. Because the jury's verdict did not state the basis on which it had ruled for Mrs. Harris on her § 1983 claim, a new trial was ordered.

The city petitioned for certiorari, arguing that the Sixth Circuit's holding represented an impermissible broadening of municipal liability under § 1983. We granted the petition.

* * *

III

In *Monell v. New York City Dept. of Social Services*, we decided that a municipality can be found liable under § 1983 only where the municipality itself causes the constitutional violation at issue. Respondeat superior or vicarious liability will not attach under § 1983. "It is only when the 'execution of the government's policy or custom . . . inflicts the injury' that the municipality may be held liable under § 1983." *Springfield v. Kibbe* (quoting *Monell, supra*).

Thus, our first inquiry in any case alleging municipal liability under § 1983 is the question whether there is a direct causal link between a municipal policy or custom and the alleged constitutional deprivation. The inquiry is a difficult one; one that has left this Court deeply divided in a series of cases that have followed *Monell*; one that is the principal focus of our decision again today.

A

Based on the difficulty that this Court has had defining the contours of municipal liability in these circumstances, petitioner urges us to adopt the rule that a municipality can be found liable under § 1983 only where "the policy in question [is] itself unconstitutional." Whether such a rule is a valid construction of § 1983 is a question the Court has left unresolved. Under such an approach, the outcome here would be rather clear: we would have to reverse and remand the case with instructions that judgment be entered for petitioner. There can be little doubt that on its face the city's policy regarding medical treatment for detainees is constitutional. The policy states that the city jailer "shall . . . have [a person needing medical care] taken to a hospital for medical treatment, with permission of his supervisor . . . .". It is difficult to see what constitutional guarantees are violated by such a policy.

Nor, without more, would a city automatically be liable under § 1983 if one of its employees happened to apply the policy in an unconstitutional manner, for liability would then rest on respondeat superior. The claim in this case, however, is that if a concededly valid policy is unconstitutionally applied by a municipal employee, the city is liable if the employee has not been adequately trained and the constitutional wrong has been caused by that failure to train. For reasons explained below, we conclude, as have all the Courts of Appeals that have addressed this issue, that there are limited circumstances in which an allegation of a "failure to train" can be the basis for liability under § 1983. Thus, we reject petitioner's contention that only unconstitutional policies are actionable under the statute.

B

Though we agree with the court below that a city can be liable under § 1983 for inadequate training of its employees, we cannot agree that the District Court's jury instructions on this issue were proper, for we conclude that the Court of Appeals provided an overly broad rule for when a municipality can be held liable under the "failure to train" theory. Unlike the question whether a municipality's failure to train employees can ever be a basis for § 1983 liability—on which the Courts of Appeals have all agreed—there is substantial division among the lower courts as to what degree of fault must be evidenced by the municipality's inaction before liability will be permitted. We hold today that the inadequacy of police training may serve as the basis for § 1983 liability only where the failure to train amounts to deliberate indifference to the rights of persons with whom the police come into contact.[8] This rule is most consistent with

our admonition in *Monell* and *Polk County v. Dodson*, that a municipality can be liable under § 1983 only where its policies are the "moving force [behind] the constitutional violation." Only where a municipality's failure to train its employees in a relevant respect evidences a "deliberate indifference" to the rights of its inhabitants can such a shortcoming be properly thought of as a city "policy or custom" that is actionable under § 1983. As JUSTICE BRENNAN's opinion in *Pembaur v. Cincinnati* (plurality) put it: "Municipal liability under § 1983 attaches where—and only where—a deliberate choice to follow a course of action is made from among various alternatives" by city policymakers. Only where a failure to train reflects a "deliberate" or "conscious" choice by a municipality—a "policy" as defined by our prior cases—can a city be liable for such a failure under § 1983.

Monell's rule that a city is not liable under § 1983 unless a municipal policy causes a constitutional deprivation will not be satisfied by merely alleging that the existing training program for a class of employees, such as police officers, represents a policy for which the city is responsible. That much may be true. The issue in a case like this one, however, is whether that training program is adequate; and if it is not, the question becomes whether such inadequate training can justifiably be said to represent "city policy." It may seem contrary to common sense to assert that a municipality will actually have a policy of not taking reasonable steps to train its employees. But it may happen that in light of the duties assigned to specific officers or employees the need for more or different training is so obvious, and the inadequacy so likely to result in the violation of constitutional rights, that

---

[8] The "deliberate indifference" standard we adopt for section 1983 "failure to train" claims does not turn on the degree of fault (if any) that a plaintiff must show to make out a constitutional violation. For example, this Court has never determined what degree of culpability must be shown before the particular constitutional violation asserted in this case—a denial of the due process right to medical care while in detention—

is established. Indeed, in *Revere v. Massachusetts General Hospital*, we reserved decision on the question whether something less than the Eighth Amendment's "deliberate indifference" test may be applicable to claims by detainees asserting violations of the due process right to medical care while in custody.

We need not resolve the question left open in *Revere* for two reasons. First, petitioner has conceded that, as the case comes to us, we must assume that respondent's constitutional right to receive medical care was denied by city employees—whatever the nature of that right might be. Second, the proper standard for determining when a municipality will be held liable under section 1983 for constitutional wrongs does not turn on any underlying culpability test that determines when such wrongs have occurred.

the policymakers of the city can reasonably be said to have been deliberately indifferent to the need. In that event, the failure to provide proper training may fairly be said to represent a policy for which the city is responsible, and for which the city may be held liable if it actually causes injury.

In resolving the issue of a city's liability, the focus must be on adequacy of the training program in relation to the tasks the particular officers must perform. That a particular officer may be unsatisfactorily trained will not alone suffice to fasten liability on the city, for the officer's shortcomings may have resulted from factors other than a faulty training program. It may be, for example, that an otherwise sound program has occasionally been negligently administered. Neither will it suffice to prove that an injury or accident could have been avoided if an officer had had better or more training, sufficient to equip him to avoid the particular injury-causing conduct. Such a claim could be made about almost any encounter resulting in injury, yet not condemn the adequacy of the program to enable officers to respond properly to the usual and recurring situations with which they must deal. And plainly, adequately trained officers occasionally make mistakes; the fact that they do says little about the training program or the legal basis for holding the city liable.

Moreover, for liability to attach in this circumstance the identified deficiency in a city's training program must be closely related to the ultimate injury. Thus in the case at hand, respondent must still prove that the deficiency in training actually caused the police officers' indifference to her medical needs. Would the injury have been avoided had the employee been trained under a program that was not deficient in the identified respect? Predicting how a hypothetically well-trained officer would have acted under the circumstances may not be an easy task for the factfinder, particularly since matters of judgment may be involved, and since officers who are well trained are not free from error and perhaps might react very much like the untrained officer in similar circumstances. But judge and jury, doing their respective jobs, will be adequate to the task.

To adopt lesser standards of fault and causation would open municipalities to un-precedented liability under § 1983. In virtually every instance where a person has had his or her constitutional rights violated by a city employee, a § 1983 plaintiff will be able to point to something the city "could have done" to prevent the unfortunate incident. See *Oklahoma City v. Tuttle* (opinion of REHNQUIST, J.). Thus, permitting cases against cities for their "failure to train" employees to go forward under § 1983 on a lesser standard of fault would result in de facto respondeat superior liability on municipalities—a result we rejected in *Monell*. It would also engage the federal courts in an endless exercise of second-guessing municipal employee-training programs. This is an exercise we believe the federal courts are ill suited to undertake, as well as one that would implicate serious questions of federalism.

Consequently, while claims such as respondent's—alleging that the city's failure to provide training to municipal employees resulted in the constitutional deprivation she suffered—are cognizable under § 1983, they can only yield liability against a municipality where that city's failure to train reflects deliberate indifference to the constitutional rights of its inhabitants.

IV

The final question here is whether this case should be remanded for a new trial, or whether, as petitioner suggests, we should conclude that there are no possible grounds on which respondent can prevail. It is true that the evidence in the record now does not meet the standard of § 1983 liability we have set forth above. But, the standard of proof the District Court ultimately imposed on respondent (which was consistent with Sixth Circuit precedent) was a lesser one than the one we adopt today. Whether respondent should have an opportunity to prove her case under the "deliberate indifference" rule we have adopted is a matter for the Court of Appeals to deal with on remand.

V

Consequently, for the reasons given above, we vacate the judgment of the Court of Appeals and remand this case for further proceedings consistent with this opinion.

[The concurring opinion of Justice Brennan and the concurring in part and dissenting in part opinion of Justices O'Connor, Scalia and Kennedy are omitted.]

NOTES

1. What is the liability rule of *City of Canton*? Is it broad or narrow?

2. What state of mind requirement is established by *City of Canton* for local government liability for failure to train? If it is deliberate indifference, why? Why not ordinary negligence?

3. Is this state of mind requirement imposed by section 1983 itself as a matter of statutory interpretation? If so, how can this be reconciled with *Parratt v. Taylor*, 451 U.S. 527 (1981), addressed in Chapter 3, which squarely ruled that section 1983 does not contain a state of mind requirement for the *prima facie* case?

4. Is this state of mind requirement imposed by the constitution? If so, what is the constitutional provision? Is it due process? In this regard, what is the significance of footnote 8 in *City of Canton*?

5. Whatever the source of the state of mind requirement, is it fault based? Why should this be? For an argument against using state of mind analysis for local government liability, *see*Kritchevsky, *"Or Causes to be Subjected": The Role of Causation in Section 1983 Municipal Liability Analysis*, 35 UCLA L. Rev. 1187 (1988), reprinted in *Section 1983 Anthology* 75.

6. Does *City of Canton* indicate that the plaintiff's burden in such cases is a relatively easy one? A relatively hard one? Evaluate the following language from a Seventh Circuit opinion:

> A particular officer's unsatisfactory training cannot alone suffice to attach liability to the state. An officer's faults . . . may result from factors other than the deficient training program. Nor can plaintiffs prevail merely by proving that an accident or injury could have been avoided had an officer received enhanced training forestalling the particular conduct resulting in the injury. Even adequately trained officers sometimes err, and such error says little about their training program or the legal basis for liability . . . . This is why claims alleging a constitutional deprivation due to failure to provide train-

ing . . . yield liability only if that defendant's failure to train demonstrates its "deliberate indifference" to the constitutional rights of its citizens.

Erwin v. County of Manitowoc, 872 F.2d 1292, 1298 (7th Cir. 1989).

7. What is the role of causation in failure to train cases? Does it appear to be the same as in other section 1983 cases? For the argument that causation should be determined from the perspective of the local government's agent (the "wrongdoer"), and not from that of the local government itself, *see* Brown, *Correlating Municipal Liability and Official Immunity Under Section 1983*, 1989 U. of Ill. L. Rev. 625.

8. What does *City of Canton*'s deliberate indifference standard mean? Is it, for example, primarily subjective or objective or some combination thereof?

Consider in this connection the possible relevance of the Supreme Court's important 1994 Eighth Amendment prison conditions decision in *Farmer v. Brennan*, 114 S. Ct. 1970 (1994), also noted in Chapter 3. The Court unanimously held that prison officials could be liable in damages under the Eighth Amendment for their deliberate indifference in failing to protect inmates from harm caused by other inmates. In the case before it the plaintiff federal prisoner, a transsexual with feminine characteristics, was beaten and raped shortly after he was placed in the general population. The Court defined deliberate indifference in a *subjective* manner as meaning the failure to act when prison officials actually knew of a "substantial risk of serious harm," even though an inmate did not warn them of a particular threat and even if they did not believe that harm would occur to a particular inmate. It also went on say that an "inference from circumstantial evidence" could suffice to demonstrate that prison officials had the requisite knowledge. Thus, the plaintiff's failure in *Farmer* to express concern over his own safety did not warrant dismissal of his Eighth Amendment damages action. In general, then, a prison official could be liable for denying humane conditions only if he knew that inmates faced a substantial risk of serious harm and disregarded that risk by failing to take reasonable measures to abate it.

The *Farmer* Court insisted on the essentially *subjective* nature of deliberate indifference in a prison setting with respect to *individual* liability.

It sharply distinguished the subjective nature of this kind of deliberate indifference from what it termed the different *objective* nature of the deliberate indifference inquiry in a local government failure to train context. Here, the Court explained, *City of Canton*'s inquiry was into the state of mind of a *governmental* entity, thereby calling for a focus on liability for deliberate indifference based on obviousness or constructive notice. "It would be hard to describe the *Canton* understanding of deliberate indifference, permitting liability to be premised on obviousness or constructive notice, as anything but objective." 114 S. Ct. at 1981.

Does *Farmer* change your understanding of *City of Canton* or does it just explain *City of Canton*?

9. Recall that the Supreme Court rejected a heightened pleading requirement in failure to train and other local government liability cases in *Leatherman v. Tarrant County*, 113 S. Ct. 1160 (1993).

10. Failure to train issues often arise in jail suicide cases. *See, e.g., Simmons v. City of Philadelphia*, 947 F.2d 1042 (3rd Cir. 1991) and *Rhyne v. Henderson County*, 973 F.2d 386 (5th Cir. 1992).

C. Supervisory Liability and Deliberate Indifference After *City of Canton* and *Farmer*

As we have seen, there are circumstances in which supervisors are considered to be policymakers for attribution purposes, thereby rendering a local government liable. However, whether supervisors are considered to be policymakers or not in particular cases, they may still be found liable in their individual capacities for damages regardless of the liability of the local government. The question is: what must be alleged and proved against a supervisor in order to render him or her personally liable?

We know from *Monell* that some sort of personal involvement by the supervisor in the constitutional deprivation is required. As the Court there said, "By our decision in *Rizzo v. Goode*[, 423 U.S. 362 (1976)] we would appear to have decided that the mere right to control without control or direction having been exercised and without any failure to supervise is not

enough to support section 1983 liability." *Monell v. Department of Social Services*, 436 U.S. 658, 694 n.58 (1978). In *Rizzo*, the Court rejected extensive equitable relief directed against those charged with operating the Philadelphia Police Department. Among the Court's concerns were the broad scope of the relief sought, the concomitant federal court supervision required, the federal-state relation and *the absence of any showing of personal involvement by supervisory personnel in the unconstitutional conduct of various police officers*.

Before *City of Canton*, it was not clear in the circuits whether negligence was enough for supervisory liability, although in fact most of them required at least gross negligence, if not deliberate indifference. *See e.g., Williams v. Smith*, 781 F.2d 319 (2d Cir. 1986) (gross negligence) and *Gutierrez-Rodriguez v. Cartagena*, 882 F.2d 553 (1st Cir. 1989) ("indifference that rises to the level of being deliberate, reckless or callous"). After *City of Canton*, though, it is likely that supervisory liability, like local government liability for failure to train, requires at least deliberate indifference. In this connection, the Third Circuit declared itself confident that, after *City of Canton*, "the standard of individual liability for supervisory public officials will be found to be no less stringent than the standard of liability for the public entities that they serve." *Sample v. Diecks*, 885 F.2d 1099, 1118 (3rd Cir. 1989). Indeed, deliberate indifference, rapidly turning into a "standard for all seasons," is the prevailing supervisory liability standard in the circuits.

In this connection, recall the immediately preceding discussion of deliberate indifference contrasting *City of Canton*'s deliberate indifference standard and that of the Supreme Court's 1994 prison conditions case, *Farmer v. Brennan*, 114 S. Ct. 1970 (1994). In *Farmer*, a unanimous Court emphasized the *subjective* nature of deliberate indifference for the Eighth Amendment liability of prison officials individually and distinguished it from the *objective* nature of deliberate indifference for the failure to train liability of local governments, with its focus on obviousness and constructive notice pursuant to *City of Canton*. What does this distinction indicate for deliberate indifference and supervisory liability? Is deliberate indifference in this setting governed by a subjective standard because what is at stake is the individual liability of supervisors? Or is deliberate indifference in this setting governed by an objective standard because supervisory liability is comparable to the failure to train liability of local governments?

Under any definition of deliberate indifference, could a prison supervisory official defeat a prisoner's Eighth Amendment claim of deliberate indifference by proving that the governmental entity responsible for the prison provided inadequate resources, with the result that the official was unable to remedy the allegedly unconstitutional condition of confinement? See *LaMarca v. Turner*, 995 F.2d 1526 (11th Cir. 1993), set out in Chapter 6 in connection with causation and supervisory liability.

What approach to deliberate indifference do the following pre-*Farmer* supervisory liability cases take?

1. The First Circuit, applying a deliberate indifference standard to the conduct of a police chief in a prison suicide case involving a pretrial detainee, defined it as follows: "(1) an unusually serious risk of harm (self-inflicted harm, in a suicide case), (2) defendant's actual knowledge of (or at least, willful blindness to) that elevated risk, and (3) defendant's failure to take obvious steps to address that known, serious risk." In the case before it, the court, affirming the district court, found that there was insufficient evidence to show deliberate indifference on the part of the police chief, in part because there were typical suicide prevention policies in place and some officer training. *Manarite v. City of Springfield*, 957 F.2d 953, 958 (1st Cir. 1992).

2. The First Circuit, ultimately finding the supervisory police officer not liable for the alleged assault by arresting police officers on the plaintiff, determined that the defendant's recruiting practices and training program did not demonstrate the requisite deliberate indifference. Neither was his supervision of one of the police officers reckless or deliberately indifferent to citizens' constitutional rights. In this regard, the court commented: "An important factor in determining whether a supervisor is liable to the extent he has encouraged, condoned, acquiesced, or been deliberately indifferent to the behavior of a subordinate, is whether the official was put on notice of behavior which was likely to result in the violation of the constitutional rights of citizens." Here, the five complaints against that police officer were insufficient because, among other things, they stemmed from incidents "completely unrelated to the present one." At most,

the supervisor was negligent. *Febus-Rodriguez v. Betancourt-Lebron*, 14 F.3d 87, 93 (1st Cir. 1994).

3. In *Larez v. City of Los Angeles*, 946 F.2d 630, 646 (9th Cir. 1991), a case involving a claim against a police chief for excessive use of force by police officers during a search, the Ninth Circuit approved the following supervisory liability instruction:

> [The jury could find the defendant liable in his individual capacity if he] set in motion a series of acts by others, or knowingly refused to terminate a series of acts by others, which he kn[e]w or reasonably should [have] know[n], would cause others to inflict the constitutional injury.

Whatever your approach to deliberate indifference in a supervisory liability setting, keep in mind that, as we have seen, different constitutional provisions have their own state of mind requirements independent of the section 1983 deliberate indifference standard for supervisory liability (as well as for local government liability for failure to train).

VII. Ethical Considerations

Because of the possibility of local government liability in many cases, potential conflicts of interest may arise for attorneys representing local governments at the same time they represent individual officials or employees of those governments. Why should this be? Consider in this connection the leading case of *Dunton v. City of Suffolk*, 729 F.2d 903 (2d Cir. 1984).

Dunton v. County of Suffolk, State of New York

729 F.2d 903 (2d Cir. 1984)

Meskill, Circuit Judge:

Robert Pfeiffer appeals from a judgment entered against him after a jury trial in the United States District Court for the Eastern District of New York, Glasser, J., awarding Emerson Dunton, Jr. $10,000 compensatory damages and $10,000 punitive damages on a state law battery claim. Angela Pfeiffer appeals from a judgment entered against her in the same trial, awarding Dunton $5,000 compensatory damages and $20,000 punitive damages for malicious prosecution. We reverse the judgment against Robert Pfeiffer and remand for a new trial and reverse the judgment against Angela Pfeiffer and remand to the district court with instructions to dismiss the complaint.

I

Defendant-appellant Angela Pfeiffer attended a retirement party for a fellow employee on the evening of May 20, 1981. As the party broke up, plaintiff-appellee Emerson Dunton Jr., a co-worker and attendee, accompanied Ms. Pfeiffer to her car. The accounts of the subsequent events differ; Ms. Pfeifer claims that Dunton began making improper advances while they were seated in her car, while Dunton asserts that Ms. Pfeiffer willingly participated in the maneuvers. Defendant-appellant Robert Pfeiffer, Angela's husband and also a Suffolk County police officer, came upon the scene in his patrol car, threw Dunton out of Ms. Pfeiffer's car, struck him repeatedly and left him lying in the parking lot. Dunton suffered non-disabling and non-permanent injuries from the incident.

Dunton was arrested after Angela Pfeiffer filed a criminal complaint on June 18, alleging third degree sexual abuse in violation of N.Y. Penal Law § 130.55. When the matter did not come to trial by November 16, Dunton moved to dismiss on the ground that the sixty day limit for trial had been exceeded. The motion was denied and Dunton moved for reconsideration. On December 23, the Suffolk County district court concluded that it had erred in computing the sixty day period and that sixty-seven days were actually chargeable to the prosecution. Accordingly, it granted the motion to dismiss. The Appellate Division affirmed.

On August 17, 1981, Dunton filed this action against Suffolk County, the Suffolk County Police Department and the Pfeiffers seeking $50 million compensatory damages, $50 million punitive damages and reasonable attorney's fees. Dunton alleged violations of 42 U.S.C. § 1983 by Officer Pfeiffer and his patrol car partner for the actions in the parking lot, by a desk sergeant for failing to make a report, and by Officer Pfeiffer and

other members of the police department for covering up and conspiring to cover up the incident. He also alleged that the Pfeiffers violated 42 U.S.C. § § 1983 and 1985 by conspiring to cover up the incident with Angela's malicious prosecution complaint of sexual abuse. Finally, he alleged pendent state claims of assault and battery against Robert Pfeiffer and false arrest and malicious prosecution against Angela Pfeiffer.

By local law, Suffolk County provides for the representation of its employees sued under section 1983. Robert Pfeiffer and Suffolk County were represented in this action by the office of the Suffolk County Attorney (County Attorney). An indication that this joint representation might create a conflict came in a form letter from the County Attorney to Robert Pfeiffer dated August 25, 1981 suggesting that because "plaintiff has alleged that [Pfeiffer] acted in [his] personal capacity and/or has demanded punitive damages" and because of possible counterclaims, Pfeiffer should contact private counsel "for such additional advice as may be appropriate." Angela Pfeiffer retained her own attorney.

The County Attorney's answer to Dunton's complaint included an affirmative defense that Robert Pfeiffer was acting in good faith pursuant to his official duties and responsibilities. However, it was the last time that the defense contended that Pfeiffer was acting in good faith as a police officer. The County Attorney told the jury in opening statements that Pfeiffer "acted as a husband, not even as an officer,". Similarly, he told the jury in closing statements that it was obvious Pfeiffer "was acting as an irate husband rather than a police officer," and that he acted "with the human spirit as a husband, not really as an officer," This was clearly the County Attorney's theory of the case, as he made similar statements to the trial judge.

All of Dunton's claims were dismissed by the court as meritless except for the section 1983 claim against Robert Pfeiffer and that state law claims of battery against Robert Pfeiffer and malicious prosecution against Angela Pfeiffer. The jury found Robert Pfeiffer not liable under section 1983, but awarded $10,000 compensatory and $10,000 punitive damages on the battery claim. Angela Pfeiffer was held liable for $5,000 compensatory and

$20,000 punitive damages for malicious prosecution.

Robert Pfeiffer then made a series of post-trial motions relating to the County Attorney's conflict of interest. While the district court acknowledged that there was a conflict, it denied the motions on the ground that Pfeiffer was not prejudiced thereby. It stated that even if Pfeiffer had been shown to be acting under color of state law, damages would still have been awarded for the unjustified battery, and that punitive damages would also have been awarded in any event.

II

Robert Pfeiffer appeals on the ground that the Suffolk County Attorney failed to represent his interest adequately because of the attorney's conflicting representation of Suffolk County. Specifically, Officer Pfeiffer claims that it was in his interest to assert his immunity from section 1983 liability based on good faith actions within the scope of his employment. See *Harlow v. Fitzgerald*; *Pierson v. Ray*. Pfeiffer contends that the attorney undermined the good faith immunity defense by repeatedly stating that Pfeiffer acted not as a police officer but as an "irate husband."

Municipalities commonly provide counsel for their employees and themselves when both municipality and employee are sued. The Suffolk County Attorney's representation of Officer Pfeiffer here was mandated by statute. Prior to 1978, such representation would not have caused a conflict because municipalities were not "persons" subject to section 1983 liability. See *Monroe v. Pape*. Thus, a municipality would have had not reason to give an employee less than full representation.

However, since the Supreme Court's decision in *Monell v. Department of Social Services*, municipalities can be held liable under section 1983 for employees' actions taken pursuant to municipal policy. After *Monell* the interests of a municipality and its employee as defendants in a section 1983 action are in conflict. A municipality may avoid liability by showing that the employee was not acting within the scope of his official duties, because his unofficial actions would not be pursuant to municipal policy. The employee, by contrast, may partially or completely avoid liability by showing that he was acting within the scope of his official duties. If he can show that his

actions were pursuant to an official policy, he can at least shift part of his liability to the municipality. If he is successful in asserting a good faith immunity defense, the municipality may be wholly liable because it cannot assert the good faith immunity of its employees as a defense to a section 1983 action. *Owen v. City of Independence.*

Because of the imminent threat of a serious conflict, disqualification would have been appropriate here even before any proceedings began. See *Shadid v. Jackson* (granting motion to disqualify in virtually identical case because of "high potential for conflicting loyalties"). *Cf. Armstrong v. McAlpin* (en banc) (disqualification appropriate when conflict will taint a trial by affecting attorney's presentation of a case). This conflict surfaced when the County Attorney stated that Pfeiffer was not acting under color of state law but rather as an "irate husband." This was a good defense for the county, which eventually was dismissed from the action. However, it was not in the best interest of Pfeiffer, who was ultimately found liable in his individual capacity. Pfeiffer's failure to object to the multiple representation before or during trial did not constitute a waiver. As a layman, he could not be expected to appreciate his need to prove a good faith defense. Furthermore, he was never advised that his counsel would take positions directly contrary to his interest.

The County Attorney's multiple representation in this case was inconsistent with his professional obligation to Officer Pfeiffer. It was also inconsistent with Canons 5 and 9 of the ABA Code of Professional Responsibility. A violation of Canons 5 and 9 of the Code, which call for exercising independent judgment on behalf of a client and avoiding any appearance of impropriety, provides ample grounds for disqualifying an attorney. As soon as the County Attorney began to undermine Officer Pfeiffer's good faith immunity defense by stating that Pfeiffer acted as an "irate husband" and not as a police officer, he was not only failing to act as a conscientious advocate for Pfeiffer, but was acting against Pfeiffer's interest. The seriousness of this conflict made disqualification appropriate.

Where a conflict is serious and disqualification might be warranted, the district court is under a duty to ensure that the client fully appreciates his situation. This Court has stated that [w]hen a potential or actual conflict of interest situation arises, it is the court's duty to ensure that the attorney's client, so involved, is fully aware of the nature of the conflict and understands the potential threat to the protection of his interest." *In re Taylor.*

There are at least two reasons why a court should satisfy itself that no conflict exists or at least provide notice to the affected party if one does. First, a court is under a continuing obligation to supervise the members of its Bar. E.g., *In re Taylor*; see *Musicus v. Westinghouse Electric Corp.* (per curiam) (district court obligated to take measures against unethical conduct occurring in proceedings before it). Second, trial courts have a duty "to exercise that degree of control required by the facts and circumstances of each case to assure the litigants of a fair trial." *Koufakis v. Carvel.* When a litigant's statutorily appointed counsel is acting against the litigant's interests because of a conflict that the litigant has not been informed of and cannot be expected to understand on his own, the litigant is not receiving a fair trial. *Cf. Wood v. Georgia* (divided loyalties of counsel may create due process violation).

In holding that the trial court had a duty to inform Pfeiffer of the conflict, we in no way excuse the conduct of the other attorneys here. Attorneys are officers of the court and are obligated to adhere to all disciplinary rules and to report incidents of which they have unprivileged knowledge involving violations of a disciplinary rule. See *In re Walker* (as officers of court, attorneys required to notify parties and court of error in court order). The County Attorney had to know of the serious conflict his multiple representation created, and knew or should have known that he could not fulfill his ethical obligations to the county without seriously undercutting Pfeiffer's legal position. The plaintiff's attorney should also have been aware of the problem and should have called it to the attention of the court. See *Estates Theatres, Inc. v. Columbia Pictures Industries, Inc.* ("[T]hose attorneys representing other parties to the litigation were obligated to report relevant facts [regarding conflict of interest of opponent's attorney] to the Court. . . .").

Neither do we believe that Pfeiffer waived his objections to multiple representation by failing to object before or during trial. The letter to Pfeiffer only said that there was a possibility of punitive damages, personal liability or counterclaims, and only suggested that Pfeiffer contact outside counsel. It did not say anything about the most serious conflict, that the County Attorney would take a basic position throughout the litigation which was adverse to Pfeiffer's interest. Pfeiffer presumably knew little or nothing about the law of attorney conflicts and could not be expected to discern the nature of the conflict. He would naturally rely on his attorney to protect him. See *Wood v. Georgia* (lawyer on whom conflict-of-interest charge focuses is unlikely to concede that his actions were improper).

The district court acknowledged that there was a conflict in Pfeiffer's representation but denied the motion for a new trial in the mistaken belief that the conflict was not prejudicial. We do not agree. If Pfeiffer's first trial had been fair, he might have escaped liability altogether. The county had agreed to indemnify Pfeiffer for compensatory damages. If the jury found that Pfeiffer was acting in good faith as a police officer, it might not have awarded punitive damages. We believe that because the jury never had a chance to consider Pfeiffer's good faith immunity defense, Pfeiffer did not receive the fair trial to which he was entitled. See *Turner v. Gilbreath* (reversing trial court's failure to grant new trial); see also *Jedwabny v. Philadelphia Transportation Co.* (affirming trial court's decision to grant new trial); *In re Estate of Richard* (violation of Code of Professional Responsibility that prevents a fair trial constitutes reversible error).

The conflict of interest not only prejudiced Pfeiffer, it may also have resulted in an improper benefit to the municipal defendants. The claim that Pfeiffer acted under color of state law was never presented to the jury in the trial below. If Pfeiffer had the opportunity to contend that he did act under color of state law but was immune from liability based on good faith actions within the scope of his duties, Suffolk County or the Police Department may still have been found liable under section 1983. While Dunton did not cross-appeal on this issue, this Court may consider questions of law not raised by the parties in order to prevent injustice. Because the liability of the County and the Police Department were not determined in a fair trial, failure to reinstate those parties in the action would work an injustice on Dunton, who did not create the conflict of interest at issue here.

Accordingly, we vacate the judgment against Robert Pfeiffer and the orders dismissing' Suffolk County and the Suffolk County Police Department and remand the entire cause of action against them for a new trial.

* * *

NOTES

1. Is it primarily the plaintiff's attorney's responsibility to raise the conflict of interest issue? The local government's attorney's responsibility? What does *Dunton* indicate?

2. Could there be an ethical problem even where the local government is not sued? The Sixth Circuit in *Gordon v. Norman*, 788 F.2d 1194 (6th Cir. 1986), suggested that the answer is yes, although it did not find one in the case before it. Still, it warned that the bar should be concerned about such ethical issues and possible malpractice liability.

3. Why not simply respond to *Dunton* and *Gordon* by getting different counsel for the local government and for the individual defendants? What are some of the practical obstacles to doing this?

4. This kind of ethical issue is (or should be) extensively addressed in professional responsibility courses taught at most law schools. Our purpose here is to alert you to the fact that it arises quite often in the section 1983 setting.

CHAPTER SIX

"[S]ubjects or Causes to be Subjected . . .": Causation

The issue of causation is fundamental to every section 1983 claim. Causation provides the bridge between culpable conduct and injury that most observers deem necessary as a matter of fairness to support liability. E.g. Weinrib, *Causation and Wrongdoing*, 63 Chi.-Kent L. Rev. 407 (1987). Money damages are not recoverable unless the defendant is found to have caused the plaintiff to be deprived of some right secured by the constitution or laws of the United States, and that deprivation is the cause of some legally cognizable harm.

Causation has a long and rich history in the context of common law tort. Hundreds of law review articles and books explore the nuances of causation in tort. Under the traditional approach, causation is divided into two separate inquires: cause in fact and proximate cause. Conduct is viewed as the cause in fact of an injury if it is a necessary condition for its occurrence. *Restatement (Second) of Torts* § 432 (1965). Common law courts invoke the familiar "but for" or "substantial factor" tests in determining whether a defendant's conduct is a cause in fact of the plaintiff's injury. P. Keeton, D. Dobbs, R. Keeton, and D. Owen, *Prosser and Keeton on Torts* § 41 (5th ed. 1985). Proximate or legal cause addresses limitations on liability for conduct that is the cause in fact of harm. *Id.* at § 42. The problems posed by thin skulls, intervening forces, and unforeseeable consequences are considered under the umbrella of proximate cause.

While the general contour of common law tort rules of causation is longstanding, constitutional tort litigation is of comparatively recent origin. Perhaps it is not surprising that the familiar common law lexicon often appears in court decisions that discuss causation in the constitutional tort context. Although common law tort doctrine may provide a convenient starting point for discussing constitutional tort causation issues, it is not controlling. Through-out this chapter, the student should consider whether the constitutional foundation of most section 1983 litigation justify the adoption of standards of causation different from those applied in the common law context.

I. Cause in Fact

Most section 1983 opinions employ the familiar "but for" test to determine cause in fact. That is, the defendant's conduct may be considered the cause in fact of the plaintiff's injury if the harm would not have occurred "but for" the defendant's unconstitutional conduct. For example, a jury could find that the defendants' delay in cutting down the body of an inmate found hanging in his cell was the cause in fact of his death when an expert testified that the inmate had a 95% chance of survival had resuscitation efforts been initiated immediately. *Heflin v. Stewart County*, 958 F.2d 709 (6th Cir. 1992). On the other hand, a deficiencies in a county's policy of processing arrest warrants was not the cause of the plaintiffs' illegal arrests when "corrective measures that might reasonably have been required . . . would [not] have prevented" the detention. *Hvorick v. Shealan*, 847 F.Supp. 1414, 1424 (N.D. Ill. 1994).

The "but for" test is problematic in that it is impossible to know with absolute certainty "what would have happened" if the defendant had acted differently. Courts must determine how much leeway to give juries to decide this inherently speculative question. The rigor with which courts scrutinize evidence of causation necessarily reflects subtle, but significant, policy choices. Plaintiffs benefit from rules that give juries considerable discretion, while rules demanding strict proof favor defendants. See Malone, *Ruminations on Cause in Fact*, 9 Stan.

L. Rev. 60 (1956). The following cases should be examined with this point in mind. Consider how the courts deal with the uncertainty inherent in the but for test.

A. Mixed Motives

Mt. Healthy City School District Board of Education v. Doyle

429 U.S. 274 (1976)

Mr. Justice **Rehnquist** delivered the opinion of the Court.

Respondent Doyle sued petitioner Mt. Healthy Board of Education in the United States District Court for the Southern District of Ohio. Doyle claimed that the Board's refusal to renew his contract in 1971 violated his rights under the First and Fourteenth Amendments to the United States Constitution. After a bench trial the District Court held that Doyle was entitled to reinstatement with backpay. The Court of Appeals for the Sixth Circuit affirmed the judgment, and we granted the Board's petition for certiorari to consider an admixture of jurisdictional and constitutional claims.

. . .

Doyle was first employed by the Board in 1966. He worked under one-year contracts for the first three years, and under a two-year contract from 1969 to 1971. In 1969 he was elected president of the Teachers' Association, in which position he worked to expand the subjects of direct negotiation between the Association and the Board of Education. During Doyle's one-year term as president of the Association, and during the succeeding year when he served on its executive committee, there was apparently some tension in relations between the Board and the Association.

Beginning early in 1970, Doyle was involved in several incidents not directly connected with his role in the Teachers' Association. In one instance, he engaged in an argument with another teacher which culminated in the other teacher's slapping him. Doyle subsequently refused to accept an apology and

insisted upon some punishment for the other teacher. His persistence in the matter resulted in the suspension of both teachers for one day, which was followed by a walkout by a number of other teachers, which in turn resulted in the lifting of the suspensions.

On other occasions, Doyle got into an argument with employees of the school cafeteria over the amount of spaghetti which had been served him; referred to students, in connection with a disciplinary complaint, as "sons of bitches"; and made an obscene gesture to two girls in connection with their failure to obey commands made in his capacity as cafeteria supervisor. Chronologically the last in the series of incidents which respondent was involved in during his employment by the Board was a telephone call by him to a local radio station. It was the Board's consideration of this incident which the court below found to be a violation of the First and Fourteenth Amendments.

In February 1971, the principal circulated to various teachers a memorandum relating to teacher dress and appearance, which was apparently prompted by the view of some in the administration that there was a relationship between teacher appearance and public support for bond issues. Doyle's response to the receipt of the memorandum—on a subject which he apparently understood was to be settled by joint teacher-administration action—was to convey the substance of the memorandum to a disc jockey at WSAI, a Cincinnati radio station, who promptly announced the adoption of the dress code as a news item. Doyle subsequently apologized to the principal, conceding that he should have made some prior communication of his criticism to the school administration.

Approximately one month later the superintendent made his customary annual recommendations to the Board as to the rehiring of nontenure teachers. He recommended that Doyle not be rehired. The same recommendation was made with respect to nine other teachers in the district, and in all instances, including Doyle's, the recommendation was adopted by the Board. Shortly after being notified of this decision, respondent requested a statement of reasons for the Board's actions. He received a statement citing "a notable lack of tact in handling professional matters which leaves much doubt as to your sincerity in establishing good school relationships." That general statement was followed by references to the radio station incident and to the obscene-gesture incident.

The District Court found that all of these incidents had in fact occurred. It concluded that respondent Doyle's telephone call to the radio station was "clearly protected by the First Amendment," and that because it had played a "substantial part" in the decision of the Board not to renew Doyle's employment, he was entitled to reinstatement with backpay. The District Court did not expressly state what test it was applying in determining that the incident in question involved conduct protected by the First Amendment, but simply held that the communication to the radio station was such conduct. The Court of Appeals affirmed. . .

We . . . accept the District Court's finding that [Doyle's] communication [with the radio station] was protected by the First and Fourteenth Amendments. We are not, however, entirely in agreement with that court's manner of reasoning from this finding to the conclusion that Doyle is entitled to reinstatement and back pay.

The District Court made the following "conclusions" on this aspect of the case:

"1) If a non-permissible reason, e.g., exercise of First Amendment rights, played a substantial part in the decision not to renew—even in the face of other permissible grounds—the decision may not stand (citations omitted).

"2) A non-permissible reason did play a substantial part. That is clear from the letter of the Superintendent immediately following the Board's decision, which stated two reasons—the one, the conversation with the radio station clearly protected by the First Amendment. A court may not engage in any limitation of First Amendment rights based on 'tact'—that is not to say that the 'tactfulness' is irrelevant to other issues in this case."

At the same time, though, it stated that

"[i]n fact, as this Court sees it and finds, both the Board and the Superintendent were faced with a situation in which there did exist in fact reason. . .independent of any First Amendment rights or exercise thereof, to not extend tenure."

Since respondent Doyle had no tenure, and there was therefore not even a state-law requirement of "cause" or "reason" before a decision could be made not to renew his employment, it is not clear what the District Court meant by this latter statement. Clearly the Board legally *could* have dismissed respondent had the radio station incident never come to its attention. One plausible meaning of the court's statement is that the Board and the Superintendent not only could, but in fact *would* have reached that decision had not the constitutionally protected incident of the telephone call to the radio station occurred. We are thus brought to the issue whether, even if that were the case, the fact that the protected conduct played a "substantial part" in the actual decision not to renew would necessarily amount to a constitutional violation justifying remedial action. We think that it would not.

A rule of causation which focuses solely on whether protected conduct played a part, "substantial" or otherwise, in a decision not to rehire, could place an employee in a better position as a result of the exercise of constitutionally protected conduct than he would have occupied had he done nothing. The difficulty with the rule enunciated by the District Court is that it would require reinstatement in cases where a dramatic and perhaps abrasive incident is inevitably on the minds of those responsible for the decision to rehire, and does indeed play a part in that decision—even if the same decision would have been reached had the incident not occurred. The constitutional principle at stake is sufficiently vindicated if such an employee is placed in no worse a position than if he had not engaged in the conduct. A borderline or marginal candidate should not have the employment question resolved against him because of constitutionally protected conduct. But that same candidate ought not to be able, by engaging in such conduct, to prevent his employer from assessing his performance record and reaching a decision not to rehire on the basis of that record, simply because the protected conduct makes the employer more certain of the correctness of its decision.

This is especially true where, as the District Court observed was the case here, the current decision to rehire will accord "tenure." The long-term consequences of an award of tenure are of great moment both to the employee and to the employer. They are too significant for us to hold that the Board in this case would be precluded, because it considered constitutionally protected conduct in deciding not to rehire Doyle, from attempting to prove to a trier of fact that quite apart from such conduct Doyle's record was such that he would not have been rehired in any event.

In other areas of constitutional law, this Court has found it necessary to formulate a test of causation which distinguishes between a result caused by a constitutional violation and one not so caused. We think those are instructive in formulating the test to be applied here.

In *Lyons v. Oklahoma* the Court held that even though the first confession given by a defendant had been involuntary, the Fourteenth Amendment did not prevent the State from using a second confession obtained 12 hours later if the coercion surrounding the first confession had been sufficiently dissipated as to make the second confession voluntary. In *Wong Sun v. United States* the Court was willing to assume that a defendant's arrest had been unlawful, but held that "the connection between the arrest and the statement [given several days later] had 'become so attenuated as to dissipate the taint.' *Nardone v. United States*." *Parker v. North Carolina* held that even though a confession be assumed to have been involuntary in the constitutional sense of the word, a guilty plea entered over a month later met the test for the voluntariness of such a plea. The Court in *Parker* relied on the same quoted language from *Nardone*, supra, as did the Court in *Wong Sun*, supra. While the type of causation on which the taint cases turn may differ somewhat from that which we apply here, those cases do suggest that the proper test to apply in the present context is one which likewise protects against the invasion of constitutional rights without commanding undesirable consequences not necessary to the assurance of those rights.

Initially, in this case, the burden was properly placed upon respondent to show that his conduct was constitutionally protected, and that this conduct was a "substantial factor"— or, to put it in other words, that it was a "motivating factor" in the Board's decision not to rehire him. Respondent having carried that burden, however, the District Court

should have gone on to determine whether the Board had shown by a preponderance of the evidence that it would have reached the same decision as to respondent's re-employment even in the absence of the protected conduct.

We cannot tell from the District Court opinion and conclusions, nor from the opinion of the Court of Appeals affirming the judgment of the District Court, what conclusion those courts would have reached had they applied this test. The judgment of the Court of Appeals is therefore vacated, and the case remanded for further proceedings consistent with this opinion.

So ordered.

NOTES

1. *Mt. Healthy* establishes a two-part test of causation in so-called mixed motive cases. The plaintiff must first prove by a preponderance of the evidence that the adverse action taken against her was motivated "in substantial part" by constitutionally impermissible factors, such as protected speech or racial discrimination. If the plaintiff fails to discharge this burden, the defendant will prevail. E.g., *Garrett v. Barnes*, 961 F.2d 629 (7th Cir. 1992); *Erickson v. Pierce County*, 960 F.2d 801 (9th Cir. 1992) (plaintiffs in both cases failed to prove that termination of employment was substantially motivated by political affiliation). If the plaintiff proves that the adverse action was substantially motivated by unconstitutional factors, the burden shifts to the defendant to prove by a preponderance of the evidence that the same action would have been taken even in the absence of the constitutionally impermissible motive. Thus, even though religious discrimination played a substantial part in the decision to terminate the studies of a doctoral student, the student could not recover damages when the defendant proved that the student would have been dismissed because of his poor research skills regardless of the religious discrimination. *Al-Zubaidi v. Ijaz*, 917 F.2d 1347 (4th Cir. 1990). See generally S. Nahmod, *Civil Rights and Civil Liberties Litigation* §§ 3.25 & 4.03 (3d ed. 1991) (collecting cases). The Supreme Court has applied the *Mt. Healthy* test in a variety of contexts other than section 1983. See *Price Waterhouse v. Hopkins*, 490 U.S. 228 (1990)

(Title VII employment discrimination); *NLRB v. Transportation Management Corp.*, 462 U.S. 393 (1983) (unfair labor practice). Cf. *Carey v. Piphus*, 435 U.S. 247 (1978) (plaintiff cannot recover damages for injuries caused by his suspension from public schools without a hearing if he would have been suspended had a proper hearing been held).

2. Litigation in mixed motive cases often focuses on the second part of the *Mt. Healthy* test and the nature of the defendant's burden. How is a defendant to prove or a fact finder to determine whether the same action would be taken without regard to the constitutionally impermissible factor? In *North Mississippi Communications, Inc. v. Jones*, 951 F.2d 652 (5th Cir. 1992), a county government had been placing legal notices in the county's largest newspaper. After the plaintiff-newspaper published a series of articles critical of various county board activities, the county began placing legal notices in a smaller rival newspaper. The plaintiff-newspaper discharged its burden of proving that the county's decision to place legal notices with the rival newspaper was substantially motivated by a desire to retaliate against the newspaper's editorial policies. The district court also found, however, that the county would have given "the bulk" of the legal ads to the rival newspaper anyway, because the plaintiff-newspaper had broken two bid agreements. The fifth circuit court of appeals concluded that this finding did not satisfy the second part of the *Mt. Healthy* test. The court explained:

> the defendant may not prevail "by offering a legitimate and sufficient reason for its decision if that reason did not motivate it at the time of the decision;" nor may it prevail "by merely showing that at the time of the decision it was motivated only in part by a legitimate reason".

951 F.2d at 656–57 (quoting *Price Waterhouse v. Hopkins*, 490 U.S. 228, 248 (1989)). Rather, the county's burden was to prove by a preponderance of the evidence, which of the 252 individual advertisements would have been placed with the rival newspaper even in the absence of the retaliatory motive. Is it possible to dissect motive so cleanly? See also *White Plains Towing Corp. v. Patterson*, 991 F.2d 1049 (2d Cir. 1993) (termination of the government's contract with a towing company was

substantially motivated by unconstitutional retaliation against the plaintiff for publicly criticizing defendants; as a matter of law, however, defendants met their burden of proving that the contract would have been terminated anyway, because of consumer complaints about the plaintiff's services).

3. The precise scope of the *Mt. Healthy* rule is subject to debate. Some commentators have argued that the first part of the *Mt. Healthy* test addresses liability while the second merely addresses remedy. That is, a plaintiff who fails to prove that constitutionally impermissible factors (e.g., retaliation against the exercise of free speech) played a substantial part in the decision to terminate her employment fails to establish any constitutional violation. Hence there is no basis for imposing liability under section 1983. However, where unconstitutional considerations do substantially motivate the decision, but the defendant proves that the same decision would have been made for legitimate reasons, some commentators maintain that there has been a violation of constitutional rights, but that certain remedies are inappropriate. The issue is whether the defendant's discharge of its burden under the second part of the *Mt. Healthy* test means that there is no constitutional violation or merely that the plaintiff cannot recover for the economic loss resulting from the dismissal. The theoretical distinction between "no liability" and "no remedy" could produce significant practical consequences. For example, if the second test of *Mt. Healthy* only limits remedy, the plaintiff could recover for the emotional distress stemming from the unconstitutional retaliation as distinguished from the loss of wages resulting from the dismissal. If so, an award of attorney fees might be available. See S. Nahmod, *Civil Rights and Civil Liberties Litigation* § 4.03 (3d ed. 1991) (arguing that the second part of the *Mt. Healthy* test "goes to remedy and not to the existence of a constitutional violation."); M. Weber, *Beyond* Price Waterhouse v. Hopkins: *A New Approach to Mixed Motive Discrimination*, 68 N.C. L. Rev. 495, 523–24 (1990); Wolly, What Hath *Mt. Healthy* Wrought?, 41 Ohio St. L.J. 385, 392 (1980).

In *Price Waterhouse v. Hopkins*, 490 U.S. 228 (1989), a plurality of the Supreme Court indicated that a defendant who was substantially motivated by constitutionally impermissible factors, but proves that the same decision would have been made for legitimate reasons, avoids all liability. That is, a defendant who discharges its burden under the second part of the *Mt. Healthy* test avoids all liability on the merits—not merely a particular remedy such as back pay or reinstatement. Although *Price Waterhouse* involved a Title VII claim, the court was construing the same rule announced for section 1983 cases in *Mt. Healthy.*

In 1991, Congress amended Title VII by adding a new section that provides:

> an unlawful employment practice is established when the complaining party demonstrates that race. . .was a motivating factor for any employment practice even though other factors also motivated the practice.

42 U.S.C. § 2000e–2(m).

How does this amendment affect the *Mt. Healthy* test? See S. Nahmod, *Civil Rights and Civil Liberties Litigation* § 4.03 (3d ed. 1991) (1993 Supp.) ("This amendment brings Title VII in line with the position set out . . . [in] the Treatise: that the second part of the *Mount Healthy* test goes to remedy and not liability and that, consequently, a § 1983 defendant who carries on this part has *not* prevailed on the merits."). Should an amendment to Title VII affect a rule of causation developed in the context of section 1983?

4. What other approaches might be taken to resolve the issue of causation in mixed motive cases? Consider various models that have developed in common law contexts.

(a) Motive is often a critical issue in the common law torts of intentional interference with contract, defamation, and malicious prosecution. Specifically, whether certain conduct is tortious or privileged may turn on the motive of the defendant. As in *Mt. Healthy*, the motive of the defendant is often disputed. Many courts apply a "dominant purpose" test in such cases. E.g., *Alyeska Pipeline Service Co. v. Aurora Air Service, Inc.*, 604 P.2d 1090 (Alaska 1979) (interference with contract); *Nodar v. Galbreath*, 462 So.2d 803 (Fla. 1984) (defamation); *Nesmith v. Alford*, 318 F.2d 110 (5th Cir. 1963) (malicious prosecution). See generally P. Keeton, D. Dobbs, R. Keeton, and D. Owen, *Prosser and Keeton on the Law of Torts*

1094 (5th ed. 1984) ("It may be suggested that [with regard to interference with contract], as in the case of mixed motives in the exercise of a privilege in defamation and malicious prosecution, the court may well look to the predominant purpose underlying the defendant's conduct."); *Restatement (Second) of Torts* § 668 (1976) ("To subject a person to liability for malicious prosecution, the proceedings must have been initiated primarily for a purpose other than that of bringing an offender to justice.") How is a "dominant purpose" test similar to or different from that adopted by the Court in *Mt. Healthy*? Would the county in *North Mississippi Communications, Inc. v. Jones*, discussed in note 2 above, have a better chance of prevailing under a "dominant purpose" test or the *Mt. Healthy* test?

(b) Could the mixed motive termination of Doyle be analogized to the concurrent causation cases in common law tort where two forces combine to produce an injury? The paradigm example of such a case is where two independent fires combine to destroy the plaintiff's property. Under prevailing common law principles, each fire would be considered a cause in fact of the injury. Thus, a railroad which negligently ignites one fire that combines with a second fire of independent origin and burns the plaintiff's property may be held liable for the resulting injury even if the second fire alone would have burned the plaintiff's property anyway. E.g., *Anderson v. Minneapolis, St. Paul & Sault Ste. Marie Ry.*, 146 Minn. 430, 179 N.W. 45 (1920). See generally *Restatement (Second) of Torts* § 432(2) (1965). This common law rule developed as an exception to the but for test and is predicated on the belief that holding the wrongdoer responsible in such situations provides needed deterrence of future misconduct, vindicates the plaintiff's rights, and compensates the plaintiff for her injuries. See Carpenter, *Concurrent Causation*, 83 Pa. L. Rev. 941, 949–52 (1935). If a railroad can not escape common law tort liability by proving that the plaintiff's property would have burned just the same through other causes, why can the defendants escape constitutional tort liability in cases like *Mt. Healthy* by proving that plaintiff would have been terminated for legitimate reasons? Does *Mt. Healthy* provide less protection against invasions of constitutional rights than the common law provides for invasions of common law rights? If so, what policy considerations might explain this result?

(c) Many states have embraced principles of proportional recovery through a variety of legal doctrines, including comparative fault, the modification of joint and several liability, market share liability, and allowing recovery for "loss of chance". See generally, Makdisi, *Proportional Liability: A Comprehensive Rule to Apportion Tort Damages Based on Probability*, 67 U.N.C. L. Rev. 1063 (1989). Could these developments in the traditional tort context be adapted to mixed motive constitutional tort claims? If both constitutionally permissible and impermissible factors motivate a decision, should a claimant be allowed to recover a proportion of the resulting damages? In *Mt. Healthy*, could the fact finder rationally assign percentages to the extent that the protected speech and rude gestures contributed to the decision to not rehire Doyle?

5. As illustrated by the various common law doctrines described in the preceding note, legal standards for determining whether conduct causes injury are rife with policy choices. For a classic discussion of the role of policy in fashioning cause in fact doctrine in common law tort, see Malone, *Ruminations on Cause in Fact*, 9 Stan. L. Rev. 60 (1956). To what extent do the *constitutional* underpinnings of most section 1983 claims affect the policy choices regarding causation standards? On the one hand, the fundamental nature of constitutional rights might support causation rules that greatly protect the civil liberties of individuals. On the other hand, constitutional rules are purposefully less susceptible to democratic modification than are common law rules. This characteristic of section 1983 litigation might counsel for principles of causation that better preserve legislative and executive discretion. Does *Mt. Healthy* strike an appropriate balance between the competing interests of the individual and government? See Eaton, *Causation in Constitutional Torts*, 67 Iowa L. Rev. 443, 454–61 (1982).

6. Suppose a government is actually motivated by racial discrimination in firing an employee, but later learns of a permissible ground for the decision. Should "after-acquired evidence" affect the defendant's liability under section 1983? In one recent case, a jailer named Washington alleged he was fired because of his race. After his termination, the Sheriff's department learned that Washington had falsified his employment application by stating that he had not been convicted of an offence other than a minor traffic violation. In fact, Washington had been convicted of criminal trespass and third-degree assault. The Sheriff's department submitted two uncontroverted affidavits stating that the facts of Washington's convictions, if known during the time of Washington's employment, would have led to his immediate discharge. Is the Sheriff's department entitled to summary judgment? See, *Washington v. Lake County*, 969 F.2d 250 (7th Cir. 1992). Cf. *McKennon v. Nashville Banner Publishing Co.*, 9 F.3d 539 (6th Cir. 1993), *cert. granted*, 114 S.Ct. 2099 (1994) (defendant-employer was granted summary judgment in an age discrimination case when after acquired evidence of violations of work rules provided a legitimate basis for firing a 62 year old secretary). Are after-acquired evidence cases different from mixed motive cases? Do the same policy considerations that support the second part of the *Mt. Healthy* test apply with equal force when the legitimate reason was not an actual motivating factor at the time of the decision? For a thorough analysis of these issues, see Rebecca White and Robert Brussack, *The Proper Role of After-Acquired Evidence in Employment Discrimination Litigation*, 35 B.C. L. Rev. 49 (1993).

B. Governmental and Supervisory Liability

Chapter Five addressed issues pertaining to the liability of governmental entities and supervisory personnel for the constitutional violations committed by others. A brief review of those materials may help set the stage for considering the issue of causation in that context. In *Monell v. Department of Social Services*, 436 U.S. 658 (1978), the court held that cities were "persons" that could be sued under section 1983, but that liability could not be based on principles of respondeat superior. The latter ruling was grounded in the "subjects, or causes to be subjected" language of the statute. The court viewed principles of vicarious liability as inconsistent with the requirement of causation set forth in section 1983. *Monell*, 436 U.S. at 691. Instead, plaintiffs must prove that governmental policy or custom was "the moving force" behind the unconstitutional conduct of municipal employees. *Monell*, 436 U.S. at 694. A plurality of the court later emphasized that "[a]t the very least, there must be an affirmative link between the policy and the particular constitutional violation alleged." *City of Oklahoma City v. Tuttle*, 471 U.S. 808, 823 (1985).

Phrases like "moving force" and "affirmative link" provide little concrete guidance as to how to evaluate the causal relationship between governmental policy and a violation of constitutional rights. The court elaborated on this issue in *City of Canton v. Harris*, 489 U.S. 378 (1989). The plaintiff alleged that she was denied her rights under the due process clause of the fourteenth amendment to medical care while in police custody. The city's liability was based on its alleged failure to train the police force. After ruling that inadequate training could be considered a "policy", the court addressed the issue of causation.

> Moreover, for liability to attach in this circumstance the identified deficiency in a city's training program must be closely related to the ultimate injury. Thus, in the case at hand, respondent must still prove that the deficiency in training actually caused the police officers' indifference to her medical needs. Would the injury have been avoided had the employee been trained under a program that was not deficient in the identified respect? Predicting how a hypothetically well-trained officer would have acted under the circumstances may not be an easy task for the factfinder, particularly since matters of judgment may be involved, and since officers who are well trained are not free from error and perhaps might react very much like the untrained officer in similar circumstances. But judge and jury, doing their respective jobs, will be adequate to the task.

City of Canton, 489 U.S. at 391.

Supervisors also are not vicariously liable for the unconstitutional actions of the police offi-

cers, prison guards or others whom they supervise. E.g., *Rizzo v. Goode*, 423 U.S. 362, 376 (1976) (supervisory liability requires a showing of "direct responsibility" for the unconstitutional actions of subordinates). Yet lower courts routinely uphold liability when the supervisor is shown to have been deliberately indifferent to the plight of the person deprived of her constitutional rights. E.g., *Larez v. City of Los Angeles*, 946 F.2d 630 (9th Cir. 1991) (police chief held liable for use of excessive force by police officers); *Guitierez-Rodriguez v. Cartagena*, 882 F.2d 553 (1st Cir. 1989) (supervisor and chief of police held liable for excessive force by subordinate). See generally S. Nahmod, *Civil Rights and Civil Liberties Litigation* § 3.23 (3d ed. 1991) (collecting cases). As with governmental liability, however, the deliberate indifference of the supervisor must cause the unconstitutional conduct of the subordinate.

How is a factfinder to determine whether a city's policy or a supervisor's conduct caused someone to violate another's constitutional rights? The following two cases illustrate how lower courts address this issue of causation in the context of governmental and supervisory liability.

1. Causation and Municipal Policy

Buffington v. Baltimore County

913 F.2d 113 (4th Cir. 1990)

Phillips, Circuit Judge

I

At about 4:30 a.m. on March 19, 1987, David Buffington, Jr., was awakened by the sound of his father's car pulling out of the driveway of his parents' house, next door to his. Knowing that his younger brother, James Buffington, 24, was the only person home that night, and that James did not have a valid driver's license, David rushed next door and discovered a handwritten suicide note and guns missing from his father's gun closet, which had been forced open. David immediately called the police emergency line, then set off in search of his brother. Officer Lewis Harvey of the Wilkens precinct of the Baltimore County Police Department, responding to a broadcast over the police radio describing James as suicidal, went to David's house and met David's wife, Kathryn, who showed him the suicide note. Kathryn described James' history of emotional problems and drug and alcohol abuse, particularly as a teenager. These problems had led to a number of encounters with the Wilkens precinct police, and in fact Officer Harvey acknowledged to Kathryn that he knew of James' background. Acting Shift Lieutenant Joseph Gribbin soon arrived at the house and also read the note. Officer Harvey called the Wilkens station and advised that James was suicidal and armed.

The county police apprehended James at 5:47 a.m. When he was seized, James appeared to be intoxicated and had in his possession two rifles and three handguns, all loaded. At 6:25 a.m., Officer Harvey called Kathryn Buffington and informed her that James had been found and was being held at the Wilkens station in protective custody. He told her that James had said that he had not committed suicide "because he couldn't decide which gun to use." David Buffington returned from his search minutes later and called Officer Harvey to confirm that James was being held and to remind him of James' history of emotional problems. David stressed his sense that James was at extreme risk of committing suicide. Officer Harvey stated that preparations were currently being made to take James to Greater Baltimore Medical Center for an emergency psychiatric evaluation. On Officer Harvey's advice, David decided to press criminal charges against his brother in order to enable the police to hold James in custody in the event that the hospital would not take him on an emergency commitment basis. At the time he spoke to David, Officer Harvey had already prepared the paperwork for arrest and charging.

From the time he was first brought into the station, Buffington was handcuffed to a rail beside the booking desk in the receiving room of the police station so he could be observed by the desk officers. Several police officers testified at trial that it was standard practice to handcuff suicidal detainees to the rail by the booking desk rather than place them in the lockup, where they might be able, quietly and

unnoticed, to hang themselves. At approximately 6:15 a.m. that morning, Officers Donald Gaigalas and Ronald Tucker had taken over as desk officers, relieving Officers William Maeser and Patrick Kamberger from that post. Officer Gaigalas, at about 6:25 a.m., unhitched Buffington from the rail and took him to an isolation cell, without removing any of his clothing. Although there were numerous detainees in the male lock-up, Gaigalas placed Buffington alone in the female lockup area, and made no provision to keep him under observation. At 7:15 a.m., Buffington was found, hanged from the cell's horizontal bars by a noose fashioned from his pants.

David and Barbara Buffington, as James' parents, and Barbara as James' personal representative, then brought this action alleging claims of constitutional violation under 42 U.S.C. § 1983, and pendent state claims under the wrongful death and survival statutes. Named as defendants were Baltimore County, Chief of Police Cornelius Behan, Sergeant Daniel Yuska, Corporal Joseph Gribbin, Captain Kenneth Kramer, and Officers Lewis Harvey, Donald Gaigalas, Ronald Tucker, and William Maeser.

There was conflicting evidence at trial about Buffington's emotional state while handcuffed to the rail and about how much the desk officers knew concerning Buffington's intention to commit suicide. Outgoing desk officer Kamberger testified that Buffington told him that he wanted to shoot himself, and Kamberger further stated that he passed this information on to Officer Tucker when Tucker and Gaigalas took over at the desk. Tucker denied that Kamberger told him this. Officer Gaigalas admitted that he knew Officer Harvey was preparing forms for Buffington's emergency commitment. Though he later equivocated on the point, Gaigalas admitted in original testimony that he knew Buffington was suicidal before he took him to the cell. Gaigalas also admitted that a prior deposition statement that he did not know that Buffington was suicidal and was being held for emergency psychiatric treatment had been "deliberately and knowingly false."

At trial, the Buffingtons presented expert testimony about the County's deficiencies in suicide prevention at correctional facilities. Since 1977, there had been 57 suicide attempts in the County jails, twelve of which had been "successful." Although the County had adopted in 1984 one of the nationally recognized suicide prevention standards, known as "CALEA" (Commission on Accreditation for Law Enforcement Agencies), it did not have any written policies or regulations implementing the standards. As noted, however, the department's officers did operate under a "standing order" that suicidal detainees should remain handcuffed to the rail by the front desk. The evidence at trial also showed that County police officers received no training in identifying suicidal detainees and in preventing suicide attempts. Dr. Joseph Rowan, one of the Buffingtons' experts on jail and lockup suicide prevention, testified that "I strongly feel that this is the worst case of handling of a suicide case that I have ever seen."

After a first trial ended in mistrial, a second jury found Officers Tucker and Gaigalas liable under § 1983 for deliberate indifference to Buffington's serious need for some measure of suicide prevention. The County, through its policymaker Chief Behan, and Behan himself were found liable under § 1983 on the theory that their failure to train county police officers in suicide prevention evidenced a deliberate indifference to the rights of suicidal detainees. The jury awarded a total of $185,000 in damages against the appellants. Following denial of the defendants' motions for j.n.o.v. and alternatively for a new trial, the court awarded over $430,000 in attorneys' fees and costs to plaintiffs. . . .

These appeals followed. . . .

IV

Appellant Baltimore County argues separately that it was entitled in any event to judgment as a matter of law on the § 1983 claim against it. Specifically, the County contends that the district court erred in submitting that claim to the jury because there was no evidence that its failure to train its officers in suicide prevention proximately caused Buffington's suicide. We agree that under the Supreme Court's decision in *City of Canton v. Harris*, the judgment against the County on the § 1983 claim must be reversed.

In *Canton*, the Supreme Court outlined the circumstances under which a municipality can be held liable under § 1983 for constitutional violations resulting from a policy of failing to

train municipal employees. Under general principles of § 1983, a municipality can be liable only when the municipality itself, through one of its policies or customs, causes the constitutional violation; municipal liability cannot be premised on respondeat superior or vicarious liability. *Monell v. New York City Dep't of Social Servs.* Moreover, the municipal policy or custom must be the direct cause of—the "moving force" behind—the constitutional violation. *Polk County v. Dodson.* The *Canton* Court, addressing the peculiar context of a claim that a municipality's policy of omission, i.e., its failure to train, was the cause of the constitutional violation, considered both the degree of fault and the causal link required under § 1983 to sustain that type claim. The Court held first that § 1983 requires a showing that the failure to train amounts to "deliberate indifference to the rights of persons with whom the police come in contact." *Canton.* This degree of fault was thought necessary to reconcile the failure-to-train theory of liability, which alleges a policy of omission, with the principle that § 1983 municipal liability can attach only when the municipality's policy represents "a deliberate choice [by the municipality's authorized policy-makers] to follow a course of action . . . made from among various alternatives." *Pembaur v. City of Cincinnati.* In addition to the "deliberate indifference" culpability standard, the Court explained that a direct causal link must exist between a specific deficiency in training and the particular violation alleged: "the identified deficiency in [a] training program must be closely related to the ultimate injury." *Canton.* The pertinent question on causation will be "Would the injury have been avoided had the employee been trained under a program that was not deficient in the identified respect?" Id. It will not

> suffice to prove that an injury or accident could have been avoided if an officer had had better or more training, sufficient to equip him to avoid the particular injury-causing conduct. Such a claim could be made about almost any encounter resulting in injury, yet not condemn the adequacy of the program to enable officers to respond properly to the usual and recurring situations with which they must deal.

Id.

We do not think the evidence was sufficient under *Canton* to permit a jury to find that a policy of failure to train officers in suicide prevention actually and proximately caused the particular harm that occurred here. Immediately before the suicide, Buffington was handcuffed to the rail by the precinct's booking desk, in conformance with the standard procedure used as a matter of policy for suicidal detainees at the precinct. Buffington would have remained handcuffed there until moved to the hospital but for desk officer Gaigalas's decision, unchecked by his fellow desk officer Tucker, to take him to an isolation cell without removing any of his clothing, arranging for monitoring, or taking some other preventive measure. It may well be, as the Buffingtons contend, that better suicide prevention training, closer adherence to national standards on jail suicide prevention, written regulations, or some combination of these would have served to avoid what occurred here. But *Canton* has made clear that municipal liability under § 1983 may not rest on such proof. This particular injury would have been avoided by the individual desk officers taking the minimal preventive step of following the precinct's official policy and customary practice of keeping Buffington handcuffed to the rail, i.e., by showing more than the deliberate indifference that the jury found.[3] In so holding, we need not determine whether the Wilkens precinct's standards and procedures for handling suicidal detainees necessarily met constitutional standards in all possible respects. Rather, in light of *Canton*'s instruction on causation, we hold only that the normal practice of handcuffing such detainees to the rail, which was a part of those procedures, was "sufficient to equip [Gaigalas and

Tucker] to avoid the particular injury causing conduct" in this case. *Canton*[.]

V

. . .

For the foregoing reasons, we affirm the judgments against Officers Tucker and Gaigalas, [and] reverse the judgments against Chief Behan and Baltimore County on both the § 1983 and state law claims. . .

AFFIRMED IN PART; REVERSED IN PART; VACATED AND REMANDED IN PART

NOTES

1. What is the precise holding in *Buffington*? Did the court reverse the jury verdict against the county because there was insufficient evidence that its failure to train county police officers in suicide prevention reflected deliberate indifference to the rights of suicidal detainees; or that the deliberately indifferent policy (if there was one) was not the cause in fact of Buffington's suicide; or that the actions of officers Gaigalas and Tucker were a superseding cause of Buffington's death. Did Buffington present evidence that could support a finding that the county did not adequately train its police officers in suicide prevention? Was there evidence that Buffington's suicide would not have occurred had better training policies been in place? What additional evidence is needed to support a jury verdict?

2. The rejection of principles of vicarious liability in *Monell v. Department of Social Services*, 436 U.S. 658 (1978), requires courts to determine whether a governmental policy or custom causes another person to deprive the plaintiff of a constitutional right. Recall that the Supreme Court in *City of Canton* framed the causation issue in terms of a "but for" test ("Would the injury have been avoided had the employee been trained under a program that was not deficient in the identified respect?", 489 U.S. at 391 (1989)). In the context of common law torts, commentators have long recognized the inherent uncertainty in the hypothetical nature of the but for test. E.g., Leon Green, *The Causal Relation Issue in Negligence Law*, 60 Mich. L. Rev. 543 (1962); Thode, *The Indefensible Use of the Hypothetical Case to*

---

[3] Indeed, the district court has held and the Buffingtons themselves, in their appellate brief, have acknowledged that it was Gaigalas's critical dereliction that directly caused this suicide. The court stated that it was not "necessary for the police officers at Wilkens Police Station to obtain a Ph.D. in order to refrain from placing a known suicidal person in an isolated jail cell with his pants on. A semi-clear head and a normal degree of common sense would have sufficed." Similarly, the Buffingtons' statement of facts notes that "this suicide was the direct, proximate, and inevitable result of the utter failure of Gaigalas and Tucker to constantly observe James while he was in their custody." Brief of Appellees at 10.

Determine Cause in Fact, 46 Tex. L. Rev. 423 (1968). This uncertainty is heightened when causal question concerns the effect of a hypothetical change in the defendant's policy on the actions or inactions of third parties. How is a jury to determine how a police officer would have acted if trained differently? The Court in *City of Canton* acknowledged that "predicting how a hypothetically well-trained officer would have acted under the circumstances may not be an easy task for the factfinder", but expressed confidence the "judge and jury, doing their respective jobs, will be adequate to the task." *City of Canton*, 489 U.S. at 391. For an interesting discussion of how courts cope with the uncertainty of causation, see Strassfeld, *If. . . : Counterfactuals in the Law*, 60 Geo. Wash. L. Rev. 340 (1992).

3. The causal relationship is most easily found in section 1983 claims where the alleged constitutional violation follows from the implementation of an official policy which itself is unconstitutional. For example, the plaintiff in *Monell* challenged the constitutionality of the city's policy of compelling pregnant employees to take unpaid leaves of absences before such leaves were required for medical reasons. Once the compulsory maternity leave policy is found to be unconstitutional, the causal connection between that policy and the violation of the plaintiff's constitutional rights is apparent. As noted by Professor Kritchevsky,

> [w]hen an unconstitutional policy is proved, courts generally assume that the policy alone caused the injury. The courts assume that the violation of the plaintiff's constitutional rights occurred because the state actor was following a municipal policy, and not because of any improper personal motive.

Kritchevsky, *"Or Causes to be Subjected": The Role of Causation in Section 1983 Municipal Liability Analysis*, 35 U.C.L.A. Law Rev. 1187, 1208 (1988), reprinted in Nahmod, *A Section 1983 Civil Rights Anthology* 75.

4. As a practical matter, the critical question in cases like *Buffington* is whether the evidence is sufficient to submit the issue of causation to the jury. Can a plaintiff ever offer direct evidence of what would have happened if training or supervision had been different? What additional evidence might be presented to support

the jury's finding that the county's policies or customs caused officers Tucker and Gaigalas to violate the constitutional rights of James Buffington? In *Vineyard v. County of Murray*, 990 F.2d 1207 (11th Cir. 1993), the court upheld a judgment against a county and its Sheriff when two deputies used excessive force against a pretrial detainee. The county's policies of inadequate training, discipline and supervision were found to have caused the constitutional violation. In affirming the judgment, the court stated:

> The testimony of Professor White supports the jury's finding of causation. When asked to assume [the plaintiff's] version of what occurred at the hospital to be true, Professor White offered his opinion that these events would not have occurred if the county policies were such that officers knew they must report any confrontation, that others could call the Sheriff's Department to report complaints to the department, and that the department would investigate the complaints.

Vineyard, 990 F.2d at 1213.

A more critical assessment of expert testimony appears in *Berry v. City of Detroit*, 25 F.3d 1342 (6th Cir. 1994). In *Berry*, a jury awarded the plaintiff $6 million for the death of her son who was shot by a Detroit police officer. The plaintiff claimed that the city's customary failure to discipline its police officers amounted to deliberate indifference to the rights of its citizens. In support of her claim, the plaintiff offered the testimony of a former sheriff who purported to be an expert in "police policies and practices." In reversing the lower court's judgment, the court of appeals offered the following criticism of the testimony of the expert witness:

> If there is some formal training that would allow one to testify from a scientific standpoint on how failure to discipline officer "A" would impact on the conduct of his peer, officer "B," it is clear that [the plaintiff's expert] does not have such training. Thus, for this kind of testimony to be admissible, a foundation would have to have been laid based upon the witness's firsthand familiarity with disciplining police officers and the effect of lax discipline on the entire force. . . .

If . . . [plaintiff's expert] had testified that when he became sheriff there were "x" number of incidents involving alleged excessive force, but two years after he instituted a training program, there were "x - y" incidents, we would have a starting point. If he then said that after the training program was in place, he increased the regularity and severity of discipline for infractions and incidents fell to "x - y2," then at least there would be some basis for his opinions. . .

. . .

The danger in doing what the trial judge did here is that there is no such "field" as "police policies and practices." . . . This term . . . is so broad as to be devoid of meaning. It is like declaring an attorney an expert in the "law.". . .

With all due respect to [the plaintiff's expert], his credentials . . . do not qualify him to know any more about what effect claimed disciplinary shortcomings would have on the future conduct of 5,000 different police officers than does any member of the jury. . .

Berry, 25 F.3d at 1350 and 1352.

Why is the expert opinion in *Vineyard* sufficient to support the jury verdict, while the testimony of the plaintiff's expert in *Berry* and that of Dr. Rowan in *Buffington* were not sufficient to support jury verdicts? Is expert testimony essential in these cases?

5. Consider the observations of Professor Malone:

The judge enjoys an extensive power either to dismiss the plaintiff's claim because he has failed to make out a case on the issue of causation or to refer the question of cause freely to the jury for its consideration. There is language available that can make either decision sound thoroughly plausible. . . .

[Selecting the appropriate standard] is not carried on in a vacuum by some philosopher meditating upon the niceties of etiology. For the judge the choice is purposeful, and his purpose is the administration of justice in the very special controversy before him . . .

At this point matters of policy and estimates of factual likelihood become hopelessly involved with each other.

Malone, *Ruminations on Cause in Fact*, 9 Stan. L. Rev. 60, 68, 72 (1956). To what extent are decisions like *Mt. Healthy* and *Buffington* the product of "policy" or "estimates of factual likelihood?"

6. Consider the following approaches found in common law tort cases for dealing with the uncertainty of causation:

(a) Some courts reframe the but for test in terms of "substantial factor." That is, causality is established if the defendant's conduct is a substantial factor in producing the plaintiff's injury. See Strassfeld, *If. . . : Counterfactuals in the Law*, 60 Geo.Wash. L. Rev. 340, 353–57 (1992).

(b) Many courts afford juries great latitude in determining causation when the defendant's conduct created a risk of the very injury suffered by the plaintiff. Consider the case of *Reynolds v. Texas & Pacific Ry. Co.*, 37 La. Ann. 694 (1885) cited in many torts casebooks. The plaintiff was an overweight woman who fell down the unlighted steps leading to the train platform. The defendant argued that she might have fallen even if it had been broad daylight. In affirming a judgment for the plaintiff, the court stated "where the negligence of the defendant greatly multiplies the chances of accident to the plaintiff, and is of a character naturally leading to its occurrence, the mere possibility that it might have happened without the negligence is not sufficient to break the chain of cause and effect between the negligence and the injury." *Reynolds*, 37 La. Ann. at 698.

(c) In some instances courts formally shift the burden of proof on causation to the defendant. For example, in *Haft v. Lone Palm Hotel*, 3 Cal. 3d 756, 478 P.2d 465, 91 Cal.Rptr. 745 (1970), a father and son drowned in a pool where defendants failed to comply with a statute requiring the hotel to provide a lifeguard or post a sign indicating that no lifeguard was on duty. The court shifted the burden of proof on the issue of causation to the defendant because the defendant's negligence "deprived the present plaintiffs of a means of definitively establishing the facts leading to the drownings." *Haft*, 478 P.2d at 771.

Should any of these approaches apply in section 1983 cases? How would *Buffington* be analyzed under these approaches?

7. Should courts adapt the *Mt. Healthy* test to address governmental liability? If the plaintiff establishes that a governmental policy or custom was a substantial factor in producing the constitutional violation, should the burden shift to the defendant to prove that the same injury would have occurred in any event? As a matter of policy, who should bear the burden of explaining what would have happened if the government's policy had been different?

8. Some decisions allow juries considerable leeway in assessing the causal connection between municipal training and supervision policies and police misconduct. See *Gentile v. County of Suffolk*, 926 F.2d 142, 152 (2d Cir. 1991) (plaintiff need not prove that individual defendants knew of and acted on county's policy not to discipline police and prosecutors for misconduct; the jury could "reasonably infer" causation from proof of policy and custom); *Bielevicz v. Dubinon*, 915 F.2d 845, 851 (3rd Cir. 1990) (jury could find that plaintiffs' arrests were caused by a municipal custom of tolerating arrests for public intoxication without probable cause; "[a]s long as the causal link is not too tenuous, the question whether the municipal policy or custom proximately caused the constitutional infringement should be left to the jury."); *Bordanaro v. McLeod*, 871 F.2d 1151 (1st Cir. 1989) (custom of breaking down doors without a warrant to arrest suspected felons created risk of fourth amendment violation; jury could find causal relationship between the policy and the violation).

9. How should a jury be instructed on the issue of causation? Consider the following instruction:

It is not enough to say, oh, that was bad police administration, that was sloppy, that was a violation of an ordinance or whatever. You have to show that there was a causal relationship, likely causal relationship; that is, the plaintiffs have to persuade you by a preponderance of the evidence that there was a causal relationship between whatever policies were

adopted and the harm that the plaintiffs suffered.

What is required under the Supreme Court's rulings in these matters is an affirmative link, an affirmative link between the conduct of the city and its supervisory officials and the harm that befell the plaintiffs.

. . .

When I say "caused". . .I'm talking about whether the policy or the acts complained of were a moving force of the violation, whether there is an affirmative link between the conduct complained of and the harm suffered.

Bordanaro v. McLeod, 871 F.2d 1151, 1165–66 (1st Cir. 1989) (no error in giving this instruction). Does this instruction accurately state the applicable legal standards? Does it provide guidance to the jury? How would you instruct a jury on causation?

2. Causation and Supervisory Liability

LaMarca v. Turner

995 F.2d 1526 (11th Cir. 1993)

Tjoflat, Chief Judge:

This is a suit brought by ten present and former inmates of Glades correctional Institution (GCI), a Florida prison. They seek individually, under 42 U.S.C. § 1983 (1988), money damages for cruel and unusual punishment they allege they suffered because of the deliberate indifference of a former superintendent of the institution, Randall Turner. The plaintiffs still housed at GCI also seek an injunction, on behalf of all present and future inmates at the prison, against the current superintendent, Chester Lambdin, to correct certain allegedly unconstitutional conditions of confinement.

. . .

The magistrate judge, operating under S.D. Fla. Mag. J. R. 1(f), commenced the bench trial. At the plaintiffs' request, the magistrate judge bifurcated the proceeding, indefinitely postponing consideration of the claim for injunctive relief. The trial, therefore, considered only the damages claims against Turner. The following is a brief statement of the facts the court found.

. . .

[The magistrate described how the physical design of the facility and the failure of guards to conduct patrols in the interior of the dorms facilitated acts of violence and sexual assaults. Even inmates placed in protective confinement were often assaulted.]

Inmates in the general population could gain access to the confinement area by crawling under a poorly maintained fence or with the permission of the guard in charge of the area. These confinements, therefore, failed to insulate inmates from their tormentors.

. . .

Turner, in a July 16, 1981 letter to his superior, described the prevailing atmosphere at GCI: "On an almost daily basis I feel that our security staff is simply being tolerated by the inmate population rather than being in control of the operation of the institution." The presence of contraband (weapons, alcohol, and drugs), corruption of GCI's staff, inmate violence, and homosexual activity were accepted as part of prison life.

While a minimal level of contraband may be an unavoidable aspect of prison life, excessive quantities of contraband flowed freely into and within the prison. Prison officials made "little or no effort . . . to control illicit activity at GCI, resulting in readily-available contraband." Inmates carried knives and openly used drugs. The contraband problem was compounded by staff corruption, as prison officials contributed to, and apparently profited from, the contraband, and utilized prisoners to "control" and punish other prisoners.

GCI's staff permitted regular, unsupervised showings of hard-core pornographic movies. As Dr. Swanson, an expert witness for the plaintiffs, testified, these movies "would only serve to maximize the possibility of sexual and other violence." Indicative of this observation, during the movies, "[s]ounds of inmates screaming and crying could be heard."

When alerted to specific dangers, prison staff often looked the other way rather than protect inmates. Rather than offer to help, the staff suggested that the inmates deal with their problems "like men," that is, use physical force against the aggressive inmate.[10]

Several management problems persisted during Turner's tenure as superintendent: low morale among the prison's staff, high employee turnover (leading to a less experienced staff), high vacancy rates for staff positions, and inadequate supervision of employees.[11]
. . .

In sum, as the court concluded, "Turner's overall laxity in managing and controlling his staff" directly contributed to an unconstitutional condition of confinement at GCI consisting of an undeterred atmosphere of violence.

For purposes of this appeal, the appellants concede the credibility of the plaintiffs' accounts of the alleged assaults. A group of inmates, one brandishing a bush ax, made an unsuccessful attempt sexually to assault La-Marca in a dorm. Inmates raped Saunders in a small bathroom adjacent to the confinement area; he reported the incident but officials did not investigate and refused his request for a medical examination. Inmates repeatedly attacked Johnson while he was in protective confinement. Inmates raped Aldred and Durranoe in shower areas. Aldred reported the incident to an officer, but there was no investigation. Bronson was sexually assaulted with the handle of a baseball bat on GCI's recreation field. Cobb was stabbed by an inmate who, because of his cooperation with

---

[10] The acceptance of this condition might be best illustrated by LaMarca's story (taken as credible by the district court) that when he asked a guard for protection, the guard gave him a knife.

[11] In a survey, when GCI's staff were asked, "'Did you receive instructions or guidelines on the responsibilities and supervisory functions of your job when you became supervisor?,' they answered with a 'resounding no.'" The Department of Corrections, Office of Inspector General observed that "we fail to understand and appreciate laxity, in some instances, the disregard for established procedures." The court found that when staff engaged in egregious conduct, "so gross that immediate action should have been taken," Turner did not act. This "underscored the day-to-day operation of GCI with its staff not controlled, by Superintendent Turner."

guards in conducting illicit activities, was protected.

. . .

II.

Turner challenges the court's determination that he was deliberately indifferent to the plaintiffs' safety in violation of the Eighth Amendment and 42 U.S.C. § 1983. He asserts that the plaintiffs failed to make out a case of liability against him—in particular, he claims that the evidence does not support the district court's findings of fact—and that the court applied the wrong legal standard in determining liability. We conclude that although the record contains sufficient evidence upon which the district court could find liability, the court failed to make certain essential findings of fact and erred in its legal analysis. Consequently, we return this case to the district court for further consideration.

. . .

[The court concluded that there was sufficient evidence to support lower court's determinations that (1) the conditions at GCI inflicted unnecessary pain and suffering upon the plaintiffs; and (2) Turner was deliberately indifferent to the conditions at GCI. With regard to the finding of deliberate indifference, the court cited evidence that Turner had actual knowledge of an unreasonable risk of violence and failed to take certain measures (within budget constraints) to improve the security at GCI.]

[S]ection 1983 "requires proof of an affirmative causal connection between the actions taken by a particular person 'under color of state law' and the constitutional deprivation." *Williams [v. Bennett]*. . . Section 1983 thus focuses our inquiry on whether an official's acts or omissions were the cause—not merely a contributing factor—of the constitutionally infirm condition.

"A causal connection may be established by proving that the official was personally involved in the acts that resulted in the constitutional deprivation." *Zatler v. Wainwright*. Because the analysis focuses on the defendant's conduct, the doctrine of respondeat superior does not apply. Whether a defendant actually controls, or fails properly to supervise a subordinate, however, may prove to be relevant inquiries.

If a plaintiff establishes a causal link between the defendant's acts or omissions and the infirm condition, the defendant is "precluded from contending that the unconstitutional condition was not at least a proximate cause of . . . injuries" that arose from that condition. *Williams*. This is not to say that a plaintiff need not show a causal link between the constitutionally infirm condition and the alleged injuries. Rather, the finding that a prison condition offends the Eighth Amendment presupposes the distinct likelihood that the harm threatened will result. The wrong in Eighth Amendment cases is the deliberate indifference to a constitutionally infirm condition; that wrong must, in turn, have been the proximate cause of the plaintiffs' injuries, here the injuries brought about by the assaults.

In *Doe v. Sullivan County*, the Sixth circuit addressed causation under section 1983 arising from allegations of "systematic deficiencies" in a prison's protection of inmates similar to those in the instant case. The plaintiff presented evidence of overcrowding, dark cells, insufficient staff, lack of mental and physical evaluations, and inadequate surveillance. Additionally, a penological expert testifying for the plaintiff concluded that there was a pattern of violence among inmates at the prison and that because of the plaintiff's slight build and mental disability, prison officials should have placed him in protective custody. In reviewing the sufficiency of the evidence to show causation, the Sixth Circuit concluded "that more is required than [a] naked assertion that the assault would not have occurred but for the offensive conditions. To hold otherwise would effectively transform the causality requirement from a substantive element of proof into one of pleading." Id. at 550. In this case, the plaintiffs presented evidence to support their allegations that Turner "was in a position to take steps that could have averted" the alleged unconstitutional condition at GCI, "but, through [deliberate] indifference, [he] failed to do so." *Williams*.

The plaintiffs presented evidence supporting five conditions of confinement that were under Turner's control and that together created an unconstitutional risk of violence at GCI: (1) a "prevalence of . . . weapons" at GCI, (2) the lack of adequate patrols, (3) the lack of adequate reporting procedures for rapes and assaults, (4) the presence of "obvious and rampant indicia of homosexual activity," and (5) a lack of supervision of officers leading to corruption and incompetence. *LaMarca*. The evidence supports the plaintiffs' assertion that Turner could have brought GCI within constitutional norms through more diligent supervision of his officers, by establishing and enforcing rules and procedures to eliminate specific sources of danger to prisoners, and through low-cost modifications to GCI's physical plant. In particular, Turner could have taken significant steps to eliminate the highly permissive atmosphere at GCI both as to officers shirking their duties and as to prisoners engaging in extortion, harassment, sexual activity, and sexual and other assaults.

[T]he evidence strongly supports a finding that, even within the constraints he faced, Turner had the means substantially to improve prisoner safety at GCI. This evidence also supports findings that Turner knew that the actions he undertook would be insufficient to provide inmates with reasonable protection from violence, and that other means were available to him which he nevertheless disregarded. Such evidence provides the necessary causal link between Turner and the infirm conditions at GCI.

Finally, the evidence shows a link between the unconstitutional conditions and the plaintiffs' injuries. The record supports the district court's finding "that due to [their] very nature as acts of violence, the rapes that occurred are not isolated incidents of sexual conduct, but rather flow directly from the lawless prison conditions at GCI. . . . [These conditions created] the background and climate which . . . preordained homosexual rapes and other inmate assaults." *LaMarca*. The evidence thus permits a finding of a causal link between the objectively intolerable conditions at GCI and the plaintiffs' injuries.

. . .

Turner also challenges the court's findings as to causation, i.e., whether his deliberate indifference caused the alleged constitutionally infirm condition, and whether the condition caused the assaults. The district court incorrectly stated that an official must "accomplish[] what [can] be accomplished within the limits of his authority." *LaMarca*. As our

discussion of Turner's deliberate indifference and causation indicates. . . merely showing that an official had the means to correct a constitutional infirmity will not suffice. For the plaintiffs to demonstrate the requisite causal nexus, Turner must not only have had the means to correct the alleged constitutional infirmities, but also must have at least recklessly disregarded the inadequacy of the approach he took, the availability of other approaches, and their capacity to provide a cure. . . . This approach ensures that we do not question the direction taken by officials in performing the complex and arduous task of running prisons. Thus, we must revisit our analysis of Turner's subjective intent to ensure that only evidence probative of causation in the Eighth Amendment context will, be considered.

The district court did not identify the potential solutions that Turner actually or recklessly disregarded. Additionally, the court's causation inquiry was not circumscribed by the knowledge Turner possessed at the time of each alleged assault, a particularly important consideration since the district court found that conditions slowly, but continuously, improved during Turner's tenure as superintendent. Instead, the court assumed that Turner actually knew, or should have known, of these measures. Thus, even though the plaintiffs' evidence supports a finding of causation . . . the court's finding that the solutions available to Turner were sufficient may have erroneously charged him with an Eighth Amendment duty he did not have. The court must, therefore, reconsider the issue of causation and determine whether Turner knowingly or recklessly disregarded any corrective measures. If he did, the court must then determine whether, taken as a whole, these measures would have eliminated the infirm conditions for which he was responsible.

[The court's discussion of a variety of other issues is omitted.]

We remand the judgments favoring LaMarca, Johnson, and Saunders for reconsideration . . .

IT IS SO ORDERED.

NOTES

1. As discussed in Chapter 5, supervisors may be held liable in their individual capacities if their deliberate indifference causes another to be deprived a constitutional right. The same conduct may also subject a governmental entity to liability if the supervisor is acting as a "policymaker" for the government. In *Larez v. City of Los Angeles*, 946 F.2d 630 (9th Cir. 1991), for example, a jury found that the plaintiffs' constitutional rights were violated by an unreasonable search executed through the use of excessive force by police officers. The defendants included the Chief of Police and the City of Los Angeles. The Chief of Police was held liable in his individual capacity because he condoned, ratified and encouraged the excessive use of force. The Chief's conduct also subjected the City to liability because the Chief was an "official policymaker" for the City on police matters. *Larez*, 946 F.2d at 646–48. It is important to remember, however, that the supervisor in his individual capacity may enjoy a qualified immunity, but the city does not. Compare *Owen v. City of Independence*, 445 U.S. 622 (1980) discussed in Chapter 5, with the cases discussed in Chapter 8, infra.

2. *LaMarca* discusses the issue of causation in the context of individual capacity supervisor liability. The basic causal inquiry presented in *LaMarca* is similar to that presented in the governmental policy or custom cases. When can the deliberate indifference of a supervisor be said to cause a constitutional violation? It has been suggested that the standards established in *City of Canton v. Harris*, 489 U.S. 378 (1989) for governmental liability also apply to claims against supervisors in their individual capacity. See S. Nahmod, *Civil Rights and Civil Liberties Litigation* § 3.23 (3d ed. 1991). Is this still correct (if it ever was) in light of the Supreme Court's Eighth Amendment-deliberate indifference decision in *Farmer v. Brennan*, 114 S. Ct. 1970 (1994), set out in Chapter 3 and discussed both there and in Chapter 5? Recall that the Court in *Farmer* sharply distinguished between the subjective nature of deliberate indifference for individual liability purposes and the objective nature of deliberate indifference for governmental liability purposes. Does this mean that the causation standards are similarly different depending on whether the context is

individual or governmental liability? Or does *Farmer*'s distinction govern only state of mind?

However you answer these particular questions, is *LaMarca* consistent with *City of Canton* and *Buffington* with regard to causation?

3. What must the plaintiff prove regarding causation in cases like *LaMarca*? Must the defendant's conduct be a cause of the constitutionally infirm condition? Must the constitutionally infirm condition be a cause of the plaintiff's injury? Is the evidence of causation in *LaMarca* circumstantial or direct? Does the court's discussion adequately distinguish causation from the level of culpability necessary to support a section 1983 claim?

4. During a period of urban unrest, the mayor issues a proclamation instructing the police to "shoot to kill" anyone engaged in unlawful activity. A police officer thereafter shoots a fleeing 12 year old boy suspected of committing a misdemeanor. Assuming that the officer used excessive force, what would be the causation issues presented by claims against the mayor and city? What sort of evidence would you try to present as counsel for the plaintiff or defendants? See *Palmer v. Hall*, 517 F.2d 705 (5th Cir. 1975).

II. Proximate or Legal Cause

A. Remote Consequences

Martinez v. California

444 U.S. 277 (1980)

Mr. Justice **Stevens**

The two federal questions that appellants ask us to decide are (1) whether the Fourteenth Amendment invalidates a California statute granting absolute immunity to public employees who make parole-release determinations, and (2) whether such officials are absolutely immune from liability in an action brought under the federal Civil Rights Act of 1871, 42 U. S. C. § 1983. We agree with the California Court of Appeal that the state statute is valid when applied to claims arising under state law, and we conclude that appellants have not alleged a claim for relief under federal law.

The case arises out of the murder of a 15-year-old girl by a parolee. Her survivors brought this action in a California court claiming that the state officials responsible for the parole-release decision are liable in damages for the harm caused by the parolee.

The complaint alleged that the parolee, one Thomas, was convicted of attempted rape in December 1969. He was first committed to a state mental hospital as a "Mentally Disordered Sex Offender not amenable to treatment" and thereafter sentenced to a term of imprisonment of 1 to 20 years, with a recommendation that he not be paroled. Nevertheless, five years later, appellees decided to parole Thomas to the care of his mother. They were fully informed about his history, his propensities, and the likelihood that he would commit another violent crime. Moreover, in making their release determination they failed to observe certain "requisite formalities." Five months after his release Thomas tortured and killed appellants' decedent. We assume, as the complaint alleges, that appellees knew, or should have known, that the release of Thomas created a clear and present danger that such an incident would occur. Their action is characterized not only as negligent, but also as reckless, willful, wanton and malicious. Appellants prayed for actual and punitive damages of $2 million.

The trial judge sustained a demurrer to the complaint and his order was upheld on appeal. After the California Supreme Court denied appellants' petition for a hearing, we noted probable jurisdiction.

. . .

[The Court ruled that a California statute conferring absolute immunity on parole officials was constitutional as applied to claims arising under state law.]

We turn then to appellants' § 1983 claim that appellees, by their action in releasing Thomas, subjected appellants' decedent to a deprivation of her life without due process of law. It is clear that the California immunity statute does not control this claim even though the federal cause of action is being asserted in the state courts. We also conclude that it is not necessary for us to decide any question concerning the immunity of state parole officials as a matter of federal law because, as we recently held in *Baker v. McCollan*, "[the] first inquiry in any § 1983 suit . . . is whether the plaintiff has been deprived of a right 'secured by the Constitution and laws'" of the United States. The answer to that inquiry disposes of this case.

Appellants contend that the decedent's right to life is protected by the Fourteenth Amendment to the Constitution. But the Fourteenth Amendment protected her only from deprivation by the "State . . . of life . . . without due process of law." Although the decision to release Thomas from prison was action by the State, the action of Thomas five months later cannot be fairly characterized as state action. Regardless of whether, as a matter of state tort law, the parole board could be said either to have had a "duty" to avoid harm to his victim or to have proximately caused her death . . . we hold that, taking these particular allegations as true, appellees did not "deprive" appellants' decedent of life within the meaning of the Fourteenth Amendment.

Her life was taken by the parolee five months after his release. He was in no sense an agent of the parole board. Further, the parole board was not aware that appellants' decedent, as distinguished from the public at large, faced any special danger. We need not and do not decide that a parole officer could never be deemed to "deprive" someone of life by action taken in connection with the release of a prisoner on parole. But we do hold that at least under the particular circumstances of this parole decision, appellants' decedent's death is too remote a consequence of the parole officers' action to hold them responsible under the federal civil rights law. Although a § 1983 claim has been described as "a species of tort liability," *Imbler v. Pachtman*, it is perfectly clear that not every injury in which a state official has played some part is actionable under that statute.

The judgment is affirmed.

So ordered.

NOTES

1. What is the state action alleged to have violated the plaintiffs' constitutional rights? Was

the allegedly reckless decision to release Thomas a cause in fact of the death of the plaintiffs' daughter? Was the death of plaintiffs' daughter a foreseeable consequence of the allegedly reckless parole decision? In what sense was the death of the plaintiffs' daughter "too remote a consequence" of the decision to release Thomas on parole? Would the murder be too remote if it occurred two months after release? The same day? See *Janan v. Trammell*, 785 F.2d 557, 560 (6th Cir. 1986) ("We do not believe that the Supreme Court intended to provide us with a due process timetable such that a five month gap does not deprive one of due process while a two month gap automatically does. We decline to place such weight on the temporal factor."); *Commonwealth Bank & Trust Co. v. Russell*, 825 F.2d 12 (3rd Cir. 1987) (brief interval between escape and murder does not take the case out of the rule in *Martinez*; the same "causal nexus" is missing). But see *Reed v. Gardner*, 986 F.2d 1122, 1127 (7th Cir. 1993) ("Despite the two hour time lapse between and distance between the place [where the police left a car in the custody of an allegedly intoxicated person] and the car accident, the events are not sufficiently attenuated to relieve the defendants of § 1983 liability."). Would it have made any difference in *Martinez* if the plaintiff was not just a member of the general public but was an individually identifiable potential victim? Compare *Jones v. Phyfer*, 761 F.2d 642 (11th Cir. 1985) (furloughed prisoner attacked a woman who had previously been victimized by prisoner; *Martinez* controls) with *Hardmon v. County of Lehigh*, 613 F.Supp. 649 (E.D. Pa. 1985) (furloughed prisoner attacked a child whom correctional officials knew had been threatened by the prisoner; *Martinez* distinguished).

2. The Supreme Court in *Martinez* notes that state courts might address the question of the defendants' liability in terms of duty or proximate cause. The *Martinez* court, however, invokes proximate cause terminology when it speaks of remote consequences. In the subsequent case of *DeShaney v. Winnebago County Department of Social Services*, 489 U.S. 189 (1989) the Court used an affirmative duty analysis to explain why welfare officials could not be held liable under section 1983 for the beating of a child by his father. Are the controlling issues presented by the two cases fundamentally different? Does it matter whether the limitation on liability is phrased in terms of duty or proximate cause? Tort scholars have long recognized that "[i]t is quite possible to state every question which arises in connection with "proximate cause" in the form of a single question: was the defendant under a duty to protect the plaintiff against the event which did in fact occur." P. Keeton, D. Dobbs, R. Keeton, and D. Owen, *Prosser and Keeton on Torts* 274 (5th ed. 1984). Several noted scholars advocate using a duty analysis because it provides a more open and direct way for judges to resolve the policy choices that underlie the question of the extent of liability. See L. Green, *The Rationale of Proximate Cause* 11–43 (1927); Thode, *Tort Analysis: Duty-Risk v. Proximate Cause and the Rational Allocation of Functions Between Judge and Jury*, 1977 Utah L. Rev. 1. Consider the comments of Professor Nahmod,

> The § 1983 proximate cause question of the extent of liability could conceivably be dealt with primarily as a question of the scope of the constitutional duty breached, thereby largely eliminating the terminology of proximate cause and the concomitant jury role. Doing so could, however, result in "overloading" the constitutional inquiry by making it determinative not only of the constitutionally required standard of conduct, but also of the ultimate liability, a remedial issue. Thus it is probably better that courts in appropriate § 1983 cases continue to use the language of proximate cause.

S. Nahmod, *Civil Rights and Civil Liberties Litigation* § 3.24, p. 250 (3d ed. 1991). How would the constitutional inquiry be "overloaded" by analyzing the extent of government officials' liability in terms of the scope of duty?

3. Courts in discussing section 1983 proximate cause issues often rely on principles developed in the context of common law torts. E.g., *Stevenson v. Koskey*, 877 F.2d 1435 (9th Cir. 1989) (probation officer is not liable for the unforeseeable actions of prison officials); *Hibma v. Odegaard*, 769 F.2d 1147 (7th Cir. 1985) ("Though the deputies' actions set in motion the events which led to [the plaintiff's] confinement at the Green Bay Reformatory, the duty of protection assumed by the Wisconsin Prison System and the criminal acts of other inmates formed superseding causes which prevent the

deputies action from being a legal cause" of an assault); *Johnson v. Greer*, 477 F.2d 101 (5th Cir. 1973) (defendant who participated in the unconstitutional involuntary confinement of the plaintiff in a state hospital is not liable for the unforeseeable injury to the plaintiff's shoulder that occurred when orderlies attempted to medicate the plaintiff). The proper rule of proximate cause in section 1983 cases, however, is a matter of federal—not state—law. Cf. *Stokes v. Bullins*, 844 F.2d 269, 276 (5th Cir. 1988) ("We differ with the [district] court's and the parties' characterization of the issue of causation as governed by state law. This cannot be, because "cause" is part of the definitional language of § 1983 and has been construed by the Supreme Court without reference to specific state law."). Thus, courts may be guided by common law principles in establishing federal rules of proximate cause governing section 1983 claims, but are not bound by decisions of state courts. See Eaton, *Causation in Constitutional Torts*, 67 Iowa L. Rev. 443, 446–52 (1982).

B. Intervening Acts

Barts v. Joyner

865 F.2d 1187 (11th Cir. 1989)

Edmondson, Circuit Judge:

[Scarlet Barts reported to the sheriff's office that Billy Floyd had been shot and killed by an unknown intruder. Barts referred to Floyd as her father, although she was not related to him. Barts became a suspect when information she provided Deputy Joyner "didn't sound right". Captain Blount instructed Joyner to pick up Barts for questioning.]

Barts then was again read her *Miranda* rights, and Joyner and Blount questioned her for about three hours. Barts finally told Joyner that Floyd had come in while she was in the bathroom and started kissing her all over. She said that when she struggled with him he left. Barts admitted that she had shot Floyd when he came at her again. Defendants arrested Barts for the murder of Billy Floyd.

Barts was tried and convicted of second degree murder. Her attorney stated that she was unable to give him any details of the killing because she always became too upset. Barts served eight months of a twenty-five year sentence before her release on appellate bond. She finally was able to tell a psychologist and then her attorneys that she shot Floyd because he had raped her and she thought he was attempting to do so again. Barts was granted a new trial because of her inability to communicate with her attorneys due to Rape Trauma Syndrome and because of her corresponding incompetence to stand trial. Barts was acquitted at her second trial.

Barts brought an action under 42 U.S.C. sec. 1983 against Joyner and Blount individually and in their capacities as deputy sheriffs of Jefferson County, Florida alleging that Barts' detention and transportation to the sheriff's station was an unlawful seizure within the meaning of the fourth amendment. A jury awarded Barts damages of $175,000 from each defendant.

[The court held that Joyner and Blount were entitled to qualified immunity in their individual capacities.]

Joyner and Blount have not argued on appeal that their conduct in seizing and initially detaining Barts satisfied the fourth amendment, but have instead argued that various defenses bar the action against them even if they violated the Constitution. Because the case comes to us in this way and because we decide constitutional issues as a last resort, we need not and do not decide whether the Constitution was violated, but accept as a given the district court's judgment finding and concluding that the Constitution was violated.

Although we conclude that defendants are entitled to the benefit of qualified immunity under *Harlow [v. Fitzgerald]*, this does not require that the judgment be totally reversed. The judgment in this case was against defendants in both their official and individual capacities. Appellants have never contended that the judgment is not in conformity with the pleadings, proof, and issues in the district court. Harlow's qualified immunity is no defense to an action brought against someone in his official capacity. *Fitzgerald v. McDaniel.* The judgment of liability against defendants in their official capacity stands; and we must turn to a consideration of damages.

Damages

No one disputes that the confession, when linked to the other information[6] available to the police, was sufficient to justify a lawful arrest. Once the officers were faced with probable cause to arrest, they had a duty to arrest Barts. Her detention became at that time consistent with the fourth amendment. Therefore, we hold that defendants can be liable only for the damages suffered by Barts during the approximately three hours she spent at police headquarters before she confessed and for any damages directly resulting from that detention.[8]

We reject plaintiff's contention that she is entitled to damages for her criminal trials, conviction, incarceration, and the resulting aggravation of her Rape Trauma Syndrome. The intervening acts of the prosecutor, grand jury, judge and jury—assuming that these court officials acted without malice that caused them to abuse their powers—each break the chain of causation unless plaintiff can show that these intervening acts were the result of deception or undue pressure by the defendant policemen. See *Smiddy v. Varney*. . . Plaintiff introduced no evidence that the intervening acts of the prosecutor, grand jury, judge or jury were caused by any deception or undue pressure by Joyner or Blount.

Barts argues that *Malley v. Briggs* means that a judge's decision—even in the absence of deception or undue pressure on the judge— will not always break the causal chain that began with police misconduct. This view of *Malley* is correct; but we question whether *Malley's* holding extends beyond its facts. In Malley, the court held that a police officer

---

[6] For example, by the time Barts admitted shooting Billy Floyd, police had discovered that the caliber of Barts' missing gun matched the caliber of the bullets used in the shooting; and Captain Blount had observed that Barts' "black man intruder" story was inconsistent with the physical evidence at the crime scene. Of course, Barts had already said that she, Billy Floyd and the intruder were the only people there when Billy was shot.

[8] If it appears on retrial that at the sheriff's station the police officers had probable cause to arrest even before Barts confessed, the time of detention that might justify damages should be reduced accordingly.

---

submitting affidavits in application for arrest warrant (or search warrant) may be held liable for damages resulting from arrest (or search) under the authority of the warrant when no reasonable police officer could have believed that the affidavits established probable cause, and the action of the judge issuing the warrant does not break the causal chain. *Malley* never considered the question of whether, once an arrest has incorrectly occurred, later independent decisions of prosecutors, juries and judges to prosecute, indict, convict, and sentence would break the chain of causation for damages that might relate to the original unlawful seizure. But we believe that these independent acts must break the causal connection and that Barts' extended detention was caused by these public authorities and not by Joyner and Blount.

In *Malley*, the police initiated the arrest and were the sole source of the information available to the judge approving the warrant. When the police apply for a warrant and a judge approves a warrant, they use the same legal standard; and the police have as much or more information at that time than does the judge. Arresting suspects is police business. The police have it within their power to avoid the damage caused by a false arrest simply by not seeking the warrant. Thus, because the police have control over the damages, it makes sense to hold the police responsible for damages caused directly by the initial arrest when the police acted clearly unlawfully in arresting someone or in seeking a warrant to arrest someone. Such liability punishes and deters conduct over which the police have control.

Once someone is arrested and then substantial evidence of the suspect's guilt comes to light, the police can do little or nothing to stop further proceedings. Holding the police responsible for damage due to these later proceedings makes little sense. Prosecuting, indicting, finding ultimate guilt, and sentencing criminal defendants are not the business of the police. In addition, arresting police officers do not ordinarily control all the information available to the prosecutor, the grand jury, the trial jury and trial judge. The decisions to prosecute, to indict, to convict, and to sentence are independent from and involve considerations different from the original decision to arrest and result in different harm to a person than the harm caused by the original arrest.

Criminal procedure from arrest to sentencing involves a division of power and duties among several entities, each of which has the responsibility to make its own decisions. To hold that the decisions of the prosecutor, juries and judge do not break the chain of proximate causation trivializes the importance of these post-arrest decisions, which do not merely pass on the correctness of the seizure or arrest by police but which, based on all the information then available to these court officials, determine the likelihood that a potential defendant is guilty of violating the law. Plaintiff has directed our attention to no precedent either under section 1983 or the common-law tort of false arrest in which a recovery has been allowed against arresting officers for everything, including time served in prison following a conviction, that followed the improper seizure or arrest; we will not create that precedent in the absence of a showing that the police officers deceived the court officials or unduly pressured them or that the court officials themselves acted with malice and the police joined with them.

We REVERSE the judgment against defendants in their individual capacities and VACATE the judgment against defendants in their official capacities and REMAND for a new trial on the question of damages due from defendants in their official capacities.

NOTES

1. The court in *Barts* reaches the proximate cause issue despite its ruling on qualified immunity because the judgment was against the defendants in both their official and individual capacities. Suits against named persons in their official capacity are treated as suits against the governmental entity for which they work. Thus, when the court states that Joyner and Blount are not entitled to qualified immunity in their official capacities, it is because local governments do not enjoy such immunity. *Owen v. City of Independence*, 445 U.S. 622 (1980). Moreover, the conduct of Joyner and Blount could not give rise to liability in their official capacities unless it reflected the official policy or custom of the county. *Pembaur v. City*

of Cincinnati, 475 U.S. 469 (1986). The court in *Barts* did not address whether Joyner and Blount were "policymakers" of the county. See Chapter 5.

2. The plaintiffs in *Malley v. Briggs*, 475 U.S. 335 (1986) brought a section 1983 action against a state trooper who obtained an arrest warrant on the basis of information obtained from a court-authorized wire tap. The warrant itself was issued by a state judge. The plaintiffs alleged that the trooper violated their fourth amendment rights by presenting the judge with a complaint and a supporting affidavit which failed to establish probable cause. The district court directed a verdict for the trooper on the grounds that the judge in issuing the arrest warrants "broke the causal chain" between the trooper's filing of a complaint and the plaintiffs' arrest. The district court also held that an officer who believes the facts stated in his affidavit are true and who submits them to a neutral magistrate is entitled to qualified immunity. The court of appeals reversed, holding that qualified immunity does not apply unless the trooper has an objectively reasonable basis for believing the facts alleged in his affidavit are sufficient to establish probable cause. The Supreme Court affirmed the circuit court's decision with regard to immunity. In the course of the opinion the Court noted

> Petitioner has not pressed the argument that in a case like this the officer should not be liable because the judge's decision to issue the warrant breaks the causal chain between the application for the warrant and the improvident arrest. It should be clear, however, that the District Court's "no causation" rationale in this case is inconsistent with our interpretation of § 1983. As we stated in *Monroe v. Pape*, 365 U.S. 167, 187 (1961), § 1983 "should be read against the background of tort liability that makes a man responsible for the natural consequences of his actions." Since the common law recognized the causal link between the submission of a complaint and an ensuing arrest, we read § 1983 as recognizing the same causal link.

Malley v. Briggs, 475 U.S. at 344 n.7. Is the structure of the Eleventh Circuit's analysis in *Barts* consistent with *Malley*? Why is it that the judge's decision to issue a warrant does not break the chain of causation in *Malley*, but the decisions of the prosecutor, grand jury, judge and jury do so in *Barts*? Is the relevant distinction the number of independent reviews of the evidence in *Barts* or the quality of the review? When asked to issue an arrest warrant, does a judge apply a qualitatively lesser level of independent review than does a grand jury when deciding whether to indict?

3. The effect of third party conduct on the scope of a defendant's liability is, perhaps, the most common proximate cause issue that arises in section 1983 cases. The alleged intervening force may be the conduct of other government officials as in *Barts*, or it may be the conduct of private actors. Common law courts often frame the intervening cause analysis in terms of reasonable foreseeability. The defendant remains liable for harms produced by foreseeable intervening causes, but is not responsible for harms produced by unforeseeable intervening causes. See P. Keeton, D. Dobbs, R. Keeton and D. Owen, *Prosser and Keeton on Torts* § 44 (5th ed. 1984). A few section 1983 cases measure the scope of liability in terms of the foreseeability of the intervening actor's conduct. Thus, in *Duncan v. Nelson*, 466 F.2d 939 (7th Cir. 1972), police officers who coerced a confession from a suspect were not held liable for the plaintiff's nine year incarceration because it was not foreseeable that a judge would improperly admit the confession into evidence. "To find that these [police officers], who knew or should have known this confession was inadmissible, would foresee that the trial judge would erroneously admit this unlawful confession is untenable." *Duncan*, 466 F.2d at 942. Is it really "untenable" that a police officer could foresee that a coerced confession could lead to a criminal conviction and incarceration? See also *Anderson v. Nosser*, 456 F.2d 835 (5th Cir. 1972) (en banc) (whether the police chief who violated the plaintiffs' constitutional rights in the course of an arrest was liable for subsequent mistreatment that occurred in a state prison turned on whether the prison conditions were foreseeable).

The analysis in *Barts* and similar cases focuses less on foreseeability and more on the independent responsibility of prosecutors, judges and others to protect the accused from the risk of an improper conviction. These cases are analogous to common law decisions in which responsibility for protecting the plaintiff is shifted from the defendant to some third party. E.g., *Pittsburgh Reduction Co. v. Horton*, 87 Ark. 576, 113 S.W. 647 (1908) (defendants who negligently allowed dynamite caps to get into the hands of children were not responsible for injuries occurring after the parents seized control of the dynamite caps). See generally, *Restatement (Second) of Torts* § 452(2) (1965). Several constitutional tort decisions hold that the independent decisions of prosecutors, grand juries and others breaks the chain of causation between an illegal arrest and subsequent injury. E.g., *Hand v. Gary*, 838 F.2d 1420 (5th Cir. 1988). Many courts buttress this principle with a rebuttable presumption of independent judgment. E.g., *Smiddy v. Varney*, 665 F.2d 261 (9th Cir. 1981); *McLaughlin v. Alban*, 775 F.2d 389 (D.C. Cir. 1985). The presumption may be rebutted by evidence that the defendant-officers knowingly concealed from prosecutors or misrepresented to them material facts likely to influence the decision to prosecute. E.g., *Jones v. City of Chicago*, 856 F.2d 985 (7th Cir. 1988); *Dellums v. Powell*, 566 F.2d 167 (D.C. Cir. 1977).

Is the shifting of responsibility from the arresting officer to others in the criminal justice system consistent with the deterrent or compensatory goals of section 1983? What is the impact of immunities on the ultimate assessment of liability in cases like *Barts*? If the evidence obtained from the unconstitutional seizure and questioning of Barts should not have been considered, does she have a section 1983 claim against the prosecutor, grand jury or judge? What immunities would they have? See Chapters 7 and 8.

4. What consequences of an unconstitutional arrest should be compensable in a section 1983 action? Should a person arrested without probable cause be allowed to recover the attorney fees incurred in defending the criminal charges? See *Borunda v. Richmond*, 885 F.2d 1384 (9th Cir. 1988) (yes). Should detectives that "frame" a suspect be held liable for a sexual assault that occurs during incarceration? See *Himba v. Odegaard*, 769 F.2d 1147 (7th Cir. 1985) (no—superseding cause analysis).

What are the foreseeable consequences of unconstitutional prison overcrowding? Should officials in charge of an unconstitutionally overcrowded jail be held liable for injuries suffered by one inmate when another inmate sets a fire? See *Marsh v. Barry*, 824 F.2d 1139 (D.C. Cir.

1987) (prison officials would not be held responsible if the fire was an isolated act of violence, but could be held liable if the fire was set during a riot; riot-related fire is a foreseeable risk of overcrowding). The outcomes of individual cases may turn on fine factual nuances. Compare *Best v. Essex County*, 986 F.2d 54 (3rd Cir. 1993) (connection between overcrowding and inmate pouring boiling water on plaintiff is "far too attenuated") with *Ryan v. Burrlington County*, 708 F. Supp. 623 (D. N.J.) aff'd, 889 F.2d 1286 (3rd Cir. 1989) (allowing recovery by prisoner assaulted by another inmate in an overcrowded jail). Whether a particular consequence is foreseeable is generally a question of fact for the jury. E.g., *Glover v. Alabama Dept. of Corrections*, 734 F.2d 691 (11th Cir. 1984) (jury could find that a prison official's statement that the plaintiff-inmate's life is worth 5 or 6 packs of cigarettes was the proximate cause of the next day attack on the plaintiff).

5. Some decisions appear to analyze the legal effect of the plaintiff's conduct on the defendant's liability in terms of proximate cause. For example, in *Cameron v. City of Pontiac*, 813 F.2d 782 (6th Cir. 1987), a criminal suspect was struck by a car when attempting to evade an allegedly unconstitutional arrest. Dismissal of the section 1983 claim was upheld on proximate cause grounds. "Clearly, the use of firearms by the officers in the attempted apprehension of Cameron was not, as a matter of law, the proximate cause of his death. He was killed when he, at his own election, ran onto a high speed freeway. The district court was correct in concluding that this was unforeseeable, and that it would be an absurd result to permit recovery for a felon's unwise choice of an escape route." *Cameron*, 813 F.2d at 786. Should a jury determine whether the plaintiff's conduct was foreseeable? See *White v. Roper*, 901 F.2d 1501 (9th Cir. 1990) (a jury could find that it is foreseeable that an inmate would resist being placed in the cell of another inmate known to be dangerous; injuries sustained when jail officials subdued the resisting plaintiff could be found to be a proximate result of the defendant's deliberate indifference to the inmate's safety); *Parker v. District of Columbia*, 850 F.2d 708 (D.C. Cir. 1988) (upholding a jury finding that the plaintiff's conduct in resisting arrest was not a superseding cause breaking the chain of causation between the City's

failure to train and supervise police and individual officer's use of excessive force).

6. The common law "thin skull" rule has been applied in a number of section 1983 cases. E.g., *Niehus v. Liberio*, 973 F.2d 526 (7th Cir. 1992) (thin skull rule applied when excessive force aggravated preexisting injury); *Pieczynski v. Duffy*, 875 F.2d 1331 (7th Cir. 1989) (upholding an award of $95,000 in compensatory damages for "petty" political harassment when the evidence indicated that the emotional distress aggravated a preexisting back injury; the tortfeasor takes his victim as he finds her). Cf. *Blackburn v. Snow*, 771 F.2d 556 (1st Cir. 1985) (the plaintiff can recover for extensive psychological injuries caused by being subjected to unconstitutional strip search; circumstances in the plaintiff's family background rendered her extremely vulnerable to such distress); *McCulloch v. Glasgow*, 620 F.2d 47 (5th Cir. 1980) (allowing recovery for heart attack arguably triggered by procedural due process violation).

7. Professor Jeffries advocates a "risk rule" limitation on the scope of liability for constitutional torts. Under this view, "compensation for violations of constitutional rights should encompass only constitutionally relevant injuries—that is, injuries within the risks that the constitutional prohibition seeks to avoid." Jeffries, *Damages for Constitutional Violations: The Relation of Risk to Injury in Constitutional Torts*, 75 Va. L. Rev. 1461 (1989). By way of example, Jeffries considers a hypothetical case in which an adult bookstore is shut down under a zoning ordinance later held to violate the first amendment. As a result of the government's enforcement of the unconstitutional ordinance, the owner of the bookstore suffered significant economic loss. According to Jeffries, the free speech clause of the first amendment is a "systemic right", primarily concerned with protecting society (not specific persons) from a "contraction of social discourse". Jeffries would deny the bookstore owner a recovery for lost profits because these are wholly unrelated to the constitutionally relevant concerns of the first amendment.

Professor Nahmod criticizes Jeffries' proposal on several grounds. Nahmod, *Constitutional Damages and Corrective Justice: A Different View*, 76 Va. L. Rev. 997 (1990). Nahmod maintains that the distinction between "systemic" and "individual" constitutional rights is not clear nor administratively workable.

In response to the adult bookstore hypothetical, Nahmod argues that the relevant harm includes the economic injury to the owner. "[H]e suffers from this contraction as a member of society (whether he knows or cares about it) and because it is his bookstore that can no longer contribute to social discourse. In addition, his interests in individual self-fulfillment has been harmed, because he can no longer sell books and magazines as well as provide nude dancing." Nahmod would award compensatory damages for all foreseeable harm resulting from unconstitutional conduct and use cause-in-fact and superseding cause doctrine to limit liability.

Which is the better approach? Why? An edited version of both the Jeffries and Nahmod articles appears in S. Nahmod, *A Section 1983 Civil Rights Anthology* at 154 and 161.

CHAPTER SEVEN

"Every Person": Absolute Immunity

Suppose that a plaintiff properly pleads and proves all of the requisite elements of the section 1983 cause of action for damages against an individual defendant. Does it follow that the defendant will be held liable? Somewhat surprisingly, the answer is "no" despite the broad "person" language of section 1983. Indeed, it turns out that when certain defendants are sued for damages, they are treated, essentially for policy reasons, as if they are not "persons" at all and are protected by absolute immunity.

Absolute immunity is a powerful defense when it is successfully asserted. First, the defendant escapes liability even though he or she may have violated the plaintiff's constitutional rights and caused harm. Second, and equally important, absolute immunity protects the defendant from having to defend against the section 1983 action at all. As a practical matter, the absolutely immune defendant can admit the allegations of the plaintiff's complaint in the course of moving, early in the litigation, either to dismiss the complaint for failure to state a claim or for summary judgment on absolute immunity grounds.

As we shall see, privileged defendants protected by absolute immunity generally fall into four classes: state and local legislators, judges, witnesses and prosecutors. The Supreme Court has protected them by claiming to interpret section 1983 against the background of common law immunity in 1871, the year section 1983 was enacted. Significantly, though, absolute immunity only protects them when they act in particular ways: legislators must act in a legislative capacity, judges must act judicially, witnesses must in fact act in that capacity in judicial proceedings and prosecutors must act in an advocative role. If, for example, legislators, judges or prosecutors act administratively, they lose their absolute immunity (although they are still protected by qualified immunity). This approach to immunity, based not upon status but rather on *function*, is also considered in this chapter.

This chapter addresses the following questions: (1) who is protected by absolute immunity? (2) what are the reasons for absolute immunity? (3) what is the scope of absolute immunity? (4) does the functional approach also protect those who would not ordinarily be protected by absolute immunity? Also briefly considered are the burden of pleading absolute immunity and appeals from denials of absolute immunity summary judgment motions.

I. Absolute Legislative Immunity

A. *Tenney*: The Seminal Case on Absolute Legislative Immunity

Interestingly, *Tenney v. Brandhove*, 341 U.S. 367 (1951), the first Supreme Court decision dealing with immunities was handed down in 1951, ten years before *Monroe v. Pape*. *Tenney* articulated an approach to section 1983 immunities that has dominated the Court's immunities jurisprudence ever since.

Tenney v. Brandhove

341 U.S. 367 (1951)

Mr. Justice **Frankfurter** delivered the opinion of the Court.

William Brandhove brought this action in the United States District Court for the Northern District of California, alleging that he had been deprived of rights guaranteed by the Federal Constitution. The defendants are Jack B. Tenney and other members of a committee of the California Legislature, the Senate Fact-Finding Committee on Un-American Activities, colloquially known as the Tenney Committee. Also named as defen-

225

dants are the Committee and Elmer E. Robinson, Mayor of San Francisco.

The action is based on §§ 43 and 47 (3) of Title 8 of the United States Code. These sections derive from one of the statutes, passed in 1871, aimed at enforcing the Fourteenth Amendment. Section 43 provides:

"Every person who, under color of any statute, ordinance, regulation, custom, or usage, of any State or Territory, subjects, or causes to be subjected, any citizen of the United States or other person within the jurisdiction thereof to the deprivation of any rights, privileges, or immunities secured by the Constitution and laws, shall be liable to the party injured in an action at law, suit in equity, or other proper proceeding for redress."

Section 47 (3) provides a civil remedy against "two or more persons" who may conspire to deprive another of constitutional rights, as therein defined.

Reduced to its legal essentials, the complaint shows these facts. The Tenney Committee was constituted by a resolution of the California Senate on June 20, 1947. On January 28, 1949, Brandhove circulated a petition among members of the State Legislature. He alleges that it was circulated in order to persuade the Legislature not to appropriate further funds for the Committee. The petition charged that the Committee had used Brandhove as a tool in order "to smear Congressman Franck R. Havenner as a 'Red' when he was a candidate for Mayor of San Francisco in 1947; and that the Republican machine in San Francisco and the campaign management of Elmer E. Robinson, Franck Havenner's opponent, conspired with the Tenney Committee to this end." In view of the conflict between this petition and evidence previously given by Brandhove, the Committee asked local prosecuting officials to institute criminal proceedings against him. The Committee also summoned Brandhove to appear before them at a hearing held on January 29. Testimony was there taken from the Mayor of San Francisco, allegedly a member of the conspiracy. The plaintiff appeared with counsel, but refused to give testimony. For this, he was prosecuted for contempt in the State courts. Upon the jury's failure to return a verdict this prosecution was dropped. After Brandhove refused to testify,

the Chairman quoted testimony given by Brandhove at prior hearings. The Chairman also read into the record a statement concerning an alleged criminal record of Brandhove, a newspaper article denying the truth of his charges, and a denial by the Committee's counsel—who was absent—that Brandhove's charges were true.

Brandhove alleges that the January 29 hearing "was not held for a legislative purpose," but was designed "to intimidate and silence plaintiff and deter and prevent him from effectively exercising his constitutional rights of free speech and to petition the Legislature for redress of grievances, and also to deprive him of the equal protection of the laws, due process of law, and of the enjoyment of equal privileges and immunities as a citizen of the United States under the law, and so did intimidate, silence, deter, and prevent and deprive plaintiff." Damages of $10,000 were asked "for legal counsel, traveling, hotel accommodations, and other matters pertaining and necessary to his defense" in the contempt proceeding arising out of the Committee hearings. The plaintiff also asked for punitive damages.

The action was dismissed without opinion by the District Judge. The Court of Appeals for the Ninth Circuit held, however, that the complaint stated a cause of action against the Committee and its members. We brought the case here because important issues are raised concerning the rights of individuals and the power of State legislatures.

We are again faced with the Reconstruction legislation which caused the Court such concern in *Screws v. United States* and in the *Williams* cases decided this term. But this time we do not have to wrestle with far-reaching questions of constitutionality or even of construction. We think it is clear that the legislation on which this action is founded does not impose liability on the facts before us, once they are related to the presuppositions of our political history.

The privilege of legislators to be free from arrest or civil process for what they do or say in legislative proceedings has taproots in the Parliamentary struggles of the Sixteenth and Seventeenth Centuries. As Parliament achieved increasing independence from the Crown, its statement of the privilege grew stronger. In 1523, Sir Thomas More could make only a tentative claim. In 1668, after a long and bitter struggle, Parliament finally laid the ghost of Charles I, who had prosecuted Sir John Elliot and others for "seditious" speeches in Parliament. In 1689, the Bill of Rights declared in unequivocal language: "That the Freedom of Speech, and Debates or Proceedings in Parliament, ought not to be impeached or questioned in any Court or Place out of Parliament."

Freedom of speech and action in the legislature was taken as a matter of course by those who severed the Colonies from the Crown and founded our Nation. It was deemed so essential for representatives of the people that it was written into the Articles of Confederation and later into the Constitution. Article V of the Articles of Confederation is quite close to the English Bill of Rights: "Freedom of speech and debate in Congress shall not be impeached or questioned in any court or place out of Congress . . . ." Article I, § 6, of the Constitution provides: ". . . for any Speech or Debate in either House, [the Senators and Representatives] shall not be questioned in any other Place."

The reason for the privilege is clear. It was well summarized by James Wilson, an influential member of the Committee of Detail which was responsible for the provision in the Federal Constitution. "In order to enable and encourage a representative of the public to discharge his public trust with firmness and success, it is indispensably necessary, that he should enjoy the fullest liberty of speech, and that he should be protected from the resentment of every one, however powerful, to whom the exercise of that liberty may occasion offence."

The provision in the United States Constitution was a reflection of political principles already firmly established in the States. Three State Constitutions adopted before the Federal Constitution specifically protected the privilege. The Maryland Declaration of Rights, Nov. 3, 1776, provided: "That freedom of speech, and debates or proceedings, in the legislature, ought not to be impeached in any other court or judicature." Art. VIII. The Massachusetts Constitution of 1780 provided: "The freedom of deliberation, speech and debate, in either house of the legislature, is so essential to the rights of the people, that it cannot be the foundation of any accusation or

prosecution, action, or complaint, in any other court or place whatsoever." Chief Justice Parsons gave the following gloss to this provision in *Coffin v. Coffin*:

"These privileges are thus secured, not with the intention of protecting the members against prosecutions for their own benefit, but to support the rights of the people, by enabling their representatives to execute the functions of their office without fear of prosecutions, civil or criminal. I therefore think that the article ought not to be construed strictly, but liberally, that the full design of it may be answered. I will not confine it to delivering an opinion, uttering a speech, or haranguing in debate; but will extend it to the giving of a vote, to the making of a written report, and to every other act resulting from the nature, and in the execution, of the office; and I would define the article as securing to every member exemption from prosecution, for every thing said or done by him, as a representative, in the exercise of the functions of that office, without inquiring whether the exercise was regular according to the rules of the house, or irregular and against their rules."

The New Hampshire Constitution of 1784 provided: "The freedom of deliberation, speech, and debate, in either house of the legislature, is so essential to the rights of the people, that it cannot be the foundation of any action, complaint, or prosecution, in any other court or place whatsoever."

It is significant that legislative freedom was so carefully protected by constitutional framers at a time when even Jefferson expressed fear of legislative excess. For the loyalist executive and judiciary had been deposed, and the legislature was supreme in most States during and after the Revolution. "The legislative department is every where extending the sphere of its activity, and drawing all power into its impetuous vortex." Madison, The Federalist, No. XLVIII.

As other States joined the Union or revised their Constitutions, they took great care to preserve the principle that the legislature must be free to speak and act without fear of criminal and civil liability. Forty-one of the forty-eight States now have specific provisions in their Constitutions protecting the privilege.

Did Congress by the general language of its 1871 statute mean to overturn the tradition of legislative freedom achieved in England by Civil War and carefully preserved in the formation of State and National Governments here? Did it mean to subject legislators to civil liability for acts done within the sphere of legislative activity? Let us assume, merely for the moment, that Congress has constitutional power to limit the freedom of State legislators acting within their traditional sphere. That would be a big assumption. But we would have to make an even rasher assumption to find that Congress thought it had exercised the power. These are difficulties we cannot hurdle. The limits of §§ 1 and 2 of the 1871 statute—now §§ 43 and 47 (3) of Title 8— were not spelled out in debate. We cannot believe that Congress—itself a staunch advocate of legislative freedom—would impinge on a tradition so well grounded in history and reason by covert inclusion in the general language before us.

We come then to the question whether from the pleadings it appears that the defendants were acting in the sphere of legitimate legislative activity. Legislatures may not of course acquire power by an unwarranted extension of privilege. The House of Commons' claim of power to establish the limits of its privilege has been little more than a pretense since *Ashby v. White*. This Court has not hesitated to sustain the rights of private individuals when it found Congress was acting outside its legislative role.

The claim of an unworthy purpose does not destroy the privilege. Legislators are immune from deterrents to the uninhibited discharge of their legislative duty, not for their private indulgence but for the public good. One must not expect uncommon courage even in legislators. The privilege would be of little value if they could be subjected to the cost and inconvenience and distractions of a trial upon a conclusion of the pleader, or to the hazard of a judgment against them based upon a jury's speculation as to motives. The holding of this Court in *Fletcher v. Peck*, that it was not consonant with our scheme of government for a court to inquire into the motives of legislators, has remained unquestioned.

Investigations, whether by standing or special committees, are an established part of representative government. Legislative committees have been charged with losing sight of their duty of disinterestedness. In times of political passion, dishonest or vindictive motives are readily attributed to legislative conduct and as readily believed. Courts are not the place for such controversies. Self-discipline and the voters must be the ultimate reliance for discouraging or correcting such abuses. The courts should not go beyond the narrow confines of determining that a committee's inquiry may fairly be deemed within its province. To find that a committee's investigation has exceeded the bounds of legislative power it must be obvious that there was a usurpation of functions exclusively vested in the Judiciary or the Executive. The present case does not present such a situation. Brandhove indicated that evidence previously given by him to the committee was false, and he raised serious charges concerning the work of a committee investigating a problem within legislative concern. The Committee was entitled to assert a right to call the plaintiff before it and examine him.

It should be noted that this is a case in which the defendants are members of a legislature. Legislative privilege in such a case deserves greater respect than where an official acting on behalf of the legislature is sued or the legislature seeks the affirmative aid of the courts to assert a privilege. In *Kilbourn v. Thompson* this Court allowed a judgment against the Sergeant-at-Arms, but found that one could not be entered against the defendant members of the House.

We have only considered the scope of the privilege as applied to the facts of the present case. As Mr. Justice Miller said in the *Kilbourn* case: "It is not necessary to decide here that there may not be things done, in the one House or the other, of an extraordinary character, for which the members who take part in the act may be held legally responsible." We conclude only that here the individual defendants and the legislative committee were acting in a field where legislators traditionally have power to act, and that the statute of 1871 does not create civil liability for such conduct.

The judgment of the Court of Appeals is reversed and that of the District Court affirmed. Mr. Justice **Douglas**, dissenting.

I agree with the opinion of the Court as a statement of general principles governing the liability of legislative committees and members of the legislatures. But I do not agree that all abuses of legislative committees are solely for the legislative body to police.

We are dealing here with a right protected by the Constitution—the right of free speech. The charge seems strained and difficult to sustain; but it is that a legislative committee brought the weight of its authority down on respondent for exercising his right of free speech. Reprisal for speaking is as much an abridgment as a prior restraint. If a committee departs so far from its domain to deprive a citizen of a right protected by the Constitution, I can think of no reason why it should be immune. Yet that is the extent of the liability sought to be imposed on petitioners under 8 U.S.C. § 43.

It is speech and debate in the legislative department which our constitutional scheme makes privileged. Included, of course, are the actions of legislative committees that are authorized to conduct hearings or make investigations so as to lay the foundation for legislative action. But we are apparently holding today that the actions of those committees have no limits in the eyes of the law. May they depart with impunity from their legislative functions, sit as kangaroo courts, and try men for their loyalty and their political beliefs? May they substitute trial before committees for trial before juries? May they sit as a board of censors over industry, prepare their blacklists of citizens, and issue pronouncements as devastating as any bill of attainder?

No other public official has complete immunity for his actions. Even a policeman who exacts a confession by force and violence can be held criminally liable under the Civil Rights Act, as we ruled only the other day in *Williams v. United States.* Yet now we hold that no matter the extremes to which a legislative committee may go it is not answerable to an injured party under the civil rights legislation. That result is the necessary consequence of our ruling since the test of the statute, so far as material here, is whether a constitutional right has been impaired, not whether the domain of the committee was traditional. It is one thing to give great leeway to the legislative right of speech, debate, and investigation. But when a committee perverts its power, brings down on an individual the whole weight of government for an illegal or corrupt purpose,

the reason for the immunity ends. It was indeed the purpose of this civil rights legislation to secure federal rights against invasion by officers and agents of the states. I see no reason why any officer of government should be higher than the Constitution from which all rights and privileges of an office obtain.

[The concurring opinion of Justice **Black** is omitted.]

NOTES

1. What is the Court's approach to interpreting section 1983's "person" language?
2. Is the Court's reliance on the Speech or Debate Clause convincing? What of the common law background?
3. According to the Court, if Congress had intended that absolute legislative immunity *not* apply to section 1983, what should Congress have done?
4. What are the policy considerations underlying absolute legislative immunity? Do they play any real role in *Tenney*? If *Tenney* is a statutory interpretation case, *should* such policy considerations play a role?
5. Suppose the plaintiff could in fact prove that the defendants knowingly violated his First Amendment rights by interrogating and prosecuting him? Would the result be any different?
6. If legislators are to be protected by absolute immunity, does the allegedly unconstitutional conduct of the defendants in *Tenney* itself present an easy or hard case for such immunity?

B. The Functional Approach of *Lake Country Estates*: Local and Regional Legislators

After *Tenney*, at least two major questions were left open. First, which legislators are protected by absolute immunity? After all, *Tenney* deals with state legislators. What of local legislators like city council members and aldermen? Second, what kind of conduct is protected by absolute immunity? The Supreme Court's 1979 decision in *Lake Country Estates, Inc. v.*

Tahoe Regional Planning Agency, 440 U.S. 391 (1979), effectively answered both questions.

Lake Country Estates involved a section 1983 action against an interstate-compact planning agency and its officers. The basis of the suit was the agency's adoption of a land use ordinance and general plan that allegedly destroyed the value of the plaintiffs' property. The Court, in an opinion by Justice Stevens, first found that the defendants' conduct had been undertaken *under color of state law* within the meaning of section 1983, even though federal approval was required and had been given for the interstate compact. Thus, a section 1983 cause of action was stated. The Court next concluded that the Eleventh Amendment did not bar suits in federal court against the planning agency and also suggested that the agency was a suable person under its decision in *Monell v. Department of Social Services*.

Finally, the Court held that the individual officers of the interstate planning agency were absolutely immune from section 1983 damages liability for actions taken in their legislative (as distinct from executive) capacities. Repeating *Tenney v. Brandhove*'s assertion that "[o]ne must not expect uncommon courage even in legislators," the Court reasoned that it was for the public good that regional legislators, as well as federal and state legislators, be protected by an absolute immunity. It then remanded for determination of whether the defendants acted in a legislative capacity, that is, "in a capacity comparable to that of members of a state legislature."

Justices Brennan, Marshall, and Blackmun dissented on the immunity issue and argued that the individual defendants should not have *Tenney*'s absolute immunity protection. Justice Blackmun specifically questioned whether the defendants were even properly characterizable as "regional legislators":

> Their duties are not solely legislative; they possess some executive powers. They are not in equipoise with other branches of government, and the concept of separation of powers has no relevance to them. They are not subject to the responsibility and the brake of the electoral process. And there is no provision for discipline within the body, as the Houses of Congress and the state legislatures possess.

The Court expressly left open the question of the relevance of *Lake Country Estates* for the immunity of local legislators. However, Justice Marshall, in his dissent, asserted that "the majority's reasoning in this case leaves little room to argue that municipal legislators stand on a different footing than their regional counterparts." In his view, the Court applied a functional test for absolute immunity to the defendants in *Lake Country Estates*, a test which, if applied to the legislative acts of local legislators, would in all likelihood lead to the same result.

1. After *Lake Country Estates*, should absolute immunity protect the following acts of local legislators: enacting an ordinance? reducing the number of liquor licenses? budget making? *See Aitchison v. Raffiani*, 708 F.2d 96 ((3rd Cir. 1983) (enacting ordinance), *Reed v. Village of Shorwood*, 704 F.2d 943 (7th Cir. 1983) (liquor license reduction) and *Rateree v. Rockett*, 852 F.2d 946 (7th cir 1988) (budget making), all of which applied absolute immunity.

2. What if a city's high-ranking executive vetoes an ordinance or votes to enter into a contract? *See Hernandez v. City of Lafayette*, 643 F.2d 1188 (5th Cir. 1981) (ordinance veto) and *Healy v. Town of Pembroke*, 831 F.2d 980 (11th Cir. 1987) (vote to contract), both of which applied absolute immunity. What additional factor is present in these two cases?

3. Because local legislators often perform non-legislative functions, it is sometimes difficult for courts to distinguish acts protected by absolute immunity from those that are not. One bright line, in theory at least, is between legislative and administrative acts, the latter being unprotected by absolute immunity. For example, the discharge of a local legislator's aide was found not protected by absolute immunity because it was administrative in nature. *Gross v. Winter*, 876 F.2d 165 (D.C. Cir. 1989). Similarly, judges who promulgated a personnel rule were found not protected by legislative immunity because their conduct was administrative. *Gutierrez v. Municipal Court*, 838 F.2d 1031 (9th Cir. 1988).

4. What factors do you consider significant in determining whether challenged conduct is legislative in nature? Consider the following, all of which have played some role in the cases:

> a. Was the challenged conduct a general policy or overall plan, or was it administrative

in nature because it was not based on legislative facts and its impact was particularized?

b. Was the challenged conduct the adoption of prospective, legislative-type rules or was it the enforcement of such rules?

c. Was the challenged conduct the formulation of a policy or did it involve monitoring and administering, thereby being executive in nature?

c. Under state law, was the proper legislative procedure used in connection with the challenged conduct so that it was legislative in nature, or was the challenged conduct not a proper exercise of legislative powers?

See generally S. Nahmod, 2 *Civil Rights and Civil Liberties Litigation: The Law of Section 1983* 19–20 (3 ed. 1991).

5. Evaluate the following Fifth Circuit cases.

In *Hughes v. Tarrant County*, 948 F.2d 918 (5th Cir. 1991), the plaintiff state court clerk sued county commissioners for unconstitutionally refusing to pay for attorney's fees incurred in contempt proceedings brought against him. Ruling against the commissioners, the Fifth Circuit rejected the argument that their refusal to pay was a decision regarding the allocation of county monies and was thus legislative in nature. Instead, after canvassing the case law in the circuits, the court relied on a distinction between legislative facts and administrative facts and determined that the challenged decision "was based on specific facts of an individual situation related to the [plaintiff and] did not purport to establish a general policy; it was particular to [plaintiff]." Thus, it was administrative in nature.

Compare *Calhoun v. St Bernard Parish*, 937 F.2d 172 (5th Cir. 1991), where the plaintiff developer sued parish police jurors who adopted a series of construction moratoria that delayed his housing project. The Fifth Circuit held that the defendants were protected by absolute legislative immunity even though their challenged conduct was not the initial enforcement of a zoning code but rather spot zoning. The court relied for this determination on *Shelton v. City of College Station*, 780 F.2d 475 (5th Cir. 1986), which "held that the denial of a request for a variance from a zoning ordinance was a legislative decision" because it involved legislative facts. 937 F.2d at 174. According to the Fifth Circuit, the same was true in this case.

Calhoun is one of many examples of a legislative immunity case arising in the land use regulation setting.

C. A Note on Prospective Relief

As we shall see, neither judges nor prosecutors are absolutely immune from prospective relief liability, in marked contrast to their absolute immunity from damages liability. *See Pulliam v. Allen*, 466 U.S. 522 (1984) (judges) and *Supreme Court v. Consumers Union*, 446 U.S. 719 (1980) (prosecutors). However, state legislators are different in that they are protected from both. The Supreme Court so held in *Supreme Court v. Consumers Union*, noted above. *Consumers Union* involved a section 1983 suit against, among others, the Supreme Court of Virginia and its chief justice (in his official capacity) challenging on First Amendment grounds the Virginia Supreme Court's disciplinary rule for lawyer advertising. A three-judge district court held the challenged rule unconstitutional and enjoined the defendants from enforcing it. Defendants' argument that absolute immunity protected them both from declaratory or injunctive relief was rejected.

In an opinion by Justice White, the Supreme Court vacated and remanded. It first found that the Virginia Supreme Court acted in a legislative capacity in promulgating lawyer disciplinary rules. In fact, "the Virginia Court is exercising the State's 'entire legislative power' with respect to regulating the Bar, and its members are the *State's legislators* for the purpose of issuing the Bar Code." The Court then discussed its decision in *Eastland v. United States Servicemen's Fund*, 421 U.S. 491 (1975), which held that the Speech or Debate Clause immunizes members of Congress from suits for both prospective relief and damages. The Court reasoned, citing *Tenney v. Brandhove*, that *Eastland*'s concern with interference with the federal legislative function through injunctive relief was equally applicable to state legislators sued under section 1983 for prospective relief. Thus, because the Virginia Supreme Court had acted in a legislative capacity in promulgating the challenged rule, it and its members were absolutely immune from suit.

Nevertheless, the Court, after expressly leaving open the question of whether judicial immunity bars prospective relief, held that the Virginia Supreme Court and its chief justice could be sued for injunctive relief in their *enforcement* capacities (as distinguished from their legislative and judicial capacities) like other enforcement officers and agencies. The Court here referred to the Virginia Supreme Court's "independent authority of its own to initiate proceedings against attorneys," and affirmed that prosecutors, despite their absolute immunity from liability for damages, could be sued for injunctive and declaratory relief.

1. *Consumers Union*, which obviously takes a functional approach, makes clear that state legislators are absolutely immune from prospective relief liability (although prosecutors are not). Does this double-barreled immunity for state legislators make sense? If it does, should it protect *local* legislators as well?

2. Do state of mind requirements for particular constitutional violations also serve to protect against injunctive relief? Consider, for example, the Supreme Court's important 1994 decision in *Waters v. Churchill*, 114 S. Ct — (1994), revg, 977 F.2d 1114 (7th Cir. 1993), a First Amendment employment case, also noted in Chapter 3.

In *Waters*, the relevant question presented in the petition for certiorari was the following: "May public employer that terminates employee based on credible, substantiated reports of unprotected, insubordinate speech be held liable for retaliatory discharge under First Amendment if it is later shown that reports were inaccurate and that employee actually spoke on protected matters of public concern, when employer's ignorance of protected speech is result of incomplete investigation?" There was no opinion for the Court in *Waters* but the plurality, in an opinion by Justice O'Connor, adopted a reasonableness requirement under which an employee may not be dismissed or otherwise disciplined unless the employer had a reasonable basis for believing that the speech was either disruptive or that it involved a matter of purely private concern outside the scope of the First Amendment. There was thus a First Amendment duty to conduct a reasonable investigation into the nature and content of the speech, although not a full-scale investigation. Subjective good faith, standing alone, was not

sufficient to avoid liability. In short, First Amendment protection depended on what the employer reasonably believed the nature and content of the speech to be, and not on what the speech actually was.

Justice Scalia, in an opinion joined by Justices Kennedy and Thomas, concurred in the result. *Id* at —. He maintained that reasonableness was not the appropriate standard because it would subject public employers to "intolerable legal uncertainty." Rather, a public employer should be liable under the First Amendment only where it retaliated against the employee for speaking on a matter of public concern; there was no duty to investigate. Justices Stevens and Blackmun dissented, *id* at —, arguing that the plurality did not go far enough in providing First Amendment protection to employee speech. In their view, what was determinative was the *actual* nature and content of the speech, not what the public employer thought, reasonably or otherwise, it was.

The *Waters* plurality standard staked out the middle ground between an intent requirement on the one hand (Justice Scalia's position) and a kind of strict liability approach on the other (Justices Stevens and Blackmun). Does it follow from this kind of negligence standard that section 1983 plaintiffs seeking reinstatement will not get their jobs back if they are unable to prove by a preponderance of the evidence that the defendant public employers acted unreasonably with respect to investigating the nature and content of their speech, even though it turns out that the speech was such that it was in fact nondisruptive speech on a matter of public concern? If so, is that fair?

Is *Waters* a qualified immunity case in disguise? Should the Court have dealt with it on that ground and adopted the First Amendment approach of Justices Stevens and Blackmun so that the reasonableness inquiry would be relevant not to the state of mind requirement for the prima facie First Amendment cause of action but rather to the objective reasonableness inquiry called for by qualified immunity? Wouldn't that have avoided the non-reinstatement harshness inasmuch as qualified immunity is relevant only to damages liability of individuals (although not that of local governments)? Qualified immunity is addressed in Chapter 8, state of mind requirements for particular constitutional violations are considered in Chapter 3, local government liability is addressed in Chapter 5 and remedies in general are dealt with in Chapter 9.

II. Absolute Judicial Immunity

A. The Common Law Immunity Background in 1871: *Bradley*

Consider *Bradley v. Fisher*, 80 U.S. 335 (1871), on which much absolute judicial immunity doctrine is premised. *Bradley* involved a criminal court judge of the District of Columbia who was sued for damages by a lawyer whom he removed from practice before his court without notice and the opportunity to defend. The Court elaborately set out the general absolute judicial immunity rules, *id.* at 351–52 (emphasis added):

> [J]udges of courts of superior or general jurisdiction are not liable to civil actions for their judicial acts, even when such acts are in excess of their jurisdiction, and are alleged to have been done maliciously or corruptly. *A distinction must be here observed between excess of jurisdiction and the clear absence of all jurisdiction over the subject-matter. Where there is clearly no jurisdiction over the subject-matter any authority exercised is a usurped authority, and for the exercise of such authority, when the want of jurisdiction is known to the judge, no excuse is permissible. But where jurisdiction over the subject-matter is invested by law in the judge, or in the court which he holds, the manner and extent in which the jurisdiction shall be exercised are generally as much questions for his determination as any other questions involved in the case, although upon the correctness of his determination in these particulars the validity of his judgments may depend.* Thus, if a probate court, invested only with authority over wills and the settlement of estates of deceased persons, should proceed to try parties for public offences, jurisdiction over the subject of offences being entirely wanting in the court, and this being necessarily known to its judge, his commission would afford no protection to him in the exercise of the usurped authority. But if on the other hand a judge of a criminal court, invested with general criminal jurisdiction over offences committed within a certain district, should hold a particular act to be a public offence, which is not by the law made an offence, and proceed to the arrest and trial of a party charged with such act, or should sentence a party convicted to a greater punishment than that authorized by the law upon its proper construction, no personal liability to civil action for such acts would attach to the judge, although those acts would be in excess of his jurisdiction, or of the jurisdiction of the court held by him, for these *are particulars for his judicial consideration, whenever his general jurisdiction over the subject-matter is invoked.* Indeed some of the most difficult and embarrassing questions which a judicial officer is called upon to consider and determine relate to his jurisdiction, or that of the court held by him, or the manner in which the jurisdiction shall be exercised. And the same principle of exemption from liability which obtains for errors committed in the ordinary prosecution of a suit where there is *jurisdiction of both subject and person,* applies in cases of this kind, and for the same reasons.

In applying these principles to the facts before it, the Supreme Court in *Bradley* observed that, while the defendant judge had the power to remove a lawyer from the bar, this should not ordinarily be done without notice and an opportunity to explain and defend. Nevertheless, even though the defendant judge erred in not giving plaintiff such notice, this action constituted at most an excess of jurisdiction but "did not make the act any less a judicial act . . . . It was not as though the court had proceeded without any jurisdiction whatever over its attorneys." Thus, the defendant judge was absolutely immune from liability for damages for the allegedly wrongful disbarment.

1. Why did the case before the Court not involve the "clear absence of all jurisdiction?"

2. What does "jurisdiction" mean"? Is it limited to subject matter jurisdiction? Does it include personal jurisdiction?

3. Is the language of jurisdiction helpful in this setting?

4. How would you describe the margin for judicial error articulated in *Bradley?*

B. *Pierson:* The Seminal Case on Absolute Judicial Immunity

The jurisdiction language of *Bradley* was combined with the common law background approach of *Tenney* in *Pierson v. Ray*, 386 U.S. 547 (1967), the seminal section 1983 absolute judicial immunity case. In *Pierson*, the plaintiffs had been arrested by the defendant police officers in 1961 and then convicted and given the maximum sentence by the defendant municipal police justice for violating a Mississippi breach of the peace statute. This statute was held unconstitutional by the Supreme Court as applied to similar facts four years later but prior to the Court's decision in *Pierson*. After plaintiffs had been vindicated in a trial de novo, they sued the defendants for damages under section 1983 as well as for false arrest and imprisonment at common law.

In holding that the police justice was absolutely immune from liability for damages under section 1983, the Court compared judicial immunity at common law to legislative immunity. Following *Tenney's* approach, the Court stated:

> The legislative record gives no clear indication that Congress meant to abolish wholesale all common-law immunities . . . . The immunity of judges for acts within the judicial role is equally well established [as absolute legislative immunity], and we presume that Congress would have specifically so provided had it wished to abolish the doctrine.

As to the scope and application of the doctrine, the Court observed that the only act of the police justice was to find plaintiffs guilty. It then went on to hold that judges are absolutely immune from liability for damages

> for acts committed within their judicial jurisdiction . . . even when the judge is accused of acting maliciously and corruptly . . . . It is a judge's duty to decide all cases within his judicial jurisdiction that are brought before him, including controversial cases that arouse the most intense

feelings in the litigants. His errors may be corrected on appeal, but he should not have to fear that unsatisfied litigants may hound him with litigation charging malice or corruption. Imposing such a burden on judges would contribute not to principled and fearless decision making but to intimidation.

1. As a matter of policy, is absolute judicial immunity as defensible as absolute legislative immunity?

2. Is absolute judicial immunity defensible as a matter of legislative history? Justice Douglas argued in dissent in *Pierson* that section 1983's legislative history indicated that it was to apply to judges. He stated: "It was recognized [in 1871] that certain members of the judiciary were instruments of oppression and were partially responsible for the wrongs to be remedied." It has also been argued that absolute judicial immunity was not as well established at common law as absolute legislative immunity. *See Note, Developments in the Law—Section 1983 and Federalism*, 90 Harv. L. Rev. 1133, 1201 (1977). *See also* Kates, *Immunity of State Judges Under the Federal Civil Rights Acts: Pierson v. Ray Reconsidered*, 65 Nw. U. L. Rev. 615 (1970). Should these historical considerations make a difference? For the argument that the Court's historical methodology is seriously flawed, *see* Matasar, *Personal Immunities Under Section 1983: The Limits of the Court's Historical Analysis*, 40 Ark. L. Rev. 741 (1987), reprinted in *Section 1983 Anthology* 86.

3. Is absolute judicial immunity defensible as a matter of economic analysis? It has been asserted that the answer is yes. *See* Cass, *Damage Suits Against Public Officers*, 129 U. Pa. L. Rev. 110 (1981), reprinted in *Section 1983 Anthology* 96. Under this view, although "judges lack any significant incentive, intrinsic to the judicial process, for responding to the parties' (and ultimately the society's) interests in minimizing costs on the one hand and benefits on the other," they nevertheless generally reach appropriate decisions because of the seriousness with which they approach their job. There also are review mechanisms available to correct improper initial decisions. Most significantly, the cost of assessing liability is likely to be extraordinarily high because "the same difficult decisions must be repeated."

4. On its facts, is *Pierson* an easy or hard absolute judicial immunity case? How does it compare with *Stump v. Sparkman*, the next case?

C. The Broad Scope of Absolute Judicial Immunity: *Stump*

Stump v. Sparkman

435 U.S. 349 (1978)

Mr. Justice **White** delivered the opinion of the Court.

This case requires us to consider the scope of a judge's immunity from damages liability when sued under 42 U.S.C. § 1983.

I

The relevant facts underlying respondents' suit are not in dispute. On July 9, 1971, Ora Spitler McFarlin, the mother of respondent Linda Kay Spitler Sparkman, presented to Judge Harold D. Stump of the Circuit Court of DeKalb County, Ind., a document captioned "Petition To Have Tubal Ligation Performed On Minor and Indemnity Agreement." The document had been drafted by her attorney, a petitioner here. In this petition Mrs. McFarlin stated under oath that her daughter was 15 years of age and was "somewhat retarded," although she attended public school and had been promoted each year with her class. The petition further stated that Linda had been associating with "older youth or young men" and had stayed out overnight with them on several occasions. As a result of this behavior and Linda's mental capabilities, it was stated that it would be in the daughter's best interest if she underwent a tubal ligation in order "to prevent unfortunate circumstances. . . ." In the same document Mrs. McFarlin also undertook to indemnify and hold harmless Dr. John Hines, who was to perform the operation, and the DeKalb Memorial Hospital, where the operation was to take place, against all causes of action that might arise as a result of the performance of the tubal ligation.

The petition was approved by Judge Stump on the same day. He affixed his signature as "Judge, DeKalb Circuit Court," to the statement that he did "hereby approve the above Petition by affidavit form on behalf of Ora Spitler McFarlin, to have Tubal Ligation performed upon her minor daughter, Linda Spitler, subject to said Ora Spitler McFarlin covenanting and agreeing to indemnify and keep indemnified Dr. John Hines and the DeKalb Memorial Hospital from any matters or causes of action arising therefrom."

On July 15, 1971, Linda Spitler entered the DeKalb Memorial Hospital, having been told that she was to have her appendix removed. The following day a tubal ligation was performed upon her. She was released several days later, unaware of the true nature of her surgery.

Approximately two years after the operation, Linda Spitler was married to respondent Leo Sparkman. Her inability to become pregnant led her to discover that she had been sterilized during the 1971 operation. As a result of this revelation, the Sparkmans filed suit in the United States District Court for the Northern District of Indiana against Mrs. McFarlin, her attorney, Judge Stump, the doctors who had performed and assisted in the tubal ligation, and the DeKalb Memorial Hospital. Respondents sought damages for the alleged violation of Linda Sparkman's constitutional rights; also asserted were pendent state claims for assault and battery, medical malpractice, and loss of potential fatherhood.

* * *

[The district court found absolute immunity applicable, but the Seventh Circuit disagreed and reversed. The Supreme Court in turn reversed]

II

The governing principle of law is well established and is not questioned by the parties. As early as 1872, the Court recognized that it was "a general principle of the highest importance to the proper administration of justice that a judicial officer, in exercising the authority vested in him, [should] be free to act upon his own convictions, without apprehension of personal consequences to himself."

Bradley v. Fisher. For that reason the Court held that "judges of courts of superior or general jurisdiction are not liable to civil actions for their judicial acts, even when such acts are in excess of their jurisdiction, and are alleged to have been done maliciously or corruptly." Later we held that this doctrine of judicial immunity was applicable in suits under § 1 of the Civil Rights Act of 1871, 42 U.S.C. § 1983, for the legislative record gave no indication that Congress intended to abolish this long-established principle. *Pierson v. Ray.*

The Court of Appeals correctly recognized that the necessary inquiry in determining whether a defendant judge is immune from suit is whether at the time he took the challenged action he had jurisdiction over the subject matter before him. Because "some of the most difficult and embarrassing questions which a judicial officer is called upon to consider and determine relate to his jurisdiction. . .," *Bradley*, the scope of the judge's jurisdiction must be construed broadly where the issue is the immunity of the judge. A judge will not be deprived of immunity because the action he took was in error, was done maliciously, or was in excess of his authority; rather, he will be subject to liability only when he has acted in the "clear absence of all jurisdiction."

We cannot agree that there was a "clear absence of all jurisdiction" in the DeKalb County Circuit Court to consider the petition presented by Mrs. McFarlin. As an Indiana Circuit Court Judge, Judge Stump had "original exclusive jurisdiction in all cases at law and in equity whatsoever . . .;" jurisdiction over the settlement of estates and over guardianships, appellate jurisdiction as conferred by law, and jurisdiction over "all other causes, matters and proceedings where exclusive jurisdiction thereof is not conferred by law upon some other court, board or officer." This is indeed a broad jurisdictional grant; yet the Court of Appeals concluded that Judge Stump did not have jurisdiction over the petition authorizing Linda Sparkman's sterilization.

In so doing, the Court of Appeals noted that the Indiana statutes provided for the sterilization of institutionalized persons under certain circumstances, but otherwise contained no express authority for judicial approval of tubal ligations. It is true that the

statutory grant of general jurisdiction to the Indiana circuit courts does not itemize types of cases those courts may hear and hence does not expressly mention sterilization petitions presented by the parents of a minor. But in our view, it is more significant that there was no Indiana statute and no case law in 1971 prohibiting a circuit court, a court of general jurisdiction, from considering a petition of the type presented to Judge Stump. The statutory authority for the sterilization of institutionalized persons in the custody of the State does not warrant the inference that a court of general jurisdiction has no power to act on a petition for sterilization of a minor in the custody of her parents, particularly where the parents have authority under the Indiana statutes to "consent to and contract for medical or hospital care or treatment of [the minor] including surgery." The District Court concluded that Judge Stump had jurisdiction under § 33-4-4-3 to entertain and act upon Mrs. McFarlin's petition. We agree with the District Court, it appearing that neither by statute nor by case law has the broad jurisdiction granted to the circuit courts of Indiana been circumscribed to foreclose consideration of a petition for authorization of a minor's sterilization.

* * *

We conclude that the Court of Appeals, employing an unduly restrictive view of the scope of Judge Stump's jurisdiction, erred in holding that he was not entitled to judicial immunity. Because the court over which Judge Stump presides is one of general jurisdiction, neither the procedural errors he may have committed nor the lack of a specific statute authorizing his approval of the petition in question rendered him liable in damages for the consequences of his actions.

The respondents argue that even if Judge Stump had jurisdiction to consider the petition presented to him by Mrs. McFarlin, he is still not entitled to judicial immunity because his approval of the petition did not constitute a "judicial" act. It is only for acts performed in his "judicial" capacity that a judge is absolutely immune, they say. We do not disagree with this statement of the law, but we cannot characterize the approval of the petition as a nonjudicial act.

Respondents themselves stated in their pleadings before the District Court that Judge Stump was "clothed with the authority of the state" at the time that he approved the petition and that "he was acting as a county circuit court judge." They nevertheless now argue that Judge Stump's approval of the petition was not a judicial act because the petition was not given a docket number, was not placed on file with the clerk's office, and was approved in an ex parte proceeding without notice to the minor, without a hearing, and without the appointment of a guardian ad litem.

This Court has not had occasion to consider, for purposes of the judicial immunity doctrine, the necessary attributes of a judicial act; but it has previously rejected the argument, somewhat similar to the one raised here, that the lack of formality involved in the Illinois Supreme Court's consideration of a petitioner's application for admission to the state bar prevented it from being a "judicial proceeding" and from presenting a case or controversy that could be reviewed by this Court. *In re Summers.* Of particular significance to the present case, the Court in *Summers* noted the following: "The record does not show that any process issued or that any appearance was made. . . . While no entry was placed by the Clerk in the file, on a docket, or in a judgment roll, the Court took cognizance of the petition and passed an order which is validated by the signature of the presiding officer." Because the Illinois court took cognizance of the petition for admission and acted upon it, the Court held that a case or controversy was presented.

Similarly, the Court of Appeals for the Fifth Circuit has held that a state district judge was entitled to judicial immunity, even though "at the time of the altercation [giving rise to the suit] Judge Brown was not in his judge's robes, he was not in the courtroom itself, and he may well have violated state and/or federal procedural requirements regarding contempt citations." *McAlester v. Brown.* Among the factors relied upon by the Court of Appeals in deciding that the judge was acting within his judicial capacity was the fact that "the confrontation arose directly and immediately out of a visit to the judge in his official capacity."

The relevant cases demonstrate that the factors determining whether an act by a judge is a "judicial" one relate to the nature of the act itself, i.e., whether it is a function normally performed by a judge, and to the expectations of the parties, i.e., whether they dealt with the judge in his judicial capacity. Here, both factors indicate that Judge Stump's approval of the sterilization petition was a judicial act. State judges with general jurisdiction not infrequently are called upon in their official capacity to approve petitions relating to the affairs of minors, as for example, a petition to settle a minor's claim. Furthermore, as even respondents have admitted, at the time he approved the petition presented to him by Mrs. McFarlin, Judge Stump was "acting as a county circuit court judge." We may infer from the record that it was only because Judge Stump served in that position that Mrs. McFarlin, on the advice of counsel, submitted the petition to him for his approval. Because Judge Stump performed the type of act normally performed only by judges and because he did so in his capacity as a Circuit Court Judge, we find no merit to respondents' argument that the informality with which he proceeded rendered his action nonjudicial and deprived him of his absolute immunity.

* * *

The Indiana law vested in Judge Stump the power to entertain and act upon the petition for sterilization. He is, therefore, under the controlling cases, immune from damages liability even if his approval of the petition was in error. Accordingly, the judgment of the Court of Appeals is reversed, and the case is remanded for further proceedings consistent with this opinion.

Mr. Justice **Stewart**, with whom Mr. Justice **Marshall** and Mr. Justice **Powell** join, dissenting.

It is established federal law that judges of general jurisdiction are absolutely immune from monetary liability "for their judicial acts, even when such acts are in excess of their jurisdiction, and are alleged to have been done maliciously or corruptly." *Bradley v. Fisher.* It is also established that this immunity is in no way diminished in a proceeding under 42 U.S.C. § 1983. But the scope of judicial immunity is limited to liability for "judicial acts" and I think that what Judge Stump did on July 9, 1971, was beyond the pale of anything that could sensibly be called a judicial act.

Neither in *Bradley v. Fisher* nor in *Pierson v. Ray* was there any claim that the conduct in question was not a judicial act, and the Court thus had no occasion in either case to discuss the meaning of that term. Yet the proposition that judicial immunity extends only to liability for "judicial acts" was emphasized no less than seven times in Mr. Justice Field's opinion for the Court in the *Bradley* case. *Cf. Imbler v. Pachtman.* And if the limitations inherent in that concept have any realistic meaning at all, then I cannot believe that the action of Judge Stump in approving Mrs. McFarlin's petition is protected by judicial immunity.

The Court finds two reasons for holding that Judge Stump's approval of the sterilization petition was a judicial act. First, the Court says, it was "a function normally performed by a judge." Second, the Court says, the act was performed in Judge Stump's "judicial capacity." With all respect, I think that the first of these grounds is factually untrue and that the second is legally unsound.

* * *

In sum, what Judge Stump did on July 9, 1971, was in no way an act "normally performed by a judge." Indeed, there is no reason to believe that such an act has ever been performed by any other Indiana judge, either before or since.

* * *

It seems to me, rather, that the concept of what is a judicial act must take its content from a consideration of the factors that support immunity from liability for the performance of such an act. Those factors were accurately summarized by the Court in *Pierson v. Ray*:

"[I]t 'is. . . for the benefit of the public, whose interest it is that the judges should be at liberty to exercise their functions with independence and without fear of consequences.'. . . It is a judge's duty to decide all cases within his jurisdiction that are brought before him, including controversial cases that arouse the most intense feelings in the litigants. His errors may be corrected on appeal, but he should not have to fear

that unsatisfied litigants may hound him with litigation charging malice or corruption. Imposing such a burden on judges would contribute not to principled and fearless decision-making but to intimidation."

Not one of the considerations thus summarized in the *Pierson* opinion was present here. There was no "case," controversial or otherwise. There were no litigants. There was and could be no appeal. And there was not even the pretext of principled decisionmaking. The total absence of any of these normal attributes of a judicial proceeding convinces me that the conduct complained of in this case was not a judicial act.

* * *

[The dissenting opinion of Justice **Powell** is omitted; Justice **Brennan** did not participate.]

NOTES

1. Is *Stump* an easy or hard case in which to find absolute judicial immunity applicable? Why?

2. Does *Stump* retain the language of jurisdiction that we saw in *Bradley* and *Pierson*? If so, how is it applied in *Stump*? What does it add?

3. What of the argument that the judge acted in the clear absence of all *personal* jurisdiction?

4. What does the Court mean by a "judicial act?" Is the challenged judicial conduct in *Stump* a judicial act? Can there be a *judicial act* in the clear absence of all jurisdiction? Can there be a *nonjudicial act* which is only in excess of jurisdiction? Is *Stump* wrong because what the defendant did was not correctable on appeal? *See* Rosenberg, Stump v. Sparkman: *The Doctrine of Judicial Impunity*, 64 Va. L. Rev. 833 (1978).

5. Is a judicial punch in the mouth protected by absolute judicial immunity? Why not? *See Gregory v. Thompson*, 500 F.2d 59 (9th Cir. 1974) (judge's physical assault on plaintiff not a judicial act).

6. Suppose a judge is accused of ordering a police officer to use excessive force to bring an attorney to him in his courtroom. In *Mireles v. Waco*, 112 S. Ct. 286 (1991) (per curiam), the Supreme Court summarily found absolute immunity applicable to such a case. It noted that the plaintiff was dealing with the defendant in the latter's judicial capacity because the plaintiff was called into the courtroom in connection with a pending case. While the defendant's alleged direction to use excessive force was not a normal judicial function, this was to put the inquiry at too particular a level. Under *Stump*, the inquiry was into the nature or function of the act, not the "act itself." The Court explained: "In other words, we look to the particular act's relation to a general function normally performed by a judge, in this case the function of directing police officers to bring counsel in a pending case before the court."

The Court also rejected the argument that the challenged conduct was transformed into an executive act through its implementation by a police officer. It went on to conclude that the defendant did not act in the clear absence of all jurisdiction because his conduct, even if legally erroneous, was in aid of his jurisdiction.

What do all of these cases suggest about the scope of absolute judicial immunity? Do you suppose that there is an impulse toward judicial self-preservation at work here?

D. The Functional Approach to Judicial Immunity as a Double-Edged Sword: Judges, Court Reporters and Prison Disciplinary Hearing Officers

We saw earlier in connection with absolute legislative immunity that the Supreme Court has adopted a functional approach to immunities. The Court explained it this way in *Forrester v. White*, 484 U.S. 219, 224 (1988), a judicial immunity case:

Running through our cases, with fair consistency, is a "functional" approach to immunity questions other than those that have been decided by express constitutional or statutory enactment. Under that approach, we examine the nature of the functions with which a particular official or class of officials has been lawfully entrusted, and we seek to evaluate the effect that exposure to liability would likely have

on the appropriate exercise of those functions. Officials who seek exemption for personal liability have the burden of showing that such an exemption is justified by overriding considerations of public policy, and the Court has recognized a category of "qualified immunity" that avoids unnecessarily extending the scope of the traditional concept of absolute immunity.

The Court applied this functional approach in *Forrester* itself and held that absolute judicial immunity did *not* protect a state judge accused of violating equal protection by firing a probation officer because of her sex. According to the Court, this conduct was administrative in nature, not judicial. It was true that such administrative conduct was important to the operation of a sound judicial system and also that suits by disgruntled former employees could interfere with judicial decision making. However, these considerations did not warrant absolute judicial immunity for administrative conduct.

1. Will there be many cases in which it will be difficult to distinguish between judicial and non-judicial acts for absolute immunity purposes?

2. Do judges engage in non-judicial acts to the same extent that local legislators engage in non-legislative acts? To the same extent that prosecutors engage in non-advocative acts?

3. What about others whose functions are closely related to the judicial process, such as court reporters? Consider *Antoine v. Byers & Anderson*, 113 S. Ct 2167 (1993), *revg* 950 F.2d 1471 (9th Cir. 1991), where the Supreme Court ruled unanimously that absolute judicial immunity did not protect a court reporter accused of failing to provide a criminal trial transcript in a timely manner to the plaintiff, which delayed his appeal for over four years. The Ninth Circuit had found absolute immunity applicable, reasoning that preparing a trial transcript was part of the appellate judicial function which was "inextricably intertwined with the adjudication of claims." 950 F.2d at 1476. Reversing in an opinion by Justice Stevens, the Supreme Court first noted that there was no history of common law immunity for professional court reporters because they did not exist when the common law doctrine of judicial immunity developed. It then rejected the defendant's proposed analogy to common law judges who made handwritten notes during trial. For one thing, those notes were not verbatim reports of trials. For another, even if a judge were to make such verbatim notes, under the functional approach it was likely that this conduct would be characterized as administrative in nature and hence protected only by qualified immunity. The Court went on to emphasize that court reporter did not perform quasi-judicial functions because they did not really exercise discretion. And finally, there was no real demonstration that court reporters needed absolute immunity so that they could do their jobs: cases like this one were relatively rare.

Is *Antoine* consistent with the functional approach? What does *Antoine* indicate about the respective roles of the common law of immunity and policy considerations in absolute immunity determinations? Is *Antoine* comparable to the Court's refusal in *Burns v. Reed*, considered later in this chapter, to confer absolute judicial immunity on a prosecutor for rendering legal advice to law?

4. What about those officials whose acts appear quasi-judicial in nature? Are they protected by absolute judicial immunity under the functional approach? Consider *Cleavinger v. Saxner*, 474 U.S. 193 (1985), where the Court held that members of a federal prison's disciplinary committee who heard cases involving inmate rule infractions were protected by qualified immunity, not absolute immunity. Such persons were not functionally comparable to judges: they were not independent, were not professional hearing officers, and were under pressure to resolve disputes in favor of the institution. In addition, there often were few procedural safeguards available in the prison disciplinary context. Thus, according to the Court, such defendants should be treated the same way as school board members who adjudicate and who, under *Wood v. Strickland*, 420 U.S. 308 (1975), were protected only by qualified immunity.

What is the significance of the Court's reliance in *Cleavinger* on the incentive structure of federal prison disciplinary committees? Why should the objectivity of the decisionmaking process be considered relevant to characterizing that process functionally as judicial in nature?

Compare *Cleavinger* to *Shelly v. Johnson*, 849 F.2d 228 (6th Cir. 1988) (per curiam),

where, despite *Cleavinger*, the Sixth Circuit held that Michigan prison hearing officers were absolutely immune from damages liability for acts done in their official capacity. Under Michigan law, prison hearing officers were professionals in the nature of administrative law judges who were required to be attorneys and were not simply prison employees subordinate to prison wardens. Additionally, their adjudicatory functions were specified in the law, their decisions were in writing and supported by findings of fact, and judicial review was available. For these reasons, they were entitled to the protection of absolute judicial immunity consistent with their independence and authority as full-time judicial officers. The Sixth Circuit distinguished *Cleavinger v. Saxner* on the ground that the prison disciplinary committee members sued there were not similarly exercising independent authority pursuant to quasi-judicial procedures.

E. *Pulliam* and Prospective Relief

It was observed earlier in the discussion of absolute legislative immunity and *Supreme Court v. Consumers Union* that judges, unlike state legislators, are not protected from prospective relief. This applies even to judicial acts engaged in with unquestioned jurisdiction. However, *Consumers Union* expressly left that question open. It was only in *Pulliam v. Allen*, 466 U.S. 522 (1984) that the Court finally put this matter to rest.

Pulliam involved a section 1983 prospective relief action against a magistrate accused of unconstitutionally imposing bail on persons arrested for nonjailable offenses under Virginia law and of incarcerating those persons if they could not meet the bail. The district court found for the plaintiffs, enjoined the practice, and awarded attorney's fees against the defendant magistrate under 42 U.S.C. section 1988. The Fourth Circuit affirmed, as did the Supreme Court in a opinion by Justice Blackmun.

The Court first addressed the issue of judicial immunity from prospective relief liability. Acknowledging that there were no injunctions against common law judges, the Court nevertheless found a parallel in the collateral relief available against judges through the use of "the

King's prerogative writs," especially prohibition and mandamus. It next observed that it had never declared an absolute judicial immunity rule for prospective relief, that the prevailing approach in the circuits was that there was no such immunity, and that the absence of such immunity had not had a "chilling effect" on judicial independence. Further, Article III limitations on injunctive relief against a judge, together with equitable requirements in general, both assured that injunctive relief against judges would be sparingly granted and provided sufficient safeguards of comity and federalism. Finally, there was no indication that Congress in enacting section 1983 intended to provide absolute judicial immunity from prospective relief. Indeed, all indications in the legislative history were to the contrary.

As to attorney's fees under section 1988, the Court simply noted that it was for Congress, not the Court, to provide for judicial immunity from attorney's fees awards. Since section 1988 was intended to provide fees in actions to enforce section 1983, it applied as well to judges successfully sued for prospective relief.

Chief Justice Burger and Justices Rehnquist and O'Connor joined in a dissenting opinion by Justice Powell. They contended that, under the common law, judges were absolutely immune from prospective relief liability as well as from damages liability. Both kinds of immunity were necessary to protect judicial independence from the burdens of litigation. In addition, they rejected the majority's reliance on prerogative writs as misplaced: such writs were used "only to control the proper exercise of jurisdiction, they posed no threat to judicial independence and implicated none of the policies of judicial immunity." Finally, the dissenters argued that the effect on judicial independence of section 1983 prospective relief suits would be aggravated by the possibility of attorney's fees awards under section 1988.

Attorney's fees, a topic of immense practical significance, are addressed in Chapter 12. For present purposes, consider the following questions.

1. Why should judges, but not state legislators, be subject to prospective relief actions?

2. Will it ordinarily be easy for a section 1983 plaintiff to secure prospective relief against a judge? Do Article III requirements pose special problems in this regard?

3. What of institutional and equitable constraints on such relief? See *In re Justices of the Supreme Court*, 695 F.2d 17 (1st Cir. 1982) (pre-*Pulliam* case refusing to grant prospective relief against the justices of the Puerto Rico Supreme Court on institutional grounds) and *Sterling v. Calvin*, 874 F.2d 571 (8th Cir. 1989) (refusing to grant prospective relief against state trial judge on equitable grounds)

F. A Note on Witness Immunity and Its Connection to Judicial Immunity: *Briscoe*

In *Briscoe v. LaHue*, 460 U.S. 325 (1983), a case closely related to the Supreme Court's judicial immunity decisions, the Court ruled that police officer witnesses accused of perjury at criminal trials are absolutely immune from damages liability. *Briscoe* involved consolidated cases in which the plaintiffs sued police officers and a private party for allegedly testifying falsely at their respective criminal trials and thereby violating plaintiffs' rights to due process and to trial by an impartial jury. The Seventh Circuit held that all these defendants were entitled to absolute immunity in connection with their testimony. Upon review, the Supreme Court affirmed in an opinion by Justice Stevens. The Court observed that when section 1983 was enacted, the common law background of absolute lay witness immunity was well established. The underlying policy was the prevention of witness self-censorship. Similarly, judges are absolutely immune under section 1983 for the protection of the judicial process itself. Thus, whether a police officer witness is like a lay witness or like an official playing an important role in the judicial process, the police officer witness is entitled to absolute immunity. The Court also found nothing in section 1983's legislative history to compel a different conclusion.

The Court rejected the contention that there should be an exception for police officer witness immunity on the ground that the policy reasons for lay witness immunity do not apply with the same force to police officers who testify as part of their official duties. The Court took a functional approach to absolute immunity, as opposed to a status approach. Justices Brennan, Marshall, and Blackmun dissented, arguing that police officer witnesses accused of perjury are not entitled to absolute immunity.

1. In light of the Supreme Court's solicitude for the judicial process and its emphasis on the 1871 common law, is *Briscoe* a surprising decision?

2. Should absolute witness immunity protect law enforcement officers for their testimony in pretrial adversarial proceedings?

3. Should absolute witness immunity protect a witness at a grand jury proceeding? Compare *Kincaid v. Eberle*, 712 F.2d 1023 (7th Cir. 1983) (per curiam) (yes) and *Anthony v. Baker*, 767 F.2d 657 (10th Cir. 1985) (no).

4. Can *Briscoe* be end-run by alleging an *extrajudicial conspiracy* to present false testimony? The Tenth Circuit answered in the negative, explaining that "[i]nstead of suing state witnesses for perjured testimony, a [criminal] defendant could simply transform the perjury complaint into an allegation of a conspiracy to do the same." *Miller v. Glanz*, 948 F.2d 1562, 1571 (10th Cir. 1991).

III. Absolute Prosecutorial Immunity

A. *Imbler*: The Seminal Absolute Prosecutorial Immunity Case

Imbler v. Pachtman

424 U.S. 409 (1976)

Mr. Justice **Powell** delivered the opinion of the Court.

The question presented in this case is whether a state prosecuting attorney who acted within the scope of his duties in initiating and pursuing a criminal prosecution is amenable to suit under 42 U.S.C. § 1983 for alleged deprivations of the defendant's consti-

tutional rights. The Court of Appeals for the Ninth Circuit held that he is not. We affirm.

I

* * *

. . . In April 1972, Imbler filed a civil rights action, under 42 U.S.C. § 1983 and related statutes, against [prosecutor] Pachtman, [a] police fingerprint expert, and various other officers of the Los Angeles police force. He alleged that a conspiracy among them unlawfully to charge and convict him had caused him loss of liberty and other grievous injury. He demanded $2.7 million in actual and exemplary damages from each defendant, plus $15,000 attorney's fees.

. . . The gravamen of his complaint against Pachtman was that he had "with intent, and on other occasions with negligence" allowed Costello [a witness] to give false testimony as found by the District Court, and that the fingerprint expert's suppression of evidence was "chargeable under federal law" to Pachtman. In addition Imbler claimed that Pachtman had prosecuted him with knowledge of a lie detector test that had "cleared" Imbler, and that Pachtman had used at trial a police artist's sketch of Hasson's killer made shortly after the crime and allegedly altered to resemble Imbler more closely after the investigation had focused upon him.

* * *

II

Title 42 U.S.C. § 1983 provides that "[e]very person" who acts under color of state law to deprive another of a constitutional right shall be answerable to that person in a suit for damages. The statute thus creates a species of tort liability that on its face admits of no immunities, and some have argued that it should be applied as stringently as it reads. But that view has not prevailed.

* * *

The decision in *Tenney* established that § 1983 is to be read in harmony with general principles of tort immunities and defenses rather than in derogation of them. Before today the Court has had occasion to consider the liability of several types of government officials in addition to legislators. The common-law absolute immunity of judges for "acts committed within their judicial jurisdiction," see *Bradley v. Fisher*, was found to be preserved under § 1983 in *Pierson v. Ray*. In the same case, local police officers sued for a deprivation of liberty resulting from unlawful arrest were held to enjoy under § 1983 a "good faith and probable cause" defense co-extensive with their defense to false arrest actions at common law. We found qualified immunities appropriate in two recent cases.[13] In *Scheuer v. Rhodes*, we concluded that the Governor and other executive officials of a State had a qualified immunity that varied with "the scope of discretion and responsibilities of the office and all the circumstances as they reasonably appeared at the time of the action. . . .". Last Term in *Wood v. Strickland*, we held that school officials, in the context of imposing disciplinary penalties, were not liable so long as they could not reasonably have known that their action violated students' clearly established constitutional rights, and provided they did not act with malicious intention to cause constitutional or other injury. In *Scheuer* and in *Wood*, as in the two earlier cases, the considerations underlying the nature of the immunity of the respective officials in suits at common law led to essentially the same immunity under § 1983.

III

This case marks our first opportunity to address the § 1983 liability of a state prosecuting officer. The Courts of Appeals, however, have confronted the issue many times and under varying circumstances. Although the precise contours of their holdings have been unclear at times, at bottom they are virtually unanimous that a prosecutor enjoys absolute immunity from § 1983 suits for damages when he acts within the scope of his prosecutorial duties. These courts sometimes have described the prosecutor's immunity as a form of "quasi-judicial" immunity and referred to it as derivative of the immunity of judges recognized in *Pierson v. Ray*. Petitioner focuses upon the "quasi-judicial" characteriza-

---

[13] The procedural difference between the absolute and the qualified immunities is important. An absolute immunity defeats a suit at the outset, so long as the official's actions were within the scope of the immunity. The fate of an official with qualified immunity depends upon the circumstances and motivations of his actions, as established by the evidence at trial. See *Scheuer v. Rhodes*; *Wood v. Strickland*.

tion, and contends that it illustrates a fundamental illogic in according absolute immunity to a prosecutor. He argues that the prosecutor, as a member of the executive branch, cannot claim the immunity reserved for the judiciary, but only a qualified immunity akin to that accorded other executive officials in this Court's previous cases.

Petitioner takes an overly simplistic approach to the issue of prosecutorial liability. As noted above, our earlier decisions on § 1983 immunities were not products of judicial fiat that officials in different branches of government are differently amenable to suit under § 1983. Rather, each was predicated upon a considered inquiry into the immunity historically accorded the relevant official at common law and the interests behind it. The liability of a state prosecutor under § 1983 must be determined in the same manner.

A

The function of a prosecutor that most often invites a common-law tort action is his decision to initiate a prosecution, as this may lead to a suit for malicious prosecution if the State's case misfires. The first American case to address the question of a prosecutor's amenability to such an action was *Griffith v. Slinkard*. The complaint charged that a local prosecutor without probable cause added the plaintiff's name to a grand jury true bill after the grand jurors had refused to indict him, with the result that the plaintiff was arrested and forced to appear in court repeatedly before the charge finally was nolle prossed. Despite allegations of malice, the Supreme Court of Indiana dismissed the action on the ground that the prosecutor was absolutely immune.

The *Griffith* view on prosecutorial immunity became the clear majority rule on the issue. The question eventually came to this Court on writ of certiorari to the Court of Appeals for the Second Circuit. In *Yaselli v. Goff*, the claim was that the defendant, a Special Assistant to the Attorney General of the United States, maliciously and without probable cause procured plaintiff's grand jury indictment by the willful introduction of false and misleading evidence. Plaintiff sought some $300,000 in damages for having been subjected to the rigors of a trial in which the court ultimately directed a verdict against the Government. The District Court dismissed the complaint, and the Court of Appeals affirmed. After reviewing the development of the doctrine of prosecutorial immunity, that court stated:

"In our opinion the law requires us to hold that a special assistant to the Attorney General of the United States, in the performance of the duties imposed upon him by law, is immune from a civil action for malicious prosecution based on an indictment and prosecution, although it results in a verdict of not guilty rendered by a jury. The immunity is absolute, and is grounded on principles of public policy."

After briefing and oral argument, this Court affirmed the Court of Appeals in a per curiam opinion.

The common-law immunity of a prosecutor is based upon the same considerations that underlie the common-law immunities of judges and grand jurors acting within the scope of their duties. These include concern that harassment by unfounded litigation would cause a deflection of the prosecutor's energies from his public duties, and the possibility that he would shade his decisions instead of exercising the independence of judgment required by his public trust. One court expressed both considerations as follows:

"The office of public prosecutor is one which must be administered with courage and independence. Yet how can this be if the prosecutor is made subject to suit by those whom he accuses and fails to convict? To allow this would open the way for unlimited harassment and embarrassment of the most conscientious officials by those who would profit thereby. There would be involved in every case the possible consequences of a failure to obtain a conviction. There would always be a question of possible civil action in case the prosecutor saw fit to move dismissal of the case. . . . The apprehension of such consequences would tend toward great uneasiness and toward weakening the fearless and impartial policy which should characterize the administration of this office. The work of the prosecutor would thus be impeded and we would have moved away from the desired objec-

tive of stricter and fairer law enforcement." *Pearson v. Reed.*

B

The common-law rule of immunity is thus well settled. We now must determine whether the same considerations of public policy that underlie the common-law rule likewise countenance absolute immunity under § 1983. We think they do.

If a prosecutor had only a qualified immunity, the threat of § 1983 suits would undermine performance of his duties no less than would the threat of common-law suits for malicious prosecution. A prosecutor is duty bound to exercise his best judgment both in deciding which suits to bring and in conducting them in court. The public trust of the prosecutor's office would suffer if he were constrained in making every decision by the consequences in terms of his own potential liability in a suit for damages. Such suits could be expected with some frequency, for a defendant often will transform his resentment at being prosecuted into the ascription of improper and malicious actions to the State's advocate. Further, if the prosecutor could be made to answer in court each time such a person charged him with wrongdoing, his energy and attention would be diverted from the pressing duty of enforcing the criminal law.

Moreover, suits that survived the pleadings would pose substantial danger of liability even to the honest prosecutor. The prosecutor's possible knowledge of a witness' falsehoods, the materiality of evidence not revealed to the defense, the propriety of a closing argument, and—ultimately in every case—the likelihood that prosecutorial misconduct so infected a trial as to deny due process, are typical of issues with which judges struggle in actions for post-trial relief, sometimes to differing conclusions. The presentation of such issues in a § 1983 action often would require a virtual retrial of the criminal offense in a new forum, and the resolution of some technical issues by the lay jury. It is fair to say, we think, that the honest prosecutor would face greater difficulty in meeting the standards of qualified immunity than other executive or administrative officials. Frequently acting under serious constraints of time and even information, a prosecutor inevitably makes many decisions that could engender colorable claims of constitutional deprivation. Defending these decisions, often years after they were made, could impose unique and intolerable burdens upon a prosecutor responsible annually for hundreds of indictments and trials.

The affording of only a qualified immunity to the prosecutor also could have an adverse effect upon the functioning of the criminal justice system. Attaining the system's goal of accurately determining guilt or innocence requires that both the prosecution and the defense have wide discretion in the conduct of the trial and the presentation of evidence. The veracity of witnesses in criminal cases frequently is subject to doubt before and after they testify, as is illustrated by the history of this case. If prosecutors were hampered in exercising their judgment as to the use of such witnesses by concern about resulting personal liability, the triers of fact in criminal cases often would be denied relevant evidence.

The ultimate fairness of the operation of the system itself could be weakened by subjecting prosecutors to § 1983 liability. Various post-trial procedures are available to determine whether an accused has received a fair trial. These procedures include the remedial powers of the trial judge, appellate review, and state and federal post-conviction collateral remedies. In all of these the attention of the reviewing judge or tribunal is focused primarily on whether there was a fair trial under law. This focus should not be blurred by even the subconscious knowledge that a post-trial decision in favor of the accused might result in the prosecutor's being called upon to respond in damages for his error or mistaken judgment.

We conclude that the considerations outlined above dictate the same absolute immunity under § 1983 that the prosecutor enjoys at common law. To be sure, this immunity does leave the genuinely wronged defendant without civil redress against a prosecutor whose malicious or dishonest action deprives him of liberty. But the alternative of qualifying a prosecutor's immunity would disserve the broader public interest. It would prevent the vigorous and fearless performance of the prosecutor's duty that is essential to the proper functioning of the criminal justice system. Moreover, it often would prejudice defendants in criminal cases by skewing post-conviction judicial decisions that should be made

with the sole purpose of insuring justice. With the issue thus framed, we find ourselves in agreement with Judge Learned Hand, who wrote of the prosecutor's immunity from actions for malicious prosecution:

"As is so often the case, the answer must be found in a balance between the evils inevitable in either alternative. In this instance it has been thought in the end better to leave unredressed the wrongs done by dishonest officers than to subject those who try to do their duty to the constant dread of retaliation." *Gregoire v. Biddle.*

We emphasize that the immunity of prosecutors from liability in suits under § 1983 does not leave the public powerless to deter misconduct or to punish that which occurs. This Court has never suggested that the policy considerations which compel civil immunity for certain governmental officials also place them beyond the reach of the criminal law. Even judges, cloaked with absolute civil immunity for centuries, could be punished criminally for willful deprivations of constitutional rights on the strength of 18 U.S.C. § 242, the criminal analog of § 1983. The prosecutor would fare no better for his willful acts. Moreover, a prosecutor stands perhaps unique, among officials whose acts could deprive persons of constitutional rights, in his amenability to professional discipline by an association of his peers. These checks undermine the argument that the imposition of civil liability is the only way to insure that prosecutors are mindful of the constitutional rights of persons accused of crime.

IV

It remains to delineate the boundaries of our holding. [T]he Court of Appeals emphasized that each of respondent's challenged activities was an "integral part of the judicial process." The purpose of the Court of Appeals' focus upon the functional nature of the activities rather than respondent's status was to distinguish and leave standing those cases, in its Circuit and in some others, which hold that a prosecutor engaged in certain investigative activities enjoys, not the absolute immunity associated with the judicial process, but only a good-faith defense comparable to the policeman's. We agree with the Court of Appeals that respondent's activities were intimately associated with the judicial phase of the criminal process, and thus were functions to which the reasons for absolute immunity apply with full force. We have no occasion to consider whether like or similar reasons require immunity for those aspects of the prosecutor's responsibility that cast him in the role of an administrator or investigative officer rather than that of advocate. We hold only that in initiating a prosecution and in presenting the State's case, the prosecutor is immune from a civil suit for damages under § 1983. The judgment of the Court of Appeals for the Ninth Circuit accordingly is

Affirmed.

[The concurring opinion of Justices **White**, **Brennan** and **Marshall** is omitted; Justice **Stevens** did not participate.]

NOTES

1. Is *Imbler* consistent with the Court's interpretive approaches in the legislative and judicial immunity cases? Does the result in *Imbler* follow from the 1871 common law background? Does it follow from the policy considerations we have seen?

2. What precisely is the challenged prosecutorial conduct in *Imbler*?

3. What does it mean to describe protected prosecutorial conduct as that of an advocate "intimately associated with the judicial phase of the criminal process?" What else do prosecutors do besides participate as advocates in criminal proceedings?

4. Does the Court draw any bright line between protected advocative conduct and other kinds of prosecutorial conduct that are unprotected? Is it even possible to draw a bright line? Recall the functional approach of *Lake Country Estates* for legislators and of *Forrester v. White* for judges. *See* Note, *Delimiting the Scope of Proscutorial Immunity from Section 1983 Damage Suits*, 52 N.Y.U. L. Rev. 173 (1977).

5. Where is the line between the advocative and investigative conduct of a prosecutor? Is it important to draw that line? Why? Is it relevant that, as Chapter 8 indicates, police officers engaged in law enforcement activities are ordinarily protected only by qualified immunity?

It took the Supreme Court over fifteen years to confront these questions. In *Buckley v.*

Fitzsimmons, 113 S. Ct. 2606 (1993), the Court held that prosecutors accused of fabricating evidence for the purpose of creating probable cause to arrest were not protected by absolute immunity. The Court emphasized several factors in addition to the absence at common law of prosecutorial immunity for such conduct. First, the challenged conduct occurred prior to the existence of probable cause to arrest. And second, such conduct was identical to that ordinarily engaged in by police officers.

6. Once absolute prosecutorial immunity for advocative conduct is accepted, is *Imbler* an easy or hard case?

7. Should absolute prosecutorial immunity protect a prosecutor accused of conspiring to bring false criminal charges? Accused of withholding evidence favorable to the plaintiff and of instructing a witness to testify falsely? Accused of having the plaintiff indicted and, at the criminal trial, suborning perjury and filing false affidavits? Are these easy or hard cases?

8. Should absolute prosecutorial immunity protect communications to the media? In *Buckley v. Fitzsimmons*, 113 S. Ct. 2606 (1993), the Supreme Court said no. In addition to noting that such conduct was not protected by absolute immunity at common law, the Court applied a functional approach, reasoning that such conduct was clearly not advocative in nature.

9. Should absolute prosecutorial immunity protect the giving of legal advice to police officers and others? *See Burns v. Reed*, set out next.

B. *Burns*: The Prosecutor as Legal Advisor

Burns v. Reed

111 S. Ct. 1934 (1991)

Justice **White** delivered the opinion of the Court.

The issue in this case is whether a state prosecuting attorney is absolutely immune from liability for damages under 42 U.S.C. § 1983 for giving legal advice to the police and for participating in a probable cause hearing.

The Court of Appeals for the Seventh Circuit held that he is. We reverse in part.

* * *

II

* * *

The Court in *Imbler* declined to accord prosecutors only qualified immunity because, among other things, suits against prosecutors for initiating and conducting prosecutions "could be expected with some frequency, for a defendant often will transform his resentment at being prosecuted into the ascription of improper and malicious actions to the State's advocate"; lawsuits would divert prosecutors' attention and energy away from their important duty of enforcing the criminal law; prosecutors would have more difficulty than other officials in meeting the standards for qualified immunity; and potential liability "would prevent the vigorous and fearless performance of the prosecutor's duty that is essential to the proper functioning of the criminal justice system,". The Court also noted that there are other checks on prosecutorial misconduct, including the criminal law and professional discipline.

The Court therefore held that prosecutors are absolutely immune from liability under § 1983 for their conduct in "initiating a prosecution and in presenting the State's case," insofar as that conduct is "intimately associated with the judicial phase of the criminal process". Each of the charges against the prosecutor in *Imbler* involved conduct having that association, including the alleged knowing use of false testimony at trial and the alleged deliberate suppression of exculpatory evidence. The Court expressly declined to decide whether absolute immunity extends to "those aspects of the prosecutor's responsibility that cast him in the role of an administrator or investigative officer rather than that of an advocate." It was recognized, though, that "the duties of the prosecutor in his role as advocate for the State involve actions preliminary to the initiation of a prosecution and actions apart from the courtroom."

Decisions in later cases are consistent with the functional approach to immunity employed in *Imbler*. These decisions have also emphasized that the official seeking absolute immunity bears the burden of showing that such immunity is justified for the function in question. The presumption is that qualified rather than absolute immunity is sufficient to protect government officials in the exercise of their duties. We have been "quite sparing" in our recognition of absolute immunity, and have refused to extend it any "further than its justification would warrant."

III

We now consider whether the absolute prosecutorial immunity recognized in *Imbler* is applicable to (a) respondent's participation in a probable cause hearing, which led to the issuance of a search warrant, and (b) respondent's legal advice to the police regarding the use of hypnosis and the existence of probable cause to arrest petitioner.

A

We address first respondent's appearance as a lawyer for the State in the probable cause hearing, where he examined a witness and successfully supported the application for a search warrant. The decision in *Imbler* leads to the conclusion that respondent is absolutely immune from liability in a § 1983 suit for that conduct.

Initially, it is important to determine the precise claim that petitioner has made against respondent concerning respondent's role in the search warrant hearing. An examination of petitioner's complaint, the decisions by both the District Court and Seventh Circuit, and the questions presented in the Petition for a Writ of Certiorari in this Court reveals that petitioner has challenged only respondent's participation in the hearing, and not his motivation in seeking the search warrant or his conduct outside of the courtroom relating to the warrant.

* * *

Petitioner's challenge to respondent's participation in the search warrant hearing is similar to the claim in *Briscoe v. LaHue*. There, the plaintiff's § 1983 claim was based on the allegation that a police officer had given perjured testimony at the plaintiff's criminal trial. In holding that the officer was entitled to absolute immunity, we noted that witnesses were absolutely immune at common law from subsequent damages liability for their testimony in judicial proceedings "even if the witness knew the statements were false and made them with malice."

Like witnesses, prosecutors and other lawyers were absolutely immune from damages liability at common law for making false or defamatory statements in judicial proceedings (at least so long as the statements were related to the proceeding), and also for eliciting false and defamatory testimony from witnesses. See also *King v. Skinner*, Lofft 55, 56, 98 Eng. Rep. 529, 530 (K. B. 1772), where Lord Mansfield observed that "neither party, witness, counsel, jury, or Judge can be put to answer, civilly or criminally, for words spoken in office."

This immunity extended to "any hearing before a tribunal which performed a judicial function." W. Prosser, Law of Torts § 94, pp. 826–827 (1941). In *Yaselli v. Goff*, for example, this Court affirmed a decision by the Court of Appeals for the Second Circuit in which that court had held that the common-law immunity extended to a prosecutor's conduct before a grand jury.

In addition to finding support in the common law, we believe that absolute immunity for a prosecutor's actions in a probable cause hearing is justified by the policy concerns articulated in *Imbler*. There, the Court held that a prosecutor is absolutely immune for initiating a prosecution and for presenting the State's case. The Court also observed that "the duties of the prosecutor in his role as advocate for the State involve actions preliminary to the initiation of a prosecution."

The prosecutor's actions at issue here—appearing before a judge and presenting evidence in support of a motion for a search warrant—clearly involve the prosecutor's "role as advocate for the State," rather than his role as "administrator or investigative officer," the protection for which we reserved judgment in *Imbler*. Moreover, since the issuance of a search warrant is unquestionably a judicial act, appearing at a probable cause hearing is "intimately associated with the judicial phase of the criminal process." It is also connected with the initiation and conduct of a prosecution, particularly where the hearing occurs after arrest, as was the case here.

As this and other cases indicate, pretrial court appearances by the prosecutor in support of taking criminal action against a suspect present a substantial likelihood of vexatious litigation that might have an untoward effect on the independence of the prosecutor. Therefore, absolute immunity for this function serves the policy of protecting the judicial process, which underlies much of the Court's decision in *Imbler*. Furthermore, the judicial process is available as a check on prosecutorial actions at a probable cause hearing. "The safeguards built into the judicial system tend to reduce the need for private damages actions as a means of controlling unconstitutional conduct." *Butz*.

Accordingly, we hold that respondent's appearance in court in support of an application for a search warrant and the presentation of evidence at that hearing are protected by absolute immunity.

B

Turning to respondent's acts of providing legal advice to the police, we note first that neither respondent nor the court below has identified any historical or common-law support for extending absolute immunity to such actions by prosecutors. Indeed, the Court of Appeals stated that its "review of the historical or common law basis for the immunity in question does not yield any direct support for the conclusion that a prosecutor's immunity from suit extends to the act of giving legal advice to police officers."

The Court of Appeals did observe that Indiana common law purported to provide immunity "'whenever duties of a judicial nature are imposed upon a public officer.'" The court then reasoned that giving legal advice is "of a judicial nature" because the prosecutor is, like a judge, called upon to render opinions concerning the legality of conduct. We do not believe, however, that advising the police in the investigative phase of a criminal case is so "intimately associated with the judicial phase of the criminal process," that it qualifies for absolute immunity. Absent a tradition of immunity comparable to the common-law immunity from malicious prosecution, which formed the basis for the decision in *Imbler*, we have not been inclined to extend absolute immunity from liability under § 1983.

The United States, as amicus curiae, argues that the absence of common-law support here should not be determinative because the office of public prosecutor was largely unknown at

English common law, and prosecutors in the 18th and 19th centuries did not have an investigatory role, as they do today. We are not persuaded. First, it is American common law that is determinative, and the office of public prosecutor was known to American common law. Second, although "the precise contours of official immunity" need not mirror the immunity at common law, we look to the common law and other history for guidance because our role is "not to make a freewheeling policy choice," but rather to discern Congress' likely intent in enacting § 1983. "We do not have a license to establish immunities from § 1983 actions in the interests of what we judge to be sound public policy." *Tower v. Glover.* Thus, for example, it was observed that "since the statute [§ 1983] on its face does not provide for any immunities, we would be going far to read into it an absolute immunity for conduct which was only accorded qualified immunity in 1871."

The next factor to be considered—risk of vexatious litigation—also does not support absolute immunity for giving legal advice. The Court of Appeals asserted that absolute immunity was justified because "a prosecutor's risk of becoming entangled in litigation based on his or her role as a legal advisor is as likely as the risks associated with initiating and prosecuting a case." We disagree. In the first place, a suspect or defendant is not likely to be as aware of a prosecutor's role in giving advice as a prosecutor's role in initiating and conducting a prosecution. But even if a prosecutor's role in giving advice to the police does carry with it some risk of burdensome litigation, the concern with litigation in our immunity cases is not merely a generalized concern with interference with an official's duties, but rather is a concern with interference with the conduct closely related to the judicial process. Absolute immunity is designed to free the judicial process from the harassment and intimidation associated with litigation. That concern therefore justifies absolute prosecutorial immunity only for actions that are connected with the prosecutor's role in judicial proceedings, not for every litigation-inducing conduct.

The Court of Appeals speculated that anything short of absolute immunity would discourage prosecutors from performing their "vital obligation" of giving legal advice to the police. But the qualified immunity standard is today more protective of officials than it was at the time that Imbler was decided. "As the qualified immunity defense has evolved, it provides ample support to all but the plainly incompetent or those who knowingly violate the law." *Malley.* Although the absence of absolute immunity for the act of giving legal advice may cause prosecutors to consider their advice more carefully, "'where an official could be expected to know that his conduct would violate statutory or constitutional rights, he should be made to hesitate.'" Indeed, it is incongruous to allow prosecutors to be absolutely immune from liability for giving advice to the police, but to allow police officers only qualified immunity for following the advice. Ironically, it would mean that the police, who do not ordinarily hold law degrees, would be required to know the clearly established law, but prosecutors would not.

The United States argues that giving legal advice is related to a prosecutor's roles in screening cases for prosecution and in safeguarding the fairness of the criminal judicial process. That argument, however, proves too much. Almost any action by a prosecutor, including his or her direct participation in purely investigative activity, could be said to be in some way related to the ultimate decision whether to prosecute, but we have never indicated that absolute immunity is that expansive. Rather, as in *Imbler*, we inquire whether the prosecutor's actions are closely associated with the judicial process. Indeed, we implicitly rejected the United States' argument in *Mitchell*, where we held that the Attorney General was not absolutely immune from liability for authorizing a warrantless wiretap. Even though the wiretap was arguably related to a potential prosecution, we found that the Attorney General "was not acting in a prosecutorial capacity" and thus was not entitled to the immunity recognized in *Imbler*.

As a final basis for allowing absolute immunity for legal advice, the Court of Appeals observed that there are several checks other than civil litigation to prevent abuses of authority by prosecutors. Although we agree, we note that one of the most important checks, the judicial process, will not necessarily restrain out-of-court activities by a prosecutor that occur prior to the initiation of a prosecution, such as providing legal advice to the police. This is particularly true if a suspect is not eventually prosecuted. In those circumstances, the prosecutor's action is not subjected to the "crucible of the judicial process."

In sum, we conclude that respondent has not met his burden of showing that the relevant factors justify an extension of absolute immunity to the prosecutorial function of giving legal advice to the police.

IV

For the foregoing reasons, we affirm in part and reverse in part the judgment of the Court of Appeals.

[The opinion by Justices **Scalia** and **Blackmun**, joined in part by Justice **Marshall**, which concurs in part and dissents in part, is omitted.]

NOTES

1. What are the specific challenged acts in *Burns*? Which are protected by absolute prosecutorial immunity and which by qualified immunity?

2. After *Imbler*, is it surprising that absolute prosecutorial immunity protects the conduct of a prosecutor at a probable cause hearing?

3. Why should the giving of legal advice *not* be protected by absolute prosecutorial immunity? Isn't that activity closely related to the decision to prosecute and the judicial process?

4. Does *Burns* tell us what the line is between advocative and investigative conduct? If the test is, in *Burns*'s words, "whether the prosecutor's actions are closely associated with the judicial process," does that not create such uncertainty and unpredictability that the policies underlying absolute prosecutorial immunity are undermined?

5. Since *Burns* adheres to the now-familiar functional approach, does it necessarily follow that in cases involving many different allegedly unconstitutional acts of prosecutors, each and every one of those acts must be measured for absolute prosecutorial immunity?

6. Under the functional approach, even non-prosecutors who engage in prosecutorial functions may be protected by absolute prosecutorial immunity. *See Millspaugh v. County Department of Public Welfare*, 937 F.2d 1172 (7th Cir.

1991) (applying absolute prosecutorial immunity to certain acts of a social worker in initiating and participating in proceedings to determine whether plaintiffs' children should be removed from their home and placed in foster homes).

C. Circuit Court Cases

Evaluate the following cases.

1. After finding that grand jurors were protected by absolute judicial immunity for issuing a report of their findings that allegedly violated the constitutional rights of the plaintiff who was not a target of the grand jury investigation and was not prosecuted in any way, the Eighth Circuit in *DeCamp v. Douglas County Franklin Grand Jury*, 978 F.2d 1047, 1053 (8th Cir. 1992), went on to rule that the prosecutors who allegedly co-authored the grand jury report were protected by absolute prosecutorial immunity. It stated that a grand jury report explaining why an indictment was not returned was important to the overall judicial system. Thus, the prosecutors' help to the grand jury was intimately connected to the judicial process. The Eighth Circuit also emphasized the grand jury's need to receive accurate legal advice for prosecutors.

Judge Heaney dissented on the prosecutorial immunity issue. He argued that in this kind of case there was no common law support for absolute immunity, that there was no real risk of vexatious litigation and that it was unlikely that the challenged conduct would be checked otherwise. He also contended that the prosecutors' acts were not so closely tied to the judicial process to warrant absolute immunity.

2. Affirming the district court's denial of summary judgment for the defendant prosecutors in connection with witness interviews, the Third Circuit in *Kulwicki v. Dawson*, 969 F.2d 1454, 1465 (3rd Cir. 1992), commented that although "the line between quasi-judicial and investigative activity is far from clear," some courts "look to the occurrence of the activity relative to the filing of the complaint. Evidence gleaned prior to the filing is deemed investigative . . . [while] [e]vidence obtained at or after the filing is likely to be connected with an existing prosecution, and is absolutely protected." In the case before it, the complaint on its face suggested investigation rather then prosecution, and thus, even though facts might later be developed to challenge this characterization, at this time the district court would be affirmed. The Third Circuit went on to rule that the allegations that one of the prosecutors caused the publication of criminal charges against him and that another prosecutor held a press conference, all of which harmed the plaintiff, were protected only by qualified immunity. Communication the press was administrative in nature. Finally, the further claim that one of the defendants allegedly manufactured evidence was protected by absolute prosecutorial immunity.

3. In *Pfeiffer v. Hartford Fire Ins Co*, 929 F.2d 1484 (10th Cir. 1991), the plaintiff doctor sued several state attorneys who participated in a state medical board's investigation and prosecution of the plaintiff. He alleged that: (1) they failed to investigate the charges against him reasonably; (2) they coerced him into giving up his practice in exchange for keeping the board's proceedings confidential and for not filing sexual assault charges against him; and (3) they permitted newspaper reporters access to his files and otherwise generated "wrongful publicity." As to the first allegation, there was absolute immunity because the investigation occurred after the board had decided to file a complaint and "[t]here is no question in this circuit that prosecutors are absolutely immune from liability for allegedly failing to conduct an adequate, independent investigation of matters referred to them for prosecution." *Id.* at 1490. As to the second allegation, the offers made by the defendants to the plaintiff were comparable to plea bargaining which was absolutely immune because of its close association with the judicial process. As to the third, the information at issue was protected by absolute immunity because it was "collected and prepared in the course of prosecutorial activities immune from suit under section 1983." In addition, this information was not confidential. The Tenth Circuit went on to distinguish other circuits' decisions holding that prosecutors' statements to the press were not absolutely protected on the ground that such cases dealt with confidential information from grand jury proceedings or statements made in connection with prosecutorial involvement in investigative activities. *Id.* at 1493.

4. In *Houston v. Partee*, 978 F.2d 362 (7th Cir. 1992), the court confronted the question of whether prosecutorial failure to disclose exculpatory evidence discovered after the plaintiffs were convicted but while their criminal appeals were pending was protected by absolute immunity. The Seventh Circuit rejected the argument that absolute prosecutorial immunity somehow attached to the appeal despite the fact that the defendants were not themselves involved in the appeal. It emphasized that there was no such protection at common law, there was no real risk of vexatious litigation, absolute immunity in this kind of case would not interfere with the prosecutor's conduct in judicial proceedings and there were few safeguards available to prevent the abuses alleged here. In short, "[m]aking prosecutors answer for their post-prosecution acts that were not related to the prosecution will not hamper them in initiating a prosecution or in presenting the state's case." *Id.* at 368.

D. A Note on Prospective Relief

As we saw earlier in this chapter, prosecutors, like judges but unlike state legislators, are not absolutely immune from prospective relief. *Supreme Court v. Consumers Union*, 446 U.S. 719 (1980), makes this very clear. Recall also that even though such relief is theoretically available, often there will be Article III and equitable hurdles to overcome.

IV. Procedural Aspects of Absolute Immunity

A. The Burden of Pleading

Since absolute immunity is an affirmative defense, one would expect that a defendant claiming the immunity has the burden of pleading it. And since federal courts are notice pleading jurisdictions, one would expect that the plaintiff in a section 1983 case need only allege enough to alert the defendant to the basis for the claim. But it is not that simple.

Consider that the Fifth Circuit, after an extended discussion of the Federal Rules of Civil Procedure and expressions of concern with loosely drafted complaints, announced in

Elliott v. Perez, 751 F.2d 1472, 1482 (5th Cir. 1985):

> Once a complaint against a defendant state legislator, judge, or prosecutor (or similar officer) adequately raises the likely issue of [absolute] immunity the district court should on its own require of the plaintiff a detailed complaint alleging with particularity all material facts on which he contends he will establish his right to recovery, which will include detailed facts supporting the contention that the plea of immunity cannot be sustained.

However, recall from Chapter 5 that in *Leatherman v. Tarrant County*, 113 S. Ct. 1160 (1993), the Supreme Court unanimously rejected a heightened pleading requirement in local government liability failure to train cases. While it specifically left the immunity-pleading issue open, probably because of Justice Kennedy's concurring opinion in *Siegert v. Gilley*, 111 S.Ct. 1789, 1795 (1991) in which he approved heightened pleading requirements in certain circumstances, the tone and reasoning of *Leatherman* suggest that these requirements are now seriously questionable.

Interestingly, in *Burns-Toole v. Byrne*, 11 F.3d 1270 (5th Cir. 1994), a post-*Leatherman* case where the plaintiff sued members of the Texas State Board of Dental Examiners alleging religious discrimination, the Fifth Circuit found no need to reexamine its heightened pleading requirement and affirmed the district court's grant of summary judgment for the defendants. The court "decline[d] this invitation" to revisit *Elliott v. Perez* because in this case, plaintiff had no evidentiary basis for her charges even "[u]nder the most generous standard applicable to a motion for summary judgment." *Id* at 1275.

B. A Note on Appeal From Denial of an Absolute Immunity Motion to Dismiss or for Summary Judgment

As we will see in more detail in Chapter 8 when we consider qualified immunity, it turns out that the Supreme Court has modified the final judgment rule and the Federal Rules of Appellate Procedure to allow for immediate appeal from a district court's denial of a motion to dismiss or for summary judgment grounded on absolute or qualified immunity. *Mitchell v. Forsyth*, 472 U.S. 511 (1985). The Court reasoned in *Mitchell* that inasmuch as both absolute and qualified immunity are immunities from suit itself (and from having to defend them), immediate appeals must be permitted in order to make these immunities from suit meaningful.

In light of *Mitchell*, should it come as any surprise that some federal courts, like the Fifth Circuit in *Elliott v. Perez*, have amended the Federal Rules of Civil Procedure by requiring fact-specific pleading in certain section 1983 cases?

CHAPTER EIGHT

"Every Person": Qualified Immunity

Suppose that a plaintiff properly pleads and proves all of the elements of a section 1983 cause of action against an individual defendant. We saw in Chapter 7 that certain classes of individual defendants are protected by absolute immunity and are thereby treated as if they were not suable "persons" under section 1983. You will recall that these privileged defendants included state and local legislators, judges, witnesses and prosecutors. You will also remember that the Supreme Court has developed a functional approach to absolute immunity.

What happens if the defendant is unprotected by absolute immunity? It turns out that those individual defendants (officials and employees of state and local governments) who are not protected by absolute immunity are protected by qualified immunity.

Qualified immunity, when successfully asserted, is almost as powerful a defense as absolute immunity. Qualified immunity began as a two-part test for immunity from liability but, in a series of important decisions, has been converted by the Supreme Court into an "objective reasonableness" test which in many respects is the functional equivalent of absolute immunity. Thus, as we shall see, a qualified immunity defense motion to dismiss or for summary judgment effectively stops a plaintiff's discovery on the case in chief. In addition, when a federal district court denies such a motion, an interlocutory appeal is available even though there has obviously been no final judgment.

This chapter considers the following questions: (1) what are the elements and scope of qualified immunity? (2) what are the reasons for qualified immunity? (3) how is qualified immunity dealt with at the trial level and on appeal? (4) who is protected by qualified immunity?

I. The Origins of Qualified Immunity

A. *Pierson*: The Seminal Qualified Immunity Case and the Two-Part Test

Pierson v. Ray

386 U.S. 547 (1967)

Mr. Chief Justice **Warren** delivered the opinion of Court.

These cases present issues involving the liability of local police officers and judges under § 1 of the Civil Rights Act of 1871, 17 Stat. 13, now 42 U.S.C. § 1983. Petitioners were members of a group of 15 white and Negro Episcopal clergymen who attempted to use segregated facilities at an interstate bus terminal in Jackson, Mississippi, in 1961. They were arrested by respondents Ray, Griffith, and Nichols, policemen of the City of Jackson, and charged with violating § 2087.5 of the Mississippi Code, which makes guilty of a misdemeanor anyone who congregates with others in a public place under circumstances such that a breach of the peace may be occasioned thereby, and refuses to move on when ordered to do so by a police officer. Petitioners waived a jury trial and were convicted of the offense by respondent Spencer, a municipal police justice. They were each given the maximum sentence of four months in jail and a fine of $200. On appeal petitioner Jones was accorded a trial de novo in the County Court, and after the city produced its evidence the court granted his motion for a directed verdict. The cases against the other petitioners were then dropped.

Having been vindicated in the County Court, petitioners brought this action for damages in the United States District Court for the Southern District of Mississippi, Jackson Division, alleging that respondents had violated § 1983, and that respondents were liable at common law for false arrest and imprisonment. A jury returned verdicts for respondents on both counts. On appeal, the Court of Appeals for the Fifth Circuit held that respondent Spencer was immune from liability under both § 1983 and the common law of Mississippi for acts committed within his judicial jurisdiction. As to the police officers, the court noted that § 2087.5 of the Mississippi Code was held unconstitutional as applied to similar facts in *Thomas v. Mississippi*. Although Thomas was decided years after the arrest involved in this trial, the court held that the policemen would be liable in a suit under § 1983 for an unconstitutional arrest even if they acted in good faith and with probable cause in making an arrest under a state statute not yet held invalid. The court believed that this stern result was required by *Monroe v. Pape*. Under the count based on the common law of Mississippi, however, it held that the policemen would not be liable if they had probable cause to believe that the statute had been violated, because Mississippi law does not require police officers to predict at their peril which state laws are constitutional and which are not. Apparently dismissing the common-law claim, the Court of Appeals reversed and remanded for a new trial on the § 1983 claim against the police officers because defense counsel had been allowed to cross-examine the ministers on various irrelevant and prejudicial matters, particularly including an alleged convergence of their views on racial justice with those of the Communist Party. At the new trial, however, the court held that the ministers could not recover if it were proved that they went to Mississippi anticipating that they would be illegally arrested because such action would constitute consent to the arrest under the principle of volenti non fit injuria, he who consents to a wrong cannot be injured.

We granted certiorari to consider whether a local judge is liable for damages under § 1983 for an unconstitutional conviction and whether the ministers should be denied recovery against the police officers if they acted with the anticipation that they would be illegally arrested. We also granted the police officers' petition to determine if the Court of Appeals correctly held that they could not assert the defense of good faith and probable cause to an action under § 1983 for unconstitutional arrest.

* * *

We find no difficulty in agreeing with the Court of Appeals that Judge Spencer is immune from liability for damages for his role in these convictions. The record is barren of any proof or specific allegation that Judge Spencer played any role in these arrests and convictions other than to adjudge petitioners guilty when their cases came before his court. Few doctrines were more solidly established at common law than the immunity of judges from liability for damages for acts committed within their judicial jurisdiction, as this Court recognized when it adopted the doctrine, in *Bradley v. Fisher*. This immunity applies even when the judge is accused of acting maliciously and corruptly, and it "is not for the protection or benefit of a malicious or corrupt judge, but for the benefit of the public, whose interest it is that the judges should be at liberty to exercise their functions with independence and without fear of consequences." It is a judge's duty to decide all cases within his jurisdiction that are brought before him, including controversial cases that arouse the most intense feelings in the litigants. His errors may be corrected on appeal, but he should not have to fear that unsatisfied litigants may hound him with litigation charging malice or corruption. Imposing such a burden on judges would contribute not to principled and fearless decision-making but to intimidation.

We do not believe that this settled principle of law was abolished by § 1983, which makes liable "every person" who under color of law deprives another person of his civil rights. The legislative record gives no clear indication that Congress meant to abolish wholesale all common-law immunities. Accordingly, this Court held in *Tenney v. Brandhove* that the immunity of legislators for acts within the legislative role was not abolished. The immunity of judges for acts within the judicial role is equally well established, and we presume that Congress would have specifically so provided had it wished to abolish the doctrine.

The common law has never granted police officers an absolute and unqualified immunity, and the officers in this case do not claim that they are entitled to one. Their claim is rather that they should not be liable if they acted in good faith and with probable cause in making an arrest under a statute that they believed to be valid. Under the prevailing view in this country a peace officer who arrests someone with probable cause is not liable for false arrest simply because the innocence of the suspect is later proved. Restatement, Second, Torts § 121 (1965); 1 Harper & James, The Law of Torts § 3.18, at 277–278 (1956). A policeman's lot is not so unhappy that he must choose between being charged with dereliction of duty if he does not arrest when he has probable cause, and being mulcted in damages if he does. Although the matter is not entirely free from doubt, the same consideration would seem to require excusing him from liability for acting under a statute that he reasonably believed to be valid but that was later held unconstitutional, on its face or as applied.

The Court of Appeals held that the officers had such a limited privilege under the common law of Mississippi, and indicated that it would have recognized a similar privilege under § 1983 except that it felt compelled to hold otherwise by our decision in *Monroe v. Pape. Monroe v. Pape* presented no question of immunity, however, and none was decided. . . . As we [said in *Monroe*], § 1983 "should be read against the background of tort liability that makes a man responsible for the natural consequences of his actions." Part of the background of tort liability, in the case of police officers making an arrest, is the defense of good faith and probable cause.

We hold that the defense of good faith and probable cause, which the Court of Appeals found available to the officers in the common-law action for false arrest and imprisonment, is also available to them in the action under § 1983. This holding does not, however, mean that the count based thereon should be dismissed. The Court of Appeals ordered dismissal of the common-law count on the theory that the police officers were not required to

predict our decision in *Thomas v. Mississippi*. We agree that a police officer is not charged with predicting the future course of constitutional law. But the petitioners in this case did not simply argue that they were arrested under a statute later held unconstitutional. They claimed and attempted to prove that the police officers arrested them solely for attempting to use the "White Only" waiting room, that no crowd was present, and that no one threatened violence or seemed about to cause a disturbance. The officers did not defend on the theory that they believed in good faith that it was constitutional to arrest the ministers solely for using the waiting room. Rather, they claimed and attempted to prove that they did not arrest the ministers for the purpose of preserving the custom of segregation in Mississippi, but solely for the purpose of preventing violence. They testified, in contradiction to the ministers, that a crowd gathered and that imminent violence was likely. If the jury believed the testimony of the officers and disbelieved that of the ministers, and if the jury found that the officers reasonably believed in good faith that the arrest was constitutional, then a verdict for the officers would follow even though the arrest was in fact unconstitutional. The jury did resolve the factual issues in favor of the officers but, for reasons previously stated, its verdict was influenced by irrelevant and prejudicial evidence. Accordingly, the case must be remanded to the trial court for a new trial.

It is necessary to decide what importance should be given at the new trial to the substantially undisputed fact that the petitioners went to Jackson expecting to be illegally arrested. We do not agree with the Court of Appeals that they somehow consented to the arrest because of their anticipation that they would be illegally arrested, even assuming that they went to the Jackson bus terminal for the sole purpose of testing their rights to unsegregated public accommodations. The case contains no proof or allegation that they in any way tricked or goaded the officers into arresting them. The petitioners had the right to use the waiting room of the Jackson bus terminal, and their deliberate exercise of that right in a peaceful, orderly, and inoffensive manner does not disqualify them from seeking damages under § 1983.

The judgment of the Court of Appeals is affirmed in part and reversed in part, and the cases are remanded for further proceedings consistent with this opinion.

[The dissenting opinion of Justice **Douglas** on the issue of judicial immunity is omitted.]

NOTES

1. Is qualified immunity based on an inquiry into section 1983's legislative history? Is it based on policy considerations? Is it based on a combination of each?

2. Why is absolute immunity not applicable to police officers? Can the Court's absolute immunity cases be reconciled with *Pierson*?

3. What precisely is the challenged police conduct in *Pierson*?

4. State the two parts of *Pierson*'s qualified immunity test. What are the respective roles of judge and jury regarding each? For an early critique of the subjective part of *Pierson*'s qualified immunity test, *see* Theis, *"Good Faith" as a Defense to Suits for Police Deprivations of Individual Rights*, 59 Minn. R. Rev. 991 (1975).

5. Is *Pierson* an easy or hard case in which to find the police officers qualifiedly immune from damages liability?

6. Does *Pierson*'s two-part test govern only police officers—consider the use of the probable cause standard—or is it intended to be generally applicable?

B. A Note on the Application and Further Elaboration of the Two-Part Test to Governors, Mental Health Officials, Prison Officials and School Officials

After *Pierson*, the Court made clear that the two-part qualified immunity test applied to all those state and local government officials and employees not covered by absolute immunity. Thus, qualified immunity governed the conduct of governors, *Scheuer v. Rhodes*, 416 U.S. 232 (1974); mental health officials, *O'Connor v. Donaldson*, 422 U.S. 563 (1975); prison offi-

cials, *Procunier v. Navarette*, 434 U.S. 555 (1978); and school officials, *Wood v. Strickland*, 420 U.S. 308 (1975).

Wood v. Strickland is especially significant because it explicated the two-part test in considerable detail. The following extensive quote from *Wood* is set out because it is necessary for understanding the Supreme Court's later decision in *Harlow v. Fitzgerard*, which we consider next.

The official himself must be acting sincerely and with a belief that he is doing right, but an act violating a student's constitutional rights can be no more justified by *ignorance or disregard of settled, indisputable law* on the part of one entrusted with supervision of students' daily lives than by the presence of actual malice. To be entitled to a special exemption from the categorical remedial language of § 1983 in a case in which his action violated a student's constitutional rights, a school board member, who has voluntarily undertaken the task of supervising the operation of the school and the activities of the students, must be held to a standard of conduct based not only on permissible intentions, but also on *knowledge of the basic, unquestioned constitutional rights of his charges.* Such a standard imposes neither an unfair burden upon a person assuming a responsible public office requiring a high degree of intelligence and judgment for the proper fulfillment of its duties, nor an unwarranted burden in light of the value which civil rights have in our legal system. Any lesser standard would deny much of the promise of § 1983. Therefore, *in the specific context of school discipline, we hold that a school board member is not immune from liability for damages under § 1983 if he knew or reasonably should have known that the action he took within his sphere of official responsibility would violate the constitutional rights of the student affected, or if he took the action with the malicious intention to cause a deprivation of constitutional rights or other injury to the student.* That is not to say that school board members are "charged with predicting the future course of constitutional law." . . . A compensatory award will be appropriate only if the school board member has acted with such an impermissible motivation or with such disregard of the student's clearly established constitutional rights that his action cannot reasonably be characterized as being in good faith.

Wood v. Strickland, 420 U.S. at 321–22 (emphasis added).

1. Does *Wood* retain the two-part test of *Pierson*? Does *Wood* change it in any way?

2. What is the objective part of the qualified immunity inquiry after *Wood*?

3. What does the Court mean when it speaks of "settled, indisputable law?" Who determines this issue in litigation?

4. Does *Wood* in any sense impose a duty on the part of state and local government officials and employees to know the law? If so, isn't qualified immunity thereby made more pro-plaintiff?

5. What is the subjective part of the qualified immunity inquiry after *Wood*? What is the role of a defendant's actual knowledge? Of a defendant's "malicious intention?" Who determines this issue in litigation?

6. Suppose a defendant, pursuant to Rule 56 of the Federal Rules of Civil Procedure, moves for summary judgment based on *Wood's* qualified immunity test and persuades the court that he or she did not violate "settled, indisputable law." After *Wood*, is that defendant entitled to summary judgment? What more, if anything, must that defendant demonstrate in order to prevail on the motion for summary judgment? Is the defendant likely to be successful at this stage of the litigation? Why or why not?

7. Suppose the defendant's qualified immunity motion for summary judgment is denied. What happens next?

II. The Transformation of Qualified Immunity

A. *Harlow*

By far the most important qualified immunity case, at both the theoretical and practical levels, is *Harlow v. Fitzgerald*, 457 U.S. 800 (1982). *Harlow* and its progeny continue to generate a great deal of controversy and confusion.

Harlow v. Fitzgerald

457 U.S. 800 (1982)

Justice **Powell** delivered the opinion of the Court.

The issue in this case is the scope of the immunity available to the senior aides and advisers of the President of the United States in a suit for damages based upon their official acts.

I

In this suit for civil damages petitioners Bryce Harlow and Alexander Butterfield are alleged to have participated in a conspiracy to violate the constitutional and statutory rights of the respondent A. Ernest Fitzgerald. Respondent avers that petitioners entered the conspiracy in their capacities as senior White House aides to former President Richard M. Nixon. As the alleged conspiracy is the same as that involved in *Nixon v. Fitzgerald*, the facts need not be repeated in detail.

Respondent claims that Harlow joined the conspiracy in his role as the Presidential aide principally responsible for congressional relations. At the conclusion of discovery the supporting evidence remained inferential. As evidence of Harlow's conspiratorial activity respondent relies heavily on a series of conversations in which Harlow discussed Fitzgerald's dismissal with Air Force Secretary Robert Seamans. The other evidence most supportive of Fitzgerald's claims consists of a recorded conversation in which the President later voiced a tentative recollection that Harlow was "all for canning" Fitzgerald.

Disputing Fitzgerald's contentions, Harlow argues that exhaustive discovery has adduced no direct evidence of his involvement in any wrongful activity. He avers that Secretary Seamans advised him that considerations of efficiency required Fitzgerald's removal by a reduction in force, despite anticipated adverse congressional reaction. Harlow asserts he had no reason to believe that a conspiracy existed. He contends that he took all his actions in good faith.

* * *

Together with their codefendant Richard Nixon, petitioners Harlow and Butterfield moved for summary judgment on February

12, 1980. In denying the motion the District Court upheld the legal sufficiency of Fitzgerald's *Bivens* (*Bivens v. Six Unknown Fed. Narcotics Agents*) claim under the First Amendment and his "inferred" statutory causes of action under 5 U.S.C. § 7211 and 18 U.S.C. § 1505. The court found that genuine issues of disputed fact remained for resolution at trial. It also ruled that petitioners were not entitled to absolute immunity.

Independently of former President Nixon, petitioners invoked the collateral order doctrine and appealed the denial of their immunity defense to the Court of Appeals for the District of Columbia Circuit. The Court of Appeals dismissed the appeal without opinion. Never having determined the immunity available to the senior aides and advisers of the President of the United States, we granted certiorari.

II

As we reiterated today in *Nixon v. Fitzgerald*, our decisions consistently have held that government officials are entitled to some form of immunity from suits for damages. As recognized at common law, public officers require this protection to shield them from undue interference with their duties and from potentially disabling threats of liability.

Our decisions have recognized immunity defenses of two kinds. For officials whose special functions or constitutional status requires complete protection from suit, we have recognized the defense of "absolute immunity." The absolute immunity of legislators, in their legislative functions, and of judges, in their judicial functions, now is well settled. Our decisions also have extended absolute immunity to certain officials of the Executive Branch. These include prosecutors and similar officials, see *Butz v. Economou*, executive officers engaged in adjudicative functions, and the President of the United States, see *Nixon v. Fitzgerald*.

For executive officials in general, however, our cases make plain that qualified immunity represents the norm. In *Scheuer v. Rhodes*, we acknowledged that high officials require greater protection than those with less complex discretionary responsibilities. Nonetheless, we held that a governor and his aides could receive the requisite protection from qualified or good-faith immunity. In *Butz v. Economou*,

we extended the approach of *Scheuer* to high federal officials of the Executive Branch. Discussing in detail the considerations that also had underlain our decision in *Scheuer*, we explained that the recognition of a qualified immunity defense for high executives reflected an attempt to balance competing values: not only the importance of a damages remedy to protect the rights of citizens, but also "the need to protect officials who are required to exercise their discretion and the related public interest in encouraging the vigorous exercise of official authority." Without discounting the adverse consequences of denying high officials an absolute immunity from private lawsuits alleging constitutional violations—consequences found sufficient in *Spalding v. Vilas*, and *Barr v. Matteo*, to warrant extension to such officials of absolute immunity from suits at common law—we emphasized our expectation that insubstantial suits need not proceed to trial:

> "Insubstantial lawsuits can be quickly terminated by federal courts alert to the possibilities of artful pleading. Unless the complaint states a compensable claim for relief . . ., it should not survive a motion to dismiss. Moreover, the Court recognized in *Scheuer* that damages suits concerning constitutional violations need not proceed to trial, but can be terminated on a properly supported motion for summary judgment based on the defense of immunity. . . . In responding to such a motion, plaintiffs may not play dog in the manger; and firm application of the Federal Rules of Civil Procedure will ensure that federal officials are not harassed by frivolous lawsuits."

Butz continued to acknowledge that the special functions of some officials might require absolute immunity. But the Court held that "federal officials who seek absolute exemption from personal liability for unconstitutional conduct must bear the burden of showing that public policy requires an exemption of that scope." This we reaffirmed today in *Nixon v. Fitzgerald*.

III

A

Petitioners argue that they are entitled to a blanket protection of absolute immunity as an incident of their offices as Presidential aides.

In deciding this claim we do not write on an empty page. In *Butz v. Economou*, the Secretary of Agriculture—a Cabinet official directly accountable to the President—asserted a defense of absolute official immunity from suit for civil damages. We rejected his claim. In so doing we did not question the power or the importance of the Secretary's office. Nor did we doubt the importance to the President of loyal and efficient subordinates in executing his duties of office. Yet we found these factors, alone, to be insufficient to justify absolute immunity. "[The] greater power of [high] officials," we reasoned, "affords a greater potential for a regime of lawless conduct." Damages actions against high officials were therefore "an important means of vindicating constitutional guarantees." Moreover, we concluded that it would be "untenable to draw a distinction for purposes of immunity law between suits brought against state officials under [42 U.S.C.] § 1983 and suits brought directly under the Constitution against federal officials."

Having decided in *Butz* that Members of the Cabinet ordinarily enjoy only qualified immunity from suit, we conclude today that it would be equally untenable to hold absolute immunity an incident of the office of every Presidential subordinate based in the White House. Members of the Cabinet are direct subordinates of the President, frequently with greater responsibilities, both to the President and to the Nation, than White House staff. The considerations that supported our decision in *Butz* apply with equal force to this case. It is no disparagement of the offices held by petitioners to hold that Presidential aides, like Members of the Cabinet, generally are entitled only to a qualified immunity.

* * *

Even if they cannot establish that their official functions require absolute immunity, petitioners assert that public policy at least mandates an application of the qualified immunity standard that would permit the defeat of insubstantial claims without resort to trial. We agree.

A

The resolution of immunity questions inherently requires a balance between the evils inevitable in any available alternative. In situations of abuse of office, an action for damages may offer the only realistic avenue for vindication of constitutional guarantees. It is this recognition that has required the denial of absolute immunity to most public officers. At the same time, however, it cannot be disputed seriously that claims frequently run against the innocent as well as the guilty—at a cost not only to the defendant officials, but to society as a whole. These social costs include the expenses of litigation, the diversion of official energy from pressing public issues, and the deterrence of able citizens from acceptance of public office. Finally, there is the danger that fear of being sued will "dampen the ardor of all but the most resolute, or the most irresponsible [public officials], in the unflinching discharge of their duties." *Gregoire v. Biddle*.

In identifying qualified immunity as the best attainable accommodation of competing values, in *Butz*, as in *Scheuer*, we relied on the assumption that this standard would permit "[insubstantial] lawsuits [to] be quickly terminated." Yet petitioners advance persuasive arguments that the dismissal of insubstantial lawsuits without trial—a factor presupposed in the balance of competing interests struck by our prior cases—requires an adjustment of the "good faith" standard established by our decisions.

B

Qualified or "good faith" immunity is an affirmative defense that must be pleaded by a defendant official. Decisions of this Court have established that the "good faith" defense has both an "objective" and a "subjective" aspect. The objective element involves a presumptive knowledge of and respect for "basic, unquestioned constitutional rights." *Wood v. Strickland*. The subjective component refers to "permissible intentions." Characteristically, the Court has defined these elements by identifying the circumstances in which qualified immunity would not be available. Referring both to the objective and subjective elements, we have held that qualified immunity would be defeated if an official "knew or reasonably should have known that the action he took within his sphere of official responsibility would violate the constitutional rights of the [plaintiff], or if he took the action with the malicious intention to cause a deprivation of constitutional rights or other injury . . . ." .

The subjective element of the good-faith defense frequently has proved incompatible with our admonition in *Butz* that insubstantial claims should not proceed to trial. Rule 56 of the Federal Rules of Civil Procedure provides that disputed questions of fact ordinarily may not be decided on motions for summary judgment. And an official's subjective good faith has been considered to be a question of fact that some courts have regarded as inherently requiring resolution by a jury.

In the context of *Butz'* attempted balancing of competing values, it now is clear that substantial costs attend the litigation of the subjective good faith of government officials. Not only are there the general costs of subjecting officials to the risks of trial—distraction of officials from their governmental duties, inhibition of discretionary action, and deterrence of able people from public service. There are special costs to "subjective" inquiries of this kind. Immunity generally is available only to officials performing discretionary functions. In contrast with the thought processes accompanying "ministerial" tasks, the judgments surrounding discretionary action almost inevitably are influenced by the decisionmaker's experiences, values, and emotions. These variables explain in part why questions of subjective intent so rarely can be decided by summary judgment. Yet they also frame a background in which there often is no clear end to the relevant evidence. Judicial inquiry into subjective motivation therefore may entail broad-ranging discovery and the deposing of numerous persons, including an official's professional colleagues. Inquiries of this kind can be peculiarly disruptive of effective government.

Consistently with the balance at which we aimed in *Butz*, we conclude today that bare allegations of malice should not suffice to subject government officials either to the costs of trial or to the burdens of broad-reaching discovery. We therefore hold that government officials performing discretionary functions, generally are shielded from liability for civil damages insofar as their conduct does not violate clearly established statutory or constitutional rights of which a reasonable person would have known.[30]

Reliance on the objective reasonableness of an official's conduct, as measured by reference to clearly established law, should avoid excessive disruption of government and permit the resolution of many insubstantial claims on summary judgment. On summary judgment, the judge appropriately may determine, not only the currently applicable law, but whether that law was clearly established at the time an action occurred. If the law at that time was not clearly established, an official could not reasonably be expected to anticipate subsequent legal developments, nor could he fairly be said to "know" that the law forbade conduct not previously identified as unlawful. Until this threshold immunity question is resolved, discovery should not be allowed. If the law was clearly established, the immunity defense ordinarily should fail, since a reasonably competent public official should know the law governing his conduct. Nevertheless, if the official pleading the defense claims extraordinary circumstances and can prove that he neither knew nor should have known of the relevant legal standard, the defense should be sustained. But again, the defense would turn primarily on objective factors.

By defining the limits of qualified immunity essentially in objective terms, we provide no license to lawless conduct. The public interest in deterrence of unlawful conduct and in compensation of victims remains protected by a test that focuses on the objective legal reasonableness of an official's acts. Where an official could be expected to know that certain conduct would violate statutory or constitutional rights, he should be made to hesitate; and a person who suffers injury caused by such conduct may have a cause of action. But where an official's duties legitimately require action in which clearly established rights are not implicated, the public interest may be better served by action taken "with indepen-

[30] This case involves no issue concerning the elements of the immunity applicable to state officials sued for constitutional violations under 42 U.S.C. section 1983. We have found previously, however, that it would be "untenable to draw a distinction for purposes of immunity law between suits brought against state officials under section 1983 and suits brought directly under the constitution against federal officials."

dence and without fear of consequences." *Pierson v. Ray.*

* * *

V

The judgment of the Court of Appeals is vacated, and the case is remanded for further action consistent with this opinion.

Justice **Brennan**, with whom Justice **Marshall** and Justice **Blackmun** join, concurring.

I agree with the substantive standard announced by the Court today, imposing liability when a public-official defendant "knew or should have known" of the constitutionally violative effect of his actions. This standard would not allow the official who actually knows that he was violating the law to escape liability for his actions, even if he could not "reasonably have been expected" to know what he actually did know. Thus the clever and unusually well-informed violator of constitutional rights will not evade just punishment for his crimes. I also agree that this standard applies "across the board," to all "government officials performing discretionary functions." I write separately only to note that given this standard, it seems inescapable to me that some measure of discovery may sometimes be required to determine exactly what a public-official defendant did "know" at the time of his actions. In this respect the issue before us is very similar to that addressed in *Herbert v. Lando*, in which the Court observed that "[to] erect an impenetrable barrier to the plaintiff's use of such evidence on his side of the case is a matter of some substance, particularly when defendants themselves are prone to assert their [good faith] . . . .". Of course, as the Court has already noted, summary judgment will be readily available to public-official defendants whenever the state of the law was so ambiguous at the time of the alleged violation that it could not have been "known" then, and thus liability could not ensue. In my view, summary judgment will also be readily available whenever the plaintiff cannot prove, as a threshold matter, that a violation of his constitutional rights actually occurred. I see no reason why discovery of defendants' "knowledge" should not be deferred by the trial judge pending decision of any motion of defendants for summary judgment on grounds such as these.

[The various concurring and dissenting opinions of Justices **Brennan**, **Marshall**, **Blackmun**, and **Rehnquist**, and Chief Justice **Burger**, are omitted.]

NOTES

1. Is *Harlow* a section 1983 case? What difference does it make? Does the Court intend *Harlow* to govern section 1983 cases?

2. Does *Harlow* at all rely on section 1983's legislative history? If not, what is the decision based on?

3. Why does *Harlow* eliminate the subjective part of the qualified immunity test? After *Harlow*, is a defendant's state of mind ever relevant to qualified immunity?

4. What, if anything, does *Harlow* do to the objective part of the qualified immunity test? What does "objective reasonableness" mean? What is "clearly settled law?" Who decides and by what standards? Does the jury have any role in this determination?

5. After *Harlow*, does qualified immunity function more like absolute immunity than previously? If so, was this intentional?

6. What do you make of the Court's use of cost-benefit analysis as a justification for changing the qualified immunity test? How much weight does the Court give to society's interest in constitutional compliance? To the individual's interest in being compensated for constitutional harm? For the argument that *Harlow* overstates the costs of liability for constitutional violations, *see* Nahmod, 2 *Civil Rights and Civil Liberties Litigation: The Law of Section 1983* 112–14 (3d ed. 1991).

In general, does qualified immunity make sense from an economic perspective, or might enterprise liability be preferable? Is the typical government official likely to capture the benefits of exposing others to risks like the hypothetical reasonable private person in the usual common law torts situation? What effect does your answer have on the appropriate function of qualified immunity and its relation to overdeterrence? *See* Cass, *Damage Suits Against Public Officers*, 129 U. Pa. L. Rev. 1110 (1981), *reprinted in Section 1983 Anthology* 96.

7. After *Harlow*, what is the connection between discovery and qualified immunity? If discovery is ordinarily not to be allowed before the qualified immunity motion for summary judgment is disposed of, how is a plaintiff to develop evidence of material issues of fact in dispute within the meaning of Rule 56 of the Federal Rules of Civil Procedure so as to defeat the defendant's motion? Consider the following material on summary judgment practice.

B. A Note on *Celotex* and Summary Judgment Practice Under Rule 56

In *Celotex Corp v. Catrett*, 477 U.S. 317 (1986), the Supreme Court held that in cases where the nonmoving party will bear the burden of proof at trial on a dispositive issue, "a summary judgment motion may properly be made in reliance solely on the 'pleadings, depositions, answers to interrogatories, and admissions on file.' " Such a motion is properly supported, within the meaning of Rule 56(e) of the Federal Rules of Civil Procedure. The Court found "no express or implied requirement in Rule 56 that the moving party support its motion with affidavits or other similar materials *negating* the opponent's claim." It noted that, of course, the moving party "bears the initial responsibility of informing the district court of the basis for its motion. . . ." However, the moving party is not required to produce evidence showing the absence of a genuine issue of material fact regarding an issue as to which the nonmoving party will bear the burden of proof at trial. "Instead, . . . the burden on the moving party may be discharged by 'showing'—that is, by pointing out to the District Court—that there is an absence of evidence to support the nonmoving party's case."

Once the moving party does this, the burden shifts to the nonmoving party to designate "specific facts showing that there is a genuine issue for trial." The nonmoving party at this point may not rely merely on unsupported or conclusory allegations in his or her pleadings. If the nonmoving party does not demonstrate the existence of a genuine issue of material fact in dispute with respect to the disputed element of the party's case, summary judgment is appropriate.

1. As a general matter, does *Celotex* favor the moving or non-moving party?

2. More particularly, where a section 1983 defendant makes a qualified immunity summary judgment motion, does *Celotex* favor the plaintiff or the defendant?

C. *Anderson: Harlow* Modified?

After *Harlow*, it was clear that the reformulated qualified immunity test was designed to function as an immunity from suit, much like absolute immunity. However, important questions remained. One, adverted to earlier, was the matter of fairness to plaintiffs who were forced to defend against qualified immunity motions for summary judgment in advance of any discovery. Another was the meaning of "clearly settled law." From the perspective of plaintiffs, it is obviously preferable to describe clearly settled law as generally as possible. In contrast, it is obviously preferable from the perspective of defendants to insist on a case on all fours.

These and other matters are addressed in *Anderson v. Creighton*, one of the progeny of *Harlow*.

Anderson v. Creighton

483 U.S. 635 (1987)

Justice **Scalia** delivered the opinion of the Court.

The question presented is whether a federal law enforcement officer who participates in a search that violates the Fourth Amendment may be held personally liable for money damages if a reasonable officer could have believed that the search comported with the Fourth Amendment.

I

Petitioner Russell Anderson is an agent of the Federal Bureau of Investigation. On November 11, 1983, Anderson and other state and federal law enforcement officers conducted a warrantless search of the home of respondents, the Creighton family. The search was conducted because Anderson believed that

Vadaain Dixon, a man suspected of a bank robbery committed earlier that day, might be found there. He was not.

The Creightons later filed suit against Anderson in a Minnesota state court, asserting among other things a claim for money damages under the Fourth Amendment, see *Bivens v. Six Unknown Fed. Narcotics Agents*. After removing the suit to Federal District Court, Anderson filed a motion to dismiss or for summary judgment, arguing that the *Bivens* claim was barred by Anderson's qualified immunity from civil damages liability. See *Harlow v. Fitzgerald*. Before any discovery took place, the District Court granted summary judgment on the ground that the search was lawful, holding that the undisputed facts revealed that Anderson had had probable cause to search the Creighton's home and that his failure to obtain a warrant was justified by the presence of exigent circumstances. [On appeal, the Eighth Circuit reversed.]

* * *

II

When government officials abuse their offices, "action[s] for damages may offer the only realistic avenue for vindication of constitutional guarantees." *Harlow v. Fitzgerald*. On the other hand, permitting damages suits against government officials can entail substantial social costs, including the risk that fear of personal monetary liability and harassing litigation will unduly inhibit officials in the discharge of their duties. Our cases have accommodated these conflicting concerns by generally providing government officials performing discretionary functions with a qualified immunity, shielding them from civil damages liability as long as their actions could reasonably have been thought consistent with the rights they are alleged to have violated. See, e. g., *Malley v. Briggs* (qualified immunity protects "all but the plainly incompetent or those who knowingly violate the law") (police officers applying for warrants are immune if a reasonable officer could have believed that there was probable cause to support the application); *Mitchell v. Forsyth* (officials are immune unless "the law clearly proscribed the actions" they took). Somewhat more concretely, whether an official protected by qualified immunity may be held personally liable for an allegedly unlawful official action generally

turns on the "objective legal reasonableness" of the action, *Harlow*, assessed in light of the legal rules that were "clearly established" at the time it was taken.

The operation of this standard, however, depends substantially upon the level of generality at which the relevant "legal rule" is to be identified. For example, the right to due process of law is quite clearly established by the Due Process Clause, and thus there is a sense in which any action that violates that Clause (no matter how unclear it may be that the particular action is a violation) violates a clearly established right. Much the same could be said of any other constitutional or statutory violation. But if the test of "clearly established law" were to be applied at this level of generality, it would bear no relationship to the "objective legal reasonableness" that is the touchstone of *Harlow*. Plaintiffs would be able to convert the rule of qualified immunity that our cases plainly establish into a rule of virtually unqualified liability simply by alleging violation of extremely abstract rights. *Harlow* would be transformed from a guarantee of immunity into a rule of pleading. Such an approach, in sum, would destroy "the balance that our cases strike between the interests in vindication of citizens' constitutional rights and in public officials' effective performance of their duties," by making it impossible for officials "reasonably [to] anticipate when their conduct may give rise to liability for damages." *Davis v. Scherer*. It should not be surprising, therefore, that our cases establish that the right the official is alleged to have violated must have been "clearly established" in a more particularized, and hence more relevant, sense: The contours of the right must be sufficiently clear that a reasonable official would understand that what he is doing violates that right. This is not to say that an official action is protected by qualified immunity unless the very action in question has previously been held unlawful; but it is to say that in the light of pre-existing law the unlawfulness must be apparent.

Anderson contends that the Court of Appeals misapplied these principles. We agree. The Court of Appeals' brief discussion of qualified immunity consisted of little more than an assertion that a general right Anderson was alleged to have violated—the right to be free from warrantless searches of one's home unless the searching officers have probable cause and there are exigent circumstances—was clearly established. The Court of Appeals specifically refused to consider the argument that it was not clearly established that the circumstances with which Anderson was confronted did not constitute probable cause and exigent circumstances. The previous discussion should make clear that this refusal was erroneous. It simply does not follow immediately from the conclusion that it was firmly established that warrantless searches not supported by probable cause and exigent circumstances violate the Fourth Amendment that Anderson's search was objectively legally unreasonable. We have recognized that it is inevitable that law enforcement officials will in some cases reasonably but mistakenly conclude that probable cause is present, and we have indicated that in such cases those officials—like other officials who act in ways they reasonably believe to be lawful—should not be held personally liable. The same is true of their conclusions regarding exigent circumstances.

It follows from what we have said that the determination whether it was objectively legally reasonable to conclude that a given search was supported by probable cause or exigent circumstances will often require examination of the information possessed by the searching officials. But contrary to the Creightons' assertion, this does not reintroduce into qualified immunity analysis the inquiry into officials' subjective intent that *Harlow* sought to minimize. The relevant question in this case, for example, is the objective (albeit fact-specific) question whether a reasonable officer could have believed Anderson's warrantless search to be lawful, in light of clearly established law and the information the searching officers possessed. Anderson's subjective beliefs about the search are irrelevant.

The principles of qualified immunity that we reaffirm today require that Anderson be permitted to argue that he is entitled to summary judgment on the ground that, in light of the clearly established principles governing warrantless searches, he could, as a matter of law, reasonably have believed that the search of the Creightons' home was lawful.

* * *

The general rule of qualified immunity is intended to provide government officials with the ability "reasonably [to] anticipate when their conduct may give rise to liability for damages." *Davis v. Scherer*. Where that rule is applicable, officials can know that they will not be held personally liable as long as their actions are reasonable in light of current American law. That security would be utterly defeated if officials were unable to determine whether they were protected by the rule without entangling themselves in the vagaries of the English and American common law. We are unwilling to Balkanize the rule of qualified immunity by carving exceptions at the level of detail the Creightons propose. We therefore decline to make an exception to the general rule of qualified immunity for cases involving allegedly unlawful warrantless searches of innocent third parties' homes in search of fugitives.

For the reasons stated, we vacate the judgment of the Court of Appeals and remand the case for further proceedings consistent with this opinion.[6]

Justice **Stevens**, with whom Justice **Brennan** and Justice **Marshall** join, dissenting.

This case is beguiling in its apparent simplicity. The Court accordingly represents its task as the clarification of the settled principles of qualified immunity that apply in damages suits brought against federal officials. Its opinion, however, announces a new rule of

---

[6] Noting that no discovery has yet taken place, the Creightons renew their argument that, whatever the appropriate qualified immunity standard, some discovery would be required before Anderson's summary judgment motion could be granted. We think the matter somewhat more complicated. One of the purposes of the *Harlow* qualified immunity standard is to protect public officials from the "broad-ranging discovery" that can be "peculiarly disruptive of effective government." For this reason, we have emphasized that qualified immunity questions should be resolved at the earliest possible stage of a litigation. Thus, on remand, it should first be determined whether the actions the Creightons allege Anderson to have taken are actions that a reasonable officer could have believed lawful. If they are, then Anderson is entitled to dismissal prior to discovery. If they are not, and if the actions Anderson claims he took are different from those the Creightons allege (and are actions that a reasonable officer could have believed lawful), then discovery may be necessary before Anderson's motion for summary judgment on qualified immunity grounds can be resolved. Of course, any such discovery should be tailored specifically to the question of Anderson's qualified immunity.

law that protects federal agents who make forcible nighttime entries into the homes of innocent citizens without probable cause, without a warrant, and without any valid emergency justification for their warrantless search. The Court stunningly restricts the constitutional accountability of the police by creating a false dichotomy between police entitlement to summary judgment on immunity grounds and damages liability for every police misstep, by responding to this dichotomy with an uncritical application of the precedents of qualified immunity that we have developed for a quite different group of high public office holders, and by displaying remarkably little fidelity to the countervailing principles of individual liberty and privacy that infuse the Fourth Amendment. Before I turn to the Court's opinion, it is appropriate to identify the issue confronted by the Court of Appeals. It is now apparent that it was correct in vacating the District Court's award of summary judgment to petitioner in advance of discovery.

I

The Court of Appeals understood the principle of qualified immunity as implemented in *Harlow v. Fitzgerald*, to shield government officials performing discretionary functions from exposure to damages liability unless their conduct violated clearly established statutory or constitutional rights of which a reasonable person would have known. Applying this principle, the Court of Appeals held that respondents' Fourth Amendment rights and the "exigent circumstances" doctrine were "clearly established" at the time of the search. Moreover, apparently referring to the "extraordinary circumstances" defense left open in *Harlow* for a defendant who "can prove that he neither knew nor should have known of the relevant legal standard," the Court determined that petitioner could not reasonably have been unaware of these clearly established principles of law. Thus, in reviewing the Court of Appeals' judgment rejecting petitioner Anderson's claim to immunity, the first question to be decided is whether *Harlow v. Fitzgerald* requires immunity for a federal law enforcement agent who advances the fact-specific claim that a reasonable person in his position could have believed that his particular conduct would not violate rights that he

concedes are clearly established. A negative answer to that question is required, both because *Harlow* provides an inappropriate measure of immunity when police acts that violate the Fourth Amendment are challenged, and also because petitioner cannot make the showing required for *Harlow* immunity. Second, apart from the particular requirements of the *Harlow* doctrine, a full review of the Court of Appeals' judgment raises the question whether this Court should approve a double standard of reasonableness—the constitutional standard already embodied in the Fourth Amendment and an even more generous standard that protects any officer who reasonably could have believed that his conduct was constitutionally reasonable.

* * *

NOTES

1. What is the qualified immunity test after *Anderson*? How, if at all, is it different from that of *Harlow*?

2. How fact-specific is the clearly settled law inquiry after *Anderson*? Is a case on all fours now required? If not, what *is* required? Is the objective reasonableness standard of *Harlow* and *Anderson* unnecessarily defendant-protective? *See* Rudovsky, *The Qualified Immunity Doctrine in the Supreme Court: Judicial Activism and the Restriction of Constitutional Rights*, 138 U. Pa. L. Rev. 23 (1989).

3. If *Anderson* requires a fact-specific inquiry into what a reasonable officer could have believed about the constitutionality of his or her conduct, does this foreclose *any* inquiry into the defendant's state of mind? What if a defendant public official has superior knowledge? *See* Kinports, *Qualified Immunity in Section 1983 Cases: The Unanswered Questions*, 23 Ga. L. Rev. 597 (1989).

4. If *Anderson* requires a more fact-specific inquiry, what does this suggest about the viability of *Harlow*'s directive to the parties not to engage in any discovery until a defendant's qualified immunity summary judgment motion is dealt with?

5. In this connection, does *Anderson* permit any discovery after such a summary judgment motion is filed? If so, is it limited in any way?

6. On the qualified immunity merits, the question in *Anderson* was whether a reasonable police officer in the defendant's circumstances could have believed that he was violating the Fourth Amendment when he searched the plaintiffs' home without a warrant. The Fourth Amendment requires probable cause and exigent circumstances for such searches. Consider that probable cause calls for a threshold inquiry into whether the police officer reasonably believed that a crime was committed. Does it follow from *Anderson*, therefore, that a police officer gets "two bites" at the objective reasonableness apple: the first relating to the Fourth Amendment violation, and the second relating to qualified immunity?

Justice Stevens, dissenting in *Anderson*, must have meant this when he accused the majority of adopting a "double standard, explaining": "By double standard I mean a standard that affords a law enforcement official two layers of insulation from liability or other adverse consequences, such as suppression of evidence." *Anderson v. Creighton*, 483 U.S. at 659. But what is wrong with "two layers of insulation from liability?" Doesn't every defendant in a section 1983 case have both the possibility of prevailing on the merits and the possibility of prevailing on qualified immunity?

7. Conversely, are there situations where a finding that a defendant violated the plaintiff's constitutional rights is tantamount to a determination that the defendant violated clearly settled law because the constitutional rights violated were so well-settled? Can you think of any examples? Is racial discrimination one such case?

8. After *Anderson*, what are the respective roles of judge and jury regarding qualified immunity? Since *Anderson* requires a fact-specific inquiry, does it follow that the jury has a say in the qualified immunity outcome? *Should it have a role in deciding what clearly settled law is?* In deciding whether a reasonable official in the defendant's circumstances could have known that he or she was violating the plaintiff's constitutional rights? In deciding what in fact happened between the parties? See *Hunter v. Bryant*, discussed later in connection with the procedural aspects of qualified immunity.

9. Should a plaintiff bringing a section 1983 damages action against state or local government officials or employees in their individual capacities *ever* argue that his or her case raises an important constitutional issue of *first impression*? Is your answer different if the damages action is brought only against a local government? See Chapter 5 on local government liability.

D. *Siegert*: The Qualified Immunity Inquiry into the Merits of the Prima Facie Case

The qualified immunity inquiry with its focus on clearly settled law raises an important practical point. Courts can avoid deciding the constitutional merits of the cases before them by assuming *arguendo* that a constitutional violation has occurred and then ruling that the law was not clearly settled at the time of the challenged conduct. Indeed, after *Harlow* and *Anderson*, many courts did, and have continued to do, just that. If that's so, how, apart from dicta, prospective relief actions or criminal proceedings, are relevant constitutional law principles to become clearly settled? Does the Supreme Court's 1991 decision in *Siegert v. Gilley*, noted next, partly ameliorate this problem?

Siegert v. Gilley, 111 S. Ct. 1789 (1991), involved a substantive due process action brought under *Bivens v. Six Unknown Named Agents*, 403 U.S. 388 (1971), against a federal official who allegedly in bad faith wrote a highly unfavorable reference letter regarding the plaintiff. This letter cost the plaintiff the new job for which he was seeking to obtain the necessary credentials, as well as other federal service positions he thereafter sought. According to the District of Columbia Circuit, *which assumed a violation of the plaintiff's constitutional rights*, the plaintiff's allegation of subjective bad faith, which was an essential element of the constitutional claim, did not survive its heightened pleading standard of specific, direct evidence of illicit intent (and not merely circumstantial evidence). Such pleading was necessary, the District of Columbia Circuit maintained, to survive a defense motion to dismiss or for summary judgment based on qualified immunity.

The Supreme Court granted certiorari, apparently to deal with qualified immunity and its relation to the District of Columbia Circuit's heightened pleading standard. However, rather than resolving the case on this ground, the Court instead ruled that, assuming the allegations to be true, the plaintiff did not allege the violation of a constitutional right at all. It found that plaintiff had not alleged the deprivation of a liberty interest but only impairment of future employment opportunities. This was not a constitutional violation but at most the basis for a defamation action. Thus, plaintiff lost at an "analytically earlier stage of the inquiry into qualified immunity." The Court emphasized the importance of this inquiry in connection with the qualified immunity entitlement of government officials and employees not to stand trial or bear discovery-related burdens of litigation.

1. After *Siegert*, is it clear that courts should not necessarily assume violations of constitutional rights that are seriously questionable in order to get to the qualified immunity issues?

2. What is the concern of the Court in *Siegert*?

3. Is an inquiry into the merits of the prima facie case now an element of the qualified immunity inquiry?

4. Is the substantive due process result in *Siegert* consistent with the Court's view of substantive due process in other section 1983 contexts? Recall *Graham v. Connor*, addressed in Chapter 3.

III. The Clearly Settled Law Inquiry

A. What is Clearly Settled Law?

Anderson v. Creighton teaches that the clearly settled law inquiry must be made at a fairly fact-specific level but that a case on all fours is not required. But what *is* required? Obviously, courts exercise considerable discretion when they make the clearly settled law determination.

For example, the Third Circuit rejected a strict clearly settled law standard

in favor of a more flexible approach requiring some factual correspondence and demanding that officials apply well developed legal principles to the instant case . . . . The standard involves an

inquiry into the general legal principles governing analogous factual situations, if any, and a subsequent determination whether the official should have related this established law to the instant situation. This approach eliminates unexpected liability for public officials as well as prevents the occurrence of a mere "factual wrinkle" in an area of clearly established law from barring suit altogether.

Hicks v. Feeney, 770 F.2d 375, 379–80 (3rd Cir. 1985). In contrast, the Seventh Circuit cautioned:

We must be wary both of using hindsight to make an untidy body of case law seem clear and directive at the time the public official was called on to act, and of imagining that public officials have the training and experience in extracting legal rules from case law that appellate judges have.

Colaizzi v. Walker, 812 F.2d 304 (7th Cir. 1987).

Evaluate the following cases.

1. The plaintiff, a nine year old boy, sued a police officer for holding a gun to his head in a threatening manner while searching the boy's residence in 1989. Affirming the district court's denial of the defendant's qualified immunity motion to dismiss, the court observed that qualified immunity could be lost even in the absence of a case on point. There was a 1981 Third Circuit decision indicating that such unwarranted and unprovoked conduct shocked the conscience, and there had since been no case to the contrary. In addition, the Supreme Court's 1985 decision in *Tennessee v. Garner*, 471 U.S. 1 (1985), supported this determination. The court concluded: "It would create perverse incentives indeed if a qualified immunity defense could succeed against those types of claims that have not previously arisen because the behavior alleged is so egregious that no like case is on the books." *McDonald v. Haskins*, 966 F.2d 292 (7th Cir. 1992).

2. The plaintiff, a former assistant fire chief, alleged that he was demoted or constructively discharged in early 1988 because of his speech in violation of the First Amendment. The Sixth Circuit found that the defendant city officials were protected by qualified immunity. The court, which had ruled in a prior appeal that the

defendants violated the plaintiff's First Amendment rights, relied heavily on the fact that in that earlier appeal it had referred to "the current somewhat imprecise standard" dealing with speech of a public employee. The Sixth Circuit also observed that the district court in the same case had previously held that the plaintiff's speech was merely personal opinion and not a matter of public concern. *Meyers v. City of Cincinnati*, 979 F.2d 1154 (6th Cir. 1992).

Judge Ryan dissented in *Meyers. Id.* at 1157. He argued that the majority relied overmuch on its prior comment about imprecision in this area: "I believe the majority has mistaken the lack of clarity at the boundaries of the law for uncertainty regarding its very core." *Id.* at 1158. He also discounted the district court opinion which, he pointed out, the Sixth Circuit had readily reversed previously. Finally, he went through the relevant case law and determined that the plaintiff's speech was clearly of public concern in early 1988 and that the defendants had no significant fire-fighting interest that would outweigh the plaintiff's interest. Therefore, the defendants should have known that they were violating the plaintiff's First Amendment rights at that time.

3. In *Greenberg v. Kmetko*, 922 F.2d 382, 385 (7th Cir. 1991), a case involving clearly settled First Amendment law regarding balancing of the relevant interests in employee discharge-type cases, the Seventh Circuit stated:

> Principles of immunity relieve social service workers and other staffers from having to decide, at their financial peril, how judges will balance these interests in the years to come. Governmental employees must obey the law in force at the time but need not predict its evolution, need not know that in the fight between broad and narrow readings of a precedent the broad reading will become ascendent.

Judge Cudahy concurred, *id.* at 385, commenting: "[T]he facts [in such cases] are also important because the law of qualified immunity, as it has developed in this circuit, has tended to find qualified immunity in almost any case of first impression."

4. The plaintiff, a mandatory release parolee, sued prison officials under the Due Process Clause for conditioning his parole in November 1990 on a requirement that he have monthly injections of an antipsychotic drug. Ruling in favor of the defendants, the Seventh Circuit found qualified immunity applicable. Even though the Supreme Court had ruled sixth months earlier in *Washington v. Harper*, 494 US 210 (1990) that antipsychotic drugs could not be forcibly administered without certain procedural protections, that decision did not "speak directly of the actions of parole agents." The Seventh Circuit continued: "A parole agent or parole supervisor would not necessarily find [*Washington v. Harper*] to establish clearly the need for any procedural requirement prior to adding antipsychotic drug treatment as a condition of parole." *Felce v. Fiedler*, 974 F.2d 1484, 1501 (7th Cir. 1992).

B. Whose Decisions Determine Clearly Settled Law?

Apart from what constitutes clearly settled law, whose decisions are relevant to this determination? The easiest case is one in which there is a Supreme Court case on point. Also relatively easy is one in which the particular circuit has spoken definitively on the issue. If there is no circuit case law on the issue, then one would look to the district court case law in the forum state or specific district for a relevant case. If there is no relevant federal case law, the highest state appellate court of the forum state may have addressed the particular federal constitutional issue of concern.

The Sixth Circuit articulated the following guidelines:

> Our review of the Supreme Court's decisions and of our own precedents leads us to conclude that, in the ordinary instance, to find a clearly established constitutional right, a district court must find binding precedent by the Supreme Court, its court of appeals or itself. In an extraordinary case, it may be possible for the decisions of other courts to clearly establish a principle of law. For the decisions of other courts to provide such "clearly established Law," these decisions must both point unmistakably to the unconstitutionality of the conduct complained of and be so clearly foreshadowed by applicable direct authority as to leave no doubt in the mind of a reason-

able officer that his conduct, if challenged on constitutional grounds, would be found wanting . . . . [A] mere handful of decisions of other circuit and district courts, which are admittedly novel, cannot form the basis for a clearly established constitutional right in this circuit.

Ohio Civil Service Employees Assn. v. Seiter, 858 F.2d 1171, 1177–78 (6th Cir. 1988). Under these guidelines, how often do you think an "extraordinary case" will arise in which "the decisions of other courts" will establish clearly settled law?

Consider the following cases.

1. In *Gutierrez v. Municipal Court*, 838 F.2d 1031, 1049 (9th Cir. 1988), an Hispanic-American employee of a judicial department challenged an English-only rule for its employees. The court considered the defendant judges' qualified immunity arguments based on clearly settled law in March 1984, when the rule was adopted. The Ninth Circuit first found that there was no clearly settled law regarding the facial validity of the rule, despite the fact that in 1980 the EEOC had issued guidelines that English-speaking rules were presumed to be invalid in the absence of clear business necessity. What was determinative was the somewhat earlier decision of the Fifth Circuit upholding an English-speaking rule as well as the fact that the EEOC guidelines remained largely untested. The Ninth Circuit thus avoided deciding "whether, in the absence of decisional law, EEOC guidelines and decisions can constitute clearly established law." *Id.* at 1049.

2. In *Johnson-El v. Schoemehl*, 878 F.2d 1043, 1949 (8th Cir. 1989), the Eighth Circuit rejected the defendant prison officials' "per se rule" argument

that for the law to be law to be clearly established, the specific acts of these officials must be particularly proscribed by decisions rendered by this Circuit or another court with direct jurisdiction over the institution. This rule would enable a jail official to claim immunity where several other circuit, district or state courts had condemned similar practices on the basis of the federal constitution, so long as a Missouri court, or the district court for the Eastern District of Missouri or the Eighth Circuit had not yet done so.

3. Although the plaintiff newspaper and students succeeded in their First Amendment challenge to a university's antisolicitation regulation as applied to newspapers with commercials, the Fifth Circuit found that qualified immunity protected the individual defendants. The challenged regulation became effective on January 15, 1988, and shortly before that similar regulations of a different university had been upheld by a district court in the circuit. Even though the prior case may not have been correctly decided, it demonstrated that the defendants in this case did not violate clearly settled law when they enforced the challenged regulation. *Hays County Guardian v. Supple*, 969 F.2d 111 (5th Cir. 1992).

C. Are Some Constitutional Violations Automatically Violations of Clearly Settled Law as Well?

It is always important to keep the prima facie case distinct from affirmative defenses like absolute and qualified immunity. For example, the roles of court and jury will often depend on whether it is the prima facie case or immunities that are being addressed. Nevertheless, there are circumstances in which the prima facie case and qualified immunity are closely intertwined. Thus, we have already seen a Supreme Court case, *Siegert v. Gilley*, in which the Court made the question of the existence of a constitutional violation a part of the qualified immunity inquiry.

Such circumstances also include those cases where the constitutional right allegedly violated is so clearly settled in its application to wide-ranging fact situations that the finding of a constitutional violation in a particular case dictates a finding as a matter of law that the defendant violated clearly settled law as well. Racial discrimination cases involving equal protection violations are a good example, at least where the discrimination is directed against blacks. On the other hand, there may be constitutional violations so fact-dependent that violations of clearly settled law are hard to come by.

Consider the following cases.

1. The plaintiff inmate sued various prison officials alleging that they were deliberately indifferent to his medical needs in violation of his Eighth Amendment rights. The Ninth Circuit affirmed the district court's denial of summary judgment to three of the defendants, finding that there were material issues of fact in dispute. In the course of its discussion, the court, citing *Albers v. Whitley*, 743 F.2d 1372 (9th Cir. 1984), *revd on other grounds*, 475 U.S. 312 (1986), declared: "A finding of deliberate indifference necessarily precludes a finding of qualified immunity; prison officials who *deliberately* ignore the serious medical needs of inmates cannot claim that it was not apparent to a reasonable person that such actions violated the law." *Hamilton v. Endell*, 981 F.2d 1062, 1066 (9th Cir. 1992).

2. In *Street v. Parham*, 929 F.2d 537 (10th Cir. 1991), the plaintiff sued law enforcement officers alleging that excessive force had been used against him. The Tenth Circuit ruled that the district court erred in instructing the jury on qualified immunity after it had previously instructed the jury to consider whether the force used was reasonably necessary under the circumstances. The jury determined that the force used was in fact unreasonable but found for the defendants on qualified immunity grounds. According to the Tenth Circuit, the jury, in making the excessive force determination, effectively evaluated all of the aspects of an excessive force claim, including qualified immunity. This necessarily included a finding that there were no exculpatory extraordinary circumstances. The court concluded: "No officer could reasonably believe that the use of unreasonable force did not violate clearly settled law. . . . This is one of the rare instances where the determination of liability and the availability of qualified immunity depend on the same findings." *Id.* at 540.

3. Dealing with the clearly established law issue, the Seventh Circuit in *Benson v. Allphin*, 786 F.2d 268 (7th Cir. 1986), suggested that where the applicable constitutional rule itself involves a balancing of interests and is thus fact-dependent, then the facts of the case under consideration must closely correspond to the facts of the relevant case law in order to satisfy the clearly settled law requirement. It gave as examples the due process requirements applicable to government employee discharge cases and the First Amendment standards applicable to government employees. Using this approach, the Seventh Circuit ruled

that the conduct of the defendants in discharging the plaintiff in alleged violation of the First Amendment was protected by qualified immunity while other and later allegedly conspiratorial conduct was not.

4. The plaintiffs, white male owned contractors, challenged as violative of equal protection New York's law providing for minority business set-asides for wholly state-funded highway construction projects. Dealing with qualified immunity, the Second Circuit stated: "The question on which this defense hinges is whether it was clear even before [*City of Richmond v. J A Croson Co*, 488 U.S. 469 (1989)] that state affirmative action set-aside plans had to be narrowly tailored to a compelling government interest and that a record of prior discrimination within a locality was an absolute necessity before minority preferences could be implemented." Finding qualified immunity applicable to the defendants, state officials, the court ruled regarding their pre-*Croson* conduct that it was objectively reasonable for them to believe that their enforcement of New York's program was consistent with equal protection. As to the defendants' post-*Croson* conduct, they were similarly protected by qualified immunity. Although *Croson* mandated the applicability of strict scrutiny to such plans, their validity was to be determined on a case by case basis. For this reason the New York program would not have been regarded by reasonable state officials as clearly unconstitutional. *Harrison & Burrowes Bridge Constructors, Inc v. Cuomo*, 981 F.2d 50, 61 (2d Cir. 1992).

IV.   Procedural Aspects of Qualified Immunity

A.   A Note on Pleading

As we saw in Chapter 5, the unanimous opinion of the Supreme Court in *Leatherman v. Tarrant County*, 113 S. Ct 1160 (1993), which rejected a heightened pleading requirement in local government liability failure to train cases, appears to call into question the viability of the Fifth Circuit's heightened pleading requirement for individual liability cases as set out in *Elliott v. Perez*, 751 F.2d 472 (5th Cir. 1985). However, in *Burns-Toole v. Byrne*, 11 F.3d 1270 (5th Cir. 1994), a post-*Leatherman* case, the Fifth Circuit found no need to reexamine its heightened pleading requirement and to revisit *Elliott v. Perez* because in the case before it, the plaintiff had no evidentiary basis for her charges even "[u]nder the most generous standard applicable to a motion for summary judgment." *Id.* at 1275.

Leatherman is discussed in connection with local government liability in Chapter 5.

B. Burden of Proof and Clearly Settled Law

Elder v. Holloway, 975 F.2d 1388, 1390 (9th Cir. 1992), *superseding* 951 F.2d 1112 (9th Cir. 1991), *revd*, 114 S. Ct. 1019 (1994), raised this question:

> [W]hether a summary judgment on qualified immunity in favor of a law enforcement officer which was properly granted on the record presented to the district court, should nevertheless be reversed because there are legal authorities that plaintiff did not present to the district court or to us on appeal which suggest that, contrary to what the district court found, the law was clearly established at the time of the incident.

Answering in the negative, the Ninth Circuit ruled that because the plaintiff had what it called the "burden of proof" on this issue, the district court should be affirmed. It concluded: "We therefore hold that in opposing an official's request for judgment based on qualified immunity, the plaintiff's burden includes identifying the universe of relevant statutory or decisional law from which the court can determine whether the right allegedly violated was clearly established." 975 F.2d at 1393.

Thereafter, the Ninth Circuit denied the plaintiff's petition for rehearing and rejected the suggestion for rehearing en banc. Five judges vigorously dissented from the denial of the suggestion for rehearing in lengthy opinions by Judges Kozinski and Reinhardt. 984 F.2d 991 (9th Cir. 1993). Among other things, they argued that the panel decision "has taken quite an extraordinary step . . . [and] has held that in raising a pure question of law a party may rely on appeal only on those authorities which it cited to the district court." *Id* at 992. Judge

Reinhardt pointedly added: "[I]t is civil rights plaintiffs who once again are the object of hostile and discriminatory treatment by the federal courts." *Id* at 1000.

The Supreme Court unanimously reversed the Ninth Circuit in an opinion by Justice Ginsburg. *Elder v. Holloway*, 114 S. Ct 1019 (1994). It held that "appellate review of qualified immunity dispositions is to be conducted in light of all relevant precedent, not simply those cited to or discovered by the district court." *Id.* at 1021. It disagreed with the Ninth Circuit's characterization of the existence of clearly settled law as an issue of "legal facts"; rather, it was an issue of law to be reviewed *de novo* on appeal. The Court reasoned that the Ninth Circuit's approach did not aid in the primary purpose of qualified immunity—the protection of public officials from undue interference with their duties—"because its operation is unpredictable in advance of the district court's adjudication. Nor does the rule further the interests on the other side of the balance: deterring public officials' unlawful actions and compensating victims of such conduct." *Id.* at 1022–23.

1. Did *Elder* warrant the expenditure of these judicial resources in the Ninth Circuit and the Supreme Court? Isn't it a very easy case on the merits? After all, isn't the issue of the *existence* of clearly settled law an issue of law not implicating evidentiary considerations, and aren't such issues of law reviewable *de novo* on appeal unless waived at trial?

2. Is attorney error the real issue here? If so, does *Elder* cut only in favor of a *plaintiff* whose attorney failed at trial to submit relevant precedent showing the existence of clearly settled law? What if a *defendant* lost his qualified immunity summary judgment motion because his attorney erroneously failed to submit relevant precedent demonstrating that the law was *not* clearly settled? On appeal, may the defendant correct this error?

C. The Roles of Court and Jury in the Qualified Immunity Determination

The clear thrust of *Harlow* and its progeny is to encourage courts to decide the qualified immunity issue as quickly as possible so as to spare defendants the need to defend. This raises important questions about the respective roles of court and jury in the qualified immunity determination. Surely the court decides whether there is case law relevant to the clearly settled law inquiry. After all, the jury has no expertise about such legal matters. But what of the question, especially crucial after the Supreme Court's decision in *Anderson v. Creighton*, of whether a reasonable officer in the defendant's position could have known that he or she was violating clearly settled law? Does the jury have any role here?

Hunter v. Bryant

112 S.Ct. 534 (1991)

Per Curiam.

On May 3, 1985, respondent James v. Bryant delivered two photocopies of a handwritten letter to two administrative offices at the University of Southern California. The rambling letter referred to a plot to assassinate President Ronald Reagan by "Mr. Image," who was described as "Communist white men within the National Council of Churches." The letter stated that "Mr. Image wants to murder President Reagan on his up and coming trip to Germany," that "Mr. Image had conspired with a large number of U.S. officials in the plot to murder President Reagan" and others, and that "Mr. Image (NCC) still plans on murdering the President on his trip to Germany in May, 1985." President Reagan was traveling in Germany at the time.

A campus police sergeant telephoned the Secret Service, and agent Brian Hunter responded to the call. After reading the letter, agent Hunter interviewed University employees. One identified James Bryant as the man who had delivered the letter and reported that Bryant had "told her 'he should have been assassinated in Bonn.'" Another employee said that the man who delivered the letter made statements about "'bloody coups'" and "'assassination,'" and said something about "'across the throat'" while moving his hand horizontally across his throat to simulate a cutting action.

Hunter and another Secret Service agent, Jeffrey Jordan, then visited a local address

that appeared on the letter. Bryant came to the door and gave the agents permission to enter. He admitted writing and delivering the letter, but refused to identify "'Mr. Image'" and answered questions about "'Mr. Image'" in a rambling fashion. Bryant gave Hunter permission to search the apartment, and the agent found the original of the letter. While the search was underway, Jordan continued questioning Bryant, who refused to answer questions about his feelings toward the President or to state whether he intended to harm the President.

Hunter and Jordan arrested Bryant for making threats against the President, in violation of 18 U.S.C. § 871(a). Bryant was arraigned and held without bond until May 17, 1985, when the criminal complaint was dismissed on the Government's motion.

Bryant subsequently sued agents Hunter and Jordan, the United States Department of the Treasury, and the Director of the Secret Service, seeking recovery under the Federal Tort Claims Act and alleging that the agents had violated his rights under the Fourth, Fifth, Sixth, and Fourteenth Amendments. See *Bivens v. Six Unknown Fed. Narcotics Agents*. The District Court dismissed all defendants other than agents Hunter and Jordan and all causes of action other than Bryant's Fourth Amendment claims for arrest without probable cause and without a warrant. The court denied the agents' motion for summary judgment on qualified immunity grounds.

On appeal, a Ninth Circuit panel held that the agents were entitled to qualified immunity for arresting Bryant without a warrant because, at that time, the warrant requirement was not clearly established for situations in which the arrestee had consented to the agents' entry into a residence.

However, the panel divided on the question of whether the agents were entitled to immunity on the claim that they had arrested Bryant without probable cause. The majority concluded that the agents had failed to sustain the burden of establishing qualified immunity because their reason for arresting Bryant— their belief that the "'Mr. Image'" plotting to kill the President in Bryant's letter could be a pseudonym for Bryant—was not the most reasonable reading of Bryant's letter:

"Even accepting the 'alter ego' theory that by warning what Mr. Image was going to do, Mr. Bryant was in fact communicating what he himself planned to do, the letter read in its entirety does not appear to make a threat against the president. Most of the letter does not even talk about President Reagan. A more reasonable interpretation of the letter might be that Bryant was trying to convince people of the danger Mr. Image and the conspiracy posed rather than that Bryant was speaking through Mr. Image."

Our cases establish that qualified immunity shields agents Hunter and Jordan from suit for damages if "a reasonable officer could have believed [Bryant's arrest] to be lawful, in light of clearly established law and the information the [arresting] officers possessed." *Anderson v. Creighton.* Even law enforcement officials who "reasonably but mistakenly conclude that probable cause is present" are entitled to immunity. Moreover, because "the entitlement is an immunity from suit rather than a mere defense to liability," *Mitchell v. Forsyth,* we repeatedly have stressed the importance of resolving immunity questions at the earliest possible stage in litigation.

The decision of the Ninth Circuit ignores the import of these decisions. The Court of Appeals' confusion is evident from its statement that "whether a reasonable officer could have believed he had probable cause is a question for the trier of fact, and summary judgment . . . based on lack of probable cause is proper only if there is only one reasonable conclusion a jury could reach." This statement of law is wrong for two reasons. First, it routinely places the question of immunity in the hands of the jury. Immunity ordinarily should be decided by the court long before trial. See *Mitchell.* Second, the court should ask whether the agents acted reasonably under settled law in the circumstances, not whether another reasonable, or more reasonable, interpretation of the events can be constructed five years after the fact.

Under settled law, Secret Service agents Hunter and Jordan are entitled to immunity if a reasonable officer could have believed that probable cause existed to arrest Bryant. Probable cause existed if "at the moment the arrest was made . . . the facts and circumstances within their knowledge and of which they had

reasonably trustworthy information were sufficient to warrant a prudent man in believing" that Bryant had violated 18 U.S.C. § 871.

When agents Hunter and Jordan arrested Bryant, they possessed trustworthy information that Bryant had written a letter containing references to an assassination scheme directed against the President, that Bryant was cognizant of the President's whereabouts, that Bryant had made an oral statement that "'he should have been assassinated in Bonn,'" and that Bryant refused to answer questions about whether he intended to harm the President. On the basis of this information, a magistrate ordered Bryant to be held without bond.

These undisputed facts establish that the Secret Service agents are entitled to qualified immunity. Even if we assumed, arguendo, that they (and the magistrate) erred in concluding that probable cause existed to arrest Bryant, the agents nevertheless would be entitled to qualified immunity because their decision was reasonable, even if mistaken.

The qualified immunity standard "gives ample room for mistaken judgments" by protecting "all but the plainly incompetent or those who knowingly violate the law." *Malley v. Briggs.* This accommodation for reasonable error exists because "officials should not err always on the side of caution" because they fear being sued. *Davis.* Our national experience has taught that this principle is nowhere more important than when the specter of Presidential assassination is raised.

The petition for a writ of certiorari is granted, the judgment of the Court of Appeals is reversed, and the case is remanded for further proceedings consistent with this opinion.

It is so ordered.

* * *

Justice **Scalia**, concurring in the judgment.

In my view the Ninth Circuit's opinion purported to apply the standard for summary judgment that today's opinion demands. Its error was in finding, on the facts before it, that the standard was not met. Since I think it worthwhile to establish that this Court will not let such a mistake stand with respect to those who guard the life of the President, I concur in the summary reversal.

Justice **Stevens**, dissenting.

The question in this case is not whether a reasonable officer could have believed that respondent posed a threat to the life of the President. Those "who guard the life of the President,", properly rely on the slightest bits of evidence—nothing more than hunches or suspicion—in taking precautions to avoid the ever-present danger of assassination. Mere suspicion is obviously a sufficient justification for a host of protective measures such as, for example, careful surveillance of a person like respondent. The question that is presented, however, is whether a reasonable trained law enforcement officer could have concluded that the evidence available to petitioners at the time they arrested respondent constituted probable cause to believe that he had committed the crime of threatening the life of President Reagan.

* * *

The District Court denied the petitioners' motion for summary judgment seeking dismissal on the ground of qualified immunity because it decided that further fact finding was necessary. On such a motion, the court was of course required to resolve any disputed question of fact against the moving parties. In my opinion the Court of Appeals correctly stated the governing standards when it wrote:

"Qualified immunity is an affirmative defense for which the government official bears the burden of proof. As with all summary judgment motions, the evidence should be viewed in the light most favorable to Bryant as the nonmoving party; to prevail on their motion for summary judgment, the defendants must show that they were reasonable in their belief that they had probable cause. Bryant, however, bears the burden of proving that the right which the defendants allegedly violated was clearly established at the time of their conduct. . . .

". . . In order for a secret service agent reasonably to have believed he had cause to arrest Bryant, the agent must have been reasonable in his belief that Bryant's words and the context in which he delivered them were a serious threat against the president.

"Whether a reasonable officer could have believed he had probable cause is a question for the trier of fact, and summary judgment or a directed verdict in a § 1983 action based on lack of probable cause is proper only if there is only one reasonable conclusion a jury could reach. Because qualified immunity protects government officials from suit as well as from liability, it is essential that qualified immunity claims be resolved at the earliest possible stage of litigation. This necessarily expands the factfinding role that must be played by the district court judge. In some cases, district courts will be able to establish entitlement to qualified immunity before trial and, sometimes, even before discovery. . . . In some cases, however, further development of the record will be necessary. In this case it was proper for the court to require further development of the facts to determine whether the secret service reasonably could have interpreted the letter as violating § 871."

Like JUSTICE SCALIA, I am satisfied that the Court of Appeals applied the correct legal standard when it affirmed the District Court's refusal to grant summary judgment in favor of petitioners. When the Court of Appeals opinion is read in its entirety, that conclusion is inescapable. Unlike JUSTICE SCALIA, however, I am also satisfied that when the proper legal standards are applied to this record, with the evidence examined in the light most favorable to the nonmoving party, petitioners have not yet established that a reasonable officer could have concluded that he had sufficient evidence to support a finding of probable cause at the time of respondent's arrest. I also think it unwise for this Court, on the basis of its de novo review of a question of fact, to reject a determination on which both the District Court and the Court of Appeals agreed.

Accordingly, I respectfully dissent.

Justice **Kennedy**, dissenting.

Petitioners in this case are agents of the Secret Service. Among the questions presented are the proper interpretation of 18 U.S.C. § 871(a), which prohibits mail threats against the President, and the proper standard for summary judgment on grounds of qualified immunity. Whether implied or expressed, our resolution of these questions will be parsed by the Service and by later courts. The importance of these questions suggests that we should not dispose of them in summary fashion.

For the reasons stated in today's per curiam opinion and in the dissent by Judge Trott in the Court of Appeals, I must agree that the holding of the Court of Appeals is open to serious question. The majority opinion of that court seems not to have considered all of the facts on which the agents relied, in particular the statements made by Bryant and his responses (or non-responses) to the agents' questions. This calls in question its determination that qualified immunity has not been established on summary judgment.

To reverse in this case, however, the Court considers an issue on which some doubt has been expressed, which is whether the Court of Appeals applied the correct legal standard to resolve the qualified immunity issue on summary judgment. Two members of the Court disagree with the statement in the per curiam opinion that the Court of Appeals misstated the law. Given this disagreement, as well as the precedential weight that later courts will accord to all of the questions presented in the case and addressed here in express terms or by clear implication, the case does not lend itself to summary disposition. I would set the case for full briefing and oral argument.

For these reasons, I dissent from the judgment of summary reversal in this case.

[Justice **Thomas** did not participate.]

NOTES

1. Why should it be the court and not the jury that decides whether a reasonable officer in the defendant's position could have known that he or she was violating clearly settled law? After all, couldn't the court instruct the jury as to what the settled law was and then leave it to the jury to decide what a reasonable officer could have known? Isn't this the kind of thing that is done in the ordinary negligence case, for example? Why should section 1983 and qualified immunity be any different?

2. What if the court denies a qualified immunity summary judgment motion on the ground that there are material issues of fact in dispute? Does this now give the jury a role?

3. What is really at stake in *Hunter*? Is the issue one of judicial control? For a thoughtful pre-*Hunter* analysis, *see* Note, *Qualified Immunity and Allocation of Decision-Making Functions Between Judge and Jury?* 90 *Colum. L. Rev.* 1045 (1990).

4. In *Mahoney v. Kesery*, 976 F.2d 1054 (7th Cir. 1992), the Seventh Circuit dealt with a pre-*Hunter* Fourth Amendment unlawful arrest case in which it stated that the issue of immunity and the issue on the merits was the same—probable cause. It suggested that the qualified immunity question was not whether the defendant police officer had probable cause to think he had probable cause because, after all, "probable cause [was not] independent of what the arresting officer could reasonably have known." *Id.* at 1057. The court next went on to discuss whether in such cases the determination of immunity should be postponed until the trial on the merits at which time the judge would render his own immunity decision (which was done in this case) or whether the jury should decide the issue. After considering the pro's and con's and characterizing the matter as "a fearful tangle," *id.* at 1059, the Seventh Circuit concluded that it did not have to resolve the issue because here both the judge and the jury had decided the key issue—probable cause—against the defendant. Finally, in upholding the jury's verdict for the plaintiff, the court reviewed the determination of probable cause *as a factual matter* under the clear error standard.

Does *Hunter* now clear up this "fearful tangle?"

5. In a pre-*Hunter* case where the plaintiff sued corrections officers for firing him in alleged violation of his First Amendment rights, the Eleventh Circuit overturned jury verdicts for two defendants because the district court improperly submitted qualified immunity to the jury. The jury was told to determine whether the defendants violated clearly settled law and, if so, to decide further whether a reasonable person in their position would have known it. This was not harmless error because there was a general verdict. The Eleventh Circuit went on to instruct that where a district court concludes that defendants are not entitled to qualified immunity, the jury should get the case without any reference to qualified immunity. However, "[i]f there are disputed issues of fact concerning qualified immunity that must be resolved by a full trial and which the district court determines that the jury should resolve, special interrogatories would be appropriate." *Stone v. Peacock*, 968 F.2d 1163, 1166 (11th Cir. 1992).

Does *Stone* present a workable qualified immunity procedure for both court and jury? Under *Stone*, who decides whether there was clearly settled law? Who decides whether a reasonable officer in the defendant's position should have known he or she was violating clearly settled law? Who decides material issues of fact in dispute?

6. Reacting to the Supreme Court's decision in *Hunter v. Bryant*, the Ninth Circuit reversed the district court's ruling that whether the defendant federal marshalls' decision to strip search the plaintiff protesters in alleged violation of the Fourth Amendment was reasonable was for the jury. The district court had already ruled for qualified immunity purposes that the law governing strip searches was clearly settled but left the reasonableness question to the jury. The Ninth Circuit read *Hunter* as expressly rejecting what the district court had done. Thus, the question "whether the officer could reasonably have believed he was acting properly in light of clearly established law" was for the trial court alone. *Act Up!/Portland v. Bagley*, 971 F.2d 298, 301 (9th Cir. 1992), *superseded* 988 F.2d 868 (9th Cir. 1993).

Thereafter in *Act Up*, the Ninth Circuit reaffirmed this view in an opinion superseding the earlier one. *Act Up!/Portland v. Bagley*, 988 F.2d 868 (9th Cir. 1993), *superseding* 971 F.2d 298 (9th Cir. 1992). It stated, in reliance on *Hunter*, that it was remanding the case

> to determine whether there exists a genuine issue of material fact underlying the qualified immunity question. If, as appears from the record before us, there is no such issue, then the court should determine whether a reasonable officer in Appellants' position could have thought that the circumstances gave rise to individualized reasonable suspicion that Appellees were carrying contraband, and if so, whether a reasonable officer in Appellants' position could have thought that the manner in which they were searched complied with *Vaughan [v. Ricketts*, 859 F.2d 736 (9th Cir. 1988)]. If, and only if, it answers either of these questions in the negative, the case should go to the jury to

> determine whether the searches violated the Fourth Amendment or, if summary judgment on that issue is appropriate, damages. If the court finds that a genuine issue of underlying fact does exist, it should postpone the qualified immunity determination until the facts have been determined at trial.

988 F.2d at 873–74.

Judge Norris dissented at length in *Act Up* from the failure of the Ninth Circuit to hear the case en banc. *Id* at 874. He argued that the court had misread *Hunter*, a case decided without briefs or argument, as overruling the qualified immunity law of a majority of the circuits. Among many points he maintained that *Act Up* "divides the decision-making process between judge and jury in such a way that will cause procedural nightmares for district judges and civil rights litigants." He also accused the Ninth Circuit of reading *Hunter* "in a way that attributes to the [Supreme] Court an act of judicial arrogance and, indeed, irresponsiblity. The Supreme Court rarely, if ever, makes new law in summary reversals, and it did not do so in *Hunter*." *Id*. He further contended that *Hunter* itself had contributed to this misreading by the Ninth Circuit: "*Hunter* is hardly a model of clarity." *Id*. at 882.

Is Judge Norris correct?

D. Interlocutory Appeals and *Mitchell*

As we have seen, qualified immunity has been transformed by the Supreme Court into the virtual equivalent of absolute immunity. Like absolute immunity, qualified immunity often protects a defendant from having to stand trial at all. This aspect of qualified immunity is exemplified in the emphasis of *Harlow* and its progeny on the primary role of the court in the qualified immunity determination, and by an insistence that the qualified immunity determination take place before discovery which, if it is permitted at all, must be limited to the qualified immunity issue. As it turns out, this aspect of qualified immunity is also reflected in the Supreme Court's important immunity-interlocutory appeal decision in *Mitchell v. Forsyth*, 472 U.S. 511 (1985).

Mitchell v. Forsyth

472 U.S. 511 (1985)

Justice **White** delivered the opinion of the Court.

This is a suit for damages stemming from a warrantless wiretap authorized by petitioner, a former Attorney General of the United States. The case presents three issues: whether the Attorney General is absolutely immune from suit for actions undertaken in the interest of national security; if not, whether the District Court's finding that petitioner is not immune from suit for his actions under the qualified immunity standard of *Harlow v. Fitzgerald* is appealable; and, if so, whether the District Court's ruling on qualified immunity was correct.

[As to the first issue, the Court found qualified immunity, not absolute immunity, applicable.]

* * *

III

Although 28 U.S.C. § 1291 vests the courts of appeals with jurisdiction over appeals only from "final decisions" of the district courts, "a decision 'final' within the meaning of § 1291 does not necessarily mean the last order possible to be made in a case." *Gillespie v. United States Steel Corp.* Thus, a decision of a district court is appealable if it falls within "that small class which finally determine claims of right separable from, and collateral to, rights asserted in the action, too important to be denied review and too independent of the cause itself to require that appellate consideration be deferred until the whole case is adjudicated." *Cohen v. Beneficial Industrial Loan Corp.*.

A major characteristic of the denial or granting of a claim appealable under *Cohen's* "collateral order" doctrine is that "unless it can be reviewed before [the proceedings terminate], it never can be reviewed at all." *Stack v. Boyle.* When a district court has denied a defendant's claim of right not to stand trial, on double jeopardy grounds, for example, we have consistently held the court's decision appealable, for such a right cannot be effectively vindicated after the trial has occurred. Thus, the denial of a substantial claim of absolute immunity is an order appealable before final judgment, for the essence of absolute immunity is its possessor's entitlement not to have to answer for his conduct in a civil damages action.

At the heart of the issue before us is the question whether qualified immunity shares this essential attribute of absolute immunity—whether qualified immunity is in fact an entitlement not to stand trial under certain circumstances. The conception animating the qualified immunity doctrine as set forth in *Harlow v. Fitzgerald*, is that "where an official's duties legitimately require action in which clearly established rights are not implicated, the public interest may be better served by action taken 'with independence and without fear of consequences.'". As the citation to *Pierson v. Ray* makes clear, the "consequences" with which we were concerned in *Harlow* are not limited to liability for money damages; they also include "the general costs of subjecting officials to the risks of trial—distraction of officials from their governmental duties, inhibition of discretionary action, and deterrence of able people from public service." *Harlow*. Indeed, *Harlow* emphasizes that even such pretrial matters as discovery are to be avoided if possible, as "[inquiries] of this kind can be peculiarly disruptive of effective government."

With these concerns in mind, the *Harlow* Court refashioned the qualified immunity doctrine in such a way as to "permit the resolution of many insubstantial claims on summary judgment" and to avoid "[subjecting] government officials either to the costs of trial or to the burdens of broad-reaching discovery" in cases where the legal norms the officials are alleged to have violated were not clearly established at the time. Unless the plaintiff's allegations state a claim of violation of clearly established law, a defendant pleading qualified immunity is entitled to dismissal before the commencement of discovery. Even if the plaintiff's complaint adequately alleges the commission of acts that violated clearly established law, the defendant is entitled to summary judgment if discovery fails to uncover evidence sufficient to create a genuine issue as to whether the defendant in fact committed those acts. *Harlow* thus recognized an entitlement not to stand trial or face the other burdens of litigation, conditioned on the resolution of the essentially legal question whether the conduct of which the plaintiff complains violated clearly established law. The entitlement is an immunity from suit rather than a mere defense to liability; and like an absolute immunity, it is effectively lost if a case is erroneously permitted to go to trial. Accordingly, the reasoning that underlies the immediate appealability of an order denying absolute immunity indicates to us that the denial of qualified immunity should be similarly appealable: in each case, the district court's decision is effectively unreviewable on appeal from a final judgment.

An appealable interlocutory decision must satisfy two additional criteria: it must "conclusively determine the disputed question," *Coopers & Lybrand v. Livesay,* and that question must involve a "[claim] of right separable from, and collateral to, rights asserted in the action," *Cohen.* The denial of a defendant's motion for dismissal or summary judgment on the ground of qualified immunity easily meets these requirements. Such a decision is "conclusive" in either of two respects. In some cases, it may represent the trial court's conclusion that even if the facts are as asserted by the defendant, the defendant's actions violated clearly established law and are therefore not within the scope of the qualified immunity. In such a case, there will be nothing in the subsequent course of the proceedings in the district court that can alter the court's conclusion that the defendant is not immune. Alternatively, the trial judge may rule only that if the facts are as asserted by the plaintiff, the defendant is not immune. At trial, the plaintiff may not succeed in proving his version of the facts, and the defendant may thus escape liability. Even so, the court's denial of summary judgment finally and conclusively determines the defendant's claim of right not to stand trial on the plaintiff's allegations, and because "[there] are simply no further steps that can be taken in the District Court to avoid the trial the defendant maintains is barred," it is apparent that "*Cohen's* threshold requirement of a fully consummated decision is satisfied" in such a case. *Abney v. United States.*

Similarly, it follows from the recognition that qualified immunity is in part an entitlement not to be forced to litigate the consequences of official conduct that a claim of immunity is conceptually distinct from the merits of the plaintiff's claim that his rights have been violated. An appellate court reviewing the denial of the defendant's claim of immunity need not consider the correctness of the plaintiff's version of the facts, nor even determine whether the plaintiff's allegations actually state a claim. All it need determine is a question of law: whether the legal norms allegedly violated by the defendant were clearly established at the time of the challenged actions or, in cases where the district court has denied summary judgment for the defendant on the ground that even under the defendant's version of the facts the defendant's conduct violated clearly established law, whether the law clearly proscribed the actions the defendant claims he took. To be sure, the resolution of these legal issues will entail consideration of the factual allegations that make up the plaintiff's claim for relief; the same is true, however, when a court must consider whether a prosecution is barred by a claim of former jeopardy or whether a Congressman is absolutely immune from suit because the complained of conduct falls within the protections of the Speech and Debate Clause. In the case of a double jeopardy claim, the court must compare the facts alleged in the second indictment with those in the first to determine whether the prosecutions are for the same offense, while in evaluating a claim of immunity under the Speech and Debate Clause, a court must analyze the plaintiff's complaint to determine whether the plaintiff seeks to hold a Congressman liable for protected legislative actions or for other, unprotected conduct. In holding these and similar issues of absolute immunity to be appealable under the collateral order doctrine, the Court has recognized that a question of immunity is separate from the merits of the underlying action for purposes of the *Cohen* test even though a reviewing court must consider the plaintiff's factual allegations in resolving the immunity issue.

Accordingly, we hold that a district court's denial of a claim of qualified immunity, to the extent that it turns on an issue of law, is an appealable "final decision" within the meaning of 28 U.S.C. § 1291 notwithstanding the absence of a final judgment.

IV

The Court of Appeals thus had jurisdiction over Mitchell's claim of qualified immunity, and that question was one of the questions presented in the petition for certiorari which we granted without limitation. Moreover, the purely legal question on which Mitchell's claim of immunity turns is "appropriate for our immediate resolution" notwithstanding that it was not addressed by the Court of Appeals. We therefore turn our attention to the merits of Mitchell's claim of immunity.

Under *Harlow v. Fitzgerald*, Mitchell is immune unless his actions violated clearly established law. Forsyth complains that in November 1970, Mitchell authorized a warrantless wiretap aimed at gathering intelligence regarding a domestic threat to national security—the kind of wiretap that the Court subsequently declared to be illegal. The question of Mitchell's immunity turns on whether it was clearly established in November 1970, well over a year before *Keith* was decided, that such wiretaps were unconstitutional. We conclude that it was not.

* * *

V

We affirm the Court of Appeals' denial of Mitchell's claim to absolute immunity. The court erred, however, in declining to accept jurisdiction over the question of qualified immunity; and to the extent that the effect of the judgment of the Court of Appeals is to leave standing the District Court's erroneous decision that Mitchell is not entitled to summary judgment on the ground of qualified immunity, the judgment of the Court of Appeals is reversed.

[The various concurring and dissenting opinions of Chief Justice **Burger**, Justices **O'Connor**, **Stevens**, **Brennan** and **Marshall** are omitted; Justices **Powell** and **Rehnquist** did not participate.]

NOTES

1. Does immunity fit comfortably within *Cohen*'s collateral order doctrine or does the Court strain to put it there?

2. Is *Mitchell* based on statutory interpretation? Is it a policy construct? Is it both?

3. Is *Mitchell* substantive or procedural? Does it only govern proceedings in federal courts, or does it govern state court proceed-

ings as well by virtue of the Supremacy Clause? Compare *Anderson v. City of Hopkins*, 393 N.W.2d 363 (Minn. 1986) (following *Mitchell*) and *Klindtworth v. Burkett*, 477 N.W. 2d 176 (N.D. 1991) (holding that *Mitchell* does not govern). See Chapter 11 on section 1983 state court actions.

4. Is the qualified immunity result in *Mitchell* consistent with the fact-specific approach of *Anderson v. Creighton*?

5. What happens to the district court's jurisdiction over the section 1983 claim against an individual defendant who files a notice of appeal from the denial of a qualified immunity motion for summary judgment? See *Apostol v. Gallion*, 870 F.2d 1335 (7th Cir. 1989) (district court is ousted of jurisdiction in such a case).

6. Suppose that even though a notice of appeal is filed, the district court, at the urging of the plaintiff and over the objection of the defendant, proceeds to trial nevertheless, with the result that the plaintiff "prevails" at trial and is awarded attorney's fees under 42 U.S.C. § 1988? Consider the following Tenth Circuit cases.

In *Stewart v. Donges*, 915 F.2d 572 (10th Cir. 1990) (*Stewart I*), and *Stewart v. Donges*, 979 F.2d 179 (10th Cir. 1992) (*Stewart II*), sued a police officer, among others, claiming that his Fourth Amendment rights were violated. The defendant moved for summary judgment based on qualified immunity, which was denied by the district court. The defendant then filed his notice of appeal pursuant to *Mitchell* but, despite the protests of the defendant, the district court allowed the plaintiff to go to trial against the defendant, with the result that the jury found for the plaintiff. Thereafter, the defendant argued on appeal to the Tenth Circuit that the district court was ousted of jurisdiction over the claim against him once his notice of appeal was filed. The Tenth Circuit agreed in *Stewart I*, ruling the trial null and void, and vacated and remanded to the district court. The parties then settled the case for $42,500, followed by an attorney's fees award of over $354,000 to the prevailing plaintiff. This fees award included substantial fees for time spent both in the null and void trial and in preparation for it.

On appeal of this fees award in *Stewart II*, the Tenth Circuit again reversed the district court. It held that the plaintiff was not entitled to any fees whatever either for the trial or the trial preparation. The trial was null and void and without legal effect and it was therefore inappropriate to characterize the plaintiff as a prevailing party regarding its outcome. Also, it did not serve as a catalyst for the eventual settlement. Furthermore, even if the plaintiff were somehow considered to be a prevailing plaintiff with regard to the trial, there were special circumstances that rendered unjust a fees award for the trial and trial preparation. For one thing, *Mitchell* was designed to protect the defendant from trial and all of its burdens, which should include attorney's fees. In addition, the plaintiff was at fault in pressing the district court to proceed to trial while the defendant, who objected, should not have been expected to do more. If the plaintiff believed that the *Mitchell* appeal was frivolous, then he could have asked the district court to so certify, which he did not do. Judge Logan concurred in part and dissented in part. *Id.* at 185. He contended that the plaintiff was entitled to some fees for trial preparation.

What sort of message does *Stewart II* send to the parties and the district court in a section 1983 case where the defendant files a notice of appeal from the district court's denial of a qualified immunity summary judgment motion? Is *Stewart II* a case of overkill? Is a case like *Stewart II* likely to arise again?

V. Who Is Protected by Qualified Immunity?

A. A Refresher Note on the Functional Approach

We saw in Chapter 7 in connection with absolute immunity that the Supreme Court has developed what is called a functional approach to section 1983 immunities under which function, not status, is determinative. For example, judges are protected by absolute immunity from damages liability for their judicial acts but not for their administrative acts. The latter are protected only by qualified immunity. *Forrester v. White*, 484 U.S. 219 (1988).

We also learned in Chapter 7 that there are circumstances in which certain state and local government officials and employees who are ordinarily protected only by qualified immunity can secure absolute immunity protection be-

cause their challenged conduct is legislative, judicial or prosecutorial in nature. For example, in *Reed v. Village of Shorwood*, 704 F.2d 943 (7th Cir. 1983), plaintiffs, bar owners, sued numerous village officials and others for allegedly destroying their business in violation of due process. As to the conduct of the village's mayor in his capacity as local liquor control commissioner, the Seventh Circuit ruled that he acted in a judicial capacity when he suspended and revoked plaintiffs' liquor license, and was thus absolutely immune in this regard. Similarly, the mayor and members of the village's board of trustees were absolutely immune for their legislative conduct in reducing the number of certain liquor licenses in the village.

Consequently, the functional approach is central to an understanding of section 1983 immunities. Its application can either reduce an individual defendant's scope of protection from absolute immunity to qualified immunity or, conversely, enlarge an individual defendant's scope of protection from qualified immunity to absolute immunity.

B. The Status of Private Persons Who Act Under Color of Law

It is a condition of section 1983 liability that a defendant act under color of law. Ordinarily a section 1983 defendant is a state or local government official as to whom color of law (and its companion, state action) presents no difficulty. However, as Chapter 2 demonstrates, there are cases in which private persons can be sued for damages under section 1983 under at least three theories. The private person may be accused of using state attachment procedures to the detriment of the plaintiff in violation of the Fourteenth Amendment. Or the private person may be accused of conspiring with state or local government officials in violation of the Fourteenth Amendment. Or the private person may be doing the state's work. In all three cases color of law is present. *See Lugar v. Edmondson Oil Co.*, 457 U.S. 922 (1982) (use of state attachment procedures); *Dennis v. Sparks*, 449 U.S. 24 (1980) (conspiracy); and *West v. Atkins*, 487 U.S. 42 (1988) (private physician under contract with the state to provide service to prisoners).

The interesting question is whether such private defendants are protected by qualified immunity. After all, if a primary purpose of qualified immunity is to protect persons from unexpected developments in constitutional law, then private defendants, like government officials and employees, should also be protected. Indeed, before the Supreme Court's 1992 decision in *Wyatt v. Cole*, considered next, this was the majority rule in the circuits. *See* Comment, *Private Party Immunities to Section 1983 Suits*, 57 U. Chi. L. Rev. 1323 (1990).

On the other hand, if qualified immunity is intended primarily to promote independent governmental decisionmaking, then perhaps it ought not to apply to private persons. The First Circuit made this point in a pre-*Wyatt* case in which it rejected the qualified immunity defense raised by a private person who allegedly conspired with a qualifiedly immune official defendant:

> Private parties simply are not confronted with the pressures of office, the often split-second decision-making or the constant threat of liability facing police officers, governors and other public officials. Whatever factors of policy and fairness militate in favor of extending some immunity to private parties acting in concert with state officials were resolved by Congress in favor of those who claim a deprivation of constitutional rights.

Downs v. Sawtelle, 574 F.2d 1, 15–16 (1st Cir. 1978).

The Supreme Court addressed these matters in *Wyatt v. Cole*, 112 S. Ct. 1827 (1992).

Wyatt v. Cole

112 S.Ct. 1827 (1992)

Justice **O'Connor** delivered the opinion of the Court. In *Lugar v. Edmondson Oil Co.* we left open the question whether private defendants charged with 42 U.S.C. § 1983 liability for invoking state replevin, garnishment, and attachment statutes later declared unconstitutional are entitled to qualified immunity from suit. We now hold that they are not.

I

This dispute arises out of a soured cattle partnership. In July 1986, respondent Bill Cole sought to dissolve his partnership with petitioner Howard Wyatt. When no agreement could be reached, Cole, with the assistance of an attorney, respondent John Robbins II, filed a state court complaint in replevin against Wyatt, accompanied by a replevin bond of $18,000.

At that time, Mississippi law provided that an individual could obtain a court order for seizure of property possessed by another by posting a bond and swearing to a state court that the applicant was entitled to that property, and that the adversary wrongfully took and detained or wrongfully detained" the property. The statute gave the judge no discretion to deny a writ of replevin.

After Cole presented a complaint and bond, the court ordered the County Sheriff to seize 24 head of cattle, a tractor, and certain other personal property from Wyatt. Several months later, after a postseizure hearing, the court dismissed Cole's complaint in replevin and ordered the property returned to Wyatt. When Cole refused to comply, Wyatt brought suit in Federal District Court, challenging the constitutionality of the statute and seeking injunctive relief and damages from respondents, the County Sheriff, and the deputies involved in the seizure.

* * *

II

Title 42 U.S.C. § 1983 provides a cause of action against every person who, under color of any statute . . . of any State . . . subjects, or causes to be subjected, any citizen . . . to the deprivation of any rights, privileges, or immunities secured by the Constitution and laws . . . ." The purpose of § 1983 is to deter state actors from using the badge of their authority to deprive individuals of their federally guaranteed rights and to provide relief to victims if such deterrence fails.

In *Lugar v. Edmondson Oil Co.*, the Court considered the scope of § 1983 liability in the context of garnishment, prejudgment attachment, and replevin statutes. In that case, the Court held that private parties who attached a debtor's assets pursuant to a state attachment statute were subject to § 1983 liability if the statute was constitutionally infirm. Noting that our garnishment, prejudgment attachment, and replevin cases established that private use of state laws to secure property could constitute "state action" for purposes of the Fourteenth Amendment, the Court held that private defendants invoking a state-created attachment statute act "under color of state law" within the meaning of § 1983 if their actions are fairly attributable to the State.". This requirement is satisfied, the Court held, if two conditions are met. First, the "deprivation must be caused by the exercise of some right or privilege created by the State or by a rule of conduct imposed by the State or by a person for whom the State is responsible." Second, the private party must have "acted together with or . . . obtained significant aid from state officials" or engaged in conduct otherwise chargeable to the State." The Court found potential § 1983 liability in *Lugar* because the attachment scheme was created by the State and because the private defendants, in invoking the aid of state officials to attach the disputed property, were "willful participants in joint activity with the State or its agents."

Citing *Lugar*, the District Court assumed that Cole, by invoking the state statute, had acted under color of state law within the meaning of § 1983, and was therefore liable for damages for the deprivation of Wyatt's due process rights. With respect to Robbins, the court noted that while an action taken by an attorney in representing a client "does not normally constitute an act under color of state law . . . an attorney is still a person who may conspire to act under color of state law in depriving another of secured rights." The court did not determine whether Robbins was liable, however, because it held that both Cole and Robbins were entitled to qualified immunity from suit at least for conduct prior to the statute's invalidation.

Although the Court of Appeals did not review whether, in the first instance, Cole and Robbins had acted under color of state law within the meaning of § 1983, it affirmed the District Court's grant of qualified immunity to respondents. In so doing, the Court of Appeals followed one of its prior cases, *Folsom Investment Co. v. Moore*, in which it held that a § 1983 defendant who has invoked an attachment statute is entitled to an immunity

from monetary liability so long as he neither knew nor reasonably should have known that the statute was unconstitutional." The court in Folsom based its holding on two grounds. First, it viewed the existence of a common law probable cause defense to the torts of malicious prosecution and wrongful attachment as evidence that Congress in enacting § 1983 could not have intended to subject to liability those who in good faith resorted to legal process." Although it acknowledged that a defense is not the same as an immunity, the court maintained that it could transform a common law defense extant at the time of § 1983's passage into an immunity." Second, the court held that while immunity for private parties is not derived from official immunity, it is based on the important public interest in permitting ordinary citizens to rely on presumptively valid state laws, in shielding citizens from monetary damages when they reasonably resort to a legal process later held to be unconstitutional, and in protecting a private citizen from liability when his role in any unconstitutional action is marginal." In defending the decision below, respondents advance both arguments put forward by the Court of Appeals in *Folsom*. Neither is availing.

III

Section 1983 "creates a species of tort liability that on its face admits of no immunities." *Imbler v. Pachtman*. Nonetheless, we have accorded certain government officials either absolute or qualified immunity from suit if the "tradition of immunity was so firmly rooted in the common law and was supported by such strong policy reasons that 'Congress would have specifically so provided had it wished to abolish the doctrine.'" *Owen v. City of Independence* (quoting *Pierson v. Ray*). If parties seeking immunity were shielded from tort liability when Congress enacted the Civil Rights Act of 1871—§ 1 of which is codified at 42 U.S.C. § 1983—we infer from legislative silence that Congress did not intend to abrogate such immunities when it imposed liability for actions taken under color of state law. Additionally, irrespective of the common law support, we will not recognize an immunity available at common law if § 1983's history or purpose counsel against applying it in § 1983 actions.

In determining whether there was an immunity at common law that Congress intended to incorporate in the Civil Rights Act, we look to the most closely analogous torts—in this case, malicious prosecution and abuse of process. At common law, these torts provided causes of action against private defendants for unjustified harm arising out of the misuse of governmental processes.

Respondents do not contend that private parties who instituted attachment proceedings and who were subsequently sued for malicious prosecution or abuse of process were entitled to absolute immunity. And with good reason; although public prosecutors and judges were accorded absolute immunity at common law, such protection did not extend to complaining witnesses who, like respondents, set the wheels of government in motion by instigating a legal action. *Malley v. Briggs* (In 1871, the generally accepted rule was that one who procured the issuance of an arrest warrant by submitting a complaint could be held liable if "the complaint was made maliciously and without probable cause").

Nonetheless, respondents argue that at common law, private defendants could defeat a malicious prosecution or abuse of process action if they acted without malice and with probable cause, and that we should therefore infer that Congress did not intend to abrogate such defenses when it enacted the Civil Rights Act of 1871. We adopted similar reasoning in *Pierson v. Ray*. There, we held that police officers sued for false arrest under § 1983 were entitled to the defense that they acted with probable cause and in good faith when making an arrest under a statute they reasonably believed was valid. We recognized this defense because peace officers were accorded protection from liability at common law if they arrested an individual in good faith, even if the innocence of such person were later established.

The rationale we adopted in *Pierson* is of no avail to respondents here. Even if there were sufficient common law support to conclude that respondents, like the police officers in *Pierson*, should be entitled to a good-faith defense, that would still not entitle them to what they sought and obtained in the courts below: the qualified immunity from suit accorded government officials under *Harlow v. Fitzgerald*.

In *Harlow*, we altered the standard of qualified immunity adopted in our prior § 1983 cases because we recognized that "[t]he subjective element of the good-faith defense frequently [had] prove[n] incompatible with our admonition . . . that insubstantial claims should not proceed to trial." Because of the attendant harms to government effectiveness caused by lengthy judicial inquiry into subjective motivation, we concluded that "bare allegations of malice should not suffice to subject government officials either to the costs of trial or to the burdens of broad-reaching discovery." Accordingly, we held that government officials performing discretionary functions are shielded from "liability for civil damages insofar as their conduct [did] not violate clearly established statutory or constitutional rights of which a reasonable person would have known." This wholly objective standard, we concluded, would "avoid excessive disruption of government and permit the resolution of many insubstantial claims on summary judgment."

That *Harlow* "completely reformulated qualified immunity along principles not at all embodied in the common law" *Anderson v. Creighton*, was reinforced by our decision in *Mitchell v. Forsyth*. *Mitchell* held that *Harlow* established an "*immunity from suit* rather than a mere defense to liability," which, like an absolute immunity, "is effectively lost if a case is erroneously permitted to go to trial." Thus, we held in *Mitchell* that the denial of qualified immunity should be immediately appealable.

It is this type of objectively determined, immediately appealable immunity that respondents asserted below. But, as our precedents make clear, the reasons for recognizing such an immunity were based not simply on the existence of a good-faith defense at common law, but on the special policy concerns involved in suing government officials. Reviewing these concerns, we conclude that the rationales mandating qualified immunity for public officials are not applicable to private parties.

Qualified immunity strikes a balance between compensating those who have been injured by official conduct and protecting government's ability to perform its traditional functions. Accordingly, we have recognized qualified immunity for government officials where it was necessary to preserve their ability to serve the public good or to ensure that talented candidates were not deterred by the threat of damage suits from entering public service. See, e. g., *Wood v. Strickland* (denial of qualified immunity to school board officials would contribute not to principled and fearless decision-making but to intimidation'") (quoting *Pierson*); *Butz v. Economou* (immunity for Presidential aides warranted partly to protect officials who are required to exercise their discretion and the related public interest in encouraging the vigorous exercise of official authority"); *Mitchell* (immunity designed to prevent the distraction of officials from their governmental duties, inhibition of discretionary action, and deterrence of able people from public service'") (quoting *Harlow*). In short, the qualified immunity recognized in *Harlow* acts to safeguard government, and thereby to protect the public at large, not to benefit its agents.

These rationales are not transferable to private parties. Although principles of equality and fairness may suggest, as respondents argue, that private citizens who rely unsuspectingly on state laws they did not create and may have no reason to believe are invalid should have some protection from liability, as do their government counterparts, such interests are not sufficiently similar to the traditional purposes of qualified immunity to justify such an expansion. Unlike school board members, or police officers, or Presidential aides, private parties hold no office requiring them to exercise discretion; nor are they principally concerned with enhancing the public good. Accordingly, extending *Harlow* qualified immunity to private parties would have no bearing on whether public officials are able to act forcefully and decisively in their jobs or on whether qualified applicants enter public service. Moreover, unlike with government officials performing discretionary functions, the public interest will not be unduly impaired if private individuals are required to proceed to trial to resolve their legal disputes. In short, the nexus between private parties and the historic purposes of qualified immunity is simply too attenuated to justify such an extension of our doctrine of immunity.

For these reasons, we can offer no relief today. The question on which we granted certiorari is a very narrow one: "Whether

private persons, who conspire with state officials to violate constitutional rights, have available the good faith immunity applicable to public officials." The precise issue encompassed in this question, and the only issue decided by the lower courts, is whether qualified immunity, as enunciated in *Harlow*, is available for private defendants faced with § 1983 liability for invoking a state replevin, garnishment or attachment statute. That answer is no. In so holding, however, we do not foreclose the possibility that private defendants faced with § 1983 liability under *Lugar v. Edmondson Oil Co.*, could be entitled to an affirmative defense based on good faith and/or probable cause or that § 1983 suits against private, rather than governmental, parties could require plaintiffs to carry additional burdens. Because those issues are not fairly before us, however, we leave them for another day.

IV

As indicated above, the District Court assumed that under *Lugar v. Edmondson Oil Co.*, Cole was liable under § 1983 for invoking the state replevin under bond statute, and intimated that, but did not decide whether, Robbins also was subject to § 1983 liability. The Court of Appeals never revisited this question, but instead concluded only that respondents were entitled to qualified immunity at least for conduct prior to the statute's invalidation. Because we overturn this judgment, we must remand since there remains to be determined, at least, whether Cole and Robbins, in invoking the replevin statute, acted under color of state law within the meaning of *Lugar*. The decision of the Court of Appeals is reversed and the case is remanded for proceedings consistent with this opinion.

* * *

The **Chief Justice**, with whom Justice **Souter** and Justice **Thomas** join, dissenting.

The Court notes that we have recognized an immunity in the § 1983 context in two circumstances. The first is when a similarly situated defendant would have enjoyed an immunity at common law at the time § 1983 was adopted. The second is when important public policy concerns suggest the need for an immunity. Because I believe that both requirements, as explained in our prior decisions, are satisfied here, I dissent.

First, I think it is clear that at the time § 1983 was adopted, there generally was available to private parties a good-faith defense to the torts of malicious prosecution and abuse of process. See *Malley v. Briggs* (noting that the generally accepted rule at common law was that a person would be held liable if the complaint was made maliciously and without probable cause"); *Pierson v. Ray* (noting that at common law a police officer sued for false arrest can rely on his own goodfaith in making the arrest). And while the Court is willing to assume as much, it thinks this insufficient to sustain respondents' claim to an immunity because the "qualified immunity" respondents' seek is not equivalent to such a "defense".

But I think the Court errs in suggesting that the availability of a good-faith common law defense at the time of § 1983's adoption is not sufficient to support their claim to immunity. The case on which respondents principally rely, *Pierson*, considered whether a police officer sued under § 1983 for false arrest could rely on a showing of good-faith in order to escape liability. And while this Court concluded that the officer could rely on his own good faith, based in large part on the fact that a good-faith defense had been available at common law, the Court was at best ambiguous as to whether it was recognizing a "defense" or an "immunity." Any initial ambiguity, however, has certainly been eliminated by subsequent cases; there can be no doubt that it is a qualified immunity to which the officer is entitled. Similarly, in *Wood v. Strickland*, we recognized that, "although there have been differing emphases and formulations of the common-law immunity," the general recognition under state law that public officers are entitled to a good-faith defense was sufficient to support the recognition of a § 1983 immunity.

Thus, unlike the Court, I think our prior precedent establishes that a demonstration that a good-faith defense was available at the time § 1983 was adopted does, in fact, provide substantial support for a contemporary defendant claiming that he is entitled to qualified immunity in the analogous § 1983 context. While we refuse to recognize a common law immunity if § 1983's history or purpose coun-

sel against applying it, I see no such history or purpose that would so counsel here.

Indeed, I am at a loss to understand what is accomplished by today's decision—other than a needlessly fastidious adherence to nomenclature—given that the Court acknowledges that a good-faith defense will be available for respondents to assert on remand. Respondents presumably will be required to show the traditional elements of a good-faith defense— either that they acted without malice or that they acted with probable cause. The first element, "maliciousness," encompasses an inquiry into subjective intent for bringing the suit. This quite often includes an inquiry into the defendant's subjective belief as to whether he believed success was likely. But the second element, probable cause," focuses principally on objective reasonableness. Thus, respondents can successfully defend this suit simply by establishing that their reliance on the attachment statute was objectively reasonable for someone with their knowledge of the circumstances. But this is precisely the showing that entitles a public official to immunity. *Harlow v. Fitzgerald* (official must show his action did not "violate clearly established statutory or constitutional rights of which a reasonable person would have known").

Nor do I see any reason that this "defense" may not be asserted early in the proceedings on a motion for summary judgment, just as a claim to qualified immunity may be. Provided that the historical facts are not in dispute, the presence or absence of "probable cause" has long been acknowledged to be a question of law. And so I see no reason that the trial judge may not resolve a summary judgment motion premised on such a good-faith defense, just as we have encouraged trial judges to do with respect to qualified immunity claims. Thus, private defendants who have invoked a state attachment law are put in the same position whether we recognize that they are entitled to qualified immunity or if we instead recognize a good-faith defense. Perhaps the Court believes that the defense" will be less amenable to summary disposition than will the "immunity;" perhaps it believes the defense will be an issue that must be submitted to the jury. While I can see no reason why this would be so (given that probable cause is a legal question), if it is true, today's decision will only manage to increase litigation costs needlessly for hapless defendants.

This, in turn, leads to the second basis on which we have previously recognized a qualified immunity—reasons of public policy. Assuming that some practical difference will result from recognizing a defense but not an immunity, I think such a step is neither dictated by our prior decisions nor desirable. It is true, as the Court points out, that in abandoning a strictly historical approach to § 1983 immunities we have often explained our decision to recognize an immunity in terms of the special needs of public officials. But those cases simply do not answer—because the question was not at issue—whether similar (or even completely unrelated) reasons of public policy would warrant immunity for private parties as well.

I believe there are such reasons. The normal presumption that attaches to any law is that society will be benefitted if private parties rely on that law to provide them a remedy, rather than turning to some form of private, and perhaps lawless, relief. In denying immunity to those who reasonably rely on presumptively valid state law, and thereby discouraging such reliance, the Court expresses confidence that today's decision will not "unduly impair," the public interest. I do not share that confidence. I would have thought it beyond peradventure that there is strong public interest in encouraging private citizens to rely on valid state laws of which they have no reason to doubt the validity.

Second, as with the police officer making an arrest, I believe the private plaintiff's lot is "not so unhappy" that he must forgo recovery of property he believes to be properly recoverable through available legal processes or to be "mulcted in damages" *Pierson*, if his belief turns out to be mistaken. For as one Court of Appeals has pointed out, it is at least passing strange to conclude that private individuals are acting " under color of law" because they invoke a state garnishment statute and the aid of state officers, but yet deny them the immunity to which those same state officers are entitled, simply because the private parties are not state employees. *Buller*. While some of the strangeness may be laid at the doorstep of our decision in *Lugar*, there is no reason to proceed still further down this path. Our § 1983 jurisprudence has gone very far afield

indeed, when it subjects private parties to greater risk than their public counterparts, despite the fact that § 1983's historic purpose was "to prevent state officials from using the cloak of their authority under state law to violate rights protected against state infringement."

Because I find today's decision dictated neither by our own precedent nor by any sound considerations of public policy, I dissent.

[The concurring opinion of Justice **Kennedy** is omitted.]

NOTES

1. What is the *precise* holding in *Wyatt*? Is it broad or narrow?

2. Is the holding in *Wyatt* based on legislative history? On policy?

3. What is the relation between malicious prosecution and section 1983 qualified immunity for private persons?

4. Is *Wyatt*'s approach consistent with the Court's approach in its other immunity cases?

C.   Tension with the Functional Approach?

In *Wyatt* the private defendant functioned solely as a private individual in using the challenged state attachment procedure. Suppose, however, that a private defendant acts under color of law in a governmental capacity? Should he or she still be unprotected by qualified immunity? What does the functional approach suggest? What does the reasoning in *Wyatt* suggest?

Consider the following cases.

1. In *Rodriques v. Furtado*, 950 F.2d 805 (1st Cir. 1991), a pre-*Wyatt* decision, the First Circuit ruled that a private physician who conducted a vaginal search of a drug suspect pursuant to warrant was a state actor. It stated: "The scope and motivation for the search were established solely by the state's investigatory goals and justified solely by the search warrant. [Defendant's] role in the search was purely that of an auxiliary to normal police search procedures." *Id.* at 814. Next, the court observed that in its circuit private persons were ordinarily not entitled to qualified immunity. However, in this case the defendant was entitled to claim qualified immunity because, unlike those situations where private persons initiate action and seek to employ state apparatus, here, "state officials were the initiating parties and they pressed a private citizen into assisting their efforts." *Id.* at 815. Finally, the court found that the defendant was protected by qualified immunity because he relied on an objectively reasonable and facially valid warrant. It was not necessary for him to determine whether it was based on probable cause.

The First Circuit in *Rodriques* relied for its conclusion that the defendant was entitled to claim qualified immunity on the unfairness to the defendant if he were not protected by qualified immunity while the police officers who had him conduct the vaginal search would be so protected. It also spoke about the public policy supporting this result: section 1983 liability in this case "could deter [private physicians] from assisting in the execution of valid warrants." *Id.* at 815.

2. The First Circuit followed *Rodriques* in *Frazier v. Bailey*, 957 F.2d 920 (1st Cir. 1992), another pre-*Wyatt* case, and held that social workers, whose private agency-employers were under contract with the state to perform duties of the state, were entitled to claim qualified immunity. It reasoned that they were like the private physician in *Rodriques* who similarly was compelled to act. The First Circuit characterized *Rodriques* as a case in which the defendant was under a court order.

3. In still another pre-*Wyatt* case, *Felix de Santana v. Eligio Velez*, 956 F.2d 16 (1st Cir. 1992), the First Circuit distinguished *Rodriques* and found qualified immunity inapplicable to the private defendants there. In *de Santana*, the plaintiff alleged that private defendants *conspired* with a district attorney to indict plaintiff for perjury. The First Circuit explained that private individuals who voluntarily utilized the state for their own selfish purposes should not be allowed to claim qualified immunity.

4. In *Burrell v. Bd of Trustees of Ga Military College*, 970 F.2d 785 (11th Cir. 1992), a post-*Wyatt* case, the Eleventh Circuit was confronted with the question of the applicability of qualified immunity to alleged section 1983 co-conspirators. Without dealing broadly with the scope of *Wyatt*, the court followed the First

Circuit's lead in *Felix de Santana v. Velez*, noted above, and held that private defendants accused of conspiring with government officials are not protected by qualified immunity. Here, unlike cases in which private defendants acted pursuant to government contract or were under a court order, defendants like these accused of conspiracy should not be protected by qualified immunity as a matter of policy." "[P]ublic policy clearly counsels against employing the qualified immunity defense to encourage private individuals to redress their differences with another person by conspiring with public officials to deprive that person of his or her constitutional rights." 970 F.2d at 796.

Are these cases consistent with *Wyatt*? With one another? With the functional approach? Is there something unique about section 1983 conspiracy claims?

D. The Aftermath of *Wyatt*

In *Wyatt v. Cole*, 994 F.2d 1113 (5th Cir. 1993), on remand from the Supreme Court in *Wyatt v. Cole*, the Fifth Circuit followed the suggestion made in the different opinions in *Wyatt* and found that the private defendants sued for violating procedural due process in their use of a state attachment statute were protected from damages liability because the plaintiff did not show that they either knew or should have known that the state attachment statute was unconstitutional. It relied on the background of tort liability and immunity and on the analogy to malicious prosecution and abuse of process referred to by the justices in *Wyatt*. The Fifth Circuit declared: "[W]e now hold that plaintiffs seeking to hold private actors liable under *Lugar v. Edmondson Oil Co* must demonstrate that the defendants failed to act in good faith in invoking the unconstitutional state procedures." *Id.* at 1115 (citation omitted). While the Fifth Circuit characterized this as a "good faith" defense by analogy to malicious prosecution and abuse of process, this defense apparently contains both an objective component ("should have known") and a subjective component ("knew").

1. Are there any real differences between the qualified immunity denied private party defendants using state attachment procedures and the so-called "good faith" defense set out by the Fifth Circuit in *Wyatt v. Cole* on remand? Is one difference the inclusion of a subjective element in the "good faith" defense? Is another the availability (or not) of a *Mitchell v. Forsyth* interlocutory appeal?

2. Is the Fifth Circuit's "good faith" defense really a *defense* or must the plaintiff plead and prove that the defendant either knew or should have known that the statute relied on was unconstitutional? If the latter, as suggested by some of the Fifth Circuit's language, then these elements are part of the prima facie case and must be pleaded and proved by the plaintiff, and we are not talking about a defense at all. What should the rule be and why? Does it make any real difference?

3. What is the constitutional violation alleged in *Wyatt*? Is it procedural due process? Whatever the constitutional violation, does it have any bearing on the question of whether the Fifth Circuit on remand articulated the elements of the prima facie case or a defense?

E. Concluding questions

As you evaluate private party immunity together with all of the other rather complex and important qualified immunity doctrines addressed in this chapter, consider whether the Supreme Court has been successful in converting qualified immunity into the functional equivalent of absolute immunity. Do these doctrines in fact operate in a manner consistent with the Court's insistence that, to the extent possible, defendants be spared the need to defend against constitutional tort actions? Are the extensive judicial and litigation resources that are required to implement the Court's immunity rules, including those for summary judgment and interlocutory appeals, resources well spent? Are the Court's immunity rules fair to constitutional tort plaintiffs? To defendants? Are they consistent with corrective justice? Would you change these rules if you could? If so, how?

CHAPTER NINE

"Shall be Liable to the Party Injured in an Action at Law, Suit in Equity or Other Proper Proceeding for Redress": Constitutional Tort Remedies

Once the plaintiff has proven a constitutional violation committed under color of state law and has overcome all defenses, the parties' attention turns to remedial issues. This chapter addresses the distinctive problems that arise when courts must grapple with remedial issues in the section 1983 context. The chapter is divided into two parts. The first, and longer section addresses damages, both compensatory and punitive. The second section contains some materials bearing on the standards for determining the availability of injunctive or declaratory relief for constitutional violations in the constitutional tort context.

I. Damages

In the common law of torts, the typical remedy is an award of money damages aimed at making the plaintiff whole for the wrong done him by the defendant, and in proper circumstances an award of punitive damages designed to punish and deter egregious wrongdoing. In studying the materials in this section, consider whether and to what extent the principles of damages developed in ordinary tort law ought to govern recovery for constitutional wrongs as well.

A. Compensatory Damages

Carey v. Piphus

435 U.S. 247 (1978)

Mr. Justice **Powell** delivered the opinion of the Court.

In this case, brought under 42 U.S.C. § 1983, we consider the elements and prerequisites for recovery of damages by students who were suspended from public elementary and secondary schools without procedural due process. The Court of Appeals for the Seventh Circuit held that the students are entitled to recover substantial nonpunitive damages even if their suspensions were justified, and even if they do not prove that any other actual injury was caused by the denial of procedural due process. We disagree, and hold that in the absence of proof of actual injury, the students are entitled to recover only nominal damages.

I

Respondent Jarius Piphus was a freshman at Chicago Vocational High School during the 1973–1974 school year. On January 23, 1974, during school hours, the school principal saw Piphus and another student standing outdoors on school property passing back and forth what the principal described as an irregularly shaped cigarette. The principal approached the students unnoticed and smelled what he believed was the strong odor of burning marihuana. He also saw Piphus try to pass a packet of cigarette papers to the other student. When the students became aware of the principal's presence, they threw the cigarette into a nearby hedge.

The principal took the students to the school's disciplinary office and directed the assistant principal to impose the "usual" 20-day suspension for violation of the school rule against the use of drugs. The students protested that they had not been smoking marihuana, but to no avail. Piphus was allowed to remain at school, although not in class, for the remainder of the school day while the assistant principal tried, without success, to reach his mother.

A suspension notice was sent to Piphus' mother, and a few days later two meetings were arranged among Piphus, his mother, his sister, school officials, and representatives from a legal aid clinic. The purpose of the meetings was not to determine whether Piphus had been smoking marihuana, but rather to explain the reasons for the suspension. Following an unfruitful exchange of views, Piphus and his mother, as guardian ad litem, filed suit against petitioners in Federal District Court under 42 U.S.C. § 1983 and its jurisdictional counterpart, 28 U.S.C. § 1343, charging that Piphus had been suspended without due process of law in violation of the Fourteenth Amendment. The complaint sought declaratory and injunctive relief, together with actual and punitive damages in the amount of $3,000. Piphus was readmitted to school under a temporary restraining order after eight days of his suspension . . .

The District Court held that [Piphus and another plaintiff in a companion case] . . . had been suspended without procedural due process . . . [T]he District Court declined to award damages because:

"Plaintiffs put no evidence in the record to quantify their damages, and the record is completely devoid of any evidence which could even form the basis of a speculative inference measuring the extent of their injuries. Plaintiffs' claim for damages therefore fails for complete lack of proof."

The court also stated that the students were entitled to declaratory relief and to deletion of the suspensions from their school records, but for reasons that are not apparent the court failed to enter an order to that effect. Instead, it simply dismissed the complaints. No finding was made as to whether respondents would have been suspended if they had received procedural due process . . .

[T]he Court of Appeals reversed and remanded. It first held that the District Court erred in not granting declaratory and injunctive relief. It also held that the District Court should have considered evidence submitted by respondents after judgment that tended to prove the pecuniary value of each day of school that they missed while suspended. The court said, however, that respondents would not be entitled to recover damages representing the value of missed school time if petitioners showed on remand "that there was just cause for the suspension[s] and that therefore [respondents] would have been suspended even if a proper hearing had been held."

Finally, the Court of Appeals held that even if the District Court found on remand that respondents' suspensions were justified, they would be entitled to recover substantial "non-punitive" damages simply because they had been denied procedural due process . . . [T]he court stated that such damages should be awarded "even if, as in the case at bar, there is no proof of individualized injury to the plaintiff, such as mental distress. . . ." We granted certiorari to consider whether, in an action under § 1983 for the deprivation of procedural due process, a plaintiff must prove that he actually was injured by the deprivation before he may recover substantial "nonpunitive" damages.

II

. . .

The legislative history of § 1983 . . . demonstrates that it was intended to "[create] a species of tort liability" in favor of persons who are deprived of "rights, privileges, or immunities secured" to them by the Constitution.

Petitioners contend that the elements and prerequisites for recovery of damages under this "species of tort liability" should parallel those for recovery of damages under the common law of torts. In particular, they urge that the purpose of an award of damages under § 1983 should be to compensate persons for injuries that are caused by the deprivation of constitutional rights; and, further, that plaintiffs should be required to prove not only that their rights were violated, but also that injury was caused by the violation, in order to recover substantial damages. Unless respondents prove that they actually were injured by the deprivation of procedural due process, petitioners argue, they are entitled at most to nominal damages.

Respondents seem to make two different arguments in support of the holding below. First, they contend that substantial damages should be awarded under § 1983 for the deprivation of a constitutional right whether or not any injury was caused by the deprivation. This, they say, is appropriate both because constitutional rights are valuable in and of themselves, and because of the need to deter violations of constitutional rights. Respondents believe that this view reflects accurately that of the Congress that enacted § 1983. Second, respondents argue that even if the purpose of a § 1983 damages award is, as petitioners contend, primarily to compensate persons for injuries that are caused by the deprivation of constitutional rights, every deprivation of procedural due process may be presumed to cause some injury. This presumption, they say, should relieve them from the necessity of proving that injury actually was caused.

A

Insofar as petitioners contend that the basic purpose of a § 1983 damages award should be to compensate persons for injuries caused by the deprivation of constitutional rights, they have the better of the argument. Rights, constitutional and otherwise, do not exist in a vacuum. Their purpose is to protect persons from injuries to particular interests, and their contours are shaped by the interests they protect.

Our legal system's concept of damages reflects this view of legal rights. "The cardinal principle of damages in Anglo-American law is that of compensation for the injury caused to plaintiff by defendant's breach of duty." 2 F. Harper & F. James, *Law of Torts* § 25.1, p. 1299 (1956) (emphasis in original). The Court implicitly has recognized the applicability of this principle to actions under § 1983 by stating that damages are available under that section for actions "found . . . to have been violative of . . . constitutional rights and to have caused compensable injury. . . ." The lower federal courts appear generally to agree that damages awards under § 1983 should be determined by the compensation principle.

The Members of the Congress that enacted § 1983 did not address directly the question of damages, but the principle that damages are designed to compensate persons for injuries caused by the deprivation of rights hardly could have been foreign to the many lawyers in Congress in 1871. Two other sections of the Civil Rights Act of 1871 appear to incorporate this principle, and no reason suggests itself for reading § 1983 differently. To the extent that Congress intended that awards under § 1983 should deter the deprivation of constitutional rights, there is no evidence that it meant to establish a deterrent more formidable than that inherent in the award of compensatory damages.

B

It is less difficult to conclude that damages awards under § 1983 should be governed by the principle of compensation than it is to apply this principle to concrete cases. But over the centuries the common law of torts has developed a set of rules to implement the principle that a person should be compensated fairly for injuries caused by the violation of his legal rights. These rules, defining the elements of damages and the prerequisites for their recovery, provide the appropriate starting point for the inquiry under § 1983 as well.

It is not clear, however, that common-law tort rules of damages will provide a complete solution to the damages issue in every § 1983 case. In some cases, the interests protected by a particular branch of the common law of torts may parallel closely the interests protected by a particular constitutional right. In such cases, it may be appropriate to apply the tort rules of damages directly to the § 1983 action. In other cases, the interests protected by a particular constitutional right may not also be protected by an analogous branch of the common law of torts. In those cases, the task will be the more difficult one of adapting common-law rules of damages to provide fair compensation for injuries caused by the deprivation of a constitutional right.

Although this task of adaptation will be one of some delicacy as this case demonstrates it must be undertaken. The purpose of § 1983 would be defeated if injuries caused by the deprivation of constitutional rights went uncompensated simply because the common law does not recognize an analogous cause of action. In order to further the purpose of § 1983, the rules governing compensation for injuries caused by the deprivation of constitutional rights should be tailored to the interests protected by the particular right in question just as the common-law rules of damages themselves were defined by the interests protected in the various branches of tort law. We agree with Mr. Justice Harlan that "the experience of judges in dealing with private [tort] claims supports the conclusion that courts of law are capable of making the types of judgment concerning causation and magnitude of injury necessary to accord meaningful compensation for invasion of [constitutional] rights." *Bivens v. Six Unknown Fed. Narcotics Agents.* With these principles in mind, we now turn to the problem of compensation in the case at hand.

C

The Due Process Clause of the Fourteenth Amendment provides:

> "[N]or shall any State deprive any person of life, liberty, or property, without due process of law. . . ."

This Clause "raises no impenetrable barrier to the taking of a person's possessions," or liberty, or life. *Fuentes v. Shevin.* Procedural due process rules are meant to protect persons not from the deprivation, but from the mistaken or unjustified deprivation of life, liberty, or property. Thus, in deciding what process constitutionally is due in various contexts, the Court repeatedly has emphasized that "procedural due process rules are shaped by the risk of error inherent in the truth-finding process. . . ." *Mathews v. Eldridge.* Such rules "minimize substantively unfair or mistaken deprivations of" life, liberty, or property by enabling persons to contest the basis upon which a State proposes to deprive them of protected interests.

In this case, the Court of Appeals held that if petitioners can prove on remand that "[respondents] would have been suspended even if a proper hearing had been held," then respondents will not be entitled to recover damages to compensate them for injuries caused by the suspensions. The court thought that in such a case, the failure to accord procedural due process could not properly be viewed as the cause of the suspensions. The court suggested that in such circumstances, an award of damages for injuries caused by the suspensions would constitute a windfall, rather than compensation, to respondents. We do not understand the parties to disagree with this conclusion. Nor do we.

The parties do disagree as to the further holding of the Court of Appeals that respondents are entitled to recover substantial although unspecified damages to compensate them for "the injury which is 'inherent in the nature of the wrong,'" even if their suspensions were justified and even if they fail to prove that the denial of procedural due process actually caused them some real, if intangible, injury. Respondents, elaborating on this theme, submit that the holding is correct because injury fairly may be "presumed" to flow from every denial of procedural due process. Their argument is that in addition to protecting against unjustified deprivations, the Due Process Clause also guarantees the "feeling of just treatment" by the government. *Anti-Fascist Committee v. McGrath.* They contend that the deprivation of protected interests without procedural due process, even where the premise for the deprivation is not erroneous, inevitably arouses strong feelings of mental and emotional distress in the individual who is denied this "feeling of just treatment." They analogize their case to that of defamation per se, in which "the plaintiff is relieved from the necessity of producing any proof whatsoever that he has been injured" in order to recover substantial compensatory damages. C. McCormick, *Law of Damages* § 116, p. 423 (1935).

Petitioners do not deny that a purpose of procedural due process is to convey to the individual a feeling that the government has dealt with him fairly, as well as to minimize the risk of mistaken deprivations of protected interests. They go so far as to concede that, in a proper case, persons in respondents' position might well recover damages for mental and emotional distress caused by the denial of procedural due process. Petitioners' argument is the more limited one that such injury cannot be presumed to occur, and that plaintiffs at least should be put to their proof on the issue, as plaintiffs are in most tort actions.

We agree with petitioners in this respect. As we have observed in another context, the doctrine of presumed damages in the common law of defamation per se "is an oddity of tort law, for it allows recovery of purportedly compensatory damages without evidence of actual loss." *Gertz v. Robert Welch, Inc.* The doctrine has been defended on the grounds that those forms of defamation that are actionable per se are virtually certain to cause serious injury to reputation, and that this kind of injury is extremely difficult to prove. See id. Moreover, statements that are defamatory per se by their very nature are likely to cause mental and emotional distress, as well as injury to reputation, so there arguably is little reason to require proof of this kind of injury either. But these considerations do not support respondents' contention that damages should be presumed to flow from every deprivation of procedural due process.

First, it is not reasonable to assume that every departure from procedural due process, no matter what the circumstances or how minor, inherently is as likely to cause distress as the publication of defamation per se is to cause injury to reputation and distress. Where the deprivation of a protected interest is substantively justified but procedures are deficient in some respect, there may well be those who suffer no distress over the procedural irregularities. Indeed, in contrast to the immediately distressing effect of defamation per se, a person may not even know that procedures were deficient until he enlists the aid of counsel to challenge a perceived substantive deprivation.

Moreover, where a deprivation is justified but procedures are deficient, whatever distress a person feels may be attributable to the justified deprivation rather than to deficiencies in procedure. But as the Court of Appeals held, the injury caused by a justified deprivation, including distress, is not properly compensable under § 1983. This ambiguity in causation, which is absent in the case of defamation per se, provides additional need

for requiring the plaintiff to convince the trier of fact that he actually suffered distress because of the denial of procedural due process itself.

Finally, we foresee no particular difficulty in producing evidence that mental and emotional distress actually was caused by the denial of procedural due process itself. Distress is a personal injury familiar to the law, customarily proved by showing the nature and circumstances of the wrong and its effect on the plaintiff. In sum, then, although mental and emotional distress caused by the denial of procedural due process itself is compensable under § 1983, we hold that neither the likelihood of such injury nor the difficulty of proving it is so great as to justify awarding compensatory damages without proof that such injury actually was caused.

D

The Court of Appeals believed, and respondents urge, that cases dealing with awards of damages for racial discrimination, the denial of voting rights, and the denial of Fourth Amendment rights support a presumption of damages where procedural due process is denied. Many of the cases relied upon do not help respondents because they held or implied that some actual, if intangible, injury must be proved before compensatory damages may be recovered. Others simply did not address the issue. More importantly, the elements and prerequisites for recovery of damages appropriate to compensate injuries caused by the deprivation of one constitutional right are not necessarily appropriate to compensate injuries caused by the deprivation of another. As we have said, supra, these issues must be considered with reference to the nature of the interests protected by the particular constitutional right in question. For this reason, and without intimating an opinion as to their merits, we do not deem the cases relied upon to be controlling.

III

Even if respondents' suspensions were justified, and even if they did not suffer any other actual injury, the fact remains that they were deprived of their right to procedural due process. "It is enough to invoke the procedural safeguards of the Fourteenth Amendment that a significant property interest is at stake, whatever the ultimate outcome of a hearing. . . ."

Common-law courts traditionally have vindicated deprivations of certain "absolute" rights that are not shown to have caused actual injury through the award of a nominal sum of money. By making the deprivation of such rights actionable for nominal damages without proof of actual injury, the law recognizes the importance to organized society that those rights be scrupulously observed; but at the same time, it remains true to the principle that substantial damages should be awarded only to compensate actual injury or, in the case of exemplary or punitive damages, to deter or punish malicious deprivations of rights.

Because the right to procedural due process is "absolute" in the sense that it does not depend upon the merits of a claimant's substantive assertions, and because of the importance to organized society that procedural due process be observed, we believe that the denial of procedural due process should be actionable for nominal damages without proof of actual injury. We therefore hold that if, upon remand, the District Court determines that respondents' suspensions were justified, respondents nevertheless will be entitled to recover nominal damages not to exceed one dollar from petitioners.

The judgment of the Court of Appeals is reversed, and the case is remanded for further proceedings consistent with this opinion.

NOTES

1. *Carey* sets forth the fundamental principle governing damages in section 1983 cases. By stressing that section 1983 creates "a species of tort liability", and holding that "the basic purpose of a section 1983 damages award should be to compensate persons for injuries caused by the deprivation of constitutional rights", the Court sets up a tort framework for adjudicating damages issues. See Love, *Damages: A Remedy for the Violation of Constitutional Rights*, 67 Cal. L. Rev. 1242 (1979); Note, *Damages Awards for Constitutional Torts: A Reconsideration After* Carey v. Piphus, 93 Harv. L. Rev. 966 (1980).

Why did the Court choose tort law as the exclusive model for remedying constitutional violations? As an alternative, consider the pros and cons of supplementing the tort model with a system of bounties, under which plaintiffs who prove that their constitutional rights have been violated are awarded payments reflecting the jury's view of the value of those rights, quite apart from whether the plaintiffs can show any injury. In *Carey* and elsewhere the Court says that deterring constitutional violations and vindicating constitutional rights are the central aims of section 1983. Would the availability of such payments help to deter constitutional violations, by making it more costly for officials and governments to commit them? Would it help to vindicate constitutional rights, in situations where the right is violated but no provable harm results?

If the answer to these questions is yes, then why does the Court reject this scheme? Is it inconsistent with the language and history of the statute? Section 1983 states that a constitutional violation may be vindicated by "an action at law". But it also authorizes "other proper proceeding for redress", and it does not specify that tort principles must govern the relief available. The *qui tam* action, under which the plaintiff receives a bounty for bringing suit to enforce the law, is (and was in 1871) a well-established institution in American law. Specific statutory authorization is typically required, however. See Caminker, *The Constitutionality of* Qui Tam *Actions*, 99 Yale L.J. 341, 345–46 (1989).

In practice, federal courts apply modern tort damages principles, including controversial ones, in section 1983 cases. See, e.g., *Clark v. Taylor*, 710 F.2d 4 (1st Cir. 1983) (allowing recovery for plaintiff's fear of developing cancer as a result of defendants' wrongful administration of a drug); *Bell v. City of Milwaukee*, 746 F.2d 1205, 1250 (7th Cir. 1984) (extending consortium recovery beyond spouses to include a parent's recovery for death of his child). If the statute does not bar these innovations, should the Supreme Court authorize juries to award bounties as well? Why not?

2. The universal common law rule is that the plaintiff is entitled to one full recovery, no matter how many defendants he successfully sues. Does *Carey*, with its stress on the compensation principle, adopt this as the federal rule? Whether it necessarily follows from *Carey* or not, it is the rule in the lower federal courts. See, e.g., *Watts v. Laurent*, 774 F.2d

168, 179 (7th Cir. 1985) ("[T]he very nature of damages as compensation for injury suffered requires that once the plaintiff has been fully compensated for his injuries by one or more tortfeasors, he may not thereafter recover any additional compensation from any of the remaining tortfeasors.")

In *Gentile v. County of Suffolk*, 926 F.2d 142, 153 (2d Cir. 1991), the plaintiffs sued for a due process violation and for malicious prosecution under state tort law, with all of the claims arising out of the same prosecution. The jury awarded each plaintiff $75,000 on each of the two claims, and the second circuit affirmed.

Is this outcome consistent with the "one whole recovery" principle? The Court conceded that the jury may have "committed the error of duplicating damages here, but defendants have failed to establish this allegation with any degree of certainty . . . It would have been helpful if the district court had emphasized to the jury that it should not compensate for the same injury twice merely because it was caused by the violation of two different legal rights, one state and one federal. However, the question of duplicative damages was not raised by defendants in their requests to charge or in their objections to the court's instructions on the issue of damages, and the court correctly instructed the jury to award only those damages that would reasonably compensate plaintiffs for whatever injuries were proximately caused by defendants' unlawful actions. The policy of deferring to a jury verdict is a powerful one, even in cases in which the jury has taken action that is at first blush difficult to explain." Is the court saying that the fault lies with the defendants' lawyers?

3. Granting that monetary awards in section 1983 cases should be governed by the "principle of compensation", does the Court correctly apply that principle to the procedural due process violation at issue in *Carey*? The Court held that the plaintiffs cannot recover damages due to their suspension from school unless they show that, had a due process hearing been held, they would have escaped that punishment. Is this ruling consistent with the common law tort principle that one may recover damages only if, but for the defendant's tortious conduct, the injury would not have occurred?

Carey's requirement of a causal link between the constitutional violation and the plaintiff's

harm is not limited to procedural due process. Lack of causation can be an obstacle to the recovery of substantial damages for other constitutional violations as well. See, e.g., *Gibeau v. Nellis*, 18 F.3d 107 (2d Cir. 1994) (although guard used excessive force in striking plaintiff three times, substantial damages would be inappropriate if the jury found that the first blow was not excessive and that the plaintiff's contusion was caused by the first blow); *Butler v. Dowd*, 979 F.2d 661 (8th Cir. 1992) (upholding award of nominal damages to prisoners who could show that they were raped and that prison officials were deliberately indifferent to their safety, where the jury could also find that the rapes were not caused by the defendants' deliberate indifference but by the plaintiff's own conduct).

Causation is addressed in greater detail in chapter 6.

Suppose plaintiff Piphus loses on that issue, because the principal has conclusive proof that he was smoking marihuana. Can he still recover damages for the violation of his right to due process? Is it sufficient that he can prove emotional distress resulting from this episode, or must he show that the emotional distress was caused by the failure to give him the process that was due, and not by other events, like the suspension itself?

4. Although *Carey* places serious obstacles in the way of a plaintiff asserting a procedural due process claim, it is sometimes possible to procure substantial damages anyway. See, e.g., *Hill v. City of Pontotoc*, 993 F.2d 422, 426 (5th Cir. 1993) (affirming an award of $30,000 compensatory damages and $103,704 frontpay to a firefighter discharged without proper procedural safeguards, based on a jury finding that "had Hill's procedural due process rights been observed, that is, had Hill been given a fair opportunity to answer those charges, the City would not have fired Hill.") Compare *Stevens v. McHan*, 3 F.3d 1204, 1207 (8th Cir. 1993) ($4,000 award to a prisoner who shows that a violation of procedural due process caused him to spend eight days in administrative segregation is "arbitrary and excessive" by comparison with awards in other cases).

5. Notice the award of "frontpay" in *Hill*. A worker fired illegally is normally entitled to reinstatement. If, however, reinstatement is inappropriate, as where the post has been

eliminated or where the return of the worker would be unduly disruptive to the organization, the court may award front pay instead. Here the district court made such a finding, hence the award. See also *Haskins v. City of Boaz*, 822 F.2d 1014, 1015 (11th Cir. 1987).

May a court decline to award both reinstatement and frontpay? See *Stanley v. Chilhowee R-IV School District*, 5 F.3d 319, 321–22 (8th Cir. 1993) (yes). The court said:

> Reinstatement and frontpay are equitable remedies . . . Ordinarily reinstatement would follow a finding of section 1983 liability for nonrenewal of a teaching contract. [But here there are special circumstances.] The Chilhowee R-IV School District is extremely small; the district has only one school building, which houses all of the approximately 150–155 students in kindergarten through twelfth grade . . . The trial record bristles with extensive testimony about the tense and hostile atmosphere that exited at the school . . . [which] would make future cooperation impossible . . . [With regard to front pay] after a jury finds section 1983 liability in a loss-of-employment case, the court must attempt to make the plaintiff whole, yet the court must avoid granting the plaintiff a windfall. [Here, plaintiffs] were all probationary teachers with one-year contracts . . . The jury's award of damages compensated [them] for their lost salary and benefits for [three years]. We cannot conclude that the District Court abused its discretion in declining to award front pay, thereby limiting [their] recovery to the three school years immediately following [their] final year in the employ of the district.

Suppose Piphus cannot prove any emotional distress, but seeks to recover compensation for the inherent value of his right to due process. How much will he be permitted to recover after *Carey*? Why does the Court reject "presumed damages"? Are its reasons peculiar to the procedural context? Does the Court mean to foreclose all awards of presumed damages in constitutional tort cases? These issues are addressed in the following case.

Memphis Community School District v. Stachura

477 U.S. 299 (1986)

Justice **Powell** delivered the opinion of the Court.

This case requires us to decide whether 42 U.S.C. § 1983 authorizes an award of compensatory damages based on the factfinder's assessment of the value or importance of a substantive constitutional right.

I

Respondent Edward Stachura is a tenured teacher in the Memphis, Michigan, public schools. When the events that led to this case occurred, respondent taught seventh-grade life science, using a textbook that had been approved by the School Board. The textbook included a chapter on human reproduction. During the 1978–1979 school year, respondent spent six weeks on this chapter. As part of their instruction, students were shown pictures of respondent's wife during her pregnancy. Respondent also showed the students two films concerning human growth and sexuality. These films were provided by the County Health Department, and the Principal of respondent's school had approved their use. Both films had been shown in past school years without incident.

After the showing of the pictures and the films, a number of parents complained to school officials about respondent's teaching methods. These complaints, which appear to have been based largely on inaccurate rumors about the allegedly sexually explicit nature of the pictures and films, were discussed at an open School Board meeting held on April 23, 1979. Following the advice of the School Superintendent, respondent did not attend the meeting, during which a number of parents expressed the view that respondent should not be allowed to teach in the Memphis school system. The day after the meeting, respondent was suspended with pay. The School Board later confirmed the suspension, and notified respondent that an "administration evaluation" of his teaching methods was underway. No such evaluation was ever made. Respondent was reinstated the next fall, after filing this lawsuit.

Respondent sued the School District, the Board of Education, various Board members and school administrators, and two parents who had participated in the April 23 School Board meeting. The complaint alleged that respondent's suspension deprived him of both liberty and property without due process of law and violated his First Amendment right to academic freedom. Respondent sought compensatory and punitive damages under 42 U.S.C. § 1983 for these constitutional violations.

At the close of trial on these claims, the District Court instructed the jury as to the law governing the asserted bases for liability. Turning to damages, the court instructed the jury that on finding liability it should award a sufficient amount to compensate respondent for the injury caused by petitioners' unlawful actions:

"You should consider in this regard any lost earnings; loss of earning capacity; out-of-pocket expenses; and any mental anguish or emotional distress that you find the Plaintiff to have suffered as a result of conduct by the Defendants depriving him of his civil rights."

In addition to this instruction on the standard elements of compensatory damages, the court explained that punitive damages could be awarded, and described the standards governing punitive awards. Finally, at respondent's request and over petitioners' objection, the court charged that damages also could be awarded based on the value or importance of the constitutional rights that were violated:

"If you find that the Plaintiff has been deprived of a Constitutional right, you may award damages to compensate him for the deprivation. Damages for this type of injury are more difficult to measure than damages for a physical injury or injury to one's property. There are no medical bills or other expenses by which you can judge how much compensation is appropriate. In one sense, no monetary value we place upon Constitutional rights can measure their importance in our society or compensate a citizen adequately for their deprivation. However, just because these rights are not capable of precise evaluation does not mean that an appropriate monetary amount should not be awarded.

"The precise value you place upon any Constitutional right which you find was denied to Plaintiff is within your discretion. You

may wish to consider the importance of the right in our system of government, the role which this right has played in the history of our republic, [and] the significance of the right in the context of the activities which the Plaintiff was engaged in at the time of the violation of the right."

The jury found petitioners liable, and awarded a total of $275,000 in compensatory damages and $46,000 in punitive damages. The District Court entered judgment notwithstanding the verdict as to one of the defendants, reducing the total award to $266,750 in compensatory damages and $36,000 in punitive damages.

In an opinion devoted primarily to liability issues, the Court of Appeals for the Sixth Circuit affirmed, holding that respondent's suspension had violated both procedural due process and the First Amendment. Responding to petitioners' contention that the District Court improperly authorized damages based solely on the value of constitutional rights, the court noted only that "there was ample proof of actual injury to plaintiff Stachura both in his effective discharge . . . and by the damage to his reputation and to his professional career as a teacher. Contrary to the situation in *Carey v. Piphus* . . ., there was proof from which the jury could have found, as it did, actual and important damages."

We granted certiorari limited to the question whether the Court of Appeals erred in affirming the damages award in the light of the District Court's instructions that authorized not only compensatory and punitive damages, but also damages for the deprivation of "any constitutional right." We reverse, and remand for a new trial limited to the issue of compensatory damages.

II

Petitioners challenge the jury instructions authorizing damages for violation of constitutional rights on the ground that those instructions permitted the jury to award damages based on its own unguided estimation of the value of such rights. Respondent disagrees with this characterization of the jury instructions, contending that the compensatory damages instructions taken as a whole focused solely on respondent's injury and not on the abstract value of the rights he asserted.

We believe petitioners more accurately characterize the instructions. The damages instructions were divided into three distinct segments: (i) compensatory damages for harm to respondent, (ii) punitive damages, and (iii) additional "[compensatory]" damages for violations of constitutional rights. No sensible juror could read the third of these segments to modify the first. On the contrary, the damages instructions plainly authorized—in addition to punitive damages—two distinct types of "compensatory" damages: one based on respondent's actual injury according to ordinary tort law standards, and another based on the "value" of certain rights. We therefore consider whether the latter category of damages was properly before the jury.

III

A

We have repeatedly noted that 42 U.S.C. § 1983 creates "'a species of tort liability' in favor of persons who are deprived of 'rights, privileges, or immunities secured' to them by the Constitution." *Carey v. Piphus*, quoting *Imbler v. Pachtman*. Accordingly, when § 1983 plaintiffs seek damages for violations of constitutional rights, the level of damages is ordinarily determined according to principles derived from the common law of torts. See *Smith v. Wade, Carey v. Piphus*, cf. *Monroe v. Pape*.

Punitive damages aside, damages in tort cases are designed to provide "compensation for the injury caused to plaintiff by defendant's breach of duty." To that end, compensatory damages may include not only out-of-pocket loss and other monetary harms, but also such injuries as "impairment of reputation . . ., personal humiliation, and mental anguish and suffering." *Gertz v. Robert Welch, Inc.* See also *Carey v. Piphus* (mental and emotional distress constitute compensable injury in § 1983 cases). Deterrence is also an important purpose of this system, but it operates through the mechanism of damages that are compensatory—damages grounded in determinations of plaintiffs' actual losses. E.g., 4 Harper, James, & Gray, supra, § 25.3 (discussing need for certainty in damages determinations); D. Dobbs, *Law of Remedies* § 3.1, pp. 135–136 (1973). Congress adopted this common-law system of recovery when it established liability for "constitutional torts." Con-

sequently, "the basic purpose" of § 1983 damages is "to compensate persons for injuries that are caused by the deprivation of constitutional rights." . . .

The instructions at issue here cannot be squared with *Carey*, or with the principles of tort damages on which *Carey* and § 1983 are grounded. The jurors in this case were told that, in determining how much was necessary to "compensate [respondent] for the deprivation" of his constitutional rights, they should place a money value on the "rights" themselves by considering such factors as the particular right's "importance . . . in our system of government," its role in American history, and its "significance . . . in the context of the activities" in which respondent was engaged. These factors focus, not on compensation for provable injury, but on the jury's subjective perception of the importance of constitutional rights as an abstract matter. *Carey* establishes that such an approach is impermissible. The constitutional right transgressed in *Carey*—the right to due process of law—is central to our system of ordered liberty. See *In re Gault*. We nevertheless held that no compensatory damages could be awarded for violation of that right absent proof of actual injury. *Carey* thus makes clear that the abstract value of a constitutional right may not form the basis for § 1983 damages.

Respondent nevertheless argues that *Carey* does not control here, because in this case a substantive constitutional right—respondent's First Amendment right to academic freedom—was infringed. The argument misperceives our analysis in *Carey*. That case does not establish a two-tiered system of constitutional rights, with substantive rights afforded greater protection than "mere" procedural safeguards. We did acknowledge in *Carey* that "the elements and prerequisites for recovery of damages" might vary depending on the interests protected by the constitutional right at issue. But we emphasized that, whatever the constitutional basis for § 1983 liability, such damages must always be designed "to compensate injuries caused by the [constitutional] deprivation." That conclusion simply leaves no room for noncompensatory damages measured by the jury's perception of the abstract "importance" of a constitutional right.

Nor do we find such damages necessary to vindicate the constitutional rights that § 1983 protects. Section 1983 presupposes that damages that compensate for actual harm ordinarily suffice to deter constitutional violations. Moreover, damages based on the "value" of constitutional rights are an unwieldy tool for ensuring compliance with the Constitution. History and tradition do not afford any sound guidance concerning the precise value that juries should place on constitutional protections. Accordingly, were such damages available, juries would be free to award arbitrary amounts without any evidentiary basis, or to use their unbounded discretion to punish unpopular defendants. Cf. *Gertz*. Such damages would be too uncertain to be of any great value to plaintiffs, and would inject caprice into determinations of damages in § 1983 cases. We therefore hold that damages based on the abstract "value" or "importance" of constitutional rights are not a permissible element of compensatory damages in such cases.

B

Respondent further argues that the challenged instructions authorized a form of "presumed" damages—a remedy that is both compensatory in nature and traditionally part of the range of tort law remedies. Alternatively, respondent argues that the erroneous instructions were at worst harmless error.

Neither argument has merit. Presumed damages are a substitute for ordinary compensatory damages, not a supplement for an award that fully compensates the alleged injury. When a plaintiff seeks compensation for an injury that is likely to have occurred but difficult to establish, some form of presumed damages may possibly be appropriate. See *Carey*; cf. *Dun & Bradstreet, Inc. v. Greenmoss Builders*; *Gertz v. Robert Welch, Inc.* In those circumstances, presumed damages may roughly approximate the harm that the plaintiff suffered and thereby compensate for harms that may be impossible to measure. As we earlier explained, the instructions at issue in this case did not serve this purpose, but instead called on the jury to measure damages based on a subjective evaluation of the importance of particular constitutional values. Since such damages are wholly divorced from any compensatory purpose, they cannot be justi-

fied as presumed damages.[14] Moreover, no rough substitute for compensatory damages was required in this case, since the jury was fully authorized to compensate respondent for both monetary and nonmonetary harms caused by petitioners' conduct.

Nor can we find that the erroneous instructions were harmless. When damages instructions are faulty and the verdict does not reveal the means by which the jury calculated damages, "[the] error in the charge is difficult, if not impossible, to correct without retrial, in light of the jury's general verdict." The jury was authorized to award three categories of damages: (i) compensatory damages for injury to respondent, (ii) punitive damages, and (iii)

---

[14] For the same reason, Nixon v. Herndon, and similar cases do not support the challenged instructions. In Nixon, the Court held that a plaintiff who was illegally prevented from voting in a state primary election suffered compensable injury. Accord, Lane v. Wilson. This holding did not rest on the "value" of the right to vote as an abstract matter; rather, the Court recognized that the plaintiff had suffered a particular injury—his inability to vote in a particular election—that might be compensated through substantial money damages. See [*Nixon*] ("the petition . . . seeks to recover for private damage").

Nixon followed a long line of cases, going back to Lord Holt's decision in Ashby v. White, authorizing substantial money damages as compensation for persons deprived of their right to vote in particular elections. E.g., Wiley v. Sinkler; Wayne v. Venable. Although these decisions sometimes speak of damages for the value of the right to vote, their analysis shows that they involve nothing more than an award of presumed damages for a nonmonetary harm that cannot easily be quantified:

"In the eyes of the law [the] right [to vote] is so valuable that damages are presumed from the wrongful deprivation of it without evidence of actual loss of money, property, or any other valuable thing, and the amount of the damages is a question peculiarly appropriate for the determination of the jury, because each member of the jury has personal knowledge of the value of the right." Id.

See also Ashby v. White ("As in an action for slanderous words, though a man does not lose a penny by reason of the speaking [of] them, yet he shall have an action"). The "value of the right" in the context of these decisions is the money value of the particular loss that the plaintiff suffered—a loss of which "each member of the jury has personal knowledge." It is not the value of the right to vote as a general, abstract matter, based on its role in our history or system of government. Thus, whatever the wisdom of these decisions in the context of the changing scope of compensatory damages over the course of this century, they do not support awards of noncompensatory damages such as those authorized in this case.

damages based on the jury's perception of the "importance" of two provisions of the Constitution. The submission of the third of these categories was error. Although the verdict specified an amount for punitive damages, it did not specify how much of the remaining damages was designed to compensate respondent for his injury and how much reflected the jury's estimation of the value of the constitutional rights that were infringed. The effect of the erroneous instruction is therefore unknowable, although probably significant: the jury awarded respondent a very substantial amount of damages, none of which could have derived from any monetary loss. It is likely, although not certain, that a major part of these damages was intended to "compensate" respondent for the abstract "value" of his due process and First Amendment rights. For these reasons, the case must be remanded for a new trial on compensatory damages . . .

Justice **Marshall**, with whom Justice **Brennan**, Justice **Blackmun**, and Justice **Stevens** join, concurring in the judgment.

I agree with the Court that this case must be remanded for a new trial on damages. Certain portions of the Court's opinion, however, can be read to suggest that damages in § 1983 cases are necessarily limited to "out-of-pocket loss," "other monetary harms," and "such injuries as 'impairment of reputation . . ., personal humiliation, and mental anguish and suffering.'" I do not understand the Court so to hold, and I write separately to emphasize that the violation of a constitutional right, in proper cases, may itself constitute a compensable injury . . .

Following *Carey*, the Courts of Appeals have recognized that invasions of constitutional rights sometimes cause injuries that cannot be redressed by a wooden application of common-law damages rules. In *Hobson v. Wilson*, . . . plaintiffs claimed that defendant Federal Bureau of Investigation agents had invaded their First Amendment rights to assemble for peaceable political protest, to associate with others to engage in political expression, and to speak on public issues free of unreasonable government interference. The District Court found that the defendants had succeeded in diverting plaintiffs from, and impeding them in, their protest activities. The Court of Appeals for the District of Columbia

Circuit held that that injury to a First Amendment-protected interest could itself constitute compensable injury wholly apart from any "emotional distress, humiliation and personal indignity, emotional pain, embarrassment, fear, anxiety and anguish" suffered by plaintiffs. The court warned, however, that that injury could be compensated with substantial damages only to the extent that it was "reasonably quantifiable"; damages should not be based on "the so-called inherent value of the rights violated."

I believe that the *Hobson* court correctly stated the law. When a plaintiff is deprived, for example, of the opportunity to engage in a demonstration to express his political views, "[it] is facile to suggest that no damage is done." *Dellums v. Powell.* Loss of such an opportunity constitutes loss of First Amendment rights "'in their most pristine and classic form.'" Id., quoting *Edwards v. South Carolina.* There is no reason why such an injury should not be compensable in damages. At the same time, however, the award must be proportional to the actual loss sustained.

The instructions given the jury in this case were improper because they did not require the jury to focus on the loss actually sustained by respondent. Rather, they invited the jury to base its award on speculation about "the importance of the right in our system of government" and "the role which this right has played in the history of our republic," guided only by the admonition that "[in] one sense, no monetary value we place on Constitutional rights can measure their importance in our society or compensate a citizen adequately for their deprivation." These instructions invited the jury to speculate on matters wholly detached from the real injury occasioned respondent by the deprivation of the right. Further, the instructions might have led the jury to grant respondent damages based on the "abstract value" of the right to procedural due process—a course directly barred by our decision in Carey.

The Court therefore properly remands for a new trial on damages. I do not understand the Court, however, to hold that deprivations of constitutional rights can never themselves constitute compensable injuries. Such a rule would be inconsistent with the logic of Carey, and would defeat the purpose of § 1983 by denying compensation for genuine injuries caused by the deprivation of constitutional rights.

NOTES

1. Does the Court hold that presumed damages are unavailable in section 1983 suits brought to recover for first amendment violations? Based on the reasoning set forth in the opinion, what arguments might be advanced on either side of that question? Did the Court accurately characterize the instruction that it found faulty? Did it endorse the old cases allowing damages for loss of the right to vote? Are those cases properly viewed as presumed damages cases?

For one view, see Love, *Presumed General Damages in Constitutional Tort Litigation*, 49 W. & L. L. Rev. 67, 80 (1992) (arguing that "although the court will not recognize presumed general damages for *abstract deprivations* of constitutional rights, the Court might be willing to allow the recovery of presumed general damages for certain *intangible injuries* caused by violations of constitutional rights" such as the right to vote) (emphasis in original).

After *Stachura* some lower courts have permitted presumed damages in first amendment cases. See, e.g., Walje v. City of Winchester, 827 F.2d 10 (6th Cir. 1987) (upholding a $5,000 presumed damages award to a plaintiff government employee who was suspended in violation of his first amendment rights); City of Watseka v. Illinois Pub. Action Council, 796 F.2d 1547, 1559 (7th Cir. 1986) (presumed damages for violation of first amendment solicitation right). No cases have been found squarely holding that presumed damages are not available. The issue is rarely addressed, perhaps because plaintiffs' lawyers think that the better way to convince the jury to award large damages is to offer proof of harm rather than to resort to presumed damages, or perhaps because trial judges require that they make that choice. As a result, they may forego the opportunity to argue for an instruction on presumed damages. If this is the reason why the availability of presumed damages is hardly ever litigated in section 1983 cases, then lawyers and judges may misunderstand the nature of presumed damages. Presumed damages originated in the common law of defamation,

and in that context the plaintiff may offer evidence of damages and at the same time request an instruction on presumed damages. See McCormick, *The Measure of Damages for Defamation*, 12 N.C. L. Rev. 120 (1934).

2. Plaintiffs do sometimes recover substantial damages based on proof of harm in first amendment cases. In *Keenan v. City of Philadelphia*, 983 F.2d 459 (3rd Cir. 1992), plaintiff police officers were transferred from the Homicide Division when they complained about sexual harassment, in violation of their free speech and equal protection rights. In reviewing the award of compensatory damages, the court said: "The jury awarded Keenan, $200,000; Smith, $175,000; Gilbert, $175,000; Rosenstein, $40,000; and Gerrard, $30,000. Testimony regarding the compensable harm suffered by the plaintiffs was given by plaintiffs themselves, family members, friends, and neighbors, as well as two expert witnesses. Evidence showed 'daily' harassment of Keenan. Beyond the lay testimony, Dr. Robert Sadoff, an expert witness, stated that each plaintiff suffered emotional distress related to the transfer out of the Homicide Unit. Kenan required continuing therapy. An actuary economist . . . calculated plaintiff's economic losses which alone exceeded the jury's awards for each plaintiff. Finally, the jury was presented with some evidence that detectives in the Homicide Unit routinely doubled their salaries through overtime. Given our standard of review and the evidence produced at trial, we cannot conclude that the compensatory damages were so grossly excessive as to shock our judicial conscience." Id. at 469.

3. Putting aside the problem of interpreting the ambiguous opinion in *Stachura*, the more interesting question regarding presumed damages and constitutional violations is the normative one: *Should* presumed damages be available in section 1983 cases?

Granting the correctness of the Court's holding in *Carey*, that a violation of procedural due process is a different sort of injury for which presumed damages are not appropriate, how should courts deal with substantive rights like freedom of speech and religion, the right against unreasonable searches and seizures, the right not to be subjected to cruel and unusual punishments, and the substantive due process right against arbitrary acts by government officers? Sometimes these violations produce physical injuries, loss of a job, emotional distress, and other more or less quantifiable injuries. Should these quantifiable losses exhaust the recovery available to someone injured by substantive constitutional violations? Should persons who suffer violations that produce no such consequences go without a substantial award?

Can a person who has suffered no provable emotional distress as a result of unlawfully being forbidden to demonstrate, for example, credibly argue that he has suffered any injury? Common law courts have long allowed presumed damages for "dignitary" torts, such as assault, battery, malicious prosecution, defamation, and invasion of privacy. See D. Dobbs, Law of Remedies section 7.3 at 635 (2d ed. 1993).

4. Defamation is a lively area of contemporary tort law. Because recovery for defamation may threaten freedom of speech, presumed damages is one area that has received attention from the Supreme Court. Perhaps some useful comparisons and contrasts can be drawn between defamation and constitutional tort with respect to the role of presumed damages. The rationale for presumed damages in defamation law is that the harm done to one's reputation by a defamatory publication, especially a writing that is defamatory on its face, will likely be hard to trace. No one can tell who might read the libel and be deterred from dealing with the plaintiff. Consequently, effective compensation for the injury would be thwarted if the plaintiff were required to offer proof of actual harm. See Dun & Bradstreet v. Greenmoss Builders, Inc., 472 U.S. 749, 760–61 (1985). Does this rationale apply to denials of freedom of speech?

If violations of substantive constitutional rights do not produce harm by their insidious effects on unknown persons, it may be misleading to compare them to defamation. Does it follow that presumed damages are inappropriate? Given that the harm constitutional violations produce does not entail any impact on others, are there other grounds for favoring presumed damages in constitutional tort cases? Isn't the harm resulting from a constitutional even more inchoate, even harder to prove, and consequently more deserving of presumed damages, than the harm to reputation produced by libel per se?

5. Consider the analysis of presumed damages undertaken in Bell v. Little Axe Independent School District, 766 F.2d 1391 (1985), a pre-*Stachura* case where the court held that presumed damages were appropriate for establishment clause violations. After noting *Carey*'s holding that "a procedural due process violation does not inherently precipitate the kind of injury analogous to one of the common law torts that permitted the recovery of presumed damages", the court observed that "[o]ther constitutional deprivations, however, may fare well in such comparison—a comparison that *Carey* requires us to make." 766 F.2d at 1409.

It first distinguished the first amendment from fourth, eighth and fourteenth amendment substantive due process claims. The latter group of rights concern "the deprivation of liberty interests in bodily integrity and arrest based on probable cause. The interests at stake there can be analogized to dignitary torts, which were remediable by presumed damages at common law." The opinion then cited a number of cases in which courts allowed presumed damages for such constitutional violations. It continued:

The present case, however, involves interests that are not directly analogous to dignitary torts. The First Amendment protects "the individual's freedom to believe, to worship, and to express himself in accordance with the dictates of his own conscience." It prevents the government from intruding on these interests through repression of a particular point of view, for instance, or by favoring a particular religion at the expense of those who have different beliefs. The Establishment Clause therefore functions to preserve freedom of religious belief as well as to safeguard the social and political participation of all persons, regardless of their religious preference. Like its complementary clauses it creates a right of public participation which the government may not deny . . . [The court then discussed pre-*Carey* cases allowing presumed damages for first amendment violations.]

Carey, however, directs us to look for an analogous common law tort that permitted recovery of presumed damages. We believe that voting rights provide the appropriate analogy for First Amendment violations. Like the First Amendment, voting rights assure a person of the right to express an opinion and the right to participate in the public forum. The deprivation of the right to vote has long been awarded substantial damages without requiring proof of consequential injury . . . [The court discussed some of the cases described in footnote 14 of *Stachura*, *supra*.]

These cases uniformly recognize the inherent value of the right to vote, a right of public participation that evokes many of the same interests protected by the First Amendment, including the Establishment Clause. Just as the right to vote renders our government accountable for its political actions, the Establishment Clause renders the government accountable for its actions that cultivate religion. The Establishment Clause, if anything, is broader in its protection, since it emphatically rejects the principle of majoritarian rule. To ensure full vindication of these rights, and to deter similar violations, we believe that a plaintiff need not prove consequential injury to recover damages for the violation of a First Amendment right.

Punitive damages do not serve fully the deterrent purposes of section 1983. They are limited to reckless deprivations of constitutional rights, and are restricted by various immunity defenses as well as the ability of a defendant to pay. These restrictions, in many instances, will lead to results where a plaintiff recovers a token $1.00 as nominal damages for the violation of important constitutional rights, or where plaintiffs with comparable deprivations recover unequal amounts simply because of a fortuitous difference in defendants. With such limits on recovery, prospective plaintiffs may not be sufficiently motivated to litigate and vindicate their constitutional rights.

6. Does *Stachura* endorse *Bell*'s premise for presumed damages in first amendment cases, i.e., the proposition that presumed damages are available for violations of the right to vote?

Do you agree with *Bell* that presumed damages should be allowed for other substantive constitutional violations besides the first amendment, by analogy to dignitary torts? Are presumed damages necessary for such torts, given that the victim may suffer physical or emotional injuries that can easily be proven?

7. Should the appropriateness of presumed damages in section 1983 cases turn on whether

they would be available for an analogous common law tort? See *Parrish v. Johnson*, 800 F.2d 600 (6th Cir. 1986), where the court held that presumed damages could be recovered for a prison guard's constitutional violation in waving a knife in front of the plaintiff, but not for failing to provide proper medical care. Knife-waving could be compared to common law assault, where presumed damages could be recovered. By contrast, no presumed damages were available at common law for inadequate medical care.

Professor Nahmod is strongly critical of *Parrish*:

> For one thing, it makes common law tort doctrines determinative of section 1983 damages rules, which should be informed by such tort doctrines but not governed by them. For another, it unduly complicates the damages inquiry for courts and juries; they will have to make particularized determinations by analogy from different common law torts in each and every Eighth Amendment case.

S. Nahmod, supra, at 324.

Do you agree? Would Professor Nahmod reject the specific result reached in *Parrish*? If not, why does he criticize the case so vigorously?

8. Recall from Chapter 3 that a section 1983 suit may be brought to redress a breach of the dormant commerce clause. Should presumed damages be available in such a case? If not, what is the relevant difference between this and other substantive constitutional violations? Should presumed damages be allowed for statutory violations, brought under the "laws" clause of section 1983, as discussed in Chapter 4 supra? What factors matter in resolving this issue? Does the answer depend on the statute at issue?

Cf. *Baumgardner v. U.S. Dept. of Housing*, 960 F.2d 572, 581–83 (6th Cir. 1992) (rejecting presumed damages for a violation of the Fair Housing Act). The plaintiffs in *Baumgardner* were males charging sex discrimination. Assuming the court is right, would the same result be appropriate in a race discrimination suit brought by blacks? See, e.g., *Seaton v. Sky Realty Co.*, 491 F.2d 634 (7th Cir. 1974) (a section 1982 case in which the court awarded $500 presumed damages).

In this regard, note that in section 1983 cases based on constitutional violations, courts treat racial discrimination as a prime candidate for presumed damages. See, e.g., *Stallworth v. Shuler*, 777 F.2d 1431 (11th Cir. 1985).

9. In the defamation context the Supreme Court has restricted the availability of presumed damages. If the subject matter of the defamation is of public concern, or the plaintiff is a public figure or public official, they may be awarded only upon a showing that the defendant knew the statement was false or acted with reckless disregard of its truth or falsity. What is the relevance of this development to the role of presumed damages for constitutional torts? Do constitutional values bear on the two contexts in the same way, thereby suggesting similar limits on presumed damages in section 1983 cases?

One reason for restrictions on presumed damages in the defamation context, adverted to by *Stachura*, is that juries are "free to award arbitrary amounts without any evidentiary basis, or to use their unbounded discretion to punish unpopular defendants." 477 U.S. at 310 (citing *Gertz*). Is the danger that presumed damages would be used to punish unpopular defendants as great in the section 1983 context as it is in libel?

10. Whether and in what circumstances presumed damages are available remains an open issue, at least in the Supreme Court. That issue aside, many general principles governing section 1983 damages are simply applications of the compensation principle articulated in *Carey* and elaborated in countless common law tort cases. As in other tort cases, plaintiffs may recover for lost income, property damage, medical expenses, and pain and suffering, including humiliation and emotional distress. See, e.g., *Wade v. Orange Co. Sheriff's Office*, 844 F.2d 951 (2d Cir. 1988) (upholding a $54,000 award for humiliation and embarrassment due to racial discrimination).

Plaintiffs may recover the readily foreseeable consequential damages of the constitutional violation, such as the attorney's fees spent defending a charge brought pursuant to an unconstitutional arrest, see *Borunda v. Richmond*, 885 F.2d 1384 (9th Cir. 1988), or harm to the plaintiff's business due to an illegal search and the attendant publicity, see *BCR Transportation Co. v. Fontaine*, 727 F.2d 7 (1st Cir. 1984).

Other familiar principles also apply. Plaintiffs have an obligation take reasonable steps to mitigate damages; payments received from collateral sources do not count against their recovery; spouses of constitutional tort victims are entitled to recover consortium.

In *Green v. Johnson*, 977 F.2d 1383 (10th Cir. 1992) a prisoner successfully sued for mistreatment by guards, recovering $15,000 in compensatory damages. On appeal, he argued that the award was too low. In turning him down, the court said, among other things: "Given that plaintiff is a ward of the state, provided with room, board, and medical care, his need for financial restitution based on his injuries is substantially less than that of persons responsible for their own economic support." Id. at 1389. Is this sentence consistent with the common law collateral source rule, under which the existence of collateral sources of compensation for the plaintiff's injuries is irrelevant to the calculation of damages owed by the tortfeasor? After *Carey* are lower courts free to replace the general common law rule with a rule of their own choosing? Is it relevant that many states have enacted statutes that modify the common law rule by permitting or requiring juries to take account of collateral sources?

May the jury be instructed that, if an officer is liable, his municipal employer may indemnify him? See *Larez v. Holcomb*, 16 F.3d 1513, 1519 (9th Cir. 1994) (no, applying the common law rule).

11. While the basic principles of tort damages are well-settled in the common law, there are areas of dispute. For example, some common law courts allow parents and children to sue for consortium, while others restrict it to spouses. Some allow recovery for the fear of some future catastrophe (like developing cancer) made more likely by the defendant's breach of duty, while others require current injury. Some authorize a separate instruction to the jury on lost enjoyment of life, while others insist that this be made a part of the pain and suffering instruction.

Granted that common law damages principles apply to constitutional tort cases, how should courts in section 1983 cases address controverted issues like these? Should the federal court treat section 1983 cases as indistinguishable from other tort cases, or does the constitutional context matter, perhaps justifying a different result than the same court would reach in a common law tort case?

If the constitutional context does matter, which way does it cut? Does it justify more liberal damages awards, because constitutional rights are more vital than common law rights and hence require broader remedies for their effective enforcement? Or does the anti-democratic nature of constitutional rights mean that courts should erect a more restrictive set of remedial principles, so as to limit the intrusion of constitutional tort on majoritarian rule? Are there other arguments for or against one or the other of these approaches to constitutional remedies? Can you think of a better alternative than either of them?

12. As in common law torts, damage awards in constitutional cases are reviewable by the trial judge and appellate courts for excessiveness or (much more rarely) inadequacy. One approach to this task is to measure the amount of the award against the evidence and make an intuitive judgment as to whether the evidence reasonably supports it. See, e.g., *Hale v. Fish*, 899 F.2d 390, 403 (5th Cir. 1990) (the propriety of an award is determined "by a review of the facts of each case"). Other courts, notably the Seventh Circuit, seek a more objective standard of review. See, e.g., *Cygnar v. City of Chicago*, 865 F.2d 827 (7th Cir. 1989); *Hagge v. Bauer*, 827 F.2d 101, 109 (7th Cir. 1987). They apply a "comparability" approach, under which they look to awards made in other cases in evaluating the one at hand. See 1 Nahmod, supra, at 287; *Hagge*, supra, ("Lest we grope for objective standards of compensatory damages in thin air, comparability has developed as an element of damage award analysis.") Note that comparisons are made not only to similar cases but to cases where the injuries were of a different magnitude. In *Hagge*, for example, the court found a $75,000 award appropriate by comparing it with the awards made for lesser injuries. See 827 F.2d at 110.

Which method is better? Does the case-by-case approach result in unfairness, since different juries may accord disparate treatment to similar cases? Is there a parallel danger that the comparability approach will treat different cases similarly, by giving too much weight to superficial similarities between cases and ignoring subtle differences? Does comparability amount to an unwillingness on the part of appellate judges to take responsibility for their actions?

Does the comparability approach rest on the premise that the first few cases to consider the proper award for a certain injury more than likely reach the right results? If not, why require later cases to toe the line established in earlier ones? If so, why should earlier judges and juries be presumed more capable of reaching correct results than later ones? In any event, it is clear that the results in early cases will heavily influence appellate review of later awards, is it not?

B. Punitive Damages

Smith v. Wade

461 U.S. 30 (1983)

Justice **Brennan** delivered the opinion of the Court.

We granted certiorari in this case to decide whether the District Court for the Western District of Missouri applied the correct legal standard in instructing the jury that it might award punitive damages under 42 U.S.C. § 1983. The Court of Appeals for the Eighth Circuit sustained the award of punitive damages. We affirm.

I

The petitioner, William H. Smith, is a guard at Algoa Reformatory, a unit of the Missouri Division of Corrections for youthful first offenders. The respondent, Daniel R. Wade, was assigned to Algoa as an inmate in 1976. In the summer of 1976 Wade voluntarily checked into Algoa's protective custody unit. Because of disciplinary violations during his stay in protective custody, Wade was given a short term in punitive segregation and then transferred to administrative segregation. On the evening of Wade's first day in administrative segregation, he was placed in a cell with another inmate. Later, when Smith came on duty in Wade's dormitory, he placed a third inmate in Wade's cell. According to Wade's testimony, his cellmates harassed, beat, and sexually assaulted him.

Wade brought suit under 42 U.S.C. § 1983 against Smith and four other guards and correctional officials, alleging that his Eighth Amendment rights had been violated. At trial his evidence showed that he had placed himself in protective custody because of prior incidents of violence against him by other inmates. The third prisoner whom Smith added to the cell had been placed in administrative segregation for fighting. Smith had made no effort to find out whether another cell was available; in fact there was another cell in the same dormitory with only one occupant. Further, only a few weeks earlier, another inmate had been beaten to death in the same dormitory during the same shift, while Smith had been on duty. Wade asserted that Smith and the other defendants knew or should have known that an assault against him was likely under the circumstances . . .

[T]he District Judge . . . instructed the jury that Wade could make out an Eighth Amendment violation only by showing "physical abuse of such base, inhumane and barbaric proportions as to shock the sensibilities." Further, because of Smith's qualified immunity as a prison guard, the judge instructed the jury that Wade could recover only if the defendants were guilty of "gross negligence" (defined as "a callous indifference or a thoughtless disregard for the consequences of one's act or failure to act") or "[egregious] failure to protect" (defined as "a flagrant or remarkably bad failure to protect") Wade. He reiterated that Wade could not recover on a showing of simple negligence.

The District Judge also charged the jury that it could award punitive damages on a proper showing:

"In addition to actual damages, the law permits the jury, under certain circumstances, to award the injured person punitive and exemplary damages, in order to punish the wrongdoer for some extraordinary misconduct, and to serve as an example or warning to others not to engage in such conduct.

"If you find the issues in favor of the plaintiff, and if the conduct of one or more of the defendants is shown to be a reckless or callous disregard of, or indifference to, the rights or safety of others, then you may assess punitive or exemplary damages in addition to any award of actual damages.

". . . The amount of punitive or exemplary damages assessed against any defendant may be such sum as you believe will serve to punish that defendant and to deter him and others from like conduct."

The jury . . . found Smith liable, however, and awarded $25,000 in compensatory damages and $5,000 in punitive damages. The District Court entered judgment on the verdict, and the Court of Appeals affirmed.

In this Court, Smith attacks only the award of punitive damages. He does not challenge the correctness of the instructions on liability or qualified immunity, nor does he question the adequacy of the evidence to support the verdict of liability for compensatory damages.

II

Section 1983 . . . was intended to create "a species of tort liability" in favor of persons deprived of federally secured rights. We noted in *Carey* that there was little in the section's legislative history concerning the damages recoverable for this tort liability. In the absence of more specific guidance, we looked first to the common law of torts (both modern and as of 1871), with such modification or adaptation as might be necessary to carry out the purpose and policy of the statute. We have done the same in other contexts arising under § 1983, especially the recurring problem of common-law immunities.

Smith correctly concedes that "punitive damages are available in a 'proper' § 1983 action. . . ." Although there was debate about the theoretical correctness of the punitive damages doctrine in the latter part of the last century, the doctrine was accepted as settled law by nearly all state and federal courts, including this Court. It was likewise generally established that individual public officers were liable for punitive damages for their misconduct on the same basis as other individual defendants. See also *Scott v. Donald*, 165 U.S. 58, 77–89 (1897) (punitive damages for constitutional tort). Further, although the precise issue of the availability of punitive damages under § 1983 has never come squarely before us, we have had occasion more than once to make clear our view that they are available; indeed, we have rested decisions on related questions on the premise of such availability.

Smith argues, nonetheless, that this was not a "proper" case in which to award punitive damages. More particularly, he attacks the instruction that punitive damages could be awarded on a finding of reckless or callous disregard of or indifference to Wade's rights or safety. Instead, he contends that the proper test is one of actual malicious intent—"ill will, spite, or intent to injure." He offers two arguments for this position: first, that actual intent is the proper standard for punitive damages in all cases under § 1983; and second, that even if intent is not always required, it should be required here because the threshold for punitive damages should always be higher than that for liability in the first instance. We address these in turn.

III

Smith does not argue that the common law, either in 1871 or now, required or requires a showing of actual malicious intent for recovery of punitive damages.

Perhaps not surprisingly, there was significant variation (both terminological and substantive) among American jurisdictions in the latter 19th century on the precise standard to be applied in awarding punitive damages— variation that was exacerbated by the ambiguity and slipperiness of such common terms as "malice" and "gross negligence." Most of the confusion, however, seems to have been over the degree of negligence, recklessness, carelessness, or culpable indifference that should be required—not over whether actual intent was essential. On the contrary, the rule in a large majority of jurisdictions was that punitive damages (also called exemplary damages, vindictive damages, or smart money) could be awarded without a showing of actual ill will, spite, or intent to injure.

This Court so stated on several occasions, before and shortly after 1871 . . . [Here the Court reviewed some of its nineteenth century punitive damages cases.]

The large majority of state and lower federal courts were in agreement that punitive damages awards did not require a showing of actual malicious intent; they permitted punitive awards on variously stated standards of negligence, recklessness, or other culpable conduct short of actual malicious intent.[12]

The same rule applies today. *The Restatement (Second) of Torts* (1979), for example, states: "Punitive damages may be awarded for conduct that is outrageous, because of the defendant's evil motive or his reckless indifference to the rights of others." § 908(2) (emphasis added); see also id., Comment b. Most cases under state common law, although varying in their precise terminology, have adopted more or less the same rule, recognizing that punitive damages in tort cases may be awarded not only for actual intent to injure or evil motive, but also for recklessness, serious indifference to or disregard for the rights of others, or even gross negligence.

The remaining question is whether the policies and purposes of § 1983 itself require a departure from the rules of tort common law. As a general matter, we discern no reason why a person whose federally guaranteed rights have been violated should be granted a more restrictive remedy than a person asserting an ordinary tort cause of action. Smith offers us no persuasive reason to the contrary.

Smith's argument, which he offers in several forms, is that an actual-intent standard is preferable to a recklessness standard because it is less vague. He points out that punitive damages, by their very nature, are not awarded to compensate the injured party. He concedes, of course, that deterrence of future egregious conduct is a primary purpose of both § 1983, and of punitive damages. But deterrence, he contends, cannot be achieved unless the standard of conduct sought to be deterred is stated with sufficient clarity to enable potential defendants to conform to the law and to avoid the proposed sanction.

---

[12] In the often-cited case of Welch v. Durand, for example, the court held that punitive damages were proper where the defendant's pistol bullet, fired at a target, ricocheted and hit the plaintiff:

"In what cases then may smart money be awarded in addition to the damages? The proper answer to this question . . . seems to be, in actions of tort founded on the malicious or wanton misconduct or culpable neglect of the defendant. . . .

"In this case the defendant was guilty of wanton misconduct and culpable neglect. . . . It is an immaterial fact that the injury was unintentional, and that the ball glanced from the intended direction. . . . [If] the act is done where there are objects from which the balls may glance and endanger others, the act is wanton, reckless, without due care, and grossly negligent." Id.

. . .

[The remainder of the footnote discusses other nineteenth century cases and maintains that "Justice Rehnquist's assertion that a 'solid majority of jurisdictions' required actual malicious standard is simply untrue."]

Recklessness or callous indifference, he argues, is too uncertain a standard to achieve deterrence rationally and fairly. A prison guard, for example, can be expected to know whether he is acting with actual ill will or intent to injure, but not whether he is being reckless or callously indifferent.

Smith's argument, if valid, would apply to ordinary tort cases as easily as to § 1983 suits; hence, it hardly presents an argument for adopting a different rule under § 1983. In any event, the argument is unpersuasive. While, arguendo, an intent standard may be easier to understand and apply to particular situations than a recklessness standard, we are not persuaded that a recklessness standard is too vague to be fair or useful. In the *Milwaukee* case, 91 U.S. 489 (1876), we adopted a recklessness standard rather than a gross negligence standard precisely because recklessness would better serve the need for adequate clarity and fair application. Almost a century later, in the First Amendment context, we held that punitive damages cannot be assessed for defamation in the absence of proof of "knowledge of falsity or reckless disregard for the truth." *Gertz.* Our concern in *Gertz* was that the threat of punitive damages, if not limited to especially egregious cases, might "inhibit the vigorous exercise of First Amendment freedoms," id.—a concern at least as pressing as any urged by Smith in this case. Yet we did not find it necessary to impose an actual-intent standard there. Just as Smith has not shown why § 1983 should give higher protection from punitive damages than ordinary tort law, he has not explained why it gives higher protection than we have demanded under the First Amendment.

More fundamentally, Smith's argument for certainty in the interest of deterrence overlooks the distinction between a standard for punitive damages and a standard of liability in the first instance. Smith seems to assume that prison guards and other state officials look mainly to the standard for punitive damages in shaping their conduct. We question the premise; we assume, and hope, that most officials are guided primarily by the underlying standards of federal substantive law—both out of devotion to duty, and in the interest of avoiding liability for compensatory damages. At any rate, the conscientious officer who desires clear guidance on how to do his job

and avoid lawsuits can and should look to the standard for actionability in the first instance. The need for exceptional clarity in the standard for punitive damages arises only if one assumes that there are substantial numbers of officers who will not be deterred by compensatory damages; only such officers will seek to guide their conduct by the punitive damages standard. The presence of such officers constitutes a powerful argument against raising the threshold for punitive damages . . .

[I]n the absence of any persuasive argument to the contrary based on the policies of § 1983, we are content to adopt the policy judgment of the common law—that reckless or callous disregard for the plaintiff's rights, as well as intentional violations of federal law, should be sufficient to trigger a jury's consideration of the appropriateness of punitive damages.

IV

Smith contends that even if § 1983 does not ordinarily require a showing of actual malicious intent for an award of punitive damages, such a showing should be required in this case. He argues that the deterrent and punitive purposes of punitive damages are served only if the threshold for punitive damages is higher in every case than the underlying standard for liability in the first instance. In this case, while the District Judge did not use the same precise terms to explain the standards of liability for compensatory and punitive damages, the parties agree that there is no substantial difference between the showings required by the two instructions; both apply a standard of reckless or callous indifference to Wade's rights. Hence, Smith argues, the District Judge erred in not requiring a higher standard for punitive damages, namely, actual malicious intent.

This argument incorrectly assumes that, simply because the instructions specified the same threshold of liability for punitive and compensatory damages, the two forms of damages were equally available to the plaintiff. The argument overlooks a key feature of punitive damages—that they are never awarded as of right, no matter how egregious the defendant's conduct. "If the plaintiff proves sufficiently serious misconduct on the defendant's part, the question whether to award punitive damages is left to the jury, which may or may not make such an award." D. Dobbs, *Law of Remedies* 204 (1973) (footnote omitted).

Compensatory damages, by contrast, are mandatory; once liability is found, the jury is required to award compensatory damages in an amount appropriate to compensate the plaintiff for his loss. Hence, it is not entirely accurate to say that punitive and compensatory damages were awarded in this case on the same standard. To make its punitive award, the jury was required to find not only that Smith's conduct met the recklessness threshold (a question of ultimate fact), but also that his conduct merited a punitive award of $5,000 in addition to the compensatory award (a discretionary moral judgment).

Moreover, the rules of ordinary tort law are once more against Smith's argument. There has never been any general common-law rule that the threshold for punitive damages must always be higher than that for compensatory liability. On the contrary, both the *First* and *Second Restatements of Torts* have pointed out that "in torts like malicious prosecution that require a particular antisocial state of mind, the improper motive of the tortfeasor is both a necessary element in the cause of action and a reason for awarding punitive damages." Accordingly, in situations where the standard for compensatory liability is as high as or higher than the usual threshold for punitive damages, most courts will permit awards of punitive damages without requiring any extra showing . . .

This common-law rule makes sense in terms of the purposes of punitive damages . . . The focus is on the character of the tortfeasor's conduct—whether it is of the sort that calls for deterrence and punishment over and above that provided by compensatory awards. If it is of such a character, then it is appropriate to allow a jury to assess punitive damages; and that assessment does not become less appropriate simply because the plaintiff in the case faces a more demanding standard of actionability . . .

As with his first argument, Smith gives us no good reason to depart from the common-law rule in the context of section 1983.

V

We hold that a jury may be permitted to assess punitive damages in an action under § 1983 when the defendant's conduct is shown to be motivated by evil motive or intent, or when it involves reckless or callous indifference to the federally protected rights of others. We further hold that this threshold applies even when the underlying standard of liability for compensatory damages is one of recklessness. Because the jury instructions in this case are in accord with this rule, the judgment of the Court of Appeals is

Affirmed.

Justice **Rehnquist**, with whom The Chief Justice and Justice **Powell** join, dissenting.

. . . In my view, a forthright inquiry into the intent of the 42nd Congress and a balanced consideration of the public policies at issue compel the conclusion that the proper standard for an award of punitive damages under § 1983 requires at least some degree of bad faith or improper motive on the part of the defendant . . .

I

[I]t is useful to consider briefly the purposes of punitive damages. A fundamental premise of our legal system is the notion that damages are awarded to compensate the victim—to redress the injuries that he or she actually has suffered. In sharp contrast to this principle, the doctrine of punitive damages permits the award of "damages" beyond even the most generous and expansive conception of actual injury to the plaintiff. This anomaly is rationalized principally on three grounds. First, punitive damages "are assessed for the avowed purpose of visiting a punishment upon the defendant." Second, the doctrine is rationalized on the ground that it deters persons from violating the rights of others. Third, punitive damages are justified as a "bounty" that encourages private lawsuits seeking to assert legal rights.

Despite these attempted justifications, the doctrine of punitive damages has been vigorously criticized throughout the Nation's history. Countless cases remark that such damages have never been "a favorite of the law." . . .

Punitive damages are generally seen as a windfall to plaintiffs, who are entitled to receive full compensation for their injuries—but no more. Even assuming that a punitive "fine" should be imposed after a civil trial, the penalty should go to the State, not to the plaintiff—who by hypothesis is fully compensated. Moreover, although punitive damages are "quasi-criminal," their imposition is unaccompanied by the types of safeguards present in criminal proceedings. This absence of safeguards is exacerbated by the fact that punitive damages are frequently based upon the caprice and prejudice of jurors . . . Finally, the alleged deterrence achieved by punitive damages awards is likely outweighed by the costs—such as the encouragement of unnecessary litigation and the chilling of desirable conduct—flowing from the rule, at least when the standards on which the awards are based are ill-defined . . .

[Justice Rehnquist argued that, since the issue was one of statutory interpretation, the intent of the 42nd Congress was the key to resolving it. Accordingly, recourse to common law decisions should be limited to doctrine with which the members of that Congress would have been familiar. The availability of punitive damages should depend on the state of the law in 1871. After examining a number of cases, he concluded that at that time the Supreme Court and most state courts "took the view that the standard for an award of punitive damages included a requirement of ill will."]

V

Finally, even if the evidence of congressional intent were less clearcut, I would be persuaded to resolve any ambiguity in favor of an actual-malice standard. It scarcely needs repeating that punitive damages are not a "favorite of the law", owing to the numerous persuasive criticisms that have been leveled against the doctrine. The majority reasons that these arguments apply to all awards of punitive damages, not just to those under § 1983; while this is of course correct, it does little to reduce the strength of the arguments, and, if they are persuasive, we should not blindly follow the mistakes other courts have made.

Much of what has been said above regarding the failings of a punitive damages remedy is equally appropriate here. It is anomalous, and counter to deep-rooted legal principles and common-sense notions, to punish persons who meant no harm, and to award a windfall, in the form of punitive damages, to someone who already has been fully compensated.

These peculiarities ought to be carefully limited—not expanded to every case where a jury may think a defendant was too careless, particularly where a vaguely defined, elastic standard like "reckless indifference" gives free reign to the biases and prejudices of juries. In short, there are persuasive reasons not to create a new punitive damages remedy unless it is clear that Congress so intended.

This argument is particularly powerful in a case like this, where the uncertainty resulting from largely random awards of punitive damages will have serious effects upon the performance by state and local officers of their official duties. One of the principal themes of our immunity decisions is that the threat of liability must not deter an official's "willingness to execute his office with the decisiveness and the judgment required by the public good." *Scheuer v. Rhodes*. To avoid stifling the types of initiative and decisiveness necessary for the "government to govern," we have held that officials will be liable for compensatory damages only for certain types of conduct. Precisely the same reasoning applies to liability for punitive damages. Because punitive damages generally are not subject to any relation to actual harm suffered, and because the recklessness standard is so imprecise, the remedy poses an even greater threat to the ability of officials to take decisive, efficient action. After the Court's decision, governmental officials will be subjected to the possibility of damages awards unlimited by any harm they may have caused or the fact they acted with unquestioned good faith: when swift action is demanded, their thoughts likely will be on personal financial consequences that may result from their conduct—but whose limits they cannot predict—and not upon their official duties. It would have been difficult for the Court to have fashioned a more effective Damoclean sword than the open-ended, standardless, and unpredictable liability it creates today.

Moreover, notwithstanding the Court's inability to discern them, there are important distinctions between a right to damages under § 1983 and a similar right under state tort law. A leading rationale seized upon by proponents of punitive damages to justify the doctrine is that "the award is . . . a covert response to the legal system's overt refusal to provide financing for litigation." Yet, 42 U.S.C.

§ 1988 (1976 ed., Supp. V) provides not just a "covert response" to plaintiffs' litigation expenses but an explicit provision for an award to the prevailing party in a § 1983 action of "a reasonable attorney's fee as part of the costs." By permitting punitive damages as well as attorney's fees, § 1983 plaintiffs, unlike state tort law plaintiffs, get not just one windfall but two—one for them, and one for their lawyer. This difference between the incentives that are present in state tort actions, and those in § 1983 actions, makes the Court's reliance upon the standard for punitive damages in the former entirely inapposite: in fashioning a new financial lure to litigate under § 1983 the Court does not act in a vacuum, but, by adding to existing incentives, creates an imbalance of inducements to litigate that may have serious consequences.

The staggering effect of § 1983 claims upon the work load of the federal courts has been decried time and again. The torrent of frivolous claims under that section threatens to incapacitate the judicial system's resolution of claims where true injustice is involved; those claims which truly warrant redress are in a very real danger of being lost in a sea of meritless suits. Yet, apparently oblivious to this, the Court today reads into the silent, inhospitable terms of § 1983 a remedy that is designed to serve as a "bounty" to encourage private litigation. In a time when the courts are flooded with suits that do not raise colorable claims, in large part because of the existing incentives for litigation under § 1983, it is regrettable that the Court should take upon itself, in apparent disregard for the likely intent of the 42nd Congress, the legislative task of encouraging yet more litigation. There is a limit to what the federal judicial system can bear.

Finally, by unquestioningly transferring the standard of punitive damages in state tort actions to federal § 1983 actions, the Court utterly fails to recognize the fundamental difference that exists between an award of punitive damages by a federal court, acting under § 1983, and a similar award by a state court acting under prevailing local laws. While state courts may choose to adopt such measures as they deem appropriate to punish officers of the jurisdiction in which they sit, the standards they choose to adopt can scarcely be taken as evidence of what it is appropri-

ate for a federal court to do. When federal courts enforce punitive damages awards against local officials they intrude into sensitive areas of sovereignty of coordinate branches of our Nation, thus implicating the most basic values of our system of federalism. Moreover, by yet further distorting the incentives that exist for litigating claims against local officials in federal court, as opposed to state courts, the Court's decision makes it even more difficult for state courts to attempt to conform the conduct of state officials to the Constitution.

I dissent.

Justice **O'Connor**, dissenting.

Although I agree with the result reached in Justice Rehnquist's dissent, I write separately because I cannot agree with the approach taken by either the Court or Justice Rehnquist. Both opinions engage in exhaustive, but ultimately unilluminating, exegesis of the common law of the availability of punitive damages in 1871. Although both the Court and Justice Rehnquist display admirable skills in legal research and analysis of great numbers of musty cases, the results do not significantly further the goal of the inquiry: to establish the intent of the 42nd Congress. In interpreting § 1983, we have often looked to the common law as it existed in 1871, in the belief that, when Congress was silent on a point, it intended to adopt the principles of the common law with which it was familiar. See, e.g., *Newport v. Fact Concerts, Inc.*; *Carey v. Piphus.* This approach makes sense when there was a generally prevailing rule of common law, for then it is reasonable to assume that Congressmen were familiar with that rule and imagined that it would cover the cause of action that they were creating. But when a significant split in authority existed, it strains credulity to argue that Congress simply assumed that one view rather than the other would govern. Particularly in a case like this one, in which those interpreting the common law of 1871 must resort to dictionaries in an attempt to translate the language of the late 19th century into terms that judges of the late 20th century can understand, and in an area in which the courts of the earlier period frequently used inexact and contradictory language, we cannot safely infer anything about congressional intent from the divided contemporaneous judicial opinions. The battle of the string citations can have no winner.

Once it is established that the common law of 1871 provides us with no real guidance on this question, we should turn to the policies underlying § 1983 to determine which rule best accords with those policies. In Fact Concerts, we identified the purposes of § 1983 as pre-eminently to compensate victims of constitutional violations and to deter further violations. See also *Robertson v. Wegmann*; *Carey v. Piphus*. The conceded availability of compensatory damages, particularly when coupled with the availability of attorney's fees under § 1988, completely fulfills the goal of compensation, leaving only deterrence to be served by awards of punitive damages. We must then confront the close question whether a standard permitting an award of unlimited punitive damages on the basis of recklessness will chill public officials in the performance of their duties more than it will deter violations of the Constitution, and whether the availability of punitive damages for reckless violations of the Constitution in addition to attorney's fees will create an incentive to bring an ever-increasing flood of § 1983 claims, threatening the ability of the federal courts to handle those that are meritorious. Although I cannot concur in Justice Rehnquist's wholesale condemnation of awards of punitive damages in any context or with the suggestion that punitive damages should not be available even for intentional or malicious violations of constitutional rights, I do agree with the discussion in Part V of his opinion of the special problems of permitting awards of punitive damages for the recklessness of public officials. Since awards of compensatory damages and attorney's fees already provide significant deterrence, I am persuaded that the policies counseling against awarding punitive damages for the recklessness of public officials outweigh the desirability of any incremental deterrent effect that such awards may have. Consequently, I dissent.

NOTES

1. In the course of upholding a punitive damages award, the seventh circuit said: "The defendants correctly note that jury awards for

unconstitutional force . . . and arrest without probable cause . . . must be supported by a finding that the officers acted with the intent to harm." *Wallace v. Mulholland*, 957 F.2d 333, 337 (7th Cir. 1992). For this proposition, it cited *Hagge v. Bauer*, 827 F.2d 101, 110 (7th Cir. 1987), where the court said: "Punitive damages are appropriate when the defendant acted wantonly and willfully, or was motivated in his actions by ill will or a desire to injure."

Suppose you were a plaintiff's attorney seeking punitive damages for reckless conduct on the part of a policeman. The defense quotes *Wallace* to the effect that punitives are inappropriate unless plaintiff shows intent to harm. How would you respond? What would you say in the event the district judge seems open to the defendant's suggestion that *Wallace* implicitly overrules *Hagge*? *Wallace* does not cite *Smith v. Wade*. Should it have done so?

2. *City of Newport v. Fact Concerts*, 453 U.S. 247 (1981), decided two years before *Smith*, held that municipal governments are immune from liability for punitive damages. It relied upon both "the common law background and policy considerations."

First, the Court examined nineteenth century tort law and concluded that "[b]y the time Congress enacted what is now section 1983, the immunity of a municipal corporation from punitive damages at common law was not open to serious question." Turning to policy, the Court noted that punitive damages "are not intended to compensate the injured party, but rather to punish the tortfeasor whose wrongful action was intentional or malicious, and to deter him and others from similar extreme conduct." It declared that "punitive damages imposed on a municipality are in effect a windfall to a fully compensated plaintiff, and are likely accompanied by an increase in taxes or a reduction of public services for the citizens footing the bill. Neither reason nor justice suggests that such retribution should be visited upon the shoulders of blameless or unknowing taxpayers."

Insofar as the aim of punitive damages is deterrence of wrongdoing rather than retribution,

it is far from clear that municipal officials . . . would be deterred from wrongdoing by the knowledge that large punitive awards could be assessed based on the wealth of their municipality . . . Moreover, there is available a more effective means of deterrence. By allowing juries and courts to assess punitive damages in appropriate circumstances against the offending official . . . the statute directly advances the public's interest in preventing repeated constitutional deprivations . . .

Finally, although the benefits associated with awarding punitive damages against municipalities under section 1983 are of doubtful character, the costs may be very real [especially since statutory as well as constitutional violations may be redressed under the statute] . . . Under this expanded liability, municipalities and other units of state and local government face the possibility of having to assure compensation for persons harmed by abuses of governmental authority covering a large range of activity in everyday life. To add the burden of exposure for the malicious conduct of individual government employees may create a serious risk to the financial integrity of these governmental entities.

To what extent is the holding in *Smith v. Wade* based on the reasoning behind *City of Newport*?

3. In a footnote, *City of Newport* held out the possibility that a municipality might yet be held liable for punitives: "It is perhaps possible to imagine an extreme situation where the taxpayers are directly responsible for perpetrating an outrageous abuse of constitutional rights. Nothing of that kind is presented by this case. Moreover, such an occurrence is sufficiently unlikely that we need not anticipate it here." 453 U.S. at 267 n. 29. Can you think of circumstances that would justify an exception to the rule? Suppose the voters enacted laws mandating racial discrimination? Could the municipality defend (against punitives) on the ground that its taxpayers cannot fairly be held responsible for the actions of the voters?

See Chapter 5 for a treatment of local government liability.

4. Under the reasoning of *Smith*, is it necessary that compensatory damages be recovered in order to receive punitive damages? See *Glover v. Alabama Dept. of Corrections*, 734 F.2d 691, 694 (11th Cir. 1984) (affirming jury award of $1 in nominal damages and $25,000 in

punitive damages to plaintiff, an inmate, where the defendant official was found responsible for having encouraged another inmate to stab the plaintiff); *Davis v. Locke*, 936 F.2d 1208 (11th Cir. 1991) (affirming $1750 punitive awards against two prison guards who dropped plaintiff inmate on his head, even though no compensatory award was made).

Do *Glover* and *Davis* withstand due process objections on behalf of the defendants? See, e.g., *Pacific Mutual Life Ins. Co. v. Haslip*, 499 U.S. 1 (1991) (upholding a punitive award that was more than four times as great as the compensatory award against such a challenge, but warning that broad jury discretion "may invite extremes that jar one's constitutional sensibilities." See also *TXO Production Corp. v. Alliance Resources Corp.*, 113 S. Ct. 2711 (1993) (upholding a $10 million punitive award when compensatory damages were $19,000); *Morgan v. Woessaw, 997 F.2d 1244 (9th Cir. 1993)* (remanding a § 1983 punitive damages award for reconsideration in light of *Haslip*).

Does the fact that the plaintiff relies on the constitution in a section 1983 case mean that due process arguments against big punitive awards are stronger or weaker than in common law torts? Cf. *Johnson v. Hugo's Skateway*, 949 F.2d 1338 (4th Cir. 1991) (remanding for a determination of whether $175,000 punitive damages award for a *state* law racial harassment claim violates due process in light of *Pacific Mutual*).

5. Awards of punitive damages are reviewable for excessiveness. Some courts use a "shock the conscience" standard, e.g., *Zarcone v. Perry*, 572 F.2d 52, 56–57 ((2d Cir. 1978); some say the issue is whether the award "was so excessive as to indicate inherent passion and prejudice [of the jury]," e.g., *Auster Oil & Gas Co. v. Stream*, 835 F.2d 597, 603 (5th Cir. 1988) (overturning a $5 million award for an unconstitutional search and seizure of plaintiff's property); some ask if the award is "grossly excessive", e.g., *Fountila v. Carter*, 571 F.2d 487 (9th Cir. 1978); or "so grossly excessive as to shock the judicial conscience", e.g., *Keenan v. City of Philadelphia*, 983 F.2d 459, 472 (3rd Cir. 1992) (upholding a $1.2 million award spread over four defendants for violations of free speech and equal protection). "Whatever characterization is used, it is clear that the standard is sufficiently flexible so that, particularly where substantial punitive damages are awarded, a reviewing court in effect can do what it wants." 1 S. Nahmod, supra, at 333–34 (giving examples).

6. *Smith v. Wade* is a useful vehicle for exploring the Court's methodology in section 1983 cases. Both the majority and Justice Rehnquist's dissent in *Smith* delve deeply into nineteenth century case law, in passages we have largely omitted for the sake of saving space. In her opinion, Justice O'Connor shows some impatience with both sides. If the Court's aim is to interpret the statute, and toward that end to determine the intent of the 42nd Congress, isn't the 1871 case law highly relevant to the inquiry. Are post-1871 developments at all germane? If the analysis of 1871 law is inconclusive, should the Court resort to modern tort policy concerns? Should it employ modern constitutional policy considerations? Both?

Quite apart from the content of the law, the Court might choose between two rather different methods of statutory interpretation. First, it could approach each issue of statutory interpretation afresh, unimpeded by its decision on other issues. Or it could begin its analysis of specific problems from a set of broad principles that it applies consistently across the range of issues that may arise. (E.g., it might begin from the principle that the statute is to be construed broadly because its aim was to grant generous remedies for constitutional violations; alternatively, the first principle may be that it should be construed narrowly, because principles of federalism demand deference to state prerogatives, unless the statute clearly commands otherwise.) Which methodology is better? Why?

Based on *Smith* and the other cases in this book, how would you describe the Court's actual approach to issues of statutory interpretation in section 1983 cases? Does the Court follow a consistent approach throughout the cases, or does it seem to first decide on the result it wants to reach and then choose a theory of statutory interpretation that conveniently achieves that outcome? For a discussion of the issues raised in this note, see Wells, *The Past and the Future of Constitutional Tort*, 19 Conn. L. Rev. 53, 57–68 (1986).

7. *Smith* requires courts to give content to the term "recklessness" in the punitive damages context. Are punitive damages available when the defendant should, but does not, know that his actions violate the plaintiff's constitutional rights? Suppose the defendant knows that his actions run a serious risk of violating the plaintiff's rights? The following case addresses these issues.

Soderbeck v. Burnett County

752 F.2d 285 (7th Cir. 1985)

Posner, Circuit Judge.

Arline Soderbeck brought this suit under section 1 of the Civil Rights Act of 1871, now 42 U.S.C. § 1983, against Robert Kellberg (the Sheriff of Burnett County, Wisconsin), the three members of the county's Law Enforcement Committee, and the county itself. She alleges that she was fired from her job in the sheriff's office in violation of her rights under the First Amendment, made applicable to state action by the Fourteenth Amendment. She had been hired to work in the sheriff's department when her husband was the sheriff, but Kellberg defeated Soderbeck in a subsequent election for sheriff and the first thing he did on taking office in 1979 was to fire Mrs. Soderbeck. The jury was entitled to find that Kellberg's only reason for firing her was that she was the wife and presumed ally of his political adversary . . .

The jury brought in a verdict against . . . Sheriff Kellberg and Burnett County, of $33,375 in compensatory damages and $5,000 in punitive damages (the latter against Kellberg only) . . .

[After upholding the jury's determination of liability the court addressed the propriety of punitive damages.]

Although we therefore think the district judge was right not to disturb the jury's verdict of compensatory damages, we also think she was right to rescind the award of punitive damages. This conclusion requires us to resolve a question left unanswered by *Smith v. Wade*, 461 U.S. 30 (1983), where the Supreme Court held that punitive damages will lie for reckless as well as intentional violations of section 1983. The question is whether it is ever necessary to show that the defendant knew he was violating the plaintiff's legal rights.

In a recent section 1983 case we approved an instruction that allowed the jury to award punitive damages if it found the defendant's actions "maliciously or wantonly or oppressively done" and that defined these adverbs as follows: "An act or a failure to act is maliciously done if prompted or accompanied by ill will or spite or grudge either toward the injured person individually or toward all persons in one or more groups or categories of which the injured person is a member"; "wantonly done if done in reckless disregard or callous disregard of or indifference to the rights of one or more persons including the injured person"; "oppressively done if done in a way or manner which injures or damages or otherwise violates the rights of another person with unnecessary harshness or severity as by misuse, or abuse of authority, or power, or by taking advantage of some [weakness] or disability or misfortune of another person." *McKinley v. Trattles*, 732 F.2d 1320, 1326 n.2 (7th Cir. 1983) ("weakness" bracketed in original). This is a standard punitive-damages instruction, see 3 Devitt & Blackmar, *Federal Jury Practice and Instructions* § 85.11 (3d ed. 1977), which though not tailored to civil-rights cases is commonly used in them, see, e.g., besides *McKinley v. Trattles, Abraham v. Pekarski*, 728 F.2d 167, 172 n.2 (3rd Cir. 1984). Although the instruction conveys a mood (perhaps none too clearly to the average juror) rather than establishing precise criteria, it does imply distinct types of misconduct—though, as it seems to us, two rather than three. In the first, the defendant actually derives satisfaction from hurting the plaintiff; in the second, the defendant, while not having any particular desire to hurt the plaintiff, tramples on the plaintiff's rights, in a fashion that can fairly be called reckless, to accomplish his own aims. This distinction corresponds to the distinction in the criminal law between deliberate and reckless harm. If a man sets fire to a house intending to kill the occupants, he is a deliberate murderer; if he sets fire to a house he knows to be occupied, but does so to warm himself rather than to kill the occupants, he is a reckless murderer. But he is a murderer in either case, and would be subject to punitive damages in a suit for wrongful death. The distinction between de-

liberate and reckless wrongdoing is well captured by the Supreme Court's formulation of its holding in *Smith v. Wade*: "We hold that a jury may be permitted to assess punitive damages in an action under § 1983 when the defendant's conduct is shown to be motivated by evil motive or intent, or when it involves reckless or callous indifference to the federally protected rights of others."

Although there was some evidence in this case of personal spite by Kellberg toward the Soderbecks as well as political rivalry, and spite would bring the case within the first type of conduct for which punitive damages is a proper sanction, the special-verdict form, not challenged by the plaintiff, confined the jury to the second: "In terminating plaintiff Arline Soderbeck's employment with the Burnett County Sheriff's Department, did defendant Robert Kellberg act with reckless indifference to the plaintiff's rights not to be terminated for her associations or political activity?" (It is no doubt regrettable that the instructions to the jury did not define "reckless indifference," cf. *United States v. Hanlon*, 548 F.2d 1096, 1101–02 (2d Cir. 1977), as the legal meaning of the term is unlikely to be obvious to the average juror; but no complaint was made on that score.) This formulation allowed the jury to award punitive damages even if it found that Kellberg had fired Mrs. Soderbeck not to hurt her but just to make life easier for himself; and the district judge was quite right to hold that the evidence did not permit an award of punitive damages on this basis (that is, on the basis of recklessness).

The difference between deliberate and reckless harm is the difference between wanting to hurt someone and knowing that hurting someone is a highly likely consequence of an act undertaken for a different end. But in the latter case there must be knowledge of the danger that the defendant's act creates, which in this case is a danger of depriving a public employee of her freedom of speech; and the knowledge of this danger presupposes some knowledge of the free-speech rights of public employees.

This point can be made clearer by noting that a primary purpose (we think the primary purpose) of punitive damages, both generally and in section 1983 cases, is to deter. Unless the defendant knew that the conduct which resulted in the injury to the plaintiff was forbidden, an award of punitive damages will have no deterrent effect. This is the basis on which the Supreme Court has created a limited good-faith exception to the exclusionary rule, a rule whose current rationale is a deterrent one. See *United States v. Leon*, 468 U.S. 897 (1984).

If Kellberg had not fired but instead had arrested Mrs. Soderbeck, without any basis other than antipathy to her political connections, an award of punitive damages would clearly have been appropriate, even if no spite could be shown. Every law-enforcement officer in the United States knows—or had better learn—that the law places limits on the authority of the police. But a police officer in a small rural county, even a police chief or a sheriff, cannot be assumed to know that if he fires, on the most natural of political grounds, a clerical employee whose loyalty he has some reason to regard as a legitimate job qualification, he may be violating the law. His ignorance would not necessarily immunize him from liability for compensatory damages; Kellberg does not even argue that as the law stood when he acted, he could reasonably have believed that he was justified in what he did, and therefore is immune from all damage liability. See *Harlow v. Fitzgerald*, 457 U.S. 800, 818–19, 73 L. Ed. 2d 396, 102 S. Ct. 2727 (1982). But if we therefore assume that Kellberg should have known that he was not privileged to fire Mrs. Soderbeck, still it would not follow that his ignorance of her rights was reckless; careless is not reckless.

The words used to mark off the domain of punitive damages—words like "maliciously," "wantonly," "oppressively," "spitefully"—indicate that punitive damages, like criminal fines which they resemble, are reserved for cases where the wrongfulness of the defendant's conduct is conspicuous, implying that its wrongfulness is apparent to the person who engages in it, and not just to a lawyer. If one needed great subtlety to realize that one had strayed into the forbidden zone where punitive damages are a sanction, the deterrent effect of such damages would be distorted. Some people would stray into the zone unknowingly; as to them the threat of punitive damages would not deter. Others would steer far clear of the zone, not knowing where it began; as to them lawful as well as unlawful conduct would be deterred. We may therefore

set it down as a condition of awarding punitive damages that the defendant almost certainly knew that what he was doing was wrongful and subject to punishment. Among the types of conduct that fit this description is conduct so contrary to our society's basic ethical principles that it can safely be assumed to have been undertaken with knowledge that it was legally as well as morally wrong, including conduct that has come to be regarded as contrary to the modern civil rights, as well as the older personal liberties, of Americans.

But the discharge of public employees on political grounds is not yet regarded in the light of something contrary to natural law; nor is it widely known in nonlegal circles to be a federal constitutional tort or any other sort of tort. Hence knowledge that is forbidden cannot automatically be imputed to the individuals responsible for such discharges—especially when the individual is a minor rural official with no legal training. Burnett County in northwestern Wisconsin cannot be among the more sophisticated of the nation's counties and its sheriff cannot be presumed to be steeped in the arcana of modern constitutional law. *Elrod v. Burns* was decided only three years before Mrs. Soderbeck was fired—over a vigorous dissent of three Justices, and without a majority opinion, which suggests it was something of a novelty. *Branti* was decided after she was fired. Of course knowledge is to some extent a function of the penalties for ignorance; the heavier the sanctions for an unknowing violation of someone's rights, the more will be invested in finding out what rights people have. But if Kellberg had consulted a lawyer, he might well have been advised that he could fire Mrs. Soderbeck because she was a confidential employee; it was an arguable point, though one the jury resolved against him. And this point shows why the maxim, "ignorance of the law is no defense" (on which see Perkins & Boyce, *Criminal Law* 1029–36 (3d ed. 1982)), is a maxim of criminal law, not of civil law. The requirement of fair notice in criminal cases gives reasonable assurance that the potential violator will know whether his conduct will be unlawful; there is no similar assurance in civil cases, as this case illustrates.

Although the plaintiff was free to present evidence from which a jury might infer that Sheriff Kellberg in fact knew, or circumstanced as he was should certainly have known, that he was violating her federal constitutional rights . . . she presented no such evidence. The judge was therefore right to take the issue of punitive damages—defined as we have said in terms of "reckless indifference" to the plaintiff's rights—away from the jury. But in so holding, we wish to make clear that Kellberg's ignorance of Mrs. Soderbeck's federal rights would not matter if his firing of her had been the kind of act that anyone (or at least any sheriff) would know violated some law. In *Smith v. Wade*, the defendant Smith may not have known that he was violating the Eighth Amendment when he took no steps to protect inmate Wade from being beaten and sexually assaulted; but since Wade had placed himself in protective custody because of prior assaults against him, since another inmate in the same dormitory had recently been beaten to death while Smith was on duty, and since Smith had assigned to Wade's cell an inmate who had recently been punished for fighting, Smith ought to have known he was violating some legal duty of protection toward an inmate in his care. Just as it is not necessary in order to convict a person of a federal crime to prove that he knew the facts that confer federal jurisdiction over the offense, it is not necessary in order to justify awarding punitive damages to show that the defendant ought to have known he was violating the plaintiff's federal rights. The point in both cases is that once the defendant is shown to have engaged in plainly unlawful conduct, to require a showing that the defendant knew which sovereign's laws he was violating would simply reduce the deterrent effect of punishment by making it harder to prove a violation . . .

NOTES

1. Compare *Busche v. Burkee*, 649 F.2d 509, 520 (7th Cir. 1981), where the court upheld a $2,000 punitive damages award against an official who fired an employee in violation of the plaintiff's constitutional rights.

The record establishes that Burkee ordered Busche's discharge even though he had been repeatedly advised that he was without legal authority to do so. Both Chief of Police Bosman and Inspector of Police Trotta had informed Burkee that Busche could be terminated only after he received a hearing before the Police and Fire Commission. This intentional and considered disregard of Busche's legal rights demonstrates that Burkee acted with the 'malicious intent' necessary to support the district court's award of punitive damages. Burkee also argues [that] . . . this was a unique and isolated incident which is unlikely to recur. He properly argues that a primary function of punitive damages is to deter similar future conduct. Although Burkee may not be in a position to perpetrate such unlawful conduct again . . ., we think the district court could have reasonably concluded that an award of punitive damages in this case might deter executive officials in the future from wilfully disregarding the legal rights of public employees in situations where such disregard might seem justified (and possibly politically compelled) in the heat of the moment.

Soderbeck cited *Busche* as "a good example of a section 1983 case where punitive damages for firing a public employee were upheld".

2. *Smith, Soderbeck,* and *Busche* all identify deterrence of unconstitutional conduct as a primary aim of punitive damages. If this is so, then why not allow juries to grant them any time compensatory damages may be awarded? The same question arises in common law torts. According to some common law tort theorists, the reason is that the decision on liability may be wrong, however much we strive to get it right. The threat of a mistaken imposition of punitive damages, on top of a potentially mistaken compensatory award, would unduly deter persons from engaging in the activity that gave rise to the injury. See, e.g., Ellis, *Fairness and Efficiency in the Law of Punitive Damages*, 56 S. Cal. L. Rev. 1 (1982). When the activity is itself without social value, as where someone recklessly, or willfully and wantonly, or intentionally violates someone's rights, no such danger is present and punitive damages are appropriate.

Under this reasoning, is it sufficient for punitive damages that the defendant acted in reckless disregard of *some* law, state or federal? Or must the plaintiff show reckless disregard of constitutional rights? How does *Soderbeck* answer this question?

3. Professor Nahmod takes issue with *Soderbeck*:

> The Seventh Circuit's arcane discussion of recklessness is seriously questionable. Despite its disclaimer, the court seemed to impose a specific intent requirement for punitive damages liability which depends on the defendant's actual knowledge that he or she was violating the plaintiff's constitutional rights. Also, where the defendant has such knowledge, it is inaccurate to call the conduct reckless: rather, such conduct is better characterized as intentional in the tort sense of knowledge with substantial certainty that a particular result—here, a plaintiff's constitutional deprivations—will occur. Further, the court avoided discussing another possible kind of recklessness: where a defendant knows that he or she does *not* know the constitutionality of the proposed conduct, but still proceeds to act. Indeed, this may well describe the defendant's conduct in [*Soderbeck*] . . . Finally, imposing punitive damages liability even when the defendant did not know that he was acting unconstitutionally may still have a beneficial deterrent effect: the defendant and *others similarly situated* will have a considerable incentive to learn what the law is. Otherwise, reckless ignorance will not be discouraged.

Does Nahmod's recommendation of liability for "reckless ignorance" run the risk of over-deterring government actors? Is the availability of qualified immunity where rights are not "clearly established" a sufficient answer to this concern? Labels aside, is Nahmod's approach consistent with *Smith*'s rejection of a "gross negligence" rule in favor of recklessness? In this regard, note that the common law courts have always regarded recklessness as a harder standard for the plaintiff to meet than gross negligence.

Knowledge is a continuum. An officer may be fully aware that his actions violate someone's rights, as in *Burkee*; he may be oblivious to any risk that his actions are illegal, as may be the case in *Soderbeck*. Often, he will know that there is a greater or a lesser risk, without

knowing to a "substantial certainty". Where along the continuum is his knowledge sufficient to justify characterizing his act as "reckless"? Do you agree with Professor Nahmod that *some* states of knowledge short of substantial certainty are sufficient to justify punitive damages? Does Judge Posner disagree? According to the opinion, punitive damages are appropriate when the defendant "almost certainly knew that what he was doing was wrongful and subject to punishment."

4. In libel law, reckless disregard of the truth of the defamatory statement is a requirement for liability in some cases, and a condition for the award of punitive damages in cases where the statement relates to a matter of public concern. "[R]eckless conduct is not measured by whether a reasonably prudent man would have published, or would have investigated before publishing. There must be sufficient evidence to permit the conclusion that the defendant in fact entertained serious doubts as to the truth of his publication." *St. Amant v. Thompson*, 390 U.S. 727, 731 (1968). The Court reiterated this standard some years later in *Harte-Hanks Communications v. Connaughton*, 491 U.S. 657, 667, 688 (1989). Is *St. Amant* consistent with *Soderbeck*? If you were the plaintiff's lawyer, which would you prefer? Is *St. Amant* consistent with Nahmod's definition of recklessness? If not, could Nahmod cogently distinguish the two contexts? Should the term "recklessness" be defined differently when the role of punitive damages is to enforce constitutional rights, rather than to exact retribution for speech that crosses the constitutionally protected boundary, as is the case in libel law?

5. Is the Supreme Court's deliberate indifference decision in *Farmer v. Brennan*, set out and discussed in Chapter 3, relevant to the state of mind required for punitive damages? Recall that *Farmer* is an Eighth Amendment case and does not as such address punitive damages. In addition, recklessness may not be the same as deliberate indifference (or is it?). Still, does it follow that *Farmer* tells us nothing at all regarding the state of mind required for punitive damages liability?

6. Besides deterrence, *Smith* states that "punishment" is another aim of punitive damages. See 461 U.S. at 54. See also *City of Newport v. Fact Concerts*, 453 U.S. 247, 266–67 (1981) (equating punishment and "retribution"). What definition of recklessness is appropriate toward that end? Is punishment appropriate for defendants who are utterly (however irresponsibly) ignorant of the unconstitutionality of their conduct? Is punishment ever appropriate for a state of knowledge short of substantial certainty? Does the fact that some crimes are punishable even if the defendant did not know the law mean that punitive damages are also appropriate in such circumstances? Judge Posner in *Soderbeck* says the criminal analogy is inapposite. Why? Do you agree?

7. Occasionally common law courts say that another purpose of punitive damages is to reimburse the plaintiff for his legal fees. See *Prosser & Keeton on Torts* 9 (5th ed. 1984). Is this an appropriate function of punitives in the section 1983 context, given the Civil Rights Attorney's Fees Act of 1976? See Chapter 12.

8. Though local governments cannot themselves be held liable for punitive damages, they sometimes choose to reimburse their officers for punitive awards. In view of the deterrent and retributive aims of punitive damages, should this practice be prohibited? In *Cornwall v. City of Riverside*, 896 F.2d 398, 399 (9th Cir. 1990), the plaintiff sought to compel the individual defendants to pay the damages but the court held that "there is no federal prohibition against the city paying the punitive damages."

In *Cornwall*, a local government exercised its option under state law to pay punitive damages awards against police officers because it determined that they acted within the scope of their employment, in good faith, and in its best interests. The ninth circuit observed that this result was not in conflict with federal policy. It said that if the result were otherwise, there would be cases where punitive damages awards in favor of section 1983 plaintiffs would go unsatisfied because individual defendants could be judgment proof. Furthermore, giving the option to plaintiffs to accept or reject such payments from local governments would provide plaintiffs with an "extraordinary weapon" for negotiation purposes.

Despite the Ninth Circuit's opinion, doesn't *Cornwell* in fact undercut the punitive function of section 1983 punitive damages awards? Does it undercut their deterrent function? How would federal courts administer a contrary rule? Could they stop wealthy individuals from reimbursing police officers for punitive damages?

C. Survival, Wrongful Death, and Other Damages Issues Ordinarily Addressed by Statutes

Some state law tort damages issues are typically dealt with by statutes rather than common law rules. Early on, common law courts adopted a rule that the death of the victim extinguished the lawsuit. Legislatures in all states have enacted "wrongful death" statutes and "survival" statutes, both of which permit the case to go forward. Typically, wrongful death statutes allow certain close relatives to maintain a tort suit to recover for their losses due to the tort and the death that resulted from it. By the same token, survival statutes allow the estate of the deceased victim to recover for damages suffered by the victim before his death. The cause of death is irrelevant to the viability of a survival action, while a wrongful death action may be pursued only if the tort caused the death. See generally R. Epstein, *Cases and Materials on Torts* 789–96 (1990).

A common law rule provided for joint and several liability on the part of all defendants who, by their breach of duty, caused an indivisible injury. That rule permitted the plaintiff to satisfy his judgment by pursuing any or all of the defendants for all of it, and denied any defendant a right of contribution against other defendants. Statutes in many states have modified the rule against contribution.

How should these issues be resolved in section 1983 cases? Does the absence of federal statutes addressing them mean that courts should apply state statutes? Should they make federal common law rules? Or should courts in section 1983 cases look to the prevailing law in 1871 for answers? Consider first those statutes that govern recovery after the death of the victim.

Robertson v. Wegmann

436 U.S. 584 (1978)

Mr. Justice **Marshall** delivered the opinion of the Court.

In early 1970, Clay L. Shaw filed a civil rights action under 42 U.S.C. §1983 in the United States District Court for the Eastern

District of Louisiana. Four years later, before trial had commenced, Shaw died. The question presented is whether the District Court was required to adopt as federal law a Louisiana survivorship statute, which would have caused this action to abate, or was free instead to create a federal common-law rule allowing the action to survive. Resolution of this question turns on whether the state statute is "inconsistent with the Constitution and laws of the United States." 42 U.S.C. § 1988.[1]

I

In 1969, Shaw was tried in a Louisiana state court on charges of having participated in a conspiracy to assassinate President John F. Kennedy. He was acquitted by a jury but within days was arrested on charges of having committed perjury in his testimony at the conspiracy trial. Alleging that these prosecutions were undertaken in bad faith, . . . [Shaw filed a section 1983 action against the district attorney and others.]

Trial was set for November 1974, but in August 1974 Shaw died. The executor of his estate, respondent Edward F. Wegmann (hereafter respondent), moved to be substituted as plaintiff, and the District Court granted the motion. Petitioner and other defendants then moved to dismiss the action on the ground that it had abated on Shaw's death . . .

II

[T]he applicable survivorship rule is governed by 42 U.S.C. § 1988. This statute recognizes that in certain areas "federal law is unsuited or insufficient 'to furnish suitable

---

[1] Title 42 U.S.C. § 1988 provides in pertinent part:

"The jurisdiction in civil and criminal matters conferred on the district courts by the provisions of this chapter and Title 18, for the protection of all persons in the United States in their civil rights, and for their vindication, shall be exercised and enforced in conformity with the laws of the United States, so far as such laws are suitable to carry the same into effect; but in all cases where they are not adapted to the object, or are deficient in the provisions necessary to furnish suitable remedies and punish offenses against law, the common law, as modified and changed by the constitution and statutes of the State wherein the court having jurisdiction of such civil or criminal cause is held, so far as the same is not inconsistent with the Constitution and laws of the United States, shall be extended to and govern the said courts in the trial and disposition of the cause, and, if it is of a criminal nature, in the infliction of punishment on the party found guilty."

remedies'"; federal law simply does not "cover every issue that may arise in the context of a federal civil rights action." *Moor v. County of Alameda*, quoting 42 U.S.C. § 1988. When federal law is thus "deficient," § 1988 instructs us to turn to "the common law, as modified and changed by the constitution and statutes of the [forum] State," as long as these are "not inconsistent with the Constitution and laws of the United States." See n. 1, supra. Regardless of the source of the law applied in a particular case, however, it is clear that the ultimate rule adopted under § 1988 "'is a federal rule responsive to the need whenever a federal right is impaired.'" *Moor v. County of Alameda*, quoting *Sullivan v. Little Hunting Park, Inc.*

As we noted in *Moor v. County of Alameda*, and as was recognized by both courts below, one specific area not covered by federal law is that relating to "the survival of civil rights actions under § 1983 upon the death of either the plaintiff or defendant." State statutes governing the survival of state actions do exist, however. These statutes, which vary widely with regard to both the types of claims that survive and the parties as to whom survivorship is allowed, see W. Prosser, *Law of Torts* 900–901 (4th ed. 1971), were intended to modify the simple, if harsh, 19th-century common-law rule: "[An] injured party's personal claim was [always] extinguished . . . upon the death of either the injured party himself or the alleged wrongdoer." Under § 1988, this state statutory law, modifying the common law, provides the principal reference point in determining survival of civil rights actions, subject to the important proviso that state law may not be applied when it is "inconsistent with the Constitution and laws of the United States." Because of this proviso, the courts below refused to adopt as federal law the Louisiana survivorship statute and in its place created a federal common-law rule.

III

In resolving questions of inconsistency between state and federal law raised under § 1988, courts must look not only at particular federal statutes and constitutional provisions, but also at "the policies expressed in [them]." Of particular importance is whether application of state law "would be inconsistent with the federal policy underlying the cause of action under consideration." The instant cause of action arises under 42 U.S.C. § 1983, one of the "Reconstruction civil rights statutes" that this Court has accorded "'a sweep as broad as [their] language.'"

Despite the broad sweep of § 1983, we can find nothing in the statute or its underlying policies to indicate that a state law causing abatement of a particular action should invariably be ignored in favor of a rule of absolute survivorship. The policies underlying § 1983 include compensation of persons injured by deprivation of federal rights and prevention of abuses of power by those acting under color of state law. See, e.g., *Carey v. Piphus*; *Mitchum v. Foster*; *Monroe v. Pape*. No claim is made here that Louisiana's survivorship laws are in general inconsistent with these policies, and indeed most Louisiana actions survive the plaintiff's death. See La. Code Civ. Proc. Ann., Art. 428 (West 1960); La. Civ. Code Ann., Art. 2315 (West 1971). Moreover, certain types of actions that would abate automatically on the plaintiff's death in many States—for example, actions for defamation and malicious prosecution—would apparently survive in Louisiana. In actions other than those for damage to property, however, Louisiana does not allow the deceased's personal representative to be substituted as plaintiff; rather, the action survives only in favor of a spouse, children, parents, or siblings. But surely few persons are not survived by one of these close relatives, and in any event no contention is made here that Louisiana's decision to restrict certain survivorship rights in this manner is an unreasonable one.

It is therefore difficult to see how any of § 1983's policies would be undermined if Shaw's action were to abate. The goal of compensating those injured by a deprivation of rights provides no basis for requiring compensation of one who is merely suing as the executor of the deceased's estate. And, given that most Louisiana actions survive the plaintiff's death, the fact that a particular action might abate surely would not adversely affect § 1983's role in preventing official illegality, at least in situations in which there is no claim that the illegality caused the plaintiff's death. A state official contemplating illegal activity must always be prepared to face the prospect of a § 1983 action being filed against him. In

light of this prospect, even an official aware of the intricacies of Louisiana survivorship law would hardly be influenced in his behavior by its provisions.

It is true that § 1983 provides "a uniquely federal remedy against incursions under the claimed authority of state law upon rights secured by the Constitution and laws of the Nation." *Mitchum v. Foster*. That a federal remedy should be available, however, does not mean that a § 1983 plaintiff (or his representative) must be allowed to continue an action in disregard of the state law to which § 1988 refers us. A state statute cannot be considered "inconsistent" with federal law merely because the statute causes the plaintiff to lose the litigation. If success of the § 1983 action were the only benchmark, there would be no reason at all to look to state law, for the appropriate rule would then always be the one favoring the plaintiff, and its source would be essentially irrelevant. But § 1988 quite clearly instructs us to refer to state statutes; it does not say that state law is to be accepted or rejected based solely on which side is advantaged thereby. Under the circumstances presented here, the fact that Shaw was not survived by one of several close relatives should not itself be sufficient to cause the Louisiana survivorship provisions to be deemed "inconsistent with the Constitution and laws of the United States." 42 U.S.C. § 1988.

IV

Our holding today is a narrow one, limited to situations in which no claim is made that state law generally is inhospitable to survival of § 1983 actions and in which the particular application of state survivorship law, while it may cause abatement of the action, has no independent adverse effect on the policies underlying § 1983. A different situation might well be presented, as the District Court noted, if state law "did not provide for survival of any tort actions," or if it significantly restricted the types of actions that survive. Cf. *Carey v. Piphus* (failure of common law to "recognize an analogous cause of action" is not sufficient reason to deny compensation to § 1983 plaintiff). We intimate no view, moreover, about whether abatement based on state law could be allowed in a situation in which deprivation of federal rights caused death. [C]f. *Brazier v. Cherry* (deceased allegedly beaten to death by policemen; state survival law applied in favor of his widow and estate).

Here it is agreed that Shaw's death was not caused by the deprivation of rights for which he sued under § 1983, and Louisiana law provides for the survival of most tort actions. Respondent's only complaint about Louisiana law is that it would cause Shaw's action to abate. We conclude that the mere fact of abatement of a particular lawsuit is not sufficient ground to declare state law "inconsistent" with federal law.

Accordingly, the judgment of the Court of Appeals is

Reversed.

Mr. Justice **Blackmun**, with whom Mr. Justice **Brennan** and Mr. Justice **White** join, dissenting.

It is disturbing to see the Court, in this decision, although almost apologetically self-described as "a narrow one," cut back on what is acknowledged, to be the "broad sweep" of 42 U.S.C. § 1983. Accordingly, I dissent.

I do not read the emphasis of § 1988, as the Court does, to the effect that the Federal District Court "was required to adopt" the Louisiana statute, and was free to look to federal common law only as a secondary matter. It seems to me that this places the cart before the horse. Section 1988 requires the utilization of federal law ("shall be exercised and enforced in conformity with the laws of the United States"). It authorizes resort to the state statute only if the federal laws "are not adapted to the object" of "protection of all persons in the United States in their civil rights, and for their vindication" or are "deficient in the provisions necessary to furnish suitable remedies and punish offenses against law." Even then, state statutes are an alternative source of law only if "not inconsistent with the Constitution and laws of the United States." Surely, federal law is the rule and not the exception.

Accepting this as the proper starting point, it necessarily follows, it seems to me, that the judgment of the Court of Appeals must be affirmed, not reversed. To be sure, survivorship of a civil rights action under § 1983 upon the death of either party is not specifically covered by the federal statute. But that does not mean that "the laws of the United States" are not "suitable" or are "not adapted to the

object" or are "deficient in the provisions necessary." The federal law and the underlying federal policy stand bright and clear. And in the light of that brightness and of that clarity, I see no need to resort to the myriad of state rules governing the survival of state actions.

First. In *Sullivan v. Little Hunting Park, Inc.*, a case that concerned the availability of compensatory damages for a violation of § 1982, a remedial question, as here, not governed explicitly by any federal statute other than § 1988, Mr. Justice Douglas, writing for the Court, painted with a broad brush the scope of the federal court's choice-of-law authority:

> "[As] we read § 1988, . . . both federal and state rules on damages may be utilized, whichever better serves the policies expressed in the federal statutes. . . . The rule of damages, whether drawn from federal or state sources, is a federal rule responsive to the need whenever a federal right is impaired." 396 U.S., at 240.

The Court's present reading of § 1988 seems to me to be hyperlogical and sadly out of line with the precept set forth in that quoted material. The statute was intended to give courts flexibility to shape their procedures and remedies in accord with the underlying policies of the Civil Rights Acts, choosing whichever rule "better serves" those policies . . . I do not understand the Court to deny a federal court's authority under § 1988 to reject state law when to apply it seriously undermines substantial federal concerns. But I do not accept the Court's apparent conclusion that, absent such an extreme inconsistency, § 1988 restricts courts to state law on matters of procedure and remedy. That conclusion too often would interfere with the efficient redress of constitutional rights.

Second. The Court's reading of § 1988 cannot easily be squared with its treatment of the problems of immunity and damages under the Civil Rights Acts. Only this Term, in *Carey v. Piphus*, the Court set a rule for the award of damages under § 1983 for deprivation of procedural due process by resort to "federal common law." Though the case arose from Illinois, the Court did not feel compelled to inquire into Illinois' statutory or decisional law of damages, nor to test that law for possible "inconsistency" with the federal scheme, before embracing a federal common-law rule. Instead, the Court fashioned a federal damages rule, from common-law sources and its view of the type of injury, to govern such cases uniformly State to State.

Similarly, in constructing immunities under § 1983, the Court has consistently relied on federal common-law rules. As *Carey v. Piphus* recognizes, in attributing immunity to prosecutors, to judges, and to other officials, matters on which the language of § 1983 is silent, we have not felt bound by the tort immunities recognized in the particular forum State and, only after finding an "inconsistency" with federal standards, then considered a uniform federal rule. Instead, the immunities have been fashioned in light of historic common-law concerns and the policies of the Civil Rights Acts.

Third. A flexible reading of § 1988, permitting resort to a federal rule of survival because it "better serves" the policies of the Civil Rights Acts, would be consistent with the methodology employed in the other major choice-of-law provision in the federal structure, namely, the Rules of Decision Act. 28 U.S.C. § 1652.[7] That Act provides that state law is to govern a civil trial in a federal court "except where the Constitution or treaties of the United States or Acts of Congress otherwise require or provide." The exception has not been interpreted in a crabbed or wooden fashion, but, instead, has been used to give expression to important federal interests. Thus, for example, the exception has been used to apply a federal common law of labor contracts in suits under § 301 (a) of the Labor Management Relations Act, 1947, to apply federal common law to transactions in commercial paper issued by the United States where the United States is a party, and to avoid application of governing state law to the reservation of mineral rights in a land acquisition agreement to which the United States was a party and that bore heavily upon a federal wildlife regulatory program. See also *Auto Workers v. Hoosier Cardinal Corp.*: "[State]

law is applied [under the Rules of Decision Act] only because it supplements and fulfills federal policy, and the ultimate question is what federal policy requires." (White, J., dissenting.)

Just as the Rules of Decision Act cases disregard state law where there is conflict with federal policy, even though no explicit conflict with the terms of a federal statute, so, too, state remedial and procedural law must be disregarded under § 1988 where that law fails to give adequate expression to important federal concerns. See *Sullivan v. Little Hunting Park, Inc.* The opponents of the 1866 Act were distinctly aware that the legislation that became § 1988 would give the federal courts power to shape federal common-law rules . . .

Fourth. Section 1983's critical concerns are compensation of the victims of unconstitutional action, and deterrence of like misconduct in the future. Any crabbed rule of survivorship obviously interferes directly with the second critical interest and may well interfere with the first.

The unsuitability of Louisiana's law is shown by the very case at hand. It will happen not infrequently that a decedent's only survivor or survivors are nonrelatives or collateral relatives who do not fit within the four named classes of Louisiana statutory survivors. Though the Court surmises that "surely few persons are not survived" by a spouse, children, parents, or siblings, any lawyer who has had experience in estate planning or in probating estates knows that that situation is frequently encountered. The Louisiana survivorship rule applies no matter how malicious or ill-intentioned a defendant's action was . . . The federal interest in specific deterrence, when there was malicious intention to deprive a person of his constitutional rights, is particularly strong. Insuring a specific deterrent under federal law gains importance from the very premise of the Civil Rights Act that state tort policy often is inadequate to deter violations of the constitutional rights of disfavored groups.

The Louisiana rule requiring abatement appears to apply even where the death was intentional and caused, say, by a beating delivered by a defendant. The Court does not deny this result, merely declaiming that in such a case it might reconsider the applicability of the Louisiana survivorship statute. But

---

[7] "The laws of the several states, except where the Constitution or treaties of the United States or Acts of Congress otherwise require or provide, shall be regarded as rules of decision in civil actions in the courts of the United States, in cases where they apply."

the Court does not explain how either certainty or federalism is served by such a variegated application of the Louisiana statute, nor how an abatement rule would be workable when made to depend on a fact of causation often requiring an entire trial to prove.

It makes no sense to me to make even a passing reference, ante to behavioral influence. The Court opines that no official aware of the intricacies of Louisiana survivorship law would "be influenced in his behavior by its provisions." But the defendants in Shaw's litigation obviously have been "sweating it out" through the several years of proceedings and litigation in this case. One can imagine the relief occasioned when the realization dawned that Shaw's death might—just might—abate the action. To that extent, the deterrent against behavior such as that attributed to the defendants in this case surely has been lessened.

As to compensation, it is no answer to intimate, as the Court does that Shaw's particular survivors were not personally injured, for obviously had Shaw been survived by parents or siblings, the cause of action would exist despite the absence in them of so deep and personal an affront, or any at all, as Shaw himself was alleged to have sustained. The Court propounds the unreasoned conclusion that the "goal of compensating those injured by a deprivation of rights provides no basis for requiring compensation of one who is merely suing as the executor of the deceased's estate." But the Court does not purport to explain why it is consistent with the purposes of § 1983 to recognize a derivative or independent interest in a brother or parent, while denying similar interest to a nephew, grandparent, or legatee.

Fifth. The Court regards the Louisiana system's structuring of survivorship rights as not unreasonable. The observation, of course, is a gratuitous one, for as the Court immediately observes it does not resolve the issue that confronts us here. We are not concerned with the reasonableness of the Louisiana survivorship statute in allocating tort recoveries. We are concerned with its application in the face of a claim of civil rights guaranteed the decedent by federal law . . .

Sixth. A federal rule of survivorship allows uniformity, and counsel immediately know the answer. Litigants identically aggrieved in their federal civil rights, residing in geographically adjacent States, will not have differing results due to the vagaries of state law. Litigants need not engage in uncertain characterization of a § 1983 action in terms of its nearest tort cousin, a questionable procedure to begin with, since the interests protected by tort law and constitutional law may be quite different. Nor will federal rights depend on the arcane intricacies of state survival law—which differs in Louisiana according to whether the right is "strictly personal," whether the action concerns property damage, or whether it concerns "other damages,".

The policies favoring so-called "absolute" survivorship, viz., survivorship in favor of a decedent's nonrelated legatees in the absence of familial legatees, are the simple goals of uniformity, deterrence, and perhaps compensation. A defendant who has violated someone's constitutional rights has no legitimate interest in a windfall release upon the death of the victim. A plaintiff's interest in certainty, in an equal remedy, and in deterrence supports such an absolute rule . . .

Seventh. Rejecting Louisiana's survivorship limitations does not mean that state procedure and state remedies will cease to serve as important sources of civil rights law. State law, for instance, may well be a suitable source of statutes of limitation, since that is a rule for which litigants prudently can plan. Rejecting Louisiana's survivorship limitations means only that state rules are subject to some scrutiny for suitability. Here the deterrent purpose of § 1983 is disserved by Louisiana's rule of abatement.

It is unfortunate that the Court restricts the reach of § 1983 by today's decision construing § 1988. Congress now must act again if the gap in remedy is to be filled.

NOTES

1. *Carlson v. Green*, 446 U.S. 14 (1980), was a *Bivens* case, brought under a cause of action implied from the Eighth Amendment against federal prison officials on behalf of the estate of a prisoner who died, allegedly because of unconstitutionally inadequate medical care. Under state law the claim would not survive his death. The Court distinguished *Robertson* as follows:

There the plaintiff's death was not caused by the acts of the defendants upon which the suit was based. Moreover, Robertson expressly recognized that to prevent frustration of the deterrence goals of section 1983 (which in part also underlie Bivens actions . . .) "[a] state official contemplating illegal activity must always be prepared to face the prospect of a section 1983 action being filed against him." A federal official contemplating unconstitutional conduct similarly must be prepared to face the prospect of a Bivens action. A uniform rule that claims such as respondent's survive the decedent's death is essential if we are not to "frustrate in [an] important way the achievement" of the goals of Bivens actions.

446 U.S. at 24–25.

Does it follow that state law limitations on survival will not apply to section 1983 cases where the victim died as a result of the unconstitutional act? Or do federalism considerations require different treatment for section 1983 cases, where the defendants are typically state rather than federal officers? Is uniformity less important in section 1983 cases than in Bivens cases?

2. The Supreme Court invokes section 1988 in situations where the point at issue is typically governed by statute, but section 1983 does not speak to it. Hence, state statutes govern not only survivorship but also time-based limitations on bringing suit, Wilson v. Garcia, 471 U.S. 261 (1985), and notice of claim issues, Felder v. Casey, 487 U.S. 131 (1988). These latter topics are addressed in chapter 10, on procedural defenses to section 1983 suits. In Felder you will see that, as with survivorship, the borrowing of state law may be overridden if the Court deems the state rule to be inconsistent with the aims of section 1983.

3. Suppose a state's statute provides that once the plaintiff has died, no punitive damages will be available. Is this provision inconsistent with section 1983? See McFadden v. Sanchez, 710 F.2d 907 (2d Cir. 1983) (refusing to apply the provision in a case where the death resulted from the constitutional violation). How should the case come out if the victim fortuitously dies of other causes?

Suppose a policeman unconstitutionally shoots the plaintiff's decedent, who dies imme-

diately. The state's survival statute denies recovery when the victim of a tort dies instantly, feeling no pain and suffering between the commission of the tort and his death. Should the case be dismissed, or is this provision of the statute inconsistent with section 1983, and hence not applicable under section 1988? See Jaco v. Bloeche, 739 F.2d 239, 244 (6th Cir. 1984) (refusing to apply the statutory barrier on the ground that "to suggest that the Congress had intended that a civil rights infringement be cognizable only when the victim encounters pain and suffering before his demise, is absurd"). What is the difference between this provision and the one at issue in Robertson? Is it a stronger or a weaker case than Robertson for precluding survival of the case? Did the court in Jaco correctly understand the traditional function of a survival statute?

4. Why did the Jaco court not simply allow suit under the wrongful death statute? It said:

Ohio's wrongful death statute creates an action in tort in favor of the decedent's heirs for damages resulting from losses of prospective advantages which have been pretermitted by the death of the victim. Certainly, in a sense, the heirs are injured parties as a result of decedent's premature demise however, [sic] to arbitrarily conclude that their injuries resulted from an infringement of their civil rights would be sheer obfuscation of the issue. Simply stated, the wrongful death of the decedent resulting from a tort, which gives rise to the cause of action for the benefit of his heirs, is not equivalent to decedent's personal section 1983 claim, and decedent's administratrix is therefore without standing in the federal forum to commence an action, pursuant to sections 1983 and 1988, under either the Ohio survivor or wrongful death statute.

739 F.2d at 242–43.

Some courts have allowed recovery for wrongful death in a section 1983 suit without addressing the conceptual problem identified in Jaco. See, e.g., Williams v. Kelly, 624 F.2d 695 (5th Cir. 1980).

5. Is there a good answer to the objection to a wrongful death action raised in Jaco? Suppose the administrator of the estate of a person unconstitutionally killed by the police brings a section 1983 suit and, as part of the same

lawsuit, the dependents seek to raise a claim under the state's wrongful death statute. May the wrongful death cause of action be litigated in federal court under the doctrine of pendent jurisdiction? Under *United Mine Workers of America v. Gibbs*, 383 U.S. 715 (1966), pendent jurisdiction may be appropriate if the federal and state claims "derive from a common nucleus of operative fact," and if "considerations of judicial economy, convenience, and fairness to litigants" would be served by litigating the two claims at the same time. Is it likely that these conditions would be met in cases where the estate sought to join a wrongful death claim to the decedent's case against the police? Does it matter that the estate is the plaintiff in the decedent's case, while the plaintiffs in the wrongful death case are his dependents? See 28 U.S.C. § 1367 (authorizing pendent party jurisdiction).

If the wrongful death statute places ceilings on the recovery available to the dependents, may they successfully argue that those limits should not apply where the death was caused by a federal constitutional violation?

6. *Robertson* and the preceding notes begin from the premise that courts should look to state statutes as the measures of recovery once the victim has died. Should the Court have adopted Justice Blackmun's view that the focus should be on effective remedies for constitutional violations rather than state survival and wrongful death statutes? Why should the development of section 1983 be bound by the modern implications of ancient (and rather dubious) common law decisions? Note that the approach taken in *Robertson* requires in each case an evaluation of whether a particular state rule is consistent with the purposes of section 1983. Would it not be more straightforward to consider how to achieve an effective remedy and then implement that judgment by an appropriate set of rules, regardless of state law?

There is a more fundamental problem with reference to state law. Even liberal rules on survivorship and wrongful death leave a significant gap in coverage. They allow recovery of damages up to the death, and they allow dependents to recover for their loss of support. Even taken together, however, they do not permit recovery for the death itself, or for the full value of the life that was lost. For example, in *Bell v. City of Milwaukee*, the court pointed out that "the Wisconsin statutory scheme

creates a survival action in favor of the estate for pre-death injuries and a wrongful death action in favor of the victim's survivors, and neither type of action traditionally allows recovery of damages for loss of life itself." It went on to hold that "the application and policy of this point of Wisconsin law are inconsistent with those of section 1983 and the Fourteenth Amendment protection of life. Therefore, Wisconsin law cannot be applied to preclude the estate's recovery for loss of life . . ." 746 F.2d 1205, 1236 (7th Cir. 1984). By contrast, the Colorado Supreme Court held in *Jones v. Hildebrant*, 191 Colo. 1550 P.2d 339 (1976), that state law limitations on the kind and amount of damages were applicable to section 1983 actions.

Which view should the Supreme Court adopt? Should courts in section 1983 cases respond to the lacunae in state statutory regimes by making a federal common law of damages? Consider the following case.

Berry v. City of Muscogee

900 F.2d 1489 (10th Cir. 1990)

[An inmate in the city's custody was murdered by fellow prisoners. His estate brought suit under section 1983 and established a constitutional violation based on the city's failure to protect him. The court then addressed damages issues.]

Logan, Circuit Judge.

Applying the principles set out in § 1988 for borrowing law from another source, we are satisfied that the Oklahoma survival action alone does not meet the stated criteria. As applied to the instant case, it would provide extraordinarily limited recovery, possibly only damages to property loss, of which there were none, and loss of decedent's earnings between the time of injury and death, of which there also were none. Thus, the Oklahoma survival action is clearly deficient in both its remedy and its deterrent effect.

The more difficult question is whether the Oklahoma law on survival actions, as supplemented by Oklahoma's wrongful death statute, sufficiently meets the § 1988 criteria to satisfy the test for borrowing state law . . .

We believe a strong argument can be made that borrowing state wrongful death statutes simply provides remedial assistance "to effectuate well-established primary rules of behavior" that are enforceable under § 1983. When the alleged constitutional violation results in death, Congress, through § 1988, has authorized resort to state law to assist the broad remedial policies of § 1983 . . . Moreover, *Robertson* can be read as a strong signal by the Supreme Court that it is appropriate to look to state law survival and wrongful death statutes to supply an appropriate remedy for § 1983 violations that result in death.

On the other hand, if we were to define § 1983 remedies in terms of the state survival action, supplemented by the state wrongful death act, we place into the hands of the state the decision as to allocation of the recovery in a § 1983 case, and, indeed, whether there can be any recovery at all. In an Oklahoma wrongful death action nearly all recoverable damages are expressly funneled to the decedent's surviving spouse and children to the exclusion of decedent's creditors or the beneficiaries of the decedent's will, if he or she has one. The statute also permits recovery for loss of consortium and grief of the surviving spouse, grief and loss of companionship of the children and parents, items decedent could not have recovered had he lived to sue for himself.

Allowing the state determinations to prevail also permits the state to define the scope and extent of recovery. For instance, some states may preclude, or limit, recovery for pain and suffering or for punitive damages. In addition, some state laws may deny all recovery in particular circumstances, as when wrongful death actions must be for dependents and there are none.

In *Smith v. Wade* the Supreme Court ruled that punitive damages are recoverable in § 1983 cases. In reaching this conclusion the Court relied on the common law of torts, but not the common or statutory law of any one particular state. The rule announced in *Smith* is a general one, not one specific to Missouri (the forum state) based on state law remedies. There is no stated exception for § 1983 actions brought in states that do not permit punitive damage awards in other tort cases. Similarly, in *Memphis Community School District v. Stachura*, the Court looked to the common

law of torts to hold that the abstract value of constitutional rights is not a permissible element of compensatory damages in § 1983 cases. But it did not make the rule different for suits brought in states that might have a different notion. The Court did not rely on borrowing the law of the forum state, but instead laid down a uniform rule. In *Wilson v. Garcia*, the Supreme Court looked to state law for statutes of limitations, but it did not permit the state law to define the cause of action. These cases suggest that the Supreme Court is fashioning a federal common law of remedies for § 1983 violations.

In the case before us the recovery permitted under the Oklahoma wrongful death act duplicates, in many respects, the recovery Mark Berry might have obtained had he lived to sue for his injuries. But, as we have noted, the act permits recovery of the loss of consortium and grief of the surviving spouse, children, and parents, which Mark Berry could not have recovered had he lived. In considering whether the purposes of § 1983 are satisfied by adoption of state survival and wrongful death actions, we must consider that different states will define them differently, thus requiring individual analyses of each state's law. We might have to find that a state's law works satisfactorily in some instances, as when there are surviving dependents, but not in other cases, as when there is no one with a right to sue.

Weighing these concerns, and considering the Supreme Court's approach in *Smith, Memphis Community School District*, and *Garcia*, we conclude that supplementing a state survival action with a state wrongful death action does not satisfy the criteria of § 1988 for borrowing state law. The laws are not suitable to carry out the full effects intended for § 1983 cases ending in death of the victim; they are deficient in some respects to punish the offenses. Application of state law, at least in some instances, will be inconsistent with the predominance of the federal interest.

We therefore conclude, . . . that the federal courts must fashion a federal remedy to be applied to § 1983 death cases. The remedy should be a survival action, brought by the estate of the deceased victim, in accord with § 1983's express statement that the liability is "to the party injured." It must make available to plaintiffs sufficient damages to serve the deterrent function central to the purpose of § 1983. In accord with *Smith*, punitive damages may be recovered in appropriate cases . . . We believe appropriate compensatory damages would include medical and burial expenses, pain and suffering before death, loss of earnings based upon the probable duration of the victim's life had not the injury occurred, the victim's loss of consortium, and other damages recognized in common law tort actions.

The state wrongful death actions are not foreclosed by this approach; they remain as pendent state claims. But, of course, there can be no duplication of recovery . . .

NOTES

1. Suppose a court has adopted federal rules for damages in death cases, but the state wrongful death statute allows the plaintiff broader recovery than the federal rules would. Should the court follow state law, since it poses no threat to federal values? In *Gilmere v. City of Atlanta*, 864 F.2d 734, 738–40 (11th Cir. 1989) the court applied federal law in spite of arguably more generous state provisions (which allowed recovery for the "full value" of the decedent's life). The court relied on the compensation principle, which it thought was adequately served by the federal rule, and on the importance of maintaining uniformity of federal law. As a plaintiff's lawyer, what would you do in order to take advantage of state wrongful death rules that are more liberal than the federal rules?

2. Wrongful death statutes allow the dependents to recover sums they would have received but for the tortiously caused death. May family members sue under section 1983 for loss of the decedent's society and companionship, despite state rules limiting consortium to the spouse? *Bell*, supra, holds that the parents (but not siblings) may do so, because the unconstitutional killing is a violation of their own constitutionally-protected liberty interest in the continued society and companionship of the deceased. 746 F.2d at 1242–48. What if *Bell* is wrong on the merits of the constitutional issue, and it turns out close family members have no constitutional right to consortium. Is there any

other way for them to pursue a claim for consortium in federal court?

3. What is the relevance of state law to joint and several liability? In recent years some states have modified or abolished joint and several liability. Does *Robertson* require federal courts to follow the state rule, or is such a statute inconsistent with the purposes of section 1983, and hence not applicable under section 1988? Suppose one defendant settles with the plaintiff, who then successfully sues the other. The issue then arises whether the amount received from the settling party will count against the recovery available from the defendant who lost. Should this matter be governed by state or federal law? See 1 S. Nahmod, *Civil Rights and Civil Liberties Litigation* 277–78 (3d ed. 1991) (discussing two cases that avoided the issue by finding that the two defendants had committed different torts rather than one indivisible injury, and one that adopted state law as the federal rule and held the settlement amount could not be deducted). Suppose the relevant state law provided that the settlement amount must be deducted? Would it still be appropriate to borrow state law as the federal rule?

4. Should federal law govern contribution and indemnity issues? Nahmod thinks not, "at least to the extent they implicate the relationship among defendants alone," because these "are issues which do not demand uniformity". 1 S. Nahmod, supra, at 279. Can you think of situations in which contribution and indemnity rules may affect the vindication of federal rights or the deterrence of constitutional wrongdoing?

II. Prospective Relief

Throughout this book, you have seen that it is often important to distinguish between damages, on the one hand, and injunctive and declaratory relief on the other. Our remedial system favors damages over injunctive relief. Damages are aimed at redressing an injury that occurred in the past, and influence future conduct only indirectly, by signalling to officials that courts may impose liability on them if they violate federal law. When the plaintiff's case arises from an isolated incident that will not likely recur, he may recover only damages. When the remedy at law is inadequate, injunctive relief may be appropriate, as where a plaintiff shows that the challenged conduct will recur unless the defendant is ordered to stop it. Injunctive relief specifically directs officials to do or to refrain from particular acts, or else face not only actions for damages but fines or imprisonment for contempt of court. Declaratory relief nudges them in that direction by letting them know that an injunction will likely be forthcoming if they act contrary to the rules the court sets forth in the declaratory judgment.

In some respects, prospective relief is easier to obtain than are damages. On account of the Eleventh Amendment, damages and other forms of retrospective relief are not available against state governments unless Congress explicitly abrogates state immunity, and section 1983 does not do so. On the other hand, the principle of *Ex Parte Young* in effect permits prospective relief against them. Immunity doctrines often bar recovery of damages; only legislators are immune from prospective relief. At the same time, requests for prospective relief raise issues of their own. Some of these issues arise from efforts by Congress and the Supreme Court to channel certain kinds of litigation to the state courts. Such barriers to federal court include the Tax Injunction Act, which prohibits federal injunctions against state tax collection, the Johnson Act, which prohibits federal injunctions against state utility rate making, and the *Pullman*, *Younger*, and *Burford* abstention doctrines, which postpone or forbid federal injunctions against state action in a variety of circumstances. These doctrines are discussed in detail in courses on federal jurisdiction, and are summarized in Chapter 10.

City of Los Angeles v. Lyons illustrates some of the obstacles plaintiffs face in obtaining injunctive relief, even in cases where the abstention doctrines do not exclude them from federal court altogether.

City of Los Angeles v. Lyons

461 U.S. 95 (1983)

Justice **White** delivered the opinion of the Court.

The issue here is whether respondent Lyons satisfied the prerequisites for seeking injunctive relief in the Federal District Court.

I

This case began on February 7, 1977, when respondent, Adolph Lyons, filed a complaint for damages, injunction, and declaratory relief in the United States District Court for the Central District of California. The defendants were the City of Los Angeles and four of its police officers. The complaint alleged that on October 6, 1976, at 2 a.m., Lyons was stopped by the defendant officers for a traffic or vehicle code violation and that although Lyons offered no resistance or threat whatsoever, the officers, without provocation or justification, seized Lyons and applied a "chokehold"[1]—either the "bar arm control" hold or the "carotid-artery control" hold or both—rendering him unconscious and causing damage to his larynx. Counts I through IV of the complaint sought damages against the officers and the City. Count V, with which we are principally concerned here, sought a preliminary and permanent injunction against the City barring the use of the control holds. That count alleged that the City's police officers, "pursuant to the authorization, instruction and encouragement of Defendant City of Los Angeles, regularly and routinely apply these choke holds in innumerable situations where they are not threatened by the use of any deadly force whatsoever," that numerous persons have been injured as the result of the application of the chokeholds, that Lyons and others similarly situated are threatened with irreparable injury in the form of bodily injury and loss of life, and that Lyons "justifiably fears that any contact he has with Los Angeles Police officers may result in his being choked and strangled to death without provo-

---

[1] The police control procedures at issue in this case are referred to as "control holds," "chokeholds," "strangleholds," and "neck restraints." All these terms refer to two basic control procedures: the "carotid" hold and the "bar arm" hold. In the "carotid" hold, an officer positioned behind a subject places one arm around the subject's neck and holds the wrist of that arm with his other hand. The officer, by using his lower forearm and bicep muscle, applies pressure concentrating on the carotid arteries located on the sides of the subject's neck. The "carotid" hold is capable of rendering the subject unconscious by diminishing the flow of oxygenated blood to the brain. The "bar arm" hold, which is administered similarly, applies pressure at the front of the subject's neck. "Bar arm" pressure causes pain, reduces the flow of oxygen to the lungs, and may render the subject unconscious.

cation, justification or other legal excuse." Lyons alleged the threatened impairment of rights protected by the First, Fourth, Eighth, and Fourteenth Amendments. Injunctive relief was sought against the use of the control holds "except in situations where the proposed victim of said control reasonably appears to be threatening the immediate use of deadly force." Count VI sought declaratory relief against the City, i.e., a judgment that use of the chokeholds absent the threat of immediate use of deadly force is a per se violation of various constitutional rights.

[After proceedings in the district court and the ninth circuit, the district court granted Lyons a preliminary injunction against the use of chokeholds on persons who did not pose a threat to the police. The ninth circuit affirmed, but the injunction had not yet gone into effect, on account of stays issued by the ninth circuit and the Supreme Court.]

II

Since our grant of certiorari, circumstances pertinent to the case have changed. Originally, Lyons' complaint alleged that at least two deaths had occurred as a result of the application of chokeholds by the police. His first amended complaint alleged that 10 chokehold-related deaths had occurred. By May 1982, there had been five more such deaths. On May 6, 1982, the Chief of Police in Los Angeles prohibited the use of the bar-arm chokehold in any circumstances. A few days later, on May 12, 1982, the Board of Police Commissioners imposed a 6-month moratorium on the use of the carotid artery chokehold except under circumstances where deadly force is authorized.

Based on these events, on June 3, 1982, the City filed in this Court a memorandum suggesting a question of mootness, reciting the facts but arguing that the case was not moot. Lyons in turn filed a motion to dismiss the writ of certiorari as improvidently granted. We denied that motion but reserved the question of mootness for later consideration.

In his brief and at oral argument, Lyons has reasserted his position that in light of changed conditions, an injunctive decree is now unnecessary because he is no longer subject to a threat of injury. He urges that the preliminary injunction should be vacated. The City, on the other hand, while acknowledging that subsequent events have significantly changed the posture of this case, again asserts that the case is not moot because the moratorium is not permanent and may be lifted at any time.

We agree with the City that the case is not moot, since the moratorium by its terms is not permanent. Intervening events have not "irrevocably eradicated the effects of the alleged violation." We nevertheless hold, for another reason, that the federal courts are without jurisdiction to entertain Lyons' claim for injunctive relief.

III

It goes without saying that those who seek to invoke the jurisdiction of the federal courts must satisfy the threshold requirement imposed by Art. III of the Constitution by alleging an actual case or controversy. Plaintiffs must demonstrate a "personal stake in the outcome" in order to "assure that concrete adverseness which sharpens the presentation of issues" necessary for the proper resolution of constitutional questions. Abstract injury is not enough. The plaintiff must show that he "has sustained or is immediately in danger of sustaining some direct injury" as the result of the challenged official conduct and the injury or threat of injury must be both "real and immediate," not "conjectural" or "hypothetical."

In *O'Shea v. Littleton* we dealt with a case brought by a class of plaintiffs claiming that they had been subjected to discriminatory enforcement of the criminal law. Among other things, a county magistrate and judge were accused of discriminatory conduct in various respects, such as sentencing members of plaintiff's class more harshly than other defendants. The Court of Appeals reversed the dismissal of the suit by the District Court, ruling that if the allegations were proved, an appropriate injunction could be entered.

We reversed for failure of the complaint to allege a case or controversy. Although it was claimed in that case that particular members of the plaintiff class had actually suffered from the alleged unconstitutional practices, we observed that "[past] exposure to illegal conduct does not in itself show a present case or controversy regarding injunctive relief . . . if unaccompanied by any continuing, present adverse effects." Past wrongs were evidence bearing on "whether there is a real and immediate threat of repeated injury." But the prospect of future injury rested "on the likelihood that [plaintiffs] will again be arrested for and charged with violations of the criminal law and will again be subjected to bond proceedings, trial, or sentencing before petitioners." The most that could be said for plaintiffs' standing was "that if [plaintiffs] proceed to violate an unchallenged law and if they are charged, held to answer, and tried in any proceedings before petitioners, they will be subjected to the discriminatory practices that petitioners are alleged to have followed." We could not find a case or controversy in those circumstances: the threat to the plaintiffs was not "sufficiently real and immediate to show an existing controversy simply because they anticipate violating lawful criminal statutes and being tried for their offenses. . . ." It was to be assumed that "[plaintiffs] will conduct their activities within the law and so avoid prosecution and conviction as well as exposure to the challenged course of conduct said to be followed by petitioners."

We further observed that case-or-controversy considerations "obviously shade into those determining whether the complaint states a sound basis for equitable relief," and went on to hold that even if the complaint presented an existing case or controversy, an adequate basis for equitable relief against petitioners had not been demonstrated:

"[Plaintiffs] have failed, moreover, to establish the basic requisites of the issuance of equitable relief in these circumstances— the likelihood of substantial and immediate irreparable injury, and the inadequacy of remedies at law. We have already canvassed the necessarily conjectural nature of the threatened injury to which [plaintiffs] are allegedly subjected. And if any of the [plaintiffs] are ever prosecuted and face trial, or if they are illegally sentenced, there are available state and federal procedures which could provide relief from the wrongful conduct alleged."

Another relevant decision for present purposes is *Rizzo v. Goode*, a case in which plaintiffs alleged widespread illegal and unconstitutional police conduct aimed at minority citizens and against city residents in general. The Court reiterated the holding in *O'Shea*

that past wrongs do not in themselves amount to that real and immediate threat of injury necessary to make out a case or controversy. The claim of injury rested upon "what one of a small, unnamed minority of policemen might do to them in the future because of that unknown policeman's perception" of departmental procedures. This hypothesis was "even more attenuated than those allegations of future injury found insufficient in *O'Shea* to warrant [the] invocation of federal jurisdiction." The Court also held that plaintiffs' showing at trial of a relatively few instances of violations by individual police officers, without any showing of a deliberate policy on behalf of the named defendants, did not provide a basis for equitable relief . . .

IV

No extension of *O'Shea* and *Rizzo* is necessary to hold that respondent Lyons has failed to demonstrate a case or controversy with the City that would justify the equitable relief sought. Lyons' standing to seek the injunction requested depended on whether he was likely to suffer future injury from the use of the chokeholds by police officers. Count V of the complaint alleged the traffic stop and choking incident five months before. That Lyons may have been illegally choked by the police on October 6, 1976, while presumably affording Lyons standing to claim damages against the individual officers and perhaps against the City, does nothing to establish a real and immediate threat that he would again be stopped for a traffic violation, or for any other offense, by an officer or officers who would illegally choke him into unconsciousness without any provocation or resistance on his part. The additional allegation in the complaint that the police in Los Angeles routinely apply chokeholds in situations where they are not threatened by the use of deadly force falls far short of the allegations that would be necessary to establish a case or controversy between these parties.

In order to establish an actual controversy in this case, Lyons would have had not only to allege that he would have another encounter with the police but also to make the incredible assertion either (1) that all police officers in Los Angeles always choke any citizen with whom they happen to have an encounter, whether for the purpose of arrest, issuing a citation, or for questioning, or (2) that the City ordered or authorized police officers to act in such manner. Although Count V alleged that the City authorized the use of the control holds in situations where deadly force was not threatened, it did not indicate why Lyons might be realistically threatened by police officers who acted within the strictures of the City's policy. If, for example, chokeholds were authorized to be used only to counter resistance to an arrest by a suspect, or to thwart an effort to escape, any future threat to Lyons from the City's policy or from the conduct of police officers would be no more real than the possibility that he would again have an encounter with the police and that either he would illegally resist arrest or detention or the officers would disobey their instructions and again render him unconscious without any provocation.

Under *O'Shea* and *Rizzo*, these allegations were an insufficient basis to provide a federal court with jurisdiction to entertain Count V of the complaint . . .

The Court of Appeals . . . asserted that Lyons "had a live and active claim" against the City "if only for a period of a few seconds" while the stranglehold was being applied to him and that for two reasons the claim had not become moot so as to disentitle Lyons to injunctive relief: First, because under normal rules of equity, a case does not become moot merely because the complained of conduct has ceased; and second, because Lyons' claim is "capable of repetition but evading review" and therefore should be heard. We agree that Lyons had a live controversy with the City. Indeed, he still has a claim for damages against the City that appears to meet all Art. III requirements. Nevertheless, the issue here is not whether that claim has become moot but whether Lyons meets the preconditions for asserting an injunctive claim in a federal forum. The equitable doctrine that cessation of the challenged conduct does not bar an injunction is of little help in this respect, for Lyons' lack of standing does not rest on the termination of the police practice but on the speculative nature of his claim that he will again experience injury as the result of that practice even if continued.

The rule that a claim does not become moot where it is capable of repetition, yet evades review, is likewise inapposite. Lyons'

claim that he was illegally strangled remains to be litigated in his suit for damages; in no sense does that claim "evade" review. Furthermore, the capable-of-repetition doctrine applies only in exceptional situations, and generally only where the named plaintiff can make a reasonable showing that he will again be subjected to the alleged illegality. As we have indicated, Lyons has not made this demonstration . . .

V

Lyons fares no better if it be assumed that his pending damages suit affords him Art. III standing to seek an injunction as a remedy for the claim arising out of the October 1976 events. The equitable remedy is unavailable absent a showing of irreparable injury, a requirement that cannot be met where there is no showing of any real or immediate threat that the plaintiff will be wronged again—a "likelihood of substantial and immediate irreparable injury." *O'Shea v. Littleton.* The speculative nature of Lyons' claim of future injury requires a finding that this prerequisite of equitable relief has not been fulfilled.

Nor will the injury that Lyons allegedly suffered in 1976 go unrecompensed; for that injury, he has an adequate remedy at law. Contrary to the view of the Court of Appeals, it is not at all "difficult" under our holding "to see how anyone can ever challenge police or similar administrative practices." The legality of the violence to which Lyons claims he was once subjected is at issue in his suit for damages and can be determined there.

Absent a sufficient likelihood that he will again be wronged in a similar way, Lyons is no more entitled to an injunction than any other citizen of Los Angeles; and a federal court may not entertain a claim by any or all citizens who no more than assert that certain practices of law enforcement officers are unconstitutional . . .

We decline the invitation to slight the preconditions for equitable relief; for as we have held, recognition of the need for a proper balance between state and federal authority counsels restraint in the issuance of injunctions against state officers engaged in the administration of the States' criminal laws in the absence of irreparable injury which is both great and immediate. *O'Shea; Younger v. Harris. Mitchum v. Foster* held that suits brought under 42 U.S.C. § 1983 are exempt from the flat ban against the issuance of injunctions directed at state-court proceedings, 28 U.S.C. § 2283. But this holding did not displace the normal principles of equity, comity, and federalism that should inform the judgment of federal courts when asked to oversee state law enforcement authorities. In exercising their equitable powers federal courts must recognize "[the] special delicacy of the adjustment to be preserved between federal equitable power and State administration of its own law." The Court of Appeals failed to apply these factors properly and therefore erred in finding that the District Court had not abused its discretion in entering an injunction in this case.

As we noted in *O'Shea*, withholding injunctive relief does not mean that the "federal law will exercise no deterrent effect in these circumstances." If Lyons has suffered an injury barred by the Federal Constitution, he has a remedy for damages under § 1983. Furthermore, those who deliberately deprive a citizen of his constitutional rights risk conviction under the federal criminal laws.

Beyond these considerations the state courts need not impose the same standing or remedial requirements that govern federal-court proceedings. The individual States may permit their courts to use injunctions to oversee the conduct of law enforcement authorities on a continuing basis. But this is not the role of a federal court, absent far more justification than Lyons has proffered in this case . . .

Justice **Marshall**, with whom Justice **Brennan**, Justice **Blackmun**, and Justice **Stevens** join, dissenting . . .

There is plainly a "case or controversy" concerning the constitutionality of the city's chokehold policy. The constitutionality of that policy is directly implicated by Lyons' claim for damages against the city. The complaint clearly alleges that the officer who choked Lyons was carrying out an official policy, and a municipality is liable under 42 U.S.C. § 1983 for the conduct of its employees only if they acted pursuant to such a policy. *Monell v. New York City Dept. of Social Services*, 436 U.S. 658, 694 (1978). Lyons therefore has standing to challenge the city's chokehold policy and to obtain whatever relief a court may ultimately deem appropriate. None of our prior decisions

suggests that his requests for particular forms of relief raise any additional issues concerning his standing. Standing has always depended on whether a plaintiff has a "personal stake in the outcome of the controversy," not on the "precise nature of the relief sought." . . .

II

At the outset it is important to emphasize that Lyons' entitlement to injunctive relief and his entitlement to an award of damages both depend upon whether he can show that the city's chokehold policy violates the Constitution. An indispensable prerequisite of municipal liability under 42 U.S.C. § 1983 is proof that the conduct complained of is attributable to an unconstitutional official policy or custom. It is not enough for a § 1983 plaintiff to show that the employees or agents of a municipality have violated or will violate the Constitution, for a municipality will not be held liable solely on a theory of respondeat superior.

The Court errs in suggesting that Lyons' prayer for injunctive relief in Count V of his first amended complaint concerns a policy that was not responsible for his injuries and that therefore could not support an award of damages. Paragraph 8 of the complaint alleges that Lyons was choked "without provocation, legal justification or excuse." Paragraph 13 expressly alleges that "[the] Defendant Officers were carrying out the official policies, customs and practices of the Los Angeles Police Department and the City of Los Angeles," and that "by virtue thereof, defendant City is liable for the actions" of the officers. (Emphasis added.) These allegations are incorporated in each of the Counts against the city, including Count V . . .

III

Since Lyons' claim for damages plainly gives him standing, and since the success of that claim depends upon a demonstration that the city's chokehold policy is unconstitutional, it is beyond dispute that Lyons has properly invoked the District Court's authority to adjudicate the constitutionality of the city's chokehold policy. The dispute concerning the constitutionality of that policy plainly presents a "case or controversy" under Art. III. The Court nevertheless holds that a federal court has no power under Art. III to adjudicate

Lyons' request, in the same lawsuit, for injunctive relief with respect to that very policy. This anomalous result is not supported either by precedent or by the fundamental concern underlying the standing requirement. Moreover, by fragmenting a single claim into multiple claims for particular types of relief and requiring a separate showing of standing for each form of relief, the decision today departs from this Court's traditional conception of standing and of the remedial powers of the federal courts.

A

It is simply disingenuous for the Court to assert that its decision requires "[no] extension" of *O'Shea v. Littleton* and *Rizzo v. Goode.* In contrast to this case O'Shea and Rizzo involved disputes focusing solely on the threat of future injury which the plaintiffs in those cases alleged they faced. In O'Shea the plaintiffs did not allege past injury and did not seek compensatory relief.[13] In Rizzo, the plaintiffs sought only declaratory and injunctive relief and alleged past instances of police misconduct only in an attempt to establish the substantiality of the threat of future injury . . .

These decisions do not support the Court's holding today. As the Court recognized in *O'Shea,* standing under Art. III is established by an allegation of "'threatened or actual injury.'" Because the plaintiffs in *O'Shea, Rizzo,* [and other cases] did not seek to redress past injury, their standing to sue depended entirely on the risk of future injury they faced. Apart from the desire to eliminate the possibility of future injury, the plaintiffs in those cases had no other personal stake in the outcome of the controversies.

By contrast, Lyons' request for prospective relief is coupled with his claim for damages based on past injury. In addition to the risk that he will be subjected to a chokehold in the future, Lyons has suffered past injury. Because he has a live claim for damages, he need not

rely solely on the threat of future injury to establish his personal stake in the outcome of the controversy.[16] In the cases relied on by the majority, the Court simply had no occasion to decide whether a plaintiff who has standing to litigate a dispute must clear a separate standing hurdle with respect to each form of relief sought.

B

The Court's decision likewise finds no support in the fundamental policy underlying the Art. III standing requirement—the concern that a federal court not decide a legal issue if the plaintiff lacks a sufficient "personal stake in the outcome of the controversy as to assure that concrete adverseness which sharpens the presentation of issues upon which the court so largely depends for illumination of difficult . . . questions." As this Court stated in *Flast v. Cohen,* "the question of standing is related only to whether the dispute sought to be adjudicated will be presented in an adversary context and in a form historically viewed as capable of judicial resolution." See also *Valley Forge Christian College v. Americans United for Separation of Church and State* (standing requirement ensures that "the legal questions presented to the court will be resolved, not in the rarified atmosphere of a debating society, but in a concrete factual context conducive to a realistic appreciation of the consequences of judicial action").

Because Lyons has a claim for damages against the city, and because he cannot prevail on that claim unless he demonstrates that the

---

[13] Although counsel for the plaintiffs in O'Shea suggested at oral argument that certain plaintiffs had been exposed to illegal conduct in the past, in fact "[no] damages were sought against the petitioners . . . nor were any specific instances involving the individually named respondents set forth in the claim against these judicial officers." The Court referred to the absence of past injury repeatedly.

[16] In O'Shea itself the Court suggested that the absence of a damages claim was highly pertinent to its conclusion that the plaintiff had no standing. The Court noted that plaintiffs' "claim for relief against the State's Attorney[,] where specific instances of misconduct with respect to particular individuals are alleged," stood in "sharp contrast" to their claim for relief against the magistrate and judge, which did not contain similar allegations. The plaintiffs did seek damages against the State's Attorney. See Spomer v. Littleton. Like the claims against the State's Attorney in *O'Shea,* Lyons' claims against the city allege both past injury and the risk of future injury. Whereas in *O'Shea* the Court acknowledged the significance for standing purposes of past injury, the Court today inexplicably treats Lyons' past injury for which he is seeking redress as wholly irrelevant to the standing inquiry before us.

city's chokehold policy violates the Constitution, his personal stake in the outcome of the controversy adequately assures an adversary presentation of his challenge to the constitutionality of the policy. Moreover, the resolution of this challenge will be largely dispositive of his requests for declaratory and injunctive relief. No doubt the requests for injunctive relief may raise additional questions. But these questions involve familiar issues relating to the appropriateness of particular forms of relief, and have never been thought to implicate a litigant's standing to sue. The denial of standing separately to seek injunctive relief therefore cannot be justified by the basic concern underlying the Art. III standing requirement . . .

V

Apparently because it is unwilling to rely solely on its unprecedented rule of standing, the Court goes on to conclude that, even if Lyons has standing, "[the] equitable remedy is unavailable." . . . With the single exception of *Rizzo v. Goode*, supra,[24] all of the cases relied on by the Court concerned injunctions against state criminal proceedings. The rule of *Younger v. Harris*, that such injunctions can be issued only in extraordinary circumstances in which the threat of injury is "great and immediate," reflects the venerable rule that equity will not enjoin a criminal prosecution, the fact that constitutional defenses can be raised in such a state prosecution, and an appreciation of the friction that injunctions against state judicial proceedings may produce.

Our prior decisions have repeatedly emphasized that where an injunction is not directed against a state criminal or quasi-criminal proceeding, "the relevant principles of equity, comity, and federalism" that underlie the *Younger* doctrine "have little force." Outside the special context in which the *Younger* doctrine applies, we have held that the appropriateness of injunctive relief is governed by traditional equitable considerations. Whatev-

er the precise scope of the *Younger* doctrine may be, the concerns of comity and federalism that counsel restraint when a federal court is asked to enjoin a state criminal proceeding simply do not apply to an injunction directed solely at a police department.

If the preliminary injunction granted by the District Court is analyzed under general equitable principles, rather than the more stringent standards of *Younger v. Harris*, it becomes apparent that there is no rule of law that precludes equitable relief and requires that the preliminary injunction be set aside. "In reviewing such interlocutory relief, this Court may only consider whether issuance of the injunction constituted an abuse of discretion."

The District Court concluded, on the basis of the facts before it, that Lyons was choked without provocation pursuant to an unconstitutional city policy. Given the necessarily preliminary nature of its inquiry, there was no way for the District Court to know the precise contours of the city's policy or to ascertain the risk that Lyons, who had alleged that the policy was being applied in a discriminatory manner, might again be subjected to a chokehold. But in view of the Court's conclusion that the unprovoked choking of Lyons was pursuant to a city policy, Lyons has satisfied "the usual basis for injunctive relief, 'that there exists some cognizable danger of recurrent violation.'" The risk of serious injuries and deaths to other citizens also supported the decision to grant a preliminary injunction. Courts of equity have much greater latitude in granting injunctive relief "in furtherance of the public interest than . . . when only private interests are involved." In this case we know that the District Court would have been amply justified in considering the risk to the public, for after the preliminary injunction was stayed, five additional deaths occurred prior to the adoption of a moratorium. Under these circumstances, I do not believe that the District Court abused its discretion . . .

Under the view expressed by the majority today, if the police adopt a policy of 'shoot to kill,' or a policy of shooting 1 out of 10 suspects, the federal courts will be powerless to enjoin its continuation. The federal judicial power is now limited to levying a toll for such a systematic constitutional violation.

---

24. . . . Rizzo v. Goode does not support a decision barring Lyons from obtaining any injunctive relief, for that case involved an injunction which entailed judicial supervision of the workings of a municipal police department, not simply the sort of preventive injunction that Lyons seeks.

NOTES

1. Why did the city file a memorandum suggesting a question of mootness and then oppose a finding of mootness?

2. Does the plaintiff have standing to seek damages? Why does he not have standing to seek injunctive relief? Do the policies behind the standing requirement support the Court's premise that the plaintiff must *independently* establish standing as to his request for injunctive relief? Do *O'Shea* and *Rizzo* support that premise?

Is there any class of persons for whom the claim for injunctive relief is any more appropriate for adjudication than Lyons' own claim? Cf. *Kolender v. Lawson*, 461 U.S. 352, 355 n.3 (1983) (a person who had been stopped 15 times under a state law has standing to seek prospective relief); *City of Houston v. Hill*, 482 U.S. 451, 459 n.7 (1987) (similar). Would *Lyons* have come out differently if someone who had been arrested repeatedly had been the named plaintiff? See generally Meltzer, *Deterring Constitutional Violations by Law Enforcement Officials: Plaintiffs and Defendants as Private Attorneys General*, 88 Colum. L. Rev. 247 (1988).

3. Reread the last two sentences of Justice Marshall's dissent. Is Justice Marshall engaging in rhetorical hyperbole? As a plaintiff's lawyer, and taking the court's opinion as controlling law, could you distinguish a case in which the police routinely violated the rights of arrestees, but no individual plaintiff could show that he would likely be arrested in the future? Didn't Lyons claim that this was itself such a case? Could the problem with injunctive relief raised by the Court in *Lyons* be solved by bringing a class action?

Other than injunctive relief, with its threat of contempt if the injunction is not obeyed, is there any other way to deter such unconstitutional conduct on the part of a municipality that is undeterred by the prospect of paying compensatory damages? Would such a case be appropriate for an exception to *City of Newport*? Would criminal penalties against the officers be appropriate? In this regard, recall that the officers who beat Rodney King were tried in federal court under 18 U.S.C. § 242, the criminal counterpart of section 1983.

4. In its discussion of the equitable grounds for denying injunctive relief, the Court states that "principles of equity, comity, and federal-

ism . . . should inform the judgment of federal courts when asked to oversee state law enforcement authorities." 461 U.S. at 112. Granting that federal courts should not issue intrusive injunctions without a compelling reason for doing so, is it appropriate to reject injunctive relief before a trial on the merits, as the Court does in *Lyons*? Consider the following observations:

> Once standing is established and a constitutional violation identified, the availability of an injunction, as well as the form of injunctive relief, should depend on a calculus more complex than that employed by *Lyons*. The Court should weigh attentively the relevant statutory policy. In balancing statutory policy against competing interests, the Court should also attend more closely to particular facts to identify how deeply the various asserted interests are implicated . . . [P]laintiffs . . . [are] entitled to a balancing of the public and private interests unique to the circumstances of their situations.

Fallon, *Of Justiciability, Remedies, and Public Law Litigation: Notes on the Jurisprudence of Lyons*, 59 N.Y.U. L. Rev. 1, 72–73 (1984). Fallon contrasts such a system of case-by-case weighing of interests to the "door-closing prescriptions of *Lyons.*" Id. at 74.

Why might the Court prefer rules like the one in *Lyons* over more particularized decision making? All things considered, which approach is better, Fallon's or the Court's?

5. Does the *Lyons* barrier apply only to constitutional claims arising out of random police encounters or does it extend to other constitutional cases? In *Henschen v. City of Houston*, 959 F.2d 584 (5th Cir. 1992), plaintiffs sought a parade permit for a march on the opening day of the 1990 Economic Summit. The request was refused and the plaintiffs sued, asserting that their first amendment rights were violated and seeking damages and injunctive relief. The court began its analysis by noting that, under *Lyons*, "[j]usticiability must be analyzed separately on the issues of money damages and the propriety of injunctive relief." The court held that their damages suit could go forward, but the request for prospective injunctive relief could not. In spite of the alleged wrong done them, they could not show that they are imperiled by a present threat of unlawful speech restrictions . . . [A]ppellants . . . formed a loose confederation of community activists who coalesced to demonstrate at the 1990 Economic Summit. Upon the conclusion of the Summit, their *raison d'etre* withered . . . After [the summit] the group wholly dissolved, except for the purpose of pursuing this action. Thus, they suffer no continuing threat of harm from the City's enforcement of the parade permit scheme.

959 F.2d at 588.

If a group such as these plaintiffs asked you for advice on maintaining the request for prospective relief, what would you tell them to do?

6. County of *Riverside v. McLaughlin*, 111 S. Ct. 1661 (1991) was a class action brought on behalf of a class of persons arrested without a warrant, challenging the county's practice of combining probable cause determinations with its arraignment procedures. The substantive issue was whether probable cause determinations were made soon enough to satisfy the constitution. Before reaching the merits the Court addressed the plaintiffs' standing.

The County argued that

"the main thrust of plaintiffs' suit is that they are entitled to "prompt" probable cause determinations, and insists that this is, by definition, a time-limited violation. Once enough time has passed, the County argues, the constitutional violation is complete because a probable cause determination made after that point would no longer be "prompt." Thus, at least as to the named plaintiffs, there is no standing because it is too late for them to receive a prompt hearing and, under *Lyons*, they cannot show that they are likely to be subjected again to the unconstitutional conduct.

We reject the County's argument . . . [A]t the time the . . . complaint was filed, [some named] plaintiffs . . . had been arrested without warrants and were being held in custody without having received a probable cause determination, prompt or otherwise. Plaintiffs alleged in their complaint that they were suffering a direct and current injury as a result of this detention,

and would continue to suffer that injury until they received the probable cause determination to which they were entitled. Plainly, plaintiffs' injury was at that moment capable of being redressed through injunctive relief. The County's argument that the constitutional violation had already been 'completed' relies on a crabbed reading of the complaint. This case is easily distinguishable from Lyons, in which the constitutionally objectionable practice ceased altogether before the plaintiff filed his complaint.

Does this case represent a retreat from *Lyons*, or merely a refusal to extend its reach?

7. After *Lyons*, should a plaintiff take his case to *state* court? Would the limits on standing and the availability of injunctive relief announced in *Lyons* apply to such a case? In the last paragraph of the opinion the Court seems to say they would not. Of course, state courts are not obliged to offer more favorable terms than plaintiffs would find in federal court. See Chapter 11 for further discussion of state court section 1983 litigation.

8. Over the past forty years, courts have increasingly employed injunctive remedies as an integral part of an adjudicative model Professor Abram Chayes named "public law litigation". See Chayes, *The Role of the Judge in Public Law Litigation*, 89 Harv. L. Rev. 1281 (1976). Professor Chayes usefully contrasts the new model with traditional litigation. In the traditional model,

(1) The lawsuit is *bipolar*. Litigation is organized as a contest between two individuals or at least two unitary interests, diametrically opposed, to be decided on a winner-takes-all basis.

(2) Litigation is *retrospective*. The controversy is about an identified set of completed events: Whether they occurred, and if so, with what consequences for the legal relations of the parties.

(3) *Right and remedy are interdependent*. The scope of the relief is derived more or less logically from the substantive violation under the general theory that the plaintiff will get compensation measured by the harm caused by the defendant's breach of duty—in contract by giving the plaintiff the money he would have had

absent the breach; in tort by paying the value of the damage caused.

(4) The lawsuit is a *self-contained* episode. The impact of the judgment is confined to the parties. If plaintiff prevails there is a simple compensatory transfer, usually of money, but occasionally the return of a thing or the performance of a definite act. If defendant prevails, a loss lies where it has fallen. In either case, entry of judgment ends the court's involvement.

(5) The process is *party-initiated* and *party-controlled*. The case is organized and the issues defined by exchanges between the parties. Responsibility for fact development is theirs. The trial judge is a neutral arbiter of their interactions who decides questions of law only if they are put in issue by an appropriate move of a party . . .

The characteristic features of the public law model are very different from those of the traditional model. The party structure is sprawling and amorphous, subject to change over the course of the litigation. The traditional adversary relationship is suffused and intermixed with negotiating and mediating processes at every point. The judge is the dominant figure in organizing and guiding the case, and he draws for support not only on the parties and their counsel, but on a wide range of outsiders—masters, experts, and oversight personnel. Most important, the trial judge has increasingly become the creator and manager of complex forms of ongoing relief, which have widespread effects on persons not before the court and require the judge's continuing involvement in administration and implementation. School desegregation, employment discrimination, and prisoners' or inmates' rights cases come readily to mind as avatars of this new form of litigation."

Chayes, supra, at 1282–84.

Which model best describes constitutional tort litigation?

9. Suits for injunctive relief, especially those falling into the "public law litigation" model, raise a vast array of technical and policy issues, regarding the prerequisites for obtaining such relief, the scope of injunctive relief, the persons who may be affected by it, sanctions for violations of the decree, conditions for lifting the order, and so on. As we have chosen to focus on actions seeking monetary awards, referring to prospective relief only in order to provide context and perspective for our treatment of damages, these issues are well beyond the scope of this book. They are addressed in courses on remedies. There is at least one casebook devoted exclusively to injunctions. See O. Fiss & D. Rendleman, *Injunctions* (2d ed. 1984).

CHAPTER TEN

Procedural Defenses

This chapter explores a number of defenses to a section 1983 action that do not directly pertain to the merits of the underlying claim. A common thread running throughout these materials is the tension inherent in the dual sovereignty aspects of a federal system of government. Should state or federal law govern a particular issue? When is it appropriate for federal courts to adjudicate claims against state and local officials? Should states be given the first opportunity to redress wrongs committed by its officials against its citizens? Many of the doctrines explored in this chapter are driven by a desire to maintain an appropriate balance between federal authority to protect federal constitutional rights and a respect for state sovereignty.

Keep in mind that these doctrines are not only of theoretical importance but are of immense practical significance for litigation as well.

I. Statutes of Limitations

There are important procedural issues affecting section 1983 litigation that are not governed by a specific uniform federal rule. For example, section 1983 does not contain a specific statute of limitations. Should federal courts fashion a federal common law limitations period, or should they look to analogous state law? If the latter, which state limitations period would be most appropriate? The interplay of state and federal law is especially important in statute of limitations issues. Before turning to the cases, consider the following statute.

42 U.S.C. § 1988 provides in relevant part:

The jurisdiction in civil and criminal matters conferred on the district courts by the provisions of this Title, and of Title "CIVIL RIGHTS," and of Title "CRIMES," for the protection of all persons in the United States in their civil rights, and for their

vindication, shall be exercised and enforced in conformity with the laws of the United States, so far as such laws are suitable to carry the same into effect; but in all cases where they are not adapted to the object, or are deficient in the provisions necessary to furnish suitable remedies and punish offenses against law, the common law, as modified and changed by the constitution and statutes of the State wherein the court having jurisdiction of such civil or criminal cause is held, so far as the same is not inconsistent with the Constitution and laws of the United States, shall be extended to and govern the said courts in the trial and disposition of the cause. . . .

Of what relevance is this statute in determining the proper limitations period for section 1983 claims?

Wilson v. Garcia

471 U.S. 261 (1985)

Justice **Stevens** delivered the opinion of the Court.

In this case we must determine the most appropriate state statute of limitations to apply to claims enforceable under . . . 42 U.S.C. § 1983.

On January 28, 1982, respondent brought this § 1983 action in the United States District Court for the District of New Mexico seeking "money damages to compensate him for the deprivation of his civil rights guaranteed by the Fourth, Fifth and Fourteenth Amendments to the United States Constitution and for the personal injuries he suffered which were caused by the acts and omissions of the [petitioners] acting under color of law." The complaint alleged that on April 27, 1979, petitioner Wilson, a New Mexico State Police officer, unlawfully arrested the respondent, "brutally and viciously" beat him, and sprayed his face with tear gas; that petitioner Vigil, the Chief of the New Mexico State Police, had notice of Officer Wilson's allegedly "violent propensities," and had failed to reprimand him for committing other unprovoked attacks on citizens; and that Vigil's training and supervision of Wilson was seriously deficient.

The respondent's complaint was filed two years and nine months after the claim purportedly arose. Petitioners moved to dismiss on the ground that the action was barred by the 2-year statute of limitations contained in § 41–4–15(A) of the New Mexico Tort Claims Act. The petitioners' motion was supported by a decision of the New Mexico Supreme Court which squarely held that the Tort Claims Act provides "the most closely analogous state cause of action" to § 1983, and that its 2-year statute of limitations is therefore applicable to actions commenced under § 1983 in the state courts. *DeVargas v. New Mexico.* In addition to the 2-year statute of limitations in the Tort Claims Act, two other New Mexico statutes conceivably could apply to § 1983 claims: § 37–1–8, which provides a 3-year limitation period for actions "for an injury to the person or reputation of any person"; and § 37–1–4, which provides a 4-year limitation period for "all other actions not herein otherwise provided for." If either of these longer statutes applies to the respondent's § 1983 claim, the complaint was timely filed.

[The district court denied the motion to dismiss. It ruled that *DeVargas* was not controlling because "the characterization of the nature of the right being vindicated under § 1983 is a matter of federal, rather than state law." The court then concluded that the residual 4-year limitation period should apply. The court of appeals affirmed the district court on different grounds. The court of appeals agreed that *DeVargas* was not controlling, but held that § 1983 actions were best analogized to "an action for injury to personal rights", subject to a 3-year limitation period.]
. . .

[T]he conflict, confusion, and uncertainty concerning the appropriate statute of limitations to apply to this most important, and ubiquitous, civil rights statute provided compelling reasons for granting certiorari. 469 U.S. 815 (1984). We find the reasoning in the Court of Appeals' opinion persuasive, and affirm.

I

The Reconstruction Civil Rights Acts do not contain a specific statute of limitations governing § 1983 actions—"a void which is commonplace in federal statutory law." *Board of Regents v. Tomanio.* When Congress has not established a time limitation for a federal cause of action, the settled practice has been to adopt a local time limitation as federal law if it is not inconsistent with federal law or policy to do so. In 42 U.S.C. § 1988, Congress has implicitly endorsed this approach with respect to claims enforceable under the Reconstruction Civil Rights Acts.

The language of § 1988, directs the courts to follow "a three-step process" in determining the rules of decision applicable to civil rights claims:

> "First, courts are to look to the laws of the United States 'so far as such laws are suitable to carry [the civil and criminal civil rights statutes] into effect.' [42 U.S.C. § 1988.] If no suitable federal rule exists, courts undertake the second step by considering application of state 'common law, as modified and changed by the constitution and statutes' of the forum state. Ibid. A third step asserts the predominance of the federal interest: courts are to apply state law only if it is not 'inconsistent with the Constitution and laws of the United States.' Ibid." *Burnett v. Grattan.*

This case principally involves the second step in the process: the selection of "the most appropriate," or "the most analogous" state statute of limitations to apply to this § 1983 claim.

In order to determine the most "most appropriate" or "most analogous" New Mexico statute to apply to the respondent's claim, we must answer three questions. We must first consider whether state law or federal law governs the characterization of a § 1983 claim for statute of limitations purposes. If federal law applies, we must next decide whether all § 1983 claims should be characterized in the same way, or whether they should be evaluated differently depending upon the varying factual circumstances and legal theories presented in each individual case. Finally, we must characterize the essence of the claim in the pending case, and decide which state statute provides the most appropriate limiting principle. Although the text of neither § 1983 nor § 1988 provides a pellucid answer to any of these questions, all three parts of the inquiry are, in final analysis, questions of statutory construction.

II

Our identification of the correct source of law properly begins with the text of § 1988. Congress' first instruction in the statute is that the law to be applied in adjudicating civil rights claims shall be in "conformity with the laws of the United States, so far as such laws are suitable." This mandate implies that resort to state law—the second step in the process—should not be undertaken before principles of federal law are exhausted. The characterization of § 1983 for statute of limitations purposes is derived from the elements of the cause of action, and Congress' purpose in providing it. These, of course, are matters of federal law. Since federal law is available to decide the question, the language of § 1988 directs that the matter of characterization should be treated as a federal question. Only the length of the limitations period, and closely related questions of tolling and application, are to be governed by state law.

This interpretation is also supported by Congress' third instruction in § 1988: state law shall only apply "so far as the same is not inconsistent with" federal law. This requirement emphasizes "the predominance of the federal interest" in the borrowing process, taken as a whole. Even when principles of state law are borrowed to assist in the enforcement of this federal remedy, the state rule is adopted as "a federal rule responsive to the need whenever a federal right is impaired." *Sullivan v. Little Hunting Park, Inc.* The importation of the policies and purposes of the States on matters of civil rights is not the primary office of the borrowing provision in § 1988; rather, the statute is designed to assure that neutral rules of decision will be available to enforce the civil rights actions, among them § 1983. Congress surely did not intend to assign to state courts and legislatures a conclusive role in the formative function of defining and characterizing the essential elements of a federal cause of action.

. . .

[T]he federal interest in uniformity and the interest in having "firmly defined, easily applied rules," support the conclusion that Congress intended the characterization of § 1983 to be measured by federal rather than state standards. The Court of Appeals was therefore correct in concluding that it was not bound by the New Mexico Supreme Court's holding in *DeVargas.*

III

A federal cause of action "brought at any distance of time" would be "utterly repugnant to the genius of our laws." *Adams v. Woods.* Just determinations of fact cannot be made when, because of the passage of time, the memories of witnesses have faded or evidence is lost. In compelling circumstances, even wrongdoers are entitled to assume that their sins may be forgotten.

The borrowing of statutes of limitations for § 1983 claims serves these policies of repose. Of course, the application of any statute of limitations would promote repose. By adopting the statute governing an analogous cause of action under state law, federal law incorporates the State's judgment on the proper balance between the policies of repose and the substantive policies of enforcement embodied in the state cause of action. However, when the federal claim differs from the state cause of action in fundamental respects, the State's choice of a specific period of limitation is, at best, only a rough approximation of "the point at which the interests in favor of protecting valid claims are outweighed by the interests in prohibiting the prosecution of stale ones." *Johnson v. Railway Express Agency, Inc.*

. . .

[P]ractical considerations help to explain why a simple, broad characterization of all § 1983 claims best fits the statute's remedial purpose. The experience of the courts that have predicated their choice of the correct statute of limitations on an analysis of the particular facts of each claim demonstrates that their approach inevitably breeds uncertainty and time-consuming litigation that is foreign to the central purposes of § 1983.

Almost every § 1983 claim can be favorably analogized to more than one of the ancient common-law forms of action, each of which may be governed by a different statute of limitations. In the case before us, for example, the respondent alleges that he was injured by a New Mexico State Police officer who used excessive force to carry out an unlawful arrest. This § 1983 claim is arguably analogous to distinct state tort claims for false arrest, assault and battery, or personal injuries. Moreover, the claim could also be characterized as one arising under a statute, or as governed by the special New Mexico statute authorizing recovery against the State for the torts of its agents.

A catalog of other constitutional claims that have been alleged under § 1983 would encompass numerous and diverse topics and subtopics: discrimination in public employment on the basis of race or the exercise of First Amendment rights, discharge or demotion without procedural due process, mistreatment of schoolchildren, deliberate indifference to the medical needs of prison inmates, the seizure of chattels without advance notice or sufficient opportunity to be heard—to identify only a few. If the choice of the statute of limitations were to depend upon the particular facts or the precise legal theory of each claim, counsel could almost always argue, with considerable force, that two or more periods of limitations should apply to each § 1983 claim. Moreover, under such an approach different statutes of limitations would be applied to the various § 1983 claims arising in the same State,[32] and multiple periods of limitations would often apply to the same case.[33] There is no reason to believe that

Congress would have sanctioned this interpretation of its statute.

When § 1983 was enacted, it is unlikely that Congress actually foresaw the wide diversity of claims that the new remedy would ultimately embrace. The simplicity of the admonition in § 1988 is consistent with the assumption that Congress intended the identification of the appropriate statute of limitations to be an uncomplicated task for judges, lawyers, and litigants, rather than a source of uncertainty, and unproductive and ever-increasing litigation. Moreover, the legislative purpose to create an effective remedy for the enforcement of federal civil rights is obstructed by uncertainty in the applicable statute of limitations, for scarce resources must be dissipated by useless litigation on collateral matters.

Although the need for national uniformity "has not been held to warrant the displacement of state statutes of limitations for civil rights actions," *Board of Regents v. Tomanio*, uniformity within each State is entirely consistent with the borrowing principle contained in § 1988. We conclude that the statute is fairly construed as a directive to select, in each State, the one most appropriate statute of limitations for all § 1983 claims. The federal interests in uniformity, certainty, and the minimization of unnecessary litigation all support the conclusion that Congress favored this simple approach.

IV

After exhaustively reviewing the different ways that § 1983 claims have been characterized in every Federal Circuit, the Court of Appeals concluded that the tort action for the recovery of damages for personal injuries is the best alternative available. We agree that this choice is supported by the nature of the § 1983 remedy, and by the federal interest in ensuring that the borrowed period of limitations not discriminate against the federal civil rights remedy.

. . .

The atrocities that concerned Congress in 1871 plainly sounded in tort. Relying on this premise we have found tort analogies compelling in establishing the elements of a cause of action under § 1983, and in identifying the

---

[32] For example, compare McGhee v. Ogburn (2-year Florida statute), with Williams v. Rhoden (4-year Florida statute); Hines v. Board of Education of Covington, Ky. (1-year Kentucky statute), with Garner v. Stephens (5-year Kentucky statute); and Whatley v. Department of Education (20-year Georgia statute), with Wooten v. Sanders (2-year Georgia statute).

[33] For example, in Polite v. Diehl the plaintiff alleged that police officers unlawfully arrested him, beat him and sprayed him with mace, coerced him into pleading guilty to various offenses, and had his automobile towed away. The court held that a 1-year false arrest statute of limitations applied to the arrest claim, a 2-year personal injuries statute applied to the beating and coerced-plea claims, and a 6-year statute for

actions seeking the recovery of goods applied to the towing claim. . . .

immunities available to defendants. As we have noted, however, the § 1983 remedy encompasses a broad range of potential tort analogies, from injuries to property to infringements of individual liberty.

Among the potential analogies, Congress unquestionably would have considered the remedies established in the Civil Rights Act to be more analogous to tort claims for personal injury than, for example, to claims for damages to property or breach of contract. The unifying theme of the Civil Rights Act of 1871 is reflected in the language of the Fourteenth Amendment that unequivocally recognizes the equal status of every "person" subject to the jurisdiction of any of the several States. The Constitution's command is that all "persons" shall be accorded the full privileges of citizenship; no person shall be deprived of life, liberty, or property without due process of law or be denied the equal protection of the laws. A violation of that command is an injury to the individual rights of the person.

. . .

Had the 42d Congress expressly focused on the issue decided today, we believe it would have characterized § 1983 as conferring a general remedy for injuries to personal rights.

The relative scarcity of statutory claims when § 1983 was enacted makes it unlikely that Congress would have intended to apply the catchall periods of limitations for statutory claims that were later enacted by many States. Section 1983, of course, is a statute, but it only provides a remedy and does not itself create any substantive rights. Although a few § 1983 claims are based on statutory rights most involve much more. The rights enforceable under § 1983 include those guaranteed by the Federal Government in the Fourteenth Amendment: that every person within the United States is entitled to equal protection of the laws and to those "fundamental principles of liberty and justice" that are contained in the Bill of Rights and "lie at the base of all our civil and political institutions." These guarantees of liberty are among the rights possessed by every individual in a civilized society, and not privileges extended to the people by the legislature.

Finally, we are satisfied that Congress would not have characterized § 1983 as providing a cause of action analogous to state remedies for wrongs committed by public officials. It was the very ineffectiveness of state remedies that led Congress to enact the Civil Rights Acts in the first place. Congress therefore intended that the remedy provided in § 1983 be independently enforceable whether or not it duplicates a parallel state remedy. *Monroe v. Pape.* The characterization of all § 1983 actions as involving claims for personal injuries minimizes the risk that the choice of a state statute of limitations would not fairly serve the federal interests vindicated by § 1983. General personal injury actions, sounding in tort, constitute a major part of the total volume of civil litigation in the state courts today, and probably did so in 1871 when § 1983 was enacted. It is most unlikely that the period of limitations applicable to such claims ever was, or ever would be, fixed in a way that would discriminate against federal claims, or be inconsistent with federal law in any respect.

V

In view of our holding that § 1983 claims are best characterized as personal injury actions, the Court of Appeals correctly applied the 3-year statute of limitations governing actions "for an injury to the person or reputation of any person." N.M. Stat. Ann. § 37–1–8 (1978). The judgment of the Court of Appeals is affirmed.

It is so ordered.

Justice **Powell** took no part in the consideration or decision of this case.

[The dissenting opinion of Justice **O'Connor** is omitted.]

NOTES

1. When and to what extent should federal courts look to state law under section 1988? When would state law be considered "inconsistent with the Constitution and laws of the United States"? Why are federal courts free to ignore state supreme court determinations as to which state statute of limitations is most appropriate? The majority characterizes the issue as one of statutory construction. Is the Court's conclusion that a single state statute of limitations should govern all section 1983 cases most strongly supported by the language of section 1988, its legislative history, or contemporary policy?

2. Unlike New Mexico, many states do not provide a single limitations period for "the tort action for the recovery of damages for personal injuries." It is common for states to have one or more limitations period for certain intentional torts, and a residual or general limitations period for all other personal injury actions. In such instances, which limitations period controls the section 1983 claim? In *Owens v. Okure*, 488 U.S. 235 (1989), the Court held that residual or general limitations period for personal injury actions should govern section 1983 claims. Thus, New York's three-year general personal injury statute of limitations governed the plaintiff's excessive force section 1983 claim, rather than the one-year period for intentional torts. Would it matter if the general personal injury limitations period is shorter than the period for intentional torts? Should it matter that many section 1983 claims require evidence of "deliberate indifference", a standard more closely analogous to intentional torts than to negligence? The *Owens* Court emphasized that choosing a state's residual limitations period was appropriate only where "state law provides multiple statutes of limitations for personal injury actions and the residual one embraces either explicitly or by judicial construction, unspecified personal injury actions." *Owens*, 488 U.S. at 250 n.12.

3. Are states free to enact special statutes of limitations exclusively for section 1983 claims? In 1987, Utah enacted a statute imposing a 2 year limitations period for section 1983 claims (Utah Code Ann. § 78–12–28(3)), the same as provided for claims under state law against state officials for violations of official duties. The residual statute of limitations for personal injuries in Utah is 4 years. Utah Code Ann. § 78–12–25(3). Is the specific statute of limitations for section 1983 claims the "most analogous" limitations period under *Wilson* and *Owens*? Is a specific statute of limitations of two years for section 1983 claims "consistent" with federal law and policy? Is it relevant that the special limitations period for section 1983 claims is the same as applicable to similar claims against state officials under state law? The Tenth Circuit Court of Appeals recently struck down the Utah statute. *Arnold v. Duchesne County*, 26 F.3d 982 (10th Cir. 1994).

The court held that the statute was inconsistent with federal law and policy. Among the reasons cited by the court was that the special limitations period was "at least partially motivated by . . . [a desire] to reduce the number of [prisoner section 1983] suits." *Arnold*, 26 F.3d 988. Would the outcome in *Arnold* be different if the special statute of limitations for section 1983 claims was longer than the residual personal injury statute of limitations?

4. The *Wilson* decision forced the circuit courts to reexamine many of their earlier rulings regarding which limitations period governed section 1983 claims. In some instances, the residual personal injury statute of limitations was shorter than the more specific provision the court had been applying. E.g., *McDougal v. County of Imperial*, 942 F.2d 668 (9th Cir. 1991) (before *Wilson*, landowner's section 1983 claim was subject to a 3 year statute of limitations for violations of statute; after *Wilson*, the same claim was subject to a 1 year limitations period). A recurring question was whether *Wilson* was to be given retroactive effect. In *Saint Francis College v. Al-Khazraji*, 481 U.S. 604 (1987), the Supreme Court upheld a lower court ruling that *Wilson* was not to be applied retroactively so as to bar a claim that was timely under the clearly settled law in effect when the suit was filed. A more difficult retroactivity issue was raised in cases where the limitations period was not settled on the day the suit was filed, or when the suit was not filed until after *Wilson* was decided. The lower courts were divided on this issue. Compare *Ridgway v. Wapello County*, 795 F.2d 646 (8th Cir. 1986) (*Wilson* not applied retroactively) with *Bartholomew v. Fischl*, 782 F.2d 1148 (3rd Cir. 1986) (*Wilson* applied retroactively). The Supreme Court recently announced a rule that strongly supports the retroactive application of decisions like *Wilson*. In *Harper v. Virginia Department of Taxation*, 113 S. Ct. 2510, 2417 (1993), Justice Thomas wrote for the majority:

> When this Court applies a rule of federal law to the parties before it, that rule is the controlling interpretation of federal law and must be given full retroactive effect in all cases still open on direct review as to all events, regardless of whether such events predate or postdate our announcement of the rule. . .[W]e now prohibit the erection of selective temporal

barriers to the application of federal law in noncriminal cases.

5. Under *Wilson*, the governing limitations period for section 1983 claims necessarily will vary from state to state. In most jurisdictions, the limitations period is 2 or 3 years. E.g., *Street v. Vose*, 936 F.2d 38 (1st Cir. 1991) (Massachusetts 3 year limitations period); *Leon v. Murphy*, 988 F.2d 303 (2d Cir. 1993) (New York 3 year limitations period); *Genty v. Resolution Trust Corp.*, 937 F.2d 899 (3rd Cir. 1991) (New Jersey 2 year limitations period). In California, however, the limitations period is only one year. *McDougal v. County of Imperial*, 942 F.2d 668 (9th Cir. 1991). Is there a principled reason why a civil rights claimant should have three years in which to file her suit in New York, but only one year in California?

6. The issue of when a cause of action "accrues" for purposes of the statute of limitations is determined by federal law. *Delaware State College v. Ricks*, 449 U.S. 250 (1980). In *Ricks*, a college professor complained that he was denied tenure because of his national origin. The Court ruled that his claim accrued (and the limitations period began to run) on the date was notified of the tenure decision, not when his contract expired. *Ricks* held that as a matter of federal law, the section 1983 claim accrued on the date of the challenged conduct. Suppose that on the date of the challenged conduct, the plaintiff did not have reason to know that the defendants' decision was unconstitutionally discriminatory. Should the cause of action accrue when the plaintiff discovers the impermissible discriminatory motive? The Supreme Court applied such a discovery rule in a medical malpractice claim brought under the Federal Tort Claims Act. In *United States v. Kubrick*, 444 U.S. 111 (1979), the Court held that a cause of action accrues when the patient is, or reasonably should be, aware of an injury and its probable cause, but not necessarily the possibility of negligence. Suppose an African-American is denied a liquor license by the defendant in 1979 and a white couple is granted a license for the same location in 1981. Would the African-American's section 1983 claim of alleged racial discrimination accrue on the date his application was denied, or on the date the white application was granted? See *Calhoun v. Alabama Alcoholic Beverage Control Board*, 705 F.2d 422, 425

(11th Cir. 1983) ("the statute does not begin to run until the facts which would support a cause of action are apparent or should be apparent to a person with a reasonably prudent regard for his rights.").

7. Suppose a plaintiff complains of a series of racially discriminatory episodes occurring over a number of years and culminating in her discharge from employment. Can the plaintiff bring an action for all the alleged misconduct if only the discharge occurred within the limitations period? See *Hull v. Cuyahoga Valley Board of Education*, 926 F.2d 505 (6th Cir. 1991) (the plaintiff can bring all of her claims as part of a "continuing violation" of her civil rights). See also *Velazquez v. Chardon*, 736 F.2d 831 (1st Cir. 1984) (continuing violation theory does not apply unless a discriminatory act occurs within the limitation period).

With regard to conspiracies, the statute of limitations begins to run from the occurrence of the last overt act. E.g., *Buford v. Tremayne*, 747 F.2d 445 (8th Cir. 1984); *Gibson v. United States*, 781 F.2d 1334 (9th Cir. 1986).

8. Though accrual is governed by federal law, the tolling of the limitations period is controlled by state law. *Board of Regents v. Tomanio*, 446 U.S. 478 (1980) (rejecting the application of a federal tolling rule). Historically, many states have tolled the running of the statute of limitations for minors, the insane and the imprisoned. Such state tolling rules have enabled inmates to bring actions against prison officials many years after the challenged conduct occurred. See *Hardin v. Straub*, 490 U.S. 536 (1989) (applying the Michigan tolling statute). Perhaps in response to decisions like *Hardin*, some states modified their tolling statutes for claims by inmates against prison officials. Suppose a state eliminates its tolling provisions for claims by inmates against prison officials, but retains it for claims by inmates against all other defendants. Would such a statute be considered "inconsistent" with the purposes of section 1983, and hence not controlling? See *Dixon v. Chrans*, 986 F.2d 201 (7th Cir. 1993) (Illinois law is "inconsistent" with the purposes of section 1983 and will not be applied to section 1983 claims; subsequently, Illinois completely abolished the tolling rule for prison inmates).

9. Suppose police officers fraudulently conceal the identity of the officers who used excessive force in arresting the plaintiff. Should state or federal law control whether the limitation period is tolled? See *Smith v. City of Chicago Heights*, 951 F.2d 834 (7th Cir. 1992) (applying a federal rule of "equitable tolling" when the state fraudulent concealment statute did not apply). Is the application of a federal rule of equitable tolling consistent with *Tomanio* cited in the preceding note? Could any apparent inconsistency be avoided by characterizing equitable tolling as an aspect of accrual which, as discussed in note 6, is governed by federal law?

10. Many states have laws that require that notice be given within a short time of injury in order to bring tort claims against local governments or their officials. Should such notice of claim statutes apply to section 1983 claims brought in federal or state court? In *Felder v. Casey*, 487 U.S. 131, 138 (1988), the Supreme Court concluded that Wisconsin's four-month notice-of-claim statute "conflicts both in its purpose and effects with the remedial objectives of § 1983" and therefore could not be applied to section 1983 claims brought in state court. See Chapter 11 infra.

II. Release-Dismissal Agreements

The statute of limitations materials illustrate one type of federal-state conflict in section 1983 litigation: whether federal or state law should control a particular issue. The absence of a uniform federal statute of limitations creates the need for federal courts to borrow from and apply state law. The procedural defenses addressed in the remainder of this chapter implicate an additional type of federal-state conflict: to what extent should state proceedings affect a subsequent section 1983 claim? For example, many section 1983 claims arise from alleged infringements of constitutional rights occurring in the course of a state criminal investigation or prosecution. Challenges to the constitutionality of a search or arrest often are raised first in state court as a defense to the criminal prosecution. The case below considers whether the terms of an agreement dismissing state criminal charges can effectively bar a section 1983 suit pertaining to the legality of the arrest and prosecution.

Town of Newton v. Rumery

480 U.S. 386 (1987)

Justice **Powell** announced the judgment of the Court and delivered the opinion of the Court with respect to Parts I, II, III-A, IV, and V, and an opinion with respect to Part III-B, in which **The Chief Justice**, Justice **White**, and Justice **Scalia** join.

The question in this case is whether a court properly may enforce an agreement in which a criminal defendant releases his right to file an action under 42 U.S.C. § 1983 in return for a prosecutor's dismissal of pending criminal charges.

I

In 1983, a grand jury in Rockingham County, New Hampshire, indicted David Champy for aggravated felonious sexual assault. Respondent Bernard Rumery, a friend of Champy's, read about the charges in a local newspaper. Seeking information about the charges, he telephoned Mary Deary, who was acquainted with both Rumery and Champy. Coincidentally, Deary had been the victim of the assault in question and was expected to be the principal witness against Champy. The record does not reveal directly the date or substance of this conversation between Rumery and Deary, but Deary apparently was disturbed by the call. On March 12, according to police records, she called David Barrett, the Chief of Police for the town of Newton. She told him that Rumery was trying to force her to drop the charges against Champy. Rumery talked to Deary again on May 11. The substance of this conversation also is disputed. Rumery claims that Deary called him and that she raised the subject of Champy's difficulties. According to the police records, however, Deary told Chief Barrett that Rumery had threatened that, if Deary went forward on the Champy case, she would "end up like" two women who recently had been murdered in Lowell, Massachusetts. Barrett arrested Rumery and accused him of tampering with a witness. . .

Rumery promptly retained Stephen Woods, an experienced criminal defense attorney. Woods contacted Brian Graf, the Deputy County Attorney for Rockingham County. He warned Graf that he "had better [dismiss] these charges, because we're going to win them and after that we're going to sue." After further discussions, Graf and Woods reached an agreement, under which Graf would dismiss the charges against Rumery if Rumery would agree not to sue the town, its officials, or Deary for any harm caused by the arrest. All parties agreed that one factor in Graf's decision not to prosecute Rumery was Graf's desire to protect Deary from the trauma she would suffer if she were forced to testify. . . .

Woods drafted an agreement in which Rumery agreed to release any claims he might have against the town, its officials, or Deary if Graf agreed to dismiss the criminal charges (the release-dismissal agreement). After Graf approved the form of the agreement, Woods presented it to Rumery. Although Rumery's recollection of the events was quite different, the District Court found that Woods discussed the agreement with Rumery in his office for about an hour and explained to Rumery that he would forgo all civil actions if he signed the agreement. Three days later, on June 6, 1983, Rumery returned to Woods' office and signed the agreement. The criminal charges were dropped.

Ten months later, on April 13, 1984, Rumery filed an action under § 1983 in the Federal District Court for the District of New Hampshire. He alleged that the town and its officers had violated his constitutional rights by arresting him, defaming him, and imprisoning him falsely. The defendants filed a motion to dismiss, relying on the release-dismissal agreement as an affirmative defense. Rumery argued that the agreement was unenforceable because it violated public policy. . . .

[The District Court rejected Rumery's argument and dismissed the § 1983 action on the basis of the release-dismissal agreement. The Court of Appeals reversed, holding that all such agreements are per se invalid.]

Because the case raises a question important to the administration of criminal justice, we granted the town's petition for a writ of certiorari. We reverse.

II

We begin by noting the source of the law that governs this case. The agreement purported to waive a right to sue conferred by a federal statute. The question whether the

policies underlying that statute may in some circumstances render that waiver unenforceable is a question of federal law. We resolve this question by reference to traditional common-law principles, as we have resolved other questions about the principles governing § 1983 actions. The relevant principle is well established: a promise is unenforceable if the interest in its enforcement is outweighed in the circumstances by a public policy harmed by enforcement of the agreement.

III

The Court of Appeals concluded that the public interests related to release-dismissal agreements justified a per se rule of invalidity. We think the court overstated the perceived problems and also failed to credit the significant public interests that such agreements can further. Most importantly, the Court of Appeals did not consider the wide variety of factual situations that can result in release-dismissal agreements. Thus, although we agree that in some cases these agreements may infringe important interests of the criminal defendant and of society as a whole, we do not believe that the mere possibility of harm to these interests calls for a per se rule.

A

Rumery's first objection to release-dismissal agreements is that they are inherently coercive. He argues that it is unfair to present a criminal defendant with a choice between facing criminal charges and waiving his right to sue under § 1983. We agree that some release-dismissal agreements may not be the product of an informed and voluntary decision. The risk, publicity, and expense of a criminal trial may intimidate a defendant, even if he believes his defense is meritorious. But this possibility does not justify invalidating all such agreements. In other contexts criminal defendants are required to make difficult choices that effectively waive constitutional rights. For example, it is well settled that plea bargaining does not violate the Constitution even though a guilty plea waives important constitutional rights. . .[3]

---

[3] We recognize that the analogy between plea bargains and release-dismissal agreements is not complete. The former are subject to judicial oversight. Moreover, when the State enters a plea bargain with a

. . .

In many cases a defendant's choice to enter into a release-dismissal agreement will reflect a highly rational judgment that the certain benefits of escaping criminal prosecution exceed the speculative benefits of prevailing in a civil action. Rumery's voluntary decision to enter this agreement exemplifies such a judgment. Rumery is a sophisticated businessman. He was not in jail and was represented by an experienced criminal lawyer, who drafted the agreement. Rumery considered the agreement for three days before signing it. The benefits of the agreement to Rumery are obvious: he gained immunity from criminal prosecution in consideration of abandoning a civil suit that he may well have lost.

Because Rumery voluntarily waived his right to sue under § 1983, the public interest opposing involuntary waiver of constitutional rights is no reason to hold this agreement invalid. Moreover, we find that the possibility of coercion in the making of similar agreements insufficient by itself to justify a per se rule against release-dismissal bargains. If there is such a reason, it must lie in some external public interest necessarily injured by release-dismissal agreements.

B

. . . [T]he Court of Appeals held that all release-dismissal agreements offend public policy because it believed that these agreements "temp prosecutors to trump up charges in reaction to a defendant's civil rights claim, suppress evidence of police misconduct, and leave unremedied deprivations of constitutional rights." We can agree that in some cases there may be a substantial basis for this concern. It is true, of course, that § 1983 actions to vindicate civil rights may further significant public interests. But it is important to remember that Rumery had no public duty to institute a § 1983 action merely to further

the public's interest in revealing police misconduct. Congress has confined the decision to bring such actions to the injured individuals, not to the public at large. Thus, we hesitate to elevate more diffused public interests above Rumery's considered decision that he would benefit personally from the agreement.

We also believe the Court of Appeals misapprehended the range of public interests arguably affected by a release-dismissal agreement. The availability of such agreements may threaten important public interests. They may tempt prosecutors to bring frivolous charges, or to dismiss meritorious charges, to protect the interests of other officials.[4] But a per se rule of invalidity fails to credit other relevant public interests and improperly assumes prosecutorial misconduct.[5]

The vindication of constitutional rights and the exposure of official misconduct are not the only concerns implicated by § 1983 suits. No one suggests that all such suits are meritorious. Many are marginal and some are frivolous. Yet even when the risk of ultimate liability is negligible, the burden of defending such lawsuits is substantial. Counsel may be retained by the official, as well as the governmental entity. Preparation for trial, and the trial itself, will require the time and attention of the defendant officials, to the detriment of their public duties. In some cases litigation will extend over a period of years. This diversion of officials from their normal duties and the inevitable expense of defending even unjust claims is distinctly not in the public interest. To the extent release-dismissal agreements protect public officials from the burdens of defending such unjust claims, they further this important public interest.

_____

[4] Actions taken for these reasons properly have been recognized as unethical. See ABA Model Code of Professional Responsibility, Disciplinary Rule 7–105 (1980).

[5] Prosecutors themselves rarely are held liable in § 1983 actions. See Imbler v. Pachtman (discussing prosecutorial immunity). Also, in many States and municipalities—perhaps in most—prosecutors are elected officials and are entirely independent of the civil authorities likely to be defendants in § 1983 suits. There may be situations, of course, when a prosecutor is motivated to protect the interests of such officials or of police. But the constituency of an elected prosecutor is the public, and such a prosecutor is likely to be influenced primarily by the general public interest.

_____

criminal defendant, it receives immediate and tangible benefits, such as promptly imposed punishment without the expenditure of prosecutorial resources. Also, the defendant's agreement to plead to some crime tends to ensure some satisfaction of the public's interest in the prosecution of crime and confirms that the prosecutor's charges have a basis in fact. The benefits the State may realize in particular cases from release-dismissal agreements may not be as tangible, but they are not insignificant.

A per se rule invalidating release-dismissal agreements also assumes that prosecutors will seize the opportunity for wrongdoing. . . . Our decisions . . .uniformly have recognized that courts normally must defer to prosecutorial decisions as to whom to prosecute. The reasons for judicial deference are well known. Prosecutorial charging decisions are rarely simple. In addition to assessing the strength and importance of a case, prosecutors also must consider other tangible and intangible factors, such as government enforcement priorities. Finally, they also must decide how best to allocate the scarce resources of a criminal justice system that simply cannot accommodate the litigation of every serious criminal charge.[6] Because these decisions "are not readily susceptible to the kind of analysis the courts are competent to undertake," we have been "properly hesitant to examine the decision whether to prosecute."

Against this background of discretion, the mere opportunity to act improperly does not compel an assumption that all—or even a significant number of—release-dismissal agreements stem from prosecutors abandoning "the independence of judgment required by [their] public trust," Imbler v. Pachtman.[7] Rather, tradition and experience justify our belief that the great majority of prosecutors will be faithful to their duty. . . .

Because release-dismissal agreements may further legitimate prosecutorial and public interests, we reject the Court of Appeals'

holding that all such agreements are invalid per se.

IV

Turning to the agreement presented by this case, we conclude that the District Court's decision to enforce the agreement was correct. . . .[I]t is clear that Rumery voluntarily entered the agreement. Moreover, in this case the prosecutor had an independent, legitimate reason to make this agreement directly related to his prosecutorial responsibilities. The agreement foreclosed both the civil and criminal trials concerning Rumery, in which Deary would have been a key witness. She therefore was spared the public scrutiny and embarrassment she would have endured if she had had to testify in either of those cases. Both the prosecutor and the defense attorney testified in the District Court that this was a significant consideration in the prosecutor's decision.

In sum, we conclude that this agreement was voluntary, that there is no evidence of prosecutorial misconduct, and that enforcement of this agreement would not adversely affect the relevant public interests.[10]

V

We reverse the judgment of the Court of Appeals and remand the case to the District Court for dismissal of the complaint.

It is so ordered.

Justice **O'Connor**, concurring in part and concurring in the judgment.

I join in Parts I, II, III-A, IV, and V of the Court's opinion. . . .

[T]he dangers of the release-dismissal agreement do not preclude its enforcement in all cases. The defendants in a § 1983 suit may establish that a particular release executed in

---

[6] In 1985, the federal district courts disposed of 47,360 criminal cases. Of these, only 6,053, or about 12.8%, ended after a trial. Annual Report of the Director of the Administrative Office of the U.S. Courts 374 (1985). As we have recognized, if every serious criminal charge were evaluated through a full-scale criminal trial, "the States and the Federal Government would need to multiply by many times the number of judges and court facilities," Santobello v. New York.

[7] Of course, the Court has found that certain actions are so likely to result from prosecutorial misconduct that it has "'[p]resumed' an improper vindictive motive," United States v. Goodwin. E. g., Blackledge v. Perry (holding that it violates the Due Process Clause for a prosecutor to increase charges in response to a defendant's exercise of his right to appeal). But the complexity of pretrial decisions by prosecutors suggests that judicial evaluation of those decisions should be especially deferential. Thus, the Court has never accepted such a blanket claim with respect to pretrial decisions.

[10] We note that two Courts of Appeals have applied a voluntariness standard to determine the enforceability of agreements entered into after trial, in which defendants released possible § 1983 claims in return for sentencing considerations. See Bushnell v. Rossetti, Jones v. Taber. We have no occasion in this case to determine whether an inquiry into voluntariness alone is sufficient to determine the enforceability of release-dismissal agreements. We also note that it would be helpful to conclude release-dismissal agreements under judicial supervision. Although such supervision is not essential to the validity of an otherwise-proper agreement, it would help ensure that the agreements did not result from prosecutorial misconduct.

exchange for the dismissal of criminal charges was voluntarily made, not the product of prosecutorial overreaching, and in the public interest. But they must prove that this is so; the courts should not presume it as I fear portions of Part III-B of the plurality opinion may imply.

. . .

Against the convincing evidence that Rumery voluntarily entered into the agreement and that it served the public interest, there is only Rumery's blanket claim that agreements such as this one are inherently coercive. While it would have been preferable, and made this an easier case, had the release-dismissal agreement been concluded under some form of judicial supervision, I concur in the Court's judgment, and all but Part III-B of its opinion, that Rumery's § 1983 suit is barred by his valid, voluntary release.

Justice **Stevens**, with whom Justice **Brennan**, Justice **Marshall**, and Justice **Blackmun** join, dissenting.

The question whether the release-dismissal agreement signed by respondent is unenforceable is much more complex than the Court's opinion indicates. A complete analysis of the question presented by this case cannot end with the observation that respondent made a knowing and voluntary choice to sign a settlement agreement. Even an intelligent and informed, but completely innocent, person accused of crime should not be required to choose between a threatened indictment and trial, with their attendant publicity and the omnipresent possibility of wrongful conviction, and surrendering the right to a civil remedy against individuals who have violated his or her constitutional rights. Moreover, the prosecutor's representation of competing and possibly conflicting interests compounds the dangerous potential of release-dismissal agreements. . . .

I

Respondent is an innocent man. As a matter of law, he must be presumed to be innocent.

. . .

From respondent's point of view, it is unquestionably true that the decision to sign the release-dismissal agreement was, as the

Court emphasizes, "voluntary, deliberate, and informed." It reflected "a highly rational judgment that the certain benefits of escaping criminal prosecution exceed the speculative benefits of prevailing in a civil action." As the plurality iterates and reiterates, respondent made a "considered decision that he would benefit personally from the agreement." I submit, however, that the deliberate and rational character of respondent's decision is not a sufficient reason for concluding that the agreement is enforceable. Otherwise, a promise to pay a state trooper $ 20 for not issuing a ticket for a traffic violation, or a promise to contribute to the police department's retirement fund in exchange for the dismissal of a felony charge, would be enforceable. . . .

Thus, even though respondent's decision in this case was deliberate, informed, and voluntary, this observation does not address two distinct objections to enforcement of the release-dismissal agreement. The prosecutor's offer to drop charges if the defendant accedes to the agreement is inherently coercive; moreover, the agreement exacts a price unrelated to the character of the defendant's own conduct.

II

When the prosecutor negotiated the agreement with respondent, he represented three potentially conflicting interests. His primary duty, of course, was to represent the sovereign's interest in the evenhanded and effective enforcement of its criminal laws. In addition, as the covenant demonstrates, he sought to represent the interests of the town of Newton and its Police Department in connection with their possible civil liability to respondent. Finally, as the inclusion of Mary Deary as a covenantee indicates, the prosecutor also represented the interest of a potential witness who allegedly accused both respondent and a mutual friend of separate instances of wrongdoing.

If we view the problem from the standpoint of the prosecutor's principal client, the State of New Hampshire, it is perfectly clear that the release-dismissal agreement was both unnecessary and unjustified. For both the prosecutor and the State of New Hampshire enjoy absolute immunity from common-law and § 1983 liability arising out of a prosecutor's decision to initiate criminal proceedings. . . .

The record in this case indicates that an important reason for obtaining the covenant was "[t]o protect the police department." There is, however, an obvious potential conflict between the prosecutor's duty to enforce the law and his objective of protecting members of the Police Department who are accused of unlawful conduct. The public is entitled to have the prosecutor's decision to go forward with a criminal case, or to dismiss it, made independently of his concerns about the potential damages liability of the Police Department. It is equally clear that this separation of functions cannot be achieved if the prosecutor may use the threat of criminal prosecution as a weapon to obtain a favorable termination of a civil claim against the police. . . .When release agreements are enforceable, consideration of the police interest in avoiding damages liability severely hampers the prosecutor's ability to conform to the strictures of professional responsibility in deciding whether to prosecute. In particular, the possibility that the suspect will execute a covenant not to sue in exchange for a decision not to prosecute may well encourage a prosecutor to bring or to continue prosecutions in violation of his or her duty to "refrain from prosecuting a charge that the prosecutor knows is not supported by probable cause." ABA Model Rules of Professional Conduct, Rule 3.8(a) (1984).[16]

. . .

The prosecutor's potential conflict of interest increases in magnitude in direct proportion to the seriousness of the charges of police wrongdoing. . . .

. . .[T]here is a potential conflict between the public interest represented by the prosecutor and the private interests of a recalcitrant witness. As a general matter there is no reason to fashion a rule that either requires or permits a prosecutor always to defer to the interests of a witness. The prosecutor's law enforcement responsibilities will sometimes diverge from those interests; there will be cases in which the prosecutor has a plain duty to obtain critical testimony despite the desire of the witness to remain anonymous or to avoid a courtroom confrontation with an offender. There may be other cases in which a witness has given false or exaggerated testimony for malicious reasons. It would plainly be unwise for the Court to hold that a release-dismissal agreement is enforceable simply because it affords protection to a potential witness.

. . .

It may well be true that a full development of all the relevant facts would provide a legitimate justification for enforcing the release-dismissal agreement. In my opinion, however, the burden of developing those facts rested on the defendants in the § 1983 litigation, and that burden has not been met by mere conjecture and speculation concerning the emotional distress of one reluctant witness.

III

Because this is the first case of this kind that the Court has reviewed, I am hesitant to adopt an absolute rule invalidating all such agreements.[22] I am, however, persuaded that

---

[16] See also ABA Model Code of Professional Responsibility, Disciplinary Rule 7–103 (1980) ("A public prosecutor or other government lawyer shall not institute or cause to be instituted criminal charges when he knows or it is obvious that the charges are not supported by probable cause"), and Ethical Consideration 7–14 ("A government lawyer who has discretionary power relative to litigation should refrain from instituting or continuing litigation that is obviously unfair"); ABA Standards for Criminal Justice 3–3.9(a) (2d ed. 1980) ("It is unprofessional conduct for a prosecutor to institute, or cause to be instituted, or to permit the continued pendency of criminal charges when it is known that the charges are not supported by probable cause").

[22] It seems likely, however, that the costs of having courts determine the validity of release-dismissal agreements will outweigh the benefits that most agreements can be expected to provide. A court may enforce such an agreement only after a careful inquiry into the circumstances under which the plaintiff signed the agreement and into the legitimacy of the prosecutor's objective in entering into the agreement. This inquiry will occupy a significant amount of the court's and the parties' time, and will subject prosecutorial decision-making to judicial review. But the only benefit most of these agreements will provide is another line of defense for prosecutors and police in § 1983 actions. This extra protection is unnecessary because prosecutors already enjoy absolute immunity and because police have been afforded qualified immunity. Thus, the vast majority of "marginal or frivolous" § 1983 suits can be dismissed under existing standards with little more burden on the defendants than is entailed in defending a release-dismissal agreement. Moreover, there is an oddly suspect quality to this extra protection; the

the federal policies reflected in the enactment and enforcement of § 1983 mandate a strong presumption against the enforceability of such agreements and that the presumption is not overcome in this case by the facts or by any of the policy concerns discussed by the plurality. . . . [T]he plurality's decision seems to rest on the unstated premise that § 1983 litigation imposes a net burden on society. If that were a correct assessment of the statute, it should be repealed. Unless that is done, however, we should respect the congressional decision to attach greater importance to the benefits associated with access to a federal remedy than to the burdens of defending these cases.

. . .

Accordingly, although I am not prepared to endorse all of the reasoning of the Court of Appeals, I would affirm its judgment.

NOTES

1. Given the division of the Court, what is the precise holding of *Rumery*? Does the section 1983 plaintiff have the burden of proving that the release-dismissal agreement is invalid, or does the section 1983 defendant bear the burden of establishing its validity? What are the relevant factors to consider? Which facts most strongly support enforcement of the release-dismissal agreement in *Rumery*?

2. *Rumery* envisions a case-by-case determination of the enforceability of release-dismissal agreements. The outcome in any particular case will depend on its specific facts. Thus, generalizations are of limited value. Nonetheless, most post-*Rumery* lower court opinions have focused on the same three factors: (1) voluntariness; (2) indications of prosecutorial overreaching: and (3) public policy. E.g., *Hill v. City of Cleveland*, 12 F.3d 575 (6th Cir. 1993); *Vallone v. Lee*, 7 F.3d 196 (11th Cir. 1993); *Cain v. Darby Borough*, 7 F.3d 377 (3rd Cir.

1993) (en banc). Does the vague term "public policy" have any independent content?

3. A determination of voluntariness may be influenced by a number of factors. One court summarized these factors as follows

the sophistication of the signer, cost/benefit considerations by the signer, and the circumstances of the signing, i.e, whether the signer is in custody at the time of the signing. . . .

Additional factors in determining voluntariness are: whether the signer was represented by counsel, the time with which the signer considered the document, and whether the signer's attorney drafted the document. Courts also consider whether the signer expressed any unwillingness, and whether the release is clear on its face.

Woods v. Rhodes, 994 F.2d 494, 499–500 (8th Cir. 1993) (citations omitted). Several courts have emphasized the coercive aspects of incarceration in finding that particular release agreements were not voluntary. E.g., *Vallone v. Lee*, 7 F.3d 196 (11th Cir. 1993) (affirming a verdict for the plaintiff; the jury found that a release agreement was not voluntary because the inmate's release from jail on bail was improperly conditioned on signing the release); *Hall v. Ochs*, 817 F.2d 920 (1st Cir. 1987) (forcing plaintiff to sign release to get out of jail was not voluntary and therefore not enforceable). However, the fact that the signer is in custody does not render the release agreement involuntary *per se*, if other factors suggest otherwise. *Berry v. Peterson*, 887 F.2d 635 (5th Cir. 1989) (emphasizing that the plaintiff was represented by competent counsel).

4. A few post-*Rumery* decisions have refused to enforce release agreements that were found (or assumed) to be voluntary, when there was evidence of prosecutorial overreaching or other public policy concerns. In *Cain v. Darby Borough*, 7 F.3d 377 (3rd Cir. 1993) (en banc), the plaintiff signed a release-dismissal agreement in exchange for a recommendation by prosecutors that she be enrolled in an alternative sentencing program known as ARD. The local district attorney's office had a "blanket policy" of requiring the execution of a release from every ARD petitioner who might have a civil rights claim against government officials. The court held that the release agreement

agreement is one that a public official signs, presumably in good faith, but that a court must conclude is invalid unless that official proves otherwise. In most cases, if social and judicial resources are to be expended at all, they would seem better spent on an evaluation of the merits of the § 1983 claim rather than on a detour into the enforceability of a release-dismissal agreement.

violated public policy so that she could proceed with her section 1983 claim. The court reasoned that the "blanket policy" was "wholly and patently unrelated to the goals of ARD. . . .[I]t may allow unqualified criminal defendants to be admitted into ARD if they sign releases and at the same time exclude the otherwise qualified because they did not. . . .The policy does not distinguish between frivolous and meritorious litigation; it indiscriminately curtails both." *Cain*, 7 F.3d at 383.

In *Lynch v. City of Alhambra*, 880 F.2d 1122 (9th Cir. 1989), an off-duty deputy marshall alleged that he was roughed up by city police officers investigating a crime. The police officers claimed that Lynch was injured in the course of resisting arrest. Lynch was not threatened with prosecution for resisting arrest until after he initiated his civil claims against the city. Lynch released his section 1983 claims in exchange for non-prosecution of the criminal charges. Despite finding that Lynch voluntarily entered into the release-dismissal agreement, the court of appeals held the agreement may violate public policy. Police records indicated that Lynch's arrest was "questionable", and perhaps "invalid". Under these circumstances, the court of appeals directed the district court to determine whether the defendants used the threat of criminal prosecution for the impermissible purpose of suppressing civil rights claims.

5. Courts of appeals are in general agreement that *Rumery* places the burden on the section 1983 defendant to prove that the release-dismissal agreement is enforceable. E.g., *Coughlen v. Coots*, 5 F.2d 970 (6th Cir. 1993); *Lynch v. City of Alhambra*, 880 F.2d 1122 (9th Cir. 1989); *Cain v. Darby Borough*, 7 F.3d 377 (3rd Cir. 1993) (en banc). Is the validity of the release agreement susceptible to summary adjudication? Are voluntariness, prosecutorial overreaching, and public policy questions of fact or law? Are they issues to be decided by the district court or a jury? In two cases, courts of appeals reversed jury verdicts for the plaintiffs, holding that the release-dismissal agreements in question were enforceable as a matter of law. In each case, a dissenting judge would have left the determination of voluntariness to the jury. *Woods v. Rhodes*, 994 F.2d 494 (8th Cir. 1993); *Berry v. Peterson*, 887 F.2d 635 (5th Cir. 1989). See also *Coughlen v. Coots*, 5 F.3d 970 (6th Cir. 1993) (district court must make

"specific determinations" regarding voluntariness, prosecutorial overreaching, and public policy); *Vallone v. Lee*, 7 F.3d 196 (11th Cir. 1993) (upholding a jury finding that the release agreement was not voluntary).

Suppose that a release-dismissal agreement is negotiated during the course of a criminal trial at the suggestion of the presiding judge. In addition to the entry of a judgment of acquittal of the criminal charges, the oral agreement called for the government to pay for the medical expenses and property damage occasioned by the arrest. The agreement was never reduced to writing and the criminal defendants/section 1983 plaintiffs never submitted any bills for payment. Although they were represented by defense counsel at the time the oral agreement was negotiated, the criminal defendants/section 1983 plaintiffs claim they did not understand the nature and terms of the purported agreement. Are the section 1983 defendants entitled to summary judgment on the basis of the oral release-dismissal agreement? See *Livingstone v. North Belle Vernon Borough*, 12 F.3d 1205 (3rd Cir. 1993) (en banc) (disputed issue of voluntariness precluded summary judgment).

Are there any steps that a prosecutor could take to reduce the vulnerability of a release-dismissal agreement to a subsequent challenge?

6. Is the merit of the section 1983 claim relevant to the determination of the enforceability of the release-dismissal agreement? In *Coughlen v. Coots*, 5 F.3d 970, at 974 (6th Cir. 1993), the court commented that "the existence of substantial evidence of police misconduct. . .could be probative of the motives of the prosecutor for seeking such an agreement, as well as the degree to which enforcing the agreement would serve the public interest."

7. Quite often, a person is represented by counsel in the criminal matter at the time he executes the release-dismissal agreement. In *Lynch*, *Vallone*, and *Cain*, attorneys for the criminal defendants recommended that their clients sign release agreements that were later found to have been involuntary, involve prosecutorial misconduct, or violate public policy. Why would a criminal defense attorney advise a client to sign such a document? Consider the observations of Professor Kreimer:

Defense lawyers also have an economic interest in encouraging the execution of release-dismissal agreements, which risks coloring the advice tendered to a client. Many private defense lawyers are paid a flat rate in advance, a system that provides an incentive to avoid protracted litigation whenever possible. . . . Moreover, relatively few defense lawyers handle plaintiff's civil rights litigation. They thus have little economic incentive to preserve civil rights claims for they would not handle claims if they are brought. Public defenders suffer from their own incentives to dispose of cases rapidly and are often entirely barred from private litigation.

Kreimer, *Releases, Redress, and Police Misconduct: Reflections on Agreements to Waive Civil Rights Actions in Exchange for Dismissal of Criminal Charges*, 136 U. Pa. L. Rev. 851, 874–75 (1988) (footnotes omitted), reprinted in Nahmod, *A Section 1983/Civil Rights Anthology* 287. What are the ethical obligations of the criminal defense attorney vis-a-vis the civil section 1983 claim?

8. Consider the following Ethics Opinion issued by the Colorado Bar Association

> It is improper for a public prosecutor to require that a defendant, as a condition of charging or sentencing concessions, release governmental agencies or their agents from actual or potential civil claims which arise from the same transactions as the criminal episode. It is also improper for a city attorney to make such a request of a public prosecutor.

Colorado Bar Association, Ethics Opinion No. 62 (November 20, 1982), reprinted at 12 Colorado Lawyer 455 (1983). The Colorado Bar Association substantially based its opinion on the American Bar Association Ethical Consideration 7–21, which states that "[t]hreatening to use, or using, the criminal process to coerce adjustment of private claims or controversies is a subversion of [the civil adjudicative] process." See also, Bartholomy, *An Ethical Analysis of the Release-Dismissal Agreement*, N.D. J. of L. Ethics & Pub. Pol. 331 (1993).

After having considered the arguments in *Rumery* and the post-*Rumery* lower court opinions, is such an across-the-board prohibition preferable to a case-by-case assessment of the validity of release-dismissal agreements?

III.   Issue and Claim Preclusion

Many section 1983 actions concern claims or issues that were or might have been first raised in state judicial or administrative proceedings. Mr. Rumery, for example, could have challenged the constitutionality of his arrest in the trial of the state criminal charges brought against him. Instead, Rumery signed a release-dismissal agreement that disposed of both the state criminal charges and the federal section 1983 claim. Many other section 1983 claimants, however, have participated in some state judicial or administrative proceeding before filing their section 1983 suit. For example, a section 1983 plaintiff who claims to be the victim of an illegal search may have raised this issue in a motion to suppress evidence in his state court criminal trial; or a state worker who believes she was fired from her job for a constitutionally impermissible reason may have raised this issue in a state administrative forum before filing the section 1983 action. This section explores the effect of prior state judicial or administrative proceedings on subsequent section 1983 actions in federal court.

The preclusive effect of prior proceedings on subsequent litigation often is referred to in terms of res judicata and collateral estoppel. The Supreme Court first addressed the preclusive effect of state court proceedings on subsequent section 1983 suits in *Allen v. McCurry*, 449 U.S. 90 (1980). There the Court explained the policies underlying res judicata and collateral estoppel as follows:

> The federal courts have traditionally adhered to the related doctrines of res judicata and collateral estoppel. Under res judicata, a final judgment on the merits of an action precludes the parties or their privies from relitigating issues that were or could have been raised in that action. Under collateral estoppel, once a court has decided an issue of fact or law necessary to its judgment, that decision may preclude relitigation of the issue in a suit on a different cause of action involving a party to the first case. As this Court and other courts have often recognized,

res judicata and collateral estoppel relieve parties of the cost and vexation of multiple lawsuits, conserve judicial resources, and, by preventing inconsistent decisions, encourage reliance on adjudication.

In recent years, this Court has reaffirmed the benefits of collateral estoppel in particular, finding the policies underlying it to apply in contexts not formerly recognized at common law. Thus, the Court has eliminated the requirement of mutuality in applying collateral estoppel to bar relitigation of issues decided earlier in federal-court suits and has allowed a litigant who was not a party to a federal case to use collateral estoppel "offensively" in a new federal suit against the party who lost on the decided issue in the first case. But one general limitation the Court has repeatedly recognized is that the concept of collateral estoppel cannot apply when the party against whom the earlier decision is asserted did not have a "full and fair opportunity" to litigate that issue in the earlier case.

The federal courts generally have also consistently accorded preclusive effect to issues decided by state courts. Thus, res judicata and collateral estoppel not only reduce unnecessary litigation and foster reliance on adjudication, but also promote the comity between state and federal courts that has been recognized as a bulwark of the federal system. . . .

Allen v. McCurry, 449 U.S. at 94–96 (citations and footnotes omitted).

With this background in mind, consider whether a federal court in a section 1983 case should be bound by the actual or potential resolution of a particular claim or issue in some prior state proceeding. Should the preclusive effect of a prior state proceeding be determined by state or federal law? Should it make any difference whether the prior proceeding was judicial or administrative in nature? Should it make any difference whether the section 1983 claimant had any choice in participating in the prior state proceeding?

Migra v. Warren City School District Board of Education

465 U.S. 75 (1984)

Justice **Blackmun** delivered the opinion of the Court.

This case raises issues concerning the claim preclusive effect[1] of a state-court judgment in the context of a subsequent suit, under 42 U.S.C. §§ 1983 and 1985 (1976 ed., Supp. V), in federal court.

I

. . .

[Dr. Ethel D. Migra was employed by the defendants to serve as the supervisor of elementary education. The Board initially voted to renew Dr. Migra's contract, but then later voted not to renew it. Dr. Migra filed suit in state court alleging breach of contract by the Board and wrongful interference by individual members with her contract of employment. The state trial court ruled in favor of Dr.

---

[1] The preclusive effects of former adjudication are discussed in varying and, at times, seemingly conflicting terminology, attributable to the evolution of preclusion concepts over the years. These effects are referred to collectively by most commentators as the doctrine of "res judicata." See Restatement (Second) of Judgments, Introductory Note before ch. 3 (1982); 18 C. Wright, A. Miller, & E. Cooper, Federal Practice and Procedure § 4402 (1981). Res judicata is often analyzed further to consist of two preclusion concepts: "issue preclusion" and "claim preclusion." Issue preclusion refers to the effect of a judgment in foreclosing relitigation of a matter that has been litigated and decided. See Restatement, supra, § 27. This effect also is referred to as direct or collateral estoppel. Claim preclusion refers to the effect of a judgment in foreclosing litigation of a matter that never has been litigated, because of a determination that it should have been advanced in an earlier suit. Claim preclusion therefore encompasses the law of merger and bar. See id., Introductory Note before § 24.

This Court on more than one occasion has used the term "res judicata" in a narrow sense, so as to exclude issue preclusion or collateral estoppel. See, e. g., Allen v. McCurry; Brown v. Felsen. When using that formulation, "res judicata" becomes virtually synonymous with "claim preclusion." In order to avoid confusion resulting from the two uses of "res judicata," this opinion utilizes the term "claim preclusion" to refer to the preclusive effect of a judgment in foreclosing litigation of matters that should have been raised in an earlier suit. For a helpful explanation of preclusion vocabulary, see Wright et al., supra, § 4402.

Migra on the breach of contract claim and "reserved and continued" the "issue of conspiracy". On Dr. Migra's motion, the trial court dismissed without prejudice "the issue of conspiracy and individual board member liability." The lower court's ruling on the breach of contract issue was affirmed by the Ohio Court of Appeals.]

[Dr. Migra then filed an action in federal court alleging that] the Board's actions were intended to punish her for the exercise of her First Amendment rights. She also claimed that the actions deprived her of property without due process and denied her equal protection. Her federal claim thus arose under the First, Fifth, and Fourteenth Amendments and 42 U.S.C. §§ 1983 and 1985 (1976 ed., Supp. V). She requested injunctive relief and compensatory and punitive damages. Answers were filed in due course and shortly thereafter the defendants moved for summary judgment on the basis of res judicata and the bar of the statute of limitations.

The District Court granted summary judgment for the defendants and dismissed the complaint. The United States Court of Appeals for the Sixth Circuit, by a short unreported order, affirmed. Because of the importance of the issue, and because of differences among the Courts of Appeals, we granted certiorari.

II

The Constitution's Full Faith and Credit Clause[4] is implemented by the federal full faith and credit statute, 28 U.S.C. § 1738. That statute reads in pertinent part:

"Such Acts, records and judicial proceedings or copies thereof, so authenticated, shall have the same full faith and credit in every court within the United States and its Territories and Possessions as they have by law or usage in the courts of such State, Territory or Possession from which they are taken."

It is now settled that a federal court must give to a state-court judgment the same preclusive effect as would be given that judgment under the law of the State in which the judgment was rendered. In *Allen v. McCurry* this Court said:

"Indeed, though the federal courts may look to the common law or to the policies supporting res judicata and collateral estoppel in assessing the preclusive effect of decisions of other federal courts, Congress has specifically required all federal courts to give preclusive effect to state-court judgments whenever the courts of the State from which the judgments emerged would do so. . . ." Id., at 96.

. . . Accordingly, in the absence of federal law modifying the operation of § 1738, the preclusive effect in federal court of petitioner's state-court judgment is determined by Ohio law.

In *Allen*, the Court considered whether 42 U.S.C. § 1983 modified the operation of § 1738 so that a state-court judgment was to receive less than normal preclusive effect in a suit brought in federal court under § 1983. In that case, the respondent had been convicted in a state-court criminal proceeding. In that proceeding, the respondent sought to suppress certain evidence against him on the ground that it had been obtained in violation of the Fourth Amendment. The trial court denied the motion to suppress. The respondent then brought a § 1983 suit in federal court against the officers who had seized the evidence. The District Court held the suit barred by collateral estoppel (issue preclusion) because the issue of a Fourth Amendment violation had been resolved against the respondent by the denial of his suppression motion in the criminal trial. The Court of Appeals reversed. That court concluded that, because a § 1983 suit was the respondent's only route to a federal forum for his constitutional claim,[5] and because one of § 1983's underlying purposes was to provide a federal cause of action in situations where state courts were not adequately protecting individual rights, the respondent should be

---

[4] "Full Faith and Credit shall be given in each State to the public Acts, Records, and judicial Proceedings of every other State. And the Congress may by general Laws prescribe the Manner in which such Acts, Records and Proceedings shall be proved, and the Effect thereof." U.S. Const., Art. IV, § 1.

[5] The respondent had not asserted that the state courts had denied him a "full and fair opportunity" to litigate his search and seizure claim; he therefore was barred by Stone v. Powell from seeking a writ of habeas corpus in federal district court.

allowed to proceed to trial in federal court unencumbered by collateral estoppel. This Court, however, reversed the Court of Appeals, explaining:

> "[N]othing in the language of § 1983 remotely expresses any congressional intent to contravene the common-law rules of preclusion or to repeal the express statutory requirements of the predecessor of 28 U.S.C. § 1738. . . . Section 1983 creates a new federal cause of action. It says nothing about the preclusive effect of state-court judgments.
>
> "Moreover, the legislative history of § 1983 does not in any clear way suggest that Congress intended to repeal or restrict the traditional doctrines of preclusion. . . . [T]he legislative history as a whole . . . lends only the most equivocal support to any argument that, in cases where the state courts have recognized the constitutional claims asserted and provided fair procedures for determining them, Congress intended to override § 1738 or the common-law rules of collateral estoppel and res judicata. Since repeals by implication are disfavored . . . much clearer support than this would be required to hold that § 1738 and the traditional rules of preclusion are not applicable to § 1983 suits."

Allen therefore made clear that issues actually litigated in a state-court proceeding are entitled to the same preclusive effect in a subsequent federal § 1983 suit as they enjoy in the courts of the State where the judgment was rendered.

The Court in *Allen* left open the possibility, however, that the preclusive effect of a state-court judgment might be different as to a federal issue that a § 1983 litigant could have raised but did not raise in the earlier state-court proceeding. 449 U.S., at 97, n.10. That is the central issue to be resolved in the present case. Petitioner did not litigate her § 1983 claim in state court, and she asserts that the state-court judgment should not preclude her suit in federal court simply because her federal claim could have been litigated in the state-court proceeding. Thus, petitioner urges this Court to interpret the interplay of § 1738 and § 1983 in such a way as to accord state-court judgments preclusive effect in § 1983 suits only as to issues actually litigated in state court.

It is difficult to see how the policy concerns underlying § 1983 would justify a distinction between the issue preclusive and claim preclusive effects of state-court judgments. The argument that state-court judgments should have less preclusive effect in § 1983 suits than in other federal suits is based on Congress' expressed concern over the adequacy of state courts as protectors of federal rights. *Allen* recognized that the enactment of § 1983 was motivated partially out of such concern, but *Allen* nevertheless held that § 1983 did not open the way to relitigation of an issue that had been determined in a state criminal proceeding. Any distrust of state courts that would justify a limitation on the preclusive effect of state judgments in § 1983 suits would presumably apply equally to issues that actually were decided in a state court as well as to those that could have been. If § 1983 created an exception to the general preclusive effect accorded to state-court judgments, such an exception would seem to require similar treatment of both issue preclusion and claim preclusion. Having rejected in *Allen* the view that state-court judgments have no issue preclusive effect in § 1983 suits, we must reject the view that § 1983 prevents the judgment in petitioner's state-court proceeding from creating a claim preclusion bar in this case.

Petitioner suggests that to give state-court judgments full issue preclusive effect but not claim preclusive effect would enable litigants to bring their state claims in state court and their federal claims in federal court, thereby taking advantage of the relative expertise of both forums. Although such a division may seem attractive from a plaintiff's perspective, it is not the system established by § 1738. That statute embodies the view that it is more important to give full faith and credit to state-court judgments than to ensure separate forums for federal and state claims. This reflects a variety of concerns, including notions of comity, the need to prevent vexatious litigation, and a desire to conserve judicial resources.

In the present litigation, petitioner does not claim that the state court would not have adjudicated her federal claims had she presented them in her original suit in state court. Alternatively, petitioner could have obtained a federal forum for her federal claim by litigating it first in a federal court.[7] Section 1983, however, does not override state preclusion law and guarantee petitioner a right to proceed to judgment in state court on her state claims and then turn to federal court for adjudication of her federal claims. We hold, therefore, that petitioner's state-court judgment in this litigation has the same claim preclusive effect in federal court that the judgment would have in the Ohio state courts.

III

. . . [The Court went on to hold that it was unclear whether the District Court's dismissal was based on an application of Ohio or federal law.]

Our holding today makes clear that Ohio state preclusion law is to be applied to this case. Prudence also dictates that it is the District Court, in the first instance, not this Court, that should interpret Ohio preclusion law and apply it.

The judgment of the Court of Appeals, accordingly, is vacated, and the case is remanded to that court so that it may instruct the District Court to conduct such further proceedings as are required by, and are consistent with, this opinion.

It is so ordered.

[The concurring opinion of Justice White, in which Chief Justice Burger and Justice Powell joined, is omitted].

---

[7] The author of this opinion was in dissent in *Allen*. The rationale of that dissent, however, was based largely on the fact that the § 1983 plaintiff in that case first litigated his constitutional claim in state court in the posture of his being a defendant in a criminal proceeding. In this case, petitioner was in an offensive posture in her state-court proceeding, and could have proceeded first in federal court had she wanted to litigate her federal claim in a federal forum.

In the event that a § 1983 plaintiff's federal and state-law claims are sufficiently intertwined that the federal court abstains from passing on the federal claims without first allowing the state court to address the state-law issues, the plaintiff can preserve his right to a federal forum for his federal claims by informing the state court of his intention to return to federal court on his federal claims following litigation of his state claims in state court. See, e. g., England v. Louisiana State Board of Medical Examiners.

NOTES

1. As reflected in the first footnote of the Court's opinion, the precise meaning and usage of the phrases "res judicata" and "collateral estoppel" have sometimes varied. In a subsequent opinion, the Court more succinctly differentiated between the two concepts as follows:

> [W]e utilize the term "res judicata" to refer to the effect of a judgment on the merits in barring a subsequent suit between the same parties or their privies that is based on the same claim. By contrast, "[u]nder collateral estoppel, once a court has decided an issue of fact or law necessary to its judgment, that decision may preclude relitigation of the issue in a suit on a different cause of action involving a party to the first case."

McDonald v. City of West Branch, 466 U.S. 284, 287 n.5 (1984) (quoting *Allen v. McCurry*, 449 U.S. 90, 94 (1980). (*citations omitted*).

2. Following *Allen* and *Migra*, federal courts applying state law have found that a variety of section 1983 claims and issues are precluded by prior state civil or criminal proceedings. E.g., *Hubbert v. City of Moore*, 923 F.2d 769 (10th Cir. 1991) (Under Oklahoma law, a probable cause finding in a criminal proceeding resulting in an acquittal collaterally estops consideration of that issue in a section 1983 case in federal court); *Baker v. McCoy*, 739 F.2d 381 (8th Cir. 1984) (prior state ruling in a criminal case that the plaintiff's confession was voluntary and not the result of alleged beatings by police officers had a collateral estoppel effect under Missouri law on section 1983 damages action against police officers); *Mears v. Town of Oxford*, 762 F.2d 368 (4th Cir. 1985) (land developer's section 1983 suit challenging a local land use ordinance was barred by res judicata under Maryland law; claims raised in the section 1983 action were actually decided or could have been raised in prior state court litigation); *Hernandez v. City of Lafayette*, 699 F.2d 734 (5th Cir. 1983) (section 1983 action challenging a zoning decision is barred under the Louisiana law of res judicata; prior state court suit actually decided the issue of whether the defendant's refusal to rezone the plaintiff's property was a denial of property without due process).

3. The cases dealing with wrongful death and survivorship actions (chapter 9) and statutes of limitations invoke 42 U.S.C. § 1988 to justify reliance on state law. *Migra* and *Allen* cite 28 U.S.C. § 1738 to explain why the preclusive effect of prior state judicial proceedings is determined by state law. Are there any differences in how and to what extent these statutes direct federal courts to apply state law in section 1983 actions?

4. *Migra* makes clear that if state law so provides, res judicata will preclude a subsequent consideration of constitutional claims that could have been but were not actually litigated in a prior state judicial proceeding. In *Vandenplas v. City of Muskego*, 753 F.2d 555 (7th Cir. 1985), the plaintiffs' filed an action in state court seeking to enjoin a condemnation order. The plaintiffs' unsuccessfully argued in state court that the order was "unreasonable" under Wisconsin law, but did not directly challenge the order on federal constitutional grounds. Because the plaintiffs' could have raised federal constitutional claims in state court, res judicata applied to bar the subsequent federal section 1983 suit challenging the constitutionality of the Wisconsin condemnation statute on its face and as applied to the plaintiffs.

5. State law often places specific limitations on the use of collateral estoppel and res judicata. These limitations, which vary from state to state, will determine the preclusive effect of prior state proceedings on subsequent section 1983 litigation. Some states limit the application of collateral estoppel to litigation between the "same parties". Thus, under Massachusetts law, a determination of probable cause in a criminal case does not preclude a section 1983 claim against individual police officers for an alleged illegal arrest, search and seizure. *B.C.R. Transport Co. v. Fontaine*, 727 F.2d 7 (1st Cir. 1984). Some states preclude relitigation of only those issues or claims that were actually litigated and decided on its merits in the prior litigation. If the ruling in the prior suit did not actually decide the issue or claim in question, it may be litigated in the subsequent section 1983 action. E.g., *Davenport v. North Carolina Department of Transportation*, 3 F.3d 89, 97 (4th Cir. 1993) ("we believe these procedural and substantive differences between the state administrative claim [for wrongful discharge without just cause] and the section 1983 claims [for politically motivated discharge in violation of the first amendment] would cause them to be treated as different

claims for res judicata purposes by the North Carolina courts."); *Wade v. City of Pittsburgh*, 765 F.2d 405 (3rd Cir. 1985) (under Pennsylvania law, prior summary judgment for the defendant on state law immunity did not preclude section 1983 claim as immunity does not address the merits).

6. As reflected in the immediately preceding note, in some states the preclusive effect of a prior state proceeding may turn on determining precisely what was actually decided in that proceeding. What is decided when a person pleads guilty to a criminal charge? Should a guilty plea to a criminal charge bar a subsequent section 1983 claim alleging the police conducted an illegal search of his apartment? In *Haring v. Prosise*, 462 U.S. 306 (1983) a unanimous court ruled that such a section 1983 claim was not barred on the grounds of collateral estoppel. The Court began its analysis by noting that the preclusive effect of the state court judgment is governed by state law. It then offered three reasons why the doctrine of collateral estoppel would not be invoked in this case under Virginia law.

> First, the legality of the search of Prosise's apartment was not actually litigated in the criminal proceedings. . . . Second, the criminal proceedings did not actually decide against Prosise any issue on which he must prevail in order to establish his § 1983 claim. . .[The] question [of guilt] is simply irrelevant to the legality of the search under the Fourth Amendment or to Prosise's right to compensation from state officials under § 1983.
>
> Finally, . . . a determination that the county police officers engaged in no illegal police conduct would not have been essential to the trial court's acceptance of Prosise's guilty plea. . . .Neither state nor federal law requires that a guilty plea in state court be supported by legally admissible evidence where the accused's valid waiver of his right to stand trial is accompanied by a confession of guilt.

Haring v. Prosise, 462 U.S. at 316. The Court further rejected the argument that the guilty plea constituted a waiver of any claim involving a fourth amendment violation under federal law. *Prosise*, 462 U.S. at 319.

Why did the prior state court ruling in the suppression hearing preclude the section 1983 claim in *Allen v. McCurry*, 449 U.S. 90 (1980), while the guilty plea in *Prosise* did not have such a preclusive effect? As a matter of policy, should a guilty plea preclude a section 1983 claim arising from events pertaining to the investigation and arrest of the plaintiff? Why or why not? See generally Shapiro, *Should a Guilty Plea Have Preclusive Effect?*, 70 Iowa L. Rev. 27 (1984).

Can the prosecuting attorney handling the criminal case take any steps to insulate police officers and local governments from subsequent section 1983 claims? See *Town of Newton v. Rumery*, 480 U.S. 386 (1987) discussed *supra*.

University of Tennessee v. Elliot

478 U.S. 788 (1986)

Justice **White** delivered the opinion of the Court.

A state Administrative Law Judge determined that petitioner University of Tennessee (hereafter petitioner or University) was not motivated by racial prejudice in seeking to discharge respondent. The question presented is whether this finding is entitled to preclusive effect in federal court, where respondent has raised discrimination claims under various civil rights laws, including Title VII of the Civil Rights Act of 1964, 78 Stat. 253, as amended, 42 U.S.C. § 2000e et seq., and 42 U.S.C. § 1983.

I

In 1981, petitioner informed respondent, a black employee of the University's Agricultural Extension Service, that he would be discharged for inadequate work performance and misconduct on the job. Respondent requested a hearing under the Tennessee Uniform Administrative Procedures Act, Tenn. Code Ann. § 4–5–101 et seq. (1985), to contest his proposed termination. Prior to the start of the hearing, respondent also filed suit in the United States District Court for the Western District of Tennessee, alleging that his proposed discharge was racially motivated and seeking relief under Title VII and other civil

rights statutes, including 42 U.S.C. § 1983. The relief sought included damages, an injunction prohibiting respondent's discharge, and classwide relief from alleged patterns of discrimination by petitioner.

. . .

[Pursuant to state law, a hearing was conducted over a five month period involving more than 100 witnesses and 150 exhibits.] The focus of the hearing was on 10 particular charges that the University gave as grounds for respondent's discharge. Respondent denied these charges, which he contended were motivated by racial prejudice, and also argued that the University's subjecting him to the charges violated his rights under the Constitution, Title VII, and other federal statutes. The ALJ held that he lacked jurisdiction to adjudicate respondent's federal civil rights claims, but did allow respondent to present, as an affirmative defense, evidence that the charges against him were actually motivated by racial prejudice and hence not a proper basis for his proposed discharge.

After hearing extensive evidence, the ALJ found that the University had proved some but not all of the charges against respondent, and that the charges were not racially motivated. Concluding that the proposed discharge of respondent was too severe a penalty, the ALJ ordered him transferred to a new assignment with supervisors other than those with whom he had experienced conflicts. Respondent appealed to the University's Vice President for Agriculture, who affirmed the ALJ's ruling. The Vice President stated that his review of the record persuaded him that the proposed discharge of respondent had not been racially motivated.

Respondent did not seek review of these administrative proceedings in the Tennessee courts; instead, he returned to federal court to pursue his civil rights claims. There, petitioner moved for summary judgment on the ground that respondent's suit was an improper collateral attack on the ALJ's ruling, which petitioner contended was entitled to preclusive effect. The District Court agreed, holding that the civil rights statutes on which respondent relied "were not intended to afford the plaintiff a means of relitigating what plaintiff has heretofore litigated over a five-month period."

Respondent appealed to the United States Court of Appeals for the Sixth Circuit, which reversed the District Court's judgment. . . .

II

Title 28 U.S.C. § 1738 governs the preclusive effect to be given the judgments and records of state courts, and is not applicable to the unreviewed state administrative fact-finding at issue in this case. However, we have frequently fashioned federal common-law rules of preclusion in the absence of a governing statute. Although § 1738 is a governing statute with regard to the judgments and records of state courts, because § 1738 antedates the development of administrative agencies it clearly does not represent a congressional determination that the decisions of state administrative agencies should not be given preclusive effect. Accordingly, we will consider whether a rule of preclusion is appropriate, first with respect to respondent's Title VII claim, and next with respect to his claims under the Constitution and the Reconstruction civil rights statutes.

III

. . . [The Court held that Congress did not intend for unreviewed state administrative proceedings to have a preclusive effect in Title VII actions in federal court. Rather, Congress intended a claimant to have a trial de novo in federal court on the Title VII claim in which the final findings of state administrative agencies would be entitled to substantial weight.]

. . . On the basis of our analysis in Kremer [v. Chemical Construction Corp.] and Chandler [v. Roudebush] of the language and legislative history of Title VII, we conclude that the Sixth Circuit correctly held that Congress did not intend unreviewed state administrative proceedings to have preclusive effect on Title VII claims.

IV

This Court has held that § 1738 requires that state-court judgments be given both issue and claim preclusive effect in subsequent actions under 42 U.S.C. § 1983. *Allen v. McCurry* (issue preclusion); *Migra v. Warren City School District Board of Education* (claim preclusion). Those decisions are not controlling in this case, where § 1738 does not apply; nonetheless, they support the view that

Congress, in enacting the Reconstruction civil rights statutes, did not intend to create an exception to general rules of preclusion. . . .

The Court's discussion in *Allen* suggests that it would have reached the same result even in the absence of § 1738. We also see no reason to suppose that Congress, in enacting the Reconstruction civil rights statutes, wished to foreclose the adaptation of traditional principles of preclusion to such subsequent developments as the burgeoning use of administrative adjudication in the 20th century.

We have previously recognized that it is sound policy to apply principles of issue preclusion to the fact-finding of administrative bodies acting in a judicial capacity. In a unanimous decision in *United States v. Utah Construction & Mining Co.*, we held that the fact-finding of the Advisory Board of Contract Appeals was binding in a subsequent action in the Court of Claims involving a contract dispute between the same parties. We explained:

> "Although the decision here rests upon the agreement of the parties as modified by the Wunderlich Act, we note that the result we reach is harmonious with general principles of collateral estoppel. Occasionally courts have used language to the effect that res judicata principles do not apply to administrative proceedings, but such language is certainly too broad. When an administrative agency is acting in a judicial capacity and resolves disputed issues of fact properly before it which the parties have had an adequate opportunity to litigate, the courts have not hesitated to apply res judicata to enforce repose." Id., at 421–422 (1966) (footnotes omitted).

Thus, *Utah Construction* . . . teaches that giving preclusive effect to administrative fact-finding serves the value underlying general principles of collateral estoppel: enforcing repose. This value, which encompasses both the parties' interest in avoiding the cost and vexation of repetitive litigation and the public's interest in conserving judicial resources is equally implicated whether factfinding is done by a federal or state agency.

Having federal courts give preclusive effect to the factfinding of state administrative tribunals also serves the value of federalism. Significantly, all of the opinions in *Thomas v.*

Washington Gas Light Co. express the view that the Full Faith and Credit Clause compels the States to give preclusive effect to the factfindings of an administrative tribunal in a sister State. The Full Faith and Credit Clause is of course not binding on federal courts, but we can certainly look to the policies underlying the Clause in fashioning federal common-law rules of preclusion. "Perhaps the major purpose of the Full Faith and Credit Clause is to act as a nationally unifying force," and this purpose is served by giving preclusive effect to state administrative factfinding rather than leaving the courts of a second forum, state or federal, free to reach conflicting results.[7] Accordingly, we hold that when a state agency "acting in a judicial capacity . . . resolves disputed issues of fact properly before it which the parties have had an adequate opportunity to litigate," *Utah Construction & Mining Co.*, federal courts must give the agency's factfinding the same preclusive effect to which it would be entitled in the State's courts.

The judgment of the Court of Appeals is affirmed in part and reversed in part, and the case is remanded for further proceedings consistent with this opinion.

It is so ordered.

Justice **Marshall** took no part in the consideration or decision of this case.

Justice **Stevens**, with whom Justice **Brennan** and Justice **Blackmun** join, concurring in part and dissenting in part.

. . . [Justice Stevens concurred with the majority that 28 U.S.C. § 1738 does not require that state administrative rulings be given full faith and credit in subsequent federal litigation. He further agreed that petitioner's claims under Title VII were not precluded by the unreviewed state administrative rulings. He then addressed whether the unreviewed state administrative rulings should have a preclusive effect on claims and issues brought under section 1983.]

Preclusion of claims brought under the post-Civil War Acts does not advance the objectives typically associated with finality or federalism. In the employment setting which concerns us here, precluding civil rights claims based on the Reconstruction-era statutes fails to conserve the resources of either the litigants or the courts, because the complainant's companion Title VII claim will still go to federal court under today's decision.[1] Nor does preclusion show respect for state administrative determinations, because litigants apprised of this decision will presumably forgo state administrative determinations for the same reason they currently forgo state judicial review of those determinations—to protect their entitlement to a federal forum.

. . .

. . . Due respect for the intent of the Congress that enacted the Civil Rights Act of 1871, as revealed in the voluminous legislative history of that Act, should preclude the Court from creating a judge-made rule that bars access to the express legislative remedy enacted by Congress.

Accordingly, I respectfully dissent from Part IV of the Court's opinion.

---

[1] "The difficulties that will be encountered with this schizophrenic approach [ruling that state administrative findings may establish preclusion as to the claims under these Civil Rights Acts, at the same time as the same issues are relitigated as to the Title VII claim] are obvious. A way out of these difficulties remains to be found. As to any issues that must be retried, with perhaps inconsistent results, it may prove better simply to retry the issues as to all statutory claims. Application of preclusion as to part of the case saves no effort, does not prevent the risk of inconsistent findings, and may distort the process of finding the issues. The opportunity for repose is substantially weakened by the remaining exposure to liability. Insistence on preclusion in these circumstances has little value, and more risk than it may be worth." 18 C. WRIGHT, A. MILLER, & E. COOPER, FEDERAL PRACTICE AND PROCEDURE § 4471, p. 169 (Supp. 1985).

Moreover, in this case, and presumably in many other cases as well, even the § 1983 claim may be litigated in federal court, at least to the extent of determining whether the complainant was afforded a full and fair opportunity to litigate before the state administrative tribunal.

NOTES

1. In *Kremer v. Chemical Construction*, 456 U.S. 461 (1982), the Court, applying 28 U.S.C. § 1738, gave full faith and credit to a New York

---

[7] Congress of course may decide, as it did in enacting Title VII, that other values outweigh the policy of according finality to state administrative factfinding. See Part III, supra.

court decision upholding a state administrative agency's decision rejecting the plaintiff's claim of employment discrimination. Under New York law, a judicially reviewed administrative ruling precluded relitigation of the same question. The Court relied on this state rule of preclusion in holding that the plaintiff was barred from bringing his Title VII claim in federal court in the face of his unsuccessful appeal of an adverse agency ruling. Under *Kremer*, a Title VII claim may be precluded by a prior judicially reviewed state administrative proceeding, while under *Elliot* the Title VII claim is subject to a trial *de novo* in federal court if the prior state administrative proceeding was not reviewed by a court. The different preclusive potential of judicially reviewed and unreviewed agency rulings is justified in terms of the language and legislative history of Title VII. *Elliot*, 478 U.S. at 795–96. Given the often limited scope of judicial review of agency action, does this different treatment make sense as a matter of policy?

2. As discussed in *Migra*, 28 U.S.C. § 1738 directs federal courts to determine the preclusive effect of a prior state court proceeding according to state law. *Elliot*, on the other hand, applies federal common law rules of preclusion to a prior unreviewed state administrative proceeding. The preclusive effect of prior federal proceedings is also determined by federal common law. E.g., *Nagle v. Lee*, 807 F.2d 435 (5th Cir. 1987). Federal and state rules of preclusion may differ from one another. For example, some states limit the application of collateral estoppel to prior proceedings involving the same parties, while mutuality of parties is not required under federal common law rules of preclusion. Compare *B.C.R. Transportation Co., v. Fontaine*, 727 F.2d 7 (1st Cir. 1984) (mutuality of parties required under Massachusetts law) with *Parklane Hosiery Co. v. Shore*, 439 U.S. 322 (1979) (mutuality of parties not required under federal common law rules of preclusion). Is the potential for differences among the states and between federal and state rules of preclusion a healthy aspect of federalism? Would uniform rules of preclusion better serve the purposes of federal civil rights legislation?

3. Suppose a woman filed a complaint with a state agency claiming that she was terminated from her employment because of her race, color, and gender. The state agency issued an order concluding that there was "no probable cause to believe that the employer engaged in the unlawful discriminatory practice complained of." The plaintiff did not appeal the adverse agency ruling until after the 60 day period allowed by statute had expired. Her appeal was dismissed by the state court on statute of limitations grounds. She then filed a civil rights suit in federal court. For res judicata purposes under state law, a dismissal on statute of limitations grounds is considered a final judgment on the merits. How would you frame the defendant's motion for summary judgment based on claim or issue preclusion? How would you frame the plaintiff's response? Is the preclusive effect of the prior state proceeding determined by state or federal law? Does it matter whether the federal claim is based on Title VII or section 1983? Cf. *Bray v. New York Life Insurance*, 851 F.2d 60 (2d Cir. 1988) (Title VII claim is barred by prior state proceedings).

4. Should the preclusive effect of the prior state proceeding depend on who initiated the proceeding? In both *Migra* and *Elliot*, the plaintiffs chose to challenge their respective adverse employment decisions in state forums. Suppose that the collateral estoppel argument was made against a party who was a defendant in the prior state proceeding. Should the party who did not select the state forum be precluded from having a federal court pass on the fact issues crucial to the resolution of the federal claim? Justice Blackmun, who authored the majority opinion in *Migra*, made the following argument in his dissent in *Allen v. McCurry*:

A state criminal defendant cannot be held to have chosen "voluntarily" to litigate his Fourth Amendment Claim in the state court. The risk of conviction puts pressure upon him to raise all possible defenses. . .To hold that a criminal defendant who raises a Fourth Amendment claim at his criminal trial "freely and without reservation submits his federal claims for decision by the state courts,". . .is to deny reality. The criminal defendant is an involuntary litigant in the state tribunal. . .To force him to a choice between forgoing either a potential defense or a federal forum for his constitutional civil claim is fundamentally unfair.

449 U.S. at 115–16 (1980). See also footnote 7 in *Migra, supra*. Does this argument apply with equal force to a defendant in a state civil

proceeding? Does the judicial or administrative nature of the state forum bear on the question? The special problems posed by litigating section 1983 claims in state court are considered in the next chapter.

5. Should a determination in an arbitration proceeding that there was "just cause" to terminate the plaintiff's employment preclude a subsequent section 1983 action alleging he was discharged for exercising his first amendment rights? In *McDonald v. City of West Branch*, 466 U.S. 284 (1984), a unanimous Court held that a federal court should not afford res judicata or collateral estoppel effect to arbitration rulings. Since arbitration is not a "judicial proceeding", 28 U.S.C. § 1738 does not require that it be given full faith and credit. Moreover, the Court declined to fashion a federal rule of preclusion because

> First, an . . . arbitrator may not . . . have the expertise required to resolve the complex legal questions that arise in § 1983 actions. . . .
>
> Second, because an arbitrator's authority derives solely from the contract. . .an arbitrator may not have the authority to enforce § 1983. . . .
>
> Third, [a union may have control over how the grievance is presented, and] may present the employee's grievance less vigorously, or make different strategic choices, than would the employee. . . .
>
> Finally, arbitral factfinding is generally not equivalent to judicial factfinding.

McDonald, 466 U.S. at 290–91. However, the arbitration award can be used as evidence in the subsequent federal proceedings.

IV. Exhaustion of Remedies

As is evident from the preceding section, plaintiffs sometimes choose to pursue state judicial or administrative remedies prior to instigating a section 1983 suit. Should they be required to do so? Requiring exhaustion of state remedies would reduce federal intrusions upon state sovereignty by allowing states to redress wrongs committed by its officials without federal court intervention. Moreover, providing compensation under state tort law could

avoid the unnecessary adjudication of federal constitutional issues.

As will be recalled from Chapter 1, the Court in the seminal case of *Monroe v. Pape*, 365 U.S. 167 (1961), emphatically rejected this proposition. The Court reviewed the legislative history of section 1983 and concluded that Congress intended to provide a federal remedy in federal court even where a state remedy was theoretically adequate. "It is no answer that the State has a law which if enforced would give relief. The federal remedy is supplementary to the state remedy, and the latter need not first be sought and refused before the federal one is invoked." *Monroe*, 365 U.S. at 183.

This aspect of *Monroe* was reaffirmed in *Patsy v. Board of Regents*, 457 U.S. 496 (1982), where the court held that the plaintiff did not have to exhaust her state administrative remedies before filing a section 1983 action. Together, *Monroe* and *Patsy* clearly establish that there is no general principle of exhaustion of judicial or administrative remedies as a prerequisite to bringing a section 1983 action. There are, however, a limited number of situations where exhaustion of state remedies may be required, or where other legal doctrine produce exhaustion-like consequences. The following notes briefly explore these situations.

NOTES

1. Congress has enacted legislation that requires persons institutionalized in state or local correctional facilities to exhaust their state administrative remedies in certain circumstances. Civil Rights of Institutionalized Persons Act (CRIPA), 42 U.S.C. § 1997e. Exhaustion may be ordered only when the applicable administrative procedures have been certified by the United States Attorney General or are determined by the court to comply substantially with specified minimum acceptable standards. These standards include: (1) an advisory role for the inmates; (2) time limits for written replies to inmate grievances; (3) priority processing of emergency grievances; (4) safeguards to avoid reprisals; and (5) independent review of the disposition of grievances. 28 C.F.R. § 40.1 et seq..

CRIPA has had little impact on prisoner section 1983 claims. Very few states have attempted to have their administrative griev-ance procedures certified by the Attorney Gen-eral and, when pressed, courts often find that the state's remedies do not comply with the minimum standards set forth in the Act. See e.g., *Lewis v. Meyer*, 815 F.2d 43 (7th Cir. 1987) (inmate's section 1983 suit against a prison social worker was improperly dismissed by the district court; state procedures had not been certified by the Attorney General and they appeared to be out of compliance with CRIPA minimum standards because of the absence of an inmate advisory role). Should exhaustion of administrative remedies be required if the in-mate brings his section 1983 claim in state court? See *Casteel v. Vaade*, 481 N.W.2d 476 (Wis. 1992) (the inmate need not exhaust his administrative remedies to bring a § 1983 claim in state court; Wisconsin's Inmate Review System does not on its face comply with CRIPA standards). Where exhaustion of state reme-dies is required under CRIPA, the inmate's section 1983 suit should be continued, not dismissed, while administrative remedies are pursued. *Gartrell v. Gaylor*, 981 F.2d 254 (5th Cir. 1993); *Francis v. Marquez*, 741 F.2d 1127 (9th Cir. 1984). See generally Lay, *Exhaustion of Grievance Procedures for State Prisoners Under Section 1997e of the Civil Rights Act*, 71 Iowa L. Rev. 935 (1986).

2. Habeas corpus is the traditional remedy for a person who is illegally confined. By statute, a state inmate must exhaust his state remedies before seeking a writ of habeas corpus in federal court. 28 U.S.C. § 2254(b). By contrast, inmates generally do not have to exhaust state remedies before bringing a sec-tion 1983 action challenging the constitutionali-ty of prison procedures or conditions. A recur-ring and troublesome issue concerns the proper characterization of a prisoner's complaint. Sup-pose a prisoner alleges that he has been deprived of good behavior time credits without due process. Should this suit be characterized as one seeking a writ of habeas corpus (in which case the inmate must exhaust his state remedies), or a section 1983 challenge to prison procedures (in which case there is no exhaus-tion requirement)? The Supreme Court in *Preis-er v. Rodriquez*, 411 U.S. 475, 500 (1973) ruled that this claim fell under the heading of habeas corpus and set down the following guiding principle:

> when a state prisoner is challenging the very fact or duration of his physical im-prisonment, and the relief he seeks is a determination that he is entitled to imme-diate release or a speedier release from that imprisonment, his sole federal reme-dy is a writ of habeas corpus.

Lower federal courts have since struggled with the application of that principle. See S. Nahmod, *Civil Rights and Civil Liberties Litiga-tion* § 9.13 (3d ed. 1991) (collecting cases). Suppose a prisoner claims that he is being unconstitutionally denied admission into a work release program. Is his remedy a writ of habeas corpus or section 1983? Judge Posner ana-lyzed the issue as follows:

> If the prisoner is seeking what can fairly be described as a quantum change in the level of custody—whether outright free-dom, or freedom subject to the limited reporting and financial constraints of bond or parole or probation, or the run of the prison in contrast to the approximation to solitary confinement that is disciplinary segregation—then habeas corpus is his remedy. But if he is seeking a different program or location or environment, then he is challenging the conditions rather than the fact of his confinement and his remedy is under civil rights law, even if, as will usually be the case, the program or location or environment that he is chal-lenging is more restrictive than the alter-native that he seeks.

Graham v. Broglin, 922 F.2d 379, 381 (7th Cir. 1991). The court went on to hold that this complaint should be considered under section 1983. Id.

3. The Supreme Court recently addressed the section 1983-habeas corpus problem in *Heck v. Humphrey*, 114 S. Ct. 114 S. Ct. 2364, (1994). Heck had been convicted of voluntary manslaughter and, while serving his sentence, brought a section 1983 action against two prosecutors and an investigator. Heck alleged that the defendants conducted an arbitrary investigation, knowingly destroyed exculpatory evidence, and caused an illegal voice identifica-tion procedure to be used at his trial. Although Heck sought monetary relief, he did not ask for an injunction or release from custody.

The Supreme Court affirmed the lower courts' dismissal of Heck's suit. All nine justices agreed that regardless of the relief sought, Heck was in fact challenging the legality of his conviction. Justice Scalia, speaking for five justices, characterized Heck's claim as one most analogous to common law malicious prosecution. An essential element of malicious prosecution is the termination of the prior criminal proceeding in favor of the accused. Borrowing from that principle, Justice Scalia wrote

We hold that, in order to recover damages for allegedly unconstitutional conviction or imprisonment, or for other harm caused by actions whose unlawfulness would render a conviction or sentence invalid, a § 1983 plaintiff must prove that the conviction or sentence has been reversed on direct appeal, expunged by executive order, declared invalid by a state tribunal authorized to make such determination, or called into question by a federal court's issuance of a writ of habeas corpus . . . A claim for damages bearing that relationship to a conviction or sentence that has not been so invalidated is not cognizable under § 1983. Thus, when a state prisoner seeks damages in a § 1983 suit, the district court must consider whether a judgment in favor of the plaintiff would necessarily imply the invalidity of his conviction or sentence; if it would, the complaint must be dismissed unless the plaintiff can demonstrate that the conviction or sentence has already been invalidated. But if the district court determines that the plaintiff's action, even if successful, will not demonstrate the invalidity of any outstanding criminal judgment against the plaintiff, the action should be allowed to proceed in the absence of some other bar to the suit.

Heck, 114 S. Ct. at 2372–73 (footnotes omitted).

Justice Souter, writing for four justices, adopted a more narrow position. He would require proof of a favorable termination of the prior criminal prosecution only in such cases where the plaintiff was " 'in custody' for habeas purposes." *Heck*, 114 S. Ct. at 2379 (Souter, J., concurring). The "in custody" limitation would allow section 1983 damages actions for

unconstitutional conviction or imprisonment to be brought by those who cannot invoke federal habeas jurisdiction, such as a person who was convicted of a crime, fined but not incarcerated.

Suppose Heck did not find out that the defendants destroyed exculpatory evidence until after he had served out his entire sentence. Could he bring a section 1983 claim? Should he be able to bring such a claim? Does Justice Scalia's opinion limit substantive constitutional protection? Is the majority's treatment of the malicious prosecution claim in *Heck* consistent within its approach in *Albright v. Oliver*, 114 S. Ct. 807 (1994) (noted in chapter 3) and *Wyatt v. Cole*, 112 S. Ct. 1827 (1992) (reprinted in Chapter 8)? What is the appropriate role of common law tort principles in defining the reach of section 1983?

What is a "favorable termination" of the criminal charges? Suppose a man, charged with harassing and threatening his wife, successfully completes the state's accelerated pretrial rehabilitation program resulting in the dismissal of the criminal charges without an adjudication of guilt and erasing all records of the charges. Could he then bring a section 1983 claim against the arresting officer since the charges were ultimately dismissed and the record erased? See *Roesch v. Otarola*, 980 F.2d 950, 853 (2d Cir. 1992) ("a dismissal pursuant to the Connecticut accelerated pretrial rehabilitation program is not a termination in favor of the accused for purposes of a civil rights suit.").

4. The Tax Injunction Act, 28 U.S.C. § 1341, restricts federal court jurisdiction in actions seeking an injunction against "the assessment, levy or collection of any tax under State law where a plain, speedy and efficient remedy may be had in the courts of such State". In *Fair Assessment in Real Estate Ass'n, Inc. v. McNary*, 454 U.S. 100, 107 (1981), the Court drew on the policies underlying the Act to hold that "the principle of comity bars federal courts from granting damages relief" in a suit brought pursuant to section 1983 alleging constitutional violations in the administration of a local property tax system. The holding was qualified by the requirement that "plain, adequate, and complete" state remedies be available. The plaintiff must demonstrate that the state remedy is inadequate, and even burdensome state procedures have been deemed sufficient. E.g., *Winicki v. Mallard*, 783 F.2d 1567 (11th Cir. 1986)

(Florida procedure would have required the filing of 67 class actions in 67 counties to recover millions of dollars in tax collected under a statute since declared to be unconstitutional; *Fair Assessment* applied). The practical effect of the Tax Injunction Act and *Fair Assessment* is to channel federal constitutional challenges to state and local tax systems to state courts. E.g., *Pryzina v. Ley*, 813 F.2d 821 (7th Cir. 1987) (suit for damages arising from Wisconsin's allegedly unconstitutional tax assessments and refund collections is barred by the comity principle set forth in *Fair Assessment*). See generally Bravemen, *Fair Assessment and Federal Jurisdiction in Civil Rights Cases*, 45 U. Pitt. L. Rev. 351 (1984).

Are tax cases distinctive? Why do principles of comity require a plaintiff to pursue her adequate state remedy for an unconstitutional tax, though she may proceed directly in federal court under section 1983 for a claim arising from an unreasonable search or seizure?

The Tax Injunction Act on its face applies only to suits filed in federal courts. Can a plaintiff challenge the constitutionality of a tax in state court under section 1983 and thereby avail herself of the attorney's fee provision? Do principles of comity have any relevance when the suit is brought in state court? Several states have refused to entertain § 1983 challenges to state taxes or have conditioned such claims on the exhaustion of state administrative remedies. E.g., *Zarda v. State*, 826 P.2d 1365 (Kan. 1992) (plaintiff must exhaust state administrative remedies before bringing section 1983 suit in state court); *Hogan v. Musolf*, 471 N.W.2d 216 (Wis. 1991) (same); *L.L. Bean Inc. v. Bracey*, 817 S.W.2d 292 (Tenn. 1991) (state law provides the exclusive basis for challenging state taxes in state court; state courts may not entertain section 1983 claim). Are these rulings consistent with the principle that state courts cannot discriminate against § 1983 claims filed in state courts? See Chapter 11. In upholding a lower court's decision to not consider a section 1983 challenge to a state tax, the South Carolina Supreme Court commented that "[s]tate remedies for asserting rights may not be circumvented by invoking § 1983". *Spencer v. South Carolina Tax Comm'n*, 316 S.E.2d 386, 389 (S.C. 1984). This decision was affirmed by an equally divided Supreme Court. *Spencer v. South Carolina Tax Comm'n*, 471 U.S. 82 (1985). In a subsequent opinion, however, the Court remarked that "whether state courts must assume jurisdiction over [section 1983 suits challenging state taxation] is not entirely clear", and noted that the affirmance in *Spencer* by an equally divided court "is not entitled to precedential value." *Arkansas Writers' Project, Inc. v. Ragland*, 481 U.S. 221, 234 n.7 (1987).

See generally Note, *Clarifying Comity: State Court Jurisdiction and Section 1983 State Tax Challenges*, 103 Harv. L. Rev. 1888 (1990) reprinted in S. Nahmod, *A Section 1983 Civil Rights Anthology* 250.

5. Suppose a person is charged with a crime in state court under a statute that is alleged to be unconstitutional. Can the state-court criminal defendant secure injunctive relief from prosecution in a section 1983 action filed in federal court? Section 1983 on its face speaks of the availability of equitable relief, with no apparent exception for declaratory judgments or injunctions. How would the availability of such a section 1983 action impact upon state criminal proceedings? The Court addressed these issues in *Younger v. Harris*, 401 U.S. 37 (1971), holding that a federal district court could not enjoin a pending state criminal prosecution notwithstanding the allegations that the prosecution and criminal statute inhibited the exercise of first amendment rights by the criminal defendant. The Court justified this ruling on several grounds. First, the constitutional issues could be adjudicated in the state criminal prosecution so that the section 1983 plaintiff/criminal defendant had an adequate remedy at law and would not suffer an irreparable injury if denied equitable relief. *Younger*, 401 U.S. at 45. Moreover, principles of "comity" and "Our Federalism," require a "proper respect for state functions" and a commitment to protect federal rights "in ways that will not unduly interfere with legitimate activities of the States." *Younger*, 401 U.S. at 44.

The *Younger* rule has been applied when the federal suit was filed before the state criminal proceeding. *Hicks v. Miranda*, 422 U.S. 332 (1975). It has been extended to administrative and private civil proceedings implicating important state interests. *Ohio Civil Rights Comm'n v. Dayton Christian Schools, Inc.*, 477 U.S. 619 (1986) (*Younger* barred suit to enjoin pending state administrative proceedings); *Pennzoil Co. v. Texaco, Inc.*, 481 U.S. 1 (1987) (*Younger* barred suit to enjoin the execution of state judgment pending appeal to state appellate courts).

Should the *Younger* rule apply when the section 1983 plaintiff seeks damages and not injunctive or declaratory relief? Does a damage remedy interfere with state functions in a qualitatively different way than an injunction? In *Deakins v. Monaghan*, 484 U.S. 193 (1988), the Court considered whether the *Younger* doctrine required dismissal of a 1983 claims for damages brought by plaintiffs who were the subjects of an ongoing state grand jury investigation. While not resolving the issue completely, the Court stated

> We need not decide the extent to which the *Younger* doctrine applies to a federal action seeking only monetary relief, however, because even if the *Younger* doctrine requires abstention here, the District Court has no discretion to dismiss rather than to stay claims for monetary relief that cannot be redressed in the state proceeding.

Deakins, 484 U.S. at 202. *Deakins* suggests that while *Younger* does not require outright dismissal, it permits (but does not compel) district courts to stay federal 1983 damages actions where those damages claims cannot be redressed in the state proceedings.

For commentary on the *Younger* doctrine, see Althouse, *How to Build a Separate Sphere: Federal Courts and State Power*, 100 Harv. L. Rev. 1485 (1987); Laycock, *Federal Interference with State Prosecutions: The Need for Prospective Relief*, 1977 Sup. Ct. Rev. 193; Wells, *The Role of Comity in the Law of Federal Courts*, 60 N.C. L. Rev. 59 (1981).

6. In *Railroad Commission v. Pullman*, 312 U.S. 496 (1941), the plaintiff filed a suit in federal court alleging that a state agency's order violated state law and various federal constitutional provisions. The state law claim turned on an unresolved issue of state law whose resolution might avoid the need to deal with the federal constitutional claims. The Supreme Court fashioned a rule of "abstention", under which lower federal courts abstain from deciding the federal issues while the parties seek a decision in state court on the unresolved issue of state law. The federal court retains jurisdiction pending such a state court determination.

In a subsequent opinion, the Supreme Court protected the interest of the plaintiff in having a federal forum for his federal claims. Under *England v. Louisiana State Board of Medical Examiners*, 375 U.S. 411 (1964), a plaintiff who is forced to state court under *Pullman*-abstention can preserve his right to a federal forum by informing the state court of his intention to return to the federal court on his federal claims. Should an *England*-type reservation apply in situations that do not technically fall within the *Pullman* abstention doctrine? See *Bradley v. Pittsburgh Board of Education*, 913 F.2d 1064 (3rd Cir. 1990) (plaintiff's state court appeal of school board's decision to terminate his employment did not preclude his section 1983 claim pending in federal court when he expressly reserved his right to have the federal court decide the federal constitutional issues). Is *Bradley* consistent with *Younger*?

7. A category of section 1983 cases producing exhaustion-like consequences involves challenges to the enforcement of allegedly unconstitutional land use regulations. The typical complaint alleges that the regulation in question so greatly restricts what an owner can do with her property as to constitute a "taking" under the fifth and fourteenth amendments. The Supreme Court has held that under certain conditions land use regulations can amount to a taking, thereby triggering a constitutional obligation to provide just compensation. E.g., *Dolan v. City of Tigard*, 114 S. Ct. 2309 (1994) (a city's conditioning of its approval of petitioner's request for a zoning variance on dedication of a flood plain and bicycle/pedestrian easement was a taking requiring just compensation). *Lucas v. South Carolina Coastal Council*, 112 S. Ct. 2886 (1992) (South Carolina Beachfront Management Act that denied all economically beneficial or productive use of land may constitute a taking). Cf. *Nollan v. California Coastal Commission*, 483 U.S. 825 (1987) (California law conditioning the issuance of a building permit on the granting of a public access easement constituted a taking).

A section 1983 claim of this nature is not "ripe", however, until the governmental entity charged with implementing the regulation has reached a "final decision". Thus, a constitutional challenge to a zoning ordinance was dismissed on ripeness grounds when the plaintiff had not applied for a variance. *Williamson County Regional Planning Commission v. Ham-*

ilton Bank, 473 U.S. 172 (1985). Justice Brennan explained that until the plaintiff applies for and receives a final ruling on a request for a variance, a court cannot determine whether the plaintiff has been denied all reasonable beneficial use of the property. *Williamson*, 473 U.S. at 194. Moreover, a taking is unconstitutional only if "just compensation" is not provided. A plaintiff must pursue available state procedures to determine whether the government will provide just compensation.

Thus, a court cannot pass on either the "taking" or "just compensation" issue until the plaintiff has pursued available state procedures. Although conceptually different from exhaustion, the ripeness doctrine applied in this context produces exhaustion-like consequences.

See also *MacDonald, Sommer & Frates v. Yolo County*, 477 U.S. 340 (1986) (without a final and authoritative determination by the planning commission as to how the land use regulation at issue will be applied to the plaintiff's property, the court cannot determine whether a "taking" has occurred or whether the county failed to provide "just compensation").

8. A somewhat analogous situation arises in the procedural due process context. Recall that *Parratt v. Taylor*, 451 U.S. 527 (1981) and its progeny hold that the availability of post-deprivation remedies under state law may satisfy the demands of "due process" under some circumstances. See Chapter 3. Where this principle applies, a deprivation of life, liberty or property in not unconstitutional because adequate post-deprivation state remedies provide due process. The Supreme Court has acknowledged the similarity between *Parratt* and the ripeness requirement in takings cases. See *Williamson Planning Comm'n v. Hamilton Bank*, 473 U.S. 172, 195 (1985) ("The recognition that a property owner has not suffered a violation of the Just Compensation Clause until the owner has unsuccessfully attempted to obtain just compensation through the procedures provided by the State for obtaining such compensation is analogous to the Court's holding in *Parratt v. Taylor*, 451 U.S. 527 (1981).").

CHAPTER ELEVEN

Litigating Section 1983 Claims in State Courts

A distinctive feature of American government is the existence, in each state, of parallel judicial systems, one organized under federal law, the other a creature of state law. Unless Congress provides otherwise, the state systems may decide cases arising under federal substantive law. While *Monroe v. Pape* establishes the principle that persons complaining of unconstitutional treatment by state officers have access to federal court, that case was decided against a background of remedial law in which state courts were presumed to be available to hear such cases. Recall the holding in *Monroe*: Even if state courts are open to the plaintiff, the unconstitutional conduct is "under color of" state law, and he may proceed in federal court. Although most section 1983 cases go to federal courts, state courts have concurrent jurisdiction over section 1983 claims, and some plaintiffs prefer to litigate in state court.

The complexities of our federal system generate some interesting issues for state court adjudication of section 1983 cases: May state courts refuse to hear section 1983 cases? Why might a plaintiff prefer state (or federal) court? How do the terms upon which the litigation is conducted differ depending on the choice of a state or federal forum? To what extent are state courts required to forego their normal practices for the sake of the federal rights at stake in section 1983 cases?

One important point to keep in mind throughout these materials is that the defendant may thwart the plaintiff's preference for state court. Even if suit is brought in state court, the defendant may remove a section 1983 case to federal court under 28 U.S.C. § 1441(a).

I. Must State Courts Hear Section 1983 Claims?

Howlett v. Rose

496 U.S. 356 (1990)

Stevens, J., delivered the opinion for a unanimous Court . . .

42 U.S.C. § 1983 creates a remedy for violations of federal rights committed by persons acting under color of state law. State courts as well as federal courts have jurisdiction over § 1983 cases. The question in this case is whether a state law defense of "sovereign immunity" is available to a school board otherwise subject to suit in a Florida court even though such a defense would not be available if the action had been brought in a federal forum.

I

Petitioner, a former high school student, filed a complaint in the Circuit Court for Pinellas County, Florida, naming the School Board of Pinellas County and three school officials as defendants. He alleged that an assistant principal made an illegal search of his car while it was parked on school premises and that he was wrongfully suspended from regular classes for five days. Contending that the search and subsequent suspension violated rights under the Fourth and Fourteenth Amendments of the Federal Constitution and under similar provisions of the State Constitution, he prayed for damages and an order expunging any reference to the suspension from the school records . . .

The school board . . . contended that the court was without jurisdiction to hear the federal claims—but not the state claims—because the Florida waiver of sovereign immunity statute did not extend to claims based on § 1983. The Circuit Court dismissed the complaint with prejudice . . . [and] [t]he District Court of Appeal affirmed . . . It held that the availability of sovereign immunity in a § 1983 action brought in state court is a matter of state law, and that Florida's statutory waiver of sovereign immunity did not apply to § 1983 cases . . . The Florida Supreme Court denied review. In view of the importance of the question decided by the Court of Appeal, we granted certiorari . . .

II

. . . As [the District Court of Appeal] construed the law, Florida has extended absolute immunity from suit not only to the State and its arms but also to municipalities, counties, and school districts who might otherwise be subject to suit under § 1983 in federal court. That holding raises the concern that the state court may be evading federal law and discriminating against federal causes of action. The adequacy of the state law ground to support a judgment precluding litigation of the federal claim is itself a federal question which we review de novo. Whether the constitutional rights asserted by petitioner were "'given due recognition by the [Court of Appeal] is a question as to which the [petitioner is] entitled to invoke our judgment, and this [he has] done in the appropriate way. It therefore is within our province to inquire not only whether the right was denied in express terms, but also whether it was denied in substance and effect, as by putting forward non-federal grounds of decision that were without any fair or substantial support.'" *Staub v. City of Baxley.*

III

Federal law is enforceable in state courts not because Congress has determined that federal courts would otherwise be burdened or that state courts might provide a more convenient forum—although both might well be true—but because the Constitution and laws passed pursuant to it are as much laws in the States as laws passed by the state legislature. The Supremacy Clause makes those laws "the supreme Law of the Land," and charges state courts with a coordinate responsibility to enforce that law according to their regular modes of procedure . . . As Alexander Hamilton expressed the principle in a classic passage: "In every case in which they were not expressly excluded by the future acts of the national legislature, [state courts] will of course take cognizance of the causes to which those acts may give birth. This I infer from the nature of judiciary power, and from the general genius of the system. The judiciary power of every government looks beyond its own local or municipal laws, and in civil cases lays hold of all subjects of litigation between parties within its jurisdiction, though the causes of dispute are relative to the laws of the most distant part of the globe. Those of Japan, not less than of New York, may furnish the objects of legal discussion to our courts. When in addition to this we consider the State governments and the national governments, as they truly are, in the light of kindred systems, and as parts of ONE WHOLE, the inference seems to be conclusive, that the State courts would have a concurrent jurisdiction in all cases arising under the laws of the Union, where it was not expressly prohibited." *The Federalist No. 82*, p. 132 (E. Bourne ed. 1947) (emphasis added).

Three corollaries follow from the proposition that "federal" law is part of the Law of the Land in the State:

1. A state court may not deny a federal right, when the parties and controversy are properly before it, in the absence of "valid excuse." . . .

2. An excuse that is inconsistent with or violates federal law is not a valid excuse: the Supremacy Clause forbids state courts to dissociate themselves from federal law because of disagreement with its content or a refusal to recognize the superior authority of its source . . .

3. When a state court refuses jurisdiction because of a neutral state rule regarding the administration of the courts, we must act with utmost caution before deciding that it is obligated to entertain the claim . . . The requirement that a state court of competent jurisdiction treat federal law as the law of the land does not necessarily include within it a requirement that the State create a court competent to hear the case in which the

federal claim is presented. The general rule "bottomed deeply in belief in the importance of state control of state judicial procedure, is that federal law takes the state courts as it finds them." Hart, [*The Relations Between State and Federal Law*,] 54 Colum. L. Rev. [489], 508. The States thus have great latitude to establish the structure and jurisdiction of their own courts. In addition, States may apply their own neutral procedural rules to federal claims, unless those rules are pre-empted by federal law. See *Felder v. Casey*.

These principles are fundamental to a system of federalism in which the state courts share responsibility for the application and enforcement of federal law. In *Mondou [v. New York, N.H. & H.R.Co.]*, for example, we held that rights under the Federal Employers' Liability Act (FELA) "may be enforced, as of right, in the courts of the States when their jurisdiction, as prescribed by local laws, is adequate to the occasion." The Connecticut courts had declined cognizance of FELA actions because the policy of the federal act was "not in accord with the policy of the State" and it was "inconvenient and confusing" to apply federal law. We noted, as a matter of some significance, that Congress had not attempted "to enlarge or regulate the jurisdiction of state courts or to control or affect their modes of procedure," and found from the fact that the state court was a court of general jurisdiction with cognizance over wrongful death actions that the court's jurisdiction was "appropriate to the occasion". "The existence of the jurisdiction created an implication of duty to exercise it," which could not be overcome by disagreement with the policy of the federal act.

In *McKnett [v. St. Louis & San Francisco R. Co.]*, the state court refused to exercise jurisdiction over a FELA cause of action against a foreign corporation for an injury suffered in another State. We held "while Congress has not attempted to compel states to provide courts for the enforcement of the Federal Employers' Liability Act, the Federal Constitution prohibits state courts of general jurisdiction from refusing to do so solely because the suit is brought under a federal law." Because the state court had "general jurisdiction of the class of actions to which that here brought belongs, in cases between litigants situated like those in the case at bar," the

refusal to hear the FELA action constituted discrimination against rights arising under federal laws in violation of the Supremacy Clause.

We unanimously reaffirmed these principles in *Testa v. Katt*. We held that the Rhode Island courts could not decline jurisdiction over treble damages claims under the federal Emergency Price Control Act when their jurisdiction was otherwise "adequate and appropriate under established local law." The Rhode Island court had distinguished our decision in *McKnett* and *Mondou* on the grounds that the federal act was a "penal statute," which would not have been enforceable under the Full Faith and Credit Clause if passed by another State. We rejected that argument. We observed that the Rhode Island court enforced the "same type of claim" arising under state law and claims for double damages under federal law. We therefore concluded that the court had "jurisdiction adequate and appropriate under established local law to adjudicate this action." The court could not decline to exercise this jurisdiction to enforce federal law by labeling it "penal." The Policy of the Federal Act was to be considered "the prevailing policy in every state" which the state court could not refuse to enforce "'because of conceptions of impolicy or want of wisdom on the part of Congress in having called into play its lawful powers.'"

On only three occasions have we found a valid excuse for a state court's refusal to entertain a federal cause of action. Each of them involved a neutral rule of judicial administration. In *Douglas v. New York, N.H. & H.R. Co.* the state statute permitted discretionary dismissal of both federal and state claims where neither the plaintiff nor the defendant was a resident of the forum state.[19] In *Herb [v. Pitcairn]*, the city court denied jurisdiction over a FELA action on the grounds that the cause of action arose outside its territorial jurisdiction. Although the state court was not free to dismiss the federal claim

---

[19] We wrote: "It may very well be that if the Supreme Court of New York were given no discretion, being otherwise competent, it would be subject to a duty. But there is nothing in the Act of Congress that purports to force a duty upon such Courts as against an otherwise valid excuse. Second Employers' Liability Cases, 223 U.S. 1, 56, 57." 279 U.S., at 387–388.

"because it is a federal one," we found no evidence that the state court "construed the state jurisdiction and venue laws in a discriminatory fashion." Finally, in *Missouri ex rel. Southern R. Co. [v. Mayfield]* we held that a state court could apply the doctrine of forum no conveniens to bar adjudication of a FELA case if the State "enforces its policy impartially so as not to involve a discrimination against Employers' Liability Act suits."

IV

The parties disagree as to the proper characterization of the District Court of Appeal's decision. Petitioner argues that the court adopted a substantive rule of decision that state agencies are not subject to liability under § 1983. Respondent, stressing the court's language that it had not "opened its own courts for federal actions against the state," argues that the case simply involves the court's refusal to take cognizance of § 1983 actions against state defendants. We conclude that whether the question is framed in pre-emption terms, as petitioner would have it, or in the obligation to assume jurisdiction over a "federal" cause of action, as respondent would have it, the Florida court's refusal to entertain one discrete category of § 1983 claims, when the court entertains similar state law actions against state defendants, violates the Supremacy Clause.

If the District Court of Appeal meant to hold that governmental entities subject to § 1983 liability enjoy an immunity over and above those already provided in § 1983, that holding directly violates federal law. The elements of, and the defenses to, a federal cause of action are defined by federal law. A State may not, by statute or common law, create a cause of action under § 1983 against an entity whom Congress has not subjected to liability. Since this Court has construed the word "person" in § 1983 to exclude States, neither a federal court or a state court may entertain a § 1983 action against such a defendant. Conversely, since the Court has held that municipal corporations and similar governmental entities are "persons," a state court entertaining a § 1983 action must adhere to that interpretation . . . "By including municipalities with the class of 'persons' subject to liability for violation of the Federal Constitution and laws, Congress—the supreme sover-

eign on matters of federal law—abolished whatever vestige of the State's sovereign immunity the municipality possessed." . . .

Federal law makes governmental defendants that are not arms of the State, such as municipalities, liable for their constitutional violations. Florida law, as interpreted by the District Court of Appeal, would make all such defendants absolutely immune from liability under the federal statute. To the extent that the Florida law of sovereign immunity reflects a substantive disagreement with the extent to which governmental entities should be held liable for their constitutional violations, that disagreement cannot override the dictates of federal law . . .

If, on the other hand, the District Court of Appeal meant that § 1983 claims are excluded from the category of tort claims that the Circuit Court could hear against a school board, its holding was no less violative of federal law. This case does not present the questions whether Congress can require the States to create a forum with the capacity to enforce federal statutory rights or to authorize service of process on parties who would not otherwise be subject to the court's jurisdiction.[20] The State of Florida has constituted the Circuit Court for Pinellas County as a court of general jurisdiction. It exercises jurisdiction over tort claims by private citizens against state entities (including school boards), of the size and type of petitioner's claim here, and it can enter judgment against them. That court also exercises jurisdiction over § 1983 actions against individual officers and is fully competent to provide the remedies the federal statute requires. Petitioner has complied with all the state law procedures for invoking the jurisdiction of that court.

The mere facts, as argued by respondent's amici, that state common law and statutory law do not make unlawful the precise conduct that § 1983 addresses and that § 1983 actions "are more likely to be frivolous than are other

---

[20] Virtually every State has expressly or by implication opened its courts to § 1983 actions and there are no state court systems that refuse to hear § 1983 cases. See S. STEINGLASS, SECTION 1983 LITIGATION IN STATE COURTS 1–3, and App. E (1989) (listing cases). We have no occasion to address in this case the contentions of respondent's amici, that the States need not establish courts competent to entertain § 1983 claims.

suits," clearly cannot provide sufficient justification for the State's refusal to entertain such actions. These reasons have never been asserted by the State and are not asserted by the school board. More importantly, they are not the kind of neutral policy that could be a "valid excuse" for the state court's refusal to entertain federal actions. To the extent that the Florida rule is based upon the judgment that parties who are otherwise subject to the jurisdiction of the court should not be held liable for activity that would not subject them to liability under state law, we understand that to be only another way of saying that the court disagrees with the content of federal law. Sovereign immunity in Florida turns on the nature of the claim—whether the duty allegedly breached is discretionary—not on the subject matter of the dispute. There is no question that the Circuit Court, which entertains state common law and statutory claims against state entities in a variety of their capacities, ranging from law enforcement to schooling to the protection of individuals using parking lots, has jurisdiction over the subject of this suit. That court cannot reject petitioner's § 1983 claim because it has chosen, for substantive policy reasons, not to adjudicate other claims which might also render the school board liable. The federal law is law in the State as much as laws passed by the state legislature . . .

The argument by amici that suits predicated on federal law are more likely to be frivolous and have less of an entitlement to the State's limited judicial resources warrants little response. A State may adopt neutral procedural rules to discourage frivolous litigation of all kinds, as long as those rules are not pre-empted by a valid federal law. A State may not, however, relieve congestion in its courts by declaring a whole category of federal claims to be frivolous. Until it has been proven that the claim has no merit, that judgment is not up to the States to make . . .

The judgment of the Court of Appeal is reversed and the case is remanded for further proceedings not inconsistent with this opinion . . .

NOTES

1. After *Howlett*, suppose someone injured by the state police tries to sue the state itself in state court under section 1983. Could the state successfully assert sovereign immunity and have the case dismissed? The answer is yes, but the reason is not that sovereign immunity is a "valid excuse" for state court refusals to hear section 1983 cases. *Will v. Michigan Dept. of State Police*, 491 U.S. 58 (1989), which may be found in Chapter 5, holds that state governments (including state agencies like the state police, state universities, and state departments of taxation, welfare, agriculture, and the like) are not "persons" within the coverage of section 1983. By contrast, local governments, and local school boards like the one sued in *Howlett*, are "persons" subject to suit. See *Monell v. Dept. of Social Servs.*, 436 U.S. 658 (1978).

The distinction between local and state governments may seem artificial and arbitrary. The explanation for it lies in the nuances of eleventh amendment law. Long ago the Supreme Court held that the states' immunity from suit in federal court did not extend to municipal governments. *Lincoln County v. Luning*, 133 U.S. 529 (1890). Historically, the distinction makes some sense, as local governments began as private associations, which gradually took on more and more governmental tasks, finally ending up as governmental bodies.

In recent years the Court has ruled that Congress may abrogate the states' immunity, but only if the statutory language is sufficiently explicit. In *Quern v. Jordan*, 440 U.S. 332 (1979) it ruled that section 1983 did not abrogate the immunity. *Will* ruled that the holding of *Quern* could not be evaded by bringing suit in state court. But this whole line of Eleventh Amendment doctrine is irrelevant to suits against local governmental bodies like the school board sued in *Howlett*, for *Lincoln County* places them outside the scope of eleventh amendment protection in any event.

2. Although *Will* establishes that state governments may not be sued in state court under section 1983, it would be an (understandable) error to conclude that they always may assert sovereign immunity against suit in their own courts. Quite apart from section 1983, plaintiffs may have success with other theories of recovery. One alternative is illustrated by *McKesson Corp. v. Div. of Alcoholic Beverages and Tobacco*, 496 U.S. 18 (1990). The issue was whether the state could be made to refund taxes illegally collected. The state court had refused to order

relief, citing "equitable considerations." The Supreme Court held that "the due process clause . . . obligates the state to provide meaningful backward-looking relief to rectify any unconstitutional deprivation." Does this amount to a holding that the due process clause itself requires the state to provide a meaningful "backward-looking" remedy where necessary to enforce constitutional rights effectively?

3. How broad is the *McKesson* principle? Does it extend only to tax cases? Suppose that, after *McKesson*, someone injured by the state police sues the state in state court, abjuring section 1983 and maintaining instead that the due process clause requires the state to recognize a cause of action to recover damages for unconstitutional deprivation of liberty by the state government. Can *McKesson* be distinguished as a tax refund case? As a case where an "equitable" remedy was sought and the Supreme Court merely found that the "equitable" grounds offered for denying it were insufficient? Can the state remove the case to federal court under 28 U.S.C. § 1441 (a) and then successfully assert an eleventh amendment defense? See S. Steinglass, *Section 1983 Litigation in the State Courts* § 24.4(a) [maintaining that the federal court should remand the case under 28 U.S.C. § 1447(c) (directing that a case be remanded if "it appears that the district court lacks subject matter jurisdiction")].

4. The scope of *McKesson* awaits further elucidation by the Supreme Court. Whether the suit described in the preceding paragraph would succeed or not, keep in mind that section 1983 is not the only avenue for pursuing relief on federal grounds in state court. State law might authorize a cause of action to vindicate federal rights. See, e.g., Note, *State Incorporation of Federal Law: A Response to the Demise of Implied Federal Rights of Action*, 94 Yale L.J. 1144 (1985); S. Steinglass, *Section 1983 Litigation in State Courts* § 15.2(e). State law may provide more effective remedies than a section 1983 suit. See, e.g., *Bell v. City of Milwaukee*, 746 F.2d 1205, 1271 (7th Cir. 1984) (relying on state law to require a municipal defendant to indemnify its officers for punitive damages assessed against them).

Of course, the availability of this recourse will vary from state to state.

5. What kinds of reasons for refusing to hear section 1983 cases will be deemed "valid excuses" after *Howlett*? Would a state court be able to argue that it has a state law of standing to sue that is narrower than the federal law of standing, and that a suit that could be brought in federal court must be dismissed for lack of standing in state court? In Illinois, for example, "a contract purchaser whose contract is contingent upon rezoning cannot contest a zoning decision in the Illinois courts . . . [O]nly the owner of the property has standing to pursue such an action." *Village of Arlington Heights v. Metropolitan Housing Corp.*, 429 U.S. 252, 262, n.8 (1977). *Arlington Heights* was brought in federal district court, and the Supreme Court held that "[s]tate law of standing . . . does not govern such determinations in the federal courts." Id. But suppose a contract purchaser chose to sue under section 1983 in state court, alleging that the zoning decision violated his constitutional rights. Would the state standing rule trip him up? See Fletcher, *The "Case or Controversy" Requirement in State Court Adjudication of Federal Questions*, 78 Cal. L. Rev. 263, 291–93 (1990) (interpreting the *Arlington Heights* footnote as giving an affirmative answer, and arguing that "this is the wrong answer").

6. *Kish v. Wright*, 562 P.2d 625 (Utah 1977), approved dismissal of a section 1983 case on grounds of forum non conveniens, provided suit could be filed in federal court. The suit was brought by a Utah prisoner in a Utah state court against Utah prison officials. The court did not explain why Utah state court would be an inconvenient forum. Is this case good law after *Howlett*? The court relied on *Missouri ex rel. Southern Ry. v. Mayfield*, 340 U.S. 1 (1950), which is discussed in *Howlett*. Do you think the reliance was justified? See S. Steinglass, *Section 1983 Litigation in State Courts* § 11.5 (no). Suppose the plaintiff is injured in an altercation with the police in Chicago but moves to California and decides to bring suit in California state court. Assuming he can obtain personal jurisdiction in California, would a dismissal on forum non conveniens grounds be appropriate? How is this case different from *Kish*?

7. In *Moore v. Sims*, 442 U.S. 415 (1979), local authorities in Houston seized the Sims's children and brought child neglect charges against the Sims in state court, in an effort to place the children in a foster home. The parents then instituted a section 1983 suit in federal court, challenging on constitutional grounds the

Texas statutes allowing children to be taken without a prompt hearing. Citing the principle of comity favoring federal deference to pending state proceedings, the Supreme Court held that the federal suit must be dismissed because the parents could raise their constitutional claims in the state proceeding by making a counterclaim under section 1983. The district court, however, had suggested that the state court hearing the custody proceeding could not adjudicate the Sims' constitutional challenge. See 442 U.S. at 439 & n.10 (Stevens, J., dissenting).

What if it turns out that the majority in *Moore* misunderstood state law? The state court charged with making determinations of child abuse is (in this hypothetical) a specialized court that has no jurisdiction under state law to hear constitutional objections to procedures used to seize children: Is that a valid excuse for dismissing the counterclaim? See S. Steinglass, *Section 1983 Litigation in State Courts* § 11.4.

NOTES ON THE CHOICE BETWEEN FEDERAL AND STATE COURTS

1. Most plaintiffs prefer to litigate constitutional claims in federal court. Why? Consider the reasons set forth by Professor Neuborne in his classic article, *The Myth of Parity*, 90 Harv. L. Rev. 1105, 1115–16, 1120–21 (1977). Professor Neuborne, a plaintiffs' civil liberties lawyer, prefers to litigate in federal court for three sets of reasons. First, he believes that "the level of technical competence which the federal district court is likely to bring to the legal issues involved generally will be superior to that of a given state trial forum. Stated bluntly, in my experience, federal trial courts tend to be better equipped to analyze complex, often conflicting lines of authority and more likely to produce competently written, persuasive opinions than are state trial courts." In addition, he notes that "there are several factors, unrelated to technical competence—which, lacking a better term, I call a court's psychological set—that render it more likely that an individual with a constitutional claim will succeed in federal district court than in a state trial court." These include a tradition of federal enforcement of the constitution, greater receptivity to effective enforcement of Supreme Court pronouncements, the isolation of federal courts from the undesirable

practical consequences of upholding constitutional claims, and the upper- and upper-middle class backgrounds of federal judges. Third, Neuborne thinks that "the federal judiciary's insulation from majoritarian pressures makes federal court structurally preferable to state trial court as a forum in which to challenge powerful local interests."

2. Why, then, does any plaintiff ever take his case to state court? In his treatise, *Section 1983 Litigation in State Courts*, Professor Steinglass identifies a variety of considerations that may so incline plaintiffs' lawyers. This note and those that follow discuss some of the more important ones. He contends that finding a sympathetic judge is more important to the plaintiff than obtaining the most talented one. Whatever the general rule regarding the "psychological set" of federal and state judges, in a given set of circumstances the plaintiff may find the available state judges more attractive than their federal counterparts. In this regard, keep in mind that Neuborne wrote in 1977, before the Reagan and Bush administrations appointed large numbers of conservative judges to the federal bench. S. Steinglass, *Section 1983 Litigation in State Courts* § 7.2.

In an era when the Supreme Court is dominated by conservative justices, is it possible that plaintiffs' lawyers might prefer state courts *just because* state judges are less familiar with recent constitutional developments than their federal counterparts?

3. Quite apart from the attorney's comparative evaluation of the judges' likely responses to his client's arguments, there may be a federal circuit court precedent on point that threatens the plaintiff's recovery. Even sympathetic federal judges would ordinarily follow the unfavorable precedent. Except for Supreme Court rulings, state judges are not bound by federal decisions. Only by filing in state court (and hoping the defendant fails to remove) could the plaintiff hope to win such a case. S. Steinglass, supra, at § 5.4.

Should state courts be required to follow federal circuit court precedents? On the one hand, requiring them to do so would make federal law more uniform. See S. Steinglass at p. 5–27. At the same time, we may benefit from contributions to federal law-making from a variety of sources, each learning from the others. See Bator, *The State Courts and Federal Constitutional Litigation*, 22 Wm. & Mary L.

Rev. 605, 634 (1981); Cover & Alienikoff, *Dialectical Federalism: Habeas Corpus and the Court*, 86 Yale L.J. 1035 (1977).

4. The plaintiff may prefer (or avoid) state court because of the process by which jurors are selected. "Federal jurors are chosen from multi-county areas that are generally more diverse than the single county or city from which state juries are typically chosen." S. Steinglass, supra, at § 7.3(a). Hence, "[l]awyers representing members of racial or ethnic minorities in urban areas often choose state courts to obtain a jury that includes persons with similar minority backgrounds." Id. at § 7.3(a)(4).

Attorneys often conduct the voir dire in state court, while federal judges keep them on a short leash. As a result, Steinglass maintains, "lawyers representing unpopular parties or parties advancing unpopular claims should welcome the state court practice of permitting extensive questioning of prospective jurors about their knowledge of the case and the parties as well as their views on the issues." Id.

In federal court, the jury must reach a unanimous verdict unless the parties agree otherwise. In contrast, thirty states permit split votes. According to Steinglass, "plaintiffs raising federal claims may prefer state courts, where they can prevail with less than a unanimous vote, to federal courts, where the presence of a single hold-out juror can result in a hung jury." Is this an important factor in section 1983 litigation? According to Steinglass, "it is likely that the existence of strongly held views by jurors concerning the parties and issues in such controversial cases may create less room for compromise verdicts that find liability but split the amount of damages." Id. at § 7.3(c).

If Steinglass is right, why has there been no rush to file section 1983 cases in state courts?

5. Besides the considerations discussed in the previous note, persons seeking to litigate both federal and state claims may find it convenient to take them all to state court. *Monroe v. Pape*, and thousands of other section 1983 cases, illustrate that arguably unconstitutional official conduct may also violate state law. Consequently, section 1983 plaintiffs not uncommonly seek to raise both federal and state claims for recovery. They may encounter obstacles to litigating the state claims in federal court. Article III of the Constitution does not authorize federal courts to hear state law cases unless the parties are citizens of different states. Apart from the diversity jurisdiction, federal courts normally may only hear claims arising under federal law. Even so, plaintiffs with both state and federal claims may litigate their whole case in federal court if the conditions for "pendent jurisdiction" are met. The terms of the doctrine are set out in *United Mine Workers of America v. Gibbs*, 383 U.S. 715 (1966):

> Pendent jurisdiction, in the sense of judicial *power*, exists whenever there is a claim "arising under . . . [federal law]", and the relationship between that claim and the state claim permits the conclusion that the entire action before the court comprises but one constitutional "case." The federal claim must have substance sufficient to confer subject matter jurisdiction on the court. [In other words, it must not be frivolous.] The state and federal claims must derive from a common nucleus of operative fact. But if, considered without regard to their federal or state character, a plaintiff's claims are such that he would ordinarily be expected to try them all in one judicial proceeding, then, assuming substantiality of the federal issues, there is *power* in federal courts to hear the whole.

> That power need not be exercised in every case in which it is found to exist. It has consistently been recognized that pendent jurisdiction is a doctrine of discretion, not of plaintiff's right. Its justification lies in considerations of judicial economy, convenience, and fairness to litigants; if these are not present a federal court should hesitate to exercise jurisdiction over state claims, even though bound to apply state law to them. Needless decisions of state law should be avoided both as a matter of comity and to promote justice between the parties, by procuring for them a surer-footed reading of applicable law. Certainly, if the federal claims are dismissed before trial, even though not insubstantial in a jurisdictional sense, the state claims should be dismissed as well. Similarly, if it appears that the state issues substantially predominate, whether in terms of proof, of the scope of the issues raised, or of the comprehensiveness of the remedy sought, the state claims may be dis-

missed without prejudice and left for resolution to state tribunals. There may, on the other hand, be situations in which the state claim is so closely tied to questions of federal policy that the argument for pendent jurisdiction is particularly strong . . . Finally, there may be reasons independent of jurisdictional considerations, such as the likelihood of jury confusion in treating divergent legal theories of relief, that would justify separating state and federal claims for trial. If so, jurisdiction should ordinarily be refused.

The doctrine is now codified at 28 U.S.C. § 1367. Note that one of the major grounds for dismissing the state claim comes up when the federal claim has been dismissed before trial, e.g., where the defendant successfully asserts official immunity. See 28 U.S.C. § 1367(c)(3).

6. Suppose a police car collided with the plaintiff's car. According to the plaintiff, the officers then yanked him from his car and beat him up. He wishes to sue under state negligence law for the original accident and under section 1983 for the beating. Can he bring both claims in federal court? Note that if the facts needed to make out the state law claim are substantially different from the constitutional claim, federal courts will lack constitutional power to hear the state claim.

Of course, the unavailability of federal court for both claims does not mean that they can both be brought in one state court action. If the claims are sufficiently different, or if the jury would be confused by trying them both at once, state procedural rules may require bifurcation in any event. Someone who prefers federal court for the federal claim may find that proceeding in state court with that claim offers few advantages in terms of convenience, and therefore may choose to try the federal claim in federal court and the state claim in state court.

This possibility aside, a plaintiff who values the convenience of litigating all of his claims in one forum will often be able to do so in state court when federal pendent jurisdiction is lacking.

7. Pendent jurisdiction may be unavailable for another reason. In *Pennhurst State School and Hospital v. Halderman*, 465 U.S. 89 (1984) the Supreme Court held that federal courts may not grant injunctive relief against state officers on state law grounds, on account of the eleventh amendment prohibition on federal suits against state governments. *Pennhurst* overturned seventy five years of the contrary practice, under which federal courts faced with a request to enjoin state action would first look to state law and only if no state ground were available turn to the constitution. See *Siler v. Louisville & Nashville R. Co.*, 213 U.S. 175, 191–93 (1909) (authorizing that practice). After *Pennhurst*, plaintiffs seeking injunctive relief on both state and federal grounds must either bifurcate the case between state and federal court or bring the whole case in state court. See Chemerinsky, *State Sovereignty and Federal Court Power: The Eleventh Amendment after* Pennhurst v. Halderman, 12 Hastings Const. L.Q. 643 (1985); Shapiro, Comment, *Wrong Turns: The Eleventh Amendment and the* Pennhurst *Case*, 98 Harv. L. Rev. 61 (1984).

8. Recall that defendants may remove section 1983 suits filed in state court. 28 U.S.C. § 1441(a). Do the considerations bearing on the decision whether to remove parallel those that may influence the plaintiff's initial decision where to file? Are there additional considerations defendants may take into account?

When the plaintiff files in state court on account of the convenience of trying the whole case in one place and the defendant removes the federal part of it to federal court, the plaintiff may then seek pendent jurisdiction over the state claims. Should the federal court simply apply the *Gibbs* criteria in determining whether to hear the state claim, or should it consider also the defendant's action in removing to federal court as a factor weighing in favor of pendent jurisdiction?

Recall that there are two potential obstacles to pendent jurisdiction. First, the state claims may not arise out of the same nucleus of operative fact as the federal claims. If this is so, then there is a constitutional barrier to hearing the state claims. But other reasons for not hearing the state claims are within the district court's discretion. The recent statute codifying pendent jurisdiction states that the district court "may" decline to exercise pendent jurisdiction if, for example, the court has dismissed the federal claims. 28 U.S.C. § 1367(c).

The statute does not mention the situation envisioned in this note. Does that omission doom the plaintiff's effort to obtain pendent jurisdiction where a discretionary factor might otherwise preclude it?

9. Federal courts may adjudicate a dispute only if it is a "case" within the meaning of Article III. The plaintiff must meet certain "justiciability" requirements in order to get his issues heard. He must establish that he has standing to raise the issues he tenders, and that the dispute is ripe and has not yet become moot. While standing, ripeness, and mootness apply to the federal courts, the Supreme Court does not require that the state courts abide by those doctrines, and some do not. See, e.g., *ASARCO, Inc. v. Kadish,* 490 U.S. 605 (1989) (holding that once the state court grants relief the defendants have suffered an "injury" sufficient to give them standing to seek review in the Supreme Court). Indeed, many state courts hear claims that have become moot, if there is a strong public interest in resolving the issue. See Fletcher, *The "Case or Controversy" Requirement in State Court Adjudication of Federal Questions*, 78 Calif. L. Rev. 263, 300 n.168 (1990). Consequently, a plaintiff who fears he will be denied access to federal court may find state court more accommodating.

Professor Fletcher thinks this rule should be overturned, and replaced with a regime under which state courts adjudicating questions of federal law must dismiss cases that do not meet federal justiciability standards. He argues that the federal doctrine on justiciability serves a good purpose in identifying cases fit for resolution, that the change would help the Supreme Court to fulfill its role as the final arbiter of federal law, and that "a common 'case or controversy' requirement . . . would treat the two courts as genuine partners in the business of adjudicating federal law." Fletcher, supra, 78 Calif. L. Rev. at 282–84.

Professor Herman disagrees, pointing out that the Article III requirements by their terms apply only to federal courts. See Herman, *Beyond Parity: Section 1983 and the State Courts*, 54 Brooklyn L. Rev. 1057, 1115 (1989), reprinted in *Section 1983 Civil Rights Anthology* 239.

Who is right?

10. Why don't defendants simply remove all cases of this sort to federal court, where they can then have them dismissed? Professor Steinglass thinks that removal should be unavailable, because "[l]ike the eleventh amendment, the 'case or controversy' requirement is a subject matter jurisdictional limitation on the power of the federal courts, and federal courts

do not have jurisdiction within the meaning of [28 U.S.C.] section 1447(c) when this requirement is not met." S. Steinglass, supra, at § 24.4(b). See *Maine Ass'n of Independent Neighborhoods v. Commissioner, Maine Dep't of Human Servs.*, 876 F.2d 1051 (1st Cir. 1989) (taking this view); cf. *Int'l Primate Protection League v. Adm'rs of Tulane Educ. Fund*, 111 S. Ct. 1700, 1710 (1991) (suggesting that the Court may take this view).

In *Neighborhoods* and *Primate Protection League*, the requirements of Article III were lacking. But standing doctrine also includes "prudential" limitations on the cases federal courts will hear. For example, "injury in fact" is a constitutional requirement, while the principle that federal courts normally allow persons to assert only their own rights is a "prudential" principle that is sometimes overridden by other considerations. Strictly speaking, these prudential requirements do not go to the jurisdictional power of federal courts. Do cases like this require different treatment when defendants remove them? Consider Professor Steinglass's view:

> The better resolution . . . is to interpret the jurisdictional limitation on removal in section 1447(c) broadly and remand cases that fail to meet prudential limitations on standing. Such an approach is closer to the policy the Court generally follows in treating original and removal jurisdiction the same, and it assures that cases that meet state but not federal justiciability standards can be heard in state courts.

Suppose the removal tactic would work for the defendant. Are there reasons to go ahead in state court anyway? Is it always easy to tell whether federal standards governing ripeness, mootness, and standing have been met? From the defendant's point of view, is there any advantage to remaining in state court despite the possibility of getting the case dismissed in federal court?

11. Is the rule that state courts may employ more liberal justiciability standards than those required of federal courts consistent with Professor Fletcher's position, discussed in note 5 after *Howlett*, that a state court's holding against justiciability is not an adequate state ground for refusing to hear a federal case? Does consistency require that we either accept all of his thesis or none of it, i.e., either that state justiciability law is wholly independent of federal law, or else that, in federal cases like those filed under section 1983, there should be no separate state justiciability law?

II. The Choice Between State and Federal Law

Felder v. Casey

487 U.S. 131 (1988)

Justice **Brennan** delivered the opinion of the Court.

A Wisconsin statute provides that before suit may be brought in state court against a state or local governmental entity or officer, the plaintiff must notify the governmental defendant of the circumstances giving rise to the claim, the amount of the claim, and his or her intent to hold the named defendant liable. The statute further requires that, in order to afford the defendant an opportunity to consider the requested relief, the claimant must refrain from filing suit for 120 days after providing such notice. Failure to comply with these requirements constitutes grounds for dismissal of the action. In the present case, the Supreme Court of Wisconsin held that this notice-of-claim statute applies to federal civil rights actions brought in state court under 42 U.S.C. § 1983. Because we conclude that these requirements are pre-empted as inconsistent with federal law, we reverse.

I

[The case arose out of an altercation between Felder and some Milwaukee police officers on July 4, 1981.] . . . Nine months after the incident, petitioner filed this action in the Milwaukee County Circuit Court against the city of Milwaukee and certain of its police officers, alleging that the beating and arrest were unprovoked and racially motivated, and violated his rights under the Fourth and Fourteenth Amendments to the United States Constitution. He sought redress under 42 U.S.C. § 1983 . . . The officers moved to dismiss the suit based on petitioner's failure to comply with the State's notice-of-claim stat-

ute. That statute provides that no action may be brought or maintained against any state governmental subdivision, agency, or officer unless the claimant either provides written notice of the claim within 120 days of the alleged injury, or demonstrates that the relevant subdivision, agency, or officer had actual notice of the claim and was not prejudiced by the lack of written notice. The statute further provides that the party seeking redress must also submit an itemized statement of the relief sought to the governmental subdivision or agency, which then has 120 days to grant or disallow the requested relief. Finally, claimants must bring suit within six months of receiving notice that their claim has been disallowed.

The trial court granted the officers' motion as to all state-law causes of action but denied the motion as to petitioner's remaining federal claims. The Court of Appeals affirmed on the basis of its earlier decisions holding the notice-of-claim statute inapplicable to federal civil rights actions brought in state court. The Wisconsin Supreme Court, however, reversed. Passing on the question for the first time, the court reasoned that while Congress may establish the procedural framework under which claims are heard in federal courts, States retain the authority under the Constitution to prescribe the rules and procedures that govern actions in their own tribunals. Accordingly, a party who chooses to vindicate a congressionally created right in state court must abide by the State's procedures . . .

We granted certiorari and now reverse.

II

No one disputes the general and unassailable proposition relied upon by the Wisconsin Supreme Court below that States may establish the rules of procedure governing litigation in their own courts. By the same token, however, where state courts entertain a federally created cause of action, the "federal right cannot be defeated by the forms of local practice." *Brown v. Western R. Co. of Alabama*, 338 U.S. 294, 296 (1949). The question before us today, therefore, is essentially one of pre-emption: is the application of the State's notice-of-claim provision to § 1983 actions brought in state courts consistent with the goals of the federal civil rights laws, or does the enforcement of such a requirement instead "'stand as an obstacle to the accomplishment and execution of the full purposes and objectives of Congress'"? Under the Supremacy Clause of the Federal Constitution, "the relative importance to the State of its own law is not material when there is a conflict with a valid federal law," for "any state law, however clearly within a State's acknowledged power, which interferes with or is contrary to federal law, must yield." *Free v. Bland*, 369 U.S. 663, 666 (1962). Because the notice-of-claim statute at issue here conflicts in both its purpose and effects with the remedial objectives of § 1983, and because its enforcement in such actions will frequently and predictably produce different outcomes in § 1983 litigation based solely on whether the claim is asserted in state or federal court, we conclude that the state law is pre-empted when the § 1983 action is brought in a state court.

A

Section 1983 creates a species of liability in favor of persons deprived of their federal civil rights by those wielding state authority. As we have repeatedly emphasized, "the central objective of the Reconstruction-Era civil rights statutes . . . is to ensure that individuals whose federal constitutional or statutory rights are abridged may recover damages or secure injunctive relief." Thus, § 1983 provides "a uniquely federal remedy against incursions . . . upon rights secured by the Constitution and laws of the Nation," and is to be accorded "a sweep as broad as its language."

Any assessment of the applicability of a state law to federal civil rights litigation, therefore, must be made in light of the purpose and nature of the federal right. This is so whether the question of state-law applicability arises in section 1983 litigation brought in state courts, which possess concurrent jurisdiction over such actions, or in federal-court litigation, where, because the federal civil rights laws fail to provide certain rules of decision thought essential to the orderly adjudication of rights, courts are occasionally called upon to borrow state law. Accordingly, we have held that a state law that immunizes government conduct otherwise subject to suit under section 1983 is preempted, even where the federal civil rights litigation takes place in state court, because the application of the

state immunity law would thwart the congressional remedy, see *Martinez v. California*, 444 U.S. 277 (1980) . . .

Although we have never passed on the question, the lower federal courts have all, with but one exception, concluded that notice-of-claim provisions are inapplicable to § 1983 actions brought in federal court. See *Brown v. United States* 239 U.S. App. D.C. 345, 346, n. 6, 742 F.2d 1498, 1509 n. 6 (1984) (en banc) (collecting cases); but see *Cardo v. Lakeland Central School Dist* 592 F.Supp. 765, 772–773 (SDNY 1984). These courts have reasoned that, unlike the lack of statutes of limitations in the federal civil rights laws, the absence of any notice-of-claim provision is not a deficiency requiring the importation of such statutes into the federal civil rights scheme. Because statutes of limitation are among the universally familiar aspects of litigation considered indispensable to any scheme of justice, it is entirely reasonable to assume that Congress did not intend to create a right enforceable in perpetuity. Notice-of-claim provisions, by contrast, are neither universally familiar nor in any sense indispensable prerequisites to litigation, and there is thus no reason to suppose that Congress intended federal courts to apply such rules, which "significantly inhibit the ability to bring federal actions."

While we fully agree with this near-unanimous consensus of the federal courts, that judgment is not dispositive here, where the question is not one of adoption but of preemption. Nevertheless, this determination that notice-of-claim statutes are inapplicable to federal-court § 1983 litigation informs our analysis in two crucial respects. First, it demonstrates that the application of the notice requirement burdens the exercise of the federal right by forcing civil rights victims who seek redress in state courts to comply with a requirement that is entirely absent from civil rights litigation in federal courts. This burden, as we explain below, is inconsistent in both design and effect with the compensatory aims of the federal civil rights laws. Second, it reveals that the enforcement of such statutes in § 1983 actions brought in state court will frequently and predictably produce different outcomes in federal civil rights litigation based solely on whether that litigation takes place in state or federal court. States may not apply such an outcome-determinative law when entertaining substantive federal rights in their courts.

B

. . . Wisconsin's notice-of-claim statute is part of a broader legislative scheme governing the rights of citizens to sue the State's subdivisions. The statute, both in its earliest and current forms, provides a circumscribed waiver of local governmental immunity that limits the amount recoverable in suits against local governments and imposes the notice requirements at issue here . . . The purposes of these conditions, however, mirror those of the judicial immunity the statute replaced. Such statutes "are enacted primarily for the benefit of governmental defendants," and enable those defendants to "investigate early, prepare a stronger case, and perhaps reach an early settlement." Moreover, where the defendant is unable to obtain a satisfactory settlement, the Wisconsin statute forces claimants to bring suit within a relatively short period after the local governing body disallows the claim, in order to "assure prompt initiation of litigation." . . .

In sum, as respondents explain, the State has chosen to expose its subdivisions to large liability and defense costs, and, in light of that choice, has made the concomitant decision to impose conditions that "assist municipalities in controlling those costs." The decision to subject state subdivisions to liability for violations of federal rights, however, was a choice that Congress, not the Wisconsin Legislature, made, and it is a decision that the State has no authority to override. Thus, however understandable or laudable the State's interest in controlling liability expenses might otherwise be, it is patently incompatible with the compensatory goals of the federal legislation, as are the means the State has chosen to effectuate it . . .

This burdening of a federal right, moreover, is not the natural or permissible consequence of an otherwise neutral, uniformly applicable state rule. Although it is true that the notice-of-claim statute does not discriminate between state and federal causes of action against local governments, the fact remains that the law's protection extends only to governmental defendants and thus conditions

the right to bring suit against the very persons and entities Congress intended to subject to liability. We therefore cannot accept the suggestion that this requirement is simply part of "the vast body of procedural rules, rooted in policies unrelated to the definition of any particular substantive cause of action, that forms no essential part of 'the cause of action' as applied to any given plaintiff." On the contrary, the notice-of-claim provision is imposed only upon a specific class of plaintiffs—those who sue governmental defendants—and, as we have seen, is firmly rooted in policies very much related to, and to a large extent directly contrary to, the substantive cause of action provided those plaintiffs. This defendant-specific focus of the notice requirement serves to distinguish it, rather starkly, from rules uniformly applicable to all suits, such as rules governing service of process or substitution of parties, which respondents cite as examples of procedural requirements that penalize noncompliance through dismissal. That state courts will hear the entire § 1983 cause of action once a plaintiff complies with the notice-of-claim statute, therefore, in no way alters the fact that the statute discriminates against the precise type of claim Congress has created . . .

Respondents and their supporting amici urge that we approve the application of the notice-of-claim statute to § 1983 actions brought in state court as a matter of equitable federalism. They note that "'the general rule, bottomed deeply in belief in the importance of state control of state judicial procedure, is that federal law takes the state courts as it finds them.'" Litigants who choose to bring their civil rights actions in state courts presumably do so in order to obtain the benefit of certain procedural advantages in those courts, or to draw their juries from urban populations. Having availed themselves of these benefits, civil rights litigants must comply as well with those state rules they find less to their liking.

However equitable this bitter-with-the-sweet argument may appear in the abstract, it has no place under our Supremacy Clause analysis. Federal law takes state courts as it finds them only insofar as those courts employ rules that do not "impose unnecessary burdens upon rights of recovery authorized by federal laws." States may make the litigation of federal rights as congenial as they see fit—

not as a quid pro quo for compliance with other, uncongenial rules, but because such congeniality does not stand as an obstacle to the accomplishment of Congress' goals. As we have seen, enforcement of the notice-of-claim statute in § 1983 actions brought in state court so interferes with and frustrates the substantive right Congress created that, under the Supremacy Clause, it must yield to the federal interest. This interference, however, is not the only consequence of the statute that renders its application in § 1983 cases invalid. In a State that demands compliance with such a statute before a § 1983 action may be brought or maintained in its courts, the outcome of federal civil rights litigation will frequently and predictably depend on whether it is brought in state or federal court. Thus, the very notions of federalism upon which respondents rely dictate that the State's outcome-determinative law must give way when a party asserts a federal right in state court.

Under *Erie R. Co. v. Tompkins* when a federal court exercises diversity or pendent jurisdiction over state-law claims, "the outcome of the litigation in the federal court should be substantially the same, so far as legal rules determine the outcome of a litigation, as it would be if tried in a State court." *Guaranty Trust Co. v. York*. Accordingly, federal courts entertaining state-law claims against Wisconsin municipalities are obligated to apply the notice-of-claim provision. See *Orthmann v. Apple River Campground, Inc.* Just as federal courts are constitutionally obligated to apply state law to state claims, see *Erie*, so too the Supremacy Clause imposes on state courts a constitutional duty "to proceed in such manner that all the substantial rights of the parties under controlling federal law are protected." Garrett v. Moore-McCormack Co.
. . .

The state notice-of-claim statute is more than a mere rule of procedure: as we discussed above, the statute is a substantive condition on the right to sue governmental officials and entities, and the federal courts have therefore correctly recognized that the notice statute governs the adjudication of state-law claims in diversity actions. In Guaranty Trust, supra, we held that, in order to give effect to a State's statute of limitations, a federal court could not hear a state-law action that a state court would deem time-barred. Conversely, a state court

may not decline to hear an otherwise properly presented federal claim because that claim would be barred under a state law requiring timely filing of notice. State courts simply are not free to vindicate the substantive interests underlying a state rule of decision at the expense of the federal right . . .

[Justice **White's** concurring opinion is omitted.]

Justice **O'Connor**, with whom the **Chief Justice** joins, dissenting.

"A state statute cannot be considered 'inconsistent' with federal law merely because the statute causes the plaintiff to lose the litigation." *Robertson v. Wegmann*. Disregarding this self-evident principle, the Court today holds that Wisconsin's notice of claim statute is pre-empted by federal law as to actions under 42 U.S.C. § 1983 filed in state court. This holding is not supported by the statute whose pre-emptive force it purports to invoke, or by our precedents. Relying only on its own intuitions about "the goals of the federal civil rights laws," the Court fashions a new theory of pre-emption that unnecessarily and improperly suspends a perfectly valid state statute . . .

Wisconsin's notice of claim statute . . . serves at least two important purposes apart from providing municipal defendants with a special affirmative defense in litigation. First, the statute helps ensure that public officials will receive prompt notice of wrongful conditions or practices, and thus enables them to take prompt corrective action. Second, it enables officials to investigate claims in a timely fashion, thereby making it easier to ascertain the facts accurately and to settle meritorious claims without litigation. These important aspects of the Wisconsin statute bring benefits to governments and claimants alike, and it should come as no surprise that 37 other States have apparently adopted similar notice of claim requirements. Without some compellingly clear indication that Congress has forbidden the States to apply such statutes in their own courts, there is no reason to conclude that they are "pre-empted" by federal law. Allusions to such vague concepts as "the compensatory aims of the federal civil rights laws," which are all that the Court actually relies on, do not provide an adequate substitute for the statutory analysis that we customarily require of ourselves before we reach out to find statutory pre-emption of legitimate procedures used by the States in their own courts.

Section 1983, it is worth recalling, creates no substantive law. It merely provides one vehicle by which certain provisions of the Constitution and other federal laws may be judicially enforced. Its purpose, as we have repeatedly said, "'was to interpose the federal courts between the States and the people, as guardians of the people's federal rights.'" . . .

Congress has never given the slightest indication that § 1983 was meant to replace state procedural rules with those that apply in the federal courts. The majority does not, because it cannot, cite any evidence to the contrary . . .

Brown v. Western R. Co. of Alabama which is repeatedly quoted by the majority, does not control the present case. In *Brown*, which arose under the Federal Employers' Liability Act (FELA), this Court refused to accept a state court's interpretation of allegations in a complaint asserting a federal statutory right. Concluding that the state court's interpretation of the complaint operated to "detract from 'substantive rights' granted by Congress in FELA cases," the Court "simply held that under the facts alleged it was error to dismiss the complaint and that the claimant should be allowed to try his case." . . . In the case before us today, by contrast, the statute at issue does not diminish or alter any substantive right cognizable under § 1983. As the majority concedes, the Wisconsin courts "will hear the entire § 1983 cause of action once a plaintiff complies with the notice-of-claim statute."

Unable to find support for its position in § 1983 itself, or in its legislative history, the majority suggests that the Wisconsin statute somehow "discriminates against the federal right." The Wisconsin statute, however, applies to all actions against municipal defendants, whether brought under state or federal law. The majority is therefore compelled to adopt a new theory of discrimination, under which the challenged statute is said to "condition the right to bring suit against the very persons and entities viz., local governments and officials Congress intended to subject to liability." First, the statute erects no barrier at all to a plaintiff's right to bring a § 1983 suit

against anyone. Every plaintiff has the option of proceeding in federal court, and the Wisconsin statute has not the slightest effect on that right. Second, if a plaintiff chooses to proceed in the Wisconsin state courts, those courts stand ready to hear the entire federal cause of action, as the majority concedes. Thus, the Wisconsin statute "discriminates" only against a right that Congress has never created: the right of a plaintiff to have the benefit of selected federal court procedures after the plaintiff has rejected the federal forum and chosen a state forum instead. The majority's "discrimination" theory is just another version of its unsupported conclusion that Congress intended to force the state courts to adopt procedural rules from the federal courts.

The Court also suggests that there is some parallel between this case and cases that are tried in federal court under the doctrine of *Erie R. Co. v. Tompkins*. Quoting the "outcome-determinative" test of *Guaranty Trust Co. v. York*, the Court opines today that state courts hearing federal suits are obliged to mirror federal procedures to the same extent that federal courts are obliged to mirror state procedures in diversity suits. This suggestion seems to be based on a sort of upside-down theory of federalism, which the Court attributes to Congress on the basis of no evidence at all. Nor are the implications of this "reverse-*Erie*" theory quite clear. If the Court means the theory to be taken seriously, it should follow that defendants, as well as plaintiffs, are entitled to the benefit of all federal court procedural rules that are "outcome determinative." If, however, the Court means to create a rule that benefits only plaintiffs, then the discussion of *Erie* principles is simply an unsuccessful effort to find some analogy, no matter how attenuated, to today's unprecedented holding.

"Borrowing" cases under 42 U.S.C. § 1988, which the Court cites several times, have little more to do with today's decision than does *Erie*. Under that statute and those cases, we are sometimes called upon to fill in gaps in federal law by choosing a state procedural rule for application in § 1983 actions brought in federal court. See, e.g., *Wilson v. Garcia*; *Burnett v. Grattan*. The congressionally imposed necessity of supplementing federal law with state procedural rules might well caution us against supplanting state procedural rules with federal gaps, but it certainly offers no support for what the Court does today . . .

As I noted at the outset, the majority correctly characterizes the issue before us as one of statutory pre-emption. In order to arrive at the result it has chosen, however, the Court is forced to search for "inconsistencies" between Wisconsin's notice of claim statute and some ill-defined federal policy that Congress has never articulated, implied, or suggested, let alone enacted. Nor is there any difficulty in explaining the absence of congressional attention to the problem that the Court wrongly imagines it is solving. A plaintiff who chooses to bring a § 1983 action in state court necessarily rejects the federal courts that Congress has provided. Virtually the only conceivable reason for doing so is to benefit from procedural advantages available exclusively in state court. Having voted with their feet for state procedural systems, such plaintiffs would hardly be in a position to ask Congress for a new type of forum that combines the advantages that Congress gave them in the federal system with those that Congress did not give them, and which are only available in state courts . . .

NOTES

1. The first principle to keep in mind in connection with the scope of federal preemption of state law is that state laws that directly conflict with federal law cannot stand. For example, *Martinez v. California*, 444 U.S. 277 (1980), which is discussed in *Felder*, held that a state law immunity doctrine that gave more protection to officials than federal immunity doctrine (see Chapters 7 & 8) may not be applied in state court section 1983 actions.

Under the banner of "tort reform", many states have in recent years enacted statutes that place ceilings or other restrictions on tort damage awards, for example, by limiting the amount of punitive or non-pecuniary damages, or modifying the collateral source rule, or restricting joint and several liability. See Sanders & Joyce, *"Off to the Races": The 1980s Tort Crisis and the Law Reform Process*, 27 Hous. L. Rev. 207, 220–22 (1990) (tabulating tort reform statutes). Do these statutes apply to

section 1983 suits? Can these statutes be distinguished from the state law immunity held inapplicable to section 1983 suits in *Martinez*?

2. Where state law does not conflict directly with federal law, but only interferes with the implementation of the policies behind federal law, the preemption issue is more difficult. See Herman, *Beyond Parity: Section 1983 and the State Courts*, 54 Brooklyn L. Rev. 1057, 1092–1113 (1989), reprinted in Sections 1983 *Civil Rights Anthology* 239 (1993).

Would the Court have found the notice of claim provision unconstitutional if it applied to litigation generally, and not solely to suits against governmental defendants? Would the Court hold inapplicable to section 1983 cases a strict statute of limitations that applied across the board? See *Burnett v. Grattan*, 468 U.S. 42 (1984) (Maryland 6-month statute of limitations for filing any employment discrimination case is too short to serve the remedial purposes of section 1983). *Burnett* was litigated in the federal courts. Would it have come out differently had it been brought in state court?

3. Besides section 1983 itself, at least two lines of doctrine bear on the problem of determining the respective roles of federal and state law on collateral matters that arise in state court section 1983 cases, like the notice of claim issue in *Felder*. One consists of decisions regarding state court enforcement of other federal statutes, such as the Federal Employers' Liability Act, the Jones Act, and the Labor Management Relations Act. The other is the body of law built up in the wake of *Erie v. Tompkins* regarding federal court enforcement of state causes of action under diversity and pendent jurisdiction.

In each of these areas of doctrine, one jurisdiction generates the rights and obligations upon which the plaintiff relies while the courts of another jurisdiction provide a forum where persons may enforce those rights. No one disputes that the generative jurisdiction is in charge of defining the rights and obligations, yet the outcome of a given case may turn on a whole array of collateral issues governing such matters as pleading, proper plaintiffs, discovery, statutes of limitations, preconditions to suit, jury practice, and interlocutory appeals. The problem is to determine which of these should be governed by the law of the forum and which by the source of substantive rights. See Neuborne, *Toward Procedural Parity in Consti-*

tutional Litigation, 22 Wm. & Mary L. Rev. 725, 768–70 (1981).

4. To what extent do rulings in the *Erie* context and earlier federal-law-in-state-courts cases have *precedential* value (as opposed to persuasive value) for section 1983 litigation? How persuasive are they? See *Herman*, supra, at 1104 ("I do not think that the particular results of the FELA or diversity cases may simply be borrowed to resolve debates about choice of law in civil rights cases. The policies underlying the FELA and diversity cases, and the interpretations of the different statutory schemes are distinct and represent a balance of different interests.")

She maintains that "[t]he Congressional intent underlying the FELA is significantly different from the intent of section 1983. Congress was deemed to have contemplated nationwide uniformity as a central aim in enacting the FELA . . . Section 1983, in contrast, is aimed at the misconduct of state officials and, unlike the FELA, deals with intrastate activity." Id. at 1107. In Herman's view, "the analogy to the diversity cases is no more helpful than the analogy to the FELA cases . . ." For example, "[t]he system of statutes applicable in the two contexts is obviously different. With respect to choice of law decisions pertaining to state court, the Rules Enabling Act, the Rules of Decision Act, and even section 1988 do not apply . . ." In addition, "[t]he comity issues that troubled the Court in the *Erie* cases and that would lead to a hesitancy to apply the forum's procedural law cut the other way here." Id. at 1110–11.

5. The opinion in *Felder* indicates, and Professor Herman agrees, that FELA and *Erie* cases may be helpful. The notes that follow consider the application of rulings from both of these areas, as well as *Felder* and other section 1983 cases, to several collateral issues that may arise in state court section 1983 litigation.

(a) *Pleading Requirements*. Under Federal Rule of Civil Procedure 8(a)(2), a complaint is normally sufficient if it contains "a short and plain statement of the claim showing that the pleader is entitled to relief," without setting forth particulars or categorizing the claim in any way. Many state courts have adopted the federal rules, but others oblige plaintiffs to meet more onerous pleading requirements. Professor Neuborne describes New York practice as requiring the plaintiff "to engage in a complex

process of determining whether the claim sounds in common law mandamus . . . or whether the claim states a request for more traditional plenary common law relief." Neuborne, *Toward Procedural Parity in Constitutional Litigation*, 22 Wm & Mary L. Rev. 725, 738 (1981).

Neuborne, says that state courts should be required to follow federal pleading rules in section 1983 cases. Would the Supreme Court agree? *Felder* quotes an *Erie* case, *Guaranty Trust Co. v. York*, 326 U.S. 99, 109 (1945), to the effect that "the outcome of the litigation in the federal court should be substantially the same, so far as legal rules determine the outcome of a litigation, as it would be if tried in a state court." Do pleading rules ever affect the outcome of litigation? Certainly, in that a case might be dismissed for failure to meet the requirements. See *Brown v. Western Ry. of Alabama*, 338 U.S. 294 (1949) (reversing state court dismissal of the complaint for inadequacy); *Int'l. Soc'y for Krishna Consciousness v. City of Evanston*, 89 Ill. App. 3d 701, 411 N.E.2d 1030 (1980) (encouraging trial judges to dismiss complaints that do not meet state pleading requirements). See also S. Steinglass, *Section 1983 Litigation in State Courts* § 12.3(b).

At other places in the *Felder* opinion, the Court states that Wisconsin's notice of claim rule is objectionable because "it will frequently and predictably produce different outcomes in section 1983 litigation based solely on whether the claim is asserted in federal or state court." 487 U.S. at 139. See also 487 U.S. at 141, 151. Will a requirement that litigants meet state pleading requirements "frequently and predictably" lead to different outcomes depending on whether the case is brought in federal or state court?

Is *Felder* best read as adopting the "outcome determinative" test of *Guaranty Trust*, or does it mean that only rules that "frequently and predictably" produce different outcomes will be preempted? Notice that in the *Erie* context the rule of *Guaranty Trust* was criticized as overly rigid and was later modified. See, e.g., *Hanna v. Plumer*, 380 U.S. 460 (1965) (federal service of process rules apply in diversity cases even though they may affect the outcome).

Leatherman v. Tarrant Co. Narcotics Intelligence and Coordination Unit, 113 S. Ct. 1160

(1993) rejected the practice of some federal courts of applying heightened pleading requirements to section 1983 cases asserting claims against municipal defendants, in an effort to determine at an early stage whether the plaintiff could make out a credible "policy or custom" claim. The Court said: "Perhaps if Rules 8 and 9 were rewritten today claims against municipalities under section 1983 might be subjected to [an] added specificity requirement . . . But this is a result which must be obtained by the process of amending the Federal Rules, and not by interpretation. In the absence of such an amendment, federal courts and litigants must rely on summary judgment and control of discovery to weed out unmeritorious claims sooner rather than later." 113 S. Ct. at 1163.

Does this reasoning suggest that state as well as federal courts must allow notice pleading?

In *Brown*, supra, the Court reversed a state court's dismissal of an FELA complaint that alleged that the plaintiff stepped on a "clinker" in the railroad yards, but did not specifically allege the act of negligence complained of. The Court declared that "[s]trict local rules of pleading cannot be used to impose unnecessary burdens upon rights of recovery authorized by federal laws . . . Should this Court fail to protect federally created rights from dismissal because of over-exacting local requirements for meticulous pleadings, desirable uniformity in adjudication of federally created rights could not be achieved." 338 U.S. at 298–99.

Does it follow that state rules requiring fact pleading must give way in section 1983 cases? Compare Neuborne, supra (yes) with S. Steinglass, supra (no).

Professor Neuborne complains that arcane state pleading requirements discourage plaintiffs' lawyers unfamiliar with state procedure from filing section 1983 cases in state courts. Is that a good reason for requiring state courts to change their ways?

Professor Steinglass recognizes the differences between federal and state pleading rules but thinks that "few cases actually turn on issues of pleading," because "when issues are actually tried on theories actionable under section 1983, plaintiffs can usually amend their complaints to conform to the evidence." S. Steinglass, supra, at pp. 12–15.

(b) *Class Actions*. Many state procedural systems place significant restrictions on the use of class actions. See S. Steinglass, supra, § 8.8. Should plaintiffs with section 1983 claims be bound by those limits, or should Federal Rule 23(b) and federal principles governing class actions apply to state court section 1983 claims? In answering this question, the analytical framework of *Felder*, with its emphasis on whether the state rule will frequently and predictably affect outcomes, may be inapposite. Perhaps the focus should be on whether the broad availability of class actions in state courts is necessary to achieve the purposes of section 1983? Consider Professor Neuborne's analysis:

> Traditional cross-forum collateral rule analysis has required the forum jurisdiction to apply the collateral rules of the generative jurisdiction in defining the class of eligible plaintiffs. [He then qualifies this generalization, citing *Robertson v. Wegmann*, 436 U.S. 584 (1978) (discussed in Chapter 9) as an exception to it. In *Robertson*,] the plaintiff's death was unrelated to the defendants' acts, [so that] the survivorship rule was wholly unconnected to the policies underlying section 1983. The issue, therefore, in the context of section 1983 litigation in state court is whether the collateral rules governing the ability of a class of plaintiffs to enforce section 1983 is linked to the policies underlying section 1983 . . . or is wholly divorced from them as in *Robertson*.

Neuborne, supra, at 783. In Neuborne's view,

> the potential for class action relief should exercise substantial deterrent effect on persons contemplating activity at the margins of constitutional protection . . . Since the availability of a class action will not merely affect, but will actually control, much preincident behavior by placing direct restraints on an official's freedom of action, and since members of the typical section 1983 class are unlikely to be in a position to assert their rights individually, the availability of class relief is no less integral to the policies underlying section 1983 than the power to award attorney's fees and the ability to define immunity from suit. Accordingly, its availability

should similarly be governed by uniformly applicable federal rules.

Id. at 783–84. Do you agree? What arguments might be advanced against Neuborne's view? Is it relevant that Congress has nowhere expressed any intent to require state courts to undertake the arduous tasks associated with managing class actions?

(c) *Discovery.* State courts often follow less liberal discovery policies than federal courts do. See R. Figg, R. McCullough & J. Underwood, *Civil Trial Manual* 76–78 (1977). Professor Steinglass reports that, with some exceptions, "state courts . . . have assumed that issues involving the scope of discovery, including the applicable privileges, are matters of state law, even when state courts are entertaining section 1983 or other federal causes of action." In *Denari v. Superior Court,* 215 Cal. App. 3d 1488, 264 Cal. Rptr. 261 (1989) for example, the California Court of Appeal applied an evidentiary privilege under state law to deny a discovery request for the names of persons arrested and booked at a county jail, made by a section 1983 plaintiff seeking potential witnesses. The plaintiff had proposed testing the claim of privilege under a federal balancing test. This case, the court held, was not like *Felder:*

> The recognition of the right to privacy of all citizens of the state, along with the concomitant protection of such right in the context of civil discovery, is certainly not antagonistic to the remedial objectives of section 1983; the effect of such right does not necessarily conflict with the objectives of the civil rights tort . . . Unlike the [notice of claim statute at issue in *Felder*] our qualified protection of a privacy right does not play a conclusive role in defining the outcome of the cause of action . . . This is not to say that in a particular case the results might not differ depending upon the forum, only that the rule itself is not outcome determinative with respect to the litigation in general . . . Finally, the *Felder* Court considered whether the rule was "a neutral and uniformly applicable rule of procedure." Here, of course, the limits on discovery pursuant to the right of privacy apply in

both civil and criminal cases and are equally applicable to all parties.

215 Cal. App. 3d at 1499, 1501–02.

Does the court successfully distinguish *Felder*? Is it relevant that the evidentiary privilege it relies on is aimed at protecting the privacy of arrestees rather than, as in *Felder*, shielding the government from onerous liability? Would a state discovery rule absolutely privileging official documents pass muster?

(d) *Interlocutory appeals.* As discussed in Chapter 8, when a defendant seeks and is denied official immunity in section 1983 cases on summary judgment or in a motion to dismiss the complaint, the order is immediately appealable. *Mitchell v. Forsyth,* 472 U.S. 511 (1985). Some state courts have refused to allow interlocutory appeals of immunity denials. See S. Steinglass, supra, at § 8.11(b)(1).

Must state courts follow *Forsyth,* or may they apply their normal appellate practice to denials of immunity? Does the refusal to allow interlocutory appeals "frequently and predictably" alter the outcome of litigation, under the standard set forth in *Felder*?

In *Felder* the Court said that "[s]tates may make the litigation of federal claims as congenial as they see fit . . . because such congeniality does not stand as an obstacle to the accomplishment of Congress' goals." 487 U.S. at 151. Isn't a rule refusing interlocutory appeal more "congenial" to the federal claim than the rule in *Forsyth,* since it avoids costly delays in getting to the merits?

Is it relevant that the *Forsyth* Court characterized official immunity as "an entitlement not to stand trial or face the other burdens of litigation," not merely a defense to liability. 472 U.S. at 526. Does this mean that section 1983 grants rights to a state court defendant seeking an interlocutory appeal, and that contrary state appellate practice is not sufficiently "congenial" to those rights?

6. *Patsy v. Florida Bd. of Regents,* 457 U.S. 496 (1982) held that, absent special circumstances, litigants may file section 1983 suits in federal court without first exhausting state administrative remedies. See Chapter 10. In *Felder* the Court extended this rule to section 1983 actions filed in state courts.

> [T]he notice provision imposes an exhaustion requirement on persons who

choose to assert their federal right in state courts, inasmuch as the section 1983 plaintiff must provide the requisite notice of injury within 120 days of the civil rights violation, then wait an additional 120 days while the governmental defendant investigates the claim and attempts to settle it . . . Although it is true that the principal remedy Congress chose to provide injured persons was immediate access to *federal* courts, it did not leave the protection of such rights exclusively in the hands of the federal judiciary, and instead conferred concurrent jurisdiction on the state courts as well. Given the evil at which the federal civil rights legislation was aimed, there is simply no reason to suppose that Congress meant "to provide these individuals immediate access to the federal courts notwithstanding any provision of state law to the contrary," yet contemplated that those who sought to vindicate their federal rights in state courts could be required to seek remedies in the first instance from the very state officials whose hostility to those rights precipitated their injuries.

487 U.S. at 146–47.

CHAPTER TWELVE

Attorney's Fees

The award of attorney's fees in section 1983 litigation is a recent development of extraordinary importance. Under what is known as the "American Rule", attorney's fees generally are not awarded to the prevailing party in civil litigation in the absence of a specific authorizing statute. In *Alyeska Pipeline Service Co. v. Wilderness Society*, 421 U.S. 240 (1975), the Supreme Court reaffirmed the "American Rule" and disapproved lower court awards of attorney's fees to successful civil rights plaintiffs under principles of equity. Congress responded to *Alyeska Pipeline Service* with the enactment of The Civil Rights Attorney's Fees Award Act of 1976, 42 U.S.C. § 1988(b), which provides in pertinent part:

> In any action or proceeding to enforce a provision of sections 1981, 1982, 1983, 1985, and 1986 of this title, title IX of Public Law 92–318 [20 U.S.C. §§ 1681–1688], or title VI of the Civil Rights Act of 1964 [42 U.S.C. §§ 2000d–2000d–4], the court, in its discretion, may allow the prevailing party, other than the United States, a reasonable attorney's fee as part of the costs.

This chapter explores the contours of this relatively brief statute. It addresses three basic questions: When is a party entitled to attorney's fees? How does a court determine what is a "reasonable" fee? And what are the strategic and ethical implications of a potential fee award?

Two points should be made at the outset. First, there are dozens of federal fee shifting statutes that resemble section 1988(b). As a result, judicial constructions of other attorney's fee legislation often provides guidance in interpreting section 1988. E.g., *City of Burlington v. Dague*, 112 S. Ct. 2638, 2641 (1992) (method of calculating a "reasonable fee" under the fee shifting provisions of the Solid Waste Disposal Act, 42 U.S.C. § 7002(e) and the Clean Water Act, 33 U.S.C. § 1365(d) also applies to section 1988). Second, because of the statutory foundation of attorney's fee awards in constitutional tort litigation, court decisions often refer to legislative history and Congressional intent in addressing issues concerning the availability and computation of fees. Before turning to specific cases, consider the Senate Report that accompanied the Civil Rights Attorney's Fees Awards Act of 1976.

I. Legislative History

The Civil Rights Attorney's Fees Awards Act of 1976

Senate Report No. 94–1011

* * *

Statement

The purpose and effect of S. 2278 are simple—it is designed to allow courts to provide the familiar remedy of reasonable counsel fees to prevailing parties in suits to enforce the civil rights acts which Congress has passed since 1866. S. 2278 follows the language of Titles II and VII of the Civil Rights Act of 1964, 42 U.S.C. §§ 2000a–3(b) and 2000e–5(k), and section 402 of the Voting Rights Act Amendments of 1975, 42 U.S.C. § 1973(e). All of these civil rights law depend heavily upon private enforcement, and fee awards have proved an essential remedy if private citizens are to have a meaningful opportunity to vindicate the important Congressional policies which these laws contain.

In many cases arising under our civil rights laws, the citizen who must sue to enforce the law has little or no money with which to hire a lawyer. If private citizens are to be able to assert their civil rights, and if those who violate the Nation's fundamental laws are not to proceed with impunity, then citizens must have the opportunity to recover what it costs them to vindicate these rights in court.

Congress recognized this need when it made specific provision for such fee shifting in Titles II and VII of the Civil Rights Act of 1964:

> When a plaintiff brings an action under [Title II] he cannot recover damages. If he obtains an injunction, he does so not for himself alone but also as a "private attorney general," vindicating a policy that Congress considered of the highest priority. If successful plaintiffs were routinely forced to bear their own attorneys' fees, few aggrieved parties would be in a position to advance the public interest by invoking the injunctive powers of the Federal courts. Congress therefore enacted the provision for counsel fees—* * * to encourage individuals injured by racial discrimination to seek judicial relief under Title II." *Newman v. Piggie Park Enterprises, Inc.*, 390 U.S. 400, 402 (1968).

The idea of the "private attorney general" is not a new one, nor are attorneys' fees a new remedy. Congress has commonly authorized attorneys' fees in laws under which "private attorneys general" play a significant role in enforcing our policies. We have, since 1870, authorized fee shifting under more than 50 laws. . . .

The remedy of attorneys' fees has always been recognized as particularly appropriate in the civil rights area, and civil rights and attorneys' fees have always been closely interwoven. In the civil rights area, Congress has instructed the courts to use the broadest and most effective remedies available to achieve the goals of our civil rights laws. The very first attorneys' fee statute was a civil rights law, . . . which provided for attorneys' fees in three separate provisions protecting voting rights.

Modern civil rights legislation reflects a heavy reliance on attorneys' fees as well. In 1964, seeking to assure full compliance with the Civil Rights Act of that year, we authorized fee shifting for private suits establishing violations of the public accommodations and equal employment provisions. 42 U.S. C. §§ 2000a–3(b) and 2000e–5(k). Since 1964, every major civil rights law passed by the Congress has included, or has been amended to include, one or more fee provisions. . . .

These fee shifting provisions have been successful in enabling vigorous enforcement of modern civil rights legislation, while at the same time limiting the growth of the enforcement bureaucracy. Before May 12, 1975, when the Supreme Court handed down its decision in *Alyeska Pipeline Service Co. v. Wilderness Society*, 421 U.S. 240 (1975), many lower Federal courts throughout the Nation had drawn the obvious analogy between the Reconstruction Civil Rights Acts and these modern civil rights acts, and, following Congressional recognition in the newer statutes of the "private attorney general" concept, were exercising their traditional equity powers to award attorneys' fees under early civil rights laws as well.

These pre-*Alyeska* decisions remedied a gap in the specific statutory provisions and restored an important historic remedy for civil rights violations. However, in *Alyeska*, the United States Supreme Court, while referring to the desirability of fees in a variety of circumstances, ruled that only Congress, and not the courts, could specify which laws were important enough to merit fee shifting under the "private attorney general" theory. The Court expressed the view, in dictum, that the Reconstruction Acts did not contain the necessary congressional authorization. This decision and dictum created anomalous gaps in our civil rights laws whereby awards of fees are, according to *Alyeska*, suddenly unavailable in the most fundamental civil rights cases. For instance, fees are authorized in an employment discrimination suit under Title VII of the 1964 Civil Rights Act, but not in the same suit brought under 42 U.S.C. § 1981, which protects similar rights but involves fewer technical prerequisites to the filing of an action. Fees are allowed in a housing discrimination suit brought under Title VIII of the Civil Rights Act of 1968, but not in the same suit brought under 42 U.S.C. § 1982, a Reconstruction Act protecting the same rights. Likewise, fees are allowed in a suit under Title II of the 1964 Civil Rights Act challenging discrimination in a private restaurant, but not in suits under 42 U.S.C. § 1983 redressing violations of the Federal Constitution or laws by officials sworn to uphold the laws.

This bill, S. 2278, is an appropriate response to the *Alyeska* decision. It is limited to cases arising under our civil rights laws, a category of cases in which attorneys fees have been traditionally regarded as appropriate. It remedies gaps in the language of these civil rights laws by providing the specific authorization required by the Court in *Alyeska*, and makes our civil rights laws consistent.

It is intended that the standards for awarding fees be generally the same as under the fee provisions of the 1964 Civil Rights Act. A party seeking to enforce the rights protected by the statutes covered by S. 2278, if successful, "should ordinarily recover an attorney's fee unless special circumstances would render such an award unjust." *Newman v. Piggie Park Enterprises, Inc.*, 390 U.S. 400, 402 (1968). Such "private attorneys general" should not be deterred from bringing good faith actions to vindicate the fundamental rights here involved by the prospect of having to pay their opponent's counsel fees should they lose. . . . This bill thus deters frivolous suits by authorizing an award of attorneys' fees against a party shown to have litigated in "bad faith" under the guise of attempting to enforce the Federal rights created by the statutes listed in S. 2278. Similar standards have been followed not only in the Civil Rights Act of 1964, but in other statutes providing for attorneys' fees. . . .

In appropriate circumstances, counsel fees under S. 2278 may be awarded pendente lite. Such awards are especially appropriate where a party has prevailed on an important matter in the course of litigation, even when he ultimately does not prevail on all issues. . . . Moreover, for purposes of the award of counsel fees, parties may be considered to have prevailed when they vindicate rights through a consent judgment or without formally obtaining relief.

. . . It is intended that the amount of fees awarded under S. 2278 be governed by the same standards which prevail in other types of equally complex Federal litigation, such as antitrust cases and not be reduced because the rights involved may be nonpecuniary in nature. The appropriate standards, see *Johnson v. Georgia Highway Express*, 488 F.2d 714 (5th Cir. 1974),[*] are correctly applied in

[district court] cases . . . [that] have resulted in fees which are adequate to attract competent counsel, but which do not produce windfalls to attorneys. In computing the fee, counsel for prevailing parties should be paid, as is traditional with attorneys compensated by a fee-paying client, "for all time reasonably expended on a matter."

This bill creates no startling new remedy—it only meets the technical requirements that the Supreme Court has laid down if the Federal Courts are to continue the practice of awarding attorneys' fees which had been going on for years prior to the Court's May decision. It does not change the statutory provisions regarding the protection of civil rights except as it provides the fee awards which are necessary if citizens are to be able to effectively secure compliance with these existing statutes. There are very few provisions in our Federal laws which are self-executing. Enforcement of the laws depends on governmental action and, in some cases, on private action through the courts. If the cost of private enforcement actions becomes too great, there will be no private enforcement. If our civil rights laws are not to become mere hollow pronouncements which the average citizen cannot enforce, we must maintain the traditionally effective remedy of fee shifting in these cases.

* * *

properly; (4) the preclusion of employment by the attorney due to acceptance of the case; (5) the customary fee; (6) whether the fee is fixed or contingent; (7) time limitations imposed by the client or the circumstances; (8) the amount involved and the results obtained; (9) the experience, reputation, and ability of the attorneys; (10) the "undesirability" of the case; (11) the nature and length of the professional relationship with the client; and (12) awards in similar cases.

NOTES

1. Suppose a jury finds that a government official deprived the plaintiff of liberty and property without due process, but that this constitutional violation was not the proximate cause of any pecuniary harm. Can the plaintiff be considered a "prevailing party" under section 1988? Should the trial court award the plaintiff attorney's fees in such a case? If so, what is a "reasonable" fee? How much guid-

---

[*] [editors' note]. *Johnson* listed 12 factors relevant in determining a fee award: (1) the time and labor required; (2) the novelty and difficulty of the questions; (3) the skill requisite to perform the legal service

ance does Senate Report No. 94–1011 provide in resolving these questions?

2. What standards did Congress intend to govern the determination of the amount of a "reasonable" fee? Would the amount of a fee calculated by a contingency formula be relevant to the determination of a "reasonable" fee under section 1988? Can plaintiff's attorneys enter into contingency fee contracts with their clients in civil rights cases? How much guidance does Senate Report No. 94–1011 provide in resolving these questions?

II. When Is a Party Entitled to Attorney's Fees Under 42 U.S.C. § 1988?

Farrar v. Hobby

113 S. Ct. 566 (1992)

Justice **Thomas** delivered the opinion of the Court.

We decide today whether a civil rights plaintiff who receives a nominal damages award is a "prevailing party" eligible to receive attorney's fees under 42 U.S.C. § 1988. The Court of Appeals for the Fifth Circuit reversed an award of attorney's fees on the ground that a plaintiff receiving only nominal damages is not a prevailing party. Although we hold that such a plaintiff is a prevailing party, we affirm the denial of fees in this case.

I

. . .

[Joseph Farrar filed suit under § 1983 against the then-Lieutenant Governor of Texas, William Hobby, and others alleging that they deprived him of his liberty and property without due process through malicious prosecution aimed at closing a school he owned and operated. Prior to trial, Farrar dropped his claim for injunctive relief and increased the request for damages to $17 million.]

The case was tried before a jury in the Southern District of Texas on August 15, 1983. Through special interrogatories, the jury found that all of the defendants except Hobby had conspired against the plaintiffs but that

this conspiracy was not a proximate cause of any injury suffered by the plaintiffs. The jury also found that Hobby had "committed an act or acts under color of state law that deprived Plaintiff Joseph Davis Farrar of a civil right," but it found that Hobby's conduct was not "a proximate cause of any damages" suffered by Joseph Farrar. . . In accordance with the jury's answers to the special interrogatories, the District Court ordered that "Plaintiffs take nothing, that the action be dismissed on the merits, and that the parties bear their own costs."

The Court of Appeals . . . affirmed the failure to award compensatory or nominal damages against the conspirators because the plaintiffs had not proved an actual deprivation of a constitutional right. Because the jury found that Hobby had deprived Joseph Farrar of a civil right, however, the Fifth Circuit remanded for entry of judgment against Hobby for nominal damages.

The plaintiffs then sought attorney's fees under 42 U.S.C. § 1988. On January 30, 1987, the District Court entered an order awarding the plaintiffs $280,000 in fees, $27,932 in expenses, and $9,730 in prejudgment interest against Hobby. The court denied Hobby's motion to reconsider the fee award on August 31, 1990.

A divided Fifth Circuit panel reversed the fee award. . . . [T]he majority held that the plaintiffs were not prevailing parties and were therefore ineligible for fees under § 1988. . . .

II

. . .

[In enacting the Civil Rights Attorney's Fees Award Act of 1976, 42 U.S.C. § 1988(b)], "Congress intended to permit the . . . award of counsel fees only when a party has prevailed on the merits." Therefore, in order to qualify for attorney's fees under § 1988, a plaintiff must be a "prevailing party." Under our "generous formulation" of the term, "'plaintiffs may be considered "prevailing parties" for attorney's fees purposes if they succeed on any significant issue in litigation which achieves some of the benefit the parties sought in bringing suit.'" "[L]iability on the merits and responsibility for fees go hand in hand; where a defendant has not been prevailed against, either because of legal immunity or on the merits, § 1988 does not authorize a fee award against that defendant." *Kentucky v. Graham.*

We have elaborated on the definition of prevailing party in three recent cases. In *Hewitt v. Helms* we addressed "the peculiar-sounding question whether a party who litigates to judgment and loses on all of his claims can nonetheless be a 'prevailing party.'" Id. In his § 1983 action against state prison officials for alleged due process violations, respondent Helms obtained no relief. "The most that he obtained was an interlocutory ruling that his complaint should not have been dismissed for failure to state a constitutional claim." Id. Observing that "respect for ordinary language requires that a plaintiff receive at least some relief on the merits of his claim before he can be said to prevail," we held that Helms was not a prevailing party. Ibid. We required the plaintiff to prove "the settling of some dispute which affects the behavior of the defendant towards the plaintiff." Id.

In *Rhodes v. Stewart* (per curiam), we reversed an award of attorney's fees premised solely on a declaratory judgment that prison officials had violated the plaintiffs' First and Fourteenth Amendment rights. By the time the District Court entered judgment, "one of the plaintiffs had died and the other was no longer in custody." Id. Under these circumstances, we held, neither plaintiff was a prevailing party. We explained that "nothing in [*Hewitt*] suggested that the entry of [a declaratory] judgment in a party's favor automatically renders that party prevailing under § 1988." Id. We reaffirmed that a judgment—declaratory or otherwise—"will constitute relief, for purposes of § 1988, if, and only if, it affects the behavior of the defendant toward the plaintiff." Id. Whatever "modification of prison policies" the declaratory judgment might have effected "could not in any way have benefited either plaintiff, one of whom was dead and the other released." Ibid.

Finally, in *Texas State Teachers Assn. v. Garland Independent School Dist.*, we synthesized the teachings of *Hewitt* and *Rhodes*. "To be considered a prevailing party within the meaning of § 1988," we held, "the plaintiff must be able to point to a resolution of the dispute which changes the legal relationship between itself and the defendant." We reemphasized that "the touchstone of the prevailing party inquiry must be the material alteration of the legal relationship of the parties." Id. Under this test, the plaintiffs in *Garland* were prevailing parties because they "obtained a judgment vindicating [their] First Amendment rights [as] public employees" and "materially altered the [defendant] school district's policy limiting the rights of teachers to communicate with each other concerning employee organizations and union activities." Id.

Therefore, to qualify as a prevailing party, a civil rights plaintiff must obtain at least some relief on the merits of his claim. The plaintiff must obtain an enforceable judgment against the defendant from whom fees are sought, or comparable relief through a consent decree or settlement. Whatever relief the plaintiff secures must directly benefit him at the time of the judgment or settlement. Otherwise the judgment or settlement cannot be said to "affec[t] the behavior of the defendant toward the plaintiff." *Rhodes.* Only under these circumstances can civil rights litigation effect "the material alteration of the legal relationship of the parties" and thereby transform the plaintiff into a prevailing party. *Garland.* In short, a plaintiff "prevails" when actual relief on the merits of his claim materially alters the legal relationship between the parties by modifying the defendant's behavior in a way that directly benefits the plaintiff.

III

A

Doubtless "the basic purpose of a § 1983 damages award should be to compensate persons for injuries caused by the deprivation of constitutional rights." *Carey v. Piphus.* For this reason, no compensatory damages may be awarded in a § 1983 suit absent proof of actual injury. We have also held, however, that "the denial of procedural due process should be actionable for nominal damages without proof of actual injury." *Carey.* The awarding of nominal damages for the "absolute" right to procedural due process "recognizes the importance to organized society that [this] righ[t] be scrupulously observed" while "remain[ing] true to the principle that substantial damages should be awarded only to compensate actual injury." Thus, *Carey* obligates a court to award nominal damages when a plaintiff establishes the violation of his right to procedural due process but cannot prove actual injury.

We therefore hold that a plaintiff who wins nominal damages is a prevailing party under § 1988. When a court awards nominal damages, it neither enters judgment for defendant on the merits nor declares the defendant's legal immunity to suit. To be sure, a judicial pronouncement that the defendant has violated the Constitution, unaccompanied by an enforceable judgment on the merits, does not render the plaintiff a prevailing party. Of itself, "the moral satisfaction [that] results from any favorable statement of law" cannot bestow prevailing party status. *Hewitt.* No material alteration of the legal relationship between the parties occurs until the plaintiff becomes entitled to enforce a judgment, consent decree, or settlement against the defendant. A plaintiff may demand payment for nominal damages no less than he may demand payment for millions of dollars in compensatory damages. A judgment for damages in any amount, whether compensatory or nominal, modifies the defendant's behavior for the plaintiff's benefit by forcing the defendant to pay an amount of money he otherwise would not pay. As a result, the Court of Appeals for the Fifth Circuit erred in holding that petitioners' nominal damages award failed to render them prevailing parties.

. . .

[W]e hold that the prevailing party inquiry does not turn on the magnitude of the relief obtained. We recognized as much in *Garland* when we noted that "the *degree* of the plaintiff's success" does not affect "eligibility for a fee award."

B

Although the "technical" nature of a nominal damages award or any other judgment does not affect the prevailing party inquiry, it does bear on the propriety of fees awarded under § 1988. Once civil rights litigation materially alters the legal relationship between the parties, "the degree of the plaintiff's overall success goes to the reasonableness" of a fee award under *Hensley v. Eckerhart.* Indeed, "the most critical factor" in determining the reasonableness of a fee award "is the degree of success obtained." In this case, petitioners received nominal damages instead of the $17 million in compensatory damages that they

sought. This litigation accomplished little beyond giving petitioners "the moral satisfaction of knowing that a federal court concluded that [their] rights had been violated" in some unspecified way. We have already observed that if "a plaintiff has achieved only partial or limited success, the product of hours reasonably expended on the litigation as a whole times a reasonable hourly rate may be an excessive amount." Yet the District Court calculated petitioners' fee award in precisely this fashion, without engaging in any measured exercise of discretion. . . .

In some circumstances, even a plaintiff who formally "prevails" under § 1988 should receive no attorney's fees at all. A plaintiff who seeks compensatory damages but receives no more than nominal damages is often such a prevailing party. As we have held, a nominal damages award does render a plaintiff a prevailing party by allowing him to vindicate his "absolute" right to procedural due process through enforcement of a judgment against the defendant. In a civil rights suit for damages, however, the awarding of nominal damages also highlights the plaintiff's failure to prove actual, compensable injury. Whatever the constitutional basis for substantive liability, damages awarded in a § 1983 action "must always be designed 'to compensate injuries caused by the [constitutional] deprivation.'" *Memphis Community School Dist. v. Stachura* (quoting *Carey*) (emphasis and brackets in original). When a plaintiff recovers only nominal damages because of his failure to prove an essential element of his claim for monetary relief, the only reasonable fee is usually no fee at all. In an apparent failure to heed our admonition that fee awards under § 1988 were never intended to "'produce windfalls to attorneys,'" the District Court awarded $280,000 in attorney's fees without "consider[ing] the relationship between the extent of success and the amount of the fee award."

Although the Court of Appeals erred in failing to recognize that petitioners were prevailing parties, it correctly reversed the District Court's fee award. We accordingly affirm the judgment of the Court of Appeals.

So ordered.

Justice **O'Connor**, concurring.

If ever there was a plaintiff who deserved no attorney's fees at all, that plaintiff is Joseph

Farrar. He filed a lawsuit demanding 17 million dollars from six defendants. After 10 years of litigation and two trips to the Court of Appeals, he got one dollar from one defendant. As the Court holds today, that is simply not the type of victory that merits an award of attorney's fees.

. . .

I

Congress has authorized the federal courts to award "a reasonable attorney's fee" in certain civil rights cases, but only to "the prevailing party." 42 U.S.C. § 1988. To become a prevailing party, a plaintiff must obtain, at an absolute minimum, "actual relief on the merits of [the] claim," which "affects the behavior of the defendant towards the plaintiff," . . . Joseph Farrar met that minimum condition for prevailing party status. Through this lawsuit, he obtained an enforceable judgment for one dollar in nominal damages. One dollar is not exactly a bonanza, but it constitutes relief on the merits. And it affects the defendant's behavior toward the plaintiff, if only by forcing him to pay one dollar—something he would not otherwise have done.

Nonetheless, *Garland* explicitly states that an enforceable judgment alone is not always enough: "Beyond th[e] absolute limitation [of some relief on the merits], a technical victory may be so insignificant . . . as to be insufficient" to support an award of attorney's fees. While *Garland* may be read as indicating that this de minimis or technical victory exclusion is a second barrier to prevailing party status, the Court makes clear today that, in fact, it is part of the determination of what constitutes a reasonable fee. . . . And even if the exclusion's location is debatable, its effect is not: When the plaintiff's success is purely technical or de minimis, no fees can be awarded. Such a plaintiff either has failed to achieve victory at all, or has obtained only a pyrrhic victory for which the reasonable fee is zero. The Court's opinion today and its unanimous opinion in *Garland* are thus in accord. . . .

Consequently, the Court properly holds that, when a plaintiff's victory is purely technical or de minimis, a district court need not go through the usual complexities involved in calculating attorney's fees. . . . As a matter of common sense and sound judicial adminis-

tration, it would be wasteful indeed to require that courts laboriously and mechanically go through those steps when the de minimis nature of the victory makes the proper fee immediately obvious. Instead, it is enough for a court to explain why the victory is de minimis and announce a sensible decision to "award low fees or no fees" at all.

. . .

[In enacting § 1988(b), Congress intended] to restore the former equitable practice of awarding attorney's fees to the prevailing party in certain civil rights cases, a practice this Court had disapproved in *Alyeska Pipeline Services Co. v. Wilderness Society* . . . . That practice included the denial of fees to plaintiffs who, although technically prevailing parties, had achieved only de minimis success. . . .

Indeed, § 1988 contemplates the denial of fees to de minimis victors through yet another mechanism. The statute only authorizes courts to award fees "as part of the costs." 42 U.S.C. § 1988. As a result, when a court denies costs, it must deny fees as well; if there are no costs, there is nothing for the fees to be awarded "as part of." And when Congress enacted § 1988, the courts would deny even a prevailing party costs under Federal Rule of Civil Procedure 54(d) where the victory was purely technical. . . . Just as a pyrrhic victor would be denied costs under Rule 54(d), so too should it be denied fees under § 1988.

II

In the context of this litigation, the technical or de minimis nature of Joseph Farrar's victory is readily apparent: He asked for a bundle and got a pittance. While we hold today that this pittance is enough to render him a prevailing party, it does not by itself prevent his victory from being purely technical. . . . That is not to say that all nominal damages awards are de minimis. Nominal relief does not necessarily a nominal victory make. But, as in pre-Alyeska and Rule 54(d) practice, a substantial difference between the judgment recovered and the recovery sought suggests that the victory is in fact purely technical. . . . Here that suggestion is quite strong. Joseph Farrar asked for 17 million dollars; he got one. It is hard to envision a more dramatic difference.

The difference between the amount recovered and the damages sought is not the only consideration, however. *Carey v. Piphus* makes clear that an award of nominal damages can represent a victory in the sense of vindicating rights even though no actual damages are proved. Accordingly, the courts also must look to other factors. One is the significance of the legal issue on which the plaintiff claims to have prevailed. Petitioners correctly point out that Joseph Farrar in a sense succeeded on a significant issue—liability. But even on that issue he cannot be said to have achieved a true victory. Respondent was just one of six defendants and the only one not found to have engaged in a conspiracy. If recovering one dollar from the least culpable defendant and nothing from the rest legitimately can be labeled a victory—and I doubt that it can—surely it is a hollow one. Joseph Farrar may have won a point, but the game, set, and match all went to the defendants.

Given that Joseph Farrar got some of what he wanted—one seventeen millionth, to be precise—his success might be considered material if it also accomplished some public goal other than occupying the time and energy of counsel, court, and client. . . . Yet one searches these facts in vain for the public purpose this litigation might have served. The District Court speculated that the judgment, if accompanied by a large fee award, might deter future lawless conduct, but did not identify the kind of lawless conduct that might be prevented. Nor is the conduct to be deterred apparent from the verdict, which even petitioners acknowledge is "regrettably obtuse." Such a judgment cannot deter misconduct any more than a bolt of lightning can; its results might be devastating, but it teaches no valuable lesson because it carries no discernable meaning. . . .

III

In this case, the relevant indicia of success—the extent of relief, the significance of the legal issue on which the plaintiff prevailed, and the public purpose served—all point to a single conclusion: Joseph Farrar achieved only a de minimis victory. As the Court correctly holds today, the appropriate fee in such a case is no fee at all. Because the Court of Appeals gave Joseph Farrar everything he deserved—

nothing—I join the Court's opinion affirming the judgment below.

Justice **White**, with whom Justice **Blackmun**, Justice **Stevens**, and Justice **Souter** join, concurring in part and dissenting in part.

We granted certiorari in this case to decide whether 42 U.S.C. § 1988 entitles a civil rights plaintiff who recovers nominal damages to reasonable attorney's fees. Following our [prior] decisions. . . the Court holds that it does. With that aspect of today's decision, I agree. Because Farrar won an enforceable judgment against respondent, he has achieved a "material alteration" of their legal relationship, and thus he is a "prevailing party" under the statute.

However, I see no reason for the Court to reach out and decide what amount of attorney's fees constitutes a reasonable amount in this instance. That issue was neither presented in the petition for certiorari nor briefed by petitioners. The opinion of the Court of Appeals was grounded exclusively in its determination that Farrar had not met the threshold requirement under § 1988. At no point did it purport to decide what a reasonable award should be if Farrar was a prevailing party.

It may be that the District Court abused its discretion and misapplied our precedents by belittling the significance of the amount of damages awarded in ascertaining petitioners' fees. But it is one thing to say that the court erred as a matter of law in awarding $280,000; quite another to decree, especially without the benefit of petitioners' views or consideration by the Court of Appeals, that the only fair fee was no fee whatsoever.[1]

Litigation in this case lasted for more than a decade, has entailed a 6-week trial and given rise to two appeals. Civil rights cases often are complex, and we therefore have committed the task of calculating attorney's fees to the trial court's discretion for good reason. . . . Estimating what specific amount would be reasonable in this particular situation is not a

---

[1] In his brief to the Fifth Circuit, respondent did not argue that petitioners should be denied all fees even if they were found to be prevailing parties. Rather, he asserted that the District Court misapplied the law by awarding "excessive" fees and requested that they be reduced. See Brief for Defendant-Appellant in No. 90–2830, pp. 38–42.

matter of general importance on which our guidance is needed. Short of holding that recovery of nominal damages never can support the award of attorney's fees—which, clearly, the majority does not—the Court should follow its sensible practice and remand the case for reconsideration of the fee amount. Indeed, respondent's counsel all but conceded at oral argument that, assuming the Court found Farrar to be a prevailing party, the question of reasonableness should be addressed on remand.

I would vacate the judgment of the Court of Appeals and remand the case for further proceedings. Accordingly, I dissent.

NOTES

1. Given the division of the Court, what is the precise holding of the case? In what sense did Farrar prevail? What difference does it make to base a decision to deny attorney's fees on the rationale applied by the court of appeals (Farrar did not prevail), or that applied by a majority of the Supreme Court (Farrar did prevail, but no fee is the only reasonable fee)? Is the Court's ruling consistent with Senate Report No. 94-1011?

2. The Court in *Farrar* relies heavily on three prior cases, *Hewitt v. Helms*, 482 U.S. 775 (1987); *Rhodes v. Stewart*, 488 U.S. 1 (1988); and *Texas State Teachers Association v. Garland Independent School District*, 489 U.S. 782 (1989). In *Hewitt*, an inmate sued prison officials seeking damages and injunctive relief to redress his allegedly unconstitutional disciplinary confinement. Although the Court agreed that the plaintiff's due process rights had been violated, his claim for damages was defeated by the defendants' immunity. State correctional officials subsequently revised their disciplinary procedures. The inmate had abandoned his claim for injunctive relief because he had been released from prison on parole prior to the conclusion of the litigation. In this context, the Court concluded that the plaintiff was not a prevailing party.

In *Rhodes*, two inmates claimed that their First Amendment rights were violated by prison officials who denied them access to certain magazines. The district court agreed and entered a declaratory judgment in favor of the inmates. Prior to the entry of the declaratory judgment, however, one of the plaintiffs had died and the other had been released from custody. The Court held that the inmates could not be considered prevailing parties under these circumstances. The declaratory judgment entered by the district court was not sufficient relief to support an award of attorney's fees because it did not affect the behavior of the defendants towards the plaintiffs.

In *Garland*, individual teachers and a teachers' union sued a school district claiming that a variety of district policies violated the teachers' First Amendment rights. Some of the policies were upheld while others were found to be unconstitutional. The court of appeals held that the plaintiffs were not entitled to attorney's fees because they did not prevail on the "central issue" in the litigation. The Supreme Court reversed, holding that a fee award was appropriate when plaintiffs' prevailed on a "significant issue" and the litigation resolved a dispute which changed the legal relationship between the parties.

Collectively, how strongly do *Hewitt*, *Rhodes*, and *Garland* support the holding that although Farrar prevailed, as a matter of law the only reasonable fee is no fee?

3. Recall that the Supreme Court ruled in *Carey v. Piphus*, 435 U.S. 247 (1978), that absent proof of actual injury, the plaintiff would be entitled only to a judgment for nominal damages for a violation of procedural due process. Recall also that in *Memphis Community School Dist. v. Stachura*, 477 U.S. 299 (1986), the Court disapproved of an instruction that would allow a jury to award damages based on the value or importance of the constitutional right violated. Taken together, how would *Farrar*, *Carey*, and *Stachura* influence an attorney's decision whether to represent a plaintiff in a section 1983 procedural due process case?

4. Section 1988 makes clear that "prevailing party" status is a threshold requirement for an award of attorney's fees, and all nine justices in *Farrar* agree that a plaintiff who secures a judgment for nominal damages is a prevailing party. May a party who recovers damages under a pendent state claim be considered a prevailing party under section 1988 for purposes of attorney's fees? Compare *Carreras v. City of Anaheim*, 768 F.2d 1039 (9th Cir. 1985) (court ruled for the plaintiff on state constitutional grounds without reaching the federal constitutional issues; attorney's fees awarded) with *Mateyko v. Felix*, 924 F.2d 824 (9th Cir. 1990) (plaintiff lost all federal constitutional claims but prevailed on the pendent state tort claim; attorney's fees denied). In *Hall v. Western Production Co.*, 988 F.2d 1050 (10th Cir. 1993), a jury had awarded substantial damages to the plaintiff on a state breach of contract claim, but only nominal damages for his federal claim under the Age Discrimination in Employment Act claim. Should the plaintiff recover attorney's fees? What does *Farrar* suggest? Is *Farrar* distinguishable?

5. Should attorney's fees be awarded when the plaintiff fails to recover any money damages, but secures injunctive relief? Courts have awarded attorney's fees in such cases. E.g., *Herrington v. County of Sonoma*, 883 F.2d 739 (9th Cir. 1989). In particular cases, can injuctive relief be considered technical or *de minimis* so that it will not support a fee award? In *People Helpers Foundation v. City of Richmond*, 12 F.3d 1321 (4th Cir. 1993), a nonprofit corporation promoting housing for the developmentally disabled brought suit against the city alleging various violations of the Fair Housing Act. The plaintiff sought $4 million in damages and injunctive relief. The jury found that the city had violated the Act, awarded $1 in punitive damages, but did not award any compensatory damages. The district judge granted the plaintiff's motion for a permanent injunction enjoining the city from "coercing, harassing, intimidating or interfering" with the plaintiff. The district court also awarded the plaintiff $10,000 in attorney's fees. The court of appeals reversed the award of punitive damages, but did not disturb the injunction. The court then explained why the injunction alone could not support the award of attorney's fees:

> The injunction does not. . .restrict legitimate conduct of the City, namely the enacting of city ordinances and other policies designed to effectively administer the City. . . Following the jury verdict and entry of the permanent injunction, People Helpers is still under the direct authority of the City. . . While People Helpers did obtain some form of relief, such relief has not altered the relative position of the parties.

People Helpers Foundation, 12 F.3d at 1328–29.

Is an injunction that prohibits city officials from "harassing" the plaintiff only a technical or *de minimis* victory? What type of injunction would have supported an award of attorney's fees? Would the fee award in *People Helpers* have been justified if the plaintiff had not sought and failed to recover substantial damages?

6. After *Farrar*, can a district court ever award attorney's fees when the plaintiff seeks significant compensatory and punitive damages, but recovers only nominal damages? If so, when? In the wake of *Farrar*, several courts have denied attorney's fees to plaintiffs who recovered only nominal damages. E.g. *Willis v. City of Chicago*, 999 F.2d 284 (7th Cir. 1993) (nominal damages awarded for Fourth Amendment violation; attorney's fees denied); *Kjorlie v. Ludin*, 930 F. Supp. 1386 (D. Kan. 1993) (same). In *Cartwright v. Stamper*, 7 F.3d 106 (7th Cir. 1993), the jury found that the defendant violated the plaintiff's fourth amendment rights by entering her apartment without a warrant, but awarded only $1 nominal damages. In reversing the district court's pre-*Farrar* award of attorney's fees, the court of appeals offered these observations:

> Justice O'Connor [in *Farrar*] suggested that there are three factors courts should consider when determining whether a victory is de minimis or otherwise strictly technical: first, the difference between the judgment recovered and the recovery sought; second, the significance of the legal issue on which the plaintiff prevailed; and third, the public purpose served by the litigation. . . .
>
> The first factor is the most important of the three. . .and clearly weights in favor of classifying the [plaintiff's] victory [in this case] de minimis. . . .
>
> The jury found that Stamper violated the Fourth Amendment rights of all three of the plaintiffs. . . . This factor, therefore, suggests, albeit modestly, that the victory was more than de minimis. . . .Of the three factors, however, the significance of the issue on which the party prevailed tends to be the least weighty in classifying the victory. . .
>
> [T]he third factor.principally relates to whether the victory vindicates important

rights and deters future violations. . . .[The district] court specifically found that "the 'external benefits' or future deterrent effect of this action is limited." Order at 14. Accordingly, this factor weighs firmly in favor of finding the victory technical.

Weighing the *Farrar* factors—specifically, the weight of factors one and three, strongly suggesting a de minimis victory, against the modest weight of factor two suggesting otherwise—we conclude that the plaintiff's victory was purely technical and that the appropriate fee is no fee.

Cartwright, 7 F.3d at 109–10.

In *Gilmore v. Gregg*, 1993 U.S.Dist.Lexis 12353 (D. Kan. 1993), a jury found that the defendant used unconstitutionally excessive force in arresting the plaintiff. Although the jury found the actual damages to be $1 and refused to award punitive damages, the district judge awarded the plaintiff more than $5,000 in attorney's fees and costs. The district judge distinguished *Farrar* on the following basis:

Unlike *Farrar*. . .the verdict reflects a clear finding that defendant Gregg violated the plaintiff's constitutional right to be free of excessive force. The use of excessive force by a public servant is certainly a significant legal issue. Plaintiff's victory served the public interest by sending defendant Gregg a message that, as a police officer, he must control his temper and refrain from the use of excessive force. . .Hopefully, plaintiff's victory will deter future violations of the civil rights of other citizens.

Gilmore, 1993 U.S.Dist. Lexis 12353 at *4–5.

7. Must a plaintiff secure relief through a judicial ruling, consent decree, or settlement agreement to be considered a prevailing party for purposes of an attorney's fees award under section 1988? Suppose a religious organization files suit challenging the constitutionality of a municipal ordinance regulating the solicitation of charitable contributions. Before the district court rules on the issue, the city repeals the contested provisions, thereby rendering moot the request for declaratory and injunctive relief. Can the plaintiff be considered a "prevailing party" if the litigation was the "catalyst" or "cause" of the policy change? Prior to *Farrar*, most circuit courts had approved the awarding of attorney's fees under this so-called catalyst rule. E.g., *Nadeau v. Helgemoe*, 581 F.2d 275 (1st Cir. 1978). See S. Nahmod, *Civil Rights and Civil Liberties Litigation* § 10.02 (3d ed. 1991) (collecting cases). Does the catalyst rule survive *Farrar*? The fourth circuit court of appeals has held that it does not, reasoning

[t]here is no way. . .that *Farrar* and a broad "catalyst theory" of attorneys' fees recovery can be reconciled. . . *Farrar* [specifies that] judgments, consent decrees, and settlement agreements [are] the exclusive avenues to prevailing party status. . .[A] voluntary change in conduct must be formalized in a legally enforceable settlement agreement to transform a plaintiff into a prevailing party for purposes of § 1988.

S–1 v. State Board of Education, 6 F.3d 160, 168–169, 170, 171 (4th Cir. 1993) (opinion of J. Wilkinson) adopted as the majority opinion, 21 F.3d 49, 51 (4th Cir. 1994) (en banc).

A majority of circuit courts, however, continue to uphold fee awards under the catalyst rule after *Farrar*. According to these courts

if taken out of context some of the language in *Farrar*. . . could be viewed as inconsistent with a "catalyst theory." However, in *Farrar*, because there was in fact a judgment, the Supreme Court did not have before it a situation where the "catalyst theory" might have been applicable. . .We believe it is not likely that the Supreme Court would overturn such a wide-spread theory without even once mentioning it. . .

Baumgartner v. Harrisburg Housing Authority, 21 F.3d 541, 547 (3rd Cir. 1994). See also *Paris v. U.S. Department of Housing & Urban Development*, 988 F.2d 236 (1st Cir. 1993); *Citizens Against Tax Waste v. Westerville City School Dist.*, 985 F.2d 255 (6th Cir. 1993).

When the catalyst rule applies, the burden rests with the plaintiff to establish that the litigation caused the defendant to alter its policies in a way that benefited the plaintiff. Absent such proof, the plaintiff will not be considered a prevailing party entitled to an award of attorney's fees. E.g., *Stewart v. McGinnis*, 5 F.3d 1031 (7th Cir. 1993); *Ameri-*

can Council of the Blind v. Romer, 992 F.2d 249 (10th Cir. 1993).

8. Should attorney's fees be awarded in a case where the prevailing plaintiff was represented by a nonprofit legal service organization? Are statutory attorney's fees needed to induce representation in such a case? Does section 1988 purport to distinguish between public interest attorneys and private counsel? If attorney's fees are awarded for work performed by a nonprofit legal service organization, should the fee be based on market rates, the cost to the organization, or some other criteria? See *Blum v. Stenson*, 465 U.S. 886 (1984) (awarding attorney's fees to the Legal Aid Society based on market rates). In *Kay v. Ehrler*, 499 U.S. 432 (1991), the Court held that an award of attorney's fees under section 1988 should not be made to a lawyer who successfully represented himself in the litigation. Why award attorney's fees for work performed by the Legal Aid Society but not the *pro se* attorney?

9. Should prevailing defendants, like prevailing plaintiffs, enjoy a strong presumption of entitlement to an attorney's fee award? The Supreme Court has construed section 1988 to authorize an award of attorney's fees to a prevailing defendant "only where the suit was vexatious, frivolous, or brought to harass or embarrass the defendant." *Hensley v. Eckerhart*, 461 U.S. 424, 429 n.2 (1983). This standard was drawn from cases involving Title VII employment discrimination claims. *Christianburg Garment Co. v. EEOC*, 434 U.S. 412–421 (1978). Why would Congress impose such a double standard? What does Senate Report No. 94–1011 suggest?

10. Can a prevailing party recover attorney's fees against federal officials who violate the plaintiff's constitutional rights? Section 1988 does not expressly permit the recovery of attorney's fees against the United States or federal officials. Instead, it authorizes an award of attorney's fees to parties who prevail in claims brought under specific civil rights statutes, the most significant of which section 1983. Section 1983 claims are limited to actions taken under color of *state*—not federal—law. For this reason, section 1988 typically does not authorize a fee award against federal defendants who violate the plaintiff's constitutional rights.

Other statutes, however, may support such an award. The most important statute is the Equal Access to Justice Act (EAJA), 28 U.S.C. § 2412. The EAJA authorizes an award of attorney's fees against the "United States or any agency and any official. . .acting in his or her official capacity. . .to the same extent that any other party would be liable under the common law or under the terms of any statute which specifically provides for such award." 28 U.S.C. § 2412(b). The EAJF goes on to specify that attorney's fees are recoverable from the federal government if its prelitigation or litigation position was "not substantially justified." 28 U.S.C. § 2412(d)(1)(A). This provision can support fee awards in constitutional litigation, e.g. *United Staters v. $12,248 U.S. Currency*, 957 F.2d 1513 (9th Cir. 1991), although the "not substantially justified" requirement puts a heavier burden on the prevailing plaintiff than is imposed in cases brought against state officials under section 1983.

Does the EAJA's reference to "any statute" serve to incorporate section 1988 so as to allow the routine award of attorney's fees against federal officials who are found to have deprived plaintiffs of constitutional rights? Courts agree that the incorporation language of the EAJA authorizes an award of attorney's fees against federal defendants who violate the specific civil rights statutes listed in section 1988. See generally *Unification Church v. I.N.S.*, 762 F.2d 1077, 1080–81 (D.C. Cir. 1985); *Premachandra v. Mitts*, 753 F.2d 635, 637 n.7 (8th Cir. 1985) (en banc). Thus, attorney's fees may be awarded against federal defendants who violate 42 U.S.C. § 1981 or § 1982 for racial discrimination in transactions involving contracts or real or personal property, or who violate 42 U.S.C. § 1985 by conspiring with state actors to violate a person's civil rights. However, most courts have concluded that the EAJA does not authorize an award of attorney's fees against the United States or its officers in a pure *Bivens*-type action. Some opinions explain that *Bivens* actions are brought against the federal officers in their individual—not official—capacity, and hence are not suits against the United States for which fees are authorized by the EAJA. E.g., *Saxner v. Bensen*, 727 F.2d 669, 673 (7th Cir. 1984), aff'd on other grds. sub. nom, *Cleavinger v. Saxner*, 474 U.S. 193 (1985); *Lauritzen v. Lehman*, 736 F.2d 550 (9th Cir. 1984); *Kreines v. United States*, 812 F.Supp.

164 (N.D. Cal. 1992). Other decisions interpret the "to the same extent" language of the EAJA to mean that

> the federal government is not liable for fees under section 1988 unless it actually violates one of the statutes giving rise to fees under that section, regardless of whether a state might be liable for such fees had the state taken the same actions under color of state law as the federal government took under color of federal law.

Unification Church v. I.N.S. 762 F.2d 1077, 1080 (D.C. Cir. 1985). See also *Martin v. Heckler*, 773 F.2d 1145, 1154 (11th Cir. 1985) (en banc). Thus, although subsection b of the EAJA incorporates section 1988, it also incorporates the "under color of" state law limitation of section 1983. See Chapter 2 *supra*.

III.   What is a "Reasonable" Fee?

Once a court determines that a party prevailed with a measure of success sufficient to warrant an award of attorney's fees, it must determine what is a "reasonable" fee. The theoretical and practical components of a reasonable fee are explored in the next two cases. In the first case, the Supreme Court identifies general principles that govern this inquiry. The second case illustrates one district court's application of those principles to a partially successful challenge to a state's abortion statutes.

Hensley v. Eckerhart

461 U.S. 424 (1983)

Justice **Powell** delivered the opinion of the Court.

Title 42 U.S.C. § 1988 provides that in federal civil rights actions "the court, in its discretion, may allow the prevailing party, other than the United States, a reasonable attorney's fee as part of the costs." The issue in this case is whether a partially prevailing plaintiff may recover an attorney's fee for legal services on unsuccessful claims.

I

A

Respondents brought this lawsuit on behalf of all persons involuntarily confined at the Forensic Unit of the Fulton State Hospital in Fulton, Mo. . . .

In 1972 respondents filed a three-count complaint in the District Court for the Western District of Missouri against petitioners, who are officials at the Forensic Unit and members of the Missouri Mental Health Commission. Count I challenged the constitutionality of treatment and conditions at the Forensic Unit. Count II challenged the placement of patients in the [maximum security section of the Forensic Unit] without procedural due process. Count III sought compensation for patients who performed institution-maintaining labor.

Count II was resolved by a consent decree in December 1973. Count III largely was mooted in August 1974 when petitioners began compensating patients for labor. . . In April 1975 respondents voluntarily dismissed the lawsuit and filed a new two-count complaint. Count I again related to the constitutionality of treatment and conditions at the Forensic Unit. Count II sought damages, based on the Thirteenth Amendment, for the value of past patient labor. In July 1976 respondents voluntarily dismissed this back-pay count. Finally, in August 1977 respondents filed an amended one-count complaint specifying the conditions that allegedly violated their constitutional right to treatment.

In August 1979, following a three-week trial, the District Court held that an involuntarily committed patient has a constitutional right to minimally adequate treatment. The court then found constitutional violations in five of six general areas: physical environment; individual treatment plans; least restrictive environment; visitation, telephone, and mail privileges; and seclusion and restraint. With respect to staffing, the sixth general area, the District Court found that the Forensic Unit's staffing levels, which had increased during the litigation, were minimally adequate. Petitioners did not appeal the District Court's decision on the merits.

B

In February 1980 respondents filed a request for attorney's fees for the period from January 1975 through the end of the litigation. Their four attorneys claimed 2,985 hours worked and sought payment at rates varying from $40 to $65 per hour. This amounted to approximately $150,000. Respondents also requested that the fee be enhanced by 30 to 50 percent, for a total award of somewhere between $195,000 and $225,000. Petitioners opposed the request on numerous grounds, including inclusion of hours spent in pursuit of unsuccessful claims.

The District Court first determined that respondents were prevailing parties under 42 U.S.C. § 1988 even though they had not succeeded on every claim. It then refused to eliminate from the award hours spent on unsuccessful claims . . . Finding that respondents "have obtained relief of significant import," the District Court awarded a fee of $133,332.25. This award differed from the fee request in two respects. First, the court reduced the number of hours claimed by one attorney by 30 percent to account for his inexperience and failure to keep contemporaneous records. Second, the court declined to adopt an enhancement factor to increase the award.

The Court of Appeals for the Eighth Circuit affirmed on the basis of the District Court's memorandum opinion and order. We granted certiorari and now vacate and remand for further proceedings.

II

. . .

The amount of the fee, of course, must be determined on the facts of each case. On this issue the House Report simply refers to 12 factors set forth in *Johnson v. Georgia Highway Express, Inc.*[3] The Senate Report cites to

Johnson as well and also refers to three District Court decisions that "correctly applied" the 12 factors. One of the factors in *Johnson*, "the amount involved and the results obtained," indicates that the level of a plaintiff's success is relevant to the amount of fees to be awarded. . . .

. . .

In this case petitioners contend that "an award of attorney's fees must be proportioned to be consistent with the extent to which a plaintiff has prevailed, and only time reasonably expended in support of successful claims should be compensated." Respondents agree that a plaintiff's success is relevant, but propose a less stringent standard focusing on "whether the time spent prosecuting [an unsuccessful] claim in any way contributed to the ultimate results achieved." Both parties acknowledge the discretion of the district court in this area. We take this opportunity to clarify the proper relationship of the results obtained to an award of attorney's fees.

III

A

. . .

The most useful starting point for determining the amount of a reasonable fee is the number of hours reasonably expended on the litigation multiplied by a reasonable hourly rate. This calculation provides an objective basis on which to make an initial estimate of the value of a lawyer's services. The party seeking an award of fees should submit evidence supporting the hours worked and rates claimed. Where the documentation of hours is inadequate, the district court may reduce the award accordingly.

The district court also should exclude from this initial fee calculation hours that were not "reasonably expended." S. Rep. No. 94–1011, p. 6 (1976). Cases may be overstaffed, and the skill and experience of lawyers vary widely. Counsel for the prevailing party should make a good-faith effort to exclude from a fee request hours that are excessive, redundant, or otherwise unnecessary, just as a lawyer in

---

[3] The 12 factors are: (1) the time and labor required; (2) the novelty and difficulty of the questions; (3) the skill requisite to perform the legal service properly; (4) the preclusion of employment by the attorney due to acceptance of the case; (5) the customary fee; (6) whether the fee is fixed or contingent; (7) time limitations imposed by the client or the circumstances; (8) the amount involved and the results obtained; (9) the experience, reputation, and ability of the attorneys; (10) the "undesirability" of the case; (11) the nature

and length of the professional relationship with the client; and (12) awards in similar cases. These factors derive directly from the American Bar Association Code of Professional Responsibility, Disciplinary Rule 2–106 (1980).

private practice ethically is obligated to exclude such hours from his fee submission. "In the private sector, 'billing judgment' is an important component in fee setting. It is no less important here. Hours that are not properly billed to one's *client* also are not properly billed to one's *adversary* pursuant to statutory authority." *Copeland v. Marshall* (en banc) (emphasis in original).

B

The product of reasonable hours times a reasonable rate does not end the inquiry. There remain other considerations that may lead the district court to adjust the fee upward or downward, including the important factor of the "results obtained." This factor is particularly crucial where a plaintiff is deemed "prevailing" even though he succeeded on only some of his claims for relief. In this situation two questions must be addressed. First, did the plaintiff fail to prevail on claims that were unrelated to the claims on which he succeeded? Second, did the plaintiff achieve a level of success that makes the hours reasonably expended a satisfactory basis for making a fee award?

In some cases a plaintiff may present in one lawsuit distinctly different claims for relief that are based on different facts and legal theories. In such a suit, even where the claims are brought against the same defendants— often an institution and its officers, as in this case—counsel's work on one claim will be unrelated to his work on another claim. Accordingly, work on an unsuccessful claim cannot be deemed to have been "expended in pursuit of the ultimate result achieved." *Davis v. County of Los Angeles.* The congressional intent to limit awards to prevailing parties requires that these unrelated claims be treated as if they had been raised in separate lawsuits, and therefore no fee may be awarded for services on the unsuccessful claim.[10]

. . .Many civil rights cases will present only a single claim. In other cases the plaintiff's claims for relief will involve a common core of facts or will be based on related legal theories. Much of counsel's time will be devoted generally to the litigation as a whole,

making it difficult to divide the hours expended on a claim-by-claim basis. Such a lawsuit cannot be viewed as a series of discrete claims. Instead the district court should focus on the significance of the overall relief obtained by the plaintiff in relation to the hours reasonably expended on the litigation.

Where a plaintiff has obtained excellent results, his attorney should recover a fully compensatory fee. Normally this will encompass all hours reasonably expended on the litigation, and indeed in some cases of exceptional success an enhanced award may be justified. In these circumstances the fee award should not be reduced simply because the plaintiff failed to prevail on every contention raised in the lawsuit. Litigants in good faith may raise alternative legal grounds for a desired outcome, and the court's rejection of or failure to reach certain grounds is not a sufficient reason for reducing a fee. The result is what matters.[11]

If, on the other hand, a plaintiff has achieved only partial or limited success, the product of hours reasonably expended on the litigation as a whole times a reasonable hourly rate may be an excessive amount. This will be true even where the plaintiff's claims were interrelated, nonfrivolous, and raised in good faith. Congress has not authorized an award of fees whenever it was reasonable for a plaintiff to bring a lawsuit or whenever conscientious counsel tried the case with devotion and skill. Again, the most critical factor is the degree of success obtained.

Application of this principle is particularly important in complex civil rights litigation involving numerous challenges to institutional practices or conditions. . . .In this case, for example, the District Court's award of fees based on 2,557 hours worked may have been reasonable in light of the substantial relief

---

[10] If the unsuccessful claim is frivolous, the defendant may recover attorney's fees incurred in responding it. . . .

[11] We agree with the District Court's rejection of "a mathematical approach comparing the total number of issues in the case with those actually prevailed upon." Record 220. Such a ratio provides little aid in determining what is a reasonable fee in light of all the relevant factors. Nor is it necessarily significant that a prevailing plaintiff did not receive all the relief requested. For example, a plaintiff who failed to recover damages but obtained injunctive relief, or vice versa, may recover a fee award based on all hours reasonably expended if the relief obtained justified that expenditure of attorney time.

obtained. But had respondents prevailed on only one of their six general claims, for example the claim that petitioners' visitation, mail, and telephone policies were overly restrictive, a fee award based on the claimed hours clearly would have been excessive.

There is no precise rule or formula for making these determinations. The district court may attempt to identify specific hours that should be eliminated, or it may simply reduce the award to account for the limited success. The court necessarily has discretion in making this equitable judgment. This discretion, however, must be exercised in light of the considerations we have identified.

C

A request for attorney's fees should not result in a second major litigation. Ideally, of course, litigants will settle the amount of a fee. Where settlement is not possible, the fee applicant bears the burden of establishing entitlement to an award and documenting the appropriate hours expended and hourly rates. The applicant should exercise "billing judgment" with respect to hours worked, and should maintain billing time records in a manner that will enable a reviewing court to identify distinct claims.[12]

We reemphasize that the district court has discretion in determining the amount of a fee award. This is appropriate in view of the district court's superior understanding of the litigation and the desirability of avoiding frequent appellate review of what essentially are factual matters. It remains important, however, for the district court to provide a concise but clear explanation of its reasons for the fee award. When an adjustment is requested on the basis of either the exceptional or limited nature of the relief obtained by the plaintiff, the district court should make clear that it has considered the relationship between the amount of the fee awarded and the results obtained.

IV

. . .

---

[12] We recognize that there is no certain method of determining when claims are "related" or "unrelated." Plaintiff's counsel, of course, is not required to record in great detail how each minute of his time was expended. But at least counsel should identify the general subject matter of his time expenditures. . . .

[The District Court made] a commendable effort to explain the fee award. Given the interrelated nature of the facts and legal theories in this case, the District Court did not err in refusing to apportion the fee award mechanically on the basis of respondents' success or failure on particular issues. And given the findings with respect to the level of respondents' success, the District Court's award may be consistent with our holding today.

We are unable to affirm the decisions below, however, because the District Court's opinion did not properly consider the relationship between the extent of success and the amount of the fee award. The court's finding that "the [significant] extent of the relief clearly justifies the award of a reasonable attorney's fee" does not answer the question of what is "reasonable" in light of that level of success. We emphasize that the inquiry does not end with a finding that the plaintiff obtained significant relief. A reduced fee award is appropriate if the relief, however significant, is limited in comparison to the scope of the litigation as a whole.

V

We hold that the extent of a plaintiff's success is a crucial factor in determining the proper amount of an award of attorney's fees under 42 U.S.C. § 1988. Where the plaintiff has failed to prevail on a claim that is distinct in all respects from his successful claims, the hours spent on the unsuccessful claim should be excluded in considering the amount of a reasonable fee. Where a lawsuit consists of related claims, a plaintiff who has won substantial relief should not have his attorney's fee reduced simply because the district court did not adopt each contention raised. But where the plaintiff achieved only limited success, the district court should award only that amount of fees that is reasonable in relation to the results obtained. On remand the District Court should determine the proper amount of the attorney's fee award in light of these standards.

The judgment of the Court of Appeals is vacated, and the case is remanded for further proceedings consistent with this opinion.

It is so ordered.

Chief Justice **Burger**, concurring.

I read the Court's opinion as requiring that when a lawyer seeks to have his adversary pay the fees of the prevailing party, the lawyer must provide detailed records of the time and services for which fees are sought. It would be inconceivable that the prevailing party should not be required to establish at least as much to support a claim under 42 U.S.C. § 1988 as a lawyer would be required to show if his own client challenged the fees. A district judge may not, in my view, authorize the payment of attorney's fees unless the attorney involved has established by clear and convincing evidence the time and effort claimed and shown that the time expended was necessary to achieve the results obtained.

. . .[T]he party who seeks payment must keep records in sufficient detail that a neutral judge can make a fair evaluation of the time expended, the nature and need for the service, and the reasonable fees to be allowed.

[The opinion of Justice Brennan, concurring in part and dissenting in part, is omitted.]

NOTES

1. *Hensley* sets out the basic approach for calculating a reasonable attorney's fee. The starting point is the product of reasonable time expended times a reasonable hourly rate. This approach is commonly referred to as the "lodestar". See Alba Conte, *1 Attorney Fee Awards* § 4.02 (2d ed. 1993). Of course, the parties may disagree as to the reasonableness of time expended or the proposed hourly rate. Those points are further developed in *Jane L. v. Bangerter*, 828 F. Supp. 1544 (D. Utah 1993), *infra*. The lodestar calculation "is presumed to be the reasonable fee contemplated by § 1988." *Blum v. Stenson*, 465 U.S. 886, 897 (1984). After determining the lodestar the court may consider whether the fee should be adjusted upward or downward to account for factors which are not included in a time times rate formula.

2. In many constitutional tort suits, the plaintiff may sue several defendants and rely on several different legal theories. What guidelines does *Hensley* provide to determine what is a reasonable fee when the plaintiff prevails only against some defendants or only as to some claims? How is a district court to determine

whether a lawsuit involves "distinctly different claims" or whether it concerns "a common core of facts or . . . related legal theories," so that it "cannot be viewed as a series of discrete claims."? *Hensley*, 461 U.S. at 434–35. Suppose a plaintiff does not prevail on his claim that he was subjected to excessive force in the course of an arrest, but does prevail on his claim that the arrest was racially motivated. Are the equal protection and excessive force claims sufficiently related that an attorney's fee award can be based on the time spent on both issues? Suppose the plaintiff is also unsuccessful on his additional claim that he was maliciously prosecuted. Is the malicious prosecution claim sufficiently related to the equal protection claim that an attorney's fee award can be based on the time spent on both issues? See *Lenard v. Argento*, 808 F.2d 1242, 1246–47 (7th Cir. 1987) (equal protection and excessive force claims were sufficiently related because they both involved the arrest itself; the equal protection claim was not related to the malicious prosecution claim because the prosecution took place at a later time). Suppose a plaintiff proves that a school district's decision not to rehire her was made in retaliation for her exercise of first amendment rights, but is unsuccessful on her claim that she was denied procedural due process. Should a full award of attorney's fees be made? See *Durant v. Independent School District No. 16*, 990 F.2d 560, 566 (10th Cir. 1993) (remanded to district court for consideration).

Suppose the plaintiff sues multiple defendants, but prevails only against some of them. Does *Hensley* address the multiple defendant situation? Should an award of attorney's fees be reduced to reflect the lack of success as to some of the defendants? In *Cobb v. Miller*, 818 F.2d 1227 (5th Cir. 1987) the plaintiff sued three defendants for an alleged use of excessive force, but prevailed only against one. The magistrate reduced the attorney's fee award by 2/3, but the court of appeals reversed, characterizing the claims as interrelated. In *Buffington v. Baltimore County*, 913 F.2d 113 (4th Cir. 1990) reprinted in Chapter 6, the plaintiffs sued the mayor of Baltimore, Baltimore County, and several individual police officers in connection with the suicide of an inmate. The court of appeals reversed the jury verdict against the mayor and county, but upheld it as to some of the officers. Can the attorney's fees awarded against the officers include time spent litigating the unsuccessful claims against the county and mayor? The court of appeals remanded the attorney's fees issue to the district court to determine whether the claims against the mayor and county were "distinct" or "inextricably intermingled." *Buffington*, 913 F.2d at 128. The court of appeals intimated that even if the claims were interrelated, a reduction in fees might be appropriate because the claims against the county and mayor were considered to be more significant than those against the individual officers. *Id.* at 127–29.

3. Suppose that the lodestar fee greatly exceeds the amount of damages awarded the plaintiff. Does *Hensley* indicate that the fee must be proportional to the amount of damages recovered? In *City of Riverside v. Rivera*, 477 U.S. 561 (1986), the district court awarded the plaintiffs $245,456.25 in attorney's fees in a case in which the compensatory and punitive damages were $33,350. The Court affirmed the award calculated under the lodestar. Justice Brennan, writing for a plurality of four justices, explained:

> A rule of proportionality would make it difficult, if not impossible, for individuals with meritorious civil rights claims but relatively small potential damages to obtain redress from the courts. This is totally inconsistent with Congress' purpose in enacting § 1988. Congress recognized that private-sector fee arrangements were inadequate to ensure sufficiently vigorous enforcement of civil rights. In order to ensure that lawyers would be willing to represent persons with legitimate civil rights grievances, Congress determined that it would be necessary to compensate lawyers for all time reasonably expended on a case.
>
> . . .
>
> [H]ad respondents had to rely on private-sector fee arrangements, they might well have been unable to obtain redress for their grievances. It is precisely for this reason that Congress enacted § 1988.

City of Riverside, 477 U.S. at 578–80 (footnote omitted). Four justices argued that the size of the fee award should be proportional to the damage award. Justice Rehnquist wrote that

the District Court failed at almost every turn to apply any kind of "billing judgment" or to seriously consider the "results obtained," which we described in *Hensley* as "the important factor" in determining a "reasonable" fee award. . . .

The very "reasonableness" of the hours expended on a case by a plaintiff's attorney necessarily will depend, to a large extent, on the amount that may be expected to be recovered if the plaintiff prevails.

. . .

Nearly 2,000 attorney-hours spent on a case in which the total recovery was on $33,000 . . . and in which the District Court expressed the view that. . .juries typically were reluctant to award substantial damages against police officers, is simply not a "reasonable" expenditure of time.

City of Riverside, 477 U.S. at 590, 593, 595 (Rehnquist, J., dissenting).

Justice Powell based his decisive vote affirming the award on the "District Court's detailed findings of fact, which were approved by the Court of Appeals." *City of Riverside*, 477 U.S. at 581 (Powell, J., concurring in the judgment).

Which approach is most consistent with *Hensley*? Does *Farrar* resurrect the proportionality issue supposedly laid to rest in *City of Riverside*?

4. As reflected in S. Rep. No. 94–1011, many civil rights plaintiffs lack the resources to hire counsel on a fee for time basis. Section 1988(b) offers the prospect of attorney's fees to the prevailing plaintiff. *Farrar* illustrates, however, that civil rights litigation may be protracted and result in no fee award. Thus, attorneys who represent civil rights plaintiffs run the risk that they will receive no fee in some cases. When plaintiffs do prevail with a level of success that justifies some fee award, should the lodestar be enhanced to reflect the contingent nature of the practice? Consider the comments of Professor Leubsdorf:

> A lawyer who both bears the risk of not being paid and provides legal services is not receiving the fair market value of his work if he is paid only for the second of

these functions. If he is paid no more, competent counsel will be reluctant to accept fee award cases.

Leubsdorf, *The Contingency Factor in Attorney Fee Awards*, 90 Yale L.J. 473, 480 (1981). See also R. Posner, *Economic Analysis of Law* § 21.9 at 567–68 (4th ed. 1992).

The Supreme Court in City of *Burlington v. Dague*, 112 S. Ct. 2638 (1992), however, held that an enhancement of the lodestar for contingency is not permitted under federal fee-shifting statutes. The majority believed that a contingency enhancement was not needed to attract competent counsel and posed a danger of encouraging the filing of nonmeritorious claims.

5. Suppose the prevailing section 1983 plaintiff has a contingent fee contract with his counsel and that fees calculated under the lodestar greatly exceed those that otherwise would be payable under the contingent fee contract. Should the attorney's fees awarded the plaintiff under section 1988 be limited to the contingent fee? No, according to the court in *Blanchard v. Bergeron*, 489 U.S. 97 (1989).

Suppose, however, that the prevailing plaintiff recovered substantial damages so that a fee calculated under the contingent fee contract would be larger than one based on the lodestar. If the defendant is obligated to pay only an attorney's fees award based on the lodestar under section 1988, can the plaintiff's attorney nonetheless recover a contingent fee from her client? In *Venegas v. Mitchell*, 495 U.S. 82 (1990), a unanimous Court held that while "§ 1988 controls what the losing defendant must pay . . . [it] does not interfere with the enforceability of a contingent-fee contract." *Venegas* 495 U.S. 90. The Court explained that

> depriving plaintiffs of the option of promising to pay more than the statutory fee if that is necessary to secure counsel of their choice would not further § 1988's general purpose of enabling such plaintiffs in civil rights cases to secure competent counsel.

Is this rationale consistent with *Dague*'s rejection of a contingency enhancement?

A universal limitation on the use of contingent fee contracts is that they be "reasonable." Model Code of Professional Responsibility, DR 2–106(B)(8) (1980); ABA Model Rules of Professional Conduct, Rule 1.5(a)(8) (1993). If a contingent fee is "reasonable" for purposes of professional ethics, why is it not considered a "reasonable" award under section 1988?

6. Attorney's fees calculated as a percentage of recovery have been awarded under the "common fund" doctrine, which "allows a party who creates, preserves, or increases the value of a fund in which others have an ownership interest to be reimbursed from that fund for litigation expenses incurred, including counsel fees." *Swedish Hospital Corp. v. Shalala*, 1 F.3d 1261, 1265 (D.C. Cir. 1993). See generally Alba Conte, *1 Attorney Fee Awards* §§ 2.01–2.02 (2d ed. 1993); *Court Awarded Attorney Fees, Report of the Third Circuit Task Force*, 108 F.R.D. 237 (1985). The common fund doctrine is grounded in principles of unjust enrichment, and often applies in class action suits in which the class representative secures a monetary recovery or substantial nonpecuniary benefit for the class. See Dawson, *Lawyers and Involuntary Clients: Attorney Fees from Funds*, 82 Harv. L. Rev. 1597, 1601 (1974). Unlike a contingency fee arrangement, the percentage used to calculate fees is set by the court, and not by contract. The typical attorney's fee award calculated under the common fund doctrine ranges from 20 to 30 percent of the fund. See Alba Conte, *1 Attorney Fee Awards* § 2.08 (2d ed. 1993). The Supreme Court has embraced both the common fund doctrine and the use of the percentage-of-the-fund method of calculating a fee award. E.g., *Boeing Co. v. Van Gemert*, 444 U.S. 472 (1980) (common fund); *Sprague v. Ticonic National Bank*, 307 U.S. 161 (1939) (percentage-of-the-fund); *Central RR. & Banking Co. v. Pettus*, 113 U.S. 116 (1885) (percentage-of-the-fund).

In *Blum v. Stenson*, 465 U.S. 886 (1984), the Court distinguished the lodestar method of calculating an award of attorney's fees under fee-shifting statutes like section 1988 from the percentage-of-the-fund method used in common fund cases:

> Unlike the calculation of attorney's fees under the "common fund doctrine," where a reasonable fee is based on a percentage of the fund bestowed on the class, a reasonable fee under § 1988 reflects the amount of attorney time reasonably expended on the litigation.

Blum, 465 U.S. at 900 n.16. Several lower courts have construed this passage from *Blum* as recognizing the common fund doctrine and the percentage-of-the-fund method of calculation as an alternative basis for awarding attorney's fees in appropriate cases. E.g., *Swedish Hospital Corp. v. Shalala*, 1 F.3d 1261 (D.C. Cir. 1993) (awarding fees of $2 million under common fund doctrine even though the fee would have been $619,000 calculated on an hourly rate); *Camden I Condominium Ass'n, Inc. v. Dunkle*, 946 F.2d 768 (11th Cir. 1991) (reversing a district court award of attorney's fees under a lodestar and remanding for calculation under a percentage-of-fund approach). See generally Monique Lapointe, Note, *Attorney's Fees in Common Fund Actions*, 59 Fordham L. Rev. 843 (1991); *Court Awarded Attorney Fees, Report of the Third Circuit Task Force*, 108 F.R.D. 237, 254–59 (1985).

Jane L. v. Bangerter

828 F.Supp. 1544 (D. Utah 1993)

MEMORANDUM DECISION AND ORDER IN RE ATTORNEYS FEES

J. Thomas **Greene**, District Judge

. . .

FACTUAL BACKGROUND

Plaintiffs filed a complaint in this action on April 5, 1991, challenging the newly amended Utah Abortion Act (the "Act") and certain preexisting provisions of the Act. Utah Code Ann. §§ 76–7–301 et seq. (1990 & Supp. 1992). Prompted by the filing of this complaint, the Utah legislature revised the Act to avoid certain legal problems in a special session. On May 15, 1991, plaintiffs filed an eight count Amended Complaint alleging numerous violations of the United States Constitution and the Utah Constitution. Enforcement of the contested provisions of the Act was enjoined pending a final ruling by this court.

. . .

The final judgment in this case was entered on January 14, 1993. Both parties subsequently filed applications for attorneys' fees and costs, each claiming to be the "prevailing party" under 42 U.S.C. § 1988, and Fed. R.

Civ. P. 54(d). Plaintiffs argue that they prevailed because the alleged "core" of the Act (prohibition of elective abortion with certain exceptions), along with the spousal notification requirement, were ruled to be unconstitutional. Defendants claim to be the prevailing party because the court ruled in their favor on all of the other claims.

ANALYSIS

I. PLAINTIFFS' ATTORNEYS' FEES

. . .

There can be no doubt that plaintiffs succeeded on significant issues that brought them some of the benefits they sought in bringing this action. This court's decision that § 7–7–302(2) of the Utah Code is unconstitutional insofar as it relates to abortions before 21 weeks, as well as its ruling striking down Utah's spousal notification statute, both pertain to such significant issues.

Because plaintiffs have "prevailed" on significant issues in this action, they are entitled under § 1988 to a "reasonable attorney's fee." The first step in determining a reasonable fee is to establish a "lodestar" figure. This is done by multiplying the hours plaintiffs' counsel reasonably spent on the case by a reasonable hourly rate.

A. Reasonable Hours

Plaintiffs' burden in an application for attorneys' fees is to "prove and establish the reasonableness of each dollar, each hour, above zero." *Mares v. Credit Bureau of Raton.* To meet that burden, the Tenth Circuit requires that lawyers keep "meticulous, contemporaneous time records . . ." *Ramos v. Lamm.* In particular,

These records must reveal, for each lawyer for whom fees are sought, all hours for which compensation is requested and how those hours were allotted to specific tasks—for example, how many hours were spent researching, how many interviewing the client, how many drafting the complaint, and so on.

Id.

Before submitting a fee application to the court, the prevailing party must "make a good-faith effort to exclude from a fee request hours that are excessive, redundant, or otherwise unnecessary, just as a lawyer in private practice ethically is obligated to exclude such hours from his fee submission." *Hensley.*

Upon review of the time records, this court has determined that five of plaintiffs' counsel have not met their burden of providing time records which adequately designate how much time was allotted to specific tasks. The time records for these five attorneys represent over 50% of the total hours which were submitted by plaintiffs. For example, on 4/10/92, Janet Benshoof's time records state that she spent 16.5 hours in preparation for a hearing, attendance at the hearing, a meeting with clients, travel and "discussion." Her entry for 3/13/92 lists preparation for a hearing, attendance at the hearing, travel and "review" for a total of 14 hours. Id. Rachael Pine's entry for 3/18/92 reads: "Travel; prepare for hearing before magistrate; hearing before magistrate; press" for a total of 10 hours. Pine Declaration at A4. No attempt was made in these entries to break down time among the several different tasks performed.

In addition, it appears that with few exceptions, plaintiffs' counsel as a whole have not adequately excluded requests for "excessive, redundant, or otherwise unnecessary" hours. While some of the time plaintiffs' attorneys devoted to this case is clearly compensable, much of the time is not compensable. Hours spent on such things as unspecified "review" time, press conferences, excessive travel, and unnecessary duplicative time should be disallowed or reduced.

The Tenth Circuit imposes the task upon the district judge of distinguishing between "raw" time and "billable" time, and determining the number of hours reasonably spent. . .

In those instances where time records are not sufficiently detailed, as is the case with five attorneys in this case, the Supreme Court has offered the following guidance: "Where the documentation of hours is inadequate, the district court may reduce the award accordingly." *Hensley.*

The reasons for reducing plaintiffs' claimed compensable time are numerous. Plaintiffs' time records include unspecified or inadequately specified "review" time, excessive travel time, unnecessary and duplicative time spent in conference calls, meetings, and hearings, noncompensable public relations time, noncompensable time expended after the judgment was rendered, and noncompensable clerical or "overhead" time.

1. Review Time

"Review" is a somewhat ambiguous term that often turns up in attorneys' time records. In this case, there are several instances where plaintiffs' counsel refer to unspecified or inadequately specified "review" time. This is evidence of excess. "[T]he word 'review' seems to be a catchall category with great versatility in counsels' applications. It is also a signal for the padding of hours." Apart from the matter of "padding," however, excessive requests for "review" time may indicate that counsel have not adequately exercised billing judgment before submitting their fee application.

2. Travel Time

One category of time that is often inflated is that devoted to travel. A large amount of travel time was involved in this action because most of plaintiffs' attorneys were centered in New York City. In this regard, plaintiffs have submitted 45 travel entries which cover at least 300 hours of claimed compensable time.

Travel time is "essentially unproductive," and therefore appropriately "compensable at a reduced hourly rate." . . . .It is apparent to this court that the travel time submitted by plaintiffs' counsel is excessive. More importantly, the travel time charges were unnecessary in view of the fact that this case could have been handled adequately by local attorneys.

3. Overlapping and Duplicative Time

Another category of time in which reductions are appropriate is unnecessary duplicative time. "If the same task is performed by more than one lawyer, multiple compensation should be denied." The problem of duplication of hours is frequently encountered in cases of multiple representation because too many attorneys (all billing their time) are present at meetings, hearings, and depositions: "The more lawyers representing a side of the litigation, the greater the likelihood will be for duplication of services." . . .

In this case, among the attorneys of record for plaintiffs were three local attorneys, several attorneys from the Center for Reproductive Law and Policy, attorneys in a private nonlocal law firm, and an attorney from Planned

Parenthood Federation of America. In all, 17 lawyers and one paralegal submitted affidavits in connection with plaintiffs' request for attorneys' fees. Few of these lawyers participated in oral argument. Plaintiffs' time records indicate that an enormous amount of time, much of it duplicative, was spent discussing the case with each other on the telephone or in meetings.

As to time spent in hearings, this court determines that plaintiffs' have made excessive claims for compensation with respect to at least two occasions. Four of plaintiffs' attorneys submitted compensation requests for attending the March 13, 1992 hearing concerning the Motion to Dismiss and Motion for Summary Judgment. Seven attorneys submitted compensation requests for attending the April 10, 1992 hearing.

. . ."[T]he presence of more than two lawyers during trial or the presence of more than one lawyer at depositions and hearings must be justified to the court." [*Ramos v. Lamm*]. The court further declared that "[if] three attorneys are present at a hearing when one would suffice, compensation should be denied for the excess time." Id. (citation omitted).

Plaintiffs were obligated to eliminate this excess and duplicative time from their time records before submitting them to the court. Because plaintiffs have failed to do this, the court is compelled to make appropriate reductions itself.

4. Public Relations, Press Lobbying Etc.

In this case, plaintiffs' attorneys spent a great deal of time in public relations efforts, including press conferences, interviews, and lobbying efforts at the legislative level.

Time spent by attorneys in public relations is noncompensable. . . . Moreover, time spent on advertisements submitted or created in connection with litigation is not compensable.[8] Plaintiffs' time entries are replete with references to media and public relations matters.

5. Post Judgment Time

Plaintiffs' attorneys spent a significant block of time after this court's December 17, 1992 final decision posturing for and planning an appeal. There was also substantial time spent lobbying members of the Utah Legislature to change Utah's abortion statutes. However, it is evident that most of the hours devoted to these two activities pertained to issues upon which plaintiffs did not prevail.

This time does not fit under the rubric of "fees for a prevailing party." To the contrary, compensation for all such hours is inappropriate.

6. Preparation of Fee Application

Reasonable hours expended in preparation of a fee application are at least partially compensable, "although hours not spent representing the client are at best on the borderline of what Congress intended to be compensable." *Mares v. Credit Bureau of Raton.* Plaintiffs' attorneys spent over 130 hours on their fee application and in opposing defendants' application. In the opinion of this court, these hours are excessive, and should be reduced.

7. Clerical or Overhead Time

Plaintiffs' records also refer to time spent filing and retrieving documents, time devoted to reading background cases, and other miscellaneous matters. These hours should be eliminated or reduced. This is the sort of time that is generally absorbed by a private firm as overhead, and is therefore not properly billable to defendants.

Pursuant to the principles enunciated above, and after extensive review of plaintiffs' time records, this court determines that plaintiffs' requested hours far exceed the hours that reasonably would be required by reasonably competent attorneys in handling this litigation. . .

Because Julie Mertus failed to provide the court with any time records supporting her hours request, the court reduces her request by 90%. The court reduces by 1/3 the hours requested by the other four attorneys who failed to submit adequate time documentation. [The specific reductions in the number of

---

[8] On March 14, 1991, Janet Benshoof claims 2.75 hours for an entry which includes "ad work." This "ad work" apparently relates to her creation of an advertisement run in New York City newspapers that "In Utah, They Know How To Punish A Woman Who Has An Abortion. Shoot Her." See Lance Gurwell, Utah Congressman Blasts ACLU Over Abortion Ad, U.P.I., March 26, 1991. (available on LEXIS/NEXIS).

compensable hours are reflected in Appendix A]

. . .

B. Reasonable Hourly Rates

Appropriate hourly rates for counsel are calculated according to the "prevailing market rates in the relevant community." *Blum v. Stenson.* In determining those rates, the fee applicant should produce evidence that "the requested rates are in line with those prevailing in the community for similar services by lawyers of reasonably comparable skill, experience, and reputation." Id. . . .

Defendants have not objected to the rates requested by plaintiffs' local counsel, but take serious issue with the rates requested by the New York attorneys.[12] These rates range from a high of $355.00 per hour for Janet Benshoof[13] and $310.00 per hour for Rachel Pine,[14] to an average of around $200.00 for the other New York attorneys. The prevailing rates locally for excellent trial counsel experienced in civil rights litigation range from $135.00 to $185.00 per hour. Local rates for attorneys with less experience range from $70.00 to $125.00 per hour. Rates claimed by seasoned and highly competent counsel representing the State of Utah range from $155 per hour to $50 per hour. This court has looked to years of experience as one important factor in fixing rates. Out-of-state counsel are not entitled to premium rates based on rate structures in other communities when similar expertise—with significantly lower rates—is available locally.

The overall experience of Ms. Benshoof and Ms. Pine in litigation is not equal to that of local seasoned front-line litigators, with

more years of experience. However, their specialized backgrounds in abortion matters is a factor of importance. Accordingly, the court fixes the rate of Ms. Benshoof and Roger K. Evans, Director of Planned Parenthood, at $155.00 per hour, and that of Ms. Pine at $125.00 per hour. The court has correspondingly adjusted the rates of other plaintiffs' attorneys to reflect the rates of the relevant community. [The specific reductions in hourly rates are reflected in Appendix A.]

C. Adjustments to the Lodestar

The Supreme Court stated in *Hensley* that "the product of reasonable hours times a reasonable rate does not end the inquiry." Where a plaintiff has prevailed on only some claims, there remain two questions to address:

First, did the plaintiff fail to prevail on claims that were unrelated to the claims on which he succeeded? Second, did the plaintiff achieve a level of success that makes the hours reasonably expended a satisfactory basis for making a fee award?

Id.

With regard to the first question, this court dismissed 17 of the 28 plaintiffs in its May 22, 1992 decision because their claims were found to be without merit. *Jane L. v. Bangerter* 794 F.Supp. 1537, 1551 (D. Utah 1992) [*Jane L. II*]. Plaintiffs claim that the dismissed claims were so "inextricably intertwined" with their success on the "core issues" of this case that it is inappropriate not to compensate them for all work done on the case. The issue here is whether the unsuccessfully prosecuted claims were related or unrelated to the successfully prosecuted claims. . . .

In the opinion of this court, this case falls within the category of several separate lawsuits brought in one action. For example, challenges to the serious medical emergency statute, the spousal notification statute, and the statute banning fetal experimentation all involve completely different sets of facts. Further, the legal theories of involuntary servitude, equal protection, separation of church and state, free exercise of religion, freedom of speech, and the corresponding state constitutional claims are not interrelated with the theories behind the successfully prosecuted claims. In this case, it appears that at least in some instances, separate law firms and coun-

---

[12] Plaintiffs' lead counsel, Janet Benshoof and Rachael Pine, are currently president and director of domestic legal projects, respectively, of the Center for Reproductive Law & Policy. From the beginning of this litigation until June, 1992, they were employed as director and senior staff attorney, respectively, of the American Civil Liberties Union's Reproductive Freedom Project ("RFP"). Similarly, for much of the time for which fees are requested, Dominique Bravo, Simon Heller, Andrew Dwyer, Ellen Goetz, Julie Mertus and Margaret Martin, were employees of the RFP.

[13] Janet Benshoof has 20 years of experience in the practice of law and is experienced in abortion litigation.

[14] Rachel Pine has practiced law for 9 years and is experienced in abortion litigation.

sel were engaged to develop separate claims and theories. In all events, this court concludes that the various claims brought by plaintiffs stand independent of one another. Hence, "work on an unsuccessful claim cannot be deemed to have been 'expended in pursuit of the ultimate result achieved'" and, therefore, "no fee may be awarded for services on the unsuccessful claim." [*Hensley*] (citations omitted).

Due to the lack of specificity in plaintiffs' time records, it is impossible to determine exactly how many hours were spent on unsuccessful claims. It is apparent to the court, however, that a very substantial portion of requested time was spent on claims essentially unrelated to the successfully prosecuted claims.

With regard to the second issue identified in Hensley, the Supreme Court stated that in determining a reasonable fee, "the most critical factor is the degree of success obtained." *Hensley*. Plaintiffs achieved success on significant issues in this case by maintaining women's right to abortions before 21 weeks without undue interference by the state, and by obtaining a ruling striking down the spousal notification statute. However, in terms of what was presented and argued to the court, plaintiffs' losses were even more significant. Plaintiffs failed to persuade the court that the 21 weeks abortion cut-off date set out in § 76–7–302(3) was impermissible. This court's ruling that §§ 76–7–307 and 308 (post-viability abortion requirements for doctors) are constitutional also went against plaintiffs. Other unsuccessful statutory challenges were those brought against § 76–7–314 (criminal liability) and § 76–7–315 (serious medical emergency). Plaintiffs not only did not prevail on their state constitutional claims, but attempted to abandon them. Finally, plaintiffs prevailed on a very small percentage of their legal theories for relief on the claims in which they were successful.

In acknowledgment of the limited success of their claims, plaintiffs have voluntarily reduced their lodestar claim by 20%, from $827,484.30 to $661,987.44. Based upon reasonable compensable hours and hourly rates, the court has calculated plaintiffs' lodestar figure to be $293,741.55. The court finds that in order to reflect plaintiffs' limited success in this action, this lodestar figure should be reduced by 85% for the firm of Berle, Kass & Case, and 75% for the other plaintiffs' counsel, yielding an adjusted fee award of $69,656.37.

II. DEFENDANTS' ATTORNEYS' FEES

Defendants have submitted a request for attorneys' fees and expenses totalling $300,000.77. Prevailing defendants are granted attorneys' fees under § 1988 only in limited circumstances:

> A prevailing defendant may recover an attorney's fee only where the suit was vexatious, frivolous, or brought to harass or embarrass the defendant. See HR Rep. No. 94–1558, p. 7 (1976); *Christiansburg Garment Co. v. E.E.O.C.* ("[A] district court may in its discretion award attorney's fees to a prevailing defendant in a Title VII case upon a finding that the plaintiff's action was frivolous, unreasonable, or without foundation, even though not brought in subjective bad faith.")

Hensley v. Eckerhart. This court has determined that plaintiffs' case involved "unrelated claims," which should be treated as if they had been raised in separate lawsuits. To the extent these claims are frivolous, or meritless, defendants may receive attorneys' fees involved in responding to them under 42 U.S.C. § 1988. An additional basis for such an award is found in the inherent powers of the court. *Chambers v. NASCO, Inc.* To the extent that such claims were unreasonable and prosecuted in bad faith, defendants also may be entitled to an award under 28 U.S.C. § 1927 and Federal Rule of Civil procedure 11.

A. Defendants' Time Records and Fees

Defendants' time records are clear, concise, and specific. It is also apparent that defendants' counsel exercised appropriate billing judgment before submitting their records to the court. They did not bill for excessive travel or public relations time, and, with few exceptions, time entries for hearings, meetings, and conference calls were billed to only one attorney to avoid excessive duplicative time. Those instances where an attorney listed multiple activities under one time entry usually involved fully compensable activities. This court further finds, with one exception, that defendants' requested hourly rates are reasonable.[20]

B. Claims For Which Defendants Are Awarded Attorneys' Fees

Defendants have alleged that most of plaintiffs' lawsuit is frivolous, groundless, and/or brought in bad faith. After review of these arguments, the court concurs as to the following four claims:

1. Involuntary Servitude

In their Sixth Cause of Action, plaintiffs allege that prohibiting abortion forces women into slavery or involuntary servitude in violation of the Thirteenth Amendment of the United States Constitution. In May 1992, this court held that "it strains credulity to equate the carrying of a child to term with 'compulsory labor,' and concluded that "the argument borders on the frivolous." *Jane L. v. Bangerter* 79 F.Supp. 1537, 1549 (D. Utah 1992) [*Jane L. II*].

The frivolity or groundlessness of the Involuntary Servitude claim was not before the court at the time the May 22, 1992 Memorandum Decision and Order was issued. However, upon analysis of the historical background of the Thirteenth Amendment, along with consideration of more recent Supreme Court interpretation of the Amendment's scope, this court found at that time that the "contention that one of the purposes of the Thirteenth Amendment was to secure the right of elective abortion totally lacks merit." Id. Because plaintiffs' Thirteenth Amendment claim was frivolous and groundless, the court awards defendants attorneys' fees incurred in opposing this argument in the amount of $8,071.46.

2. Equal Protection

Plaintiffs' Fourth Cause of Action alleges that because the Utah Abortion Act primarily impinges upon women's procreative choices,

the Act discriminates on the basis of gender in violation of the Fourteenth Amendment of the United States Constitution. This court summarily disposed of the equal protection claim because plaintiffs were unable to establish that the Utah Act did anything more than "'realistically reflect[] the fact that the sexes are not similarly situated in certain circumstances.'" Id. (quoting *Michael M. v. Sonoma County Superior Court*). In addition, plaintiffs did not allege facts sufficient to support an allegation of "invidious discrimination." Accordingly, this Court finds their claim to have been without foundation. Defendants are therefore granted attorneys' fees of $5,880.37.

3. Establishment Clause

In their Fifth Cause of Action, plaintiffs alleged that the Utah Act violated the Establishment Clause of the First Amendment. Plaintiffs argued that the Act failed the three-part test set forth in *Lemon v. Kurtzman* in that (1) its preamble embodied a prohibited "religious viewpoint" concerning rights of unborn children; and (2) the Act mirrored and therefore unconstitutionally endorsed the position of the Church of Jesus Christ of Latter-Day Saints.

Similar arguments have been soundly rejected in previous Supreme Court cases. In *Harris v. McRae* the Court held that a statute does not violate the "secular purpose" prong of the Lemon test simply "because it 'happens to coincide or harmonize with the tenets of some or all religions.'" Id. (citation omitted). Subsequent cases have reaffirmed this rule. . . .Moreover, the *Harris* Court explicitly held that provisions similar to those set forth in the Act are "as much a reflection of 'traditionalist' values towards abortion, as it is an embodiment of the views of any particular religion." *Harris*. Furthermore, it is manifest that the evidence supporting the plaintiffs' argument in Harris was much more substantial than the evidence supporting plaintiffs' claim here.

Plaintiffs' allegations that the Utah Act violated the "primary effect" prong of the Lemon test were likewise frivolous and without foundation. This is even more apparent in light of the Supreme Court's ruling in *Bowen v. Kendrick* which involved legislation posing a significantly greater danger of having an unconstitutional "effect" on religion than

---

[20] Stuart Jones requests a rate of $70 per hour for work done as a law clerk. The court reduces this rate to $55 per hour. The rates asserted by several of defendants' counsel appear to be significantly understated. For example, Professor Richard Wilkins requests a rate of $50 per hour, doubtless meant to reflect a purposeful reduction in the nature of public service. Plaintiffs have not challenged the reasonableness of any of defendants' claimed hourly rates.

does the Utah Act. The "entanglement" prong of the Lemon test was inapplicable to this case.

Based on the evidence before it, and given the clear holdings of *Harris, Wallace,* and *Bowen,* this court finds that plaintiffs knew, or should have known, that their Establishment Clause claims were frivolous, and without legal or factual foundation at the time they filed their Complaint. . . .Litigating these claims wasted valuable time and resources and unnecessarily delayed the final resolution of this case. For this reason, the court awards defendants attorneys' fees of $29,879.63.

4. State Constitutional Claims

Plaintiffs brought eight causes of action based on the Federal Constitution, and eight analogous causes of action based on the Utah Constitution. Plaintiffs did not prevail on any of these state constitutional claims. For the most part, state law in this case mirrors federal law. The court has already found that several of plaintiffs' federal claims were frivolous and without foundation. It follows that the corresponding state claims were frivolous as well.

. . .

5. Fee Application

Prevailing defendants, like prevailing plaintiffs are entitled to at least partial compensation for the time spent preparing their fee application. The court awards defendants 50% of the amount requested, or $7,719.50.

III. COSTS AND EXPENSES

Both parties request reimbursement for costs and out-of-pocket expenses incurred in the course of litigation. . . .

A. Costs

Rule 54(d) of the Federal Rules of Civil Procedure states that "costs shall be allowed as of course to the prevailing party unless the court otherwise directs." (emphasis added). The word "costs" in rule 54(d) is a term of art, defined by 28 U.S.C. § 1920. . . . While this court is given broad discretion in awarding costs, "it has no discretion to award items as costs that are not set out in section 1920." *Bee v. Greaves.* Only the following items may be taxed as costs:

(1) Fees of the clerk and marshal;

(2) Fees of the court reporter for all or any part of the stenographic transcript necessarily obtained for use in the case;

(3) Fees and disbursements for printing and witnesses;

(4) Fees for exemplification and copies of papers necessarily obtained for use in the case;

(5) Docket fees under section 1923 of [Title 28];

(6) Compensation of court appointed experts, compensation of interpreters, and salaries, fees, expenses, and costs of special interpretation services under section 1828 of [Title 28].

28 U.S.C. § 1920.

. . .

1. Plaintiffs' Costs

In their memorandum in support of their application for attorneys' fees, plaintiffs requested reimbursement for the following "costs" and "expenses":

* CRLP
  (a) airfare $22,709.57
  (b) overnight courier service ... $ 2,510.31
  (c) copies, postage, phone,
       faxes, LEXIS research $13,546.49
  (d) deposition transcripts .... $ 9,223.59
  (e) court transcript costs .... $ 795.50
  (f) filing fee for complaint ...... $ 120.00
* Planned Parenthood
  (a) deposition transcript costs $ 2,765.10
* Jeffrey Oritt
  (a) notice of appeal fee .... $ 105.00
* TOTAL $51,775.56

Plaintiffs have lumped together their "costs," with "expenses" which are more appropriately sought as part of an attorney's fee under § 1988. The parties' "categorization of items is not dispositive of their recoverability," so the court will separate the claimed amounts into "costs" and "expenses."

Of the items listed above, the following are properly categorized as "costs" under Rule 54(d):

* deposition transcripts	$11,988.69
* court transcript costs	$ 795.50
* filing fee for complaint	$ 120.00
* notice of appeal fee	$ 105.00
	$13,009.19

Some of plaintiffs' identified costs are not recoverable. For instance, the Notice of Appeal filing fee pertains to claims on which plaintiffs lost, and should not be included in the taxation of costs.

2. Defendants' Costs

Defendants have filed a bill of costs amounting to $12,754.69. The items sought include court reporter fees ($1,326.50), exemplification of copies fees ($3,571.98), and deposition transcript fees ($7,856.21).

A prevailing party under Rule 54(d) is usually the one for whom judgment is entered. In this case, however, both parties were successful on some claims, and both parties have requested costs in approximately equal amounts. For these reasons, the court exercises its discretion and orders the parties to bear their own costs.

B. Expenses

Section 1988 provides that, in civil rights actions, "the court, in its discretion, may allow the prevailing party . . . a reasonable attorney's fee as part of the costs. " 42 U.S.C. 1988(b). While only those items listed under § 1920 may be awarded as "costs," other out-of-pocket expenses incurred during litigation may be awarded as "attorney's fees" under section 1988 if (1) the expenses are not absorbed as part of law firm overhead but are normally billed to a private client, and (2) the expenses are reasonable. *Bee v. Greaves* (citing *Ramos v. Lamm*).

1. Plaintiffs' Expenses

Plaintiffs request the following "expenses" under § 1988:

* airfare	$22,709.57
* overnight courier service	$ 2,510.31
* copies, postage, phone, faxes, LEXIS research	<u>$13,546.49</u>
	$38,766.37

Attorney travel expenses are normally billed to a private client and are therefore appropriately reimbursed as "attorney's fees" under § 1988. However, as has already been discussed, this case could have been handled adequately by local attorneys. The Tenth Circuit has explained that it is generally improper to award travel expenses incurred by out-of-state attorneys in traveling to the place of litigation. . .Plaintiffs' request for travel expenses is therefore denied.

As to the other out-of-pocket expenses amounting to $16,056.80, the court finds that many of these expenses are generally billed to the client. The court further finds that one-half of these expenses were reasonably incurred.

This amount is included with plaintiffs' lodestar figure and adjusted to reflect plaintiffs' limited success on the merits. Accordingly, the court adds $2,007.10 in expenses to plaintiffs' attorneys' fee award.

2. Defendants' Expenses

Defendants seek reimbursement for $3,120.75 of travel expenses incurred in relation to fighting plaintiffs' Establishment Clause and Free Exercise Clause claims. These travel expenses are normally billed to the client, and, to the extent they relate to the Establishment Clause claims, should be included in defendants' attorneys' fees award. Accordingly, the court awards defendants 50% of these travel expenses, or $1,560.37, as representing the expenses defendants incurred fighting plaintiffs' Establishment Clause claims.

Based upon the foregoing, plaintiffs' application for attorneys' fees in the amount of $700,753.813 is reduced by $629,090.34. Defendants' application for attorneys' fees of $300,000.77 is reduced by $231,135.97.

Accordingly, it is hereby

ORDERED, that plaintiffs whose claims were successfully prosecuted are entitled to an award of $71,663.47 for attorneys' fees in this action; it is

FURTHER ORDERED, that defendants are entitled to an award of $68,957.80 for attorneys' fees in this action, to be paid $53,110.33 by plaintiffs whose claims are declared to be frivolous, and $15,847.47 by plaintiffs' counsel; it is

FURTHER ORDERED, that the parties shall bear their own costs.

IT IS SO ORDERED.

APPENDIX A

Plaintiffs' Award

Name	Hours Claimed	Rate Claimed	Hours Allowed	Rate Allowed	Lodestar
J. Benshoof CRLP	451.65	$355	301.10 (67%)	$155	$46,670.50
R. Pine CRLP	353.10	$310	235.40 (67%)	$125	$29,425.00
S. Heller CRLP	117.50	$285	113.50 (97%)	$105	$11,917.50
E. Goetz CRLP	67.67	$235	65.50 (97%)	$ 95	$ 6,222.50
J. Mertus CRLP	600	$195	60.00 (10%)	$ 95	$ 5,700.00
L. Lapidus CRLP	91.00	$195	71.00 (79%)	$ 85	$ 6,035.00
D. Bravo CRLP	632.75	$125	506.20 (80%)	$ 75	$37,965.00
C. Albissa CRLP	167.55	$155	137.55 (92%)	$ 90	$12,379.50
A. Dwyer CRLP	41.65	$155	29.15 (70%)	$ 85	$ 2,477.75
D. Gans CRLP (paralegal)	47.55	$ 80	31.70 (67%)	$ 55	$ 1,743.50
R. Evans PPFA	58.75	$250	25.00 (43%)	$155	$ 3,875.00
J. McCarroll BKC	33.70	$250	26.96 (80%)	$130	$ 3,504.80
E. Gartner BKC	392.30	$160	360.90 (92%)	$ 95	$34,285.50
J. Oritt WOR	565.05	$125	376.70 (67%)	$125	$47,087.50
H. Lundgren BL	266.30	$125	177.50 (67%)	$125	$22,187.50
K. Kendell ACLU	74.00	$110	55.50 (75%)	$ 90	$ 4,995.00
M. Martin CRLP	471.00	$135	314.00 (67%)	$ 55	$17,270.00

Name	Lodestar Award	Lodestar Adjustment	Final Fee Award
CRLP	$177,806.25	−75%	$44,451.56
PPFA	$ 3,875.00	−75%	$ 968.75
Berle, Kass & Case	$ 37,790.30	−85%	$ 5,668.55
J. Oritt	$ 47,087.50	−75%	$11,771.88
J. Lundgren	$ 22,187.50	−75%	$ 5,546.88
K. Kendell	$ 4,995.00	−75%	$ 1,248.75
Expenses Awarded	$ 8,028.40	−75%	$ 2,007.10
Total	$301,769.95		$71,663.47

APPENDIX B

Defendants' Award

* Normal type—amount requested

* Bold type—amount actually awarded

Name	Inv. Serv.	Religion Claims	Eq. Prot.	State Const.	Fee App.	Total
P. Durham	**$1,123.50**	$16,779 **$7,917**				
R. Wilkins		$587.50 **$293.75**		$225 **$175**		
L. Hawkins		$3,500 **$1,750**				
C. Durham		$25,820 **$12,460**				
A. Quinn		$5,265 **$2,632.50**		$260 **$130**	$1,657.50 **$828.75**	
M. Wood		$1,486.25 **$743.13**		$2,356.25 **$2,066.25**	$2,392 **$1,196**	
K. Balmforth		$2,167.50 **$1,041.25**		$7,990 **$7,820**	$4,845 **$2,422.50**	
R. Skousen		$2,351.25 **$1,045**		$1,567.50 **$1,457.50**	$5,307 **$2,653.50**	
K. Patterson		$357 **$178.50**				
J. Bowser		$495 **$192.50**			$1,237.50 **$ 618.75**	
M. Holman	$310 **$103.33**					
M. Kelley	$4,505 **$4,391**					
J. Walker	$190 **$63.33**					
T. Anderson		$3,380 **$1,625**	**$2,892.50**			
S. Jones				$434 **$341**		
Expenses		$3,120.75 **$1,560.37**				
SJ MOTION	$2,441.70 **$2,390.30**		$3,052.13 **$2,987.87**	$3,845.68 **$3,764.72**		
Totals	8,570.20 **8,071.46**	65,309.75 **31,439**	5,944.63 **5,880.37**	16,678.43 **15,754.47**	15,440 **7,719.50**	111,943 **68,864.80**

NOTES

1. A district court's award of attorney's fees is reviewable under an abuse of discretion standard. *Hensley v. Eckerhart*, 461 U.S. 424, 437 (1983). Findings on underlying questions of fact are subject to the clearly erroneous standard. *Mares v. Credit Bureau of Raton*, 801 F.2d 1197, 1201 (10th Cir. 1986). A district court's statutory interpretation or legal analysis providing the basis for the fee award is reviewable de novo. *Homeward Bound, Inc. v. Hissom Memorial Center*, 963 F.2d 1352, 1355 (10th Cir. 1992). Given these principles, which portions of the District Court's rulings in *Jane L.*, if any, are most vulnerable to attack? What are the lessons to be learned from the District Court's rulings on attorney's fees in *Jane L.*? What message does the opinion send regarding record keeping, the advocacy of innovative legal theories, or the type of activities that an attorney should engage in when representing a client? Does the result in *Jane L.* comport with the purposes of section 1988 as elucidated in Senate Report No. 94–1011?

2. The first factor in computing the lodestar is the reasonable number of hours expended by counsel. The plaintiffs in *Jane L.* requested compensation for 4,431.52 hours of work. The District Court awarded compensation for 2,887.66 hours, a reduction of approximately 35%. Some of that reduction was attributable to inadequately documented time records. Although detailed contemporaneous records are preferred, a court may, in its discretion, base an award of attorney's fees on detailed reconstructed time records. E.g., *Carter v. Sedgwick County*, 929 F.2d 1501, 1506–07 (10th Cir. 1991) (awarding attorney's fees for all hours requested based on reconstructed time records); *Johnson v. University College*, 706 F.2d 1205, 1207 (11th Cir. 1983) ("lack of contemporaneous [time] records does not justify an automatic reduction in the hours claimed").

The District Court in *Jane L.* also reduced the time component of the lodestar because certain listed activities were vague, unnecessary or otherwise not compensable. The court specifically disallowed compensation for time spent by counsel on public relations and lobbying to change the statutes under constitutional attack. These rulings invite an examination of the variety of things lawyers do in the course of representing a client. Should lobbying and pub-

lic relations be considered a compensable part of representing the client in litigation? Consider the comments of another court:

> Where the giving of press conferences and performance of other lobbying and public relations work is directly and intimately related to the successful representation of a client, private attorneys do such work and bill their clients. Prevailing civil rights plaintiffs may do the same.

Davis v. City and County of San Francisco, 976 F.2d 1536, 1545 (9th Cir. 1992), vacated in part on other grounds, 984 F.2d 345 (9th Cir. 1993) (employment discrimination). But see *Watkins v. Fordice*, 7 F.3d 453, 458 (5th Cir. 1993) ("Because pre-litigation lobbying is not a necessary precursor to the filing of a lawsuit, the district court did not abuse its discretion when it deducted these hours during its lodestar analysis. . . .we find no abuse of discretion in the district court's exclusion of the press-conference hours. . ."). Does the legislative history of the attorney's fee statute provide insight as to the scope of activities Congress intended to be included and excluded from the calculation an attorney's fee award?

3. The second component of the lodestar is the reasonable hourly rate. *Blum v. Stenson*, 465 U.S. 886, 895 (1984) held that a reasonable fee reflects compensation at "the prevailing market rates in the relevant community. . . ." Should the "relevant community" always, or at least presumptively, be that of the forum? Under what circumstances, if any, would it be appropriate to award attorney's fees calculated on rates other than those prevailing in the forum community? See *Chrapliwy v. Uniroyal, Inc.*, 670 F.2d 760, 769 (7th Cir. 1982) ("If. . .a party does not find counsel readily available in [the forum] locality with whatever degree of skill may reasonably be required, it is reasonable that the party go elsewhere to find an attorney, and the court should make the allowance on the basis of the chosen attorney's billing rate. . ."); *Maceira v. Pagan*, 698 F.2d 38, 40 (1st Cir. 1983) (awarding attorney's fees for out-of-town counsel in a labor law case based on rates he charged in Detroit rather than prevailing rates charged in the forum jurisdiction because using an outside specialist was reasonable); *Palmigiano v. Garrahy*, 707 F.2d 636, 637 (1st Cir. 1983) (attorney's fees paid to out-of-state specialist with unique competence in prison civil rights case should be based on out-of-state rates) (dicta).

4. Once a court has fixed both the reasonable hours and reasonable rate, it should consider whether any adjustments to the lodestar are appropriate. The District Court in *Jane L.* held that the lodestar should be reduced by 75% to 85% because the plaintiffs did not prevail on a number of "unrelated" issues and achieved only a limited success overall. Courts routinely award attorney's fees for time spent on unsuccessful claims if they are "sufficiently interconnected with the causes of action upon which [the plaintiff] prevailed". *Lipsett v. Blanco*, 975 F.2d 934, 940 (1st Cir. 1992). By what standard should the "relatedness" of various claims be measured? Was plaintiffs' unsuccessful challenge of Utah's ban on fetal experimentation related, or unrelated, to their successful challenge of the spousal notification provision? Was plaintiffs' unsuccessful challenge to Utah's restrictions on post-viability abortions related, or unrelated, to their successful challenge to the state's restrictions on pre-viability abortions?

How relevant is it to the attorney's fee issue that the plaintiffs challenged the pre-viability restrictions under a variety of constitutional theories, but prevailed on only one? Should the district court's rejection of the alternative legal theories affect the amount of the attorney's fee award? See *Durant v. Independent School Dist. No. 16*, 990 F.2d 560, 566 (10th Cir. 1993) (full attorney's fees may be awarded in the court's discretion when a teacher successfully challenged her dismissal on first amendment grounds, but lost her due process claim); *Tidwell v. Fort Howard Corp.*, 989 F.2d 406, 412 (10th Cir. 1993) (plaintiffs who succeeded on an Equal Pay Act claim but did not prevail on alternative claims under Title VII and state law were entitled to a full lodestar award of attorney's fees). Is *Jane L.* consistent with *Durant* and *Tidwell*?

How does one measure the overall "degree of success" obtained by this litigation? The defendants in *Jane L.* were successful in defending the constitutionality of 6 of the 8 statutes at issue. Does this mean that the plaintiffs were only 25% successful? Is this type of mathematical approach a reliable measure of "success," or should a court attempt to determine which results were most important in a

qualitative sense? Which is more important, the upholding of the constitutionality of restrictions placed on post-viability abortions, or the invalidation of restrictions on pre-viability abortions? Is it relevant that more women are likely to be affected by pre-viability than post-viability restrictions?

5. Defendants may be awarded attorney's fees in civil rights cases only when the plaintiff's action was "vexatious, frivolous, or brought to harass or embarrass." *Hensley v. Eckerhart*, 461 U.S. 424, 429 n.2 (1983) citing *Christiansburg Garment Co. v. EEOC*, 434 U.S. 412, 421 (1978). How can courts apply this standard so as to protect governments and officials from the costs of defending patently meritless litigation without unduly chilling the advocacy of civil rights? Should a legal theory be labeled "frivolous" when it finds some support among individual jurists and legal scholars, but has not been accepted by a court? The equal protection, involuntary servitude, and establishment clause claims found to be frivolous in *Jane L.* each have such support. See Ruth Bader Ginsburg, *Speaking in a Judicial Voice*, 67 N.Y.U. L. Rev. 1185, 1199–1200 (1992) (supporting an equal protection approach to abortion law); *Webster v. Reproductive Health Services*, 492 U.S. 490, 566 (1989) (Stevens, J., concurring in part, dissenting in part) (embracing an establishment clause attack on the preamble to a Missouri abortion statute); *Roe v. Rampton*, 394 F. Supp. 677, 689 (D. Utah 1975) (Ritter, C.J., dissenting on other grounds) (characterizing compelled pregnancy as "a form of involuntary servitude"), aff'd 535 F.2d 1219 (10th Cir. 1976). On the other hand, defendants have a legitimate interest in avoiding the expense incurred in defending suits that attempt to establish new constitutional theories. At what point should the plaintiff bear the financial risk of experimenting with constitutional law? See *Vakas v. Rodriquez*, 728 F.2d 1293, 1297 (10th Cir. 1984) (unsuccessful theories having "some slight legal support" could be deemed frivolous).

6. An attorney's fee award under section 1988 may include compensation for paralegals, law clerks, and other support personnel. In *Missouri v. Jenkins*, 491 U.S. 274 (1989), the Court stated that the increasingly widespread custom of separately billing for the services of paralegals and law clerks must be taken into account so that "an attorney's fee awarded under § 1988 . . . yield[s] the same level of compensation that would be available from the market. . . ." *Jenkins*, 491 U.S. at 286.

Should expert witness fees also be awarded? In *West Virginia University Hospitals, Inc. v. Casey*, 499 U.S. 83 (1991), the Court held that expert witness expenses could not be included in an award of attorney's fees under section 1988. Limited compensation ($40 per day) for the testimonial services of expert witnesses could be assessed as "costs" under 28 U.S.C. § 1821(b). This limitation on recovery for expert witness fees was seen by many civil rights advocates as a major barrier to effective representation. In 1991, Congress amended section 1988 to authorize the court, "in its discretion," to included expert witness fees as part of the attorney's fee award. This amendment, however, only applies to claims brought pursuant to 42 U.S.C. § 1981, and not section 1983 actions.

7. Should an award of attorney's fees under section 1988 include time spent representing the claimant in forums other than the one in which the section 1983 claim was filed? Recall from Chapter 10 that *Patsy v. Board of Regents*, 457 U.S. 496 (1982), held that a civil rights plaintiff does not have to exhaust her state administrative remedies before filing a section 1983 claim. Nonetheless, suppose a plaintiff first unsuccessfully seeks redress in a state administrative forum and later prevails in her section 1983 claim. Should the time spent in the state administrative proceeding be included in calculating the attorney's fee award under section 1988? In *Webb v. County Board of Education*, 471 U.S. 234, 241–43 (1985) the Court held that such hours were not "automatically" compensable; however, a "discrete portion" of the time spent in the state administrative proceeding could be included in the section 1988 award of attorney's fees if it was "both useful and of a type ordinarily necessary to advance the [subsequent] civil rights litigation . . . ." May a plaintiff who prevails in the state administrative proceeding recover attorney's fees under section 1988? See *North Carolina Department of Transportation v. Crest Street Community Council*, 479 U.S. 12 (1986) (No; "§ 1988 does not authorize a court to award attorney's fees except in an action to enforce the listed civil rights laws."). Do these cases

encourage claimants' counsel to file a section 1983 claim in federal court before attempting to resolve the dispute on nonconstitutional grounds in a state administrative forum? Are there countervailing strategic or ethical considerations that might lead an attorney to pursue state agency remedies anyway? If so, does the result in *Crest Street* square with the purposes of section 1988?

Recall also that there are various abstention doctrines that may force a civil rights plaintiff to pursue remedies in state court before a federal court will consider her section 1983 claim. See Chapter 10. Several courts have included in their award of attorney's fees to an ultimately successful section 1983 claimant, time spent unsuccessfully representing the plaintiff in state court pursuant to an abstention doctrine. See *Bartholomew v. Watson*, 665 F.2d 910 (9th Cir. 1982); *Lampher v. Zagel*, 755 F.2d 99 (7th Cir. 1985); *Stathos v. Bowden*, 728 F.2d 15 (1st Cir. 1984). One abstaining federal court awarded fees when the case was resolved in the state court on state law grounds, thus rendering moot the section 1983 claim. *Exeter-West Greenwich Regional School v. Pontarelli*, 788 F.2d 47 (1st Cir. 1986). Are these cases consistent with *Webb* and *Crest Street Community Council*? Are they consistent with the lower court cases cited in note 4 following *Farrar*, concerning fee awards for work on pendent state claims in federal court?

IV. Strategic and Ethical Aspects of Attorney's Fee Awards

The previous sections considered when attorney's fees are recoverable and how such an award is calculated. We turn now to the strategic and ethical implications of attorney's fee awards on litigation. How might the potential availability of attorney's fees affect litigation strategy? Is the potential for an attorney's fees award likely to promote or inhibit the settlement of cases? Can the defendant structure a settlement proposal in such a way as to drive a wedge between the plaintiff and her attorney? If so, would such a proposal be ethical?

Evans v. Jeff D.

475 U.S. 717 (1986)

Justice **Stevens** delivered the opinion of the Court.

The Civil Rights Attorney's Fees Awards Act of 1976 (Fees Act) provides that "the court, in its discretion, may allow the prevailing party . . . a reasonable attorney's fee" in enumerated civil rights actions. 90 Stat. 2641, 42 U.S.C. § 1988. In *Maher v. Gagne* we held that fees may be assessed against state officials after a case has been settled by the entry of a consent decree. In this case, we consider the question whether attorney's fees must be assessed when the case has been settled by a consent decree granting prospective relief to the plaintiff class but providing that the defendants shall not pay any part of the prevailing party's fees or costs. We hold that the District Court has the power, in its sound discretion, to refuse to award fees.

I

The petitioners are the Governor and other public officials of the State of Idaho responsible for the education and treatment of children who suffer from emotional and mental handicaps. Respondents are a class of such children who have been or will be placed in petitioners' care.

On August 4, 1980, respondents commenced this action by filing a complaint against petitioners in the United States District Court for the District of Idaho. The factual allegations in the complaint described deficiencies in both the educational programs and the health care services provided respondents. These deficiencies allegedly violated the United States Constitution, the Idaho Constitution, four federal statutes, and certain provisions of the Idaho Code. The complaint prayed for injunctive relief and for an award of costs and attorney's fees, but it did not seek damages.

. . .[The District Court appointed a lawyer, Johnson, from the Idaho Legal Aid Society to represent the plaintiff. Because the Legal Aid Society was prohibited from representing persons capable of paying attorney's fees, an award of fees under section 1988 was the only potential source of payment in this case. The parties quickly settled the claims relating to educational services. This settlement, which included a waiver of attorney's fees, was approved by the District Court. The parties were unable to reach a settlement on the treatment issues. The District Court certified the class and the parties prepared for trial.]

In March 1983, one week before trial, petitioners presented respondents with a new settlement proposal. As respondents themselves characterize it, the proposal "offered virtually all of the injunctive relief [they] had sought in their complaint." Brief for Respondents 5. See App. 89. The Court of Appeals agreed with this characterization, and further noted that the proposed relief was "more than the district court in earlier hearings had indicated it was willing to grant." As was true of the earlier partial settlement, however, petitioners' offer included a provision for a waiver by respondents of any claim to fees or costs. Originally, this waiver was unacceptable to the Idaho Legal Aid Society, which had instructed Johnson to reject any settlement offer conditioned upon a waiver of fees, but Johnson ultimately determined that his ethical obligation to his clients mandated acceptance of the proposal. The parties conditioned the waiver on approval by the District Court.

After the stipulation was signed, Johnson filed a written motion requesting the District Court to approve the settlement "except for the provision on costs and attorney's fees," and to allow respondents to present a bill of costs and fees for consideration by the court. At the oral argument on that motion, Johnson contended that petitioners' offer had exploited his ethical duty to his clients—that he was "forced," by an offer giving his clients "the best result [they] could have gotten in this court or any other court," to waive his attorney's fees.

. . . [The District Court rejected the plaintiff's argument and and approved the settlement, including the waiver of attorney's fees. The Court of Appeals, however,] invalidated the fee waiver and left standing the remainder of the settlement; it then instructed the District Court to "make its own determination of the fees that are reasonable" and remanded for that limited purpose.

. . .

The importance of the question decided by the Court of Appeals, together with the conflict between its decision and the decisions of other Courts of Appeals, led us to grant certiorari. We now reverse.

II

. . .

To begin with, the Court of Appeals' decision rested on an erroneous view of the District Court's power to approve settlements in class actions. Rule 23(e) wisely requires court approval of the terms of any settlement of a class action, but the power to approve or reject a settlement negotiated by the parties before trial does not authorize the court to require the parties to accept a settlement to which they have not agreed. . . The District Court could not enforce the settlement on the merits and award attorney's fees anymore than it could, in a situation in which the attorney had negotiated a large fee at the expense of the plaintiff class, preserve the fee award and order greater relief on the merits. . . .

. . .Although respondents contend that Johnson, as counsel for the class, was faced with an "ethical dilemma" when petitioners offered him relief greater than that which he could reasonably have expected to obtain for his clients at trial (if only he would stipulate to a waiver of the statutory fee award), and although we recognize Johnson's conflicting interests between pursuing relief for the class and a fee for the Idaho Legal Aid Society, we do not believe that the "dilemma" was an "ethical" one in the sense that Johnson had to choose between conflicting duties under the prevailing norms of professional conduct. Plainly, Johnson had no ethical obligation to seek a statutory fee award. His ethical duty was to serve his clients loyally and competently. Since the proposal to settle the merits was more favorable than the probable outcome of the trial, Johnson's decision to recommend acceptance was consistent with the highest standards of our profession. . .

The defect, if any, in the negotiated fee waiver must be traced not to the rules of ethics but to the Fees Act[15] . . . .[R]espondents

argue that the statute must be construed to forbid a fee waiver that is the product of "coercion." They submit that a "coercive waiver" results when the defendant in a civil rights action (1) offers a settlement on the merits of equal or greater value than that which plaintiffs could reasonably expect to achieve at trial but (2) conditions the offer on a waiver of plaintiffs' statutory eligibility for attorney's fees. Such an offer, they claim, exploits the ethical obligation of plaintiffs' counsel to recommend settlement in order to avoid defendant's statutory liability for its opponents' fees and costs.[16]

. . .[W]e are not persuaded that Congress has commanded that all such settlements must be rejected by the District Court. Moreover, on the facts of record in this case, we are

---

[15] Even state bar opinions holding it unethical for defendants to request fee waivers in exchange for relief

on the merits of plaintiffs' claims are bottomed ultimately on § 1988. See District of Columbia Bar Legal Ethics Committee, Op. No. 147, reprinted in 113 Daily Wash. L. Rep. 389, 394–395 (1985); Committee on Professional and Judicial Ethics of the New York City Bar Association, Op. No. 82–80, p. 1 (1985); id., at 4–5 (dissenting opinion); Committee on Professional and Judicial Ethics of the New York City Bar Association, Op. No. 80–94, reprinted in 36 Record of N. Y. C. B. A. 507, 508–511 (1981); Grievance Commission of Board of Overseers of the Bar of Maine, Op. No. 17, reprinted in Advisory Opinions of the Grievance Commission of the Board of Overseers of the Bar 69–70 (1983). For the sake of completeness, it should be mentioned that the bar is not of one mind on this ethical judgment. See Final Subcommittee Report of the Committee on Attorney's Fees of the Judicial Conference of the United State Court of Appeals for the District of Columbia Circuit, reprinted in 13 Bar Rep. 4, 6 (1984) (declining to adopt flat rule forbidding waivers of statutory fees). Cf. State Bar of Georgia, Op. No. 39, reprinted in 10 Ga. St. Bar News No. 2, p. 5 (1984) (rejecting the reasoning of the Committee on Professional and Judicial Ethics of the New York City Bar Association in the context of lump-sum settlement offers for the reason, among others, that "[to] force a defendant into proposing a settlement offer wherein plaintiffs['] statutory attorney fees are not negotiated . . . [means that] meaningful settlement proposals might never be made. Such a situation undeniably . . . is inimical to the resolution of disputes between parties").

[16] See Committee on Professional and Judicial Ethics of the New York City Bar Association, Op. No. 80–94, reprinted in 36 Record of N. Y. C. B. A., at 508 ("Defense counsel thus are in a uniquely favorable position when they condition settlement on the waiver of the statutory fee: they make a demand for a benefit which the plaintiff's lawyer cannot resist as a matter of ethics and which the plaintiff will not resist due to lack of interest"). Accord, District of Columbia Bar Legal Ethics Committee, Op. No. 147, reprinted in 113 Daily Wash. L. Rep., at 394.

satisfied that the District Court did not abuse its discretion by approving the fee waiver.

III

The text of the Fees Act . . . and its legislative history nowhere suggest that Congress intended to forbid all waivers of attorney's fees—even those insisted upon by a civil rights plaintiff in exchange for some other relief to which he is indisputably not entitled[20] —anymore than it intended to bar a concession on damages to secure broader injunctive relief. Thus, while it is undoubtedly true that Congress expected fee shifting to attract competent counsel to represent citizens deprived of their civil rights, it neither bestowed fee awards upon attorneys nor rendered them nonwaivable or nonnegotiable; instead, it added them to the arsenal of remedies available to combat violations of civil rights, a goal not invariably inconsistent with conditioning settlement on the merits on a waiver of statutory attorney's fees.

In fact, we believe that a general proscription against negotiated waiver of attorney's fees in exchange for a settlement on the merits would itself impede vindication of civil rights, at least in some cases, by reducing the attractiveness of settlement. . .

Most defendants are unlikely to settle unless the cost of the predicted judgment, discounted by its probability, plus the transaction costs of further litigation, are greater than the cost of the settlement package. If fee waivers cannot be negotiated, the settlement package must either contain an attorney's fee component of potentially large and typically

uncertain magnitude, or else the parties must agree to have the fee fixed by the court. Although either of these alternatives may well be acceptable in many cases, there surely is a significant number in which neither alternative will be as satisfactory as a decision to try the entire case.

. . . We conclude, therefore, that it is not necessary to construe the Fees Act as embodying a general rule prohibiting settlements conditioned on the waiver of fees in order to be faithful to the purposes of that Act.

IV

The question remains whether the District Court abused its discretion in this case by approving a settlement which included a complete fee waiver. As noted earlier, Rule 23(e) wisely requires court approval of the terms of any settlement of a class action. The potential conflict among members of the class—in this case, for example, the possible conflict between children primarily interested in better educational programs and those primarily interested in improved health care—fully justifies the requirement of court approval.

. . . Petitioners and the amici who support them never suggest that the district court is obligated to place its stamp of approval on every settlement in which the plaintiffs' attorneys have agreed to a fee waiver. The Solicitor General, for example, has suggested that a fee waiver need not be approved when the defendant had "no realistic defense on the merits,". . . or if the waiver was part of a "vindictive effort. . .to teach counsel that they had better not bring such cases, . . ."

We find it unnecessary to evaluate this argument, however, because the record in this case does not indicate that Idaho has adopted such a statute, policy, or practice. . . .

. . .[T]he District Court. . .[found] that the extensive structural relief they obtained constituted an adequate quid pro quo for their waiver of attorney's fees. The Court of Appeals did not overturn this finding. Indeed, even that court did not suggest that the option of rejecting the entire settlement and requiring the parties either to try the case or to attempt to negotiate a different settlement would have served the interests of justice. Only by making the unsupported assumption that the respondent class was entitled to retain the favorable portions of the settlement while rejecting the

---

[20] Judge Wald has described the use of attorney's fees as a "bargaining chip" useful to plaintiffs as well as defendants. In her opinion concurring in the judgment in Moore v. National Assn. of Security Dealers, Inc., she wrote:

"On the other hand, the *Jeff D.* approach probably means that a defendant who is willing to grant immediate prospective relief to a plaintiff case, but would rather gamble on the outcome at trial than pay attorneys' fees and costs up front, will never settle. In short, removing attorneys' fees as a 'bargaining chip' cuts both ways. It prevents defendants, who in Title VII cases are likely to have greater economic power than plaintiffs, from exploiting that power in a particularly objectionable way; but it also deprives plaintiffs of the use of that chip, even when without it settlement may be impossible and the prospect of winning at trial may be very doubtful."

fee waiver could the Court of Appeals conclude that the District Court had acted unwisely.

What the outcome of this settlement illustrates is that the Fees Act has given the victims of civil rights violations a powerful weapon that improves their ability to employ counsel, to obtain access to the courts, and thereafter to vindicate their rights by means of settlement or trial. For aught that appears, it was the "coercive" effect of respondents' statutory right to seek a fee award that motivated petitioners' exceptionally generous offer. Whether this weapon might be even more powerful if fee waivers were prohibited in cases like this is another question,[34] but it is in any event a question that Congress is best equipped to answer. . . .In this case, the District Court did not abuse its discretion in upholding a fee waiver which secured broad injunctive relief, relief greater than that which plaintiffs could reasonably have expected to achieve at trial.

The judgment of the Court of Appeals is reversed.

It is so ordered.

Justice **Brennan**, with whom Justice **Marshall** and Justice **Blackmun** join, dissenting.

Ultimately, enforcement of the laws is what really counts. It was with this in mind that Congress enacted the Civil Rights Attorney's Fees Awards Act of 1976, 42 U.S.C. § 1988 (Act or Fees Act). . . .

[T]he first and most important question to be asked is what Congress' purpose was in enacting the Fees Act. We must then determine whether conditional fee waivers are consistent with this purpose.

. . .

III

. . . [B]y awarding attorney's fees Congress sought to attract competent counsel to represent victims of civil rights violations. Congress' primary purpose was to enable "private attorneys general" to protect the public interest by creating economic incentives for lawyers to represent them. The Court's assertion that the Fees Act was intended to do nothing more than give individual victims of civil rights violations another remedy is thus at odds with the whole thrust of the legislation. Congress determined that the public as a whole has an interest in the vindication of the rights conferred by the civil rights statutes over and above the value of a civil rights remedy to a particular plaintiff.

I have gone to great lengths to show how the Court mischaracterizes the purpose of the Fees Act because the Court's error leads it to ask the wrong question. Having concluded that the Fees Act merely creates another remedy to vindicate the rights of individual plaintiffs, the Court asks whether negotiated waivers of statutory attorney's fees are "invariably inconsistent" with the availability of such fees as a remedy for individual plaintiffs. Not surprisingly, the Court has little difficulty knocking down this frail straw man. But the proper question is whether permitting negotiated fee waivers is consistent with Congress' goal of attracting competent counsel. It is therefore necessary to consider the effect on this goal of allowing individual plaintiffs to negotiate fee waivers.

A

. . .[S]ince simultaneous negotiation and waiver may have different effects on the congressional policy of encouraging counsel to accept civil rights cases, each practice must be analyzed independently to determine whether or not it is consistent with the Fees Act. . . .An independent examination leads me to conclude: (1) that plaintiffs should not be permitted to waive the "reasonable fee" provided by the Fees Act; but (2) that parties may undertake to negotiate their fee claims simultaneously with the merits so long as whatever fee the parties agree to is found by

---

[34] We are cognizant of the possibility that decisions by individual clients to bargain away fee awards may, in the aggregate and in the long run, diminish lawyers' expectations of statutory fees in civil rights cases. If this occurred, the pool of lawyers willing to represent plaintiffs in such cases might shrink, constricting the "effective access to the judicial process" for persons with civil rights grievances which the Fees Act was intended to provide. H. R. Rep. No. 94–1558, p. 1 (1976). That the "tyranny of small decisions" may operate in this fashion is not to say that there is any reason or documentation to support such a concern at the present time. Comment on this issue is therefore premature at this juncture. We believe, however, that as a practical matter the likelihood of this circumstance arising is remote. See *Moore v. National Assn. of Securities Dealers, Inc.* (Wald, J., concurring in judgment).

the court to be a "reasonable" one under the Fees Act.

B

1

It seems obvious that allowing defendants in civil rights cases to condition settlement of the merits on a waiver of statutory attorney's fees will diminish lawyers' expectations of receiving fees and decrease the willingness of lawyers to accept civil rights cases. . .

. . .[I]t does not require a sociological study to see that permitting fee waivers will make it more difficult for civil rights plaintiffs to obtain legal assistance. It requires only common sense. Assume that a civil rights defendant makes a settlement offer that includes a demand for waiver of statutory attorney's fees. The decision whether to accept or reject the offer is the plaintiff's alone, and the lawyer must abide by the plaintiff's decision. See, e. g., ABA, Model Rules of Professional Conduct 1.2(a) (1984); ABA, Model Code of Professional Responsibility EC 7–7 to EC 7–9 (1982). As a formal matter, of course, the statutory fee belongs to the plaintiff,. . . and thus technically the decision to waive entails a sacrifice only by the plaintiff. As a practical matter, however, waiver affects only the lawyer. Because "a vast majority of the victims of civil rights violations" have no resources to pay attorney's fees, H. R. Rep. 1, lawyers cannot hope to recover fees from the plaintiff and must depend entirely on the Fees Act for compensation.[10] The plaintiff thus has

no real stake in the statutory fee and is unaffected by its waiver. . . .Consequently, plaintiffs will readily agree to waive fees if this will help them to obtain other relief they desire.[11]

. . .We have on numerous prior occasions held that "a statutory right conferred on a private party, but affecting the public interest, may not be waived or released if such waiver or release contravenes the statutory policy." . . .

2

. . .

[The fear that restricting fee waiver agreements will inpede settlements] is a wholly inadequate justification for the Court's result. First,. . .I agree with the Court that encouraging settlements is desirable policy. But it is judicially created policy, applicable to litigation of any kind and having no special force in the context of civil rights cases. The congressional policy underlying the Fees Act is. . .to create incentives for lawyers to devote time to civil rights cases by making it economically feasible for them to do so. . . . [P]ermitting fee waivers significantly undercuts this policy. Thus, even if prohibiting fee waivers does discourage some settlements, a judicial policy favoring settlement cannot possibly take precedence over this express congressional policy. We must implement Congress' agenda, not our own.

. . .The fact that fee waivers may produce some settlement offers that are beneficial to a few individual plaintiffs is hardly "consistent with the purposes of the Fees Act,". . .if permitting fee waivers fundamentally undermines what Congress sought to achieve. Each individual plaintiff who waives his right to statutory fees in order to obtain additional relief for himself makes it that much more difficult for the next victim of a civil rights

---

[10] Nor can attorneys protect themselves by requiring plaintiffs to sign contingency agreements or retainers at the outset of the representation. Amici legal aid societies inform us that they are prohibited by statute, court rule, or Internal Revenue Service regulation from entering into fee agreements with their clients. . .Moreover, even if such agreements could be negotiated, the possibility of obtaining protection through contingency fee arrangements is unavailable in the very large proportion of civil rights cases which, like this case, seek only injunctive relief. In addition, the Court's misconceived doctrine of state sovereign immunity, . . . precludes damages suits against governmental bodies, the most frequent civil rights defendants. Finally, even when a suit is for damages, many civil rights actions concern amounts that are too small to provide real compensation through a contingency fee arrangement. Of course, none of the parties has seriously suggested that civil rights attorneys can protect themselves through private arrangements. After all, Congress enacted the Fees Act because, after

Alyeska, it found such arrangements wholly inadequate.

[11] This result is virtually inevitable in class actions where, even if the class representative feels sympathy for the lawyer's plight, the obligation to represent the interests of absent class members precludes altruistic sacrifice. In class actions on behalf of incompetents, like this one, it is the lawyer himself who must agree to sacrifice his own interests for those of the class he represents. See, e.g., ABA, Model Code of Professional Responsibility EC 7–12 (1982).

violation to find a lawyer willing or able to bring his case. As obtaining legal assistance becomes more difficult, the "benefit" the Court so magnanimously preserves for civil rights plaintiffs becomes available to fewer and fewer individuals, exactly the opposite result from that intended by Congress.

. . .

Second,. . .the Court greatly exaggerates the effect that prohibiting fee waivers will have on defendants' willingness to make settlement offers. This is largely due to the Court's failure to distinguish the fee waiver issue from the issue of simultaneous negotiation of fees and merits claims. . . .[I]t is a prohibition on simultaneous negotiation, not a prohibition on fee waivers, that makes it difficult for the defendant to ascertain his total liability at the time he agrees to settle the merits. Thus, while prohibiting fee waivers may deter settlement offers simply because requiring the defendant to pay a "reasonable attorney's fee" increases the total cost of settlement, this is a separate issue altogether, and the Court's numerous arguments about why defendants will not settle unless they can determine their total liability at the time of settlement. . .are simply beside the point. . . .

. . .Because the parties can negotiate a fee (or a range of fees) that is not unduly high and condition their settlement on the court's approval of this fee, the magnitude of a defendant's liability for fees in the settlement context need be neither uncertain nor particularly great. . .

C

I would, on the other hand, permit simultaneous negotiation of fees and merits claims, since this would not contravene the purposes of the Fees Act. Congress determined that awarding prevailing parties a "reasonable" fee would create necessary—and sufficient—incentives for attorneys to work on civil rights cases. Prohibiting plaintiffs from waiving statutory fees ensures that lawyers will receive this "reasonable" statutory fee. Thus, if fee waivers are prohibited, permitting simultaneous fees and merits negotiations will not interfere with the Act; the lawyer will still be entitled to and will still receive a reasonable attorney's fee. Indeed, permitting simultaneous negotiations in such circumstances may even enhance

the effectiveness of the Fees Act by making it easier for a lawyer to dispose of his cases more quickly. This frees up the lawyer's time to take other cases and may enhance his reputation as an effective advocate who quickly obtains relief for clients.

IV

. . .The Court's decision in no way limits the power of state and local bar associations to regulate the ethical conduct of lawyers. Indeed, several Bar Associations have already declared it unethical for defense counsel to seek fee waivers. See Committee on Professional Ethics of the Association of the Bar of the City of New York, Op. No. 82–80 (1985); District of Columbia Legal Ethics Committee, Op. No. 147, supra n. 8, 113 Daily Washington Law Reporter, at 389. Such efforts are to be commended and, it is to be hoped, will be followed by other state and local organizations concerned with respecting the intent of Congress and with protecting civil rights.

In addition, it may be that civil rights attorneys can obtain agreements from their clients not to waive attorney's fees. Such agreements simply replicate the private market for legal services (in which attorneys are not ordinarily required to contribute to their client's recovery), and thus will enable civil rights practitioners to make it economically feasible—as Congress hoped—to expend time and effort litigating civil rights claims. . . .

NOTES

1. What are the lessons for defense counsel in *Jeff D.*? What are the lessons for plaintiff's counsel? What type of section 1983 cases are most likely to be affected by the Court's ruling? Does the availability of contingent fee agreements reduce the practical impact of *Jeff D.*? Does the common fund approach to attorney's fees (see note 6 following *Hensley*) reduce the practical impact of *Jeff D.* in class action cases?

2. Does *Jeff D.* leave open the possibility that a particular fee waiver agreement in an individual case might be invalid? In *Phillips v. Allegheny County*, 869 F.2d 234 (3rd Cir. 1989), a paraplegic patient alleged he was unconstitutionally discharged from a county medical facility. He sued the county seeking monetary and injunctive relief. The settlement agreement signed by the parties included a payment of $3,000 to the plaintiff, a modification of the county's discharge procedures, and a waiver of attorney's fees. The plaintiff then applied for attorney's fees claiming that he was in such a medically and economically desperate situation that the fee waiver should be invalidated. The district court agreed, finding that the waiver was obtained in "bad faith" and the county's behavior was "repugnant and shocking to the conscience." The court of appeals reversed, noting that the district court lacked to power to alter the settlement and that taking advantage of the plaintiff's need to settle is not bad faith. See also *National Senior Citizens Law Center v. Social Security Administration*, 849 F.2d 401 (9th Cir. 1988) (plaintiffs in a Freedom of Information Act case are not entitled to attorney's fees in the face of an express waiver even if the defendant had no defense on the merits of the suit).

3. Defense counsel must be sure that the waiver of attorney's fees is clearly stated in the settlement agreement. In *Muckleshoot Tribe v. Puget Sound Power & Light Co.*, 875 F.2d 695 (9th Cir. 1989), the parties settled a water rights dispute by a consent decree that did not expressly mention costs or attorney's fees. The district court ruled that the plaintiff had waived any claim for attorney's fees. The court of appeals reversed, stating that an intent to waive attorney's fees would not be presumed and such a waiver must be clearly expressed in the settlement agreement. See also *Ashley v. Atlantic Richfield Co.*, 794 F.2d 128 (3rd Cir. 1986) (a settlement that released the defendant from "costs" did not release a claim for attorney's fees). Cf. *Wakefield v. Mathews*, 852 F.2d 482 (9th Cir. 1988) (a settlement agreement that released the defendant from "costs or expenses of any nature whatsoever, known or unknown, fixed or contingent," was sufficiently broad to reflect an intent to include a waiver of attorney's fees).

4. Justice Brennan's dissenting opinion suggests that states may prohibit the practice of conditioning a settlement on a waiver of attorney's fees as a matter of professional ethics. Would such a state rule be preempted by federal law in light of Justice Stevens' reasoning in *Jeff D.*? As reflected in footnotes 15 and 16 of the majority opinion in *Jeff D.*, several state and local bar associations had prohibited fee waiver agreements prior to the Supreme

Court's decision. The Committee on Professional and Judicial Ethics of the New York City Bar Association subsequently withdrew its opinion in light of *Jeff D.*'s ruling that such offers were not inconsistent with the Attorney's Fees Award Act and its purposes. N.Y. Opinion No. 87–4. The California Supreme Court considered, but rejected, a proposed rule (Rule 2–400) that would have prohibited the making of settlement offers that contained fee waiver provisions in civil rights cases. See California State Bar Standing Committee on Professional Responsibility and Conduct, Formal Opinion No. 1989–114 (1989). The proposed rule would have permitted the making of a lump sum settlement offer that covered all claims including attorney's fees. For an argument that in light of *Jeff D.*, state ethics committees should not ban fee waiver agreements, see Comment, *Evans v. Jeff D. and the Proper Scope of State Ethics Decisions*, 73 Va. L. Rev. 783 (1987). For an argument that such agreements could be prohibited by ethical considerations unrelated to the policies underlying the Attorney's Fee Award Act, see Wolfram, *The Second Set of Players: Lawyers, Fee Shifting, and the Limits of Professional Discipline*, 47 Law & Contemp. Prob. 293 (1984).

5. Justice Brennan also suggests that plaintiffs' counsel might secure agreements from their clients not to waive attorney's fees. Can an attorney ethically do so? The comments to the American Bar Association, Model Rules of Professional Responsibility, M.R. 1.2 states: "The client may not be asked to agree. . .to surrender. . .the right to settle litigation that the lawyer might wish to continue." Compare *Lewis v. S.S. Baune*, 534 F.2d 1115 (5th Cir. 1976) (provision in a retainer agreement between an attorney and client that prohibits a settlement without the attorney's consent is void as against public policy) with La. Rev. Stat. Ann. § 37–218 (permitting an attorney by contract to prohibit her client from settling a case without the lawyer's written consent). For further discussion of this question, see Calhoun, *Attorney-Client Conflicts of Interest and the Concept of Non-Negotiable Fee Awards under 42 U.S.C. § 1988*, 55 Colo. L. Rev. 341 (1984).

6. Suppose the plaintiff's counsel has reason to believe the case could be settled on terms favorable to her client, if she waives any claim for attorney's fees, but that no such offer has been made by the defendant. Must or should the plaintiff's attorney raise the possibility of pursuing settlement on those terms with her client? Consider the following comments

> Even absent such an offer [from the defendant] the attorney may be obligated to discuss such a settlement [that includes a fee waiver agreement] with the client if, for example, there is reason to believe that the defense would agree to such a disposition. Failure to recognize such a situation, or use it to the client's advantage, could well be seen as a violation of the attorney's duty to act competently. . .

California State Bar Standing Committee on Professional Responsibility and Conduct, Formal Opinion No. 1989–114 (1989).

7. Rule 68 of the Federal Rules of Civil Procedure provides that an adverse party may offer to allow judgment to be taken against him or her "with costs accrued." If the offer is refused and the final judgment is less favorable than the offer, "the offeree must pay the costs incurred after the making of the offer." If the offer of judgment is accepted, the offeror must pay the "costs" accrued as of the date of the offer. The Supreme Court addressed the relationship between Rule 68 and statutory attorney's fees under section 1988 in a case styled *Marek v. Chesny*, 473 U.S. 1 (1985).

In *Marek*, three police officers, responding to a domestic disturbance, shot and killed the plaintiff's decedent. Prior to trial, the defendants offered to settle the case "for a sum, including costs now accrued and attorney's fees" of $100,000. At the time the offer was made, the plaintiff had incurred costs, including attorney's fees of $32,000. The plaintiff rejected the offer and proceeded to trial at which a jury awarded $60,000 in compensatory and punitive damages. The plaintiff's costs, including attorney's fees, after the rejection of the offer were approximately $140,000. Pursuant to section 1988, the plaintiff sought attorney's fees and costs of approximately $172,000. The district court, relying on Rule 68, refused to award the plaintiff the $140,000 in costs incurred after the rejection of the offer of settlement.

The Supreme Court first considered whether an offer of judgment that did not separate damages from costs was valid under Rule 68.

The Court held that Rule 68 allowed such lump sum offers. Nothing in the text of Rule 68 requires a bifurcation of an offer between the an amount to settle the substantive claim and an amount to cover accrued costs. Since the combined pre-offer costs, including attorney's fees ($32,000) and the damage award ($60,000), were less than the $100,000 lump sum offer, the plaintiff obtained a less favorable judgment than the offer. *Marek*, 473 U.S. at 7. Consequently, under Rule 68, the defendants were not liable for the prevailing plaintiff's post-offer "costs."

The second major issue in *Marek* was whether the post-offer "costs" for which the defendants were not liable included attorney's fees. The Court held that the term "costs" in Rule 68 included attorney's fees under section 1988. *Marek*, 473 U.S. at 9. Accordingly, the defendants were not liable for the $140,000 in costs, including attorney's fees, incurred after the plaintiff's rejection of the $100,000 settlement offer.

The majority reasoned that this result was consistent with the plain meaning of Rule 68 and the policy of encouraging settlements. Defendants typically are more concerned with the bottom line amount of payment than with the how the payment is divided between the plaintiff and her counsel. Lump sum offers allow defendants to fix their bottom line payment. Moreover, the prospect of forfeiting entitlement to post-offer attorney's fees will force plaintiffs to "think very hard" about continuing litigation after a Rule 68 offer is made. *Marek*, 473 U.S. at 11. Finally, the Court rejected the proposition that special rules should insulate civil rights plaintiffs from such tough choices. "[W]e are convinced that applying Rule 68 in the context of a § 1983 action is consistent with the policies and objectives of § 1988. Section 1988 encourages plaintiffs to bring meritorious civil rights suits; Rule 68 simply encourages settlements. There is nothing incompatible in these two objectives." *Marek*, 473 U.S. at 11.

8. What are the strategic considerations in deciding whether to make a Rule 68 offer, the size of the offer (if made), and whether or not to accept it? Suppose defense counsel estimates that a jury would likely award damages in the range of $50,000 to the victim of excessive force by police officers. Defense counsel also estimates that if the case went to trial, the plaintiff's costs, including attorney's fees, would be approximately $150,000 and his own fees would be $100,000. Should the defendant make a Rule 68 offer of judgment? If so, how much should the defendant offer? Suppose the defendant offers $30,000 (including accrued costs and attorney's fees) and the plaintiff's attorney has performed 30 hours of work compensable under section 1988 at a rate of $100 per hour. Should the offer be accepted? Does it matter whether or not the plaintiff has a contingent fee contract with his lawyer? For a detailed analysis of this hypothetical, see Simon, *Rule 68 At The Crossroads: The Relationship Between Offers of Judgment and Statutory Attorney's Fees*, 53 U. Cin. L. Rev. 889, 916–929 (1984).

9. The majority in *Marek* states that "at the time an offer is made, the plaintiff knows the amount in damages caused by the challenged conduct." *Marek*, 473 U.S. at 7. How likely is it that plaintiff will *know* what a jury will award in damages? Pain and suffering and emotional distress are notoriously difficult to value. Even in cases where economic loss is the major component of damages, valuing the claim may

be difficult. In *Herrington v. County of Sonoma*, 12 F.3d 901 (9th Cir. 1993) the county violated the plaintiffs' constitutional rights by rejecting the plaintiffs' proposed housing development. Prior to trial, the county made a Rule 68 offer of judgment for $501,000. The plaintiffs rejected the offer and proceeded to trial at which the jury awarded them $2.5 million in damages. The court of appeals vacated the damages award as excessive. On remand, the district court found that the plaintiffs' were entitled to damages of $52,123.50 and interest in the amount of $69,348.56 for a total judgment of $121,472.06. Pursuant to Rule 68, the plaintiffs' were denied an award of attorney' fees related to work performed after the date of the county's offer of judgment.

10. Consider the cumulative effect of the major decisions reprinted in this chapter on counsel's incentives to represent plaintiffs in civil rights actions. Have the Supreme Court's rulings, when viewed in this light, paid adequate heed to Senate Report No. 94–1011 and its explication of the purposes of section 1988?